PERENNIALS

PERENNIALS

The Definitive Reference With Over 2,500 Photographs

ROGER PHILLIPS & MARTYN RIX

Assisted by Peter Barnes, James Compton & Alison Rix
Layout Jill Bryan & Gill Stokoe

FIREFLY BOOKS

Acknowledgements

We would like to thank James Compton for his help with the *Labiatae* and *Kniphofia*, Peter Barnes for the ferns, Brian Mathew for photographs of *Iris* and *Acanthus*, Martin Gardner for the photographs taken in Chile, and Jacqui Hurst for help with the studio photographs.

Most of the specimens photographed in the studio came from the following gardens, and we should like to acknowledge the help we had from them, and from their staff.

The Crown Estate Commissioners at the Savill Gardens, Windsor Great Park; The Royal Botanic Garden, Edinburgh; The Royal Botanic Gardens, Kew; The Royal Horticultural Society's Garden, Wisley; University Botanic Garden, Cambridge; The Chelsea Physic Garden; Eccleston Square, London SW1; Washfield Nurseries, Hawkhurst, Sussex; Beth Chatto Gardens, Elmstead Market, Essex; Middleton House, Enfield, Middlesex; David Austin Hardy Plants; Kelways, Langport, Somerset; Green Farm Plants, Bentley, Hants; Goldbrook Plants, Hoxne, Suffolk; Hopleys Plants, Much Hadham, Herts.; Sandling Park, Hythe, Kent.

We would also like to thank the following for their help, encouragement, and for growing the perennials we photographed: Crynan Alexander, John D'Arcy, Clair and David Austin, Bill Baker, David Barker, Igor Belolipov, Alan Bloom, John Bond, Sandra Bond, Roger Bowden, Chris Brickell, Patty Carr, Beth Chatto, Duncan Donald, John Drake, Alec Duguid, Pamela Egremont, Jack Elliott, George Fuller, Martin Furness, Jim Gardiner, Martin Gardiner, Geoffrey and Kathleen Goatcher, François Goffinet, Tony Hall, Brian Halliwell, Carolyn and Alan Hardy, Harry Hay, Diana Hewitt, Nigel Holman, Tinge Horsfall, Christopher Lloyd, John Lloyd, David McClintock, Keith MacDevette, Deborah Maclean, John and Marisa Main, Brian Matthew, Philip McMillan Browse, Michael Metianu, Bob Mitchell, Shirley Moorhead, Mikinori Ogisu, Andrew Paterson, Roger Poulett, Charles and Brigid Quest-Ritson, Richard Rix, Ted Rix, Tony Schilling, Bill Smalls, Gordon Smith, Geff Stebbings, Elizabeth Strangman, Greta Sturdza, Harriot Tennant, Ann Thatcher, Piers Trehane, Rosemary Verey, Peter Yeo.

We would also like to thank Brent Elliott and the staff of the Lindley Library for all their help and patience during the preparation of the text.

A FIREFLY BOOK

First Printing

National Library of Canada Cataloguing in Publication Data

Phillips, Roger, 1932–
    Perennials: the definitive reference with over 2,500 photographs

First published in a 2 v. set: London: Pan, 1991.
Includes bibliographical references and index.
ISBN 1-55209-641-6 (bound).—ISBN 1-55209-639-4 (pbk.)

    1. Perennials. 2. Perennials—Pictorial Works. I. Rix, Martyn
II. Title.

SB434.P49 2002   635.9 32   C2001-901967-X

Publisher Cataloguing-in-Publication Data
(Library of Congress Standards)

Phillips, Roger.
    Perennials : the definitive reference with over 2,500 photographs
Roger Phillips ; and Martyn Rix. -1st ed.
[480] p. : col. photos. ; cm.
Revision of two vol. set: Early perennials, and Late perennials :
England : Macmillan, 1991.
Includes bibliographic references and index.
Summary: Comprehensive illustrated directory of 2,500 perennials,
including planting tips, design ideas and sources.
ISBN 1-55209-641-6
ISBN 1-55209-639-4 (pbk.)
1. Perennials. I. Rix, Martyn. I. Title.
    635.93221 2002 CIP   SB434.P53

Published in Canada in 2002 by
Firefly Books Ltd.
3680 Victoria Park Avenue
Willowdale, Ontario M2H 3K1

Published in the United States in 2002 by
Firefly Books (U.S.) Inc.
P.O. Box 1338, Ellicott Station
Buffalo, New York 14205

Printed in Thailand

Contents

Candelabra primulas and *Iris laevigata* at Trebah, Cornwall

Introduction

In this book we illustrate over two thousand, five hundred herbaceous perennials; only a small sample of the many thousands grown in gardens, but sufficient, we hope, to show enough of those commonly cultivated, and a selection of rarities, to satisfy the beginner and excite the specialist. We have concentrated on plants which are hardy enough to tolerate at least −5°C of frost, and remain outside during the winter. We have not covered alpine and rock garden plants, nor desert plants and succulents, nor herbaceous perennials which require protection from frost, nor annuals and biennials. These will be the subjects of later volumes in this series.

The Photographs

When shooting flowers in the garden or in the field, it is preferable to work from a tripod so that you can take advantage of the opportunity to use a slow shutter speed and thus a smaller aperture, giving a greater depth of field. In practice the best speed to use is normally 1/15 sec., although if there is a strong wind you may have to go up to 1/30th or in extremes 1/60th.

The studio shots are taken on a Bronica 120, with a normal lens, with two Bowens quad units as a light source. The field shots are taken with a Nikon FM. The film in both cases is Ektachrome 64, that used for the field shots being pushed one stop in development.

The Order

The plants are arranged in four groups by flowering time; spring, early summer, mid-summer, and late summer and autumn. Within these seasons the plants are arranged by family in a botanical order, beginning with the buttercup family (*Ranunculaceae*), and ending with grasses and ferns. Where one or two species in a genus flower at a different season from the majority of the genus, they are put with their families, though out of season, so *Iris unguicularis* is put with the rest of the irises, though it flowers in early spring. Where there are distinct groups

in a genus flowering at different seasons, as in *Anemone*, the genus appears in two separate groups. The text gives the months of flowering in the wild, as the months of flowering in gardens differ greatly in different parts of the world. The text is arranged in alphabetical order on the page.

We have chosen a traditional family order, following P. H. Davis and J. Cullen, *The Identification of Flowering Plant Families*. This is roughly similar to the order found in Clapham, Tutin and Warburg, *Flora of the British Isles*, and P. A. Munz, *A California Flora*, and differs radically from the modified system of Engler and Prantl used in the *European Garden Flora*.

The Names

The plants are called by their Latin scientific names, and English names are used for only a few familiar plants. Taking *Primula florindae* Kingdon-Ward 'Rubra' (*Primulaceae*) as an example, the scientific name of a plant is made up as follows. The first name is that of the genus, i.e. *Primula*. This is followed by the specific name which is often descriptive, or refers to the plant's habitat or collector, i.e. *florindae*, which refers to Florinda, the first wife of the plant's discoverer and collector, Frank Kingdon-Ward. (His second wife, Jean, *née* Macklin, is remembered in *Lilium*

James Compton and John D'Arcy on Carlyle's Hoek, NE Cape Province

macklinae.) The specific name is followed by the name of the author of the species, called the authority, in this case also Kingdon-Ward. The authority is usually abbreviated: the common authority, L., refers to Linnaeus, whose *Species Plantarum* (1753) is used as the starting point of scientific naming. A garden plant can also have a cultivar name, which refers to a particular variety of the species, usually a clone, but also, as here, a colour variant which is reproduced by seed. The cultivar name is indicated by single inverted commas. 'Rubra', in this case, means red. More modern cultivar names must be in a modern language, not Latin, e.g. 'Festive Skirt' or 'Gei-sho-ui', both names of Irises. The name is often followed by the name of the family, in Latin, usually ending in -*ae*. Throughout this scheme, the Latin names are put in italics, the English or cultivar names in Roman. Names of cultivars which are illustrated are put in bold in the text; other names, including English common names, are not in bold.

The names used in this revised edition mostly follow those found in the *RHS Plant Finder 2000–2001*, an excellent and convenient source of the names of cultivated plants, which is updated annually. Its advisory committee includes botanists from the Royal Horticultural Society and the Royal Botanic Garden, Kew, and it brings in specialist advisors to help with difficult genera. The *Plant Finder* is becoming a standard reference, and is now available online at www.rhs.org.uk. Plant names are likely to continue to change as evidence from DNA studies becomes available, and the changes which becomes accepted in horticultural circles will be available through the *Plant Finder*.

The Text

The text gives the country from which the species originated, its habitat, distribution and flowering times in the wild. This is intended to help the traveller who may wish to see the plant in the wild, and the gardener who can use the information to grow the plant better in his own climate and locality. We have in many cases added brief cultural notes, but these are meant only as a supplement to the descriptions of habitat, which have been made as detailed as possible, using our own experience of the plants in the wild, as well as accounts published in local floras.

The few words of description are intended to complement the photographs and help in the identification of the plant, by choosing the diagnostic characters of the species, and characters which can be seen in the photograph are usually omitted.

Measurements are given in metres and centimetres; as a guide 1m equals around 3 feet, and 2.5cm equals about 1 inch.

Hardiness

In colder climates, deciduous herbaceous plants can generally be protected with a very deep mulch. In general we have taken −20°C as the lowest temperature to mention. Plants of doubtful hardiness will usually survive better if grown in very well-drained soil and kept rather dry in winter. The figure given shows the degrees centigrade of frost which most can survive, but there are great variations of hardiness even within a single species. Again many plants are not tolerant of heat in summer, and the native habitat and locality of a species is an indication of its likely heat tolerance. Himalayan alpines and those from very wet summer climates such as New Zealand are generally least tolerant of summer heat or drought.

This table compares the minimum temperatures (in degrees Fahrenheit and Centigrade) of the hardiness zones published by the United States Department of Agriculture for North America. The Californian system, used by the *New Western Garden Book* and in other Sunset books, is more complex, but there are heat and drought rather than frost are the likely problems for growers of perennials. The climatic notes given in the *New Western Garden Book* give minimum temperatures for inland areas. This may be useful for gardeners on the West Coast.

Plant Hardiness Zones

Zone	°F	°C
1	below −50	below −45
2	−50 to −40	−45 to −40
3	−40 to −30	−40 to −34
4	−30 to −20	−34 to −29
5	−20 to −10	−29 to −23
6	−10 to 0	−23 to −16
7	0 to 10	−16 to −12
8	10 to 20	−12 to −7
9	20 to 30	−7 to −1
10	30 to 40	−1 to 4
11	above 40	above 4

Hardiness zones are based on the average annual minimum temperature for each zone. The numbers given are approximate, avoiding fractions.

A lupin garden at Chatsworth

Rodgersia podophylla in autumn colour

The Wild Origins of Herbaceous Perennials

The hardy perennials grown in gardens originate in temperate climates in all parts of the world, but the majority are from areas with cold or dry winters and wet summers. A few, mainly from central Asia or the Mediterranean areas of Europe, western Asia or south-western North America, require moist winters and springs, and tolerate dry summers, but these Mediterranean climates are especially rich in bulbs and annuals. Those that do survive in these climates are very useful, however, for climates such as southern California and southern Europe in areas or dry parts of the garden where irrigation is restricted; many of these, such as bearded irises, paeonies and gypsophila have swollen roots to survive periods of drought.

The list below gives the original habitats of some large groups of common garden perennials, and gives an indication of the sort of conditions they need for optimum growth.

Anemones, Japanese   China, on rocks, cliffs in shade, wet in summer.

Astilbes   China and Japan, on damp rocks, by streams, wet in summer.

Carnations and pinks   Southern Europe, on rocks, cliffs and old walls, dry in summer.

Delphiniums   Central Europe, in subalpine woods and meadows, in rich but well-drained soil, moist in summer.

Day-lilies (*Hemerocallis*)   China and Japan, in marshy meadows and rocky slopes, wet in summer.

Hostas   Japan and China, in woods, shady rocks and cliffs, with cloudy, wet summers.

Irises, bearded   Eastern Europe and western Asia, on rocky slopes, moist in spring, dry in summer.

Kniphofias (Red-hot poker)   South Africa, on wet peaty and sandy soils, often in marshes, wet in summer, drier in winter.

Michaelmas daisies (*Aster*)   North America, in woods and meadows, moist in summer.

Paeonies (*P. lactiflora* cvs.)   Siberia and North China, in meadows and open scrub, on deep, rich soil, with summer rain and very cold winters.

Penstemons   Mexico and North America, in many different habitats, often dry and rocky.

Primroses   Europe and western Asia, in woods and on shady rocks, usually on heavy soil, moist in summer.

Water-lilies   Europe and North America, in still water.

In the wild, herbaceous plants have to compete with trees and shrubs for water and light. Many of the early spring-flowering ones grow in deciduous woods, and flower before the leaves come on the trees. They can survive during summer with very little light and in fact they are soon scorched and killed by sun and dry wind in summer; in many cases shelter from wind is as important as summer water. Others grow in places inhospitable to tree growth, such as in dry steppe climates; they require full sun and exposure throughout the summer, and are generally tolerant of summer drought. Small areas of herbaceous perennials may be found in forest areas in very wet places along streams, on wet or dry rocks, on avalanche tracks, or on screes where landslides are frequent. Those which grow in open meadows or in mountains above the tree line must tolerate grazing, and are often spiny, poisonous or otherwise unpalatable, e.g. delphiniums, primulas, sea holly, day-lilies, etc. Because mountains attract rain, most of them need summer moisture at the root, but sun and wind on the leaves. It is mainly those from very cloudy mountains, such as the Himalayas, which tolerate summer shade in gardens, though they are often unable to survive summer heat, and so are the most difficult to grow in lowland areas with hot summers.

Propagation

The majority of perennials, i.e. those which form multiple crowns, are easily propagated by division of the clumps. This is best done in spring in wet climates, or in autumn in climates where spring and summer are rather dry. Early planting gives the divisions (or newly acquired plants) more time to become established before they have to endure the heat of summer. In wet winter climates or where irrigation is possible, spring division is better because the young plants are less likely to rot over winter. Division is simple; the clumps are dug up, and either broken apart by hand, or, if they are tough, forced apart by inserting two forks back to back, and levering the clump apart.

Anemones and *Agapanthus* with *Sedum*

A wonderful range of foliage at Barnsley House

Many plants form clumps, but instead of branching rhizomes and fibrous roots they have deep, fleshy roots which end in a rosette of leaves; oriental poppies, acanthus and Japanese anemones have root systems of this kind, and the plants are hard to move and slow to establish thereafter. Root cuttings however, succeed very well; pieces of root a few inches long should be carefully inserted in sandy soil, with the upper end of the root near the soil surface. The upper end soon grows leaves, the lower end roots. The root cuttings may be taken in autumn, and planted out in spring when well rooted. Stem cuttings are useful for plants which either have many long-lived stems from a compact rootstock, or for those which are almost shrubby at the base, and are therefore unsuitable for division. Examples which are commonly raised by cuttings which root easily are carnations and pinks, wallflowers such as 'Bowles' Mauve', origanums and diascias. The cuttings are best taken in mid-summer, and kept well shaded and humid until they have rooted; then they will have time to make an established plant before winter. Cuttings taken later often root well, but may succumb in winter before they have become established.

Seed forms the best means of increase for species which are not easily raised from cuttings or division. Usually this is best sown as fresh as possible. Large seeds of woodland plants, such as epimediums and corydalis and many primulas lose viability very quickly and should be kept moist if possible between collection and sowing. Others need a cold period after sowing before they germinate, so if sown in summer or autumn will begin to grow in the spring. Others still need first a warm, wet period, then a cold period before they germinate, and a few even need scorching by fire. It may be difficult to discover the exact conditions required for a particular species, but seed catalogues often give some guidelines, and if in doubt it is safest to sow the seed as fresh as possible, and allow seeds that do not germinate immediately to be frosted for a couple of months during the winter. Germination is then likely in the spring, or as soon as the soil warms up.

Herbaceous Perennials in the garden

The traditional place to grow perennials in a garden is in herbaceous borders. These are long and rectangular, often in pairs with a grassy path between, and backed by yew hedges. The planting is confined to deciduous herbaceous perennials, for the very good reason that they may be dug up, divided and replanted in the spring while the beds are weeded and manured. The borders are totally brown through the winter, but make a fine and colourful show from early summer onwards, any bare patches which appear in late summer being filled with annuals which have been brought on in pots. These were the great borders of Edwardian England, filled with gorgeous imperial paeonies from Kelways, the tall spires of delphiniums and clouds of gypsophila.

A lavender edging at Mottisfont

A summer border at Crathes Castle, Aberdeenshire

Few private gardens still maintain them in the traditional manner, but there are fine examples at Newby Hall in Yorkshire, and around the parterre at Pitmedden near Aberdeen.

Perennials are now more often planted in different ways; they may be in mixed borders with shrubs, annuals and bulbs; they may be grown in a meadow garden, or planted in groups in mown grass, squeezed into crevices in walls, or pinned onto rocky slopes; they may be used as groundcover, or even planted as a hedge. They will tolerate the wettest and driest places, and many thrive in waterlogged soil.

Wherever they are planted their effect depends on their suitability for a particular position in the garden, and on the careful juxtaposition of different plants (now very much an 'in' subject, called plant associations).

Plant associations in the garden

The modern interest in perennials as garden plants can be traced back to the writings of William Robinson, an Irishman from Stradbally whose book *The Wild Garden* was first published in 1870, and was immediately influential. He championed both the use of wild flowers in the garden and the planting of large

Polemonium 'Lambrook Manor'

herbaceous perennials in grass or on the edges of shrubberies, e.g. the common double red paeony, *Paeonia officinalis* 'Rubra Plena', as well as the planting of large swathes of daffodils, anemones and other bulbs. Although many of these ideas proved failures when put into practice at Robinson's own garden at Gravetye Manor in Sussex on heavy Wealden clay, they were successful in other gardens; for instance, the paeony, pulmonarias and *Epimedium alpinum* still survive from the Robinsonian plantings at Mells Park in Somerset. Robinson combined these ideas on planting with a polemic against the tender bedding plants then widely used in Victorian gardens. One of the engravings in *The Wild Garden* entitled 'A beautiful Accident' shows a grouping of Sweet Cecily (*Myrrhis odorata*), white *Campanula persicifolia* and *Campanula alliarifolia*. In a later edition in 1894, a fascinating passage gives a list of the plants G. F. Wilson grew in the then newly established Wild Garden at Wisley; many of them such as *Lilium superbum*, *Galax aphylla*, and *Gentiana asclepiadea*, grow there today. When told that Wisley was 'fascinating, but no garden', Wilson is said to have replied, 'I think of it as a place where plants from all over the world grow wild.'

Robinson's ideas were developed further by Gertrude Jekyll, an artist before she began to design gardens in the 1880s, whose influence was spread both by her writings such as *Colour Schemes in the Flower Garden*, published in 1911, and by her association with Edwin Lutyens. Many of the gardens of Lutyens' fashionable houses were designed by Jekyll, and she summed up her intentions 'to devise living pictures with simple, well-known flowers'.

Jekyll was one of the first to propose borders or beds of one colour, but at the same time acknowledged the need for flexibility: 'A blue garden, for beauty's sake, may be hungry for a group of white lilies or something of palest lemon yellow.' Some of her ideas for plant associations are worth repeating in brief here. Her spring border consisted largely of ferns, such as *Dryopteris filix-mas* interspersed with hellebores, bulbs and *Bergenia*, with patches of *Valeriana phu* 'Aurea', the pinks and the yellows kept carefully separate. She made great use of grey foliage, and bold leaf shapes such as yuccas, *Acanthus*, *Bergenia*, seakale leaves and *Aesculus parviflora*. Her plan for a grey border included much *Eryngium*, *Echinops*, *Gypsophila*, pale heliotrope (would Robinson have approved of this!), and pale mauve delphiniums. Bearded irises were combined with catmint, lupins, old roses and pinks.

INTRODUCTION

She does not seem to have liked hostas, then called *Funkia*, though several varieties were grown at that time, possibly because of their lack of subtlety. The other remarkable absentee from her lists is *Alchemilla mollis*, now universal in herbaceous gardens. It was introduced in 1874 to Austria from Ulu Dağ in Turkey, but is not mentioned by Robinson, and is also absent from Gauntlett's *Hardy Plants Worth Growing*, a remarkable catalogue, extant in the 1930s. The alchemilla was brought to the notice of gardeners by W. T. Stearn in 1948, but did not achieve real popularity until the 1960s, after it received the Award of Merit of the Royal Horticultural Society when exhibited by Sunningdale Nurseries in 1958. However, a large planting may be seen in a photograph of Hidcote, dating from the 1920s.

E. A. Bowles is certainly one of the most important writers of the early twentieth century. He was more of a plantsman than Jekyll, loving rare and unusual species and mutations for their own sakes, and popularizing them through his books and his long association with the Royal Horticultural Society.

The present-day combination of an interest in rare, unusual or ancient garden plants, and artistic planting was stimulated by Vita Sackville-West and her writing about the garden at Sissinghurst Castle, still one of the best gardens for herbaceous plants in the world. Sissinghurst combines a formal layout with informal planting, the plants used for artistic effect but in many cases also rare and interesting. Vita Sackville-West's other interest was in old-fashioned varieties of roses, and these are used to good effect in many parts of the garden. The garden at Crathes Castle in north-east Scotland is similar in its basic formality, but here there is also an excellent collection of rare shrubs, in addition to a splendid display of perennials.

A third great garden, Hidcote, created from about 1903 by an American, Lawrence Johnston, has also been very influential, as the number of perennials named after the garden shows. Johnston also had a large garden in the south of France, at Serre de la Madone, which was important for the introduction of new plants into that part of France. Hidcote's greatness springs partly from its design, of a series of hedged-in 'garden rooms', but also from its reputation as a source and proving ground for new plants.

Both Sissinghurst and Hidcote are now in the care of the National Trust (and Crathes is run by the National Trust for Scotland), and it was through his position of Gardens Adviser to the National Trust as well as through his writings from 1940 onwards that Graham Thomas has had such an influence on gardening. His books on old roses, on perennials, on ground cover and on the art of planting are all classics, bringing the tradition of Robinson, Jekyll and Sackville-West up to the present day.

The vogue for cottage gardens, using simple plants in riotous profusion, was promoted by Margery Fish, a journalist before she and her husband began gardening in middle age at Lambrook Manor. She was a woman of great enthusiasms, and described many of her ideas for striking plant associations, using numerous variegated, purple, or silver leaves. The many cultivars named after her garden show what a good eye she had for an outstanding plant. *Polemonium* 'Lambrook Manor', shown here, is one of her selections, though it did not necessarily originate in her garden.

Many other gardens and nurseries still influence the availability and demand for perennials and their use in gardens. Christopher Lloyd at Great Dixter in Sussex has popularized many plants and scorned others. In his weekly articles in *Country Life* and through his own garden, he has long been a champion of meadow gardens, and those at Great Dixter are the best that can be seen today.

Alan Bloom and his son Adrian have what is probably the largest collection of perennials in their nursery at Bressingham in Norfolk. Alan Bloom has for many years been active in introducing new plants into general cultivation, and in creating new hybrids often of genera which have not been worked on before; *Aconitum* 'Ivorine', valuable for its early flowering and low, multi-stemmed habit, was one of his raising. He was one of the first to propose informal 'Island Beds' of perennials, surrounded by grass, the heights carefully graduated so that little staking was needed. These have tall plants, chosen for their sturdiness, in the middle, and low ones around all the edges. Good examples of these beds can be seen at Bressingham Gardens.

The long border at Great Dixter, Sussex

Through her nursery, aptly called Unusual Plants, and through her garden there, her writings and lectures, Beth Chatto has a devoted following, combining plants with horizontal and vertical shapes, different foliage types and colours to excellent effect. She regularly popularizes new plants through her nursery.

In America a rather similar function is played by the White Flower Farm in Litchfield, Connecticut. Its beautiful, twice-yearly catalogues are full of interesting perennials and have careful cultivation notes for American gardens.

Americans have also been the great plant breeders of the late twentieth century, concentrating on genera such as *Hemerocallis*, *Hosta* and bearded and spuria irises. There has been an immense growth of interest in hardy perennials in North America and in Europe in the past ten years, and the people mentioned above have been only some of the most public influences on this growth.

Lysimachia ephemerum in a rose border

Trollius europaeus in Perthshire

Natural Plant Associations

The essence of a successful plant association is that the plants chosen should grow happily together, that there should be some contrasts in the textures of foliage, and that the colours of those flowers which are open at the same time should not clash. Furthermore the plants should be of similar robustness so that the weaker ones are not overwhelmed by those that are over-vigorous. Though a particular area of the garden may look best at one season, there is usually scope for many layers of planting, so that there is some interest from spring to autumn. Snowdrops, aconites and other early bulbs may be covered by summer-leafing and flowering herbaceous plants, and the spaces taken by early flowering perennials such as oriental poppies can be filled by late-flowering ones. Flower-colour schemes may be changed through the season, beginning with the bright acid yellow and blues common in spring, with cool pinks, greys and blues in summer, and finally with warm orange, reds and yellows in autumn.

Most modern suggestions for successful plant associations concentrate on producing such harmony of colour, combined with contrasting leaf textures. Those with a feeling for plant geography may like to emphasize an additional theme – to use in an area only those plants which might be found growing together in nature, or at least those which come from the same geographical area. The few examples set out below, which include bulbs and a few dwarf shrubs, could be easily reproduced in the garden.

1. **Caucasian hay meadow** This association contains many familiar herbaceous plants and bulbs, and is found both in the Caucasus proper and in northern Turkey. For rich, but well-drained soil, moist in summer. Typical species: *Galanthus, Scilla sibirica, Cyclamen coum, Iris histrioides, Omphalodes cappadocica, Helleborus orientalis, Brunnera macrophylla, Hesperis matronalis, Lilium monadelphum, Campanula lactiflora, Campanula alliarifolia, Geranium psilostemon, Geranium platypetalum,* (and other species), *Salvia forskahlii, Paeonia mlokesewitschii, Cephalaria gigantea, Telekia speciosa, Gentiana asclepiadea, Colchicum speciosum, Crocus speciosus.*

2. **North European subalpine meadow** This association is found in the foothills of the Alps, and in a depauperate form on limestone hills in northern Britain. For rich soil, moist in summer. Typical species: *Leucojum vernum, Crocus vernus,* *Erythronium dens-canis, Narcissus poeticus, Narcissus pseudo-narcissus, Geranium pratense, sylvaticum* and *pheum, Aquilegia alpina, Aquilegia atrata, Salvia glutinosa, Ranunculus aconitifolius, Trollius europaeus, Lunaria redidiva, Pulmonaria* (several species), *Campanula latifolia, Colchicum autumnale.*

3. **North American moist deciduous woodland** This association is found from southern Canada, along the Appalachian mountains south to Georgia. Mostly spring-flowering. For acid, leafy soil, moist in summer. Typical species: *Erythronium americanum, Trillium grandiflorum, Trillium erectum, Dicentra eximea* and *canadensis, Adiantum pedatum, Clintonia umbellulata, Mertensia virginica, Tierella cordifolia, Podophyllum peltatum, Phlox ovata, Vertatrum viride* (in wet places), *Lilium canadense* (wet), *Smilacina racemosa, Geranium maculatum, Actaea rubra* and *alba, Cimicifuga racemosa, Aquilegia canadensis* (in dry places), *Monarda didyma, Gillenia trifoliata, Helianthus decapetalus, Matteuccia pensylvanica.*

4. **Himalayan wet meadow** This association is found in forest clearings or above the tree line in the central and eastern Himalayas, and into western China. Summers are cool, with very heavy rainfall; winters are cold and dry. For peaty, acid or neutral soil. Typical species: *Primula* (many species), *Meconopsis* (many species), *Thalictrum chelidonii, Ligularia* species, *Polygonum macrophyllum, Euphorbia griffithii, E. shillingii* and *E. wallichiana, Rodgersia* species, *Iris clarkei* and *delavayi, Aconitum* species, *Codonopsis species, Allium wallichii, Hemerocallis forrestii, Nomocharis* species, *Rheum alexandrae.*

5. **Mediterranean dry hillside** In this habitat summers are hot and dry, winters and springs cool and wet. Dwarf shrubs such as lavenders and Cistus are common, as are annuals and bulbs of many genera. Herbaceous plants include the following: *Iris* (bearded types), *Paeonia rhodia* and *arietina, Stipa gigantea, Asphodeline lutea, Echinops ritro, Centranthus ruber, Origanum* species, *Convolvulus althaeoides, Euphorbia characias, rigida* and *myrsinites, Erysimum* and *Cheiranthus* species, *Acanthus spinosus, Phlomis lychnitis, Anchusa azurea, Dictamnus albus.*

6. **European dry woodland** This type of habitat is found in Italy and other parts of southern Europe which are dry in summer, and often have deep shade. These are difficult conditions in a garden. Plants such as the following are found naturally in these places: *Geranium macrorrhizum* and *nodosum, Lithospermum purpureocaeruleum, Epimedium alpinum, Doronicum orientale, Vinca difformis* and *V. minor, Acanthus mollis, Iris graminea, Ranunculus creticus, Cyclamen* species, *Anemone blanda, Digitalis laevigata.*

7. **Californian dry woodland** The conditions here are similar to European dry woodlands, but bulbs, especially *Erythronium* species, are common. The large proportion of bright red species in

Athyrium niponicum 'Pictum' a good form!

A valley of *Geranium clarkei*, *Nepeta* and *Pedicularis* in Kashmir

this area is a response to the importance of hummingbirds as pollinators. Herbaceous species include the following: *Aquilegia formosa*, *Dicentra formosa*, *Delphinium cardinale*, *Ipomopsis aggregata*, *Vancouveria chrysantha*, *Heuchera* species, *Iris innominata* and the *Californicae* section, *Geranium richardsoni*.

8. **Central Asian steppe**   This type of habitat extends from central Turkey eastwards across Asia to north-west China and Mongolia. Summers are hot and dry, winters cold and frozen, and so the growing season is restricted to a few weeks in autumn and a short spring. The flora is, however, very rich and includes numerous bulbs and the following drought-resistant perennials: *Paeonia anomala*, *Tulipa fosteriana* and other species, *Iris albertii* and *I. scariosa*, and *Iris spuria* in wet places, *Gypsophila paniculata*, *Eremostachys* species, *Salvia* species, *Eremurus* species (see *Bulbs*), *Limonium platyphyllum*, *Perovskia atriplicifolia*, *Althaea rugosa*, *Achillea filipendulina*, *Ligularia macrophylla*.

9. **North American prairie and grassland**   This type of habitat is found on very shallow soils and in grassy or boggy clearings east of the Appalachians, where most of the natural vegetation was forest, but more commonly in the drier Midwest. Familiar species include the following: *Phlox maculata*, *Aster novae-angliae*, *Coreopsis verticillata*, *Asclepias tuberosa* (in dry places), *Solidago* species, *Echinacea purpurea*, *Lobelia cardinalis* (by streams), *Oenothera speciosa*, *Veronicastrum virginicum*, *Helianthus* species, especially *Helianthus salicifolius*, *Lupinus perennis*.

10. **New Zealand tussock grassland**   This type of habitat is found mainly in the mountains, and particularly in South Island. It is dominated by clump forming grasses and sedges, with peaty soils, moist in the summer. The following flowering plants are found in this habitat: *Ranunculus lyallii*, *Astelia nervosa*, *Celmisia* species, especially *Celmisia spectabilis* at high altitudes, *Aciphylla* species, *Phormium cookianum*, *Acaena microphylla*, *Carex flabellata*.

11. **Western Chinese woodland**   The ancient forests of Mount Omei and other parts of western Sichuan contain numerous endemic plants as well as animals such as the Giant Panda. The woods are very dense, hot and wet in summer, drier and sunnier in winter, with several species of *Acer*, *Corylopsis*, *Styrax* and numerous other beautiful trees and shrubs. Soils are very leafy, though the underlying rock is often limestone. Some notable species are: *Epimedium acuminatum* and *E. davidii*, *Corydalis flexuosa* and other species, *Adiantum venustum*, *Anemone flaccida*, *A. davidii* and *A. tomentosa*, *Cardiocrinum yunnanense*, *Paris polyphylla*, *Meehania fargesii*, *Sanicula* species, *Paeonia mairei*, *Primula* species, *Tiarella polyphylla*, *Iris japonica* (in more open places), *Hosta* species, *Rodgersia aesculifolia*.

12. **Drakensberg grassland**   The higher parts of the Drakensberg mountains in Natal are preserved as species-rich grassland by regular careful burning in late winter. Soils are often peaty over a gravelly subsoil and afternoon thunderstorms are frequent in summer. Many of the most familiar species from this area grow along streams or in marshy places. Bulbous plants such as *Cyrtanthus*, *Dierama*, *Gladiolus*, *Moraea* and *Watsonia* are frequent. *Rhodohypoxis* are found in wet, shallow peaty soils. Herbaceous perennials include the following: *Kniphofia*, *Agapanthus*, *Diascia*, *Phygelius*, *Leonotis* (in drier places), *Glumicalyx gosoleoides*.

Colour in an early summer border

Helleborus foetidus

Helleborus foetidus
'Wester Flisk'

Helleborus vesicarius

Helleborus × nigercors

Helleborus lividus

Helleborus purpurascens

Helleborus niger

Helleborus argutifolius

Photographed 10 February. ½ life size

Helleborus niger in the University Botanic Garden, Cambridge

Helleborus × *nigercors* 'Alabaster'

Helleborus × *ericsmithii*

Helleborus lividus 'Boughton Beauty'

Helleborus argutifolius Viv. syns. *H. corsicus* Willd., *H. lividus* subsp. *corsicus* (Willd.) Tutin (*Ranunculaceae*)   Native of Corsica and Sardinia, in maquis scrub, in dry grassy glades among bracken, by streams and roadsides, flowering in January–June. Stems to 75cm, and more across in large specimens. Flowers 2.5–5cm across. Leaf segments green, with coarse spiny teeth. For well-drained soil; hardy to −10°C with shelter. Short-lived, but usually self-seeding.

Helleborus foetidus L. Stinking Hellebore Native of SW Europe, from England and Portugal to Germany and Italy, growing on rocky slopes, roadside banks and open woods, usually on limestone, flowering in January–April. Stems to 80cm, with leaves in a rosette around the inflorescence, usually glossy, very dark green; hardy to −20°C, with shelter from wind. The variety '**Wester Flisk**' has greyish-green leaves with narrower segments and the flower stalks are tinged with red; it comes true from seed. For well-drained soil in sun or part shade, and especially tolerant of dry shade.

Helleborus lividus Ait.   Native of Majorca, growing on limestone rocks and in woods and scrub, flowering in February–April. Stems to 45cm. Leaf segments marked greyish, toothless or with fine small teeth. Flowers and stems often pinkish. Hardy only to −5°C.
'**Boughton Beauty**'   A robust form of *H.* × *ericsmithii*, a hybrid combining the greater size and hardiness of *H. arguifolius* with the colour of *H. lividus*. Hardy to around −10°C.

Helleborus niger L. Christmas Rose   Native of mountain woods, usually on limestone in the E Alps and N Apennines, from S Germany and Switzerland (Ticino) to Italy and Yugoslavia, growing in conifer woods up to the *Pinus mugo* zone, and sometimes in open grassland, flowering in January–April. Flowers 4–8cm across; stems to 30cm in the tallest forms, when the flowers are fading. Many garden forms have been selected, mainly for their tall stems and large flowers. Subsp. *macranthus* (Freyn) Schiffner, from N Italy and Yugoslavia, in spite of claims made for it, is distinguished by its leaves, with spiny teeth on broadly lanceolate, greyish leaflets, and white not pink-tinged flowers, with narrower petals. Cultivation is not always easy, but a rich, limy soil, in partial shade, deeply cultivated, and protection for the buds, young leaves and roots from slugs will give a good chance of success.

Helleborus × **nigercors** J. T. Wall   This is the usual name for hybrids between *H. niger* and *H. arguifolius*, which combine the large white flowers of the former with the profusion of the latter. Unfortunately, these hybrids are sterile, and very hard to propagate vegetatively, so they are usually raised from seed by hand-pollinating *H. niger* with *H. arguifolius* pollen. The resulting seedlings, like that shown here, are closer to *H. niger*; one was named '**Alabaster**' in 1967. Other forms I have seen, closer to *H. arguifolius* with a taller stem, may have been the reciprocal cross. The cross between *H.* × *sternii* and *H.* × *niger* is called *H.* × *ericsmithii*, and may be expected to have a pinkish tinge.

Helleborus argutifolius

Helleborus purpurascens Waldst. & Kit. Native of SE Poland, Hungary and Czechoslovakia to Romania and the W Ukraine, growing in open woods and scrub, flowering in March–April, earlier in gardens in S England. Leaves deciduous, usually with 5 segments, divided to the middle into 2–5 lobes. Stems 5–20cm at flowering. Flowers greenish or purplish, sometimes glaucous outside, 5–7cm across. For a warm position in partial shade in humus-rich, but not acid, soil. Probably the hardiest species.

Helleborus vesicarius Auch.   For fruit and text see page 16.

Helleborus cyclophyllus in N Greece

Helleborus multifidus subsp. *bocconei* near Florence

Helleborus purpurascens

Helleborus atrorubens

Helleborus atrorubens Waldst. & Kit. syn. *H. dumetorum* Waldst. & Kit. subsp. *atrorubens* (Waldst. & Kit.) Merxm. & Podlech (*Ranunculaceae*)   Native of NW Yugoslavia, growing in grassy places and scrub, flowering in February–April. Leaves deciduous to 45cm, with 7–11 undivided segments. Flowers 4–5.5cm across, brownish to deep purplish, inside and out. For a warm, sheltered position. Hardy to –15°C.

Helleborus cyclophyllus Boiss.   Native of Albania, Bulgaria, S Yugoslavia and Greece, growing in woods, scrub and on grassy hillsides, flowering in February–April. Stems to 60cm; leaves deciduous, with 5–9 usually undivided ovate-lanceolate segments, hairy beneath. Flowers *c.* 6cm across, usually yellowish green, but not whitish as in *H. orientalis*. Easily grown in sun or partial shade.

Helleborus multifidus Vis. subsp. **bocconei** (Ten.) B. Mathew syn. *H. siculus* Schiffner Native of C & S Italy, and Sicily, growing in open woods and scrub in the hills, flowering in February–March. Stems to 20cm; leaves evergreen, to 42cm across, with 5–7 leaflets, hairy beneath, each divided to halfway into 3 or 5 segments. Flowers 4.5–6cm across, sweetly scented with a hint of cat, in gardens sometimes opening in late November, as in the form shown here from the hills above Florence. Easily grown in heavy limy soil in partial shade.

Helleborus multifidus Vis. subsp. **multifidus** Native of Albania and W Yugoslavia especially Dalmatia, in scrub and grassy rocky hillsides flowering in March–April. Stems to 50cm; leaves finely divided, with 9–15 segments, each divided into 3–12 lobes. Flowers 3–4 cm across, green. It is the deeply dissected leaves which are the interesting feature of this species, not the rather small flowers. It requires a warm sheltered position in the garden.

Helleborus purpurascens Waldst. & Kit. Native of Romania, Hungary, E Czechoslovakia, SE Poland and W Russia, growing on the edges of woods and scrub, often on sandy soils, flowering in March–April, earlier in gardens in S England. Plant forming eventually low mats. Stems 5–20cm at flowering; leaves deciduous, with 2–6 leaflets, hairy beneath. Flowers appearing before the leaves, 5–7cm across, purplish, reddish or greenish inside, glaucous outside. For a humus-rich, but not acid soil in partial shade.

Helleborus vesicarius Auch.   Native of N Syria and S Turkey, from SW Adiyaman, west to the Amanus and south to Mt Cassius (today Akra Dağ), on limestone rocks and in oak scrub at 550–1300m, flowering in March–May, often earlier in gardens in S England, fruiting in May–June. Plant with a long, swollen rootstock. Stems to 45cm, much branched. Flowers 16–18mm long; capsules inflated, 5–7cm long, with 1–6 large spherical seeds 5–6mm across. Deciduous in summer; leaves appearing in autumn. Easy to grow in a bulb frame, or in some other hot position, kept dry in summer. The plant is liable to die if transplanted, so is best established from pot-grown seedlings. In cultivation the unusual fruits are produced only after cross-pollination. Hardy to –10°C.

Helleborus vesicarius in fruit, near Maraş, S Turkey

Helleborus vesicarius

Helleborus viridis subsp. *occidentalis* with *Anemone nemorosa* at Postling, Kent

Helleborus viridis L. subsp. *occidentalis* (Reuter) Schiffner   Native of NW Europe, from N England (N Yorkshire and Westmorland) south to France, Spain and W Germany (with the larger-flowered and hairy-leaved subsp. *viridis* from C France and Austria to NW Italy), growing in woods and sunny banks on chalk and limestone, flowering in February–April. Stems 20–40cm; leaves deciduous, with 7–11 leaflets, glabrous beneath, narrowly elliptical, serrate. Flowers 3–5cm across, often with purple markings inside, glaucous green. A small-flowered but graceful plant, easily grown in heavy moist soil in partial shade.

Helleborus multifidus subsp. *multifidus*

Helleborus viridis subsp. *occidentalis*

17

HELLEBORUS

Helleborus orientalis
(white seedling)

'Sirius'

Seedling

Seedling

Seedling

Seedling

'Celadon'

Helleborus orientalis
wild form from
Turkey

'Aeneas'

'Dido'

Helleborus orientalis
wild form from
Turkey

Helleborus orientalis
(double seedling)

'Zodiac'

Helleborus orientalis subsp.
guttatus

Seedling

'Atrorubens'

'Picotee'

Seedling

'Queen of the Night'

'Philip Ballard'

Helleborus atrorubens
hybrid

'Cosmos'

A selection of *Helleborus hybridus* seedlings and named cultivars from Washfield Nurseries, 14 February. ⅔ life size

HELLEBORUS

Helleborus hybridus (double seedling)

Helleborus 'Cosmos'

Helleborus orientalis Lam. (*Ranunculaceae*)
Lenten Rose   Native of NE Greece and
European Turkey, eastwards along the Black
Sea coast to the S Caucasus, in Soviet Georgia,
at up to 2200m in Turkey, growing in scrub and
on the edges of woods, usually in grassy places
in heavy soil where it thrives because it is not
grazed. Flowering stems to 60cm; leaves to
60cm, evergreen except in exceptionally cold
winters, with 7–10 usually divided or forked
segments, up to 45cm across.

Flowers in Turkey or Greece, usually whitish
or greenish, rarely with pinkish edges. In the
Caucasus two other subspecies occur as well:
subsp. *abchasicus* (A. Br.) B. Mathew has deep
purple or pinkish-grey flowers, often heavily
spotted with minute spots; it is found mainly in
Abchasia in the W Caucasus, and hybridizes in
the wild with subsp. *orientalis*. The second
subspecies, subsp. *guttatus* (A. Br. & Saur) B.
Mathew has white flowers with larger reddish
spots, and is found near Tblisi in the C
Caucasus, and further east.

All forms are easily grown in rich, heavy soil
in sun or partial shade, in a warm and sheltered
position, kept moist in summer. Hardy below
−15°C, though the leaves are killed by cold
winds around −10°C. The greenish wild-
collected forms from W Turkey may start
flowering as early as November in gardens.

Numerous cultivars called *H. hybridus* have
been selected and named, concentrating on
features such as blackish-purple, white or yellow
flowers, contrasting nectaries, different degrees
of spotting, and flowers which do not hang
down. Unfortunately, the named varieties are
slow to increase and regularly cross- and self-
seed in most gardens. Some nurseries therefore
concentrate on producing good seedling strains.
A selection of such seedlings, from Washfield
Nurseries in Hawkhurst, Sussex, is shown here,
together with some named ones. Particularly
good strains have been raised by Ashwood
Nurseries.
'Aeneas'   A double-flowered form of *H.
torquatus*, found by Elizabeth Strangman in
Crna Gora, Montenegro, Yugoslavia, in 1971.
'Atrorubens' syn. 'Early Purple'   This is not
the same as *H. atrorubens* Waldst. & Kit. but is
an old *H. orientalis* subsp. *abchasicus* form,
known since 1843, with deciduous leaves, and
reddish-purple flowers, appearing earlier than
most other cultivars.
'Celadon'   Probably a hybrid with *H. odorus*,
raised by Elizabeth Strangman.
'Cosmos'   Raised by Eric Smith in *c.*1973.
'Dido'   A double *H. torquatus* found by
Elizabeth Strangman in Crna Gora,
Montenegro, Yugoslavia, in 1971.
'Old Ugly'   Raised by Elizabeth Strangman in
the 1960s. A *Helleborus viridis* hybrid.
'Philip Ballard'   Raised in 1986 by Mrs
Ballard of Malvern, Worcs, who has specialized
in breeding blacks and yellows with large
horizontal blooms.
'Pluto'   Raised by Eric Smith of the Plantsmen
in 1960. A *Helleborus torquatus* hybrid, with
purple nectaries.
'Queen of the Night'   Raised by Elizabeth
Strangman in the 1970s. Note the dark
nectaries.
'Sirius'   Scented; possibly a hybrid of *H.
odorus*, raised by Eric Smith in *c.*1974.
'Zodiac'   A strain, raised by Eric Smith in
*c.*1974.

'Old Ugly'

A white *hybridus* seedling from Boughton

A yellow seedling

A red *hybridus* seedling

'Pluto'

Helleborus hybridus is easily raised from seed,
and often self-sows around the parent plant, so
that there is a danger that these seedlings may
grow up and overwhelm the parents if they are
named cultivars. Old plants are best moved or
divided in winter or early spring while in flower,
before root growth begins; thereafter they
should not be allowed to dry out until
established.

Caltha howellii in NE California

Caltha howellii

Hylomecon japonicum

Chelidonium majus var. *grandiflorum* near Yumin, Sinjiang

Caltha howellii (Huth) Greene (*Ranunculaceae*)   Native of S Oregon and California, from Tulare Co. northwards, and in the northern coast ranges at 1500–3000m, growing in bogs and wet ground by streams, flowering in May–July according to altitude. Plants tufted, to 30cm. Leaves 3–10cm across. Petals 12–16mm long; seed pods stalked. Flowers solitary, on a leafless and unbranched stem. *C. leptosepala* DC. from W North America, from Alaska to Washington, Montana and New Mexico, differs in having the seed pods on very short stalks, and leaves longer than broad. Both require damp peaty soil, preferably by running water. Hardy to −20°C.

Caltha palustris L. King Cup, Marsh Marigold or Cowslip (in America)   Native of most of the Northern Hemisphere from Ireland southwards to Spain, and east to Siberia and Japan; and in North America from Newfoundland to South Carolina, and west to Saskatchewan, growing in marshes, wet alder woods, or by streams, flowering in March–June, according to latitude. Plant with several hollow spreading stems from a central rootstock, to 60cm high. Leaves 5–20cm across. Flowers up to 5cm, usually yellow, or white in var. *alba*, the white form which possibly belongs to var. *himalayensis* (D. Don) Mukerjee. In the Himalayas, where it is very common at 2400–4000m, from Kashmir east to Bhutan, it is commonly white-flowered; flowering in May–August, according to altitude. Easily grown in moist soil, preferably at the edge of water. 'Plena' has double flowers on a rather small plant.

Caltha polypetala Hochst. ex Lorent   Native of Bulgaria, the Caucasus, N & NW Iran and NE Turkey, growing by streams in alpine meadows at 1700–3600m, flowering April–July, usually by melting snow. Differs from *C. palustris* in having 7–10 petals, but is otherwise similar, and probably requires the same treatment in cultivation.

Caltha polypetala of gardens   This large King-cup is frequent in gardens, and usually called *polypetala*. It is, however, quite different to the wild *C. polypetala* Hochst. (q.v.) It has 5 or occasionally 6 petals, not 7–9 which is the distinguishing feature of true *C. polypetala*. The large Kingcup can be recognized by its great size, to 80cm, its creeping and rooting stems, its leaves which are 10–25cm across and its rather sparse but large flowers, 5cm or more across. It is quite different from the creeping subsp. *minor* (Mill.) Clapham from mountains in N England & Ireland, which is always smaller in leaf and flower. In its creeping stems it is also similar to var. *flabellifolia* (Pursh.) Torrey & Gray, but that does not necessarily have large flowers. Var. *barthei* Hance, from Japan, is large in size of leaf and flower, but not creeping. 'Polypetala' grows easily in wet ground or shallow water and is hardy to −20°C, probably lower.

Chelidonium majus L. (*Papaveraceae*) Greater Celandine   Native of much of S & E Europe, NW Africa, Turkey and Asia east to Japan, and naturalized in E North America, growing on rocky slopes, in woods and scrub, flowering in April–August. A short-lived perennial with a fleshy rootstock and stems to 90cm. Flowers normally 2–2.5cm, but in the plants shown

Caltha polypetala of gardens

Caltha palustris var. *alba*

Caltha polypetala in the Caucasus

Caltha palustris 'Flore Pleno'

Caltha palustris near Sellindge, Kent

here, growing in Sinjiang, 3.5cm across. This is var. *grandiflorum* (DC.) Fedde, from C Asia and NW China. A double-flowered variety is also common in cultivation, and a cut-leaved variety, var. *laciniatum* (Mill.) Syme, has deeply cut leaves. Easily grown in any garden soil, and commonly found as a weed in old gardens. Hardy. The plant contains a yellow juice, a traditional remedy for warts.

Hylomecon japonicum (Thunb.) Prantl & Kuen. (*Papaveraceae*)   Native of Honshu, Korea and NE China west to Hubei, growing in woods in valleys and on hills, flowering in April–June. Plant rather like a refined form of poppy, forming small patches, having short rhizomes, and flowering stems to 30–40cm. Flowers with petals 2–2.5cm long. Does well in leafy soil, in semi-shade or shade. Another species, *H. vernalis* Maxim., comes from E Siberia.

Stylophorum diphyllum (Mich.) Nutt. (*Papaveraceae*)   Native of E North America, from W Pennsylvania and Ohio south to Tennessee, and west to Wisconsin and Missouri, growing in damp woods, flowering in March–May. Plant with few, rather delicate stems 30–45cm tall, from a stout root. Leaves deeply and irregularly lobed, the terminal lobe not much larger than the laterals. Flowers *c*.5cm across. Capsule ovoid, with a pointed beak. Easily grown in moist, leafy soil. Hardy to −20°C.

Stylophorum lasiocarpum (Oliv.) Fedde Native of C & E China, in Hubei and Sichuan, growing in woods and scrub, flowering in May. Plant forming dense leafy clumps about 30cm high, 45cm across. Leaves dandelion-like, with a large ovate, toothed terminal segment. Flowers *c*.5cm across. Capsule narrow, cylindrical, 5–8cm long. For leafy soil, in a cool sheltered position; hardy to −15°C perhaps. This plant is cultivated in China for the medicinal properties of its thick root, which contains a red juice.

Stylophorum lasiocarpum

Stylophorum diphyllum

Trollius
'Feuertroll'

Ranunculus acris
'Flore Pleno'

Trollius
'Alabaster'

Trollius 'Helios'

Trollius europaeus

Trollius 'Superbus'

Specimens from Beth Chatto, 20 May. ⅗ life size

Trollius acaulis in Kashmir

Trollius chinensis

Trollius ranunculinus in Turkey

Trollius pumilus

Trollius yunnanensis

Ranunculus baurii from Bustervoedpad

Ranunculus acris L. 'Flore Pleno' (*Ranunculaceae*)   This is a double-flowered form of the common Meadow Buttercup which is such a feature of moist cow pastures in England and western France, flowering in May–July. It is also found wild all across Eurasia from Greenland to Japan. Stems to 100cm. Lowest leave with 3 more or less equal, deeply cut lobes. Not producing runners like *R. repens*, so unlikely to become a nuisance in gardens. The double-flowered form, shown here, has been known since 1580, and is said to have been found wild in Lancashire. Hardy to −25°C or less.

Ranunculus baurii MacOwen syn. *R. cooperi* Oliv.   Native of South Africa, in the Drakensberg, and nearby mountains in Transvaal, and NE Cape Province, at 1900–3000m, growing in marshy peaty places, seasonal pools, bogs and by streams; flowering in October–November, or April–May in gardens in the north. Plant forming clumps of fleshy deciduous leaves. Petiole to 25cm; blade peltate, *c*.8cm across with short, blunt teeth. Flowers *c*.4cm across, shining yellow, with many petals. For moist, peaty soil in full sun. Hardy to −15°C perhaps.

Trollius acaulis D. Don (*Ranunculaceae*) Native of N Pakistan to W Nepal and especially common in Kashmir, growing on moist grassy slopes at 3000–4300m, flowering by melting snow in May–June. Plant forming small clumps. Stems *c*.10cm at flowering time in the wild, soon elongating. Flowers 5cm across. For moist, peaty soil in sun or partial shade, preferably by running water. Hardy to −20°C.

Trollius chinensis Pritz. syn. *T. ledebourii* hort.   Native of N China, growing in wet meadows and by streams, flowering in June–July. Plant forming substantial clumps, with stems to 1m. Leaves deeply divided into narrow lobes. Flowers to 3.5cm across, orange-yellow, the upright narrow petals conspicuous and longer than the stamens. For rich, wet soil by streams or ponds. Hardy to −20°C or below.

Trollius × *cultorum*   A group of hybrids between *T. asiaticus*, *T. chinensis* and *T. europaeus*, about thirty of which are in cultivation at present. They flower from April to June according to variety. Shown here are:
'**Alabaster**'   A beautiful very pale greenish yellow.
'**Feuertroll**'('Fire Globe')   Rich orange yellow.
'**Helios**'   An early-flowering variety. 'Earliest of All' is another early one.
'**Superbus**'   A tall form, though not with exceptionally large flowers.
   Globeflowers require moist, rich soil in sun or partial shade to thrive and flower well. They detest drought. All are hardy to −20°C or less.

Trollius europaeus L. Globeflower   Native of Europe from Scotland and NE Ireland to Finland and N Russia, south to the Alps, Yugoslavia and Romania in the mountains; also in the Caucasus and NE North America, growing in moist or shady meadows, by rocks in streams and in open woods, flowering May–August. Stems 30–70cm, not elongating greatly during flowering. Flowers to 3cm across; nectaries yellow, as long as the stamens. For moist, rich soil in sun or partial shade. Hardy to −20°C or less.

Trollius pumilus D. Don   Native of the Himalayas from Nepal and Bhutan eastwards to Gansu and Shaanxi, growing in alpine meadows and by streams, flowering in June–August. Plant forming small clumps with stems to 30cm, but usually *c*.15cm. Leaves 5cm across. Flowers *c*.3cm across, opening flat, yellow or orange-yellow. A small plant for a moist position in sun or partial shade. Hardy to −20°C.

Trollius ranunculinus (Smith) Stearn syns. *T. caucasicus* Stev., *T. patulus* Salisb.   Native of the Caucasus, NW Iran and NE & E Turkey, by streams in alpine meadows at 2000–3000m, usually flowering near melting snow in May–June. Stem 9–70cm; at first short, elongating during flowering. Petals 5–7; flowers 2.5–3.5cm across, open, with the stamens exposed. For moist soil in full sun by running water. Hardy to −20°C.

Trollius yunnanensis (Franch.) Ulbr. Native of NE Burma and SW China, in the Dali and Lijiang mountains, in Yunnan, Sichuan and Shaanxi, growing in mountain pastures at 3000–3500cm, flowering in June–August. Height to 75cm but usually *c*.30cm, with a branched and sparsely leafy flowering stem. Leaves with 3–5 broad overlapping lobes. Flowers open, *c*.4cm across, usually without narrow, elongated petals. For moist, peaty, but well-drained soil in sun or partial shade. Hardy to −20°C. *T. stenopetalus* Stapf. is very similar and possibly only a variety of *T. yunnanensis*, but is said to differ in its 'more boldly divided leaves and narrower petals'.

Ranunculus aconitifolius beside a stream in the Valais, Switzerland

Ranunculus aconitifolius 'Flore Pleno'

Ranunculus lingua

Ranunculus aconitifolius L. (*Ranunculaceae*)
Native of Europe in the Alps, Jura and S
Carpathians south to C Italy and C Yugoslavia,
growing in subalpine meadows and by streams
at up to 2500m, flowering in June–August.
Stems to 50cm, forming a handsome clump.
Leaves 3–5 lobed, the middle lobe fully divided
from the others; pedicels 1–3 times as long as its
subtending leaf, pubescent near the top. Flowers
10–20mm across. *R. acris* 'Flore Pleno', 'Fair
Maids of France' or 'Fair Maids of Kent' has
been known in gardens since the 16th century. It
has stems up to 60cm and tight double flowers.
Both require rich moist soil in partial shade. *R.
platanifolius* L. is larger, to 130cm, with
straighter stems; leaves 5–7 lobed, the middle
lobe not fully divided from the others. Pedicels
4–5 times as long as the subtending leaves,
usually glabrous near the apex. Common in
Europe, north to Belgium, Norway and Sweden
and extending to Spain, Corsica, Sardinia,
Greece and south-western Russia, in similar
habitats. Both are hardy to −20°C, perhaps less.

Ranunculus bulbosus L. 'F.M. Burton'
The species is native of Europe, Turkey (very
rare), the Caucasus and North Africa, growing
in rather dry grassy places, meadows and
particularly on chalk downs, flowering in
April–June. A variable species divided into
several subspecies. Plant tufted with a swollen
base, sometimes also with fleshy roots. Leaves
3-partite, the middle segment usually stalked.
Flowers with reflexed sepals, and petals
7–15mm long. 'F.M. Burton', shown here, has
pale-yellow flowers.

Ranunculus constantinopolitanus (DC.)
d'Urv. **'Plenus'** syn. *R. bulbosus* 'Speciosus
Plenus'   Native of SE Europe, from Romania
and Bulgaria to Greece and Turkey, south to
Syria and east to the Crimea, the Caucasus and
Iran, growing in damp meadows, flowering in
April–June. Plant forming dense clumps.
Flowering stems 20–75cm. Basal leaves cordate
at the base with 3 deep lobes, each deeply
toothed. Petals 8–15mm long. The double-
flowered form, shown here, has been cultivated
since the 18th century, often under the name *R.
bulbosus* 'Speciosus Plenus' or 'Flore Pleno'. *R.
bulbosus*, however, has a grooved not smooth
pedicel, and a pubescent not glabrous
receptacle. Easily grown in any moist, good soil.
Hardy to −20°C.

Ranunculus cortusifolius Willd.   Native of
the Azores, Madeira and the Canaries, growing
in damp, shady places and roadsides in heather
and laurel forest, flowering in March–April.
Plant with few stems to 100cm, from a group of
several long fleshy roots. Basal leaves up to
30cm wide. Flowers to 50cm across. For rich
soil in sun or partial shade, moist in spring, dry
but shaded in summer. Hardy to −5°C perhaps.

Ranunculus creticus L.   Native of Crete,
Karpathos and Rhodes, growing on limestone
rocks under trees, at up to 400m, flowering in
March–May. A compact perennial, with few
stems to 60cm from a cluster of fleshy roots.
Basal leaves 8–15cm across. Petals 1.5–2.5cm
long. Sepals not reflexed. Easily grown in well-
drained soil in a hot, dry position, dry in

Ranunculus lyallii

Ranunculus penicillatus

Ranunculus creticus from Rhodes

summer. Hardy to −10°C perhaps. *R. cortusifolius* differs in its larger size and thick, leathery leaves.

Ranunculus lingua L. Greater Spearwort Native of most of Europe from Scotland eastwards to the Caucasus, N Turkey, and Siberia, growing in reed swamps and by ponds and canals in shallow water, flowering in June–September. Stems 50–120cm, upright from a creeping rhizome. Basal leaves ovate, or ovate-oblong, cordate, produced in autumn, absent at flowering. Stem leaves oblong-lanceolate. Flowers 2–5cm across. A handsome plant for the margins of ponds and slow streams, with a succession of flowers throughout the summer.

Ranunculus lyallii Hook. fil. Giant Buttercup Native of New Zealand, in South Island from Marlborough southwards, in subalpine meadows and by mountain streams at 450–1500m, flowering in October–January. Stems to 1.5m, though rarely more than 1m in gardens. Leaves peltate, shallowly bowl-shaped, 12–30cm across. Flowers 5–7.5cm across. *R. insignis* Hook. fil. is smaller, with slightly lobed leaves and yellow waxy flowers 2–5cm across. It grows in alpine grassland, wet cliffs and rock crevices at 1000–2000m in both islands, from East Cape to Kaikoura. Both these species need a cool position and moist peaty soil. They grow best in cool moist climates, such as Scotland. Hybrids have been made between the two species, with cream-coloured flowers, but I have never seen them.

Ranunculus penicillatus (Dumort.) Bab. syn. *R. pseudo-fluitans* (Syme) Newbould Native of N & W Europe as far south as Hungary and the Crimea, growing in fast-flowing streams, flowering in May–August. Plant often without floating leaves, with hair-like leaves longer than the internodes forming bright-green mats which are usually all submerged. Flowers with petals 10–15mm long. This species is valued in fast flowing streams because it provides cover for fish without causing silting. As can be seen here, it is also very showy when in flower, usually in May.

Ranunculus constantinopolitanus 'Plenus'

Ranunculus bulbosus 'F. M. Burton'

Ranunculus cortusifolius

Pulsatilla alpina subsp. *apiifolia* above St Luc, Valais

Pulsatilla alpina subsp. *apiifolia*

Pulsatilla alpina near Crans, Valais

Pulsatilla alpina (L.) Delarbre syn. *Anemone alpina* L. (*Ranunculaceae*)   Native of the Pyrenees and the Alps east to Austria and Yugoslavia and of the Caucasus, growing in alpine and subalpine meadows, flowering in May–August, according to altitude, soon after the snow melts. Plant forming clumps, often with many stems up to 45cm. Flowers 4–6cm across. A plant for well-drained, rich, deep, sandy and peaty soil in full sun: seed is reported to take two years to germinate, even when sown fresh. Two subspecies are recognized: subsp. *apiifolia* (syn. *Anemone sulphurea* L.) with pale yellow flowers, usually found on acid soil, and subsp. *alpina*, with white flowers, usually found on calcareous soil. Hybrids between the two are not uncommon. The closely related *P. alba* Rchb. has smaller flowers 2.5–4.3cm across, and usually glabrous leaves with terminal segments divided to the midrib. It is found from C France east to Romania and W Russia on acid soils.

Pulsatilla armena (Boiss.) Rupr. syns. *P. violacea* Rupr., *Anemone albana* Stev. subsp. *armena* (Boiss.) Smirn.   Native of N & E Turkey from Amasya and Erciyes Dağ near Kayseri eastwards to Soviet Armenia, at up to 4200m, in Turkey, flowering in May–June, often growing on volcanic soil. Flowers always nodding, 2–3.5cm long. Stems 3–20cm. Leaves finely divided, silky. Hardy to −25°C.

Pulsatilla chinensis (Bunge) Regel   Native of N China and E Siberia, growing in dry grassy places and rocky hillsides, flowering in April–May. It is common north of Beijing, near the Great Wall, and among the ruins of the Ming Tombs. Plant forming small tufts of few rosettes. Leaves expanding during flowering, finally to 15cm or more long, with flat segments up to 1cm wide. Stems 10–15cm at flowering, elongating to 30cm in fruit. Hardy to −20°C, but reported to be difficult to grow in England, possibly easier in E North America, as it needs a dry winter and spring, and a warm, humid summer.

Pulsatilla halleri (All.) Willd. syn. *Anemone halleri* All.   Native in scattered localities across Europe; five subspecies, differing mainly in their leaves, are recognized from five areas: the SW and C Alps; the Rhodope mountains; the Crimea; the W Carpathians in Poland and Czechoslovakia; SE Austria; they grow in rocky, sunny subalpine meadows at *c.*1500m. Whole plant very silky, even after flowering. Leaves simply pinnate, with 3–5 segments, the terminal segment long-stalked; flowers dark to pale violet; very silky outside. In a sixth, subsp. *grandis* (Wenderoth) Meikle, from S Germany, Austria, Czechoslovakia, and Hungary south to the Crimea, the hairs on the stem and leaves are exceptionally dense, and either silvery or brownish. 'Budapest' is (or was?) a colour form of this subspecies, with pale-blue flowers, originally collected in the Budapest area. For well-drained soil in full sun, with protection from wet in winter; hardy to −20°C or lower.

Pulsatilla chinensis at the Ming Tombs

Pulsatilla vulgaris on Royston Heath

Pulsatilla vulgaris f. rubra

Pulsatilla occidentalis on Carson Pass, E California

Pulsatilla vulgaris f. alba

Pulsatilla occidentalis Freyn. syn. *Anemone occidentalis* Wats.   Native of C California to British Columbia and Montana, growing on steep rocky slopes at 1700–3000m, flowering June–August, according to altitude; often in north-facing gullies, flowering close to melting snow. Plant tufted, with stems to 60cm, elongating during flowering. Leaves 4–8cm wide, ternate, silky, finely bipinnate into linear segments. Petals 5–8, white, bluish outside, or purplish, 2–3cm long. For well-drained, peaty soil. Hardy to –20°C.

Pulsatilla vulgaris Mill. syn. *Anemone pulsatilla* L. Pasque Flower   Native of England, especially East Anglia, and of S Sweden, east to Finland and the Ukraine, growing in dry grassland, often on chalk soils. Plant with many stems to 15cm, from a tufted rootstock, elongating during flowering to 30cm. Flowers purple, 5.5–8.5cm across, appearing with the leaves. Leaves with *c*.40 lobes. Several colour forms of *P. vulgaris* are cultivated, the commonest being f. *alba* (white) and f. *rubra* (red-flowered). Another (not shown) is 'Barton's Pink'; 'Mrs van der Elst' is also pink, but I have seen neither of them. *Pulsatilla rubra* (Lam.) Delerbre is a distinct species from C & S France and Spain, with nodding reddish-brown or blackish flowers. All require well-drained, chalky soil. Hardy to –20°C.

Pulsatilla halleri at the Col de Glaize, France

Pulsatilla armena

Pulsatilla halleri subsp. *grandis*

Anemone demissa at Lijiang

Anemone trifolia

Anemone rivularis

Anemone flaccida at Baoxing, Sichuan, with *Corydalis flexuosa*

Anemone davidii at Baoxing

Anemone sylvestris

Anemone rupicola in Kashmir

Anemone narcissiflora (yellow form)

Anemone narcissiflora (pink form)

Anemone narcissiflora near Mount Elbrus, Caucasus

Anemone tetrasepala above Lake Vishensar, Kashmir

Anemone davidii Franch. (*Ranunculaceae*)
Native of W China, in Sichuan, growing in
grassy places by streams at *c*.2000m, flowering in
May–June. Plants with creeping underground
rhizomes, forming loose colonies. Very variable
in size. Flowers up to 7cm across, but only 4cm
in the form shown here. Easily grown in moist,
peaty soil, and well established on the peat banks
at Kew. Photographed near Baoxing in late May.

Anemone demissa Hook. & Thoms. Native of
W Nepal, Sikkim and Bhutan to SW China
(Yunnan), growing in alpine meadows, grassy
clearings in forest and scrub, and on screes and
rock ledges, at 3000–4750m, flowering in May–
July, according to altitude. Plant with few silky
hairy stems from a stout rootstock, surrounded
by the remains of last year's leaf bases. Stems
10–30cm, with 3–6 flowers on short 2–4cm
pedicels. Petals 7–15mm long, white, yellow or
purple or blue! For well-drained, peaty soil in
full sun, kept moist in summer, dry in winter and
spring. Hardy to −20°C.

Anemone flaccida Schmidt. Native of E Siberia,
Sakhalin, N & W China, and Japan, growing in
shady places in ravines in loose peaty soil, and
along streams in woods, flowering in April–June.
Plant forming clumps of several stems from
short, black, creeping rhizome. Leaves rather
fleshy, divided to the base into 3 or 5 deeply
toothed lobes. Stems 15–30cm, with a pair of
sessile leaves and 1–3 flowers, 1.6–3.5cm across.
Seeds with a very short style, ripening green
while the petals are still fresh. For moist peaty
soil in shade. Hardy to −20°C or less. A modest
but attractive plant for the woodland garden.

Anemone narcissiflora L. Native of NE
Spain, the Pyrenees, the Alps, N Turkey, the
Caucasus, the Urals and mountains across

Siberia to N Japan and in W North America,
growing in grassy, peaty but well-drained
meadows, occasionally in partial shade. Flowers
produced from May (April in gardens in
England) to August according to altitude and
latitude. Very variable; flowers in umbels usually
white, pink-flushed outside, and aptly compared
by Reginald Farrer to apple blossom, but
sometimes pink or pale yellow in the Caucasus.
Stems to 40cm; seeds flattened. Easily grown in
sun or part shade, in moist soil, but rare in
gardens as it is slow to raise from seed and not
easily divided.

Anemone rivularis Buch.- Ham, ex DC.
Native of Kashmir and N India to Tibet and SW
China (Yunnan), at 1800–3060m, in meadows, in
clearings in forest, on bunds between rice fields,
by streams and in hedges, flowering from April–
August. Plant with several arching stems to 1m,
from a tufted rootstock. Flowers rather small,
1.5–3cm across, with 5–8 narrow petals often
blue outside. Clearly distinct from *A. narcissiflora*
and its relatives, by having the flowers on long
stalks of different lengths, not in an umbel.
Easily grown in moist but well-drained soil in sun
or part shade, flowering in late spring. Hardy to
−20°C perhaps.

Anemone rupicola Cambess. Native of
Afghanistan to W China (Yunnan, and more
rarely in Sichuan), growing at 2700–4800m, on
rocky slopes, screes and alpine meadows, usually
steep and north-facing, with little other
vegetation, flowering from May–August, often
near melting snow. Plant with a tufted rootstock,
and stems to 20cm. Flowers 5–8cm across. Basal
leaves 3-lobed. It is related to *A. sylvestris* and has
woolly seeds like *A. vitifolia*. A plant for moist,
well-drained soil, in a cool position, preferably
north-facing but not shaded. Hardy to −20°C.

Anemone sylvestris L. Native of Europe
from S Sweden and NE France eastwards to the
Caucasus but not in the Alps, growing in open
woods and on rocky hills, flowering in May–
June. Plant spreading by root-buds to form
dense colonies, with stems 15–50cm. Flowers
solitary, 4–7cm across, with 5–8 petals. Easily
grown in moist, leafy soil in semi-shade. Hardy
to −20°C or less.

Anemone tetrasepala Royle Native of
Afghanistan to N India, frequent in Kashmir,
growing in meadows, often among large
boulders, at 2100–3600m, flowering from June–
August. Very similar to *A. narcissiflora*, but
basal leaves deeply divided into 5 rather broad,
shallowly incised lobes. Flowers white, often
with 4 petals, but may have up to 7. Stem
30–75cm. For well-drained peaty soil,
preferably moist in summer, with a cool root-
run. Hardy to −20°C.

Anemone trifolia L. Native of N Portugal,
N & E Spain, on acid soils (subsp. *albida*
(Moriz)Tutin), and from Italy and C Austria to
Hungary and N Yugoslavia on limestone
(subsp. *trifolia*), growing in fields, wet
meadows, and open woods, flowering in April–
May, to July in the mountains.
   Plant similar to *Anemone nemorosa*, but
rhizomes less far-creeping, so forming denser
clumps. Leaves 3, each with 3 toothed but not
lobed leaflets. Flowers white, *c*.2cm across.
Anthers white and petals elliptical in subsp.
albida; anthers blue and petals ovate in subsp.
trifolia. For a moist position in leafy soil, or
partial shade. The subsp. *trifolia* is usually
found on limestone; subsp. *albida* on acid soil.
Hardy to −15°C.

Adonis chrysocyathus in Kashmir

Adonis vernalis at Wisley

Adonis volgensis in Turkey

Adonis brevistyla near Lijiang

Actaea alba (L.) Mill. syn. *A. pachypoda* Elliot (*Ranunculaceae*)   Native of E North America, from Nova Scotia south to Georgia, west to Minnesota and Missouri, growing in woods, flowering in April–June, according to latitude. Plant with few stems to 90cm from a stout rootstock, elongating to 120cm in fruit. Flowers to 10mm long, with 4–10 narrow petals, and numerous longer stamens. Fruits white, on thickened, fleshy red stalks. Easily grown in leafy soil, in shade or partial shade. Hardy to –20°C and below. Forma *rubrocarpa* (Killip) Fernald has red fruit on thickened pedicels, in contrast to *A. rubra* in which the berries are also red, but on slender stalks, in a dense inflorescence. *Actaea spicata* L. Baneberry from mountain woods in Europe from N England eastwards, and in N Turkey; has black berries.

Actaea rubra (Ait.) Willd. f. *neglecta* (Gillman) Robinson   Native of North America, from Nova Scotia south to New Jersey, and west to South Dakota and Nebraska, with subsp. *arguta* (Nutt.) Hulton from there westwards to California and Alaska, growing in woods, flowering in April–June. Plant with several stems to 80cm from a stout rootstock. Flowers similar to *A. alba*. Fruits red, on slender green stalks, or white in f. *neglecta*. For leafy soil in shade or partial shade. Hardy to –20°C and lower.

Adonis brevistyla Franch. (*Ranunculaceae*)   Native of Bhutan and W China, e.g. in Lijiang in Yunnan, growing in wet *Tsuga* forest, damp scrub, open mountainsides, and wet ravines at 2500–4110m, flowering in April–June. Plant with few stems from a stout branching root; flowering stems 20–40cm. Leaves 5–10 × 3–8cm long, much divided into flat, acuminate lobes. Petals 1.2–2.5cm × 0.5–1cm, obovate to oblanceolate, white or yellow, often bluish beneath. For moist peaty soil, sheltered from wind in shade or partial shade. Hardy to –20°C or so.

Glaucidium palmatum at the Savill Gardens, Windsor

Adonis chrysocyathus Hook. fil. & Thoms. Native of N Pakistan to W Nepal and Tibet; common in Kashmir, growing on damp grassy slopes and among rocks, often near melting snow, flowering in June–September. Plant 15–23cm in flower; taller, to 40cm, in late flower. Flowers 3–5cm across, with 16–24 petals. For well-drained, moist, sandy, peaty soil. Not common in cultivation. Photographed in Kashmir above Lake Vishensar.

Adonis vernalis L.   Native of E, C & S Europe, from France to Spain to Italy, and north to Russia and Finland, in dry stony grassland and scrub, often on limestone, flowering from April–May. Several stems from a stout, branched rootstock, to 40cm high. Flowers 4–8cm across, with 10–20 petals. Differs from *A. volgensis* in its narrower leaf lobes, fewer petals and often larger flowers. Easily grown in very well-drained, rather dry soil, in sun or part shade, but much loved by slugs, and therefore almost useless in the open garden where slugs are common. Hardy to −20°C.

Adonis volgensis Stev.   Native of Russia, SE Hungary, Romania and the Caucasus, south to Soviet Armenia and NE Turkey, in steppes and dry subalpine meadows at *c*.1800m, flowering from March–May. Flowers 30–35mm across; stems to *c*.30cm. Lobes of leaves linear-lanceolate, dentate. For well-drained, sandy soil, and tolerant of summer drought. Hardy to −25°C. Photographed on Mount Ararat in May.

Anemonella thalictroides (L.) Spach. syn. *Thalictrum thalictroides* (L.) Eames & Boivin (*Ranunculaceae*)   Native of E North America, from New Hampshire and Massachusetts, south to Florida, and west to Ontario, Minnesota and Kansas, growing in damp deciduous and mixed woods, flowering in March–June. Plant with delicate stems to 20cm from a bunch of tuberous roots. Leaves appearing after the flowering stem, with 9 stalked leaflets. Flowers to 2.5cm across, with 5–10, white or pink (f. *rosea*), petal-like sepals. A delicate plant for a loose leafy soil, in shade or partial shade.

Glaucidium palmatum Sieb. & Zucc. Native of Japan, in Hokkaido and N & C Honshu, in woods in the mountains, flowering from May–July according to altitude. Plant with few stems to 30cm, from a stout rootstock. Leaves 8–20cm long and wide, 7–11 lobed. Flowers 5–8cm across, pale mauve or rarely white in var. *leucanthum* Mak. Carpels 2, with flat, obovate winged seeds about 10mm long. For cool, moist leafy soil, in shade and shelter from drying wind. Hardy to −15°C. Similar in general appearance to *Podophyllum*, but DNA studies have shown it to belong in *Ranunculaceae*.

Hydrastis canadensis L. (*Ranunculaceae*) Orange Root   Native of E America, from Connecticut to Minnesota, and in W Ontario, Georgia, Missouri and Kansas, growing in woods, especially in the mountains, flowering in April. Stems several to 30cm from a thick yellowish horizontal rootstock. Basal leaves palmate with 5–9 lobes, 12–20cm across. Flowering stem with 2 leaves, the upper subtending the large solitary flower up to 10mm across, without petals, but with numerous stamens. For leafy soil in shade or partial shade. Hardy to −15°C, or below.

Glaucidium palmatum var. *leucanthum* in the Cruickshank Botanic Garden, Aberdeen

Actaea rubra

Actaea alba f. *rubrocarpa*

Hydrastis canadensis

Anemonella thalictroides f. *rosea*

Anemonella thalictroides near Charlottesville, Virginia

Epimedium × versicolor
'Sulphureum'

Epimedium × versicolor
'Neosulphureum'

Epimedium alpinum

Epimedium pubigerum
(from E Turkey)

Epimedium pubigerum

Epimedium × cantabrigiense

Specimens from Washfield Nurseries, Kent, 17 April. ½ life size

Epimedium alpinum L. (*Berberidaceae*)
Native of SE Europe from N & C Italy to
Austria and south to Albania, and naturalized
elsewhere in N Europe including England;
growing in shady, rocky places in the foothills
and low mountains, flowering in April–May.
Plant forming loose patches by a creeping
rhizome. Stems 15–30cm, with a single leaf
longer than the inflorescence. Leaflets 5–10,
deciduous, pubescent beneath when young,
later glabrous. Flowers 9–13mm across. Inner
sepals dark red; petals bright yellow. Easily
grown in well-drained soil in shade. Hardy to
−20°C.

Epimedium × *cantabrigiense* Stearn   A
hybrid between *E. pubigerum* and *E. alpinum*
which arose in the 1940s in the Wilderness
Garden at St John's College, Cambridge,
among W. T. Stearn's collection of *Epimedium*
species, planted out there during the war. Plant
forming a mound of firm leaves, 30–60cm tall.
Leaves evergreen, usually with 9 leaflets, to 10 ×
7cm. Flowers *c*.1cm across. Inner sepals red;
petals pale yellow, reduced to nectaries. Easily
grown in well-drained soil in partial shade.
Hardy to −20°C perhaps.

Epimedium dolichostemon Stearn   Native
of China, in E Sichuan and SW Hubei,
discovered and introduced by Mikinori Ogisu.
Plant forming small clumps of evergreen leaves.
Leaflets 3, sagittate, acuminate, with spines on
edges and tip, *c*.10cm long, 3cm wide.
Inflorescence with 2 leaflets, the main branch
overtopping the leaves, *c*.35cm high. Flowers
whitish; inner sepals 8–9mm long, slightly
reflexed. Stamens 8–9mm long, the filaments
longer than the anthers. Nectaries small and
strongly curved. A very graceful species, for
moist woodland conditions. Hardy to −15°C
perhaps. *E sagittatum* (Sieb. & Zucc.) Maxim. is
similar in habit, but has smaller flowers *c*.6mm
across, inner sepals 3–4.5mm long, and stamens
4–5mm long, the filaments shorter than the
anthers. It is native of China, in NW Hubei,
growing on shady rocks in the mountains.
Hardy to −20°C or so.

Epimedium pubigerum (DC.) Morr. &
Decne.   Native of SE Bulgaria and Turkey,
from near Istanbul eastwards along the Black
Sea coast to W Georgia, growing in woods,
scrub and hedges, flowering in April–May.
Plant forming evergreen clumps, with short
rhizomes. Stems 20–70cm, with 1–2 leaves,
shorter than the much-branched inflorescence.
Leaflets usually 9, to 8cm long, pubescent
beneath. Flowers *c*.1cm across; inner sepals pink
or white; petals yellow. Easily grown in leafy soil
in partial shade, but often damaged, as are most
Epimediums, by late frosts. Hardy to −15°C.

Epimedium × *versicolor* Morr.   A hybrid
between *E. grandiflorum* and *E. pinnatum* subsp.
colchicum, known since 1854. Plant forming a
mound of leaves to 30cm high and across.
Flowering stem leafy or leafless. Flowers 2cm
across. Petals about equal to inner sepals; spurs
6–9mm. 'Sulphureum' and 'Neosulphureum'
are two clones of this cross. 'Sulphureum'
usually has 5 leaflets, or up to 9, and a leafy
flowering stem. 'Neosulphureum' usually has 3
leaflets, brownish when young, and slightly
shorter spurs. Other hybrids of this parentage,
such as 'Versicolor' and 'Cuprea', have pinkish
or reddish sepals. All are easily grown in partial
shade and leafy soil. Hardy to −20°C.

Epimedium × *youngianum* Fisch. & Mey.
A hybrid between *E. diphyllum* and *E.
grandiflorum*, possibly of wild origin in Japan.
Plant forming small clumps of leaves, with 2–6
or 9 leaflets 2–8cm long, 1–5cm across, to 15cm
tall. Flowering stem 10–30cm. Petals obovate,
with or without spurs, which vary in size and
shape. Selected forms include 'Roseum' syn.
'Lilacinum'?; 'Violaceum' (pinkish mauve);
'Niveum' (flowers small, white); 'Yenomoto
Form' (a good white, larger than 'Niveum').
For moist leafy soil in a partially shaded
position, moist in summer. Hardy to −20°C or
less. The easiest of the smaller species.

Epimedium dolichostemon   Epimedium pubigerum

Epimedium × *versicolor* 'Neosulphureum'

Epimedium × *youngianum* 'Yenomoto Form'

Epimedium × *youngianum* 'Niveum'

Epimedium × *youngianum* 'Violaceum'

Epimedium × rubrum

Epimedium × warleyense

Epimedium perralderianum

Epimedium
× perralchicum 'Wisley'

Epimedium davidii
(p. 36)

Epimedium × perralchicum
'Fröhnleiten'

Specimens from Washfield Nurseries, Kent, 17 April. ⅔ life size

Epimedium × *perralchicum* Stearn 'Wisley' (*Berberidaceae*) A hybrid between *E. pinnatum* subsp. *colchicum* and *E. perralderianum* which appeared at Wisley where the parents were growing together. 'Fröhnleiten' is a German hybrid of similar parentage. Both clones are robust plants with good yellow flowers and evergreen leaves; leaflets spiny at the margin, the spines up to 2.5mm long. The flowering stems are leafless, and the spurs slightly upcurved. Hardy to −15°C or lower if protected by dry leaves or snow.

Epimedium perralderianum Cosson Native of Algeria, growing in oak woods and scrub and under ceders, on the north side of the Babor mountains, at 1300–1500m, flowering in March. Plant forming clumps of shining evergreen leaves, with 3 spiny-edged leaflets, up to 30cm tall. Flowering stem without leaves, *c.*20cm. Flowers 15–25mm across; inner sepals 8–11mm, obovate. For sun or partial shade, with shelter from cold winds. Hardy to −15°C.

Epimedium pinnatum Fisch. subsp. *colchicum* (Boiss.) Busch Native of NE Turkey from Trabzon eastwards to the W Caucasus, growing in pine woods and azalea and oak scrub, at up to 50m in Turkey, flowering in April. Plant forming dense clumps with short rhizomes. Leaves with 3 or 5 leaflets, broadly ovate, to 15cm long, glaucescent beneath, sparsely toothed or smooth on the margin. Inflorescence leafless, 20–40cm, glandular or glabrous. Flowers *c.*18mm across. Petals small with a dentate lamina, and a brown or yellow spur, 2mm long. Easily grown in leafy, heavy soil in semi-shade, but slow-growing. Hardy to −15°C. Subsp. *pinnatum* differs in having more, smaller and spinier leaflets, and brownish-purple spurs, *c.*1mm long. It is found in *Parrottia* and hazel scrub in the Talysh mountains in Soviet Azerbaijan, and in N Iran, both in the Talysh and the Caspian forest.

Epimedium × *rubrum* C. Morren A hybrid between *E. grandiflorum* and *E. alpinum* known since 1854. Plant with long, thin rhizomes, forming spreading clumps. Leaves red when young and when old. Flower stem to 20cm, with leaves. Inflorescence sparsely hairy or hairless. Flowers 1.8–2.5cm across. Inner sepals crimson; petals pale yellow, with short spurs. For leafy or peaty soil in partial shade; one of the most beautiful of all foliage plants for ground cover. Hardy to −15°C.

Epimedium × *warleyense* Stearn A hybrid between *E. alpinum* and *E. pinnatum* subsp. *colchicum* raised in Miss Willmott's garden at Warley Place in Essex in around 1909. Plant with a shortly creeping rhizome, forming large clumps of evergreen leaves. Flowering stems to 50cm, leafless or with 1 leaf, in April–May. Flowers 15mm across; inner sepals coppery red, petals yellow, anthers green. For any good soil in partial shade. Hardy to −15°C.

Vancouveria chrysantha Greene (*Berberidaceae*) Native of SW Oregon in Josephine Co. and N California, growing on open rocky hillsides in *Ceanothus* and *Arctostaphylos* scrub, among *Berberis* or bracken, at up to 1200m, flowering in June. Plant creeping to form open patches. Stems *c.*20–40cm. Leaflets *c.*4cm, dark green and stiff in texture, evergreen. Flowers 1–1.3cm across,

on very glandular stalks. Suitable for a warm, sheltered, and partly shaded position in sandy soil. Hardy to −10°C.

Vancouveria hexandra (Hook.) Morr. & Decne. Native of N Washington and Oregon south to C California (Mendocino Co.), growing in shady woods (usually pine or Redwood), at below 1500m, flowering in May–June. Plant creeping to form large, loose patches. Stem 10–40cm, without leaves. Leaflets up to 7.5 × 7cm, thin, not leathery, deciduous. Flowers 1–1.3cm long, to 18mm across, white; sepals, stamens and ovary glandular, but pedicels glabrous. For leafy soil in sun or partial shade. Hardy to −15°C.

Vancouveria planipetala Calloni Native of California, from Montery Co. northwards to SW Oregon, growing in Redwood forests near the coast at up to 600m, flowering in May–June. Plant with creeping rootstock and evergreen leaves, with thick, leathery leaflets, with a thickened and wavy margin, to 4cm long. Flower stem leafless to 50cm. Flowers white or purplish, 6–8mm across; sepals, stamens and ovary glabrous, but pedicels glandular. For a sunny or partially shaded, but warm, position with shelter in winter. Hardy to −10°C, perhaps.

Epimedium × *rubrum* (young leaves)

Epimedium × *rubrum*

Epimedium pinnatum subsp. *colchicum*

Vancouveria chrysantha at Washfield Nurseries

Vancouveria hexandra at Branklyn

Vancouveria planipetala

Epimedium davidii with *Sanicula* species, in mixed *Rhododendron* forest, south of Ya-an, Sichuan

Epimedium acuminatum Franch.
(*Berberidaceae*)   Native of Guizhou, Yunnan and Sichuan, especially on Emei Shan, growing in moist deciduous woods and scrub in the mountains at 1400–4000m, flowering from April–June. Plant tufted, sometimes with a creeping rhizome. Stems 25–50cm; leaflets acuminate, *c*.8–18cm long, 1.5–7cm across, glabrous and reddish when young, but bristly below when mature. Inflorescence glabrous or sparsely glandular. Flowers 3–4cm across, yellow, white, purple or pinkish. Requires moist, leafy soil in a very sheltered position. This plant was collected by Roy Lancaster (L. 575) on Mount Omei.

Epimedium davidii Franch.   Native of W Sichuan, especially Baoxing and Emei Shan, in woods, scrub and shady leafy places in rocky gorges at 1600–2340m, flowering from April–June. Plant tufted, with a slowly creeping rhizome. Stems up to 30–50cm, with leaflets 6 × 4.5cm, glaucescent beneath and thinly pubescent, with short appressed hairs. Inflorescence very glandular. Flowers 2–3cm across, yellowish. Petals with curved spurs and a long blade forming a cup 7–13mm deep.

Epimedium diphyllum (Morr. & Decne.) Lodd.   Native of Japan, in Shikoku and Kyushu, growing in woods in the mountains, flowering in April–May. Plant forming small mounds of leaves to 30cm high and across, but usually lower. Leaves usually with only 2

leaflets, evergreen, often with few spines on the edge, 2.5–5cm long, obtuse, cordate. Flowering stem leafless. Flowers white, or rarely purplish, 10–12mm across; petals without spurs. For moist, leafy soil in a sheltered position. Hardy to −15°C. *E. setosum* Koidz, has similar flowers, but is deciduous, with longer, sagittate and acute leaflets.

Epimedium grandiflorum C. Morren syn. *E. macranthum* Morr. & Decne.   Native of Honshu, Hokkaido and Kyushu, growing in moist woods in the hills, flowering in March–May. Plant forming small clumps 20–40cm high, and finally more across, from a short rhizome. Leaves deciduous, with leaflets, 3–6cm long. Flowers white or purple in f. *violaceum* (C. Morren) Stearn (syn. 'Lilacinum'). Petals with long, downward-curving spurs 1–2cm long and limb 5–8mm long. For leafy soil with shade and shelter. Hardy to −20°C. Several very attractive cultivars of this species are grown in Japan, Europe and North America. The commonest are: 'Rose Queen' (pinkish), 'White Queen' (white) and 'Nanum', a dwarf (with leaves) only 7.5cm tall. Var. *higoense* Shimizu grows on limestone rocks in Higo province, Kyushu, and has leaves minutely hairy above. *E. sempervirens* Nakai, from C Japan, is similar, but has evergreen leaves, very glaucous beneath, and white or purplish flowers.

Epimedium leptorrhizum Stearn   Native of C China, in Guizhou (Kweichow) province,

near Guiyang, growing in woods, flowering in April. Rhizome thin, 1–2mm across, long-creeping. Basal and cauline leaves 3-foliolate; leaflets narrowly ovate, long acuminate, glaucous and pubescent beneath, 3–9.5cm long. Flowers 4cm across; petals without a lamina, with a 2cm-long spur. For moist, leafy soil in cool shade, and not tolerant of drought. Hardy to −10°C perhaps.

Epimedium membranaceum K. Meyer   Native of W Sichuan, near Wenchuan, at 1800m, growing in woodland and scrub, flowering in May–July. Plant forming a mound of evergreen leaves to 40cm. Leaves with 3 leaflets, *c*.8cm long, 4.5cm across, with spiny edges, glaucous beneath. Inflorescence with 2 leaves, a repeatedly branched irregular cyme, 15–20cm, longer than the leaves, with scattered hairs. Flowers with yellow spurs 2–7cm long, and almost no petal limb, on glandular pedicels. Easily grown in leafy or peaty soil in partial shade. Hardy to −15°C.

Epimedium setosum Koidz.   Native of SW Honshu, in Shigoku district, growing in woods, flowering from April–May. Plant forming small mounds of deciduous leaves, 25–40cm high. Leaflets 6–10cm long, 3–4cm wide, acute, with long brown hairs beneath when young. Inflorescence with one leaf. Flowers white, 10–12mm across, with short spurs. For leafy soil in a partially shaded and sheltered position. Hardy to −10°C, perhaps lower.

Epimedium grandiflorum 'Rose Queen'

Epimedium diphyllum

Epimedium grandiflorum f. *violaceum*

Epimedium grandiflorum

Epimedium membranaceum

Epimedium acuminatum at Sandling Park, Kent

Epimedium setosum

Epimedium leptorrhizum at Washfield Nurseries, Kent

Achlys triphylla at the Royal Botanic Garden, Edinburgh

Caulophyllum thalictroides

Diphylleia cymosa at Sellindge, Kent

Achlys triphylla (Sm.) DC. (*Berberidaceae*)
Deerfoot, Vanilla leaf   Native of N California, in the Coast Ranges, north to British Columbia, growing in moist forests in the mountains, below 1500m, flowering in April–June. Plant forming patches by scaly, creeping rhizomes. Leaves trifoliate, with leaflets 5–10cm long. Flowering stems 25–50cm. Flowers without petals, but with 6–13 white stamens. A second very similar species, *A. japonica* Maxim., is found in N Japan, in Hokkaido and N Honshu. It appears to have fewer flowers in the spike and leaves with only 3 shallow lobes. For moist leafy soil in partial shade. Hardy to −15°C.

Caulophyllum thalictroides (L.) Michx. (*Berberidaceae*) Blue Cohosh   Native of New Brunswick south to South Carolina and Tennessee, growing in dry woods in the mountains in the south, flowering in April– May. Plant forming large patches which must be of great age, since it is slow to increase in gardens. Stem to 75cm, bearing leaflets to 7.5cm. Sepals 9, greenish-brown; petals 6, reduced to nectaries; seeds blue, berry-like. *C. thalictroides* var. *robustum* from Japan, E Siberia and China, commonly has yellowish-green flowers, but is otherwise little different. Suitable for growing in dense shade of deciduous trees. Hardy to −20°C or less.

Diphylleia cymosa Michx. (*Berberidaceae*)
Umbrella-leaf   Native from Virginia to Georgia in the Appalachians, by mountain streams, flowering from May–June. Plant with a stout rootstock forming a dense clump of stems to 1m: leaves 2, deeply 2-lobed, 10–40cm across. Flowers c.10 in an umbel. Petals 6, 1–1.5cm long. Fruits 10mm long, with blue or red pedicels. *D. grayi* Fr. Schm. and *D. sinensis* Li, from mountains in Hokkaido, Honshu, have stems 30–70cm, smaller leaves, less deeply divided, and fewer flowers often in a cyme, with fruits on green pedicels. From photographs it would appear to be less coarse as a garden plant. Easily grown in shade or partial shade and shelter in moist leafy soil. Hardy to −15°C or lower.

Jeffersonia diphylla (L.) Pers. (*Berberidaceae*)
Native of New York State and Ontario, south to Alabama and west to Wisconsin, growing in rich woods on limestone, flowering in May. Plant forming a small clump of leaves, with stems up to 20cm, lengthening in fruit. Flowers to 3.5cm across, petals 8. Capsule splitting straight across the top. Suitable for a choice position in cool leafy soil. Hardy to −20°C or less.

Jeffersonia dubia (Maxim.) Benth. & Hook. Native of Manchuria, and around Vladivostock, growing in forest and scrub, flowering in April–May. Plant forming small clumps with stems up to 20cm, and leaves to 10cm across. Flowers 2.5cm across: petals 5 or 6, rarely white. Capsule splitting obliquely. For moist peaty soil in partial shade. Hardy to −20°C.

Podophyllum hexandrum Royle syn. *P. emodi* Wall. (*Berberidaceae*)   Native of NE Afghanistan, in Nuristan, east to C China, at 2000–3500cm, growing in scrub, forest and alpine meadows, flowering in May–August. Plant forming a clump of stems from a thick rhizome, with stems up to 30cm at flowering,

Jeffersonia dubia

Jeffersonia diphylla

Podophyllum peltatum

Podophyllum hexandrum

Podophyllum peltatum in New York State, April

Podophyllum hexandrum at the Royal Botanic Gardens, Kew

later taller. Leaves unfurling after flowering, finally 12–25cm across, 3–5 lobed, variably marked with purple. Petals 6, 2.5–4cm long. Fruits reddish, 2–5cm long, edible but insipid. Var. *chinense* Wall. has larger pink flowers and more deeply divided leaves. For leafy soil in partial shade and a cool position. Hardy to −20°C.

Podophyllum peltatum L. May Apple, American Mandrake, or Wild Jalap   Native of North America, from Quebec and Ontario south to Florida and Texas, growing in moist open woods, scrub and wet meadows, flowering in April–June. Plant forming large patches with a creeping rhizome. Leaves well developed at flowering; flowers *c.*5cm across, hidden beneath the leaves. Petals 9. Easily grown in moist shady position; this plant is interesting rather than showy. Hardy to −15°C or less.

Podophyllum pleianthum Hance   Native of Taiwan, C & SE China, growing in forests at 100–2500m, flowering in March–April. Stems up to 80cm, from a short, thick rhizome. Leaves *c.*30cm across, peltate, with 6–9 shallow obtuse lobes. Flowers 5–8, with 6–9 petals up to 6cm long. Easily cultivated in leafy soil, but probably not very hardy – perhaps to −5°C. *P. versipelle* Hance, found on woods and shady rocks in Hubei, Sichuan, Yunnan and Xizang, is smaller than *P. pleianthum*, with leaves usually 15cm across, more deeply lobed, and petals 2–3.5cm long. Hardy at Kew to −10°C.

Podophyllum pleianthum at Sellindge, Kent

Dicentra spectabilis 'Alba'

Dicentra formosa
'Zestful'

Dicentra formosa

Dicentra formosa
'Langtrees'

Dicentra formosa 'Bountiful'

Dicentra spectabilis

Dicentra formosa
'Stuart Boothman'

Dicentra formosa
'Adrian Bloom'

Dicentra eximea

Specimens from Wisley, 14 April. ½ life size

Dicentra macrantha at the Royal Botanic Gardens, Kew

Dicentra formosa 'Langtrees'

Dicentra eximea 'Alba'

Dicentra cucullaria in the Blue Ridge Mountains, Virginia

Dicentra formosa in *Sequoiadendron* forest, Yosemite, California

Dicentra cucullaria (L.) Bernh. (*Papaveraceae*) Native of E North America, from Nova Scotia south to North Carolina and west to Kansas, growing in cool places in mountain woods, flowering in May–September. Plant forming dense clumps from a tuberous rhizome. Leaves very finely divided. Stems 12–25cm, little longer than the leaves. Flowers 12–16mm long, the outer petals wide-spreading at the base. For cool leafy soil in shade. Hardy to −20°C and below.

Dicentra eximia (Ker-Gawl.) DC. Native of E North America, in New York south to Georgia and Tennessee, growing in rocky places in woods in the mountains, flowering in May–September. Plant forming compact patches, without a creeping rhizome. Stems to 60cm, little longer than the leaves. Flowers 16–20mm long, narrower than those of *D. formosa* and with more reflexed outer petals, pinkish, or white in 'Alba'. For moist but well-drained soil, growing well on rock outcrops in shade. Hardy to −20°C

Dicentra formosa (Haw.) Walp. Native of W North America, in the Sierra Nevada in C California, and in the Coast Ranges, growing in Redwood and *Sequoiadendron* forest, and oak woodland, in dry or damp places in shade, at up to 2000m, flowering in March–July. Plant with fleshy creeping rootstock, forming small

patches. Leaves to 50cm, usually c.25cm. Flower stems slightly longer than the leaves; flowers 14–18mm long.
Two subspecies are recognized in the wild:
Subsp. *nevadensis* (Eastw.) Munz from Tulare Co., at up to 3000m, has finely dissected leaves and usually pale outer and creamy inner petals, flowering in July.
Subsp. *oregona* (Eastw.) Munz from the inner coast ranges in Del Norte Co. and S Oregon, has shorter stems to 25cm, and yellowish outer petals and pink-tipped inner ones. It flowers in April–May. These have been selected and hybridized in cultivation to produce several cultivars:
'Adrian Bloom' Narrowish greyish leaves and deep pink flowers.
'Alba' Flowers pure white; leaves green.
'Bountiful' Deep purplish-red flowers.
'Langtrees' is a very attractive variety with broad silver-grey leaflets and cream and pink flowers.
'Stuart Boothman' Small, with very narrow leaflet and deep-pink flowers on shorter stems.
'Zestful' Paler pinkish flowers, close to the wild type of *D. formosa*.
All grow easily in partial shade in good soil and flower all summer if kept moist. The greyer, narrower-leaved forms do well in full sun also. Hardy to −20°C, perhaps.

Dicentra macrantha Oliver Native of E China, growing in wet woods, flowering in May. Plant with long-creeping, fleshy, brittle, thin rhizomes, forming spreading patches when growing happily! Leaves with yellow stalks, to 45cm, with leaflets c.5cm long, coarsely toothed, but not lobed. Flowers c.7.5cm long. A beautiful and elegant plant, but difficult to grow. It needs shelter from any wind, and from late frost, and a moist leafy and sandy soil, with protection from slugs. Hardy to −15°C, perhaps. Another yellow-flowered species. *D. chrysantha* (Hook. & Arn.) Walp., is an upright plant to 1.5m, with masses of small, 1.3cm upward-facing flowers and finely divided, glaucous leaves. It is found in dry chaparral, especially after a burn, in S California.

Dicentra spectabilis (L.) Lemaire Bleeding Heart Native of N China, in Heilongjiang (Manchuria) (very rare), and in Korea, growing in woods, and deep shady valleys, flowering in May–July, but in spring in gardens. Plant with fleshy arching stems to 60cm, from a thick root. Flowers c.2.5cm long, red or pure white in 'Alba'. 'Gold Heart', raised by Nori and Sandra Pope at Hadspen, Somerset, has golden leaves and red flowers. Easily grown in moist sandy soil in partial shade. Hardy to −20°C and below.

Cardamine diphylla

Sanguinaria canadensis

Cardamine bulbifera

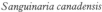

Cardamine enneaphyllos at Wisley

Cardamine laciniata in the Blue Ridge Mountains

Cardamine laciniata

Cardamine bulbifera (L.) Crantz syn.
Dentaria bulbifera L. (*Cruciferae*) Coral-root
Native of S Scotland and France eastwards to
Turkey, the Caucasus, N Iran and C Russia,
growing in wet woods of oak (in S England) or
beech, flowering in April–June. Root fleshy,
creeping underground. Stems to 70cm, with
bulbils in leaf axils. Petals 12–16mm long,
usually purplish. Easily grown, and interesting
rather than showy. Propagates quickly from
bulbils but requires moist soil to flower well.
Hardy to −20°C and less.

Cardamine diphylla (Michx.) Wood syn.
Dentaria diphylla Michx.   Native of E North
America from Nova Scotia and New Brunswick,
south to Minnesota, Kentucky and South
Carolina, growing in moist woods and
meadows, flowering in April–May. Plant with
creeping underground fleshy rhizome and
upright stems to 35cm. Stem-leaves 2, opposite,
with 3 ovate, shallowly crenate lobes. Basal
leaves 3-foliolate. Flowers white, 12–16mm
across. *C. maxima* (Nutt.) Wood is similar but
has usually 3 alternate leaves and larger purplish
flowers. For moist leafy soil in deciduous shade.
Hardy to −20°C and less.

Cardamine enneaphyllos (L.) Crantz syn.
Dentaria enneaphyllos L.   Native of the E Alps
and Carpathians to Albania and Yugoslavia,
growing in subalpine woods. Rhizome swollen,
to 6mm in diameter. Stems 20–30cm. Leaves
ternate or digitate. Petals 12–16mm, pale yellow
or white, almost equalling the stamens. For
sandy leafy soil in partial shade, moist in
summer. Hardy to −20°C.

Cardamine heptaphylla (Vill.) O.E. Schulz
syn. *Dentaria pinnata* Lam.   Native of Spain in
the Pyrenees, and France to SW Germany, W
Switzerland and NE Italy (Monte Baldo) and in
the Apennines in Italy, growing in woods in the
mountains, flowering in April–May. Rhizome
scaly, 4–10mm thick. Stems 30–60cm, usually
*c.*30cm. Leaves pinnate, leaflets varying from
3–5 pairs on lowest leaves, 2–3 pairs on upper
leaves. Flowers usually white, rarely pink or
purplish, petals 14–20mm long. For rich sandy
and leafy soil in shade or partial shade, moist in
summer. Hardy to −20°C or so.

Cardamine kitaibelii Becherer syn. *Dentaria
polyphylla* Waldst. & Kit.   Native of
Switzerland, the Apennines and Yugoslavia,
growing in scrub at up to 1700m, flowering in
April–May. Rhizome scaly, 3–6mm thick; stem
20–30cm, elongating during flowering. Leaves
pinnate with 2–6 pairs of coarsely-toothed

Cardamine kitaibelii

Cardamine pentaphyllos at Sellindge, Kent

leaflets. Petals 15–22cm. For moist, leafy soil. Hardy to −20°C.

Cardamine laciniata (Muhl.) Wood syn. *Dentaria laciniata* Muhl. Cut-leaved Toothwort Native of E North America, from Quebec south to Florida, west to Minnesota, Kansas and Louisiana, growing in moist woods, often in the mountains, flowering in April–June. Plant with short creeping underground fleshy but not scaly rhizome and upright stems to 35cm. Leaves 5–12.5cm across, 3-lobed with the lobes deeply cut and toothed. Flowers pale purplish or white, 14–18mm across. For moist leafy soil, in deciduous shade. Hardy to −20°C or less.

Cardamine microphylla (Willd.) O.E. Schulz syn. *Dentaria microphylla* Willd.   Native of the Caucasus, and recorded from Mount Ararat (Ağri Dağ) in Turkey, growing on damp screes, in shady ravines, scrub, and by mountain streams at 2000–3000m, flowering in July–September. Rhizomes scaly and creeping, so the plant forms spreading mats. Stems to 15cm. *C. quinquefolia* (Bieb.) Schmalh is very similar but has biserrate leaflets in 2–3 pairs and purple petals 14–18mm long. From Bulgaria and Romania to Turkey and the Caucasus. Beautiful but has proved shy-flowering in cultivation and rather invasive. Hardy to −20°C or less.

Cardamine pentaphyllos (L.) Crantz syn. *Dentaria digitata* Lam.   Native of Spain (in the Pyrenees) to S Germany, Austria and N Yugoslavia, growing in woods in the mountains, flowering in May–June. Rhizome scaly, 1.5–2.5mm wide. Stems 30–60cm, usually nearer 30cm. Leaves digitate or ternate, with 3–5 leaflets. Petals 18–22mm, white or pale purple. For sandy, leafy soil in partial shade, moist in summer. Hardy to −20°C or so.

Sanguinaria canadensis L. (*Papaveraceae*) Bloodroot   Native of E North America, from Nova Scotia west to Nebraska, south to Arkansas and N Florida, growing in woods and shaded slopes, in the mountains in the south, flowering in April–May. Plant slow creeping from a thick rhizome with red juice. Leaves folded and vertical before they unfold, finally 15–30cm across, variably lobed. Flowering stem *c.*10cm at flowering, petals up to 2cm long, usually 8–16, but many more in the double-flowered form which is commonly cultivated. For leafy soil in a cool position in deciduous shade. Hardy to −20°C or less. The single-flowered wild form, shown here, is more graceful than the double, but the flowers are very short-lived.

Cardamine heptaphylla at Sellindge, Kent

Cardamine microphylla near Kasbegi, C Caucasus

CARDAMINE

Cardamine pratensis in Kent

Cardamine pratensis 'Flore Pleno'

Cardamine rhaphanifolia in the Royal Botanic Garden, Edinburgh

Cardamine macrophylla at Baoxing, Sichuan

Cardamine amara by the River Don in Aberdeenshire

Cardamine amara L. (*Cruciferae*) Large Bittercress   Native of most of Europe from Scotland and Ireland to Spain and Portugal eastwards to C Asia and Siberia, by rivers, streams and in wet woods usually in trickling water, flowering in April–June. Plant with creeping rhizome and stolons, so making large patches. Stems 10–60cm, usually *c*.30cm. Petals 7–9mm across, nearly always chalky white with dark anthers, but rarely pale purple. Basal leaves with 5–9 ovate or orbicular leaflets. Easily grown in moist soil in sun or partial shade. An invasive plant for the wild garden. Hardy to −20°C or less.

Cardamine macrophylla Franch.   Native of China, in W Sichuan, growing by mountain streams and in damp woods at 2000–3000m, flowering in April–June. Rhizomes thin and fleshy, not far creeping. Stems upright, to 70cm. Basal leaves pinnate, with many pairs of

leaflets. Flowers *c*.1cm across. For moist leafy soil in shade or by water. Hardy to −15°C.

Cardamine pratensis L. Cuckoo flower, Lady's Smock   Native of most of Europe, to W Siberia and across northern North America, growing in damp meadows, by streams and in ditches, flowering from April–June. A variable plant of graceful habit, with stems 15–55cm, usually *c*.20cm, high. Roots fleshy, sometimes with stolons. Flowers pale pinkish purple, more rarely whitish, opening in the sun; petals 8–13mm. Very pretty, not invasive, and one of the best native species for damp gardens, but may require protection from wood pigeons, which eat the young buds in the spring. It is a host of the Orange Tip butterfly. The double form, '**Flore Pleno**', has been grown in gardens since at least the mid-17th century.

Cardamine rhaphanifolia Pourr. syn. *C.*

latifolia Vahl.   Native of NW Spain, the Pyrenees and S Alps to Greece, Turkey and the Caucasus, growing in streams and springs in alpine meadows, and open woods, flowering in May–July. Stems 30–70cm, several from a creeping rhizome. Leaves with 1–5 pairs of leaflets, the terminal one large, 3–7cm wide. Petals 8–12mm, pinkish purple. For moist or wet soil in full sun. Hardy to −20°C.

Cardamine trifolia L.   Native of C Europe, in the Alps and Carpathians, the Apennines and C Yugoslavia; rare in the west, growing in damp woods and shady places, flowering in April–June. Stem 20–30cm; rhizomes creeping, forming mats of leaves, simple or 3-fid. Petals 9–11mm, white or pink; anthers yellow. Fruit 20–25mm long, linear. For moist leafy soil in shade. Hardy to −20°C. Easily distinguished from the rather similar *Pachyphragma* by the fruit.

Hesperis matronalis naturalized in Aberdeenshire

Hesperis matronalis L. (*Cruciferae*) Dame's Violet   Native of the Alps, Pyrenees and SE Europe, but commonly naturalized elsewhere, also in the Caucasus and N Turkey, Siberia and Soviet C Asia, growing in mountain woods, scrub and by streams, flowering in May–July. In the wild the white-and-purple-flowered subspecies are separate, whereas in cultivation they are mixed. Stems to 120cm, usually *c.*100cm. Petals 15–25mm, usually *c.*20mm; flowers scented. A short-lived perennial, suitable for growing in damp, shady or grassy places. Hardy to –20°C. Other closely related species, differing in leaf shape and hairs, are found in Turkey and SE Europe.

Lunaria rediviva L. (*Cruciferae*) Perennial Honesty   Native of most of Europe east to Siberia, in moist, usually subalpine woods, and scrub in the mountains in the south, but not common, flowering in May–July. Stems 35–140cm, elongating during flowering. Leaves cordate. Petals 12–20mm, flowers scented. Seed pods 35–90mm long, elliptical. Hardy to –20°C. Honesty, *L. annua* L., is a biennial, with deep purple or white, unscented flowers and almost round seed pods, of which the shining septum is often dried and used for Christmas decorations.

Pachyphragma macrophyllum (Hoffm.) Busch (*Cruciferae*)   Native of NE Turkey and the W Caucasus, usually growing in wet beech forests, at up to 1900m in Turkey, flowering in April–May. Plant with a creeping rhizome, with flowering stems up to *c.*10cm and inflorescence to 15cm, soon hidden by leaves. Basal leaves large, ovate cordate, with petioles up to 18cm long. Petals 8mm long. Fruit broadly obcordate, rounded at the base 12–17mm broad. For leafy soil, in damp shade. Hardy to –15°C?

Lunaria redidiva

Cardamine trifolia

Pachyphragma macrophyllum

Erysimum 'Jubilee Gold'

Erysimum 'Bredon'

Cheiranthus
'Harpur Crewe'

Erysimum 'Mrs L. K. Elmhirst'

Erysimum concinnum

Arabis alpina subsp. caucasica 'Snowdrop'

Arabis blepharophylla

Specimens from Hopleys Nursery, 12 April. ⅓ life size

Alyssoides utriculata (L.) Medicus (*Cruciferae*) Native of France, in SW Alps, east to Romania, Greece and N Turkey, growing on rock ledges at up to 1300m in Turkey, flowering in April–June. Stems to 40cm. Leaves variably hairy, petals 14–20mm long. Fruit inflated 10–15mm in diameter. Easily recognized by the inflated seed pods.

Arabis alpina caucasica subsp. *caucasica* (Schlecht. in Willd.) Briq. syn. *A. albido* Stev. Native of SE Europe from Italy eastwards to the Caucasus, N & E Turkey, W Syria and Iran and often naturalized elsewhere, growing on rocks and cliffs, flowering in March–August. Plant forming a mat of thin stems to 1m or more across. Flowering stems 15–35cm. Flowers white with petals 12–16mm long. **'Snowdrop'** is a selected form, and a double 'Plena' is common. Pink forms are also in cultivation. Easily grown in well-drained, poor soil. Hardy to −20°C.

Arabis blepharophylla Hook. & Arn. (*Cruciferae*) Native of California, around San Francisco, growing in rocky scrub below 300m, flowering in February–April. Plant with several stems to 20cm from a central rootstock, forming small tufts. Leaves in a basal rosette, obovate to oblanceolate, obtuse, 2–8cm long. Flowers pinkish purple; petals 12–18mm long. For well-drained soil in full sun, and tolerant of some drought in summer. Hardy to −15°C.

Cheiranthus cheiri L. syn. *Erysimum cheiri* (L.) Crantz (*Cruciferae*) Wallflower Native of cliffs and rocks in Greece, Crete, W Turkey and W Syria, flowering in March–April. Plant subshrubby, with several stems to 50cm, usually c.30cm. Flowers in the wild deep yellow; petals 15–25mm long. Naturalized on walls in most of the rest of Europe; flower colour in cultivated wallflowers varies from red to pinkish or brown, yellow and cream. Although often grown as a biennial, it is a perennial, requiring very well-drained, dry soil to survive.
'Harpur Crewe' is a double-flowered form of the wild wallflower, known since the 17th century. It is a good perennial, compact and free flowering if grown in very poor limy soil. **'Bloody Warrior'** is a dark-red double. Hardy to −15°C perhaps.

Erysimum **'Bowles' Mauve'** (*Cruciferae*) A hybrid between *E. scoparium* or possibly *E. linifolium* and *Cheiranthus* of as yet unknown origin. Plant subshrubby, forming a mound of greyish leaves to 1m in diameter. Flowers produced over a long period from April onwards, c.2cm across.
'Mrs L. K. Elmhirst' is very similar to 'Bowles' Mauve' but has dark-green not greyish leaves, with a sparser coating of longer hairs. Flowers paler, with dark veins, c.2.8cm across. Both grow well in very poor soil, and are hardy to c. −15°C.

Erysimum **'Bredon'** Probably a hybrid between *Cheiranthus cheiri* and an *Erysimum*, possibly *E. helveticum* (Jacq.) DC. or *E. grandiflorum* Desf. Stems to 20cm. Buds reddish; flowers April–July.
'Jubilee Gold', similar to Bredon, has toothed leaves.

Erysimum concinnum Eastw. Native of W North America, from N California (Point Reyes) north to Oregon, growing on rocks and cliffs near the sea, flowering in March–May. Plant with a few stems to c.15cm from a central root. Leaves narrowly oblanceolate. Flowers pale yellow or creamy white, the petals 15–20mm long. A

beautiful, short-lived plant for well-drained but rich soil. Hardy to −15°C perhaps.

Erysimum **'Constant Cheer'** Growth bushy, to 30cm, but usually c.20cm. Flowers opening brownish orange, turning purple, produced over a long season in spring and summer. 'Jacob's Jacket' has rather similar colouring. Hardy to −15°C, especially in poor, well-drained soil.

Erysimum semperflorens (Schousboe) Wettst. Native of W Morocco, growing in dunes, scrub and rocky places, flowering in January–May. Plant with several upright stems to 40cm from a rather woody base. Leaves appressed-hairy; flowers c.18mm long, usually white or yellowish. For well-drained, poor soil in a warm position. *E. mutabile* Boiss. & Heldr., with which *E. semperflorens* has been confused, is endemic to Crete, growing on mountain cliffs and rocks. It has flowers which open yellow, changing to buff or purplish. Both are hardy to −15°C perhaps.

Erysimum semperflorens

Erysimum 'Bredon'

Wild Wallflower at Canterbury

Erysimum 'Constant Cheer'

Alyssoides utriculata

Erysimum 'Bowles' Mauve'

Euphorbia oblongifolia in C Caucasus

Euphorbia nicaeensis in S France

Euphorbia villosa

Euphorbia macrostegia from Iran, at Kew

Euphorbia myrsinites

Euphorbia hyberna from Co. Cork

Euphorbia denticulata near Lake Van, SE Turkey

Euphorbia rigida near Mugla, SW Turkey

Euphorbia denticulata Lam. (*Euphorbiaceae*)
Native of E Turkey, N Iraq & N Iran and
Armenia growing in open oak woods and scrub,
and on bare rocky slopes and steppes, at
800–3050m in Turkey, flowering in
April–August. Stems prostrate. Leaves
glaucous, fleshy, obovate to suborbicular, to
4cm broad. Rays 5. Glands toothed like a comb,
deep crimson. Fruits 7–8mm across. This
striking plant proved hardy in a dry, well-
drained position in Cambridge, but is difficult
to grow in climates with wet, cool summers and
warm, wet winters.

Euphorbia hyberna L. subsp. *hyberna*
Native of SW Ireland, where it is common, and
SW England, where it is very rare, to N Italy,
Spain and Portugal, growing in open woods, on
shady and rocky banks and in hedges, flowering
in April–June. Stems 30–60cm, elongating
during flowering, from a stout rootstock. Leaves
thin, oblong, obtuse, glabrous above, pilose
beneath, sometimes becoming reddish. Rays 5.
Glands suborbicular. Capsule with short and
long, slender tubercles. Easily grown in a semi-
shaded position in moist soil. The Irish form
(illustrated here) does not turn red in summer,
so the reddening is not an invariable character
of the species. Some Spanish plants, however,
do have red stems. Subsp. *insularis* (Boiss.)
Briq., with numerous axillary rays, nearly sessile
capsules and glands with thick margins, is found
in Corsica, Sardinia and NW Italy.

Euphorbia macrostegia Boiss.   Native of S
Turkey, W Syria and Lebanon, and of W & S
Iran, growing in woods, Mediterranean scrub,
and in oak scrub on limestone in the Zagros in
Iran, at 650–2100m, flowering in April–July.
Stems to 60cm. Leaves green or glaucous, thin
but tough; stem leaves to 5cm across. Floral cups
nodding 2–4cm across, often purplish. Glands
short- or medium-horned. Capsule glabrous. For

well-drained soil in sun or partial shade. Hardy to
−15°C, perhaps. This species is sometimes found
under the name *E. erubescens* Boiss.

Euphorbia myrsinites L.   Native of S
Europe from the Balearic Islands, Corsica and
North Africa, eastwards to the Crimea, Turkey
and C Asia (Turkestan), growing on rocky
slopes, open pine forest, roadside banks and
stony mountain pastures, from 450–2200m in
Turkey, flowering from April–August. Stems
prostrate, to 30cm long. Leaves obovate-
oblanceolate, glaucous, fleshy. Rays 8–13.
Glands 2-horned. Capsule conical, with 3
rounded ridges. Easily grown in well-drained
soil or hanging over a wall. Hardy to −15°C.

Euphorbia nicaeensis All.   Native of Europe
from S France and Portugal eastwards to C
Russia, Turkey and the Caucasus, on open
slopes, roadsides, rocky places, scrub and open
forest at up to 1800m in Turkey, flowering in
May–August. Stems to 80cm, often reddish.
Leaves glabrous or minutely papillose, glaucous,
leathery, lanceolate to oblong, to 1.8cm wide,
obtuse. Rays 5–18. Glands truncate or
emarginate, or with 2 short horns. Capsule
rugulose, sometimes pubescent. A variable
species, sometimes with few erect stems,
sometimes with stems numerous and
procumbent. Easily grown in dry, well-drained
soil. *E. niciciana* Borbas ex Novak is confusingly
similar, but usually has smaller seeds and
narrower, acute leaves to 8mm wide. For a dry,
sunny position. Hardy to −15°C.

Euphorbia oblongifolia (C. Koch) C. Koch
Native of N & E Turkey to the Caucasus, in
beech and spruce forests, rocky and grassy
slopes, screes, and alpine meadows at
1200–2800m in Turkey, flowering in
May–August. Stem to 1m, pubescent or nearly
glabrous. Leaves often glaucous, to 4cm across,

usually obtuse, rather thin. Raylet cups 2–3cm
across, often purplish. Glands long-horned.
Capsule smooth or with granular surface. For
good rich but sandy soil in partial shade. Hardy
to −20°C.

Euphorbia rigida M. Bieb. syn. *E.
biglandulosa*   Native of S Europe from Italy to
Albania, the W Caucasus, Greece, Turkey, W
Syria and NE Iran. It grows on rocky limestone,
shale and schist slopes, open pine forest, scrub
and overgrazed hills, at up to 2000m in Turkey,
flowering in March–August. Stems semi-
prostrate or ascending, to 60cm. Leaves
lanceolate, very acute, stiff, fleshy, glaucous,
often reddish or orange. Rays 7–16. Glands 2-
horned. Fruit cylindrical, 6–7mm in diameter.
Hardy to c.−10°C or lower, but killed by cold
winds of c.−15°C when grown in the moist
climate of S England. In drier climates it should
be hardier, especially if introduced from a cold
locality. A most attractive species, for a dry
position such as a raised bed, or for growing
hanging over a wall.

Euphorbia villosa Waldst. & Kit. syn. *E.
pilosa* auct. non L.   Native of S Europe from
Spain, France and North Africa, to Greece, the
Crimea, European Turkey, the Caucasus and W
Siberia, in damp meadows, open woods,
hedgerows and river banks, flowering in
April–June. Stems numerous, up to 120cm,
scaly below. Leaves rather thin, glabrous or
pubescent, oblong to elliptical. Rays 5 or more.
Glands suborbicular or ovate, without horns.
Capsule smooth or nearly smooth. Easily grown
in moist soil or partial shade. Hardy to −20°C,
perhaps. Formerly known, possibly not native,
from a wood near Bath, but not seen since the
1930s and probably extinct; often known as *E
pilosa* L., which name correctly belongs to a
Himalayan species.

Euphorbia cyparissias

Euphorbia griffithii 'Dixter'

Euphorbia characias
subsp. *characias*

Euphorbia polychroma

Euphorbia amygdaloides
var. *robbiae*

Euphorbia amygdaloides

Specimens from Wisley, 29 April. ²⁄₅ life size

Euphorbia amygdaloides L. (*Euphorbiaceae*) Wood Spurge   Native of Europe from Ireland and N England to Portugal and Algeria, eastwards to Poland, Turkey and the Caucasus, in woods, hedges and on grassy banks, usually in rather moist soil, at up to 2000m in Turkey, flowering in March–August. Stems tufted, more or less upright to 80cm, leafy the first year, usually flowering the second. Stems and leaves often purplish, and deep purple in '**Purpurea**' (syn. 'Rubra') which comes true from seed. Leaves oblanceolate, usually less than 2cm wide, 2.5–7cm long. Rays 5–11. Glands with 2 long horns. Capsule smooth. For moist soil in full sun, or partial shade. Individual plants are not long-lived, but seed easily. 'Variegata' has yellow-edged leaves.

Euphorbia amygdaloides L. var. *robbiae* (Turrill) Radcliffe-Smith   This variety differs from ordinary *E. amygdaloides* in its creeping underground rhizomes, forming spreading patches, and its more leathery, oblanceolate shining, nearly glabrous leaves, in a distinct rosette on the non-flowering stems. It is native of woods in NW Turkey, in the Belgrad forest in European Turkey, and as far east as Bolu in Asia. Hardy to −15°C for short periods.

Euphorbia characias L.   Native of the Mediterranean region from Portugal and Morocco eastwards to S Turkey, growing on rocky hills, in olive groves, in open forest and on roadsides, at up to 1000m in Turkey, flowering in January–May. Two subspecies are recognized; subsp. *characias*, which is mainly western, extends east to Yugoslavia and Cyrenaica; it has stems usually up to 80cm, with numerous softly hairy, greyish, usually oblanceolate leaves 3–13cm long, to 1cm wide; glands usually dark brown or reddish with short horns or emarginate. Subsp. *wulfenii* (Hoppe ex W. Koch) J. R.-Smith is taller, up to 1.8m, with a larger flowering head, and yellowish glands with long horns. It is commonest in Greece and Turkey. A large and yellow form is in cultivation as '**John Tomlinson**', collected in Greece. 'Lambrook Gold' is very similar. Both subspecies are excellent garden plants, hardy to −10°C or less if in very well-drained soil, but killed by persistent lower temperatures, especially when combined with damp.

Euphorbia cyparissias L.   Native of most of Europe except the British Isles and Scandinavia, where, however, it is often naturalized especially on sand dunes; growing in dry rocky meadows, at up to 2500m in the Alps, flowering in May–September. Plant with a creeping underground rhizome, forming large patches. Stems to 50cm, but usually less than 30cm. Leaves to 4cm long, linear. Rays 9–18. Glands with 2 horns. Easily grown in dry soil, but likely to become a nuisance with its fine, running rhizomes. Often turning orange in poor soils in summer.

Euphorbia griffithii Hook. fil.   Native of Bhutan in clearings and in scrub in pine, oak and *Rhododendron* forest at 2300–3500m, flowering in May–August. Plant with shortly creeping underground rhizome. Stems annual 40–80cm. Leaves linear or lanceolate, glabrous or pubescent in var. *bhutanica* (Fischer) Long. Bracts red or orange, glands semicircular, capsule smooth. '**Dixter**' has reddish-purple leaves, dark-red bracts and is said to have shorter stems. 'Fireglow' is the usual clone. This is most beautiful when it is planted only with greens for company, or with moisture-loving ferns such as *Matteuccia struthiopteris*, and

Euphorbia × *martinii*

Euphorbia amygdaloides 'Purpurea'

is wonderfully planted at the High Beeches where it fills a marshy valley. Hardy to −20°C or less.

E. × *martinii* Rouy   A hybrid between *E. amygdaloides* and *E. characias*, found in the wild in S France and long cultivated. It makes a clump of upright stems to *c.*60cm. A good plant for a sunny border, larger and more impressive than *E. amygdaloides* and neater and smaller than *E. characias*. Hardy to −15°C.

Euphorbia polychroma Kerner syn. *E. epithymoides* L.   Native of Europe from S Germany to the Ukraine, Bulgaria and Greece, in woods and scrub usually on limestone, flowering in April–May. Stems many from a large rootstock, 20–40cm tall. Leaves 3.0–5.0cm long, 1.1–2.5cm wide, obovate-oblong or elliptic-oblong, entire or toothed near apex, softly hairy. Raylet leaves elliptical. Rays 4–5; glands small, rounded; capsule with long, slender tubercles. There is a very beautiful purple-leaved and -stemmed form, 'Candy', syn. 'Purpurea', in cultivation, but it is rare. For good soil in partial shade. Hardy to −25°C.

Euphorbia cyparissias

Euphorbia griffithii with *Matteuccia*

Euphorbia characias 'John Tomlinson'

VIOLA

Viola blanda in New York State

Viola canadensis

Viola elatior

Viola hirta

Viola blanda Willd. (*Violaceae*) Sweet White Violet   Native of Quebec and New England, west to Minnesota, south to N Georgia in the mountains, in cool rocky woods, flowering in April–May. Plant stemless with a slender rootstock and thin, leafy runners. Leaves and flower stems from the base to *c*.5cm. Leaves ovate and cordate, with minute hairs only on the upper surface. Flowers white, slightly scented: upper petals reflexed and twisted. Seed capsules dark purple. For a cool shady position. Hardy to −20°C.

Viola canadensis L.   Native of New Brunswick, Saskatchewan, south to South Carolina, Nebraska and in the Rockies to New Mexico; growing in deciduous woods and forests in the mountains, flowering in May–July. Stems upright to 40cm, forming tufts. Leaves broadly ovate, acuminate or acute. Sepals very narrow, spreading; petals white, yellow at base. Hardy to −25°C or less.

Viola cucullata Ait. syn. *V. obliqua* Hill Native of E North America, from Quebec and Ontario, south to Georgia, growing in wet places, often in open woods, flowering in April–June. Plant spreading with a fleshy rhizome. Stems and leaves glabrous. Leaves *c*.8cm wide when full grown. Flowers violet or white with a darker throat, to 3.5cm across, not scented; hairs of the beard clavate. Cleistogamous flowers long and slender, on tall, erect peduncles, with green capsules. For good soil in a moist position in sun or partial shade. In spite of the fleshy rhizomes, this violet is easily killed by drought.

Viola elatior Fries   Native of C & E Europe, from N Italy and France east to Siberia and NW China, growing in damp meadows and scrub, flowering in April–June. Stems tufted to 50cm. Leaves lanceolate, subcordate; stipules equal to or longer than petiole. Flowers 2–2.5cm across; spur short, 2–4mm.
V. persicifolia Schreber, the fen violet, is rather similar but is usually shorter, to 25cm at most, and has stipules shorter than the petiole. It is found in fens throughout Europe, including (but very rarely) England and Ireland. For good leafy or peaty soil in sun or partial shade. Hardy to −25°C.

Viola hirta L. Hairy Violet   Native of Europe except the extreme north, eastwards to the Caucasus, Siberia and C Asia, growing in woods, grassy banks and grassland, usually on limestone, flowering in March–June. Stems and

leaves to 15cm, hairy, in a basal rosette, without creeping, stolons in summer. Flowers *c*.1.5cm across, bluish-violet, not scented. This species can be very showy in early spring, but lacks the scent of *V. odorata*. Hardy to −25°C.

Viola odorata L. Sweet Violet   Native of most of Europe except the extreme north, from the Azores and North Africa east to the Caucasus, Turkey, Syria and N Iran, growing in woods, hedges and on sunny banks, flowering in February–May. Flower stems to 5cm; leaf stalks to 12cm; plant with leaves only from the base and with creeping stolons. Leaves more or less glabrous, ovate-orbicular, obtuse. Flowers heavily scented, *c*.1.5cm across, usually deep purple or white, but reddish, pink, pale-yellow and pale-blue forms are cultivated. All sweet violets, and especially the old cultivars, respond to annual replanting in spring in rich, loose leafy soil, and much moisture in hot weather in summer. Hardy to −20°C. Numerous varieties have been cultivated in the past and some survive. 'Governor Herrick', shown here, has flowers 3–3.5cm across, from November to April.

Viola riviniana Rchb. 'Purpurea', also with purple leaves, is commonly cultivated. It has fimbriate stipules.

Viola septentrionalis Greene   Native of E North America, from NE Canada to Ontario, and south to Connecticut and N Pennsylvania, growing in moist open woods, flowering in May. Plant with a spreading and creeping, thick rhizome. Stems and leaves finely hairy. Leaves to 7.5cm wide when fully grown. Flowers deep violet to white, to 2.5cm across. Cleistogamous flowers in short but ascending peduncles, with purple capsules. For moist, leafy soil in partial shade. Hardy to −20°C.

Viola sororia Willd. syn. *V. papilionacea* Pursh Confederate Violet   Native of E North America, from Quebec west to Wyoming and south to Oklahoma and North Carolina, growing in moist meadows and shady banks, flowering in April–May. Young leaves glabrous or hairy. Leaf blades very blunt when mature. Flowers not scented, *c*.20mm across, normally violet-blue, but 'Freckles' has white flowers finely speckled with blue, and 'Albiflora' has pure white flowers. 'Priceana', syn. f. *albiflora* Grover, is the Confederate Violet, with | greyish flowers, darker towards the middle, with green centres, heavily veined with blue. Hairs of the beard not clavate. Cleistogamous flowers on short, creeping peduncles. For moist soil in sun or partial shade. Hardy to −20°C or less.

Viola suavis M. Bieb   Native of SE Europe, S Russia, Turkey, the Caucasus, C Asia, NW China and Kashmir, growing in scrub and on shady banks, often near streams, flowering in March–May. Very similar to *V. odorata* but with paler blue flowers with a white centre, more elongated leaves and underground stolons. For any good soil in sun or partial shade. Hardy to −20°C or less. This species is thought to have played a part in the breeding of some of the Sweet Violet cultivars.

Viola labradorica

Viola 'Governor Herrick'

Viola odorata in Kent

Viola odorata

Viola odorata (red form) in the Alhambra

Viola suavis in Xinjiang, NW China

Viola cucullata

Viola septentrionalis 'Alba'

Viola sororia 'Freckles'

Viola tricolor seedlings

'Jeannie'

'Martin'

'Joyce'

'Grace'

Viola gracilis 'Lutea'

Viola cornuta

'Penny Black'

'Chelsea Girl'

'Ardross Gem'

Viola corsica

'Little Liz'

'Huntercombe Purple'

'Blue Tit'

Specimens from the Savill Gardens, Windsor, 15 June. ½ life size

Viola tricolor seedling

Viola corsica

Viola cornuta 'Belmont Blue'

Viola 'Huntercombe Purple'

Viola 'Chelsea Girl'

Viola cornuta (a large form)

Viola cornuta L. (*Violaceae*) Native of the Pyrenees in France and Spain, growing on rocky mountainsides and in alpine meadows, flowering in June–August. Sometimes naturalized from gardens elsewhere in the mountains of Europe. A long-lived perennial with numerous stolons from the base, forming a dense tuft. Stems to 30cm. Spur 10–15mm, longer than the petals, which usually do not overlap. Flowers 2–3cm across, scented; pale mauve is the commonest colour, but there are also whites and an unusual pinkish grey in gardens.
'Belmont Blue', syn. 'Boughton Blue', is one of the most beautiful of the forty or so cultivars which are at present in cultivation. Its flowers are a pure and rather pale sky-blue. Also shown is an extra large-flowered form. Hardy to −20°C.

Viola corsica Nyman syn. *V. bertolonii* Salisb. Native of Corsica and Sardinia, in rocky mountain pastures at 900–1300mm, flowering in April–July. A long-lived perennial, with stems to 20cm. Flowers to 3.5cm from top to bottom: petals not overlapping, violet, rarely yellow. Spur 10–15mm. This is the plant often grown as *V. bertolonii* Salisb.; *V. bertolonii* Pio differs in having flowers more or less square in face view,

with overlapping petals. It is found throughout Italy, both in SW Alps and N Apennines and in S Italy and N Sicily.

Viola gracilis Sibth. & Sm. Native of Yugoslavia, Bulgaria, Albania, Greece and W Turkey, growing in grassy mountain woods and alpine meadows, at 1250–2000m (in Turkey), flowering in May–August. Plant forming dense mats which last several years. Stems 5–30cm, usually *c*.15cm in gardens. Leaves orbicular-ovate or oblong, crenate, upper rounded. Flowers 2–3cm from top to bottom, either violet or yellow, not bicoloured. Spur 6–7mm, straight or slightly curved. Stipules with oblanceolate, spathulate lobes. Easily grown in ordinary garden soil in full sun. The commonest form in cultivation is yellow-flowered; it has produced purple-flowered branches in my garden.

Viola × wittrockiana Gams This is the garden pansy, raised by crossing *Viola tricolor* with *Viola lutea* subsp. *sudetica* and *Viola altaica* Ker-Gawl. The large-flowered pansies, which are annuals, biennials or short-lived perennials, were bred from these species, the major development being in *c*.1800–1835, and by 1838 at least 400 show pansies had been named. The

formation of what are now called 'Violas' was started by James Grieve of Dickson's in Edinburgh in the 1860s by crossing the pansies with *V. lutea* and *V. cornuta* (q.q.v.) which are reliably perennial. In 1874, Dr Charles Stuart of Chirnside, Berwick, made hand pollinations and noted that the perennial suckering habit was produced only when *V. cornuta* was the seed parent. His perennial violas were called 'Violettas', and are similar to many of those grown today. *Viola* cultivars shown here are:
'Ardross Gem'
'Blue Tit'
'Chelsea Girl'
'Grace'
'Huntercombe Purple'
'Jeannie'
'Joyce'
'Little Liz'
'Martin' Close to *V. gracilis* (q.v.) and with a very long flowering season. Raised by J. Elliott.
'Penny Black' This black pansy is particularly short-lived, but comes true from seed. 'E. A. Bowles' syn. 'Bowles Black' has smaller flowers, shaped more like wild *V. tricolor*. 'Molly Sanderson' is a similar but neater plant, with rounded flowers above a low tuft of leaves.
Viola tricolor A striking group of seedlings, with spotted petals. (See p. 56.)

Viola lutea in Aberdeenshire, Scotland

Viola gracilis 'Lutea'

Viola 'Arkwright's Ruby'

Viola tricolor (wild form)

Viola 'Maggie Mott'

Viola gracilis Sibth. & Sm. **'Lutea'** (*Violaceae*) see p. 55.

Viola lutea Hudson   Native of W Europe, from Scotland and Ireland to Spain, east to Switzerland, in grassy meadows, usually in the hills, flowering in May–June, and sparsely later. Plant with creeping underground stolons, forming loose patches in the grass; terminal segment of stipules not large and crenate, flowers usually yellow, rarely violet or particoloured, 1.5–2.5cm across, the lower petal to 1.5cm wide. Subsp. *sudetica* (Willd.) W. Becher has thicker stems and larger flowers *c.*2.3cm across. It is found from the Alps eastwards to Czechoslovakia, and it was this subspecies that was crossed with *V. tricolor* to produce the cultivated pansy (see p. 55).

Viola pedata L. Bird's foot Violet   Native of New York to Wisconsin, south to Florida and E Texas, growing on dry rocky banks, in open deciduous woods on well-drained soil, and on the edges of ditches in acid sandy soil, flowering April–June and again in late summer and autumn. Leaves deeply divided with a narrow central lobe and 2 sets of 4 lateral lobes. Flowers to 4cm across, usually all pale bluish-purple in var. *lineariloba* DC. syn. var. *concolor* Brainerd, but often the more striking deep-purple and pale bluish bicolour, var. *pedata* syn. var. *bicolor* Pursh. One of the most beautiful species but difficult to cultivate. Requires very well-drained soil and warmth and moisture in summer. Some have recommended that it be grown on clay soil, unpoisoned by humus, and, indeed, where these photographs were taken, it was growing on the shaley banks of a newly made road in full sun. Hardy to −20°C.

Viola tricolor L. Heartsease   Native of most of Europe and Asia, south to C Turkey and east to Siberia and the Himalayas, in grassy places and arable fields, flowering in April–September. Plant usually annual, but sometimes perennial. Stipules with the terminal segment lanceolate, leaf-like, larger than the others. Flowers variably coloured, often bicoloured. The wild type shown here, from NE Scotland, is a perennial, common in the north of England and Scotland, rare in the south, growing in pastures and disturbed grassland. It forms a mat of creeping stems. Subsp. *curtisii* (E. Forster) Syme is similar, but often has yellow flowers, and is usually found on sand dunes near the sea in W Europe and the Baltic. Other perennial subspecies are found in the mountains of the Balkan peninsula and southern and central Europe.

Cultivars of *Viola* × *wittrockiana*   (p. 55).
'Arkwright's Ruby'
'Irish Molly'   Flowers greenish bronze.
'Jackanapes'
'Maggie Mott'   An old variety, grown since before 1910. Flowers 4cm across.
'Rebecca'   Flowers white, with a purplish-blue, plicata-type margin.

Viola 'Jackanapes'

Viola pedata var. lineariloba in the Blue Ridge Mountains, Virginia

Viola pedata var. pedata in Virginia

Viola 'Rebecca'

Viola 'Irish Molly'

BERGENIA

'Ballawley'

Bergenia × schmidtii

Bergenia cordifolia

'Britten'

'Admiral'

'Bach'

Bergenia purpurascens

'Brahms'

Specimens from Wisley, 28 April. ⅕ life size

Bergenia purpurascens

Bergenia (Saxifragaceae) A genus of about 7 species, closely related to Saxifraga, with a thick fleshy creeping rhizome, forming spreading patches of large leathery leaves. All flower in early spring and require rich, moist but well-drained soil in shade or partial shade. Many hybrids have been raised in gardens in Europe, and a selection are given on the following page.

Bergenia ciliata (Haw.) Sternb. Native of Afghanistan to SE Tibet, growing in woods and on shady rock ledges at 1800–4300m, flowering in March–July near melting snow. Basal leaves large, rounded, cordate at the base, entire but bristly 30cm or more across, reddish in autumn with long (c.15cm) bristly stalks. Flowers 1.5–2.5cm long, palest pink. Young leaves and flowers rather frost sensitive, doing well in cool shade. Hardy to −20°C. Bergenia ciliata f. ligulata Yeo differs in having no hairs on the leaf surface, while f. ciliata is hairy.

Bergenia cordifolia (Haw.) Sternb. Native of Siberia, in the Altai Mountains, flowering in February–March in gardens in western Europe. Leaves with blade to 30 × 20cm, obovate, bullate with wavy edges, not convex, remaining green in winter. Flowers c.2.2cm long, purplish pink. A widely grown species, introduced in the 17th century, and very tolerant of cold and heat, growing well in shady places in Mediterranean climates.

Bergenia crassifolia (L.) Fritsch Native of Siberia, Mongolia and NW China in the Altai, east to the Pacific (var. pacifica (Kom.) Nekr. shown here), and naturalized in parts of Austria and France, growing on shady north-facing mountain rocks, and in subalpine woods, flowering in March–April. Leaves 15–30cm, elliptic, obovate with sparse, bristle-like teeth, reddish brown in winter. Inflorescence to 30cm; flowers drooping. Petals 10–12mm, bright purplish pink. Hardy to −20°C or less.

Bergenia purpurascens (Hook. fil. & Thoms.) Engler Native of C Nepal, where it is common, to SW China (Yunnan), growing on rocks and open slopes at 3600–4700m. Leaves hairless, not toothed, striking deep purple in winter, blades 3–9cm long. Flowers in a dense nodding cluster 1.5–2.5cm long, on a tallish stalk to 30cm, deep pinkish purple. Hardy to −20°C, perhaps.

Bergenia stracheyi (Hook. fil. & Thoms.) Engler Native of Afghanistan to N India (Uttar Pradesh) growing on rocky alpine slopes in full exposure at 3300–4500cm. Common in W Himalayas, forming huge patches, excluding all other plants except sometimes Codonopsis (p. 354); flowering in June–August, but in early spring in gardens. Flowers pink, drooping in loose clusters, 2–2.5cm long. Leaves obovate, 5–10cm long. This species and its white form 'Alba' were the important parents of Eric Smith's hybrids which were named after composers. Bergenia hybrids are hardy, long-lived plants with evergreen leaves, many of which colour red or purple in winter. The flowers open in early spring and are often damaged by late frosts, so that some overhead protection will often prolong the flowering season. All are hardy to −25°C or less, and require a cool sheltered position in good soil.

Bergenia cultivars:
'Abendglocken' syn. 'Evening Bells' Raised by G. Arends in c.1971.
'Admiral' Raised by R. Eskuche.
'Baby Doll' Raised by zur Linden.
'Bach' Raised by Eric Smith of The Plantsman in c.1972.
'Ballawley' syn. 'Delbees' Raised at Ballawley Park, near Dublin, before 1950. Flowers April–May. Leaves, normally green, turn bronze-coloured in winter. Flower stalks bright red. Stems to 60cm. Leaves less tough and evergreen than many others, c.20cm across. Not as free-flowering as some other bergenias.
'Beethoven' Raised by Eric Smith of The Plantsman in c.1972.
'Brahms' Raised by Eric Smith of The Plantsman in c.1972.
'Britten' Raised by Jim Archibald of The Plantsman in c.1977.

Bergenia × schmidtii A hybrid between B. ciliata and B. crassifolia raised in 1875. Plant vigorous and spreading, with leaves to 23cm long, 15cm wide. Early flowering, and often the first to flower, so that the flowers are often damaged by frost. Flowering stems to 30cm.

Bergenia 'Baby Doll'

Bergenia ciliata collected by Christopher Lloyd

Bergenia stracheyi 'Alba'

Bergenia stracheyi

Bergenia crassifolia var. *pacifica*

Bergenia 'Abendglocken'

Bergenia 'Beethoven'

Lathyrus roseus at Cambridge

Lathyrus venetus

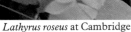

Lathyrus aureus at Cruickshank Botanic Gardens, Aberdeen

Lathyrus aureus

Lathyrus vernus

Lathyrus vernus 'Roseus'

Lathyrus vernus 'Cyaneus'

Astragalus lusitanicus Lam. syn. *Phaca boetica* L. (*Leguminosae*)   Native of the Mediterranean region, growing in rocky scrub, pine woods and abandoned fields, at up to 800m in Turkey, flowering in March–June. Stems several, upright, to 70cm. Leaves 10–18cm long. Flowers 10–20 in an upright raceme, 20–25mm long, white with a blackish or reddish hairy calyx. Plants from Spain, Portugal and NW Africa, subsp. *lusitanicus*, have leaves glabrous above, and an often dark-reddish calyx: those from the E Mediterranean, with a blackish calyx and leaves silky above, have been called subsp. *orientalis* Chater & Meikle. Cultivated since the 17th century, but very rarely seen. For a rather dry sunny border. Hardy to −15°C, perhaps.

Lathyrus aureus (Stev.) Brandza syn. *Orobus aureus* Steven (*Leguminosae*)   Native of Bulgaria and Romania to N Turkey, the Caucasus and the Crimea, growing in woods and scrub, at up to 2000m, flowering in May–July. Stems 20–60cm; leaves without tendrils, with 3–6 pairs of leaflets with brownish glands beneath. Flowers 12–25, 17–22mm long, brownish orange. Seed pods 50–70mm long, densely glandular when young.
Lathyrus gmelinii Fritsch (syn. *L. luteus* (L.) Peterm.), from the Urals and C Asia, is similar, but has yellow flowers 25–30mm long, and 2–4 pairs of leaflets. Two other species in Europe have yellowish flowers; *L. laevigatus*, found from France and Spain east to Russia, and *L. transsilvanicus* from the Carpathians, but *L. aureus* is the only one with brown glands. As a further complication, *L. aureus* is very similar to *Vicia crocea* (Desf.) B. Fedtsch., from Turkey and the Caucasus, but that has leaves folded, not rolled in the bud, unequal stipules and shorter seed pods, 27–32mm long.

Lathyrus nervosus Lam. Lord Anson's Blue Pea   Native of Tierra del Fuego (very rare), Argentina north to 37°S, Chile north to 46°S, Uruguay and S Brazil, growing in scrub, and grassy cliff-tops near the sea, flowering in December–January (May–July in the Northern Hemisphere). Plant with few climbing or creeping stems from a tufted rhizome, to 1.5m tall. Leaves sessile and stipules glabrous, glaucous, with a thickened margin. Inflorescence with 2–3 whorls of 3–4 flowers, each *c*.18mm across. For rich soil in a cool position in sun or partial shade, with water in summer. Hardy to −10°C. *L. magellanicus* Lam. is very similar, but has hairy, usually narrower, leaflets which often blacken when dried, and have a thin, membranous, not a thickened margin. It is found in W Argentina north to 40°S, in Chile north to 45°S, and in Tierra del Fuego, growing on sand dunes and shingle by the sea, and in grassland and scrub, flowering in December–February. It is possibly hardier than *L. nervosus* and is a stronger-growing plant, reaching 3m when growing well.

Lathyrus roseus Stev.   Native of the Crimea, the Caucasus, N & E Turkey and N Iran, growing in spruce and pine forest in oak and hazel scrub, flowering in May–July. Stems erect, to 60cm, from a large rootstock. Leaves without tendrils, with 1 pair of obovate leaflets, to 45mm long, 30mm across; stipules narrow, as broad as stem. Flowers 1–4 on a stalk, to 2cm across. For well-drained soil in sun or partial shade.

Lathyrus nervosus at Sissinghurst, Kent

Lathyrus nervosus at the Royal Botanic Gardens, Kew

Sophora alopecuroides in NW China

Astragalus lusitanicus near Marmaris, Turkey

Parochetus communis near Dali, Yunnan

Lathyrus venetus (Miller) Wohlf. syn. *L. variegatus* (Ten.) Gren. & Godr.   Native of S Europe, from Italy and Corsica east to C Russia and N Turkey, growing in forests, scrub and grassland, flowering in May–June. Plant tufted with numerous stems to *c*.40cm. Leaves with 2–4 pairs of acute leaflets. Flowers 10–30 in a dense raceme, 10–15mm long. Close to *L. vernus*, but usually larger, with more numerous smaller flowers and acute rather than acuminate leaflets. Easily grown in sun or partial shade in any soil. Hardy to −20°C.

Lathyrus vernus (L.) Bernh. syn. *Orobus vernus* L.   Native of most of Europe except the far south and west, from France east to the Caucasus and N Turkey and E Siberia, growing in woods and scrub, usually on limestone, flowering in April–June. Plant forming slowly spreading patches. Stems 20–40cm. Leaves 2–4 pairs, ovate, acuminate, 3.5–7cm long. Flowers 15–18mm long, usually reddish-purple, fading to blue, but other colour forms are in cultivation, e.g. 'Albus' (white); 'Caeruleus' (pure blue);

'Roseus' (pink); 'Albo-roseus' (pink and white) is probably the same as 'Variegatus'. Also a blue unfortunately named 'Cyaneus', not to be confused with *Lathyrus cyaneus* (Stev.) C. Koch, which I have seen in alpine meadows in the Caucasus, and which has only 2 pairs of linear or narrowly linear-lanceolate leaflets, and semi-sagittate stipules, pale-blue flowers and stems which creep underground through the grass. Easily grown in shade or partial shade, in any soil. Hardy to −20°C.

Parochetus communis Buch.-Ham. ex. D. Don (*Leguminoseae*)   Native of the mountains of India, the Himalayas to SW China and SE Asia, growing in ditches, on shady banks and damp forests in grassy places, at 100–4300m, flowering in May–November. Plant creeping, forming large patches. Flower stems *c*.7.5cm tall, flowers 1.3–2.5cm long. Leaflets 8–20mm long. Suitable for growing under benches in a cold greenhouse, or in a sheltered position outside. Hardy to −5°C. *Parochetus africanus* Polhill, from the mountains of tropical Africa, from Ethiopia to Malawi and Mozambique at

1500–3400m, differs at having slightly smaller flowers with very short auricles on the wings; *P. communis* is often winter-deciduous and has root tubers; *P. africanus* grows through the winter, and has no tubers.

Sophora alopecuroides L. (*Leguminosae*) Native of Asia from Turkey (around Ankara) eastwards to N China, growing in sandy deserts and waste places especially by roadsides and irrigation channels, flowering in April–July. Plant spreading by creeping underground stems, with upright flowering stems to 1m or more. Leaves silky hairy. Flowers 18–20mm, whitish, in 60–80 flowered racemes. Pods 3–10 seeded, strongly contracted between the seeds. A common plant in heavily grazed desert areas of C Asia, protected from damage by the powerful heart poison it contains. Suitable for cultivation in dry or saline areas. Hardy to −25°C.

For a late-flowering *Lathyrus* see pp. 280–281.

Asarum caudatum at Santa Barbara Botanic Garden, California

Hacquetia epipactis at Sellindge, Kent

Oxalis oregana

Oxalis acetosella

Asarum hartwegii in N California

Asarum caudatum Lindl. (*Aristolochiaceae*)
Native of W North America, from California
north to British Columbia and Montana, in the
coast ranges, growing in deep shade in
Redwood forest and pine woods, flowering in
May–July. Rhizome far-creeping, so the plant
forms wide-spreading, rather open patches.
Leaves 2–10cm long, not veined above. Flowers
hidden beneath the leaves with petals 2.5–8.5cm
long. Styles fused. For loose, leafy soil in deep
shade and useful as ground cover in such a
position. Hardy to −15°C perhaps. There are
thirty species of *Asarum* in Japan, many very
beautiful with marbled leaves, but most require
careful cultivation in a shade house. The
European Asarabacca, *A. europaeum*, has
smaller, usually round leaves.

Asarum hartwegii S. Wats.   Native of S
Oregon, south to California and Tulare Co. in
the Sierra Nevada, growing in shady woods and
scrub at 700–2000m, flowering in May–June.
Plant with a thickish, shortly creeping rhizome.
Leaves cordate, ovate, 4–10cm long, with pale
veins. Flowers hidden beneath the leaves, with
brownish, hairy petals 2.5–6.5cm long. Styles
nearly separate. For leafy soil in shade, and
tolerant of drought. Hardy to −15°C.

Aristolochia hirta L. (*Aristolochiaceae*)   Native
of W and SW Turkey and on the islands of
Chios, Lesbos and Samos southwards, growing
in rocky places, on ruins, in vineyards and pine
woods at up to 1200m, flowering in March–June.
Plant with a swollen cylindrical rootstock. Stems
15–50cm. Leaves 3–11cm long. Flowers with a
limb 1.5–8cm across, hairy outside and inside. A
strange plant, the inside of the flower looking and
smelling like mouldy meat, and attracting flies.
For well-drained, stony soil, dry in summer.
Hardy to −10°C, perhaps less.

Hacquetia epipactis (Scop.) DC.
(*Umbelliferae*)   Native of E Alps, Italy, Austria
and Poland, eastwards to Czechoslovakia and
Yugoslavia, growing in rich woods usually on
limestone at up to 1500m, flowering in
March–May. Stems 10–25cm, usually *c*.10cm,
elongating during flowering, ending in a rosette
of green bracteoles around a cluster of tiny
yellow flowers. For moist soil in shade or partial
shade. Hardy to −20°C or less.

Oxalis acetosella L. (*Oxalidaceae*) Wood
Sorrel   Native of Europe from Iceland east to
Japan and south to Spain, Italy and Greece, and
of North America east to Saskatchewan and
south to North Carolina in the mountains,
growing in moist woods, moorland and on

Pachysandra procumbens

Aristolochia hirta in an ancient theatre in SW Turkey

Pachysandra procumbens at Kew in early spring

shady rocks, flowering in April–June and intermittently to September. Leaf stalks 5–15cm. Flowers 10–16mm long, usually white with lilac veins, rarely pinkish. Needs moist leafy soil and shade in summer. Hardy to −25°C.

Oxalis oregana Nutt. Redwood Sorrel Native of C California, north to Washington, growing in Redwood forest, flowering in April–September. Leaf stalks with rusty hairs, 5–17cm long. Flowers 8–20mm long, white or pinkish veined purple with a pale centre, or 2–2.5cm long, deep-rose-purple in f. *smalliana* (Knuth) Munz. Easily grown in moist, leafy soil in shade. Hardy to −15°C.

Pachysandra procumbens Michx. (*Buxaceae*) Native of E North America from West Virginia to Kentucky, Florida and Louisiana, growing in deciduous woods, flowering April–May. Plant forming clumps or mats of creeping and ascending pubescent stems to 30cm. Leaves evergreen, though often damaged by cold winters, ovate, oval or obovate, 5–10cm long, untoothed or with few shallow teeth. Flowers in the axils of the lower scale-like leaves, male flowers on the upper part of the spike, with conspicuous stamens and anthers; female flowers few, below the male, with exposed curved styles. Capsule with 3 carpels. Hardy to −25°C.

Pachysandra terminalis Sieb. & Zucc. Native of Japan in all the islands, and China, west to Hubei and E Sichuan, growing in moist woods in the valleys and low mountains up to 2000m, flowering in April–May, fruiting in September–October; commonly planted as ground cover. Plant spreading by stolons to form a carpet of tough, upright shoots sometimes to 30cm tall, usually *c*.20cm. Leaves 5–10cm long, evergreen, leathery. Male and female flowers on separate parts of the plant, the male above, the female below. Fruits white when mature, about 1.5cm long, rare in cultivation, or never produced? 'Variegata' has leaves edged with white. Easily grown in loose, leafy soil and tolerant of dry shade. Hardy to −25°C.

Pachysandra terminalis in flower

in fruit with *Geastrum* and *Equisetum hyemale*

Pachysandra terminalis 'Variegata'

Vinca minor 'Azurea Flore Pleno'

Vinca minor 'Atropurpurea'

Vinca minor

Vinca minor 'Argenteo-variegata'

Vinca major 'Variegata'

Vinca major

Vinca difformis

Specimens from Wisley, 1 May. ⅖ life size

Vinca herbacea at the Royal Botanic Gardens, Kew

Vinca minor 'Argenteo-variegata'

Amsonia orientalis Decne. syn. *Rhazya orientalis* (Decne.) DC. (*Apocynaceae*) Native of NE Greece and NW Turkey, where it is now almost extinct, growing in grassy places, wet during winter, flowering in May–June. Plant with many stems, to 60cm from a stout woody rootstock. Leaves 3–7cm long. Flowers glabrous outside, *c.*1.2cm across. Easily grown in good garden soil. Hardy to −20°C. This species is normally known by the name *Rhazya*, but is so similar to the American *Amsonia tabernaemontana* var. *salicifolia* (q.v.) that they would probably have been considered conspecific if they had grown in the same country.

Amsonia tabernaemontana Walter Native of E North America, from New Jersey to Florida, west to Illinois, Kentucky, Missouri and Texas, growing in damp grassy places, flowering in April–July. Plant with many stems to *c.*50cm from a stout rootstock. Leaves variable in shape from ovate to lanceolate, 5–10cm long. Flowers with corolla tube pubescent outside, 1.2–1.8cm across. Hardy to −20°C or lower, and easy in good moist soil. Rarer in cultivation in Europe than *A. orientalis.*

Vinca difformis Pourret (*Apocynaceae*) Native of SW Europe from Spain, Portugal and the Azores to C Italy, and of North Africa, growing on shady banks and streamsides in woods, flowering in March–April. Plant forming mounds of evergreen stems and leaves to 1m high and more across. Leaves 2.5–7cm, ovate to lanceolate, usually narrowly lanceolate, glabrous or minutely ciliate. Flowering stems to 30cm. Flowers 3–7cm across, pale blue to nearly white. Tolerant of sun or dry shade. Probably not very hardy except in S England, requiring protection from frosts below −10°C.

Vinca erecta Regel & Schmalh. Native of C Asia in the Tien Shan and Pamir Alai, growing on loose limestone screes at 1500–2000m, flowering in April–May. Plant with many upright deciduous stems to 30cm, elongating after flowering. Flowers *c.*2.5cm across, pale blue or white. For careful cultivation in well-drained soil, and full sun, kept rather dry in summer. Hardy to −15°C.

Vinca herbacea Waldst. & Kit. Native of C Europe to Greece, SW Russia, the Caucasus, N Iran, Turkey, W Syria and N Iraq, growing in open woods, scrub, rocky slopes and screes, usually on limestone, up to 2000m in Turkey, flowering from March–May. Plant with deciduous stems to 60cm from a central rootstock. Flowering stems to 20cm upright. Leaves up to 5cm long. Flowers pale blue to purplish, 2.5–4.5cm across. One of the hardiest species, to −20°C, for dry, well-drained soil in sun or partial shade.

Vinca major L. Greater Periwinkle Native of the N Mediterranean region from SW France to Italy and Yugoslavia, but widely naturalized

Vinca difformis

Vinca difformis near Malaga, Spain

Vinca erecta near Ferghana, C Asia

Vinca major f. *alba*

Vinca major subsp. *hirsuta*

elsewhere in Europe, flowering in February–April. Stems trailing, to 2m or more, and rooting. Leaves evergreen, 2.5–9cm long, usually ovate. Flowering stems upright to 30cm. Flowers 3–5cm across, bluish purple. *Vinca major* f. *alba* has white flowers. Var. *oxyloba* Stearn has narrower leaves and narrow, violet corolla-lobes, but glabrous, or almost glabrous, young shoots. Subsp. *hirsuta* (Boiss.) Stearn is native of the S Caucasus in Georgia and along the Turkish Black Sea coast, growing in scrub at up to 200m, flowering in March–May. It has hairy petioles and young shoots and long hairs to 1mm long on the calyx lobes. Flowers violet, to 4.5cm across, with narrow lobes.

Vinca minor L. Lesser Periwinkle   Native of SW & C Europe, east to the Crimea and the Caucasus, in woods or on rocky banks, flowering in February–June. Probably not native, but long grown and naturalized in the British Isles, Scandinavia and Turkey. Stems creeping and rooting to form mats. Leaves evergreen, 1.5–4.5cm long. Flowering stems to 20cm. Flowers 2.5–3cm across. Easily grown in sun or partial shade of deciduous trees. Hardy to −20°C, with shade or snow cover. There are numerous variants (*c*.20), differing in flower colour, doubleness and leaf variegation: 'Albo-variegata' has white flowers and gold variegated leaves; 'Argenteo-variegata' has silver-edged leaves; 'Atropurpurea' has deep-purplish-red flowers, and 'Azurea Flore Pleno' has double purplish-blue flowers, both with green leaves.

Vinca major var. *oxyloba* at the Royal Botanic Gardens, Kew

Amsonia tabernaemontana

Amsonia orientalis

65

Phlox carolina 'Bill Baker' at Tidmarsh, Berks

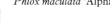

Phlox maculata 'Alpha'

Phlox 'Chattahoochee'

Phlox maculata 'Omega'

Phlox carolina L. 'Bill Baker' (*Polemoniaceae*) Native of the SE United States, in clearings and meadows, and on the edges of woods, flowering in April–May. Stems 25–50cm with sterile shoots with narrowly obovate leaves. Flowers pale purplish to pink, 2.5cm across. Leaves on inflorescence short-stemmed at base, sessile above. Close to *P. ovata*, which differs in its long-stalked leaves at the base of the flowering stem, brighter-coloured flowers and clearly stalked leaves on the sterile shoots. The clone shown here was introduced to England and distributed by Bill Baker. For clearings in woodland or partial shade, making sure that the sterile creeping stems are not swamped by stronger-growing plants. Hardy to −20°C.

Phlox 'Chattahoochee' This striking clone is considered by Wherry to be a form of *P. divaricata* subsp. *laphamii* or a hybrid with *P. pilosa*. It was collected by Mrs J. Norman Henry in the Chattahoochee valley in N Florida and forms a spreading tuft of stems up to 20cm long. Leaves are hairy and ciliate with blades lanceolate to linear, and sessile, narrower than usual for *laphamii*; the plant generally does not produce rooting creeping shoots. *P.* 'Charles Ricardo' is similar but has a white, not red, eye.

Phlox divaricata L. syn. *P. canadensis* Sweet Native of Quebec to Ontario, south to Illinois, Arkansas and South Georgia, generally east of a line from Chicago to New Orleans; subsp. *laphamii* west of the line from South Dakota and Colorado to Louisiana and E Texas. Both grow on moist wooded hills and in river valleys on wooded river flats and up to 1000m; subsp. *divaricata* on acid or neutral soils, subsp. *laphamii* on limestone soils in drier areas. Plant spreading by creeping shoots which root at the nodes. Flowering shoots 25–45cm. Leaves on sterile shoots broadly elliptic, on flowering shoots lanceolate to ovate to 5 × 2.5cm. Flowers 2–3cm across; petals usually notched in subsp. *divaricata*, pale blue, lilac to nearly white, often with a paler eye, but rounded in subsp. *laphamii* with deeper coloured often bluish flowers. 'Dirigo Ice' is a cultivar with large, shallowly notched petals.

Phlox maculata L. Meadow Phlox Native of North America, from Quebec and Vermont west to Minnesota, south to Missouri, Tennessee and North Carolina, growing in meadows, marshes and woods by streams, flowering in May–June. Stems several, often spotted and streaked with red, upright to 125cm from a shallow rootstock. Leaves dark, shining green, linear below, lanceolate above, the largest 6–13cm long, 10–25mm wide. Flowers in an elongated cylindric inflorescence, 18–25mm across. Easily grown in a normal moist herbaceous border, and should succeed also in a bog garden. Hardy to −20°C and below. A few varieties of this beautiful species are grown in gardens. Shown here are 'Alpha' mauve, and 'Omega' white with a pale-pink eye. 'Miss Lingard', pure white, often listed under *P. carolina*, and 'Rosalinde' pink, are grown in America. All these varieties are good in warm summers as they are not liable to mildew.

Phlox ovata L. Native of SE Pennsylvania south to North Carolina, on the Piedmont, and in Indiana, growing in open woods, damp grassland or rocky slopes, flowering in May–July. Stems 25–50cm, from a creeping base; lower leaves stalked, ovate to elliptic. Flowers 16–30mm across, with a pale eye. For leafy soil in partial shade. Hardy to −25°C.

Phlox paniculata L. Garden Phlox Native of North America, from New Jersey south to North Carolina, west to Ohio and south to Louisiana, growing in open woods, scrub, along streams and on hillsides, often on limestone, flowering in June–September. Plant with a short, thick rhizome and numerous, upright

Phlox ovata at Wisley

Phlox divaricata in a garden in Texas

Phlox stolonifera 'Blue Ridge'

Phlox pilosa at Coldham, Kent

Phlox divaricata 'Dirigo Ice'

stems to 2m. Leaves opposite below, often subopposite above. Flowers 1.5–2.5cm across, dull to bright purple, pink or rarely white, with narrow or round, sometimes emarginate petals. Hardy to −20°C or lower; growing best in rich, moist soil with ample moisture in summer. The three varieties shown here are close to the wild type and distinct from the large-flowered garden forms shown on p. 308–9.

Phlox pilosa L. Native of Ontario to Iowa, south to Texas and Florida, growing in grassland and scrub in rather dry soil, and formerly common on the northern prairies before they were ploughed for agriculture, flowering in April–June. Flowering stems 30–60cm, pubescent, with leaves linear below, lanceolate above, to 8cm long, 6mm wide. Flowers purplish, pink or white, 2.2cm across. For full sun and well-drained soil. Suitable for the front of a summer border.

Phlox stolonifera Sims syn. *P. reptans* Michx. Native of Pennsylvania to Georgia and Kentucky, mainly in the Appalachian mountains, growing in open deciduous woods, flowering in April–June. Plant mat-forming with creeping sterile shoots ending in a rosette of spathulate leaves. Flowering stems 15–25cm. Flowers *c*.3cm across, scented, with petals not notched. '**Blue Ridge**' is a good pale-blue form, from Virginia. '**Pink Ridge**' is pink-flowered. Easily grown in semi-shade, forming very pretty ground cover under deciduous trees. Best in slightly acid, leafy but well-drained soil. Hardy to −20°C or less.

Phlox paniculata (close to wild form) at Wallington, Northumberland

Phlox paniculata (white form)

Phlox paniculata (pink form)

Pulmonaria longifolia 'Bertram Anderson'

Pulmonaria angustifolia (left), *P. longifolia* 'Bertram Anderson' (right)

Pulmonaria officinalis

Pulmonaria angustifolia

Pulmonaria longifolia growing wild at Exbury, Hampshire

Nonea intermedia Ledeb. (*Boraginaceae*)
Native of the Caucasus and the extreme NE of
Turkey, growing in alpine meadows at *c.*2000m,
flowering in June–July. Plant forming small
tufts, without a creeping rhizome. Stems 30–
45cm. Leaves oblong, lanceolate, acuminate,
softly hairy. Flowers *c.*12mm long, 6–8mm
across, with scales and hairs in the throat of the
corolla. For moist peaty soil in sun or partial
shade. Hardy to −20°C or so. Several species of
Nonea are very similar in general appearance to
Pulmonaria, but differ in the absence of a
creeping rhizome, and in the presence of 5 hairy
scales in the throat of the corolla. *Nonea lutea*
(Desr.) DC. is a striking, *Pulmonaria*-like, pale-
yellow-flowered annual, and the perennial *N.
macrosperma* Boiss. & Held., from Turkey, also
has yellow flowers; *N. pulla* (L.) DC., from C
Europe, has blackish flowers.

Pulmonaria (*Boraginaceae*) Lungwort   These
are good garden plants for moist places between
shrubs, for the front of a border in partial shade,
for wooded gardens or for grassy banks partially
under trees. The flowers appear in spring, and
last until early summer. They are followed by
dense clumps of bold leaves, variably hairy and
often beautifully spotted with silver. In the
wild, the flowers have either long or short styles,
in the same way that primroses do; in gardens,
the species hybridize freely. Many are beautiful,
long-lived plants, which are easy to propagate,

and have been given cultivar names. As they are clones, their style length should be constant, and has therefore been noted here whenever possible. Most species, of which there are around fifteen, are mountain plants from eastern Europe. They differ in hair type as well as in leaf shape and spotting, and in flower colour. The distribution of hairs inside the corolla tube is also significant.

Pulmonaria angustifolia L. syn. *P. azurea* Besser   Native of France and Germany to Sweden and Baltic Russia, south to Italy and the northern steppes, growing in scrub and meadows, mainly in the mountains, at up to 2000m, flowering in March–May. Rhizome creeping, forming spreading mats. Stems to 30cm, usually *c.*20cm. Leaves unspotted, with equal setae, and without glands; inflorescence becoming very lax as flowering proceeds. Flowers bright blue; tube smooth inside below ring of hairs. Hardy to −20°C.

Pulmonaria longifolia (Bast.) Boreau Native of W Europe, from Spain and Portugal to W France and S England, around the New Forest and on the Isle of Wight, growing in woods and hedges, and on grassy banks, flowering in February–May. Plant clump-forming. Leaves usually spotted, lanceolate or narrowly anceolate, up to 50 × 6cm, with more or less equal setae and a few glands. Stems to 20cm; inflorescence remaining tight during flowering. Flowers usually blue; tube glabrous below ring of hairs. Shown here is the native form, growing wild in Exbury garden and in hedges and roadside banks nearby, and a striking tall form with longer, narrower leaves than the wild English form. This is 'Bertram Anderson', named after E. B. Anderson, a successful and influential grower of alpines, bulbs and other herbaceous plants in England. Hardy to −15°C perhaps.

Pulmonaria officinalis L.   Native of Holland and S Sweden south to N Italy and Bulgaria east to Romania; naturalized in places in England, growing in woods and hedges, flowering in March–May. Plant with short, creeping rhizome, finally forming patches. Leaves spotted, with lamina to 16 × 10cm, abruptly narrowed into stalk, with distinct spots and uniform setae and occasional glandular hairs. Flowers opening reddish, becoming bluish, glabrous inside below the ring of hairs. Inflorescence becoming laxer as flowering proceeds. Hardy to −20°C.

Pulmonaria rubra Schott   Native of the Carpathians in Hungary, south to Albania and Bulgaria, growing in rich, moist subalpine woods of beech and pine, usually on limestone, at 300–1600m, flowering in March–May. Plant clump-forming. Flowering stems to 30cm. Summer leaves usually unspotted; blade narrowed abruptly, to 15 × 7cm, with long and short setae and glandular hairs. Flowers red; tube hairy inside below the ring of hairs.

Pulmonaria saccharata Mill.   Native of SE France and N & C Italy in the Apennines, growing in woods and scrub, flowering from April–May. Plant clump-forming, without extending rhizome. Flowering stems to 30cm, with rather broad stem leaves. Summer leaves to 27 × 10cm, narrowed gradually into the stalk, often very heavily spotted, with more or less dense, unequal and rather fine short hairs, and long setae and glandular hairs. Flowers purplish to bluish purple, hairy inside below the ring of hairs. Hardy to −15°C, perhaps less.

Pulmonaria rubra at the Savill Gardens, Windsor

Pulmonaria saccharata from S France

Nonea intermedia in the N Caucasus

Pulmonaria officinalis
'Sissinghurst White'

'Margery Fish'

'Leopard'

Pulmonaria officinalis

'Blaues Meer'

Pulmonaria mollis

Pulmonaria rubra 'Redstart'

Pulmonaria angustifolia
'Azurea'

Pulmonaria officinalis 'Coral'

Pulmonaria rubra
'Bowles' Red'

Specimens from Wisley, 10 April. ⅔ life size

Pulmonaria officinalis 'Alba'

Pulmonaria 'Blaues Meer'

Pulmonaria 'Boughton Blue'

Pulmonaria 'Frühlingshimmel'

Pulmonaria vallarsae 'Margery Fish'

Pulmonaria 'Lewis Palmer'

Pulmonaria cultivars (*Boraginaceae*)   Some of these may be selected forms of species, but often they are hybrids of unknown parentage. Other hybrids are likely to appear in gardens where more than one species is grown, and are usually sterile; for example, narrow-leaved plants with much spotting are probably *P. longifolia × P. saccharata* and a narrow white-leaved hybrid is most likely *P. longifolia × P. vallarsae*.
The following named clones are shown here:
'Azurea'   A clone of *P. angustifolia* (short style). See p. 69.
'Blaues Meer'   Possibly a form of *P. visianii* from the E Alps, or a hybrid of *P. angustifolia* (short style).
'Boughton Blue'   Probably a hybrid between *P. officinalis* and *P. saccharata* (short style).
'Bowles' Red'   A form of *P. rubra*. Slightly spotted leaf (short style).
'Coral'   A pink-flowered clone, possibly a form of *P. officinalis*. The corolla is usually somewhat deformed and split, but very showy (long style).
'Frühlingshimmel' syn. 'Spring Beauty'   Flowers pale blue. Possibly *P. officinalis × P. saccharata* (long style).
'Leopard'   Probably *P. saccharata* or a hybrid. Leaves well spotted. Flowers red (long style).
'Lewis Palmer' syn. 'Highdown'   Probably *P. officinalis × P. saccharata* (short style). A good robust plant.
'Margery Fish'   Probably a form of *P. vallarsae* (q.v.).
'Redstart'   A form of *P. rubra* (see previous page). Leaves not spotted (long style).

'Sissinghurst White'   A white form of *P. officinalis*. Smaller and neater than 'Alba'.

Pulmonaria mollis Wulfen ex Hornem. Native of SE & C Europe, from Germany and Poland to Italy, Yugoslavia, Greece, Russia and Siberia, growing by streams, in woods and scrub at up to 1600m, flowering in April–May. Plant clump-forming, with flowering stems to 30cm. Summer leaves to 60 × 12cm; not spotted, with dense, soft, short hairs and scattered, slender, unequal setae and glandular hairs. Flowers bluish purple, very hairy below the ring of hairs. Recognized by its very soft, unspotted summer leaves. *P. vallarsae* from Italy is also softly hairy, but with shorter hairs and very spotted, sometimes almost entirely white leaves.

Pulmonaria officinalis (see previous page).

Pulmonaria vallarsae A. Kerner   Native of Italy in the S Tirol and the Apennines, growing in scrub along rivers, among rocks and gravel, at 650–1500m, flowering in March–May. Plant clump-forming. Summer leaves very heavily spotted or even white all over; lamina up to 20 × 10cm, with wavy edge, with very dense, short fine hairs and a few long setae and glandular hairs. Flower stems to 45cm, densely glandular and sticky. Flowers reddish, becoming purplish, tube hairy inside, below the ring of hairs.
'Margery Fish', with pure silver leaves, is close to this species.

Mertensia pulmonarioides

Mertensia ciliata with leaves of *Veratrum*

Mertensia simplicissima on a sandy shore in N Hokkaido, Japan

Brunnera macrophylla (Adams) Johnston
syn. *Anchusa myosotidiflora* Lehm.
(*Boraginaceae*)   Native of the Caucasus,
Georgia and NE Turkey, in spruce forest and
on grassy slopes at 500–2000m in Turkey,
flowering in March–May. Stems several, from a
stout rootstock to 50cm, elongating during the
flowering period. Leaves with long petioles to
20cm and ovate cordate blades 5–14cm long.
Flowers 3.5–7mm across. *B. orientalis* (Schenk.)
Johnston, from C Turkey to Lebanon, N Iraq
and N Iran, is glandular, with leaf blades ovate-
lanceolate or elliptic, tapering into a short stalk.
It grows on moist shady banks in pine, fir and
oak forest, flowering in April–July. The third
species in the genus is *B. siberica* Stev.
'Hadspen Cream' is a form of *B. macrophylla*
with an irregular creamy white margin to the
leaf, raised by Eric Smith in the 1960s.
'Dawson's White' syn. 'Variegata' has a wider,
paler margin to the leaf. 'Langtrees' (not
illustrated) has silver-spotted leaves. Hardy to
−15°C.

Caccinia macranthera (Banks & Sol.) Brand
var. **crassifolia** (Vent.) Brand (*Boraginaceae*)
Native of E Turkey, N Iraq and Iran, east to
Pakistan and the Pamir Alai, growing on banks,
dry hillsides and abandoned fields at up to
1900m in Turkey, flowering in April–July. Plant
with several stems to 50cm; leaves fleshy, to
10cm long. Flowers blue with tube 8–15mm and
petals 6–9mm. For dry well-drained soil in full
sun. This grows well in the Royal Botanic
Gardens, Edinburgh, in a sunny border. Hardy
to −20°C.

Mertensia ciliata (James) G. Don Mountain
Bell (*Boraginaceae*)   Native of C Oregon, east
to C Idaho and W Montana, W Colorado and
N New Mexico, growing by streams and in wet
meadows and scrub, flowering in May–August.
Rhizome short-creeping, forming clumps of
leafy stems. Flowers with tube 5-lobed, 1.3–2cm
long, narrower than *M. virginiana*. For moist,
peaty soil in full sun or slight shade. Hardy to
−20°C or less. Var. *stomatechoides* (Vell.) Jeps. is
found in moist places in coniferous forest in the
Sierra Nevada in California, from Tulare Co.
northwards to Oregon and in Nevada, at
1500–3000m. Corolla tube 6–8mm; the
expanded limb 4–10mm long.

Mertensia pulmonarioides Roth syn. *M.
virginica* (L.) DC. Virginia Cowslip, Blue Bells
Native of S Ontario to New Jersey and South
Carolina, Minnesota, Nebraska and Kansas,
growing in wet meadows and along streams,

Pentaglottis sempervirens

Caccinia macranthera

Brunnera macrophylla 'Hadspen Cream'

Brunnera macrophylla

Brunnera macrophylla 'Dawson's White'

flowering in March–May. Plant with a thick fleshy root. Stem 30–60cm. Leaves up to 15cm long, soft, fleshy. Flowers about 2.5cm long with narrow tube and expanded limb. The plant dies down soon after flowering and is completely dormant by mid-summer. For moist peaty soil in part shade or sun. Grows well in the Savill Gardens at Windsor but otherwise uncommon in gardens in Europe. It is, however, a popular and most beautiful plant for wild flower gardens in North America.

Mertensia simplicissima G. Don syn. *M. asiatica* (Takeda) Macbr. Native of Japan in N Honshu and Hokkaido, northwards to the Kurile Islands, Korea, Sakhalin and the Aleutian Islands, growing on sandy shores, flowering in May–September. Plant with prostrate flowering stems to 1m, from a rosette of glaucous leaves 3–8cm long. Flowers 8–12mm long. The closely related *M. maritima* (L.) S. F. Gray is found in northern Europe and NE North America, south to Massachusetts, usually on shingle beaches. In Britain it is becoming rare but still found in several places around the coast of Scotland and northern Ireland. Hardy to −20°C or less.

Pentaglottis sempervirens (L.) Tausch syn. *Anchusa sempervirens* L. (*Boraginaceae*) Native of SW Europe from C Portugal to SW France and naturalized in England, Ireland, Belgium and Italy, growing in damp, shady places or by roads and in hedges near the sea, flowering in April–June. A bristle-haired plant with a very deep tap root, with branched stems to 1m. Basal leaves 10–40cm, ovate-oblong, in a rosette. Flowers 8–10mm across, blue. Can become a weed if allowed to seed too freely, and the deep taproot is brittle and readily resprouts, making established plants difficult to remove. They are, however, easily killed by glycosate. Hardy to −10°C or less.

Trachystemon orientalis (L.) G. Don syn. *Borago orientalis* L. (*Boraginaceae*) Native of E Bulgaria, N Turkey and W Caucasus in wet beech forest on shady river banks and on damp rocks at up to 1000m, flowering in March–May. Rhizome creeping; flower stems emerging before the leaves, elongating during flowering to 28–40cm. Leaves ovate-cordate, with petiole 10–25cm and blade c.20 × 18cm, ovate-cordate, acuminate. Flowers with petals 4–6mm, curled back. Easy in moist shade and naturalized in several places in England. Valued for its early flowering and tolerance of neglect. Hardy to −15°C, perhaps less.

Trachystemon orientalis at Wisley

LAMIUM

Lamium galeobdolon 'Florentinum'

Lamium galeobdolon 'Hermann's Pride'

Lamium galeobdolon 'Silberteppich'

Lamium maculatum 'Beacon Silver'

Ajuga reptans 'Atropurpurea'

Lamium maculatum 'Chequers'

Lamium maculatum 'Roseum'

Lamium maculatum 'Aureum'

Ajuga reptans 'Multicolor'

Specimens from Eccleston Square, London, 12 April. ⅓ life size

Lamium galeobdolon 'Hermann's Pride'

Ajuga genevensis L. (*Labiatae*) Native of Europe from S Sweden to France (and long naturalized in England), east to European Russia, Turkey and the Caucasus, growing in scrub, in moist meadows and on steppe grassland, chalk downs and limestone grassland, flowering in May–July. Plant with creeping underground stolons. Stems 6–30cm, with white hairs. Leaves obovate with a long petiole. Flowers bright blue; upper bracts shorter than the flowers. The closely related *A. orientalis* L. from SE Europe and SW Asia differs in its more woolly stems, shorter bracts and stamens which are not exserted from the corolla which is said to be twisted through 180°. Hardy to –20°C.

Ajuga reptans L. Native of most of Europe except N Scandinavia and Russia and of North Africa eastwards to the Caucasus, Turkey and Iran, growing in woods, grassy places and on sunny banks, flowering in April–June. Flowering stems 10–30cm. Bracts ovate, tinged with blue, the upper shorter than the flowers. Flowers deep blue, rarely pink or white, 14–17mm long. Plant producing stolons at least 15cm long in summer. Forms with different leaf variegation and shape have been selected, and are usually grown for groundcover in rather dry shade, producing a mass of rosettes of rather spoon-shaped leaves.
'Atropurpurea' syn. 'Purpurea' has dark-purple leaves, with a shining surface.
'Multicolor' syns. 'Tricolor', 'Rainbow' has leaves variegated with pink and white.
'Jungle Beauty' and 'Jumbo' not shown here, are extra large with green leaves, possibly hybrids with *A. genevensis*.

Lamium album L. (*Labiatae*) White Dead Nettle Native of Europe and Asia from Turkey eastwards, though rare in the Mediterranean region, growing in hedgerows, waste places, forests, rocky slopes and by streams, and often as a weed of gardens, flowering in April–August. Plant with creeping stolons and upright flowering stems to 60cm. Flowers white 20–27mm long in whorls of 8–10. A rather weedy plant for highly cultivated parts of the garden, but very pretty on a grassy bank with forget-me-nots and primroses and other wild flowers. Hardy to –25°C or less. There is a variegated form, 'Friday', and 'Pale Peril', with new shoots gold.

Lamium galeobdolon (L.) L. syns. *Galeobdolon luteum* Hudson, *Lamiastrum galeobdolon* (L.) Ehrend & Polatschek Yellow Archangel Native of Europe from Ireland eastwards to European Russia, and south to Spain, N Turkey and the Caucasus, in wood and hedgerows on grassy banks, marshes and moist, rocky slopes, flowering in April–June. Two subspecies are common in Europe and a third is rarer. Subsp. *luteum* is commonest in N & E Europe, and is known in England only in Lincolnshire. It has leaves and bracts usually with blunt teeth, 1–2 times as long as wide, and up to 8 medium-sized (17–21mm) flowers in a whorl. It is diploid. Subspecies *montanum* (Pers.) Hayek has leaves with sharp acute teeth, upper bracts 1.8–3.5 times as long as wide, and 9–15 often large (to 2.5cm long) flowers in a whorl. It is commonest in southern Europe, and is the plant generally found wild in England and Ireland. It is tetraploid. A third subspecies, *flavidum* (F. Hermann), is also diploid, and is commonest in the central-eastern Alps, the Apennines and N Yugoslavia. It has sharply serrate or biserrate leaves, and more than 10 small flowers in a whorl. It is usually found on subalpine screes and rocky slopes.

To subsp. *argentatum* (Smejkal) Stace belongs the commonly cultivated and very rampant clone 'Florentinum' syn. 'Variegatum'. It is a native of E Europe and now widely naturalized elsewhere.
'Silberteppich' syn. 'Silver Carpet' A variety of *Lamium galeobdolon* in which the leaves are almost entirely silvery. Flowers yellow. Much less invasive than 'Variegatum' and often damaged by slugs. It is a form of subsp. *flavidum*, found by E. Pagels in Yugoslavia.
'Hermann's Pride' A much more robust form with even more beautiful silver leaves. It does not suffer from the purple-leaf disease as does 'Silberteppich'.

LAMIUM

Lamium garganicum L. subsp. *laevigatum*
Arcangeli syn. *L. longiflorum* Tenori   A very
variable species, native of Europe from S France
and NW Africa east to Romania, Turkey and
NW Iran, growing on rocks, screes, shady cliffs
and banks, often on high mountains, flowering
in March–September. Plant mat-forming, with
sprawling stems 6–45cm high. Flowers with
upper lip of corolla bifid, 26–40cm long usually
purplish pink: shown here is subsp. *laevigatum*,
one of the larger subspecies with stems more
than 10cm high, and leaves with few hairs. It is
native of the northern part of the species range.
Most distinct is subsp. *pulchrum* R. Mill from
mountains in C Turkey, in which the leaves are
densely silky and the large flowers are white
with bluish-purple veins and blotches. Easily
grown in well-drained soil.

Lamium maculatum L.   Native of most of
Europe, excluding the British Isles and
Scandinavia, and of N Iran, the Caucasus,
Turkey (mainly in the north and Amanus
Mountains), growing in woods, on banks and
subalpine meadows, flowering in
February–June. Plant with mat-forming,
creeping and rooting non-flowering stems, and
flowering stems 15–40cm tall. Leaves 1–8cm,
often with a white blotch. Flowers usually
pinkish purple, sometimes brownish purple,
pale pink or white, 20–35mm long. Easily grown
in partial shade or cool places in full sun. Hardy
to −20°C.
Lamium maculatum cultivars:
'**Album**'   Flowers white; leaves with silver
flash.
'**Aureum**'   Flowers pinkish; leaves bright
yellow-green, with silver flash.
'**Beacon Silver**' syn. 'Silbergroschen'   White
leaves and pinkish-purple flowers. Leaves often
with purple blotches caused by a disease.
'**Chequers**'   Flowers purplish pink, leaves with
silver flash – close to the commonest form of the
species.
'**Roseum**'   Flowers pale pink, leaves with
white flash. The distinction between the colour
of this and the normal variety is clearer than
appears in the photograph.
'**White Nancy**'   Leaves silver, usually without
purple blotches. Flowers white.

Lamium orvala L.   Native of N Italy and W
Austria east to W Yugoslavia and S Hungary,
growing in scrub and on the edges of woods,
flowering in April–May. Flowering stems
30–100cm, usually *c*.40cm. Leaves 4.0–15cm
long. Flowers dark purple to pink or white,
'Album' 2.5–4.5cm long. An attractive plant for
well-drained soil in partial shade, slowly
forming wide mats. Hardy to −15°C.

Meehania urticifolia (Miq.) Makino (*Labiatae*)
Native of NE China, Korea and Japan (except
Hokkaido), growing in damp woods in the
mountains, flowering in April–May. Plant with
long stolons rooting at the nodes, spreading
quickly to form a large patch. Flowering stems
upright, 15–30cm long. Leaves 2–5cm long;
flowers 4–5cm long. An attractive, early-
flowering ground cover plant for partial shade,
deciduous in cold winters. *M. cordata* (Nutt.)
Britton, native of moist woods in SW
Pennsylvania to Illinois, Tennessee and North
Carolina, is smaller, less far creeping, with
pinkish-purple flowers 2.5–3cm long, in dense
clusters. A third species, *M. montis-koyae* Ohwi,
does not have creeping stolons and is nearly
hairless. It is confined to S&W Honshu, and is
close to *M. fargesii* from W China, shown on
p. 430.

Lamium orvala and 'Album' at the Royal Botanic Gardens, Kew

Lamium maculatum 'White Nancy'

Lamium album

Lamium garganicum subsp. *laevigatum*

Meehania urticifolia at Harry Hay's, Surrey

Ajuga genevensis

Lamium galeobdolon subsp. *montanum*

Lathraea clandestina with *Equisetum*

Lathraea squamaria and *Anemone nemorosa*

Jaborosa integrifolia

Hyoscyamus aureus L. (*Solanaceae*) Native of the E Mediterranean region from Crete, Rhodes and SW Turkey east to NW Iraq and south to Egypt, growing on cliffs, old walls and ruins, at up to 1200m, flowering in February–July. An attractive, tufted plant around 60cm across with softly hairy and glandular leaves, the blade orbicular to ovate, 3–5cm long. Flowers 3–4cm across, with exserted stamens. For a hot, dry position in a wall or rock crevice. Hardy to −10°C, perhaps. *Hyoscyamus albus* L., which is also often seen on classical ruins, has greenish or yellowish flowers, and stamens not exserted. It may be annual or perennial.

Jaborosa integrifolia Lam. (*Solanaceae*) Native of S Brazil, Uruguay and NE Argentina, around Buenos Aires, growing on the pampas, in damp fields, flowering in November–December, but in May–June in gardens in the north. Plant spreading by underground rhizomes which produce rosettes of leaves *c.*15cm long on short shoots. Flowers *c.*5cm across. For well-drained soil in a warm position. Hardy to −15°C with protection in winter. Most of the 6 or 7 species of *Jaborosa* have deeply cut or toothed leaves.

Lathraea clandestina L. (*Scrophulariaceae*) Native of W Europe, from Belgium south to Spain and east to S Italy, and naturalized in England, growing in wet woods, or meadows by streams, parasitic on the roots of willow, poplar, alder or maple. A leafless plant with crowded fleshy stems to 5cm, usually less. Flowers often emerging directly from the ground, 40–50mm. Seeds large, *c.*5mm, across, expelled explosively. Can be established by sowing fresh seed near the roots of suitable trees, or by transplanting roots and soil from where the plant is growing; I suspect seed lying in the soil is thereby kept moist, and so germinates well. Hardy to −15°C.

Lathraea squamaria L. Toothwort Native of most of Europe, from Ireland eastwards to the Himalayas and south to Spain and Turkey, growing in moist woods, and parasitic on many different trees, but usually on hazel, alder or beech, flowering in March–June. A leafless plant with few fleshy stems to 30cm. Flowers 14–17mm long. Not often cultivated, but possibly seed sown on the surface roots of suitable trees would establish itself. Hardy to −20°C or less.

Mandragora autumnalis Bertol. (*Solanaceae*) Mandrake Native of the Mediterranean coastal regions, from Portugal to Turkey and North Africa and Israel, in rocky places in pine woods and olive groves (at up to 600m in Turkey), flowering from January–April (var. *microcarpa* Bertol. flowers in autumn). The deep, thick, usually forked root was the famous Mandrake, which was said to shriek when it was pulled out of the ground; the leaves are sparsely hairy and sometimes even prickly, to 40cm long when fully developed. Flowers purplish, 4–8cm across. Fruit like a small, slightly elongated tomato, yellow or orange, with a long calyx. Hardy to −15°C, perhaps. *M. officinalis* L. has hairier leaves, smaller greenish-white flowers and round yellow fruit. It is found only in N Italy and W Yugoslavia. *M. caulescens* C. B. Clarke is a remarkable species from the Himalayas at 3000–4500m, with nodding, bell-shaped flowers, *c.*2–5cm across, on leafy stems which reach 30cm high. It is

illustrated in Polunin & Stainton's *Flowers of the Himalaya.*

Phelypaea tournefortii Desf. (*Orobanchaceae*) Native of E Turkey and the S Caucasus in Georgia and Armenia, growing on mountain steppes at 1600–2600m, parasitic on *Achillea* and *Tanacetum*, flowering in June–July. Flowering stems 10–20cm, few to several, from a stout base on the root of the host. Stems and calyx glandular-pilose, with whitish hairs. Flowers to 5cm across, the petals velvety in texture. As far as I know, this exciting plant has never been cultivated successfully, but should be tried from seed sown around the roots of a suitable host, in a position in full sun, hot and dry in summer, moist in autumn and spring, and cold and dry in winter. Hardy to −20°C or less.

Physochlaina alaica Korolk. ex Kovalevsk. (*Solanaceae*) Native of Central Asia, in the Pamir-Alai, growing on rocky slopes at *c.*1800m, flowering in April–May. Stem *c.*30cm. Leaves and stem softly hairy. Flowers yellowish, *c.*2cm long, in a rounded head. For well-drained soil in sun or partial shade, kept rather dry in summer. Hardy to −20°C or less.

Physochlaina orientalis (M. Bieb.) G. Don syn. *Hyoscyamus orientalis* Bieb. Native of the Caucasus, NW Iran and NE Turkey near Gümüşane, apparently often found in the mouths of caves and in rock crevices, at *c.*1500m, flowering in May. Plant with densely and softly hairy stems to 60cm from a stout rootstock. Leaves triangular ovate 4–13cm long, long-stalked. Flowers *c.*1.5cm long, purplish. For well-drained soil in sun or part shade. Unusual and valuable for its early flowering, usually in April in S England. Although rare in gardens, it has been grown at least since 1823. *Physochlaina* is a small genus of about 4 species, mainly in C Asia. *P. praealta* (Decne.) Miers, from the Himalayas, is taller, to 120cm, with greenish-yellow, purple-veined flowers in a cluster to 10cm across.

Rehmannia glutinosa Libosch. ex Fisch. & Mey. syn. *R. chinensis* Fisch. & Mey. (*Scrophulariaceae*) Native of N China, especially the area round Beijing, where it is common on old walls in the Forbidden City and the Ming tombs, and of Korea, growing in well-drained, stony ground on roadsides and in woods, flowering in April–July. Stems 15–30cm. Leaves softly pubescent. Flowers 5–7.5cm long, reddish brown to yellow, veined with purple. Probably hardy to −25°C at least if dry, but the softly hairy leaves are susceptible to warm damp in winter, so it is often grown in a greenhouse.

Scopolia carniolica Jacq. syns. *S. tubiflora* Kreyer, *S. ?caucasica* Kolesn. ex Kreyer (*Solanaceae*) Native of Austria, Italy and Yugoslavia, eastwards to Baltic Russia and the Caucasus, growing in moist rocky beech woods at *c.*1000m, flowering in April–May. Rhizome fleshy, horizontal; stems 20–60cm, with ovate or obovate leaves, all glabrous. Flowers 1.5–2.5cm long, usually brownish-purple or brownish-orange outside, paler inside, but sometimes all greenish-yellow in var. *brevifolia* Dunal, syn. sutsp. *hladnikiana* (Koch) Nyman, shown here. Fruit a capsule, not a berry as in so many *Solanaceae* (Nightshade family).

Mandragora autumnalis at Wisley

Physochlaina orientalis at Kew

Scopolia carniolica at Wisley

Physochlaina alaica near Ferghana

Rehmannia glutinosa in woods near Beijing

Rehmannia glutinosa on a ruined Ming tomb

Hyoscyamus aureus on ancient walls near Kaş, SW Turkey

Phelypaea tournefortii near Erzurum

Doronicum carpetanum

Doronicum plantagineum with *Allium ursinum*

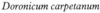
Doronicum 'Miss Mason'

Doronicum pardalianches

Doronicum carpetanum Boiss. & Reut. ex Willk. (*Compositae*)   Native of the Pyrenees, N & C Spain, N & C Portugal, growing in mountain meadows and among rocks, flowering in May–June. Plant forming large clumps of stems, 40–80cm tall. Basal leaves cordate, with long petioles. Stem leaves 6–8. Flowers 2–3 per stem, rarely more, 4–5cm across. A fine plant for a moist and partially shaded position. Hardy to −15°C, probably less.

Doronicum orientale Hoffm. syn. *D. caucasicum* M. Bieb.   Native of SE Europe, from Italy, Sicily and Yugoslavia east to Hungary and the Caucasus, and south to Turkey and Lebanon, growing in woods and scrub, in places dry in summer, at 50–1900m in Turkey, flowering in March–July, normally in April in S England. Plant spreading slowly by fleshy underground rhizomes to make wide patches. Basal leaves ovate or cordate, with a long stalk. Flower head solitary, 2.5–5cm across on a glandular and hairy stalk, 10–60cm tall, usually *c*.30cm. Stem leaves 1 or 2. For a partially shaded position, and tolerant of drought in summer, when the leaves die down. Hardy to −15°C or less.

Doronicum pardalianches L. Great Leopard's Bane   Native of W Europe from Belgium south to Spain, and east to Germany and Italy (and naturalized in Austria, Britain and Czechoslovakia), growing in woods, flowering in May–July. Plant forming spreading patches

by tubers produced at the end of underground stolons. Stems to 90cm. Basal leaves cordate, upper amplexicaul. Flower heads usually 2–6, 3–5cm across. A tall, softly hairy plant for moist soil in partial shade. Hardy to −20°C or less.

Doronicum plantagineum L.   Native of Portugal and Spain, W Italy and France, and naturalized in Britain, especially in E Scotland, in woods, meadows and heathland, flowering in April–June. Rhizome spreading and somewhat tuberous, with tufts of hairs, the plant forming extensive colonies. Stems to 80cm. Basal leaves ovate-elliptical, often weakly cordate, with a long stalk, sometimes toothed; upper leaves not amplexicaul. Flower heads 1 or 2, rarely more, 3–5cm across. Easily grown in sun or semi-shade, and very pretty naturalized in grass.

Doronicum cultivars: There are several cultivars, usually dwarf and early flowering, and often double. Shown here are:
'Miss Mason'   Stems to 45cm. Flowering in April and early May.
'Frühlingspracht' syn. 'Spring Beauty'   Stems to 45cm, usually less, with hideous double flowers.

Petasites fragrans (Vill.) C. Presl. (*Compositae*) Winter Heliotrope   Native of the Mediterranean region of Italy, Sardinia, Sicily and North Africa, in damp shady woods and gorges, flowering in December–March; commonly naturalized on roadsides in other

Doronicum 'Frühlingspracht'

Doronicum orientale near Fethiye, SW Turkey

Petasites fragrans beautiful, but unwanted at Sellindge, Kent

parts of western Europe. Flowering stem up to 50cm. Leaves to 20cm across, reniform-cordate, green but hairy beneath. Flowers strongly scented of Heliotrope, pale lilac to purple. Only the male plant is naturalized or cultivated, and the female, according to *Flora Europea*, is unknown. This plant is a terrible spreader by fleshy underground rhizomes, and is a weed in many old gardens. The flowers, however, which are freely produced in mild winters, are most welcome. Cold below −10°C will kill the top growth, but the roots survive.

Petasites palmatus (Ait.) Gray Sweet Coltsfoot   Native of North America from Newfoundland to Massachusetts, west to Alaska and south to S California along the coast, growing along streams in woods, flowering in February–April. Plant creeping by underground rhizomes. Flowering stems to 50cm, produced before the leaves. Flowers scented. Leaves 10–40cm wide, palmately lobed with 7–11 toothed lobes. For a moist, shady position. Hardy to −20°C and less. *P. japonicus* (Sieb. & Zucc.) Maxim., from Japan, Korea and China, has similar flowers, but huge orbicular leaves which may be 1.5m across, on stems 2m tall in var. *giganteus*; used by Japanese children as umbrellas.

Petasites paradoxus (Retz) Baumg. syn. *P. niveus* (Vill.) Baumb.   Native of Europe, from France and Spain in the Pyrenees, east to the Carpathians and C Yugoslavia, growing by streams in woods in the mountains, usually on limestone, near melting snow, flowering from May–July. Flowering stem up to 25cm. Leaves when mature, triangular-cordate to hastate, densely white-hairy beneath. Attractive with its pinkish-red bracts, which distinguish it from the commoner ghostly white and green *P. albus* (L.) Gaerten, also frequent in alpine woods. Both are too rampant underground for all but the wildest part of the garden.

Petasites paradoxus in the Valais

Petasites palmatus in California

Clintonia umbellulata at Washfield Nurseries

Clintonia uniflora in Yosemite, California

Clintonia andrewsiana in NW California

Clintonia borealis at Wisley

Clintonia andrewsiana Torr. (*Liliaceae*)
Native of California from Del Norte Co.
northwards to SW Oregon, in Redwood forests
in moist, shady places, flowering in May–July.
Plant without runners, forming clumps. Leaves
5 or 6, 15–25cm long, 5–12cm across. Stem
25–50cm; flowers in both terminal and lateral
umbels, deep reddish; the petals with nectaries
at the base, 10–15mm long. Berries bluish black,
8–12mm long. For semi-shade and moist peaty
or leafy soil. This species grows well in E
Scotland at the Royal Botanic Garden,
Edinburgh, and at Glendoick. Hardy to −10°C,
probably lower with a good mulch.

Clintonia borealis (Ait.) Raf.   Native to E
North America, from Newfoundland to
Manitoba south to North Carolina and
Wisconsin, growing in moist woods and scrub,
often in the mountains, flowering in May–June.
Stems creeping underground to form extensive
colonies. Leaves 2–5; stems 15–35cm, with 3–6
drooping, greenish-yellow flowers. Petals 16–
20mm long. Berries blue. For loose leafy or peaty
soil in shade or partial shade. Hardy to −25°C,
or less, but damaged by late frosts.

Clintonia umbellulata (Michx.) Morong syn.
C. umbellata Torrey   Native of E North
America, from New York and New Jersey south
to Georgia and Tennessee, growing in woods in
the hills, flowering from May–June. Stems
15–40cm, shortly creeping underground to form
dense patches. Leaves 2–5, oblong, oblanceolate
or obovate. Flowers sometimes purple-spotted,
scented, 8–12mm long. Berries black. For a
slightly moist position in partial or deciduous
shade. The fine clump shown here was growing
on acid clay in Kent. Hardy to −25°C.

Clintonia uniflora (Schultes) Kunth Bride's
Bonnet   Native of N & E California, north to
British Columbia and east to Montana, in pine
forest and under *Sequoiadendron*, at
1000–1800m in California, flowering from
May–July. Plant with slender underground
runners. Leaves 2–3, 7–15cm long; 2.5–6cm
wide. Flower stems 7–10cm; flowers solitary,
with petals pubescent, 1.8–2.2cm long. For
well-drained, moist leafy soil in part shade.
Hardy to −15°C. The fifth species of the genus,
C. udensis Trautv. & C. A. Meyer syn. *C. alpina*
Baker, from the Himalayas in N India and
Nepal east to SW China and Japan, has pale-
mauve or white flowers 6–10mm long, in a
nodding umbel of 2–6; it grows in alpine forests
and scrub, flowering in April–July.

Helonias bullata L. (*Melanthiaceae*)   Native
of E North America, from N New Jersey and S
New York south to North Carolina, growing in
swamps and bogs, flowering April–May.
Rhizome tuberous. Leaves 15–45cm long, up to
5cm wide, evergreen, crisp and shiny. Flowering
stems 4–20cm; flower heads 2–3cm long, of
25–30 minute flowers. This is the only species in
the genus and differs from *Heloniopsis* in its
smaller flowers in a tight head. For moist acid
and peaty soil. Hardy to −20°C.

Heloniopsis orientalis (Thunb.) Tanaka
(*Melanthiaceae*)   Native throughout Japan, but
commonest in the north, in Korea and Sakhalin,
growing woods, scrub and meadows in the
mountains, flowering in April–June. Leaves

Heloniopsis orientalis at Wisley

Heloniopsis orientalis var. *flavida*

Helonias bullata at Wisley

evergreen, 7–15cm long, rather leathery.
Flowering stems 10–60cm, elongating after
flowering, with 3–10 flowers. Petals 1–1.5cm
long, pink, becoming purplish or greenish in
fruit. Easily grown in a cool shady position in
leafy soil, kept moist in summer. Hardy to
−15°C. Var. *breviscapa* (Maxim.) Ohwi, in spite
of its name, differs mainly in its smaller, white
or pale pink flowers. It is found in Kyushu and
Yakushima, in the mountains. Var. *flavida*
(Nakai) Ohwi, from C Honshu, is a taller plant
with thinner leaves, and white or greenish
flowers, green in fruit. *Ypsilandra thibetica*
Franch. is very similar to Heloniopsis, but has a
nodding spike of white flowers which become
pinkish-brown as they mature.

Scoliopus bigelowii Torr. Slink Pod
(*Liliaceae*)   Native of SW Oregon and N
California, from Humboldt Co. to Santa Cruz
Co., growing in moist, shady places in Redwood
forest below 500m, flowering in February–
March. Plant with 2 broad leaves to 10cm wide,
20cm long, from a slender rootstock. Flowering
stems 3-angled, leafless, 3–12 in an umbel at
ground level, 10–20cm tall, recurving in fruit.
Flowers with greenish sepals and narrow, erect
petals, 14–17mm long, smelling of bad meat.
For careful cultivation in moist, peaty soil in
shade. Hardy to −10°C or so, and requires
protection in cold winters. A second species, *S.
hallii* Watson, from Oregon, is similar but
smaller, with unspotted leaves.

Streptopus roseus Michx. Liverberry
(*Liliaceae*)   Native of E North America, from
Newfoundland to Manitoba and south to
Georgia and Michigan, growing in moist woods,
flowering in May–July. Plant with several very
graceful and slender stems, 25–60cm tall,
branched above. Leaves ciliate. Flowers
6–12mm long; anthers forked. Berries red. For
cool leafy soil in shade or partial shade. Hardy
to −20°C or less. *S. amplexifolius* (L.) DC. from
wet subalpine woods in the Alps, eastwards to
Japan and North America, has taller stems,
amplexicaul leaves and greenish-white flowers
*c.*1cm long.

Scoliopus bigelowii at the Royal Botanic Gardens, Kew

Streptopus roseus at Cruickshank Botanic Garden, Aberdeen

Uvularia sessilifolia

Prosartes trachycarpa at the Savill Gardens, Windsor

Uvularia perfoliata

Uvularia grandiflora

Disporum bodinieri (Lvl.) Wang & Tang (*Convallariaceae*) Native of W China, in Guizhou, Yunnan and Sichuan at 1000–1800m, growing in lush, wet scrub on steep mountains, flowering in April–May. Plant with few, much-branched stems to 2m. Leaves *c.*7m long; flowers pale yellowish green, to 3cm long, with exserted stamens. For rich, moist soil in shade or partial shade. Hardy to −15°C perhaps.

Disporum cantoniense (Lour.) Merrill syn. *D. pullum* hort. Native of W China, in Yunnan to Hubei, of Japan and SE Asia, growing in open woods and scrub, flowering in May–June. Plant with few stems to 2m, elongating after flowering. Flowers on short pedicels, *c.*2.5cm long, white or reddish. For well-drained soil in shade or partial shade. Hardy to −15°C perhaps.

Disporum megalanthum Wang & Tang Native of W China, in Sichuan, growing in bamboo and *Rhododendron* scrub at 1600–2500m, flowering in May–June. Plant with few, upright stems to 30cm at flowering, elongating later. Flowers white, *c.*3cm long, stamens not exserted. Sweetly scented. Easily grown. Hardy to −15°C.

Disporum sessile subsp. *flavens* Kitagawa Native of Korea and Heilongjiang (Manchuria) growing in deciduous woods, flowering in May–June. Flowers 2cm long.

Disporum uniflorum Baker Native of W China, in Yunnan, especially near Lijiang, growing among bracken in *Rhododendron* and mixed deciduous scrub at 2000m, flowering in May. Plant with few stems to 1m, elongating after flowering. Flowers on long, *c.*6cm, pedicles, to 4cm long, stamens not exserted. For well-drained, leafy soil in sun or partial shade. Hardy to −15°C.

Prosartes smithii (Hook.) Utech, Shinwari & Kawario syn. *Disporum smithii* (Hook.) Piper (*Liliaceae*) Native of the coast ranges of California, from Santa Cruz Co. north to British Columbia, growing in cool, moist places in Redwood and evergreen forest, flowering in March–May. Stems 30–90cm, in clumps. Leaves ovate to ovate-lanceolate, rounded or subcordate at the base, 5–12cm long. Flowers 2–6 in a group, whitish, the petals 1.5–2.5cm

long. Berries obovoid, orange to red. Hardy to −15°C, perhaps less.

Prosartes trachycarpa s. Wats. syn. *Disporum trachycarpum* (S. Wats.) Benth. & Hook. Native of W North America, from British Columbia to NE Oregon and south along the Rockies from North Dakota to S Arizona and W New Mexico, at up to 3000m in Arizona, growing in woods, often along streams, flowering in May–July. Plant with several branched stems to 60cm. Leaves 4–12cm long, ovate, ciliate, glabrous above. Flowers creamy white, 9–15mm long, with exserted stamens. Style smooth. Berry yellow, becoming red. For moist, leafy soil in shade. Hardy to −20°C.

Uvularia grandiflora Smith (*Convallariaceae*) Native of Quebec to Ontario, south to Minnesota, Georgia, Tennessee and Kansas, growing in woods on rich soils, flowering in April–June. Stems to 75cm, glabrous. Leaves perfoliate, 5–13cm long, downy beneath, at least when young. Flowers 2.5–5cm, bright yellow, inner surface of petals smooth. Easily grown in well-drained but moist, leafy soil; in deciduous shade; needs protection from slugs when young. Hardy to −20°C.

Uvularia perfoliata L. Straw Bell Native of Quebec to Ontario, south to Florida and Mississippi growing in moist woods and scrub, flowering in April–June. Stems 20–60cm, glabrous. Leaves perfoliate, 5–9cm, long, glabrous and paler beneath. Flowers 2–3.5cm, pale yellow; inner surface of petals with minute glands. Easily grown in moist, leafy soil in partial shade. Hardy to −20°C or less.

Uvularia sessilifolia L. Straw Lilies Native of New Brunswick and Ontario, west to Minnesota, south to Georgia and Arkansas, growing in moist woods and scrub, flowering in May–June. Rootstock creeping; stem to 40cm, glabrous. Leaves 3.5–7.5cm, not perfoliate, glabrous, paler beneath. Flowers pale greenish yellow, 1.5–3cm long; inner surface of petals smooth. Capsule ovate, 3-angled, tapering into its stalk. Easily grown in moist, leafy soil in deciduous shade. Distinguished from *U. caroliniana* by its thin leaves and smooth stem.

Disporum bodinieri in the Min River Valley, Sichuan

Disporum bodinieri

Disporum uniflorum at Lijiang, Yunnan

Disporum sessile subsp. *flavens* at Kew

Disporum megalanthum at Wolong, Sichuan

Disporum cantoniense

Prosartes smithii

Lysichiton americanus at Chyverton, Cornwall

Symplocarpus foetidus near New York

Orontium aquaticum

Acorus calamus at Leeds Castle, Kent

Acorus calamus 'Variegatus'

Lysichiton camschatcensis

Acorus calamus L. (*Acoraceae*)   Native of Siberia, China, Japan and W North America, and naturalized from Iran and Turkey westwards since the 16th century, growing in shallow water by lakes and slow rivers; in Europe especially associated with moats and lakes around old castles. Leaves and leaf-like stems upright to 1.5m, striped in 'Variegatus', tinged pink at the base, often with wavy margins, 6–15mm wide. Flowers minute, greenish, on an apparently lateral spadix which is about 7cm long, produced in May–July. 'Variegatus' has a cleaner, longer-lasting variegation than any of the striped water irises. The plant was grown for its aromatic foliage and the Oil of Calamus extracted from the leaves and rhizomes. Hardy to −25°C. *Acorus gramineus* Solander, from India, China and Japan, is smaller, to 50cm, has evergreen leaves without a midrib and an almost erect spadix 5–10cm long. It is the dwarf form, var. *pusillus* Engl., that is generally cultivated, and the striped 'Argenteostriatus' is also common.

Lysichiton americanus Hult. & St. John (*Araceae*) Yellow Skunk Cabbage   Native of NW California, from near San Francisco in the Santa Cruz mountains, north to Alaska and east to Montana in bogs and wet woods, flowering in April–June. Leaves when mature 30–50cm tall, oblong to elliptical, short-stalked. Flowers emerging before or with the leaves, on stalks 30–50cm tall. Spathe 10–20m long, yellow. Easily grown in wet soil and valuable for its early flowering and large handsome leaves. The flowers smell unpleasant, but not foul enough to upset anyone who grows the plant well.

Lysichiton camschatcensis (L.) Schott Native of Japan, in N Honshu and Hokkaido northwards to E Siberia, Sakhalin, Kamchatka and the Kurile Islands, growing in bogs and wet places and by ponds and lakes, flowering in April–July. Like *L. americanus*, but smaller and white flowered. Mature leaves 40–80cm long. Flowers emerging before or with the leaves, on stems 10–30cm long. Spathe 8–12cm long. Flowers sweetly scented. Easily grown in moist, acid soil but rarer than *L. americanus* in gardens. Young plants of both species require protection from slugs. The probable hybrid between the two species has a pale-yellow or creamy spathe.

Orontium aquaticum L. (*Araceae*) Golden Club   Native of E North America, from Massachusetts and Kentucky south to Florida and Louisiana, growing in peaty swamps and ponds, flowering in April–June. Leaves either emerging or floating on the water surface, the blade 15–30cm long; flowering stems 15–60cm long. Spadix 2.5–5cm long. Spathe bract-like and usually dropping off before flowering. For pools and shallow water. Hardy to −20°C.

Symplocarpus foetidus (L.) Nutt. syn. *Spathyema foetida* (L.) Raf. (*Araceae*) Skunk Cabbage   Native of Nova Scotia, west to Manitoba, south to Georgia, growing in swampy woods and by streams, flowering in February–April, as soon as the frost departs the soil. Leaves 30–90cm long, *c.*30cm wide, ovate, truncate at base, developing during and after flowering into handsome rosettes. Spathe emerging before the leaves, 7.5–15cm tall, solid, fleshy, stinking. Spadix becoming large, up to 15cm in diameter when ripe in August–September. Hardy to −25°C and less.

Aquilegia canadensis near Charlottesville, Virginia

Aquilegia canadensis

Aquilegia elegantula

Aquilegia formosa var. *formosa*

Aquilegia 'Crimson Star'

Aquilegia caerulea James (*Ranunculaceae*) Native of SW Montana to N Arizona and N New Mexico, growing in the mountains at 2200–3000m, commonly in aspen groves, flowering in June–August. Stems to 90cm. Flowers 5–7.5cm across; sepals spreading, blue; petals blue or white, with spur 3–5cm, and the well-developed petal limb commonly white. This is the state flower of Colorado, where it grows on the north rim of the Grand Canyon. For a sheltered position in sun or partial shade.

Aquilegia canadensis L. Wild Columbine Native of North America from Nova Scotia to the Northwest Territories, south to Nebraska, Texas and Florida, growing in rocky woods and on shady banks and damp roadsides, flowering in April–July. Stem 25–60cm, glabrous or slightly pubescent. Leaflets deeply lobed; flowers 2.5–5cm long, including the straight spurs which are *c*.12mm long, usually scarlet, very rarely white or yellow. Sepals pointing downwards *c*.15mm long. Style and stamens exserted. Pollinated by hummingbirds. For well-drained, sandy, soil in deciduous shade, or in cool areas with some sun. Hardy to −25°C.

Aquilegia chrysantha Gray   Native of S Colorado to New Mexico, Arizona and N Mexico, growing in moist places in pine forests, scrub and along streams at 1000–3200m, flowering in April–September. Stems to 60cm. Flowers facing upwards 4–7.5cm across, with spurs 4–7cm long; sepals spreading. *Aquilegia longissima* Gray, from mountains in W Texas, S Arizona and NE Mexico, is an even more striking species with pale yellow flowers, and spurs 9–15cm long. Both require moist, well-drained soil in a warm and sheltered position.

Aquilegia 'Crimson Star'   An attractive hybrid with red and white flowers. Plants short-lived. Hardy to −15°C perhaps.

Aquilegia elegantula Greene   Native of the Rocky Mountains from SW Colorado and SE Utah to N Mexico in rocky places at *c*.3000m, flowering in June–July. Plant slender to 60cm. Flowers with spurs less than 3cm long; sepals greenish at the apex. For a warm, sheltered position. Hardy to −15°C perhaps.

Aquilegia formosa Fisch.   Native of California, north to Alaska and east to W Montana and Utah, in moist woods and damp places in scrub and on banks from near sea level to 3000m, flowering in April–August, according to altitude and latitude. Stem 50–100cm, glandular above; basal leaves, bluish, biternate; leaflets divided to about the middle. Flowers to 5cm across, spurs 10–20mm usually scarlet, with yellow limbs to the petals, 3–5mm long. Sepals 15–25mm long, spreading or reflexed. Var. *formosa* is a mountain form, found at 1000–3000m in the Sierra Nevada; var. *truncata* (Fisch. & Mey.) Baker, with glabrous or sparingly pubescent stems, and the yellow lamina only 1–2mm long, is also shown here; it grows at lower altitudes also, and is common in the coast ranges of California. For a warm position in full sun or partial shade, with moisture at the root. Hardy to −25°C.

Aquilegia olympica Boiss.   Native of the Caucasus, N & W Iran and N & E Turkey, growing in alpine meadows, scrub and spruce forest at 1700–2800m in Turkey, flowering in June–July. Plant forming small clumps with several upright stems to 60cm. Flowers with bluish sepals 25–35mm long and somewhat hooked spurs. For moist but well-drained peaty soil. Hardy to −20°C or less. The name comes

Aquilegia formosa var. *truncata*

Aquilegia formosa var. *truncata* in the Salmon Mountains, NW California

Aquilegia chrysantha

Aquilegia chrysantha in Arizona

Aquilegia ottonis subsp. *amaliae*

from Armenian Olympus, today called Keşiş Dağ in NE Turkey.

Aquilegia ottonis Orph. ex Boiss. subsp. **amaliae** (Orph. ex Boiss.) Strid   Native of NE Greece where it is common on Olimbos Or (Thessalian Mount Olympus) at 900–2300m, and possibly of neighbouring Yugoslavia and Albania, growing in damp rocky places in gorges, flowering in June–August. Plant with several flowering stems to 45cm from a tough, woody rootstock. Leaflets 1.5–3cm long. Flowers 18–28mm long, with limb of spurred petals, white, a little shorter than the blue sepals. Seed capsules 12–15mm long. The other subspecies of A. ottonis are found in the Peloponnese and in Italy. For a cool position in partial shade. Hardy to −15°C.

Aquilegia olympica

Aquilegia caerulea

'Hensol Harebell'

Aquilegia
'Long-spurred Hybrids'

Aquilegia vulgaris
'Flore Pleno'

'Olympia'
Blue and White

Aquilegia vulgaris
(reddish seedling)

'Olympia'
Red and Gold

Aquilegia
'Mrs Scott Elliott
Hybrids'

'Dwarf Fairyland
mixed'

'Hensol Harebell'

Aquilegia vulgaris
'Nora Barlow'

Specimens from Wisley, 12 May. ⅔ life size

Aquilegia 'Dwarf Fairyland Mixed'

Aquilegia 'Biedermeier Mixed'

Aquilegia 'Dragonfly hybrids'

Aquilegia 'Music' (white seedling)

Aquilegia 'Olympia' violet and yellow

Aquilegia 'Hensol Harebell'

Aquilegia 'Biedermeier mixed' A short-stemmed strain with upward-facing flowers close to *A. vulgaris*, but stems around 50cm high.

Aquilegia 'Mrs Scott Elliott hybrids' *A. caerulea* James is described on p. 86. In this strain the flowers vary somewhat in colour from the typical blue and white form. Height around 80cm.

Aquilegia 'Dwarf Fairyland mixed' A low-growing compact, many stemmed strain with stems *c*.45cm, in which the upward-facing flowers may be single or double with numerous tubular petals and short spurs. Unusual, but if not positively ugly, then lacking the grace which is one of the main charms of the Columbines.

Aquilegia 'Hensol Harebell' A hybrid strain between *A. vulgaris* and *A. alpina*. Large rich-blue flowers on branched stems to 75cm, raised at Mossdale, Castle Douglas, Scotland, by a Mrs Kennedy in the early 1900s.

Aquilegia 'Long-spurred hybrids' and **'Dragonfly hybrids'** These long-spurred hybrids, in various shades of blue, yellow, red and bicolours, are derived from the American species *A. caerulea*, *A. chrysantha* and *A. formosa*. They are good plants for a sunny position and well-drained, but not dry soil, and are generally rather short-lived perennials,

easily raised from seed. 'Long-spurred hybrids' are tall, *c*.75cm, with flowers in rather pale shades. 'McKana' hybrids are similar. 'Dragonfly' hybrids are smaller, *c*.50cm with flowers of deeper shades.

Aquilegia 'Music' A strain of medium height, *c*.60cm tall, with long-spurred flowers in various colours.

Aquilegia 'Nora Barlow' This is a variant of *A. vulgaris*, with flowers with numerous narrow petals in pale green and red. It is curious rather than beautiful, and has been in cultivation since probably the 17th century, when it was known as the 'Rose Columbine'.

Aquilegia 'Olympia' 'Blue and White', 'Red and Gold' and **'Violet and Yellow'** In these seed strains, the striking bicolours have been stabilized. Stems to 60cm.

Aquilegia vulgaris 'Flore Pleno' In this double-flowered deep purple plant the sepals are normal, but there are at least twice the usual number of petals. Other strange mutants that are known are the spurless ones, called 'Stormy Columbines', and an upside-down one, with numerous spurs facing downwards on a nodding flower, which is shown in *Gerard's Herball* (1633). It appears to be lost at present but may recur.

Aquilegia fragrans near Vishensar, Kashmir

Aquilegia fragrans

Aquilegia alpina L. (*Ranunculaceae*) Native of the Alps in France, Switzerland, Austria and Italy, and in the N Apennines, growing in open woods and on shady rocks on cliffs at 1300–2000m, flowering in July–August. Stems 15–60cm usually with 1–3 flowers, pubescent above. Flowers nodding; sepals blue, 30–45mm. Spurs 18–25mm, blue, straight or curved, limb paler 14–17mm. For moist soil in a cool shaded position. Hardy to −20°C.

Aquilegia atrata Koch Native of the Alps, from France to Austria and the Apennines, growing in subalpine hay meadows, flowering in May–July. Stems 40–80cm, densely pubescent above. Flowers nodding, deep reddish purple, 3–5cm across; sepals 15–24mm; petals with limb 8–12mm, spur 10–15mm, hooked. Easily cultivated in moist or rather dry soil in partial shade, and striking with its tall stems and almost black flowers. Hardy to −20°C.

Aquilegia bertolonii Schott syn. *A. reuteri* Boiss. Native of SE France and NW Italy, in the Alpes Maritimes and neighbouring ranges, growing in scrub on rocky hillsides at 750–1600m, flowering in June–July, in warmer places and at lower altitudes than *A. alpina*. Stems 10–30cm, glandular above; stem leaves linear, usually entire. Flowers 1–5, nodding; sepals, spurs and lamina the same colour, usually purplish blue; sepals 18–33mm; spurs 10–14mm, straight or slightly curved; limb 10–14mm. This should be tolerant of a warmer and drier position than *A. alpina*. Hardy to −15°C.

Aquilegia flabellata Sieb. & Zucc. var. *pumila* Kudo '**Mini star**' Native of Honshu and Hokkaido, north to Sakhalin, the Kurile Islands and North Korea, growing in scrub in the mountains, flowering in June–August. Flowers with limb 1.5cm, white spurs incurved, 1–5cm. An attractive plant for a sunny position. 'Mini star' is a dwarf strain with stem *c*.15cm tall. *A. flabellata* itself is not known in the wild, but has long been cultivated in Japan. It is larger, with very glaucous leaves and stems 20–50cm, with flowers 3–5cm across. A white form is also known. Hardy to −20°C perhaps.

Aquilegia fragrans Benth. Native of N Pakistan to N India (Uttar Pradesh) and frequent in Kashmir, growing in scrub and subalpine meadows at 2400–2600m, flowering in June–August. Stems 40–80cm, not much branched; whole plant glandular. Flowers pale yellowish, white or pale blue-green, scented sweetly but with a hint of cat, 3–5cm long. Sepals 2.5–3cm, spreading; spur 15–18mm, straight or hooked. A beautiful species for good, well-drained soil in sun or partial shade. Hardy to −20°C.

Aquilegia vulgaris L. Native of most of Europe from England and Ireland, Spain and Portugal to Yugoslavia, Poland and N Russia, growing in woods and meadows at up to 1700m in the Alps, flowering in May–July. Stems 30–60cm, much branched. Flowers nodding, usually purplish blue, pink or rarely reddish purple or white, *c*.5cm across, with spurs 15–22mm, and limb 10–13mm. '**William Guiness**' syn. 'Magpie' has striking flowers of blackish-purple and white. Easily grown in sun or partial shade. Hardy to −25°C or less.

Aquilegia yabeana Kitag. Native of Korea and NE China, in Heilongjiang (Manchuria), growing in the mountains, flowering in May. Plant forming a small clump of delicate stems to 60cm. Leaflets *c*.1.5cm across. Flowers pinkish purple or reddish, *c*.2.5cm across. For a cool position in leafy soil. Hardy to −20°C.

Semiaquilegia ecalcarata (Maxim.) Sprague & Hutch. (*Ranunculaceae*) Native of W China, in Gansu, W Sichuan and Shensi, growing in damp, mossy woodland and scrub, flowering in May–June. Plant forming small clumps of branching stems to 40cm; flowers *c*.2.5cm across. For moist, leafy soil in sun or partial shade. Hardy to −20°C.

Aquilegia flabellata 'Mini star'

Aquilegia alpina in the Valais, with *Geranium sylvaticum* and *Trollius*

Aquilegia vulgaris 'William Guiness'

Aquilegia atrata in the Valais

Semiaquilegia ecalcarata

Aquilegia yabeana

Aquilegia bertolonii

Thalictrum aquilegifolium in Switzerland

Thalictrum minus with plumes of *Ferulago* in C Asia

Thalictrum flavum subsp. *glaucum* at the Savill Gardens, Windsor

Thalictrum delavayi 'Hewitt's Double'

Thalictrum lucidum at Wisley

Thalictrum delavayi

Thalictrum aquilegifolium by the waterlily pool in Monet's garden, Giverny, Normandy

Thalictrum aquilegifolium L.
(*Ranunculaceae*)   Native of Europe from
France and Spain eastwards to W Russia,
Romania and Turkey (where it is rare), growing
in meadows, often in the mountains, and on
shady rocks, flowering in May–July. Stems to
150cm; leaves green; flowers with sepals which
soon fall, but conspicuous stamens; the
filaments swollen towards the apex, purplish
pink or white. An attractive plant easily grown
in good moist soil. Hardy to −25°C.

Thalictrum delavayi Franch. syn. *T.
dipterocarpum* hort. non Franch.   Native of SW
China, in Yunnan and growing in alpine
meadows and scrub, flowering in
June–September. Stems to 200cm. Leaflets 3,
lobed, to 2.5cm across. Flowers with hanging
stamens, sepals to 12mm long, purple. 'Hewitt's
Double' has flowers with petaloid stamens
forming a dense rosette. There is also a white
form in cultivation. *T. chelidonii* DC. from the
Himalayas of Bhutan and Sikkim differs in its
leaflets 1–4cm across, coarsely and bluntly
toothed. Sepals 8–15mm long, purple. Both
species are best in a cool position with moist
peaty soil. Hardy to −15°C.

Thalictrum diffusiflorum Marquand & Airy
Shaw   Native of China in SE Xizang, growing
in scrub and woods, in grassy places, at 3600m,
flowering in July. Similar to *T. chelidonii* DC.
but with smaller leaflets and flowers on a very
lax inflorescence. Stems to 3m; sepals *c*.12mm
long. For rich peaty soil. Hardy to −20°C.

Thalictrum flavum L. subsp. *glaucum*
(Desf.) Batt. syn. *T. speciosissimum* L.   Native
of Spain, Portugal and North Africa, growing in

Thalictrum diffusiflorum at Kew

damp meadows and by streams, flowering from
June to August. Stems to 150cm. Whole plant
bluish green; leaflets with prominent veins on
the underside. A most beautiful plant for the
herbaceous border or wild garden, requiring
rich, moist soil to reach full size. Subsp. *flavum*
is native of most of Europe including England,
Ireland and Scotland, east to Turkey and
Siberia, in wet meadows, fens and by rivers. It is
similar but usually rather smaller, with bright
green stems and leaves, the leaflets without
prominent veins on their underside.

Thalictrum lucidum L.   Native of C & E
Europe to Turkey and W Russia, growing in
ditches, marshes and wet meadows, flowering in
June–August. Stems to 120cm. Plant shining
green; leaflets narrowly oblong, or linear in the

upper leaves. Inflorescence with long branches.
Stamens upright, *c*.7mm long. A robust plant
forming large clumps of pointed leaflets and tall
stems with rather greenish-yellow flowers. For
moist rich soil. Hardy to −25°C.

Thalictrum minus L.   Native of Europe from
Scotland and Ireland to North Africa eastwards
to C Asia, China, Japan, with related species in
North America, growing on limestone rocks, in
chalk grassland, on sand dunes and shingle, in
damp meadows and in shady places by streams,
on mountains steppes and tundra, flowering in
May–August. Plants with small yellowish or
brownish hanging flowers and long anthers
dangling on slender filaments, well adapted for
wind pollination.

PAEONIA

Paeonia rhodia on Rhodes

Paeonia rhodia

Paeonia cambessedesii

Italy (but not recorded from Greece), to Turkey, growing in oak scrub and on rocky slopes, at up to 2000m in Turkey, flowering in June–July. Differs from subsp. *mascula* in its narrower leaflets which are hairy beneath, and usually have 12–16 segments, typically 15. Possibly less drought-tolerant than subsp. *mascula*. Hardy to –15°C.

Paeonia mascula (L.) Mill. subsp. ***mascula***
Native of Europe from France and Austria south and eastwards to Greece, the Caucasus, Turkey, N Iran and Iraq, growing in oak, pine and beech forest, often among bracken, or on rocky limestone slopes, usually north-facing, and at up to 2200m in E Turkey, flowering in April–June. Plant forming a large clump of thick, fleshy roots, with many stems to 60cm. Leaves with basically 9 elliptic leaflets, but often some are divided so there may be as many as 15, all glabrous or sparsely hairy on the veins beneath. Flowers 8–14cm across, red or pinkish. Capsules 3–5, white tomentose. Easily grown in dry, well-drained soil in full sun; in moist soils the roots are liable to slug damage. Hardy to –15°C.

Paeonia mascula subsp. ***hellenica***
Tzanoudakis   Native of Sicily, especially on mountains in the north, and of Greece, in Attica, Evvia, Andros and the C Peloponnesos (with var. *icarica* on Ikaria), growing among bracken in *Abies* forest, in scrub or on open rocky slopes, usually on schist, at 450–850m, flowering in April–May. Differs from all other subspecies in its white flowers 10–13cm across; the leaves usually have 9 segments, but may have as many as 21. Although known for many years (I took this photograph in 1968), this subspecies was only described in 1977. I have never seen it flowering in cultivation in N Europe, but Stearn's *Paeonies in Greece* records that it has been cultivated in the garden of the Goulandris Natural History Museum in Athens; it is said to come into growth very early, as does *P. rhodia*, and will require protection from late frosts. Hardy to –15°C.

Paeonia mascula subsp. ***russii*** (Biv.) Cullen & Heywood   Native of Corsica, Sardinia, Sicily, the Ionian islands and C Greece, in forests in the mountains, in vineyards and in *Quercus coccifera* scrub on rocky limestone slopes, flowering in March–May. Differs from subsp. *mascula* in having even broader, ovate to obovate leaflets, hairy beneath. The stem is usually shorter, 25–45cm, and not fully extended at flowering time, and both stems and leaves are purplish when young. Flowers 9–12cm across, usually pinkish mauve. Easily grown in a warm position and well-drained but deep, rich soil; hardy to –15°C.

Paeonia rhodia W. T. Stearn   Native of Rhodes, in open *Pinus* and *Cupressus* forest at 500–700m, flowering in February–April. Plant forming clumps of smooth, reddish stems to 50cm, and leaves with up to 29 glabrous leaflets. Flowers 7–8cm across. This species is still easily found on Rhodes. Plants grown from seed have survived in SE England for twenty years, surviving –15°C, both at the foot of a wall, and in a frame in the open. They are susceptible to botrytis, but otherwise grow and flower well. The closely related *P. clusii* Stern & Stearn from Crete and Karpathos has many more (40–80) narrower leaflets, which are usually stiffer than the soft leaves of *P. rhodia*. The white flowers are 7–10cm across. It requires similar conditions to *P. rhodia*, and hybrids between the two are in cultivation.

Paeonia cambessedesii (Willk.) Willk. (*Paeoniaceae*)   Native of the Balearic islands, in E Majorca and Minorca, growing on limestone rocks and cliffs, flowering in April. This species is now becoming rare in the wild. Stems to 45cm, but usually around 25cm. Leaves biternate, with glabrous, lanceolate leaflets, greyish shining green above, purplish beneath. Flowers 6–10cm across, with 5–8 carpels. Easily grow in a sheltered position or frame, but needs protection from late spring frosts, and too much wet in summer. The smallest and one of the most distinct species. Hardy to –10°C.

Paeonia mascula subsp. ***arietina*** (Anders.) Cullen & Heywood   Native of E Europe, from

Paeonia mascula subsp. *hellenica* in Evvia, with *Abies cephalonica*

Paeonia mascula subsp. *russii*

Paeonia mascula subsp. *mascula* near Muş, E Turkey

Paeonia mascula subsp. *arietina*

Paeonia anomala in the Maili Tau Mountains, near Yumin, NW China

Paeonia anomala

Paeonia 'Smouthii' at Kew

Paeonia anomala L. syns. *P. hybrida* Pall., *P. intermedia* C. A. Meyer   Native of Russia from the far north-west in the Kola peninsula, south to C Asia in the Tien Shan and Pamir-Alai, and east to the Altai, south to Mongolia and N China, in the W Gobi, growing in coniferous woods, on rocky hillsides among shrubs, and in dry steppe grassland, flowering in May–July. Stems to 50cm, forming clumps. Leaves biternate, with the leaflets divided into numerous narrow segments, usually 5–25mm wide; dark green above with minute bristles on the top of the veins. Flowers 7–9cm across, red. Carpels glabrous. *P. hybrida* Pall. is said to differ in its narrower leaflets, 10–15mm wide. *Paeonia intermedia* var. *intermedia* (C.A.M.) B. Fedtsch. has pubescent follicles. This should be the hardiest species, and is very beautiful with its large rather flat flowers of rich pinkish red. It will require deep, sandy, well-drained soil in full sun. Hardy to −25°C or less.

Paeonia coriacea Boiss.   Native of S Spain and Morocco in the middle Atlas, and doubtfully recorded from Corsica and Sardinia, growing in scrub and cedar forests, and among rocks and old walls, flowering in April–May. Stems to 60cm. Leaves biternate, with 9 leaflets and up to 16 segments, all glabrous beneath. Flowers 7–15cm across, usually pinkish. Carpels usually 2, 4.5cm long, glabrous, attenuate at apex. In gardens some forms of this species can appear too early and be damaged by late frosts. It requires a warm position, in rather dry soil. *P. broteroi* Boiss. & Reut., which also grows in S Spain and Portugal, differs in its softer, more divided leaves, usually red flowers and 2–4 densely tomentose carpels.

Paeonia mollis Anderson   A garden variety, probably a hybrid, known since 1818, but still in cultivation. Said to have been raised by Messrs Loddiges from seed sent by Pallas from Russia. Stem to 45cm. Leaves with narrow segments, with a bluish sheen. Flowers 7cm across, hairy beneath and said to sit down among the foliage, although that is not apparent in our illustrated specimen which was growing at Kew. Hardy to −20°C.

Paeonia officinalis L. subsp. *officinalis* Native of S France, east to Hungary and south to Albania, growing in woods, scrub and rocky slopes, usually on limestone, at up to 1800m in the S Alps, flowering in May–June. Leaves with the terminal 3 leaflets each deeply 3-lobed, and the lateral leaflets each 5-lobed; the lobes lanceolate, acuminate, pubescent beneath. Flowers 7–13cm across, red, opening flat. Easily grown in good garden soil. Hardy to −25°C. There are several cultivars of this old garden peony; the commonest is 'Rubra Plena', a huge, double very deep red, which is easily grown and long lasting in gardens and the edges of Victorian shrubberies. There is also a double white, a double pink, 'China Rose', a salmon-pink single, and 'Anemoniflora Rosea', with red, yellow-edged petaloid stamens and deep-pink petals. All except the doubles are rare in cultivation.

Paeonia mollis at Kew

Paeonia coriacea near Ronda, SE Spain

Paeonia officinalis L. subsp. *villosa* (Huth) Cullen & Heywood syn. *P. humilis* Retz var. *villosa* (Huth) F. C. Stern   Native of S France, especially around Montpelier, to C Italy, around Florence, growing in rocky places and scrub, flowering in May–June. Stems to 40cm. Lower leaves with leaflets cut into segments up to ⅓ of total leaflet length. Flowers 7–13cm across, red, opening rather flat. Carpels pubescent, 2–3. Subsp. *officinalis* differs in its more deeply divided leaflets. Subsp. *humilis* differs in its glabrous carpels. Easily grown in ordinary garden soil.

Paeonia peregrina Mill. syn. *P. decora* G. Anderson   Native of Italy (Calabria) to Romania, Greece, Bulgaria and W Turkey, growing in rough fields and scrub, among limestone rocks and in oak forests at up to 1200m, flowering in April–May. Stems to 50cm, from a clump of narrow roots with swollen ends. Lower leaves with 9 main obovate-cuneate leaflets, each divided into 3 or more pointed lobes, with minute bristles along the veins on the upper surface. Flowers usually dark red, sometimes pink, cup shaped, 9–12cm across. Carpels 1–4, with long white hairs. Easily grown in a sunny position and well-drained soil. Hardy to −20°C. Mathew & Brickell 7563.

Paeonia 'Smouthii' syn. *P. laciniata* hort.   A hybrid between *P. tenuifolia* and *P. lactiflora*, known since 1843. Plant forming large clumps, with stems *c.*60cm tall and very free-flowering in well-drained soil and full sun. The flowers are scented, and *c.*10cm across. Hardy to −20°C.

Paeonia tenuifolia L.   Native of SE Europe from Yugoslavia and Bulgaria to Romania and SW Russia in the Crimea and the neighbouring steppes near Stavropol, growing in dry grassland, flowering in May. (It is also recorded from Soviet Armenia.) Stems to 60cm. Leaves divided into filiform segments, less than 5mm wide. Flowers bright red, 6–8cm across: carpels 2–3 hairy. Easy to grow and very hardy, to −25°C or so, in full sun and well-drained soil. There is also a pale-pink cultivar, 'Rosea', and a double.

Paeonia officinalis subsp. *villosa*

Paeonia officinalis subsp. *officinalis*

Paeonia tenuifolia

Paeonia peregrina

Paeonia mlokosewitschii in Aberdeenshire, with *Berberis thunbergii* 'Atropurpurea' behind

Paeonia wittmanniana at Kew

Paeonia obovata var. *alba* at Aylburton, Gloucestershire

Paeonia mairei near Baoxing, Sichuan

Paeonia emodi Wall. (*Paeoniaceae*) Native of Pakistan and N India from Chitral to Kashmir and W Nepal, growing in forests and scrub, at 1800–2500m, flowering in April–June. Stems to 75cm. Leaves deeply dissected into lanceolate segments, which are usually glabrous. Flowers white, 2–4 per stem, 8–12cm across, with 5–10 petals. Carpels 1–2, hairy or glabrous. This is said to grow in large colonies in the wild and must be a fine sight when in flower. In cultivation it grows happily in sandy soil in a normal, moist herbaceous border. Hardy to −20°C.

Paeonia mairei Léveillé Native of China, in N Yunnan and W Sichuan, growing in steep open woods, scrub, and on mountainsides at 800–2900m, flowering in May–June. Stems 50–100cm, usually 1-flowered; leaflets long-acuminate or caudate at the apex, glabrous, thin in texture. Flowers 8–15cm across. Carpels glabrous or covered with short golden-brown hairs, 2–2.5cm long, attenuate towards the stigma. Close to *P. obovata*, but with narrower leaves, and found further south. This species should grow best in areas with a cool, moist summer in well-drained leafy soil. Hardy to −15°C.

Paeonia mlokosewitschii Lomakin Native of SE Caucasus in the valley of Lagodeki (which is now a nature reserve), growing on sunny slopes in hornbeam-oak forest, flowering in April. Stems to 60cm. Leaves biternate, with leaflets oval to obovate, often obtuse or rounded at apex, glaucous especially beneath. Flowers 8–12cm across, yellow. Carpels tomentose. Easily grown in well-drained soil in sun or partial shade. Hardy to −20°C, but the buds can be killed by late frosts, and grows well in cold parts of E Scotland. Christopher Lloyd has a memorable comment on this plant: 'It flowers for about five days in early May, and is at its ravishing best for about four hours in the middle of this period.'

Paeonia obovata Maxim. var. *alba* Saunders Native of E Siberia, N China, in Heilongjiang (Manchuria), Shaansi, Sichuan, Sakhalin and Japan, in Hokkaido, Honshu and Shikoku; growing in woods and scrub in mountains, flowering in April–June. Stem to 60cm. Young leaves purplish, biternate with rounder leaflets. Flowers white, cream or pale pinkish purple (the white form is the one usually cultivated), *c*.7cm across. Carpels glabrous. Easily grown in semi-shade in sandy, well drained but rich soil. Hardy to −20°C. Var. *willmottiae* (Stapf) Stern, from W Hubei and E Sichuan, has hairy undersides to the leaf, larger flowers, to 10.5cm across and is earlier flowering, in May in gardens in S England. *P. japonica* Mak., from Japan, Korea and Heilongjiang, also has white flowers, but short recurved stigmas.

Paeonia veitchii Lynch Native of NW China, in Gansu, Sichuan and Shensi, growing in subalpine meadows and scrub and on mountain steppes at 2500–3500m, flowering in May–June. Rhizomes creeping to form large dense clumps a metre or more across. Stems to 50cm. Leaflets cut deeply into narrow, pointed segments, with minute bristles, flowers, 2 or more per stem, pink, 5–9cm across. Carpels 2–4, hairy. Easily grown in well-drained soil in sun or part shade. There is also a white form. Hardy to −20°C. Var. *woodwardii* (Stapf & Cox) F. C. Stern, a native of Gansu and NW Sichuan, growing in yak pastures at *c*.3000m, differs from the normal variety in its shorter stems to 30cm, and leaves with longer, bristly hairs on the veins.

Paeonia wittmanniana Hartwiss ex Lindl. Native of W & S Caucasus, the Talysh in S Azerbaijan and NW Iran, and in the Elburz, growing in alpine pastures, on rocky slopes, probably among bracken, and in beech woods, at up to 1700m, flowering in April–August according to altitude. Stems to 1m. Leaves biternate with leaflets 4.5–10cm wide, acute to acuminate, glabrous and shining above, lighter green beneath, with some hairs on the veins. Flowers 10–12cm across, pale yellow. Carpels 2–3, tomentose or glabrous (var. *nudicarpa* Schipczinsky). A robust leafy plant (especially the var. *macrophylla* (Albor) Busch (which also has almost-white flowers), easily grown in rich soil in sun or partial shade among shrubs. Hardy to −15°C, perhaps less.

Paeonia emodi at Wisley, Surrey

Paeonia veitchii at Kew

Paeonia veitchii var. *woodwardii*

Double White *Paeonia lactiflora* in late May in the Old Imperial Summer Palace near Peking

'Kelways' Unique'

'Bowl of Beauty'

'Beersheba' in the paeony field at Kelways Nurseries, Langport, Somerset

***Paeonia lactiflora* cultivars**   These are the common garden paeonies which reached the peak of their popularity in Edwardian gardens, as the names Lord Kitchener and Sarah Bernhardt indicate. They were well developed as a garden flower in China by the 18th century, and first introduced to Europe in 1784. They are all very hardy, originating as they did in N China, and can tolerate −50°C or lower without damage to the roots. They prefer a rich, heavy soil, with good drainage, but moist in summer. The crowns should be planted just below the surface, with the resting buds not more than 3cm below the soil. If they are planted too deeply, they will not flower freely.

'Beersheba'   Stems to 100cm. Early flowering. Raised by Kelways.

'Bowl of Beauty'   Stems to 90cm. Flowers scented, mid- to late season. Raised by Hoogendoorn in 1949. Probably the commonest of the 'Imperial' paeonies in which the stamens are replaced by narrow petaloid filaments.

'Kelways' Unique'   Raised by Kelways.

'Lorna Doone'   Raiser not recorded.

'Madelon'   Stems to 90cm. Raised by Dessert in 1922.

'Pink Delight'   Stems to 70cm. Flowers especially beautiful and well-scented in mid- to late season. Raised by Kelways.

'White Wings'   Stems to 80cm. Raised by Hoogendoorn in 1949.

'Madelon'

'White Wings'

'Lorna Doone'

'Pink Delight'

'Ballerina'

'James Kelway'

'Barrymore'

'Shirley Temple'

'Laura Dessert'

'Festiva Maxima'

'Gleam of Light'

'Jan van Leeuwen'

'Kelway's Supreme'

'Countess of Altamont'

Specimens from Kelways Nurseries, Langport, Somerset, 26 June. ⅓ life size

Paeonia lactiflora 'Whitleyi Major'

'Duchesse de Nemours'

'White Innocence'

'Alice Harding'

Paeonia lactiflora Pallas syns. *P.* 'Whitleyi Major', *P. albiflora* Pallas (*Paeoniaceae*) *P. lactiflora* is the herbaceous paeony from which most of the large garden peonies have been bred. It is native of Siberia from south of Lake Baikal eastwards to Vladivostock and in NW China and Mongolia to near Beijing, growing on steppes and in scrub, flowering in May–June. Stems to 60cm, usually with 2 or more flowers. Leaves divided into lanceolate lobes, basically 9, but with the terminal lobes of the lateral leaflets usually further divided, glabrous or sparsely pubescent with a papillose and rough margin. Flowers 7–10cm across in the wild, white to pink; carpels 3–5, glabrous. 'Whitleyi Major' is a garden clone, similar to the wild type. For good, sandy well-drained soil, moist in summer. Hardy to −25°C or less.

'Alice Harding'　Stems to 100cm; well-scented flowers in mid-season. Raised by Lémoine in 1922.

'Ballerina'　Stems to 90cm; flowers bluish pink, fading to white in early to mid-season. Raised by Kelways.

'Barrymore'　Stems to 90cm; flowers palest pink when first open. Raised by Kelways.

'Countess of Altamont'　Stems to 100cm; flowers scented, in mid-season. Raised by Kelways.

'Duchesse de Nemours'　Stems to 80cm; very free-flowering and well scented. Raised by Canlot in 1856 .

'Festiva Maxima' Stems robust, to 90cm. Flowers scented, white with crimson blemishes. Raised by Miellez in 1851.

'Gleam of Light'　Stems to 90cm. Flowers mid- to late season. Raised by Kelways.

'Heirloom'　Rather short, with stems to 70cm. Raised by Kelways.

'Jan van Leeuwen'　Raised by van Leeuwen in 1928.

'Kelways' Supreme'　Stems to 90cm, freely branched and so with a long flowering season. Flowers palest pink fading to white. Raised by Kelways.

'Laura Dessert'　Stems to 75cm. Flowers white with yellow petaloid stamens, in early to mid-season. Raised by Dessert in 1913.

'Mme Claude Tain'　Stems to 75cm. Raised by Doriat in 1927.

'Shirley Temple'　Stems to 75cm. Very well-scented flowers, palest pink to white.

'White Innocence'　A hybrid between *P. lactiflora* and *P. emodi* raised by Dr A. P. Saunders in New York in 1947. Stems 120–150cm, arching, with several flowers, greenish in the centre.

'Heirloom'

'Mme Claude Tain'

'Knighthood'

'Magic Orb'

'Beacon Flame'

'Crimson Glory'

'Mr G. F. Hemerick'

'Kelways' Majestic'

'Inspecteur Lavergne'

'Kelways' Brilliant'

'Shimmering Velvet'

'Auguste Dessert'

'Sir Edward Elgar'

Specimens from Kelways Nurseries, Langport, Somerset, 24 June. ⅓ life size

'Sarah Bernhardt'

'Silver Flare'

'Polindra'

'Albert Crousse'

Paeonia lactiflora cultivars (continued):

'Albert Crousse' Stems to 90cm; late-flowering. Raised by Crousse in 1893.

'Auguste Dessert' Stems to 75cm. Flowers mid- or late season, with good autumn colours on the leaves. Raised by Dessert in 1920.

'Beacon Flame' Stems to 75cm. Raised by Kelways.

'Crimson Glory' Stems to 80cm. Late flowering. Raised by Sass in 1937.

'Inspecteur Lavergne' Stems to 80cm. Flowers mid- or late season. Raised by Doriat in 1924.

'Kelways' Brilliant' Stems to 90cm. Raised by Kelways.

'Kelways' Majestic' Stems to 90cm. Flowers extra large. Raised by Kelways.

'Knighthood' Raiser not recorded.

'Magic Orb' Stems to 95cm. Flowers well scented. Raised by Kelways.

'Mr G. F. Hemerick' Probably raised by van Leeuwen.

'Polindra' Raiser not recorded.

'Sarah Bernhardt' Stems to 90cm. Flowers very large, in mid- to late season. Raised by Lémoine in 1906.

'Shimmering Velvet' Stems to 85cm. Flowering season extending into summer. Raised by Kelways.

'Silver Flare' Stems to 90cm. Flowers early season. Raiser not recorded.

'Sir Edward Elgar' Flowers in mid- to late season. Stems to 75cm. Raised by Kelways.

Single paeonies in Claude Monet's garden at Giverny, in June

Corydalis flexuosa near Wolong, NW Sichuan

Corydalis cheilanthifolia

Corydalis lutea

Corydalis thyrsiflora by streams below the glacier on Lake Vishensar

Corydalis scouleri at Kew

Corydalis mucronata at Baoxing, Sichuan

CORYDALIS

Corydalis nobilis

Corydalis nobilis near Yumin, NW China

Corydalis ochroleuca

Corydalis cheilanthifolia Hemsl.
(*Fumariaceae*)   Native of China, in Hubei,
Guizhou and E Sichuan, growing among stones
by streams, flowering in April–May. Plant with
a rosette of many deeply divided fern-like leaves
to 25cm long, from a central rootstock.
Flowering stems to 20cm, upright, with *c*.20
flowers, each *c*.15mm long. Easily grown in a
cool position, in a wall or rocky place in the
shade. Hardy to −15°C or so.

Corydalis flexuosa Franch.   Native of China,
in W Sichuan, especially in the Baoxing and
Wolong valleys, growing on steep shady slopes
with *Matteuccia*, at *c*.2000m, flowering in
April–July. Plant upright from a thin rootstock
with fleshy leaf bases, and thin stolons, dormant
in summer. Leaves glaucous, sometimes marked
with purple. Stems to 40cm. Flowers *c*.2.5cm
long, blue, sometimes purplish. Capsule
slender. For moist, loose leafy soil in shade or
partial shade. Hardy to −10°C, perhaps less.
Source: CD&R 528.

Corydalis lutea (L.) DC.   Native of the
foothills of the S Alps in Switzerland, Italy and
Yugoslavia, growing on shady rocks and screes,
usually on limestone, and frequently naturalized
elsewhere, especially on old walls, flowering in
May–October. Plant forming a mound of
delicate green leaves, from a thin fleshy
rootstock. Stems to 40cm. Flowers up to 16 in a
dense, elongated raceme, yellow, 12–20mm
long. Fruits pendant; seeds shining. Easily
grown and self-seeding in shady crevices in

walls and among rocks. Hardy to −20°C.

Corydalis mucronata Franch.   Native of W
Sichuan, especially around Baoxing, growing in
shady places in woods and below wet cliffs, at
c.2000m, flowering in April–May. Stems
spreading from a thick rootstock to 40cm.
Leaves glaucous. Flowers *c*.2.5cm, opening
purplish, fading to buff, with upward-pointing
spurs and buff seed capsules. A pretty plant
with an unusual colour combination; suitable
for a shady cool place in leafy soil. Hardy to
−15°C or less?

Corydalis nobilis (L.) Pers.   Native of Soviet
C Asia, in the Saur and Tarbagatay mountains
and in China, in W Sinjiang, in the Maili
mountains near Yumin, growing in scrub and
grassy places by streams in the mountains,
flowering in April–May. A robust upright plant,
with numerous stems up to 60cm, from a
central rootstock, dormant if dry in summer.
Flowers 20–30 in a dense head, *c*.20mm long,
yellow (or white?), with a dark point on the
inner petals. For good sandy soil in full sun or
partial shade. Hardy to −20°C or less.

Corydalis ochroleuca Koch   Native of Italy
and Yugoslavia, Albania and N Greece; growing
in rocky woods, and naturalized especially on
old walls elsewhere in Europe, flowering in
May–September. Plant with several erect stems
to 40cm from a central rootstock. Leaves
glaucous. Flowers up to 14, rarely more, in a
dense raceme, creamy white, *c*.15mm long.

Fruit erect; seeds dull, not shining. A delicate
plant for growing in walls or crevices in
pavement, in sun or shade. Hardy to −15°C.
Shown here is subsp. *leiosperma* (Conr.) Hayek
which has bracts at least ⅓ as long as the
pedicels, and shiny seeds.

Corydalis scouleri Hook.   Native of W North
America from British Columbia south to N
Oregon, growing in damp shady woods,
flowering in June–July. Plant with stems to
60cm or more from a stout rootstock, forming
large clumps of delicate leaves. Flowering stems
little taller than the leaves, with short racemes of
15–35 pinkish-mauve flowers, about 2.5cm long.
The closely related *C. caseana* Gray, from NE
Oregon and California to Idaho and Colorado,
has paler pink or white flowers with purple tips,
50–200 in the raceme. For moist leafy soil in
partial shade, and a sheltered position. Hardy to
−15°C.

Corydalis thyrsiflora Prain   Native of the W
Himalayas, from Pakistan to Kashmir, where it
is very common, growing in mountain streams,
among rocks and below glaciers, at
3000–4300m, flowering in July–August. Plant
with a rosette of leaves from a deep rootstock.
Stems 15–30cm, branched, with dense terminal
flower clusters. Flowers 12–15mm long. Spur
about ½ as long as the flower. Capsule 5–7mm,
broadly ovate, with a long curved style. Not
difficult to grow in moist gritty, peaty soil in sun
or partial shade. If too shaded the plant
becomes leggy. Hardy to −20°C.

Geranium libani 'Wakehurst'

Geranium aristatum

Geranium × *monacense* var. *monacense*

Geranium monacense var. *anglicum*

Geranium reflexum

Geranium phaeum var. *phaeum*

Geranium phaeum var. *phaeum*

Geranium phaeum var. *lividum* 'Majus'

Specimens from the University Botanic Garden, Cambridge, 20 June. ⅓ life size

Geranium aristatum Freyn & Sint.
(*Geraniaceae*)   Native of S Albania, S
Yugoslavia and NW Greece growing in damp
shady places in the mountains, usually on
limestone, at 1650–2100m, flowering in June–
September. Plant tufted, with stems to 60cm,
more or less erect, glandular above. Leaves with
7 or 9 rather broad lobes. Flowers nodding;
petals 13–16mm, strongly reflexed, pale with
lilac-pink veins. Easily grown in ordinary
garden soil in partial shade.

Geranium libani Davis   Native of S Turkey
(Hatay), W Syria and Lebanon, growing in
maquis and *Abies* forest, flowering in April–
May. Leaves glossy above, appearing in
autumn, dying down in summer. Hardy to
−15°C. For a warm position, dry in summer.

Geranium × monacense Harz (syn. *G.
punctatum* hort.) var. **anglicum** Yeo   A hybrid
between *G. reflexum* and *G. phaeum* var.
lividum. Petals 11–14mm, pinkish lilac, with a
very small white base. Leaves usually
unblotched. *G. × monacense* var. *monacense* is
the hybrid between *G. reflexum* and *G. phaeum*
var. *phaeum*. Flowers purplish red with a large
pale base. Leaves often blotched.

Geranium phaeum L.   Native of Europe from
the Pyrenees and the Alps east to W Russia, N
Yugoslavia and Czechoslovakia, growing in
subalpine meadows and woods and on banks,
flowering in May–August. Naturalized
elsewhere on roadsides and by rivers, especially
commonly in E Scotland. Plant tufted with
thick rhizomes forming large clumps. Leaves
with 7–9 lobes, often spotted reddish purple,
10–20cm across. Stems 60–80cm, glandular
above. Petals 11–14mm long, pinkish, lilac to
purple or almost black; or white in the
cultivated form 'Album'. Hardy to −20°C. Var.
lividum (L'Her.) Persoon 'Majus' is a tall, large-
flowered clone of var. *lividum* with petals to
16mm long. Var. *lividum* differs from var.
phaeum in having pale flowers with a bluish
border to the white base.

Geranium pogonanthum Franch.   Native of
SW China, in Yunnan and Sichuan, and WC
and N Burma, growing in scrub, or on the edges
of forest, flowering in July–September. Plant
with stout rootstock and long creeping stems.
Leaves marbled, deeply divided into 5 or 7
lobes, with acute tips. Peduncles 4–8cm.
Flowers nodding, 2.5–3.5cm across, pink or
purple to almost white. Filaments red. For cool
moist soil in sun or shade. Hardy to −15°C.

Geranium reflexum L.   Native of Italy in the
Apennines, N Yugoslavia and N Greece,
growing in mountain meadows, shady rocks and
clearings in woods, flowering in May–June.
Plant clump-forming; stems 40–80cm. Leaves
5–7 lobed, with pointed shallowly toothed
lobes. Flowers with petals reflexed, 11–13mm
long, pink with a white base. Like *G. phaeum*
but with narrower, more strongly reflexed
petals, and with young fruits pointing
downwards. For semi-shade, and tolerant of
rather dry soil. Hardy to −15°C.

Geranium sinense Knuth   Native of W China,
in Yunnan and Sichuan, growing in alpine
meadows, flowering in August–October. Plant
with few ascending or creeping stems from a
stout rootstock. Basal leaves long-stalked,
divided to the base into 7 rather narrow lobes;
upper leaves short-stalked. Flowers up to 2cm
across, commonly visited by wasps. Hardy to
−15°C or less.

Geranium phaeum

Geranium phaeum

Geranium phaeum 'Album'

Geranium pogonanthum

Geranium sinense

Geranium sanguineum var. *striatum*

Geranium sanguineum on the Burren, Co. Clare

Geranium swatense in the Royal Botanic Garden, Edinburgh

Geranium maculatum L. (*Geraniaceae*)
Native of E North America west to Manitoba
and Kansas, growing in wet places in woods, on
wet rocks and in swamps, flowering in
April–July. Stems 50–70cm, few from a stout
rootstock. Leaves with 5 or 7 rather narrow
lobes, each toothed and lobed near the apex,
c.10cm across. Flowers pink, often very pale and
white at the base. A graceful species, useful for
its early flowering and its ability to tolerate
waterlogged soil. Hardy to −25°C or less.

Geranium oreganum Howell   Native of
Washington south to N California in meadows,
scrub or open woods at 800–1500m, in
California flowering in June–July. Stems to
60cm, spreading. Leaves 10–20cm across,
divided nearly to the base into 7 lobes, each
deeply dissected. Inflorescence loose; flowers
4.3–4.7cm across, upward-facing. An attractive
species for sun or partial shade, but with rather
a harsh colour. Hardy to −15°C.

Geranium orientalitibeticum Knuth
Native of Sichuan near Kanding (Tatsienlu),
growing in screes at 2250–3750m, flowering in
June–July. Plant growing from strings of small
underground tubers, which are pink with a
white centre. Leaves emerging in spring, dying
down in late summer, around 10cm across, pale
greenish, marbled with cream. Stems 20–35cm.
Flowers pinkish, 2.3–2.7cm across. Easily grown
in ordinary well-drained garden soil in full sun,
kept moist in early summer, and spreading to
make small patches. Hardy to −20°C.

Geranium palustre L.   Native of C & E
Europe from France and Sweden eastwards to
Russia, the Caucasus and NE Turkey, growing
in damp places, and in scrub and the edges of
woods, flowering in June–August. Stems
spreading from a central rootstock, up to about
40cm. Leaves 5–10cm across, with 7 lobes, each
with rather few deep teeth. Flowers 3–3.5cm
across, magenta with dark-purple veins. Easily
grown in any good soil, in sun or light shade.
Hardy to −20°C.

Geranium pylzowianum Maxim.   Native of
W China, in Gansu, Shaanxi, Sichuan and
Yunnan, growing in alpine meadows and rocky
places at 2400–4250m, flowering in May–June
in gardens. Plant with underground stolons and
chains of small tubers, forming slowly spreading
patches. Stems 12–25cm, rarely taller. Leaves
c.5cm across, not marbled, darker green and
more deeply divided into narrower segments
than G. orientalitibeticum. Flowers not opening
flat, with petals 1.6–2.3cm long, deep rose pink.
Easily grown in well-drained soil in a sunny
position. Hardy to −20°C.

Geranium sanguineum L. Bloody Cranesbill
Native of Europe, from NW Ireland and
Scotland eastwards to the Caucasus and N
Turkey, growing in sunny grassy places, in
scrub, among rocks, usually on limestone, and
on coastal dunes, flowering in April–August.
Stems several from a slowly increasing
rootstock, spreading or creeping to c.30cm long.
Leaves very deeply divided into 5 or 7 lobes,
each lobe further divided into 3–5 nearly to the

base. Flowers 2.5–4.2cm across, usually
purplish red, sometimes pink, especially in var.
striatum Weston syn. var. *lancastriense* (Mill.)
Druce from Walney Island off the coast of
Cumbria, NW England. Easily cultivated in sun
or, in very warm climates, in partial shade.
Low-growing, and suitable for the edge of a
border or in a path; it has an exceptionally long
flowering season. Hardy to −20°C.

Geranium swatense Schonbeck-Temesy
Native of N Pakistan, in Dir and Swat, and of
Kashmir, growing on grassy hillsides at
2000–2500m, flowering in August. Plant with
creeping but not rooting stems to 50cm from a
central rootstock. Leaves divided to ⅔ into 3
or 5 rather widely separated lobes, on stalks
c.10cm long. Flowers c.2cm across, deep pink to
white, with a white centre, on pedicels with long
soft glandular hairs. Easily grown in a sunny
position in well-drained soil. Hardy to
−20°C or less.

Geranium wlassovianum Fisch. ex Link
Native of Mongolia, NE China and E Siberia,
growing in damp grassland and scrub, flowering
in July–August in gardens. Stems to 30cm,
covered with eglandular hairs, spreading from a
stout central rootstock. Leaves short-stalked,
often brownish. Flowers usually deep purplish,
rarely pale pink, with petals 1.7–2.2cm long,
veined with deep violet. For sun or partial shade
in any ordinary soil. Hardy to −25°C.

Geranium oreganum

Geranium maculatum in the Blue Ridge Mountains, Virginia

Geranium pylzowianum

Geranium orientalitibeticum

Geranium wlassovianum

Geranium palustre

Geranium viscosissimum

Geranium ibericum subsp. jubatum

Geranium erianthum

Geranium renardii

Geranium richardsonii

Geranium himalayense 'Plenum'

Geranium himalayense

Geranium macrorrhizum 'Bevan's Variety' (p. 114)

Geranium pratense subsp. stewartianum (p. 117)

Specimens from the University Botanic Garden, Cambridge, 4 June. ⅓ life size

Geranium erianthum DC. (*Geraniaceae*)
Native of British Columbia and Alaska
westwards through the Kurile Islands to Japan
(Hokkaido) and E Siberia, growing in subalpine
meadows and scrub and on grassy slopes near
the sea, flowering in June–August. Stems to
30cm, from a compact rootstock. Leaves
divided to about ¾ into 7 or 9 lobes, each
deeply and irregularly toothed and overlapping;
non-glandular hairs appressed. Flower 2.5–
3.7cm across, often very pale blue with darker
veins, in a compact inflorescence. Hardy to
−20°C. Shown here is a plant from NE
Hokkaido.

Geranium himalayense Klotsch   Native of the
Pamirs and the Himalayas from NE
Afghanistan to C Nepal, growing in open
forests, scrub and on grassy slopes, at 2100–
4300m, flowering in May–July. Plant forming
spreading mats with underground rhizomes.
Stems to 30–45cm. Leaves to 20cm across,
divided to ¾ or ⅘, into 7 overlapping lobes,
each with blunt lobes and teeth. Flowers deep
blue, with overlapping petals, 4–6cm across, the
largest in the genus. This is a good garden plant,
tolerant of drought and a certain amount of
shade. Of the several clones in cultivation,
'Gravetye' has the largest flowers, of a good rich
blue. It is a parent, with *G. pratense*, of the
excellent hybrid 'Johnson's Blue' (see p.117).
'Plenum' syn. 'Birch Double' is a smaller plant,
with rather more purplish double flowers about
3.5cm across. Known since 1928. Hardy to
−20°C.

Geranium ibericum Cav. subsp. *jubatum*
(Handel-Mazetti) Davis   Native of N Turkey,
from Bolu to Trabzon, where it grows in scrub,
meadows, and on rocky igneous hillsides, at
1900–3000m, flowering in July and August.
Stems, with both long glandular and eglandular
hairs, to 40cm. Clump-forming, with
overlapping and deeply incised leaves with 9 or
11 lobes, to 20cm across. Flowers 4–4.8cm
across, bluish with purplish veins, facing
sideways. Subsp. *jubatum* differs from subsp.
ibericum from NE Turkey and the Caucasus in
having glandular hairs on the pedicels, like *G.
magnificum* and *G. platypetalum*. Easily grown in
well-drained soil and sun. Hardy to −20°C.

Geranium renardii Trautv.   Native of the
Caucasus, on cliffs and in rocky meadows at
c.2000m, flowering in July (June in gardens in
England). Plant with short thick rootstock
forming low mounds. Leaves to 10cm across,
greyish, strongly rugose with impressed veins,
divided halfway into 5 or 7 toothed lobes. Stems
to about 20cm. Flowers flat, 30–36mm across,
white or bluish with conspicuous blue veins.
Petals notched, well separated from each other.
Easily grown in full sun and well-drained soil.
The common clone in gardens is named 'Walter
Ingwersen', after its introducer. Hardy to
−20°C.

Geranium richardsonii Fisch. & Trautv.
Native of British Columbia, east to
Saskatchewan, south to California, South
Dakota and New Mexico, growing in damp,
grassy places and meadows, at 1000–3000m (in
California), flowering in July–August. Stems
few, much-branched, to 60cm from a thick
rootstock. Leaves slightly glossy, 5–10cm
across, deeply divided into 5 or 7 lobes each
shallowly lobed or toothed with broad teeth.
Flowers 2.4–2.8cm across, usually white,
sometimes pale pink and veined, their surface
hairy towards the centre of the flower. A
variable species, good forms of which are very

Geranium himalayense in Kashmir   *Geranium himalayense* 'Gravetye'

Geranium renardii

beautiful, as is the one shown here, collected by
Peter Yeo in Colorado in 1973. Good in moist
soil in full sun. Hardy to −20°C.

Geranium viscosissimum Fisch. & Meyer
Native of British Columbia, east to Alberta and
south to N California (at an altitude of about
1800m), South Dakota and Wyoming, growing
in open woods and meadows, flowering in May–
July. Stems 30–80cm, much-branched, very
glandular from a deep woody rootstock.
Flowers about 4.5cm across, pale pink to
pinkish purple with dark veins. Leaves 7-lobed
to about ⅘, the lobes with rather few teeth,
about 7.5cm across. For any good soil in sun or
partial shade. Hardy to −25°C.

Geranium erianthum from Japan

Geranium macrorrhizum

Geranium platypetalum from the Caucasus

Geranium 'Ann Folkard' (*Geraniaceae*) This beautiful hybrid between *G. procurrens* and *G. psilostemon* was raised by the Revd O. G. Folkard at Sleaford, Lincs., in around 1963 from seed of *G. procurrens*. It has a compact rootstock and shortly creeping stems. Leaves always bright yellowish green; flowers 3.5–4cm across, produced with great freedom. Easily grown in sun or partial shade.

Geranium canariense Reut. Native of the Canary Islands, in Tenerife, Palma, Gomera and Hierro, growing along streams and in moist partially shaded places in the laurel forest, flowering mainly in March–May. Plant with a beautiful large rosette of many wide leaves, borne on a stem up to 15cm tall in old plants. Leaf blades to 25cm across, sparsely hairy, divided to the base into three lobes, the two lateral lobes being further divided almost to the base, with the central lobe not stalked; all the lobes are deeply dissected and toothed, with curved teeth. Flowers 2.3–3.6cm across, on much-branched, glandular inflorescences from the leaf axils. This is one of the hardier of the giant Herb Roberts from the Canary Islands and Madeira, and survives outside in sheltered places in warm gardens, surviving perhaps at −5°C. The most magnificent species *G. maderense* Yeo, from Madeira, is more tender and requires greenhouse treatment. It can make a plant up to 1.5m high and across.

Geranium × *cantabrigiense* Yeo A hybrid between *G. macrorrhizum* and *G. dalmaticum*, which was raised in the University Botanic Garden, Cambridge, by Dr Helen Kiefer in 1974. It has bright-pink flowers. Other pink-flowered clones have arisen by chance in gardens. One was found in the wild in the Biokova mountains in S Yugoslavia, and is called 'Biokovo'. It has white flowers and longer runners than the Cambridge form. Plant mat-forming with stems to 30cm. Leaves up to 10cm wide; flowers 2.5–2.8cm across, like those of *G. macrorrhizum*, borne during June and July in gardens. Does well in sun, or dry areas in partial shade in hot climates. Hardy to −15°C, perhaps.

Geranium macrorrhizum L. Native of the S Alps in France and Italy and the SE Carpathians in Romania, south to Greece, growing among limestone rocks, screes, in woods and scrub, at up to 2100m in Greece, flowering in April–August. Plant with fleshy underground rootstock and thick rhizomes which creep across the ground forming dense mats. Stems to 50cm. Leaves 10–20cm across, very aromatic, and used in the past as a source of Oil of Geranium. Flowers 2–2.5cm across, magenta to pale pink or white. Easily grown in dry or moist situations in sun or shade, forming very effective, weed-smothering ground cover. Several named cultivars are grown in gardens:
'Album' Petals white; sepals and stamens pink. Introduced from the Rodope mountains in Bulgaria by Walter Ingwersen.
'Bevan's Variety' Petals deep magenta; sepals deep red. Collected by Dr Roger Bevan and distributed by Washfield Nurseries.
'Ingwersen's Variety' A pale-pink-flowered variety from Mount Koprivnik in Montenegro, introduced by Walter Ingwersen in 1929.
'Spessart' Should have dark-pink petals, although I have bought a very pale-flowered form under this name. All are hardy to −15°C.

Geranium × *magnificum* Hylander A hybrid between *G. platypetalum* and *G. ibericum* subsp. *ibericum* of unknown origin, but known to have been cultivated since 1871. This is a very good garden plant, forming large clumps and spreading also by short underground stolons. Its one drawback is its short flowering season, in June, from early to late according to district in the British Isles. Peter Yeo describes three cultivated clones of this cross in his monograph: the commonest has stems up to 70cm; leaves divided to more than ½ with about 9 major lobes. Stem with glandular and eglandular hairs. Flowers 4.5–5cm across; petals often slightly notched, purplish-blue with dark veins, slightly overlapping. This is a common cottage garden plant in E Scotland, growing exceptionally well in well-drained soil in full sun and exposure. It survives, but is much weaker and less free-flowering, in shade. Hardy to −20°C, perhaps less.

Geranium platyanthum Duthie syn. *G. eriostemon* hort. Native of E Siberia, W China in E Xizang, Sichuan and W Hubei, Korea and N Japan, growing in grassy places in the mountains and in open woods, flowering in May–June, although often in April in gardens, and intermittently later. Plant with a thick rootstock: stems few, upright to 50cm or to 1m in gardens. Flowers 2.5–3.2cm across. Leaves with 3 or 5 lobes cut to about ⅔, with shallow teeth, and with spreading hairs on the veins on the underside of the lower leaves. Photographed in Sichuan in May. This species is sometimes wrongly called *G. sinense* (q.v.) which has a smaller very purple-red flower and spreading and creeping stems, and is very late flowering. It is confusingly similar to *G. erianthum* which, however, has appressed hairs on the lower leaves, and leaf lobes deeply toothed. Hardy to −20°C.

Geranium platypetalum Fisch. & Meyer Native of the Caucasus, south to NE Turkey and NW Iran, growing in meadows and on rocky slopes in the N Caucasus and in spruce and hazel woods in Turkey, flowering in June–August. Plant forming small clumps with thick short rhizomes. Stems glandular to about 40cm. Leaves green, rugose above with 7 or 9 lobes, the main lobes divided into 3, to about ⅓. Flowers blue with darker raised veins, 30–45mm across; petals broadest at apex, and notched or slightly 3-lobed. Hardy to −20°C.

Geranium psilostemon Ledeb. syn. *G. armenum* Boiss. Native of NE Turkey and the SW Caucasus, growing in scrub, open spruce forest and the subalpine hay meadows which consist mainly of large herbaceous plants and lilies, at 400–1200m, flowering in June–September. Stems to 1.2m from a short rootstock. Leaves divided to ¾ or ⅘ into 7 lobes, each lobe deeply incised and toothed. Flowers about 3.5cm across on a much-branched inflorescence. A strong-growing species for the back of an herbaceous border or for the wild garden. It grows particularly well in the cool summer climate and well-drained soils of E Scotland. Its leaves turn red in autumn. 'Bressingham Flair' is an attractive selection, generally shorter with slightly paler flowers. It is very free-flowering. Introduced in 1973. Hardy to −20°C.

GERANIUM

Geranium × magnificum growing in shade

Geranium platyanthum above Baoxing, Sichuan

Geranium psilostemon from near Trabzon

Geranium × cantabrigiense

Geranium 'Ann Folkard' at Wakehurst Place, Sussex

Geranium canariense by a stream in the forest in Tenerife

Geranium canariense

Geranium 'Johnson's Blue'

Geranium 'Sellindge Blue'

Geranium sylvaticum 'Album'

Geranium pratense 'Plenum Violaceum' at Charleville, Co. Offaly

Geranium pratense 'Mrs Kendal Clarke'

Geranium rivulare in the Valais

Geranium clarkei in the Gadsar Valley, Kashmir

Geranium sylvaticum by the River Don, Aberdeenshire

Geranium clarkei Yeo (*Geraniaceae*)   Native of Kashmir, growing in alpine meadows and valleys in well-drained soil at 2100–4200m, flowering in July. Plant creeping with underground rhizomes. Stems to 50cm, usually *c.*30cm, spreading. Leaves cut nearly to the base into 7 lobes, each deeply dissected, to 15cm across. Flowers 4.5–5.5cm across, purplish blue, white or pale pink, with pink veins. An attractive plant, easily grown in sun or partial shade, with a long flowering season from June to September. The pale-flowered form is very distinct; the blue-flowered form can be clearly distinguished from *G. himalayense*, which has less-divided leaves with broader lobes, and sideways-facing flowers, and from *G. pratense* which has stouter upright stems. Hardy to −20°C. Photographed in the Gadsar Valley, Kashmir, where it grows in great quantity on the grassy valley floor. This is the pale form of the species, known as 'Kashmir White'.

Geranium 'Johnson's Blue'   This is almost certainly a hybrid between *G. himalayense* and *G. pratense*. It originated in a nursery in Holland in about 1950 from seed sent there by A. T. Johnson. It is shorter than *G. pratense*, more spreading, with stems to 70cm and flowers of purer blue. Petals *c.*25mm long. Because this is a sterile hybrid it has a longer flowering season than *G. pratense*, generally in June–July.

Geranium pratense L.   Native of Europe from Ireland eastwards, south to Spain and the Caucasus, east to Siberia, the Himalayas and the Altai, growing in meadows and grassy places, flowering in June–September. Plant with tufted rootstock and deep fleshy roots. Stems robust, upright, much-branched to 130cm, usually about 75cm. Leaves deeply divided into 7 or 9 lobes, each lobe further divided into narrow

pointed divisions. Flowers 3.5–4.5cm across, blue or white, usually with pinkish veins. This species is common on grassy roadsides especially on limestone in N England, flowering first in June, and again later if the verges are cut: it is thus an ideal plant for the wild garden as it can grow happily in quite rank grass. It is also good in a border, and will seed itself around an untidy garden. Many cultivars are grown, including 'Galactic' with large white flowers – there is also a double white, 'Plenum Album'.
'**Mrs Kendal Clarke**'   Which should be 'pearl-grey flushed with softest rose', but is the name often given to a pale-flowered form with white veining.
'Silver Queen' is white with a pale-blue tinge, and 'Striatum' has white flowers, spotted and streaked with blue: it comes partly true from seed.
Two good doubles are 'Plenum Caeruleum' and '**Plenum Violaceum**': the former has light-blue, loosely double, rather untidy flowers; the latter deep-purplish-blue flowers, neater, with purple petaloids surrounded by normal petals. Subsp. *stewartianum* Nasir, shown on p. 112, from Kashmir, is close to *G. clarkei*, and has narrow leaf-lobes and pinkish-purple flowers.

Geranium rivulare Villars   Native of the Alps in France, Switzerland, N Italy and Austria, growing in alpine meadows, among dwarf shrubs and rocks, and in open conifer woods, usually on acid soil, flowering in June. Plant tufted. Stems to 45cm. Leaves deeply divided into 7 to 9 lobes, each further dissected into narrow, acute elongated teeth. Flowers white with fine purplish veins, 1.5–2.5cm across. A graceful plant similar to a small, pale *G. sylvaticum*. Hardy to −20°C.

Geranium '**Sellindge Blue**'   This is probably a hybrid between *G. pratense* and *G. regelii*, which arose in the author's garden at Sellindge, Kent, in around 1986, as a seedling in a path. It forms a rounded plant with numerous glandular branching and rather floppy stems. The basal leaves are smaller than those of *G. pratense*, to 12cm across, and the flowers 3cm across, intermediate between those of *G. pratense* and *G. regelii* growing in the same garden. 'Brookside', another *G. pratense* hybrid, is very similar, with more prostrate stems and a long flowering period. Flowers a good blue, 4cm across.

Geranium sylvaticum L.   Native of most of Europe from Scotland and Ireland, east to Siberia, and south to the Caucasus and Turkey, growing in grassy places, by roads and rivers, and in open woods flowering in May–July according to locality. It is especially common in parts of N England and E Scotland, with pinkish-purple upward-facing flowers, in contrast to the purple-blue flowers of *G. pratense*. Plant with tufted rootstock and deep roots. Stems to 70cm. Leaves deeply divided into 7 or 9 lobes, each further lobed and toothed. Flowers rather crowded, 2.2–3cm across. Peter Yeo records that in NE Europe, white- and pink-flowered become commoner further north, and we saw populations in central Finland, almost entirely pink and white. Pink forms are rare among the normal purple in Scotland. The pure white form '**Album**' is very attractive and comes true from seed. 'Mayflower' is said by Yeo to have flowers of a good rich violet blue with a smaller white zone. Grows up to 60cm high, flowering in May–June. Easily grown in sun or partial shade in any good, moist, well-drained soil. Hardy to −25°C or less.

Pelargonium quercetorum at Harry Hay's, Surrey

Pelargonium endlicherianum at Nurse's Cottage, North Mundham, Sussex

Geranium magniflorum on Mont-aux-Sources, Orange Free State

Geranium brycei at Carlyle's Hoek, NE Cape

Geranium incanum var. *multifidum*

Biebersteinia multifida DC. (*Geraniaceae*) Native of Lebanon and SE Turkey, eastwards to Afghanistan and C Asia, growing in rocky places, flowering in May–June. Plant with few upright stems to 70cm, from a thick root, dormant in summer. Leaves aromatic. Flowers nodding, with petals *c.*10mm long. For a dry, well-drained position. Hardy to −15°C, or lower? *Biebersteinia orphanidis* Boiss., with small pink flowers in congested spike-like inflorescence, is found in the Peloponnese and C Turkey.

Erodium acaule (L.) Becherer & Thell. (*Geraniaceae*) Native of S Europe, from Portugal and Spain to Turkey, and around the Mediterranean, growing in dry grassy places and scrub, flowering in February–May, and until September in gardens. Plants with stems and leaves from a stout rootstock, to 25cm. Leaves to 15cm long. Petals 7–12mm, unmarked. For a well-drained sunny position. Hardy to −10°C, possibly less.

Erodium carvifolium Boiss. & Reut. Native of WC & NC Spain, especially round Soria, in pine woods and mountain meadows, at *c.*1500m, flowering in May–June. Leaves up to 10cm long, finely divided, with non-glandular hairs. Flowers to 4cm across. Easily grown in well-drained soil. Hardy to −15°C.

Erodium manescaui Cosson Native of W & C Pyrenees, mainly in France, possibly also in Spain, growing in mountain meadows, flowering in July–August. Leaves to 50cm, with deeply cut leaflets. Umbels with 5–20 flowers, the bracts green, joined to form a cup. Petals 15–20mm. Easily grown in well-drained but moist soil. Hardy to −15°C.

The African species *Geranium* Twenty-six perennials species, found mostly in the summer-rainfall areas of Africa. The four shown here are now in cultivation; the rest are described in a recent paper by Hilliard & Burtt. *G. pulchrum* has the largest flowers, as well as being the tallest.

Geranium brycei N. E. Br. (*Geraniaceae*) Native of the Drakensberg, in Lesotho, Orange Free State, Natal and the NE Cape, growing in damp and rocky, usually sunny, places, roadsides, or on open mountainsides, at 2200–3000m, flowering in December–March. Plant robust or subshrubby, up to 1m, with numerous stems, forming large mounds of silvery leaves. Leaflets 5–7, hairy on both sides, deeply lobed. Flowers in a much-branched inflorescence, pink, pale purple or bluish, 1.8–4.0cm across, the petals shallowly notched. Easily grown in a sunny position, flowering in midsummer. Hardy to −10°C.

Geranium incanum Burm. fil. var. **multifidum** (Sweet) Hilliard & Burtt   Native of Cape Province, from Port Alfred west to the Cape peninsula, growing in scrub, on dunes and in clearings in forest, flowering in September–March. Plant with stout rootstock and perennial, sometimes woody sprawling stems to 1m, often climbing through scrub. Leaves 5–7-lobed to the base, each lobe further divided and divided again into linear segments c.1mm wide, green above, silvery beneath, the margins revolute. Flowers violet to magenta, with petals 12–16 × 6–12mm; in var. *incanum*, the petals are white with dark veins, only 10–12 × 6–7mm. Although this comes from the winter rainfall area of the Cape, it is easily grown in a sunny position. Hardy to −10°C, but if killed by lower temperatures, usually appearing again, from seed?

Geranium magniflorum Knuth   Native of the Drakensberg in Lesotho, Natal and Orange Free State, growing in damp places among rocks, and on grassy slopes, at 1800–3200m, flowering in December–February. Plant with a stout rootstock and decumbent stems to around 30cm. Leaves many from the rootstock, deeply divided into 5 lobes, with each lobe further divided, green above, silvery below, the margins revolute. Flowers pink to bluish or rarely white with dark veins, 2.5–3.2cm across. This should be one of the hardiest African species, as it dies down in winter. Summer-flowering in gardens in England.

Geranium pulchrum N. E. Br.   Native of the C Drakensberg and nearby mountains in W Natal, growing in damp places and streambeds among scrub, at 1500–2285m, flowering in December–March. A robust subshrubby perennial, up to 1.2m. Leaves up to 12cm across, 5–7-lobed nearly to the base, silvery silky, especially beneath, the lobes coarsely toothed. Flowering stems much branched, hairy and glandular, with flowers 3.2–4.4cm across, pink or pale purple. This species has grown well in cultivation in the Chelsea Physic Garden in London, and is easily grown from cuttings and seed. Hardy to −10°C perhaps.

Pelargonium endlicherianum Fenzl (*Geraniaceae*)   Native of S, NE & C Turkey, Syria and Iraq (?), growing on dry limestone rocks, often in shade or partial shade at 650–1500m, flowering in June–July. Plant forming small clumps of leaves to c.6cm across. Flowering umbels on stems with few branches to 35cm; each with up to 10 flowers. Hardy to −10°C, but liable to attack by botrytis in winter. For a very well-drained, sunny position, and poor soil, so that the leaves do not grow too large.

Pelargonium quercetorum Agnew   Native of N Iraq and SE Turkey (Hakkari), growing on limestone rocks in oak and *Celtis* scrub at 1200–2000m, flowering in June, and intermittently until September in cultivation. Plant forming large mounds of leaves to 18cm tall, the blades c.12cm across: flowering umbels on stems up to 1m, with few branches and up to 30 flowers. For a dry position in full sun or partial shade, but not drought-tolerant as a seedling. Hardiness uncertain, possibly to −10°C for short periods, if kept rather dry in winter.

Geranium pulchrum on Ngeli Mountain

Biebersteinia multifida near Samarkhand

Erodium carvifolium at Corsley Mill, Warminster

Erodium acaule

Erodium manescaui

GERANIUM

Geranium × *oxonianum* 'Claridge Druce'

Geranium × *riversleaianum* 'Russell Prichard'

Geranium endressii

Geranium × *oxonianum* 'Wargrave Pink'

Geranium asphodeloides N. L. Burman subsp. *asphodeloides* (*Geraniaceae*)   Native of Sicily east to Greece, N Turkey, the Caucasus and N Iran, growing in open woods and meadows, flowering in June–October. Stems to 60cm or more, from a stout rootstock, the plant forming a mound of interlacing stems. Basal leaves divided to ¾ into 5 or 7 lobes. Flowers pale to deep pink or white, rather small, but numerous with narrow petals 10–15mm long. A distinct and quietly attractive species with a long flowering season. Subsp. *crenophilum* (Boiss.) Bornm., from Lebanon and Syria, has deep-pink flowers with broad petals; subsp. *sintenisii* (Freyn) Davis, from N Turkey, has pale-pink to purple flowers, and the whole plant is covered with red-tipped glandular hairs. Hardy to −20°C, perhaps.

Geranium collinum Willd.   Native of SE Europe, N & E Turkey, Iran and C Asia eastwards to Siberia and the NW Himalayas, growing in damp meadows and open woods, flowering in June–September. Stems spreading and sprawling to 60cm. Leaves deeply divided into 5 or 7 narrow, deeply cut lobes. Immature fruits held erect on reflexed pedicels. Flowers 25–30cm across, pinkish. A reliable plant, suitable for the wildish garden in partial shade or possibly in a moist meadow.

Geranium endressii Gay   Native of SW France and NW Spain, in the western end of the Basses Pyrénées, flowering in June–July. Rhizomes spreading underground so that the plant forms considerable patches. Stems 25–50cm. Petals bright, deep pink, darkening with age. Hardy to −15°C.

Geranium nodosum L.   Native of the Pyrenees eastwards to Italy and C Yugoslavia, growing in woods in the mountains and hills, flowering in June–October. Plant forming spreading patches, with elongated rhizomes. Leaves with 3 to 5 shallowly toothed lobes. Flowers 2.5–3cm across, bluish or purplish. A hardy and modest plant for the wild garden, tolerant of dry shade and valuable for its late flowering in hot weather. Hardy to −15°C.

Geranium × **oxonianum** Yeo 'Claridge Druce'   A hybrid between *G. endressii* and *G. versicolor*, which is fertile and now found wild in places in England. Plant strong-growing, forming mounds of deep-green leaves and flowering from May to October. Petals *c*.2.5 × 1.4mm, pink with darker veins, white at the base. All varieties of *Geranium* × *oxonianum* are good garden plants with a long flowering season, forming weed-proof clumps which are easily propagated by division. Hardy to −15°C, perhaps less.
'Thurstonianum' is a form of *G.* × *oxonianum*, known since before 1914. Petals often very narrow, 3–6mm wide, *c*.1.8cm long, often with deformed and petaloid stamens. Plant with a very long flowering season, in June–September, and tolerant of sun or shade and drought.
'Wargrave Pink' was found in the nursery of Waterer Sons and Crisp in 1930. It has several upright or spreading stems, to 50cm or more, from a branching rootstock. Leaves usually 5-lobed nearly to the base, with each lobe rather broad, shortly 3-lobed and toothed. Flowers *c*.35mm across. Easily grown in sun or partial shade.

G. × **riversleaianum** Yeo 'Mavis Simpson'   This is one of several hybrids between *G. endressii* (q.v.) and *G. traversii* from Chatham

Geranium versicolor

Geranium nodosum

Geranium collinum

Geranium × oxonianum 'Thurstonianum'

Geranium asphodeloides

Islands, New Zealand. 'Mavis Simpson' was found as a seedling at Kew. It has a stout rootstock and ascending creeping stems. Basal leaves 5–10cm across, soft and greyish, silky hairy. Flowers 2–3cm across, pale pink, with a silvery sheen. A small and low-growing plant for full sun. 'Russell Prichard' is probably the best known of the group, with magenta flowers c.3cm across. Hardy to −15°C.

Geranium versicolor L.   Native of S Europe, in C & S Italy, Sicily and Yugoslavia, south to Greece, growing in woods and on shady banks, and naturalized on roadsides and hedges in parts of England, flowering in May–October. Plant with spreading stems to 60cm from a compact rootstock. Basal leaves 5–20cm across, evergreen, deeply 5-lobed, usually with brown patches between the lobes. Flowers erect with petals broadest at the apex, deeply notched, white with a fine network of magenta veins. Easily grown in a rather dry, shady position. Hardy to −15°C.

Geranium × riversleaianum 'Mavis Simpson' at Washfield Nursery

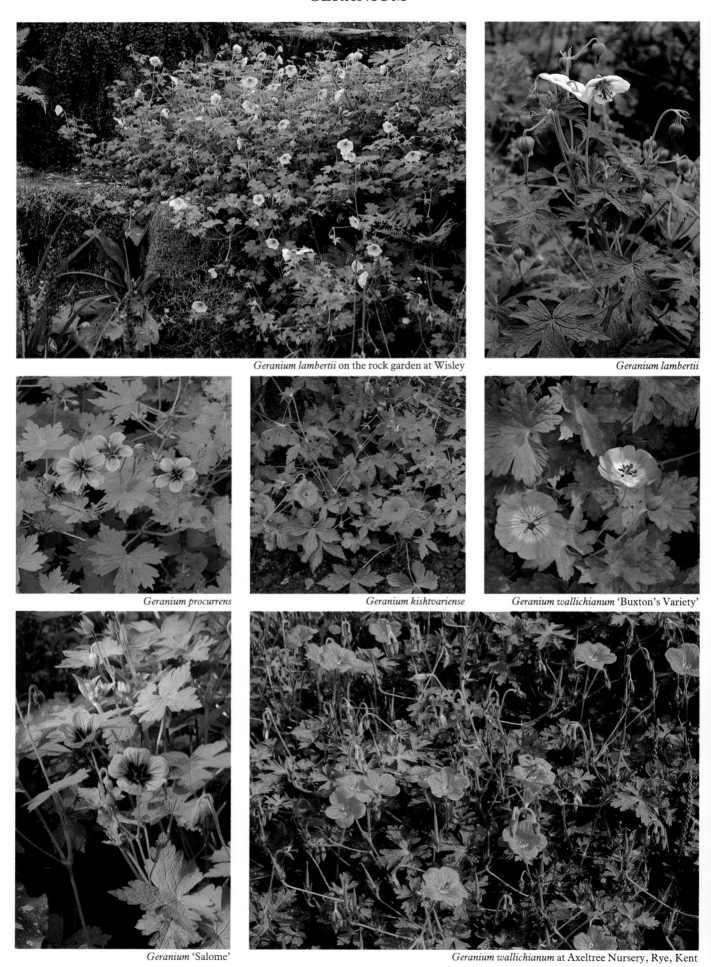

Geranium lambertii on the rock garden at Wisley

Geranium lambertii

Geranium procurrens

Geranium kishtvariense

Geranium wallichianum 'Buxton's Variety'

Geranium 'Salome'

Geranium wallichianum at Axeltree Nursery, Rye, Kent

Geranium kishtvariense Knuth (*Geraniaceae*)
Native of Kashmir, growing in grassy, open
forests and in scrub, flowering in June–
September. Plant with creeping underground
stolons, but not strong enough to be invasive;
stems creeping and forming a mound to 30cm
across. Basal leaves 5-lobed to ⅔, lobes and
teeth acute. Flowers to 4cm across, reddish
purple or intense rich pink, with a small pale
centre. Easy in a cool position in sun or partial
shade, in moist, leafy soil.

Geranium lambertii Sweet   Native of C Nepal
to Bhutan and SE Xizang, growing in clearings
in coniferous forest, and in juniper scrub at
2350–4200m, flowering in July–September.
Stems creeping from a stout rootstock to about
1m, but not rooting. Leaves divided into 5 wide
and deeply toothed lobes. Flowers 4–6cm
across, saucer-shaped, the petals elegantly
curved at their margins, pale lilac, deep pink or
white, crimson-stained at the base. A beautiful
plant for a cool position, preferably raised up so
that the nodding flowers can be seen at their
best. Very difficult to increase by division, but
comes true from seed. 'Swansdown' is the name
given to the white form; the normal form has
pale-pink flowers. The white form is sometimes
erroneously called *G. candicans* or even *G.
candidum*. Hardy to −20°C.

Geranium procurrens Yeo   A native of E
Nepal, Sikkim, and Bhutan, growing in
hemlock and fir forest at 2440–3600m, flowering
in July–September. Few long creeping and
rooting, or climbing stems are produced from a
stout rootstock. Basal leaves (produced in
spring) divided to ⅔ into 5–7 deeply toothed
lobes. Flowers, 2.3–4cm across, magenta with
black veins, to November in gardens. The
creeping stems may reach 2m in a season and
root at the nodes to form young plants, making
rampant ground cover for a cool moist area in
partial shade. This is especially useful for
growing in areas where spring-flowering bulbs
are planted, and for providing the shady root
area so enjoyed by lilies.

Geranium 'Salome'   A hybrid between *G.
lambertii* and *G. procurrens* which occurred at
Elizabeth Strangman's Washfield Nurseries at
Hawkhurst, Kent, in around 1981. It has a long
flowering season, beginning in mid-summer.
The flowers are about 4cm across, with dark-
purple veins on a cool-purple ground. The plant
dies back to a central rootstock in winter, and
so, like *G. lambertii*, is difficult to propagate.

Geranium wallichianum D. Don ex Sweet
Native of the W Himalayas from NE
Afghanistan to Kashmir, growing in subalpine
meadows and open wooded hillsides at 2400–
3600m, flowering in June–September, and into
October in gardens. Stems several from a
central rootstock, creeping to 120cm, but not
rooting; leaves and flower stalks to 30cm tall.
Leaves 5-lobed, each lobe divided to about ½.
Flowers in pairs, usually pinkish or purplish
blue, with a white centre, *c*.3.5cm across.
'Buxton's Variety' or 'Buxton's Blue' has nearly
pure blue flowers with an extra large white
centre; it is a selected form, raised by E. C.
Buxton in North Wales in *c*.1920, and comes
more or less true from seed. Some forms with
rich pinkish flowers have recently been
introduced from Kashmir. Hardy to −20°C or
lower, and grows best in a position which is cool
and moist in summer, but not heavily shaded.

Geranium species near Gadsar, Kashmir

Geranium wallichianum in open woodland in Kashmir

Helianthemum 'Henfield Brilliant'

Helianthemum nummularium in Kent

Peganum harmala

Helianthemum hybrids, *Geranium sanguineum* and *Alchemilla mollis* at Barnsley House

Ruta chalepensis at the Savill Gardens, Windsor

Haplophyllum latifolium

Dictamnus albus (pink and white forms)

Dictamnus angustifolius

Linum perenne

Linum narbonense in S France

Dictamnus albus L. (*Rutaceae*) Burning Bush
Native of Spain northwards to Italy and
Germany and east to Turkey, the Caucasus and
W Himalaya, with very closely related species in
C Asia, growing on steppes, open woods and
dry rocky places at up to 2700m, flowering in
May–July. Plant forming dense clumps, with
stems 40–80cm, glandular and aromatic.
Leaflets 6–12. Petals 2–2.5cm long, usually
pinkish, often white. The leaves are so highly
aromatic that they can be set alight on hot, still
evenings, the gases burning for a second or two.

Dictamnus angustifolius G. Don ex Sweet
Native of much of C Asia and NW China,
growing in grassy steppes and rocky woods,
flowering in May–August. Stems several,
upright, to 1m from a stout rootstock. Similar to
D. albus, but shorter, neater in habit, and with
narrower, more clearly veined petals. Hardy to
−20°C or less.

Haplophyllum latifolium Kar. & Kir.
(*Rutaceae*) Native of C Asia and NW China,
in the Tarbagatai, the Dzungarian Alatau, the
Tienshan and the Pamir Alai, growing in rich
steppes among fennels and other large herbs,
flowering in May–June. Plant with spreading,
branching stems to 60cm. Flowers *c.*1cm across.
For dry soil in full sun, hot in summer. Hardy
to −20°C or less. The genus *Haplophyllum*,
related to *Ruta*, contains many species from
E Europe to Siberia; most have yellow flowers
and entire leaves.

Helianthemum nummularium (L.) Mill. syn.
H. chamaecistus Mill. (*Cistaceae*) Rock Rose
Native of most of Europe except N Scandinavia
and Russia, of N Africa, Turkey, the Caucasus
and N Iran, growing in grassland, usually on
chalk or limestone, and dry rocky places and
dunes, flowering from May–September. A very
variable species in the wild, divided into 8
subspecies in Europe. Stems to 50cm, woody
below. Leaves to 5cm long, 1.5cm across, green
or white tomentose. Flowers red, orange, yellow
to pink or white, up to 3.5cm across. The form
found wild in Britain is subsp. *nummularium*
with yellow flowers and leaves greyish beneath.
Numerous garden varieties have been raised
from this and from subsp. *pyrenaicum*, which
has pink flowers. Large flowers with petals up to
18mm long are found in subsp. *grandiflorum*
from S Europe. *H. croceum* (Desf.) Pers. with
roundish, fleshy stellate-tomentose leaves and
variably coloured flowers has also probably had

influence in those garden hybrids with whitish
leaves. '**Henfield Brilliant**', shown here, is one
of the best, with bright orange-red flowers.
For well-drained, limy soil in full sun. Hardy
to −20°C.

Linum narbonense L. (*Linaceae*) Native of S
Europe, from NE Portugal and Spain eastwards
near the Mediterranean to Yugoslavia, Sicily
and North Africa, growing on dry hills,
flowering in May–July. Stems to 50cm. Leaves
long, acuminate, glaucous. Flowers with sepals
10–14mm, longer than the capsule; petals
2.5–4cm long, bright blue. Bracts with a papery
white margin. Very beautiful, but requiring a
warm position in full sun. Hardy to −10°C.

Linum perenne L. Perennial Flax   Native of
most of Europe from England (subsp. *anglicum*
(Mill.) Ockenden) and Spain eastwards to
Russia and C Asia, growing in grassland and
dry subalpine meadows, flowering in May–July.
Stems up to 60cm, erect, spreading or
decumbent. Flowers with petals 1–2.5cm; sepals
3.5–6mm, usually shorter than the capsule.
Bracts without a white papery margin. For dry,
well-drained soil in full sun.

Peganum harmala L. (*Zygophyllaceae*)
Native of S Europe and North Africa eastwards
to C Asia, NW China and Tibet, growing on
dry steppes, especially where grazing is heavy, at
up to 1500m in Turkey, flowering in May–July.
Plant with several branching stems to 70cm
from a tough rootstock. Leaves divided into
linear segments, greyish, very pungent. Flowers
25–40mm across. For dry soil in full sun. Hardy
to −20°C when dry. A very poisonous plant,
said to cause hallucinations, and to have been
used as a truth drug.

Ruta chalepensis L. (*Rutaceae*)   Native of the
Mediterranean area south to Arabia and
Somalia, growing in dry places on limestone,
flowering in May–June. Plant with woody base
and branching stems to 40cm. Bracts very
broad. Flowers around 1cm across, the petals
fringed with long cilia, shorter than the width of
the petal. For a dry position in full sun; hardy to
−10°C. The prostrate variety shown here is,
perhaps, the variety called 'Dimension Two'.
The familiar herb rue, *R. graveolens* L., has
petals toothed but not fringed. *Ruta angustifolia*
Pers. form the W Mediterranean area has petals
with fringes often longer than the petal width
and very narrow leaf segments.

Boykinia aconitifolia

Saxifraga stolonifera

Mukdenia rossii

Saxifraga fortunei in Hokkaido

Saxifraga spathularis

Boykinia aconitifolia Nutt. syn. *Saxifraga aconitifolia* Field (*Saxifragaceae*) Native of North America, from S West Virginia to North Carolina, Tennessee and Georgia, growing in woods in the mountains, flowering in July. Plant forming wide-spreading sheets several metres across. Stems 30–60cm; leaves *c*.15cm across, flowers 4mm across. Easily grown in a leafy soil in partial shade. Hardy to −20°C.

Lithophragma parviflorum (Hook.) Nutt. (*Saxifragaceae*) Native of the Rocky Mountains and from S California to British Columbia, growing on dry, rocky hills at 600–1800m, flowering in March–June. Roots with bulblets. Stem 20–35cm. Flowers 1–2cm across, with petals cut into 3–5 narrow lobes. For good soil, dry in summer. Hardy to −25°C. *Lithophragma affine* Gray, with stems to 60cm, is common in California and S Oregon below 1000m. It is probably less hardy.

Mukdenia rossii (Engl.) Koidz. syn. *Aceriphyllum rossii* Engl. (*Saxifragaceae*) Native of N China and Korea, growing in moist, shady places among rocks, flowering in May, usually earlier in gardens. Plant forming clumps of deeply lobed leaves with blades *c*.15cm across, flowers *c*.8mm across. For cool, moist soil in a partially shaded position. Hardy to −20°C.

Saxifraga aquatica Lapeyrouse (*Saxifragaceae*) Native of the E & C Pyrenees, growing in wet places by mountain streams at 1500–2400mm, in acid soil, flowering in June–August. Plant forming mats to 2m across

by spreading stolons. Stems 25–60cm. Leaves to 35mm across. Petals 7–9mm long. This species is like a large mossy saxifrage, and is a marsh rather than a rock plant. It requires wet, damp, acid soil by running water. *S. irrigua* M. Bieb. from the Caucasus and Crimea is similar but smaller.

Saxifraga fortunei Hook. fil. Native of Japan, Sakhalin, Korea, E Siberia and N China, growing on wet, shaded rocks by streams in the mountains and to sea level in the north, flowering in July–October. Plants forming small clumps but often solitary. Leaves 4–20cm wide. Flower stems 5–45cm tall; petals unequal, the lowest 5–15mm long. The stems are usually reddish, but the whole plant is reddish in 'Wada' and 'Rubrifolia'. The Japanese plants shown here are called var. *incisilobata* (Engl. & Irmsch) Nakai, to distinguish them from the original Chinese *S. fortunei*. 'Windsor' is a tall clone with stems to 60cm. Hardy to −15°C, perhaps less.

Saxifraga granulata L. Native of W Europe and North Africa, from Norway and Sweden, south to Spain, Sicily and Morocco and east to Yugoslavia, W Russia and Finland, growing in grassland usually on limestone or sandy soils but in damp places at high altitudes in the south, flowering in April–July. The double-flowered form, '**Flore Pleno**', has long been known in gardens. Plant dormant in summer with small bulbils. Stems 10–30cm, or rarely, to 50cm. Leaves up to 3cm across. Flowers with petals 7–16mm long, produced in late spring. Very

Saxifraga granulata near Sherborne, Dorset

Saxifraga granulata

Lithophragma parviflorum at Kew

pretty for naturalizing in a well-drained meadow as can be seen at Kew. Hardy to −20°C or less.

Saxifraga hirsuta L. Native of SW Ireland, in Kerry and Cork, and in the Pyrenees and N Spain, growing in rocky places in woods, on shady cliffs and by streams and waterfalls, flowering in May–July. Plant forming mats of loose rosettes. Leaves with lamina 15–40 × 10–50mm, and petiole 2–3 times as long, hairy all over. Petals 3.5–4mm, with a yellow patch and faint pink spots. Easily grown in a moist, shaded or partially shaded position, but not tolerant of drought. Hardy to −15°C.

Saxifraga spathularis Brot. Native of NW Spain, N Portugal and W Ireland, especially around Killarney and Killary harbour, growing on shady rocks, in woods and in shaded cliffs on acid soils, flowering in May–July. Plant forming loose clumps of rosettes. Leaves rather fleshy, the lamina 15–50 × 12–30mm, the petiole 25–55mm long with sparse, glandular hairs. Flowers with petals *c.*5mm long, each with 2 yellow and several crimson spots. S. × *urbium* D. A. Webb, the London Pride, is the hybrid S. *spathularis* × S. *umbrosa*. It has more rounded teeth on the lamina and more glandular hairs on the petiole. S. *umbrosa* L. itself, from the C Pyrenees, has leaves with a longer lamina with shallowly crenate lobes and dense hairs on the petiole. All are easily grown in moist soil in partial shade. S. × *polita*, the hybrid between S. *spathularis* and S. *hirsuta*, is also common in W Ireland. Hardy to −15°C

Saxifraga stolonifera Meeburgh syn. S. *sarmentosa* L. Mother of Thousands Native of W China (naturalized in Darjeeling), and in Japan, growing on shady cliffs and on mossy rocks at low altitudes, flowering in May–July. Plant forming rosettes of rather fleshy leaves, and spreading by long red stolons. Leaf blade 3–9cm across. Stems up to 40cm, usually *c.*25cm; flowers with the lowest petals longest, 10–20mm long. Easily grown in a moist, shady position and commonly seen as a house plant in cottage windows. Hardy to −10°C or lower in some forms.

Saxifraga granulata 'Flore Pleno'

Saxifraga aquatica at Inshriach

Saxifraga hirsuta at Littlewood Park, Aberdeenshire

Tiarella polyphylla 'Baoxing Pink' near Baoxing, Sichuan, W China

Tiarella cordifolia at the Valley Gardens, Windsor

Tiarella wherryi at Washfield Nurseries, Kent

Heuchera cylindrica 'Greenfinch', with variegated *Symphytum*

Tiarella trifoliata at Washfield Nurseries, Kent

Heuchera cylindrica Dougl. ex Hook. (*Saxifragaceae*) Native of N Nevada, Wyoming and Montana westwards to NE California and British Columbia, growing on cliffs and among rocks, flowering in April–August. Plant forming mats of wavy-edged leaves 2.5–7.5cm wide. Flower stem 15–90cm. Flowers cream or greenish, 6–13mm long, with very small or without petals. Hardy to −20°C, perhaps. For sun or partial shade in well-drained soil. 'Greenfinch' A green-flowered selection, made by Alan Bloom, with stiff upright stems around 90cm. 'Hyperion' has pinkish flowers.

Heuchera micrantha Dougl. ex Lindl. var. *diversifolia* (Rydberg) Rosendahl, Butters & Lakela syn. *H. diversifolia* Rydb. Native of North America from Vancouver Island, British Columbia and W Washington to N California, growing in rocky places at up to 800m, flowering in May–July. Plant forming mounds or small mats of leaves to 20cm high, those produced in winter nearly round, summer leaves lobed. 'Palace Purple' is striking with its blackish-purple leaves with a metallic sheen and white flowers. Hardy to −15°C perhaps.

Heuchera pilosissima Fisch. & Mey. Native of California, along the coast from San Luis Obispo Co. to Humboldt Co., growing in pine and Redwood forests below 300m, flowering in April–June. Plants with creeping rhizome. Leaves 3–7cm across, hairy. Flowering stems 20–60cm, brown-hairy, with flowers in a narrow and compact raceme. Calyx tube 3–4mm long; petals pinkish white, 2mm long. For well-drained soil in partial shade. Hardy to −15°C.

Heuchera villosa Michx. Native of E North America, from Virginia and Kentucky to Georgia and Tennessee, growing in rocky places in the mountains, flowering in June–September. Plant clump-forming; leaves 7.5–12.5cm across, with 7–9 acute lobes, the terminal lobe usually longer than wide. Flowers 2–3mm long; petals whitish; stamens exserted. For a partially shaded position and well-drained leafy soil. Hardy to −25°C or so.

Tiarella cordifolia L. (*Saxifragaceae*) Foam Flower Native of E North America from Nova Scotia to Ontario and Minnesota, south to Georgia, Indiana and Michigan, growing in rich, moist woods in the mountains, flowering in April–May. Plants forming large spreading mats, by creeping underground stolons. Leaves 5–10cm long, with scattered hairs, flowers in simple or, rarely, few branched racemes, each around 6mm across. *T. cordifolia* subsp. *collina* Wherry (see p. 131) differs in its non-creeping rhizome.

Tiarella polyphylla D. Don Native of Sikkim and Bhutan, eastwards to W China, Taiwan and Japan, growing in moist woods, on shady banks and by streams in the mountains, flowering in April–August. Plants spreading by seed, not forming dense mats. Leaves 5-lobed, cordate at base, to 7cm across, hairy and glandular beneath. Flowering stems 10–40cm, with small (4mm long) white, pinkish or green flowers in a simple or few branched, narrow raceme. An attractive plant for a cool moist shady position. Hardy to −15°C or less. This pink-flowered form is now called '**Baoxing Pink**'.

Heuchera micrantha 'Palace Purple'

Tiarella cordifolia subsp. *collina*

Heuchera villosa

Tiarella trifoliata L. Native of Oregon northwards to British Columbia and Alaska, east to N Montana and W Idaho, growing in moist woods by streams, flowering in May–July. Plant forming clumps with petioles up to 17cm high, and leaves with terminal leaflets 3–8cm long; flowering stems 25–50cm high, usually c.30cm.

Tiarella wherryi Lakela Native of Tennessee, North Carolina and Alabama, growing in shady ravines, and rocky woods, flowering in July–August. Plant without stolons, forming small patches, up to 20cm tall; leaves with 5 major acute, and other lesser blunt lobes, 7–14cm long. Flowering stems 15–35cm tall. Flowers often tinted with purple. An attractive plant for a cool sheltered position. Hardy to −15°C.

Heuchera pilosissima

Heuchera × brizoides
'Edge Hill'

Heuchera sanguinea
'Alba'

Heuchera sanguinea

Heuchera micrantha

Mitella diphylla

Tiarella cordifolia
subsp. *collina*

× *Heucherella alba*
'Bridget Bloom'

Tolmiea
'Taff's Gold'

Tellima breviflora

Heuchera cylindrica

Tellima grandiflora

Tiarella trifoliata

Tolmiea menziesii

Heuchera cylindrica

Specimens from Kew, 3 June. Life size

Heuchera × brizoides hort. ex Lémoine 'Red Spangles' (*Saxifragaceae*) *H. × brizoides* is a group of hybrids between *H. sanguinea* and *H. americana* L. (with small greenish flowers) and possibly also *H. micrantha*, raised in France in the late 19th century. 'Red Spangles' was raised by Alan Bloom in 1958. It flowers in late May and again in later summer. Stems 40–60cm tall; each flower 9mm across. Another good hybrid raised about the same time is 'Scintillation', with crimson flowers; 'Edge Hill' is a good, pink hybrid, others are white. All are good in sun or light shade. Hardy to −15°C or less.

Heuchera cylindrica Text on p. 129.

Heuchera micrantha Dougl. ex. Lindl. Native of W North America from C Oregon to C Washington in the Cascades, and east to W Idaho, growing in moist woods by creeks and falls, flowering in June. Plant forming clumps of roughly-hairy leaves usually *c*.15cm tall; flowering stems up to 1m, much branched; leaves with shallow, inconspicuous lobes, nearly round, 2–8cm long (compare 'Palace Purple' p. 129). Flowers greenish or reddish 1–3mm long; petals white or pinkish. Easily grown in sun or partial shade in moist, leafy soil. Hardy to −15°C perhaps.

Heuchera sanguinea Engelmann Native of S Arizona and N Mexico, growing on moist shady rocks, flowering in March–October. Plant forming low mats of dark-green leaves 2.5–7.5cm wide. Flowering stems 25–50cm with numerous red flowers 6–13mm long. 'Alba' is a white-flowered cultivar. Although this plant inhabits shady places in its native habitat, it requires sun or partial shade in cooler, northern climates and flowers from May onwards. Hardy to −20°C.

× Heucherella alba (Lémoine) Stearn 'Bridget Bloom' (*Saxifragaceae*) A hybrid between *Tiarella cordifolia* and *Heuchera × brizoides*, sometimes listed under *× Heucherella tiarelloides*, raised by Alan Bloom around 1958. An attractive plant forming mats of rather small leaves 4–8cm long, deeply cordate, 5–7 lobed and toothed, the terminal lobe largest. Inflorescence branched, to 45cm. Flowers with a glandular deep pink tube and calyx 6mm long, and narrowly ovate white petals *c*.4 × 1mm. For light leafy soil in partial shade, flowering from May to October. *× H. tiarelloides* (Lémoine) Wehrhahn ex Stearn was originally raised by Lémoine at Nancy in 1917. The *Tiarella* parent of 'Bridget Bloom' is usually said to be *T. cordifolia*, but Alan Bloom records that *T. wherryi* was used.

Mitella breweri Gray (*Saxifragaceae*) Native of C California, north to British Columbia and Montana, growing on damp shady slopes in conifer forest above 1800m, flowering in June–August. Plant tufted; leaves 2–6cm wide, the petioles with curled brownish-yellow hairs. Flowering stems 10–30cm tall; flowers 3mm across the tube, the petals with 5–7 hair-like lobes. *M. pentandra* Hook. is found as far north as Alaska and in the Rockies, and differs in having straight hairs on the petioles, and more rounded seeds. Both are easily grown in shady, leafy soil. Hardy to −20°C or so.

Mitella diphylla L. Native of E North America, from Quebec west to Minnesota, south to North Carolina and Missouri, growing in cool places and by streams in woods, flowering in April–May. Plant forming small

clumps. Leaves shallowly 3–5-lobed, 2.5–5cm long. Flowering stems 25–45cm tall, with a pair of rather pointed short-stalked leaves, and a narrow raceme of small flowers with white, fimbriate petals. For a cool moist position, in light leafy soil. Hardy to −25°C or below.

Tellima breviflora Rydb. (*Saxifragaceae*) Native of British Columbia and Alaska to N California, growing by streams, flowering in April–June? Very similar to, and not generally considered distinct from *T. grandiflora*, but differs in having the shorter (5mm long) calyx tube a little, not much, longer than the oblong sepals.

Tellima grandiflora (Pursh.) Dougl. Fringe Cups Native of California from San Luis Obispo Co. northwards, and in the Sierra foothills north to Alaska, growing in cool moist coniferous woods and rocky places below 1500m, flowering in April–June. Plant forming spreading clumps; basal leaves hairy, 3–7 lobed, 5–10cm wide. Flowering stems 40–80cm tall; flowers on short (1–3mm) pedicels, with petals at first whitish, later red, pinnatifid, reflexed: flower tube very broad, campanulate. For moist, shady places. Hardy to −15°C perhaps. Var. *rubra*, syn. var. *purpurea*, has purplish-red leaves.

Tiarella cordifolia subsp. *collina* (*Saxifragaceae*) Text on p.129.

Tiarella trifoliata Text on p.129.

Tolmiea menziesii (Pursh.) Torrey & Gray (*Saxifragaceae*) Native of W North America from N California (Glenn Co.) to Alaska, growing in coniferous forest below 1800m, in cool shady places, flowering in May–June. Plant forming large clumps. Leaves lobed, hairy, 3–10cm wide, pale green or spotted in 'Taff's Gold', often with young plants growing in the sinus. Flowering stems 30–80cm tall; flowers with a tube 5–6mm long, the brown recurved filiform petals 5–7mm long, and only 3 stamens. For moist, cool places in shade or semi-shade. Hardy to −15°C perhaps

Mitella breweri

Mitella diphylla in New York State

Heuchera × brizoides 'Red Spangles'

Tellima grandiflora

Tolmiea menziesii

Chloranthus sessilifolius near Ya-an, Sichuan

Houttuynia cordata

Houttuynia cordata 'Plena'

Anemopsis californica near Bishop, E California

Houttuynia cordata 'Chameleon'

Rheum 'Ace of Hearts'

Rheum ribes in Hakkari, Turkey

Rheum spiciforme in Kashmir

Anemopsis californica (Nutt.) Hook. fil. & Arnott syn. *Houttuynia californica* Benth. & Hook. (*Saururaceae*) Yerba Mansa   Native of S California and west of the Sierra Nevada, eastwards to Nevada and Texas, and south to Baja California and Mexico, in wet, often saline or alkaline fields, sometimes growing in large numbers, below 2000m, flowering in March–September. Stems 10–50cm, woolly, with one broadly ovate clasping leaf. Basal leaf blade 4–18cm, elliptic-oblong, equalling the long stalks. Petal-like bracts 1–3cm long. For warm wet soil or shallow water, probably requiring summer heat to grow well. Hardy to −15°C and below?

Chloranthus sessilifolius K. F. Wu (*Chloranthaceae*)   Native of China, growing in damp woods at *c*.1800m, flowering in April–May. Plant with 1 or 2 fleshy stems to *c*.30cm from a stout rootstock. Leaves in 2 opposite pairs, forming a whorl of 4, about 15cm long. Flowers with no petals or sepals and 3 stamens. Fruits berry-like. Hardy to −10°C, perhaps. There are at least ten *Chloranthus* species, some *Aucuba*-like shrubs, mainly found in forests in E Asia and Japan, others herbaceous perennials, grown for their scent.

Houttuynia cordata Thunb. (*Saururaceae*)   Native of Japan, China, SE Asia (to Java) and the Himalayas, west to Himachal Pradesh in N India, growing in damp shady places, woods and scrub, at up to 2400m, and as a weed in wet fields, flowering from June–July. Plant with slender creeping rhizomes and erect stems 20–50cm high. Leaves 3–8 cm long. Flowers minute in an elongated head 1–2cm long, subtended to 4–6 petal-like bracts. Easily grown in moist, shady places, creeping harmlessly between ferns. Three forms are shown here: the wild form with one whorl of bracts; a double with numerous bracts becoming smaller upwards, 'Plena', and a form with multicoloured leaves, 'Chameleon'. The leaves can be eaten like spinach, or raw, and are much collected in the mountains of W China, and sold in local markets. Hardy to −15°C, perhaps less.

Rheum 'Ace of Hearts' (*Polygonaceae*)   A hybrid between *R. kialense* and *R. palmatum*, with heart-shaped leaves, reddish-veined beneath. Flowers white or very pale pink, on stems to 125cm. For rich moist soil. Raised in c.1970 by The Plantsmen in Dorset.

Rheum alexandrae Batalin. (*Polygonaceae*) Native of W China, in W Sichuan above Kanding (Tachienlu), growing in lush marshy meadows and by streams, especially where yak have been kept, at c.4000m, flowering in June. Plant with deep roots and upright stems to 1.2m tall. Basal leaves ovate, shining-green. Bracts creamy yellow, overlapping and protecting the flowers against the monsoon. For rich, damp soil in full sun. Hardy to −20°C. *R. nobile* Hook. & Thoms. from Nepal and Bhutan grows on rock ledges at c.4000m. It has rounded basal leaves to 30cm across, and even more impressive tightly overlapping bracts on a stem to 1.5m high, but has proved very difficult to grow in gardens.

Rheum palmatum L. Native of W China, in Yunnan, W Sichuan, E Xizang and Gansu, growing in scrub and rocky places and by streams at 2500–4000m, flowering in May–June. A huge plant, from a very stout rootstock. Leaves to 100cm across, deeply lobed and toothed. Flowering stems to 3m, in late spring. Flowers usually white. 'Atrosanguineum' syn. 'Atropurpureum' has young leaves rich crimson-purple and flowers rich pink. In var. *tanguticum* Maxim., from NW China, in Gansu and N Xizang, the side shoots of the inflorescence are said to be erect, and the leaves and shoots are also red when young. This was one of the most valuable Chinese herbal drugs, and Roy Lancaster writes that it is still cultivated for medicine. All *Rheums* require very rich, moist soil, well-manured each year, to grow and flower to their full potential. Hardy to −20°C or less.

Rheum ribes L. Native of S & E Turkey south to Israel, and east to N Iraq, Armenia and NW Iran, growing in dry gorges among rocks, at 2300–2700m, flowering in May–June. Plant with a very stout, woody rhizome. Leaves to 40cm across, with stems c.15cm, prickly, the leaf blades drying crisply in summer and rustling as they blow around in the wind. The stalks are eaten raw by the locals. Flower stems 30cm. Fruits with very broad wings. For a dry position, where it is very long-lived. Hardy to −15°C, possibly less.

Rheum spiciforme Royle Native of C Asia in the Tien Shan and the Pamir Alai east to Afghanistan and Bhutan and SE Xizang, at 3600–4800m in scrub, on open slopes and among rocks, flowering from January–July. Plant with a stout rootstock and a rosette of leaves 15–30cm across, on short stalks to 18cm. Spikes 5–30cm, with flowers turning reddish as they mature. For ordinary garden soil in a well-drained position. Hardy to −20°C or less.

Rumex pseudoalpinus Höfft. syn. *R. alpinus* L. (1759 non 1753) (*Polygonaceae*) Native of the mountains of C & S Europe, from France and Spain to Poland, W Russia, the Caucasus and Turkey, and naturalized in Scotland and N England, growing in damp grassy places by old farms, and near cowsheds, at up to 2500m, flowering in June–August. Plant slowly forming large patches, with a creeping rhizome. Leaves to 40cm long and wide. Flowering stems to 1m. For very rich, cool, moist soil. Hardy to −20°C or less. The leaves were formerly used for wrapping butter, and the young shoots are edible. The red-veined dock, *R. sanguineus* L. var. *sanguineus*, is also worth growing, for its beautiful leaves.

Rheum palmatum in flower at Beth Chatto's Garden

Rheum palmatum 'Atrosanguineum'

Rheum palmatum (young leaves)

Rumex pseudoalpinus in Perthshire

Rheum alexandrae at the Savill Gardens

Silene dioica (wild form) in Aberdeenshire

Silene dioica (compact garden form)

Silene schafta

Silene fimbriata from Itkol, C Caucasus

Silene caroliniana

Lychnis flos-cuculi at Gibbon's Brook, Sellindge

Lychnis flos-cuculi L. (*Caryophyllaceae*)
Ragged Robin   Native of Europe from Iceland and Scotland, east to Siberia and the Caucasus, south to Spain, Sicily and Greece and naturalized in NE North America, growing in marshes and bogs, flowering in May–July. Plant creeping at ground level. Flowering stems upright, 30–75cm. Flowers 3–4cm across. Petals pink with 4 very thin narrow lobes or white with less deeply 2-lobed petals in subsp. *subintegra* Heyek in Greece and the Balkans. A pretty plant for a damp meadow, moist border or bog garden, especially in its double form.

Silene asterias Griseb. (*Caryophyllaceae*)
Native of Albania, Yugoslavia, Bulgaria and Greece, growing in damp places by streams at 1200–2000m, flowering in June–July. Plant forming clumps of rosettes of thin leaves to 15cm long. Stems to 100cm, with 1 or 2 pairs of leaves. Heads of flowers 4–6cm across. A striking and unusual plant for moist, peaty soil in full sun. Hardy to −20°C or less.

Silene caroliniana Walt. Wild Pink   Native of Maine south to Georgia along the mountains, west to C New York, Pennsylvania and Kentucky, growing in dry rocky or sandy places, often in shallow soil on rock outcrops, flowering in April–June. Stems 10–25cm, glandular-pubescent and sticky. Basal leaves 5–10cm long. Flowers *c*.2.5cm across. An attractive plant for poor, shallow, dry soil. Hardy to −25°C.

Silene dioica (L.) Clairv. syn. *Lychnis dioica* L.
Red Campion   Native of most of Europe, east to Bulgaria and of North Africa, growing in woods, rocky slopes, hedges and sea cliffs, flowering in March–June. Plant forming clumps of rosettes with several stems 30–90cm tall, softly hairy. Flowers 1.8–2.5cm across, bright pinkish, very rarely white. A very floriferous dwarf form is common in cottage gardens in E Scotland. It is probably subsp. *zetlandica* (Compton) Clapham, found in Orkney and Shetland; similar plants are found on coasts and mountains in other parts of Europe. It has stems *c*.30cm and is hairier with a denser inflorescence. Two double-flowered forms are also cultivated: 'Flore Pleno', an old cultivar known since the 16th century, and 'Richmond', a semi-double found in Richmond Park near London in *c*.1978. For any position that is not hot and dry. Hardy to −25°C.

Silene fimbriata Sims syns. *Oberna multifida* (Adam) Ikonn., *Silene multifida* (Adam) Rohrb. Native of the Caucasus at *c*.2000m, growing in wet subalpine birch woods, flowering in May–June. Stems 1–1.5m, swollen at the joints. Flowers *c*.2.5cm across, with a very swollen calyx. An attractive plant for the wild garden or back of a cool shaded border. Hardy to −25°C.

Silene laciniata Cav.   Native of the mountains of Mexico, with subsp. *major* Hitch. & Maguire in S California from Santa Cruz Co. southwards, growing in scrub, chaparral, and sandy places along the coast, flowering in May–July. Stems several, sprawling to 70cm from a deep taproot. Leaves linear to lanceolate, 5–10cm long. Flowers 16–30mm across, with appendages 1–1.5mm long. Capsule exserted from the calyx. *Silene californica* Durand, from S California north to Oregon, is very similar, but has broader leaves and capsules not exserted from the calyx. For dry, well-drained soil in full sun. Hardy to −10°C, possibly lower.

Silene virginica near Charlottesville, Virginia

Silene laciniata at the Royal Botanic Gardens, Edinburgh

Silene schafta S. C. Gmel. ex Hohen.   Native of the Talysh and N Iran, growing on subalpine rocks at 1500–1800m, flowering in July–August, usually in June in gardens. Stems semi-prostrate to 30cm long. Flowers *c*.2cm across, usually bright pink but paler in 'Shell Pink'. For the top of a wall or front of a border in full sun. Hardy to −20°C.

Silene virginica L.   Native of S New Jersey, W New York and SW Ontario, west to Minnesota, south to Georgia and Missouri, growing in dry woods and on roadside banks, flowering in April–September. Stem 30–60cm. Flowers 2.5–3.75cm across; petals narrow, 2-lobed or toothed at apex. A very striking plant, but seldom cultivated. For well-drained soil in partial or deciduous shade. Hardy to −20°C.

Silene asterias at Harry Hay's, Surrey

Lychnis coronaria 'Alba' with *Viola cornuta* 'Alba', delphiniums and 'Iceberg' roses

Lychnis coronaria 'Oculata'

Lychnis 'Abbotswood Rose'

Lychnis × arkwrightii hort. ex Heydt
'Vesuvius' (*Caryophyllaceae*)   A hybrid
between *L. × haageana* (*L. fulgens × L. coronata*)
and *L. chalcedonica*. Stems to 45cm. Leaves
purplish. 'Vesuvius' is a good selection, raised
in around 1912. Hardy to −15°C.

Lychnis chalcedonica L. Jerusalem Cross
Native of W Russia, from Odessa to Moscow,
and recorded also in NW China growing in
woods and scrub, flowering in June–July. Plant
with a spreading rootstock and several upright
stems to 45cm, sometimes to 1.2m in
cultivation. Flowers 10–50 in a flat-topped head,
each 1.5cm across. Petals deeply lobed. Easily
grown in good moist soil in sun or partial shade,
in a sheltered position; cultivated in gardens in
Europe since before 1593. Hardy to −20°C or
less. Several forms are grown in gardens: e.g.
'Alba' and 'Alba Plena', white single and
double; 'Rosea', a pale pink; **Carnea**, a flesh
pink; a double pink; and 'Rubra Plena', a
double red.

Lychnis coronaria (L.) Desv.   Native of
Europe from Czechoslovakia and Yugoslavia
south to NW Africa, Greece and NW Turkey,
and eastwards to the Crimea, Iran and
Turkestan, growing in scrub, woods and on
rocky sunny slopes, flowering in
May–September. Usually a rather short-lived
perennial. Stems to 100cm, much branched.
Leaves softly and densely white-hairy. Flowers
usually purplish pink, c.3cm across. Long
cultivated, and several colour forms are now
common in gardens: 'Atrosanguinea', deep
crimson; **Oculata**, white with pink eye; **Alba**,
white, and a double 'Flore Pleno'. The pale-
flowered single form comes more or less true
from seed.
'Abbotswood Rose' is probably a hybrid
between *L. coronaria* and *L. flos-jovis*, called *L. ×
walkeri*. It is shorter, to c.60cm, and more
spreading than *L. coronaria* and has flowers of a
piercing pink, with deeply emarginate petals. All
these will survive on very poor, dry sandy soils
in full sun; they will flower well, but be short-
lived in rich soil and partial shade. Hardy to
−20°C.

Lychnis flos-jovis (L.) Desv.   Native of
France, Switzerland and N Italy in the W Alps,
growing on dry sunny subalpine slopes on acid
rocks at 1000–2000m flowering in June–August.
Usually a short-lived perennial with stems
20–90cm. Leaves white hairy; flowers purplish
or scarlet, in heads of 4–10. Petals deeply lobed;
'Hort's Variety' has paler rose-pink flowers, and
there are also a white and a dwarf form. Best in
well-drained, rather poor soil. Hardy to −15°C.

Lychnis viscaria L. syn. *Viscaria vulgaris*
Bernh.   Native of Scotland and Wales, south to
Spain and east to NW Turkey, Siberia and C
Asia, growing in open sandy places, on dry
hillsides, rocks and cliffs, flowering in
May–August. Leaves narrow, not hairy, forming
mats. Stems to 90cm, usually around 40cm;
flowers purplish red, 18–20mm across.
'Splendens Plena' is a good double pink, and
there is a double white 'Splendens Alba', as well
as the normal 'Alba'. Subsp. *atropurpurea*
(Griseb.) Chater, from Romania to Yugoslavia
and Greece, differs in minor details of the calyx
and capsule stalk. For well-drained soil in full
sun. Hardy to −25°C or less.

Lychnis × *arkwrightii* 'Vesuvius'

Lychnis viscaria 'Alba'

Lychnis viscaria

Lychnis viscaria 'Splendens Plena'

Lychnis chalcedonica at Cedar Tree Cottage, Sussex

Lychnis chalcedonica 'Carnea' at Wisley

Lychnis flos-jovis at the Savill Gardens, Windsor

Lupinus nootkatensis by the River Dee, near Braemar

Lupinus nootkatensis

Lupinus polyphyllus (naturalized)

Lupinus perennis in Maine

Lupinus 'The Chatelaine'

Lupinus 'My Castle'

Lupinus 'Magnificence'

Thermopsis mollis

Thermopsis ovata in Washington State

Baptisia australis (L.) R. Br. (*Leguminosae*)
Native of N Virginia to W Pennsylvania, east to
Missouri and Kansas and south to Georgia and
Texas, growing in rich soil, flowering in June-
August. Plant forming large clumps of glabrous
upright stems to 2m tall. Leaves very short-
stalked with 3 oblanceolate leaflets. Flowers
2–2.5cm long. Seed pod inflated. For rich,
moist soil in sun or light shade. Hardy to
−20°C. *B. cinerea* (Raf.) Feon. & Schub. is
minutely hairy, with yellow flowers about 2.5cm
long; *B. leucophaea* Nutt. and *B. leucantha* T. &
G. have white flowers; all are natives of prairies
and rich meadows in SE North America.

Lupinus nootkatensis Donn ex Sims
(*Leguminosae*)   Native of NE Asia and NW
America, from British Columbia to S Alaska,
and naturalized in Norway and on the Tay,
Dee, Spey and Beauly in Scotland, growing on
shingle banks in rivers, flowering in June–July.
Stems several, erect up to 80cm. Leaflets 6–8.
Flowers bluish, 6–18mm long. This species was
introduced into cultivation in Europe as long
ago as 1795 by Archibald Menzies on Captain
Vancouver's expedition. It has since died out in
gardens, probably because it is very susceptible
to slug damage. It is, however, a fine sight in
late June on some of the best salmon rivers in E
Scotland.

Lupinus perennis L.   Native of E North
America from Maine and Ontario westwards to
Minnesota and south to Florida, Missouri and
Louisiana, growing in grassy places in dry,
sandy soil, flowering in May–June. Stems few
from a compact rootstock to 60cm. Leaves with
around 8 narrowly oblanceolate leaflets. Flowers
blue, more rarely pink or white, 12–16mm long,
without a spot on the standard. A useful species
for meadow garden on poor sandy soil; hardier
than the western *L. polyphyllus*, to −25°C, or
less.

Lupinus polyphyllus Lindl.   This is the
forerunner of the large cultivated lupins. It is a
native of coastal California from Santa Cruz
Co. of San Francisco, northwards to British
Columbia (with subsp. *superba* (Heller) Munz
inland to Nevada), growing in wet grassy
meadows, flowering in May–July. In wild forms
the stems are up to 1.5m high, with 9–17
leaflets; the flowers are blue, purple or reddish,
11–14mm long, in whorls on racemes 15–60cm
long. Good for naturalizing in sandy soil in long
grass. Hardy to −25°C.

Garden lupins   Perennial lupins were
cultivated in English gardens from about 1826

when *L. polyphyllus* was first introduced from
North America. The great strides in their
improvement took place from 1911 onwards
when George Russell, gardener to a Mrs
Michlethwaite in York, began to grow lupins on
his allotment and select, every year, the best
seedlings that appeared. It is probable that the
annual *L. hartwegii* with magenta flowers
contributed to the improved range of flower
colours in Russell's hybrids. It was not until
1937 that Russell's lupins received wide
recognition; many distinct colours are still in
cultivation, such as 'Limelight' (yellow) and the
blue-and-white bicolour 'Vogue'. 'Mrs
Michlethwaite' is named after his former
employer. Named lupin cultivars require well-
drained soil, preferably slightly acid and sandy,
without nitrogenous manure; they should not be
allowed to set seed, or the plant will be
weakened. The young shoots are also
commonly damaged by slugs. Recently Russell's
work has been continued by the Woodfield
brothers, who now produce fine lupins in a wide
range of colours and bicolours. Shown here are:
'The Chatelaine' syn. 'Schlossfrau',
'Magnificence', and 'My Castle' syn. 'Mein
Schloss'

Thermopsis mollis (Michx.) M. A. Curtis
Native of S West Virginia, E Tennessee, North
Carolina and Georgia, growing in the
mountains, flowering in July–August. Plant with
few to several erect stems, 60–90cm tall.
Stipules not leafy. Leaves stalked with 3 oval
leaflets, 2–4cm long. Flowers in an elongated
raceme, *c.*20mm long. Seed pod flat. For good
soil in sun or partial shade. Hardy to −20°C.

Thermopsis ovata (Rob.) Rydb.   Native of
Wyoming and Idaho west to Washington and
Oregon, growing in damp, grassy places, sandy
river banks, and in open woods, flowering in
May–July. Stems 60–80cm, stout, succulent.
Stipules leafy, obovate to ovate-cordate, 2–4cm
long. Leaflets obovate to broadly elliptic, 6–8cm
long. Flowers in a loose raceme. Seed pods
usually upright, 5–7cm long, silky-hairy. For any
good moist soil in sun or partial shade. Hardy to
−20°C.

Thermopsis villosa (Walt.) Fern. & Schubert
syn. *T. caroliniana* M. A. Curtis   Native of
North Carolina, Georgia and Tennessee,
growing in open woods and on river banks,
flowering in April–May. Stems 80–100cm,
stout, with few branches and leafy stipules.
Leaflets obovate, 5–8cm long. Flowers in a
compact raceme. For good soil in full sun or
partial shade. Hardy to −15°C, perhaps less.

Thermopsis villosa

Baptisia australis

Alchemilla conjuncta

Alchemilla mollis with box hedges in Gloucestershire

Alchemilla abyssinica at Harry Hay's, Surrey

Alchemilla abyssinica Fres. syn. *A. pedata* A. Rich. (*Rosaceae*)   Native of Ethiopia, particularly in the north-west, growing in grassy places and on the edges of forest. Plant spreading by runners to form patches several metres across. Leaves *c.*4cm wide. Inflorescence simple and very delicate. Hardy to −5°C, but often needs reseeding after cold winters.

Alchemilla conjuncta Babington   Native of the SW Alps and Jura in France and Switzerland, and found wild also in Scotland, growing in subalpine meadows and rocky places by streams, flowering in June–July. Plant forming spreading patches to 30cm across. Leaves blue-green above, silky-silvery beneath, the lobes joined in the lower ⅓ or so; flowering stems to 40cm. Easily grown in well-drained, moist soil in a sunny position. Hardy to −20°C or less? *A. alpina* L., which is common on granite mountains in Scotland, N England and most of Europe, is smaller, with all the leaflets separate to the base.

Alchemilla erythropoda Juz.   Native of the W Carpathians, Yugoslavia and Bulgaria eastwards to N Turkey, the Caucasus and N Iran, growing in rocky mountain meadows, flowering in May–August. Plant forming clumps up to 20cm across. Flowering stems 20–30cm, often reddish purple. Leaves bluish green, densely and softly hairy on both sides, *c.*4cm across, with characteristic deflexed hairs on the mature petioles. A small, easily grown species for a sunny position; suitable for gaps in paving

or other places near pathways. Hardy to −20°C or less.

Alchemilla glabra Neygenf.   Native of N & C Europe, including N England and Scotland, and NE North America, growing in grassy places, open woods and by streams in the mountains, usually on acid soils, flowering in May–September. Plant forming clumps with flowering stems to 60cm. Leaves *c.*8cm across, glabrous except for a few hairs on the apical part of the veins beneath. In its deep green, glabrous leaves, a contrast to *A. mollis*. *A. xanthochlora* Rothm. is similar, but has hairy stems and inflorescence, and leaves glabrous above, hairy on the veins beneath. *A. glabra* is better than *A. mollis* on damp, acid soils. Hardy to −25°C.

Alchemilla mollis (Buser) Rothm.   Native of N Greece and the E Carpathians in Romania and W Russia, south to the Caucasus, N Turkey, Armenia and N Iran, growing by streams in meadows and in fir and beech forest, flowering in June–September. Plant forming large clumps, and seeding freely. Leaves to 15cm across, hairy on both sides, lobed to ⅕. Flowering stems to 80cm long. Easily grown in sun or partial shade. Hardy to −25°C and tolerant of drought.

Cornus canadensis L. syn. *Chamaepericlymenum canadense* (L.) Asch. & Graebn. (*Cornaceae*) Bunchberry   Native of North America, from Newfoundland to Alaska,

south to West Virginia, Colorado and California, of Japan, Korea and E Siberia, growing in coniferous woods, flowering in May–July. Plant creeping underground to form extensive patches several metres across. Flowering stems 7.5–20cm, with the leaves in a whorl of *c.*6 at the top. Bracts white, 8–18mm long. Flowers minute, green. Fruits bright red and fleshy. Easily grown in peaty soil or shade or partial shade. A good companion for heathers. *C. suecica* L. is found all round the Arctic; it is a smaller, more delicate plant with 3 pairs of leaves up the stem, and blackish-purple flowers.

Gillenia trifoliata (L.) Moench syn. *Porteranthus trifoliatus* (L.) Britton (*Rosaceae*) Native of E North America, from Ontario and New York east to Michigan and south to Georgia and Missouri, growing in rocky open woods, flowering in June–July. Plant tufted with many stems to 120cm from a woody rootstock. Leaves trifoliate, the upper sessile, with leaflets to 7.5cm long. Stipules, at the base of the leaflets, small and narrow, to 8mm long. Flowers white or pinkish, with petals 1.0–1.2cm long. A most graceful and attractive plant, but I have not found it easy to establish: the young shoots are eaten by slugs and it should be planted in a position that is neither too sunny and dry, nor too shady. *G. stipulata* (Muhl.) Bergmans differs in being usually smaller, with leafy stipules about a third as long as the short-stalked leaves.

Alchemilla mollis after rain

Gillenia trifoliata

Alchemilla glabra in Aberdeenshire

Alchemilla erythropoda

Cornus canadensis

Duchesnea indica

Geum 'Mrs J. Bradshaw'

Geum coccineum

Fragaria 'Pink Panda'

Potentilla palustris

Potentilla nepalensis 'Roxana'

Potentilla 'Gibson's Scarlet'

Potentilla nepalensis 'Master Floris'

Duchesnea indica (Andrews) Focke (*Rosaceae*) Native of S & E Asia, including China and Japan, but widely naturalized in North America, from New York southwards, and south Europe, growing in damp shady woods and by streams, flowering in April–June and intermittently through the summer. Plant creeping by rooting runners, flowers yellow with petals 8mm long; fruits red, strawberry-like but insipid. *D. chrysantha* (Zoll. & Moritz) Miq. is a smaller plant with paler, pinkish-white fruit. *D. indica* is probably the hardier species, surviving to −15°C in the absence of snow cover.

Fragaria 'Pink Panda' (*Rosaceae*) A hybrid between *F. × ananassa*, a garden strawberry, and *Potentilla palustris*, the wild marsh cinquefoil, raised by Dr Jack Ellis. The original cross was made in 1966, and, after repeated backcrossing, 'Pink Panda' was selected, and introduced by Blooms in 1989. Height 10–15cm. Flowers 2–2.5cm across, often with 6 or more petals, produced in May–November, seldom fruiting. For full sun or partial shade. Hardy to −20°C.

Geum chiloense Balbis (*Rosaceae*) Native of Chile, on Chiloe Island, and around Conception, growing in damp places by mountain streams, flowering in November–January. Plant forming clumps, with flowering stems to 45cm. Flowers orange-red to purplish red. Differs from *G. coccineum* in its taller, more branched stems, and leaves in which the leaflets increase gradually in size to the apex. Hardy to −20°C, perhaps. 'Mrs J. Bradshaw' has semi-double flowers.

Geum coccineum Sibth. & Sm. syn. *G. borisii* hort. Native of the Balkan peninsula, and N Turkey, growing in wet meadows, and along streams in damp forests, at 1300–2000m flowering in May–August. Plant forming low clumps of pale green leaves with 2–4 pairs of lateral leaflets and a large terminal leaflet, 4–14cm across, orbicular-reniform. Flowering stems 10–45cm with 2–4 flowers. Petals 10–18mm long. Easily grown in moist peaty soil. Hardy to −25°C.

Potentilla nepalensis Hook. (*Rosaceae*) Native of the Himalayas from Pakistan eastwards to C Nepal, in alpine meadows and fields at 2100–2700m, flowering in June–September. Plant forming a loose mass of wiry branching stems 20–90cm long. Lower leaves with 5 leaflets. Flowers 1.3–2.5cm across, dark in any good, moist soil. 'Roxana': flowers bright pink with a red centre. 'Master Floris': flowers creamy yellow with a pink edge and dark-red centre. 'Helen Jane': flowers pale pink with dark centres. *P. nepalensis* differs from *P. atrosanguinea* by having lower leaves with 5, not 3, leaflets, and is a taller, more spreading plant with smaller flowers in a more branched inflorescence. 'Miss Willmott' (not shown) is cherry pink with a dark centre.

Potentilla palustris (L.) Scop. syn. *Comarum palustre* L. Marsh Cinquefoil Native of Europe, south to Bulgaria, eastwards to Siberia and Japan, and in North America from Greenland to New Jersey and N California, growing in wet places, by lakes, ponds and wet bogs, flowering in May–August. Plant with creeping rhizomes, forming extensive patches

Potentilla thurberi

Potentilla nepalensis 'Helen Jane'

Potentilla × *russelliana*

Potentilla 'Fireflame'

many metres across. Stems 15–45cm. Leaves bluish green with 5–7 leaflets. Petals deep purple, *c*.1cm, shorter than the purplish sepals. A plant for the wet wild garden, attractive with its greyish leaves. Hardy to −25°C.

Potentilla × *russelliana*   A hybrid between *P. atrosanguinea* and *P. nepalensis*; lower leaves with 3–5 leaflets, narrower than *P. atrosanguinea*. Some of those generally considered cultivars of *P. atrosanguinea*, e.g. 'Gibson's Scarlet', probably belong to this hybrid. The following *Potentilla* cultivars are probably either selections of *P. atrosanguinea* or hybrids between this and other species. The flowers are in various shades of red, orange or yellow, on branching stems about 45cm tall, forming spreading plants about 60cm across: 'Yellow Queen'; 'Fireflame'; 'Hamlet'; 'Gibson's Scarlet', lower leaves 3–5; 'Monsieur Rouillard'.

Potentilla thurberi A. Gray ex Lehm.   Native of C Arizona to C New Mexico and N Mexico, growing in moist clearings in conifer forest, in damp meadows and along streams, flowering in July–October. Plant tufted with many stiff stems 30–75cm tall. Leaves pinnate with 5 or 7 close, toothed leaflets, 2.5–5cm long. Flowers *c*.2.5cm across, deep velvety red with a darker centre. For a good soil in a warm position. Hardy to −25°C perhaps, growing well in New England where it flowers in June.

Waldsteinia ternata (Stephan) Fritsch (*Rosaceae*)   Native of Europe in the Carpathians in Czechoslovakia and Romania, and, rarely, in SE Austria and NW Yugoslavia, and of E Asia and E Siberia, Sakhalin and N Japan, growing in woods in the mountains, flowering in May–June. Plant forming low mats by creeping rhizomes. Leaves 3-foliolate, the leaflets 2–3cm long. Stems to 20cm, 1–7 flowered. Flowers 1.5–2cm across. Easily grown in leafy soil in partial shade where it makes very attractive ground cover. From descriptions in the floras the Japanese plants appear to be more delicate with fewer larger flowers on the stems. *W. fragarioides* (Michx.) Tratt from NE North America has similar leaves but smaller flowers 6–10mm across.

Potentilla 'Yellow Queen' with *Viola cornuta*

Potentilla 'Hamlet'

Waldsteinia ternata

Geum 'Lemon Drops'

Potentilla rupestris

Geum rivale f. *album*

Geum rossii

Potentilla atrosanguinea

Geum 'Georgenberg'

Geum montanum

Potentilla nepalensis (p. 142)

Potentilla atrosanguinea (pale form)

Specimens from Beth Chatto, Unusual Plants, 9 June. ½ life size

Geum rivale in Perthshire

Geum 'Leonard's Variety'

Geum triflorum

Geum elatum in Kashmir

Geum rivale f. album

Potentilla rupestris

Geum elatum Wall. ex D. Don (*Rosaceae*)
Native of the Himalayas from Pakistan to SE
Xizang, growing in scrub and alpine meadows
at 2700–4300m, flowering in June–August. Very
variable; as shown here a stemless plant with
congested pinnate basal leaves and single,
upright yellow flowers. At lower altitudes, a
taller plant with branched stems and nodding
yellow or more rarely reddish flowers. For well-
drained soil, in a sunny position, moist in
summer. Hardy to −20°C.

Geum 'Georgenberg' This is sometimes
quoted as *G.* × *heldreichii*, a hybrid between *G.
coccineum* and *G. montanum*, but the nodding
buds suggest that *G. rivale* or *G.* × *intermedium*
was one parent. *G. montanum* may well be the
other. The hybrid *G. rivale* × *G. montanum* is
called *G.* × *tirolense* Kerner; this is probably also
the parentage of 'Lemon Drops' from Beth
Chatto. Best in moist, peaty soil.

Geum montanum L. Native of the Pyrenees,
Alps, Corsica and Carpathians, eastwards to W
Russia and SW Greece growing in sub-alpine
meadows, at 1500–3000m, flowering in
June–July. Plant with a shortly creeping rhizome
and a rosette of leaves. Terminal leaflet *c.*6cm
long. Flowering stems 3–10cm long, 1–3
flowered. Flowers 2.5–4cm across. Easily grown
in well-drained, rather peaty soil in full sun. *G.
reptans* L. is closely related, but usually found at
a higher altitude, above 2000m; it has long
stolons and the leaves are always pinnate, with
the terminal lobe not much larger than other
lobes. Both are hardy to −25°C.

Geum rivale L. Water Avens Native of most
of Europe except the far south, of the Caucasus
and N Turkey, N Asia east to the Altai in NW
China and N America from Newfoundland to
British Columbia and south to New Jersey and
Colorado, growing in wet meadows, by streams
and in marshes, flowering in May–June. Plant
forming low mats of irregularly pinnate leaves,
with flowering stems simple or with few
branches, usually *c.*30cm, rarely up to 1m.
Stems and flowers brownish red or pinkish, pale
yellow green in *f. album*. Styles 8–9mm, hairy.
Hybrids with Herb Bennett (*G. urbanum* L.) are
common, especially in shady places by rivers.
They have taller stems with paler flowers, and
are called *G.* × *intermedium* Ehrh.
'Leonard's Variety' is probably a hybrid
between *G. rivale* and another species, possibly
G. coccineum. It has masses of stems up to 45cm
tall, with nodding flowers of pinkish orange,
with a hint of brown. All are easily grown in a
moist or partially shady border.

Geum rossii (R. Br.) Sev. Native of W North
America, from Alaska south to NE Oregon,
Nevada, New Mexico and in E Asia, growing in
arctic tundra, and on screes and stony meadows
in the mountains, flowering in June–July. Plant
forming dense clumps to 30cm across. Basal
leaves 4–10cm long. Flowering stems 8–20cm
tall. Petals 10–12mm long, yellow. Easily grown
in well-drained soil. Hardy to −20°C or lower.

Geum triflorum Pursh Native of North
America, from Newfoundland and New York
westwards to British Columbia, south to

Oregon and California and along the Rockies
south to Nevada, growing in damp places and
mountain screes, flowering in April–August,
according to altitude. Plant forming clumps to
30cm or more across. Basal leaves 5–15cm, with
up to 30 segments. Flowering stems to 30cm
tall, with 1–9 flowers. Petals pale yellow to
reddish or purplish. Easily grown in rather
damp soil. Hardy to −20°C or lower.

Potentilla atrosanguinea Lodd. syn. *P.
argyrophylla* Wall. ex Lehm. (*Rosaceae*) Native
of the Himalayas, from Afghanistan eastwards
to Sikkim, growing in scrub, and on grassy open
slopes, at 2500–4500m, flowering in
June–August. Plant with few erect or spreading
stems to 60cm. Leaves trifoliate, variably
silvery, especially beneath, with leaflets 2 × 5cm
long. Flowers red in the west, orange or yellow
(var. *argyrophylla* (Lehm.) Grierson & Long) in
the east, 2–4cm across. A useful spreading plant
for the front of a border, in cool moist soil.
Plants grown as *P. argyrophylla* commonly have
paler red flowers. Hardy to −25°C.

Potentilla rupestris L. syn. *P. foliosa* Somm. &
Lev. Native of most of Europe including
Britain, the Caucasus, Turkey and eastwards to
C Siberia, growing on dry sunny rocky slopes in
the mountains, flowering in June–July. Plant
tufted. Basal leaves pinnate, with 5–9 leaflets.
Stems 8–50cm. Flowers with petals 8–14mm
long. Easily grown in well-drained soil in full
sun. A characteristic species of dry rocky slopes
in the foothills in Europe. Hardy to −25°C.

Acaena magellanica

Acaena saccaticupula 'Blue Haze'

Acaena microphylla at Wisley, Surrey

Sanguisorba tenuifolia var. *alba* in Hokkaido

Sanguisorba canadensis at Kew

Acaena magellanica Vahl syn. *A. glaucophylla* Bitter (*Rosaceae*) Native of the Falkland Islands, South Georgia, Kerguelen Island, W Argentina and E Chile, north to 27°S, growing on sand and rocks near the sea, in scrub, open forest, moist grassland and bog at up to 1100m, flowering in November–March. Stems creeping and rooting. Leaf lamina 2–8cm long, with 5–8 pairs of leaflets. Flowering stems 7–14cm, with heads 1–3cm across, purplish when young with the unopened stamens; the spines in fruit 5–10mm long. Hardy to −15°C.

Acaena microphylla Hook. fil. Native of New Zealand, on North and South Island (var. *robusta* Allan and var. *pallideoliracea* Bitter), growing in grassland and in riverbeds, at up to 1100m, flowering in December–February. Plant creeping. Leaves green, glabrous, to 3cm long. Flower heads 2.5cm in diameter. Easily grown in rather moist soil; good for ground cover between paving stones. Hardy to −10°C.

Acaena saccaticupula Bitter 'Blue Haze' Native of New Zealand, in South Island in mountain grassland. Leaves glabrous; stipules scarious. Hardy to −15°C.

Sanguisorba alpina Bunge (*Rosaceae*) Native of the Altai, in Siberia, Sinjiang and ?Mongolia, growing in alpine meadows, flowering in June–August. Plant forming spreading clumps of very glaucous leaves, with 15–19 ovate, cordate leaflets. Flower spikes elongated, 1–5cm long. Easily grown in rich, moist soil in full sun. Very similar to *S. armena* but smaller, with blunter, more curved teeth on the leaflets.

Sanguisorba armena Boiss. Native of NE Turkey, especially around Erzurum, growing by mountain streams on treeless but grassy hills, flowering in July. Plant forming large clumps. Stems to 1.5m. Basal leaves with 15–19 ovate, cordate, strongly glaucous, leaflets. Flower spikes oblong, to 5.5cm, erect or nodding, pinkish, with long stamens. Easily grown in rich, moist soil in full or light shade. This species has bold glaucous leaves when well grown, like a smaller version of *Melianthus major*. Hardy to −25°C.

Sanguisorba canadensis L. Native of NE North America, from Newfoundland west to Michigan and south to Georgia, growing in wet meadows and swamps, flowering in July–October. Plant forming spreading clumps. Stems to 1m (or 2m!). Basal leaves green, with 7–15 ovate to oblong, cordate leaflets. Flower spikes elongated 2.5–15cm long, erect, the flowers at the base of the spike opening first. *S. stipulata* Raf. syn. *S. sitchensis* C. A. Mey from Japan is very similar, and also has narrow spikes of white flowers which open first at the base. It is a smaller plant, to 80cm, with shorter spikes 3–8cm long, usually white or greenish, rarely pinkish. Both are easily grown in good moist soil in sun or partial shade.

Sanguisorba hakusanensis Makino Native of Honshu, with varieties in Korea, and on Hokkaido, growing in alpine meadows and in moist rock crevices, flowering in June–September. Plant forming clumps with flowering stems 40–80cm. Leaflets 9–13, on stalks 3–7mm long, ovate-oblong or ovate. Flower spikes 4–10cm long, nodding, with stamens 7–10mm long, usually deep pinkish purple. Easily grown in moist soil in a cool position. Hardy to −20°C.

Sanguisorba obtusa Maxim Native of Japan, on Mount Hayachine on Honshu, growing in

Sanguisorba hakusanensis at the Royal Botanic Garden, Edinburgh

Sanguisorba alpina

Sanguisorba officinalis

Sanguisorba obtusa

Sanguisorba armena

alpine meadows, flowering in August–September. Plant forming small clumps. Stems 30–50cm. Leaflets 13–17, crowded, nearly sessile. Flower spikes 4–7cm long, nodding, with stamens 8–10mm long, usually pink, white in 'Alba'. Easily grown in moist soil in sun or partial shade. Flowering in June–July in SE England. Hardy to −20°C.

Sanguisorba officinalis L. Great Burnet Native of most of N Europe, south to Greece and Turkey, N Asia east to Japan, and North America (naturalized in Maine), growing in meadows and wet grassy places by streams, flowering in June–October. Plant forming large clumps, with stems to 1m. Basal leaves with 9–15 cordate, ovate to orbicular leaflets. Flower spikes erect, short, 1.2–2.5cm long, maroon,

blackish or flesh-red in var. *carnea* (Fisch.) Regel, from E Asia. Easily grown in moist, rich soil. Hardy to −25°C.

Sanguisorba tenuifolia Fisch. var. *alba* Trautv. & Meyer   Native of Japan, in all the islands, growing in meadows and damp places along streams, flowering in August–October. Plant forming small clumps, with stems 80–130cm. Leaflets 11–15, broadly linear to narrowly oblong, usually sessile. Flower spikes 2–7cm long, erect or nodding, narrow (6–7mm thick); flowers white with white stamens, or blood red in var. *purpurea* Trautv. & Meyer. Easily grown in moist soil in sun or partial shade. Var. *tenuifolia* grows in E Siberia, Heilongjiang (Manchuria), Korea and the north Pacific Islands. Hardy to −25°C.

Primula whitei 'Sherriff's Variety' at Sellindge, Kent

Primula heucherifolia Franch. (s. *Cortusoides*) Native of W Sichuan, growing in shady places in bamboo forest, flowering in May–June. Plant stoloniferous with creeping rhizomes. Leaves with an orbicular blade, 7–11 lobed. Stem 15–30cm, with 3–10 nodding flowers. Flowers with a coloured ring in the throat, 1–2.5cm across. For a cool shady position in well-drained soil.

Primula kaufmanniana Regel (s. *Cortusoides*) Native of C Asia, in the Tien Shan and Pamir Alai at 1000–3700m, growing in shady rocky places, flowering May–June. Plant tufted. Leaves with blade 2–8cm long and broad, 9–11 lobed, softly hairy. Stems 8–22cm, with 3–6 flowers in 1 or 2 whorls. Differs from *P. cortusoides* L. in its rounder leaves, and usually smaller flowers. Hardy to –20°C or lower.

Primula kisoana Miq. (s. *Cortusoides*) Native of C Honshu and Shikoku, growing in woods and shady places in the mountains, flowering in May, but in March–April in England. Plant stoloniferous, far-spreading. Stems 10–15cm, leaves 5–10cm across, softly hairy. Flowers 2–3cm across, with tube 15–20mm long. For semi-shade and leafy soil, in a cool, sheltered position. Hardy to –10°C.

Primula mollis Nutt. ex. Hook. syn. *P. sinomollis* Balf. fil. & Forrest (s. *Cortusoides*) Native of Bhutan, N Assam, N Burma and Yunnan, growing in shady places and scrub by streams at 2300–3300m, flowering in May–July. Plant forming rosettes of rather few softly hairy leaves, with kidney-shaped blades up to 12cm long and wide. Flowering stems to 60cm, with 2–10 whorls of 2–9 flowers. For a shady position in leafy soil. Hardy to –10°C.

Primula moupinensis Franch. (s. *Petiolaris*) Native of W Sichuan, especially above Wolong, Baoxing and Ya-an, growing in wet woods and in moss under shrubs at 2500–3000m, flowering in April–May. Similar to *P. sonchifolia*, but without scales around the resting bud, and with broader, obovate, very thin-textured leaves. Flowers lilac, *c.*2cm across. Some forms produce strawberry-like runners.

Primula ovalifolia Franch. (s. *Petiolaris*) Native of NE Yunnan, W Hubei and W Sichuan, especially in the Wolong, Baoxing and Yan-an valleys, and on Omei Shan, growing on very shady or overhanging vertical banks and rocks, at 1200–1800m, flowering in April–May. Plants solitary, up to 20cm across, not forming resting buds; leaves 3–16cm long. Flowers reddish purple, 2–2.5cm across, 2–9 in an umbel, on a delicate stem to 15cm tall. Calyx loose, expanding after flowering. For a very shaded position, humid and warm in summer, dry in winter. Hardy to –10°C perhaps.

Primula polyneura Franch. (s. *Cortusoides*) Native of W China, in Kansu, Sichuan, Yunnan, SE Xizang, growing in woods and shady places at 2300–4300m, flowering in May–June. Plant stoloniferous, spreading. Stems 10–50cm. Flowers 1–2.5cm across with a yellow, greenish-yellow or orange eye, pale pink to crimson, purple or wine-red. Easily grown in moist, leafy soil in partial shade. Probably the hardiest of this group, to –20°C.

Primula sieboldii E. Morren (s. *Cortusoides*) Native of Japan, in S Hokkaido, Honshu and Kyushu, and in Korea, NE China and E Siberia, growing in moist, grassy places by rivers, flowering in April–May. Long cultivated in Japan, with numerous colours, the original wild form being pinkish-purple. Plant with creeping underground rhizomes. Leaves 4–10cm long. Stems 15–40cm with an umbel of 7–20 flowers, 2–3cm across in cultivated forms, 2–2.5cm in the wild. Easily grown in moist, leafy soil in cool sun or partial shade. Many named varieties are in cultivation, most of which were selected in Japan.

Primula sonchifolia Franch. (s. *Petiolaris*) Native of NE Burma and China in SE Xizang, W Sichuan and Yunnan, growing in wet mountain meadows and under *Rhododendron*, at 3300–4600m, flowering in May–July, but as early as February in cultivation in S England. Plant forming tight, pointed, resting buds which may be 5cm across, and covered with scales. Leaves covered with farina at flowering time, later naked, to 35cm when fully grown. Flowers 3–20 in an umbel, pale lavender, purplish, bright blue or 'intense indigo violet', 1.5–2.5cm across, often toothed around the edge. Requires similar or wetter conditions than *P. bhutanica*.

Primula whitei W. W. Sm. syn. *P. bhutanica* Fletcher **'Sherriff's Variety'** (s. *Petiolaris*) (*Primulaceae*) Native of N Assam, E Bhutan and S Xizang, growing in coniferous and mixed forest, on damp mossy banks and under *Rhododendron* at 3000–4300m, flowering in May–June, and in February–March in England. Plant forming clusters of resting buds which open to reveal a mass of white farina-covered buds, then stemless flowers. Leaves, when mature, not floury, to 20cm long or more on well-grown specimens, oblanceolate, acute. Flowers pin-eyed in 'Sherriff's Variety', 2–3cm across, solitary or sometimes many on a short peduncle. This variety was collected by Ludlow & Sherriff in Bhutan and grown for many years in Mrs Sherriff's garden at Ascreavie, Angus; from here it was distributed to many gardens, and grows and increases easily, even in S England. Its main danger is dry heat in summer, and it should be planted so that the sun never shines directly on the leaves, e.g. on the north side of a high wall; frequent watering with a hose to wet the leaves will keep it alive during hot summers. Hardy to –25°C, but safer with snow cover.

Primula sonchifolia from Cluny, Perthshire

Primula kaufmanniana at Ferghana, C Asia

Primula ovalifolia near Wolong, Sichuan

Primula kisoana at the Savill Gardens, Windsor

Primula moupinensis above Ya-an, Sichuan

Primula sieboldii, a white cultivar

Primula polyneura

Primula heucherifolia at Baoxing, Sichuan

Primula mollis

'Peach'

'Lady Bird'

'Sparkling Wine'

'Crimson Beauty'

'Ballerina'

'Red Velvet'

'Pink Gem'

'Seaway'

'Rose Bowl'

'Rhapsody'

'Torch Light'

'Lemon Sulphur'

Specimens from Hopley's Plants, 20 April. ½ life size

Double Primrose 'Fife Yellow'

Pale yellow and flesh pink primrose in an old garden in Kent

Primula vulgaris Huds. (*s. Vernalis*) (*Primulaceae*) Primrose   The wild primrose of Europe and Turkey is usually pale yellow in colour but in many old gardens flesh-pink forms interbreed with the yellow, and the pink form is said to be common in Pembrokeshire. These are not the same as the purplish-pink subsp. *sibthorpii* from E Europe (see p.153). White primroses are common in Mallorca (subsp. *balearica*), on Andros (var. *pulchella*) and in parts of the Atlas Mountains (var. *atlantica*), as well as in cultivation. One good, neat, white form is 'Gigha' named after the island in the inner Hebrides. Forma *viridiflora* Druce is the name for the plant with a pale-green flower of somewhat leaf-like texture. It appears sporadically among populations of normal primroses, being reported from Argyll and Somerset, and may be due to infection with a fungus-like mycoplasm. It remains green in cultivation, and is not known to be particularly infectious. Hardy to −25°C.

Double Primroses   Until recently these old-fashioned double primroses were scarce and expensive, being slow to propagate and often poor growers because of virus infection; now many are being propagated by tissue culture, which produces healthy stocks at a reasonable price. Some of the old varieties are shown here, and some of the new ones, recently brought to Europe from New Zealand by Dr Barker of Hopley's Nursery and named in England by him.

Old varieties
'**Alba Plena**'   An old double white.
'**Double Red**'   A large-flowered, double, pinkish red.
'**Fife Yellow**'   An unusual brownish-yellow double. 'Double Sulphur' is paler and even more striking.
'**Red Paddy**'   syn. 'Sanguinea Plena'   Semi-double, white edge.
New varieties from Hopley's Plants, introduced in 1989:
'**Ballerina**'   Flowers often several on a stout, polyanthus-like stalk.
'**Crimson Beauty**'
'**Lady Bird**'   Flowers often several on a stout, polyanthus-like stalk.
'**Lemon Sulphur**'   Flowers often several on a stout, polyanthus-like stalk.
The following have solitary, primrose-type flowers in various colours: '**Peach**', '**Pink Gem**', '**Red Velvet**', '**Rhapsody**', '**Rose Bowl**', '**Seaway**', '**Sparkling Wine**', '**Torchlight**'.

Double Primrose 'Red Paddy'

Double Primrose 'Double Red'

Primula vulgaris 'Gigha White'

Double Primrose 'Alba Plena'

Primula vulgaris f. *viridiflora*

Primula veris subsp. *macrocalyx* in NW China

Primula veris on chalk downland, Buckinghamshire

Primula megaseifolia

Primula vulgaris subsp. *sibthorpii* at Wisley

Primula veris at Wye, Kent

Primula vulgaris

Primula luteola at Edinburgh

Primula elatior subsp. *pallasii*

Primula elatior subsp. *meyeri*

Primula elatior subsp. *elatior*

Primula juliae

Primula elatior (L.) Hill subsp. *elatior* Oxlip (s. *Vernalis*) (*Primulaceae*)   Native of N Europe, from SE England to Finland and Russia, growing in woods and meadows, flowering in April–June, according to latitude. In England it is characteristic of coppiced woods on glacial clays between London and Cambridge and into E Norfolk, growing in huge numbers in some ancient woods, replacing the common primrose. It has pale-yellow flowers on a stem to 10–30cm. Leaves 10–20cm long, with sparse, curled hairs beneath; flowers 15–25mm across, up to 20 in a 1-sided umbel. Easily grown in shade or partial shade in heavy rich and chalky soil, moist in summer. Hardy to −25°C.

Primula elatior (L.) Hill subsp. *meyeri* (Rupr.) Valentine & Lamond syn. *P. amoena* M. Bieb.   Native of the Caucasus, Georgia and NE Turkey, growing on rocks, cliff ledges, on stony, peaty, alpine meadows, on screes and in *Rhododendron* scrub at 1820–4000m, flowering in May–July. Plant forming small clumps of few rosettes. Leaves, when fully grown, 5–15cm long, usually white-woolly beneath. Flowering stem 5–15cm with up to 10 flowers of deep purple, violet-blue or pale lavender, 1.5–2.5cm across. This subspecies is rare in cultivation, but important as the parent of many of the *P.* × *pruhonicensis* hybrids. It needs careful cultivation in well-drained but moist, peaty soil, in sun or partial shade. Hardy to −20°C or less.

Primula elatior (L.) Hill subsp. *pallasii* W. W. Sm. & Forrest   Native of the Urals east to the Altai in C Asia and south to Transcaucasia and Turkey, growing in moist alpine meadows and grassy scrub, at 1900–3200m in Turkey, flowering in May–July. Leaves glabrous or nearly glabrous beneath. Flowers pale yellow, 3–6 in an umbel, similar in general appearance to subsp. *elatior*. Easily grown in heavy soil in partial or deciduous shade.

Primula juliae Kusn. (s. *Vernalis*)   Native of SE Caucasus near Lagodeki, growing in moist shady places by waterfalls, flowering in April–May. Plant forming mats of rounded leaves by its thin, creeping rhizome. Leaves 2–10cm long, the blade usually c.3cm across. Flowers pinkish with a yellow tube 2–3cm across. This dwarf and attractive species requires moist, leafy soil and a cool, shady position. It has been the parent of many hybrids (see p.154), of which *P.* 'Wanda' is probably the most familiar. *P. juliae* is named after its discoverer, Mme Julia Ludovikovna Mlokosewitsch, who also found, in the same locality, the familiar yellow paeony which bears her husband's surname.

Primula luteola Rupr. (s. *Farinosae*)   Native of E Caucasus, especially around Tuschetien, growing in moist meadows or by streams at 1400–3000m, flowering in May–June. Plant forming small clumps of a few rosettes. Leaves 10–30cm, with fine, sharp teeth. Flowering stem 15–35cm, farinose at the apex, with a rather tight umbel of 10–25 flowers. Flowers c.1–5cm across with deeply notched lobes. For moist, but well-drained soil in sun or partial shade and a cool summer climate. Hardy to −20°C or less. Related to *P. auriculata* but with a more attractive habit, and always yellow flowers.

Primula megaseifolia Boiss. & Bal. ex Boiss.   Native of NE Turkey from Trabzon eastwards to SW Georgia, growing in woods, damp gorges and on shady banks at up to 1100m, flowering in March–April, though often earlier in gardens. Plants forming small clumps. Leaves stalked, the blade cordate at the base, to 15cm long, with reddish-hairy petioles. Flowers to 9 in an umbel, pinkish, with a tube c.20mm long. For moist leafy soil in shade. This species should be heat tolerant, provided it is damp and shaded.

Primula veris L. subsp. *macrocalyx* (Bunge) Ludi   Native of S Russia and the Crimea, eastwards to Chinese Turkestan and Xinjiang and south to N Iran and Turkey, growing in scrub by streams, in mountain meadows and among rocks, flowering in May–June. Like a rather large Cowslip, but with leaves which narrow gradually into the petiole, a very large, loose, yellowish calyx, and a corolla 19–28mm across. For good soil in sun or partial shade. Very hardy, to −20°C and lower.

Primula veris L. subsp. *veris* (s. *Vernalis*) Cowslip   Native of N Europe, from Scotland, Ireland and Spain to W Russia, with other subspecies in the mountains of S Europe, the Caucasus, Italy and Turkey, C Asia as far east as the Altai, flowering in April–June. Subsp. *veris* is characteristic of dry, grassy slopes on chalk and limestone, the other subspecies of grassy alpine or subalpine meadows and scrub. Stems 10–30cm. Flowers in a one-sided umbel, 8–15mm across; larger in the other subspecies. A popular plant for meadow gardens, but requires full sun and a well-drained alkaline soil to survive well. On cold clay soils, the primrose *P. vulgaris* is more likely to succeed. Plants with large orange or red flowers are common in cultivation and probably contain genes of red-flowered polyanthus. Hardy to −20°C.

Primula vulgaris Huds. subsp. *sibthorpii* (Hoffman.) W. W. Sm. and Forrest   Native of Greece south to Euboea and Ikaria, the Crimea, Bulgaria, Transcaucasia and N Turkey; in Greece and W Turkey grows below 850m in the Mediterranean zone, on shady banks and cliffs, flowering in March–April. In the east of Turkey and Caucasus it is found in hazel groves and meadows in the mountains, at 2200m near Artvin, flowering in May. Flowers usually purplish pink, sometimes red. Leaves often similar to subsp. *vulgaris*, but reported to be more abruptly narrowed to the stalk.

Primula vulgaris Huds. subsp. *vulgaris* (s. *Vernalis*) Primrose   Native of W Europe, from Ireland to E Denmark and in the south to the Ukraine, the Crimea and Transcaucasia; also found in Lebanon, Turkey and NW Africa (var. *atlantica* Maide, usually white), growing in woods, shady cliffs and alpine meadows, usually in rather heavy soil, at up to 2100m in Turkey, flowering in January–June. Stems 3–20cm with only one flower. Leaves 2–30cm long; small leaves present at flowering, larger ones produced in early summer. Flowers 2–4cm across, yellow, occasionally white or flesh-pink. Best grown in heavy soil, with shade and moisture in summer. Hardy to −20°C.

Large polyanthus at the Savill Gardens, Windsor

Primrose hybrids   There are three main groups of Primrose hybrid cultivars in addition to *P. vulgaris*, as follows:

Primula × variabilis (*P. veris × P. vulgaris*) Generally known as Polyanthus, derived from crosses between Primrose and Cowslip. These hybrids are common in the wild where the parents grow together, and have been bred for hundreds of years to give much larger flowers in a wide range of colours, from blue and red to white and yellow.

Primula × pruhonicensis (*P. juliae × (P. elatior × P. vulgaris)*) This cross produces smaller hybrids of more refined form, usually with an umbel of flowers. *P. juliae* was introduced in 1911; the name *pruhonicensis* comes from the village of Pruhonice near Prague, where Count Ernst Silva Tarouca made a fine garden between 1886 and 1937. A pink form, shown here, is often wrongly called *Primula vulgaris sibthorpii*. Its young leaves are distinctly heart-shaped.

Primula × juliana (*P. juliae × P. elatior*) cultivars are smaller than *P. pruhonicensis*, often with only one flower per stalk. 'Wanda' is an old and popular variety of this group.

Primula × pruhonicensis
'Craddock White'   Creamy white, with flowers 2.5cm across.
'Enchantress'   Flowers larger and more solid than 'Guinevere', *c*.3cm across.
'Guinevere' syn. 'Garryard Guinevere' Probably raised by Mrs Johnson, Kinlough, Co. Leitrim, in Ireland. The original Garryarde primrose, which was named 'Appleblossom', appears to be lost. Stems to 15cm. Leaves bronze. Flowers *c*.2–5cm across.
'Lady Greer'   A delicate pale yellow, with flowers 2.5cm across.
'McWatt's Claret'   An unusual brownish red.
'Tawny Port'   A rich dark red. Flowers 2cm across. Close to 'Wanda'.
'Tomato Red'   A unique shade of orange-red. Flowers 2–5cm across.
'Wanda'   One of the oldest hybrids. Flowers *c*.2cm across.
'Wanda hose-in-hose'   A double 'Wanda' with one corolla inside the other.

Primula × polyanthus
'Crescendo Blue'   A large-flowered mid-blue, with pale-green leaves. Usually sold as F1 hybrid seeds in mixed colours.
'Duckyls Red'   Raised by Mrs Hazel Taylor at Duckyls, East Sussex. Fairly similar in habit to 'Cowichan Blue', with rather dark leaves and a small 'eye'.
'Cowichan Blue'   With medium-sized flowers, and a small 'eye' to the flower. A fine deep blue, and purple stems; the dark leaves showing the influence of *P. × pruhonicensis*. Raised by Florence Bellis in Oregon, *c*.1960, who also raised the Barnhaven strain. Height around 10cm.
'Pacific Giants Mixed'   This is a well-known strain of large-flowered polyanthus, in a wide range of colours. 'Paradise' hybrids produce a more interesting selection of colours, including bicolours and semi-doubles.

Polyanthus 'Crescendo Blue'

Polyanthus 'Duckyls Red'

Polyanthus 'Cowichan Blue'

Primula × *pruhonicensis* (pink form)

Primula × *pruhonicensis* 'Guinevere'

'McWatts Claret'

'Wanda'

'Enchantress'

'Wanda hose-in-hose'

'Tomato Red'

'Tawny Port'

'Craddock White'

'Lady Greer'

Primula waltonii at Branklyn, Perth

Primula denticulata subsp. *sinodenticulata* above Wolong, Sichuan

Primula sikkimensis

Primula alpicola var. *alba*

Primula alpicola var. *violacea*

Primula alpicola

Primula secundiflora at the Cruickshank Botanic Garden, Aberdeen

Primula florindae at Stancombe Park, Gloucestershire

Primula ioessa at the Savill Gardens, Windsor

Primula ioessa

Primula alpicola (W. W. Sm.) Stapf (s. *Sikkimensis*) (*Primulaceae*) Native of E Xizang in the Tsangpo valley and of Bhutan, near Thimpu, growing in shady bogs and moist alpine meadows at 3700–4600m, flowering in May. The flower colour is variable in the wild and the three main colours have been given variety names: var. *violacea* (Stapf) W. W. Sm., flowers purplish; var. *alba* W. W. Sm., flowers white; and var. *alpicola* syn. var. *luna* Stapf, yellow. Leaves with elliptic to oblong-elliptic blade, 2–8cm across rounded at the base, with a long stalk. Stem 15–90cm, farinose at apex with 1–4 whorls of flowers. Pedicels 1–8cm. Flowers 1.5–2.5cm long, nodding, scented. For peaty soil. Hardy to −25°C.

Primula denticulata Smith (s. *Denticulata*) Native of Afghanistan of Bhutan and SE Xizang, growing in scrub, and open grassy slopes, not always by water, at 1500–4500m, flowering in April–June. Stems 3–15cm, elongating during flowering. Flowers 1–2cm across. Leaves to 30cm after flowering. Commonly cultivated and now available in reds, magenta and pink to white, as well as the original mauvish blue. For moist soil in sun or partial shade. Hardy to −25°C. *P. denticulata* subsp. *sinodenticulata* (Balf. fil. & Forrest) W. W. Sm. & Forrest, from Burma, east to Yunnan and W Sichuan, differs merely in its usually taller stem at flowering time, as shown here.

Primula florindae Ward (s. *Sikkimensis*) Native of SE Xizang in the Tsangpo basin at *c.*4000m, growing in shady bogs by running water and in streams, flowering in June–August in gardens. One of the largest *Primula* species with leaf blades 4–20cm × 4–15cm, cordate at the base with long stalks to 30cm; stem 30–120cm with usually 1 umbel of flowers; these are up to 80, yellow or sometimes reddish or amber-orange, with a spicy scent, 1.5–2.5cm long and 1–2cm across. Easily grown in wet soil in shade or partial shade. Hardy to −25°C.

Primula ioessa W. W. Sm. from SE Xizang is similar to *P. waltoni*, but differs in its more deeply toothed leaves, with the blade alternate at the base, and often shorter flowering stems. Its flowers are pinkish, mauve or white.

Primula secundiflora Franch. (s. *Sikkimensis*) Native of Yunnan, notably in the Lijiang mountains, especially in the north and SW Sichuan and E Xizang at 3500–4000m, growing in moist meadows, flowering in June–July. Leaves 3–30cm long; blade 1–4cm broad, oblong to obovate or oblanceolate, tapering into the very short, winged stalk. Stem 10–90cm, with farina towards the apex, with 1 or rarely 2 umbels of 5–20 flowers; these are 1.5–2.5cm long, reddish purple, bell-shaped, nodding. Similar in flower colour to *P. waltoni*, but distinct in leaf. Hardy to −25°C.

Primula sikkimensis Hook. (s. *Sikkimensis*) Native of Nepal, Sikkim, Bhutan and SE Xizang, east to Yunnan and S Sichuan, growing in wet bogs and by streams at 3300–4400m, flowering in May–July, often covering large areas with a yellow carpet. Leaves with elliptic to oblanceolate blade, 2–7cm across, longer than broad, attenuate at base to a short stalk. Stem 15–90cm, farinose at apex, with 1, rarely 2, whorls of flowers. Pedicels 2–10cm. Flowers 2–3cm long, 1.5–3cm across, yellow, bell-shaped, or more tubular and creamy white in

var. *hopeana* (Balf. fil. & Cooper) from Bhutan and Xizang at 4500–5000m. For wet, peaty soil. Hardy to −25°C.

Primula waltonii Watt (s. *Sikkimensis*) Native of SE Xizang in the region south of Lhasa and Bhutan, in alpine meadows at up to 5800m, flowering in May–August. Leaves serrate with elliptic-oblong to oblanceolate blade, 2–7cm broad, long cuneate at the base, with a stalk shorter than or equalling the blade. Stem 20–70cm, with one umbel of flowers; these are 1.5–3cm long, 0.5–2cm across, pink to dark lilac or claret purple, funnel-shaped, powdered with farina inside, with a red eye. For moist but well-drained soil in a cool position in full light or partial shade. Hardy to −25°C.

Primula forrestii in the Lijiang mountains, N Yunnan

Primula nivalis

Primula nivalis near Alma Ata, in the Tien Shan

Primula capitata subsp. *sphaerocephala*

Primula capitata Hook. (s. *Capitatae*) (*Primulaceae*) Native of Sikkim, S Xizang, Bhutan, NW Burma and Yunnan, growing in scrub and grassy places, at 2900–5000m, flowering in July–September. Leaves to 13 × 2cm, rugose, denticulate, usually with farina beneath. Stems 10–45cm, farinose, with a dense head of flowers 7–10mm across. Subsp. *mooreana* W. W. Sm. & Forrest is a large form from Sikkim, commonly cultivated. Easily grown in moist, well-drained soil. Remarkable for its late flowering, often into August in gardens. Subsp. *sphaerocephala* (Balf. fil. & Forrest) W. W. Sm. & Forrest is the form from Yunnan and SE Xizang; it has leaves without farina and a globular head of more tubular flowers. Hardy to −25°C.

Primula chionantha Balf. fil. & Forrest (s. *Nivales*) subsp. *chionantha* Native of NW Yunnan, especially on the Chungtien plateau, in alpine meadows at 4000m. Leaves with blade 15–20cm long, elongating after flowering, usually with yellow farina. Stem 35–70cm with 1–4 umbels of flowers. Close to subsp. *sinopurpurea*, but always with white flowers. The easiest of the *Nivales* section to grow, in moist peaty soil in sun or partial shade. Hardy to −20°C.

Subsp. *sinopurpurea* (Balf. fil.) Richards Native of SW Xizang and W Yunnan where it is widespread, and SW Sichuan, growing in moist alpine meadows at 3000–4000m. Stems usually *c*.25cm, but to 75cm in fruit. Leaves 5–35cm long, 1.5–5cm across, with yellow farina. Flowers purplish with a white or grey eye, 2.5–3.5cm across. Not an easy species; best in wet but well-drained, peaty sandy soil in full sun.

Primula flaccida Balakrishnan syn. *P. nutans* Delavey ex Franch. non Georgi (s. *Soldanelloideae*) Native of W & E Yunnan and SW Sichuan, especially on the mountains above Dali, growing in open pine forest and rocky pastures at 3500m, flowering in June–July. Leaves to 20 × 5cm, narrowly elliptic, softly hairy. Stems to 50cm, farinose, with a dense head of flowers to 5cm long. Largest flowers 2.5cm long and across, spicily scented. The easiest and one of the largest of the section *Soldanelloideae*, easily grown in partially shaded, moist but well-drained soil. Short-lived, but easily raised from seed.

Primula forrestii Balf. fil. (s. *Bullatae*) Native of Yunnan, mainly on the east side of the Lijiang range, but also to the west in the Lankong area, growing on dry limestone rocks and cliffs in sun or partial shade, at *c*.3000m, flowering in May. Plants tufted, often forming a long-lived clump of rosettes. Leaves 6–20cm long, rather sticky, hairy and aromatic, with the blade rounded to cordate at the base. Flowers in an umbel of 10–25, on a stem 15–90cm tall. *P. bullata* Franch. is very similar, but has a farinose calyx and the leaf blade tapering into the stalk. For a vertical rock or wall face, with some overhead protection in winter. Hardy to −15°C, perhaps less if dry.

Primula nivalis Pallas (s. *Nivales*) Native of C Asia and S Siberia in the Tien Shan, Alatau

Primula vialii at Wisley

Primula tanneri subsp. *tsariensis* var. *alba*

Primula chionantha

Primula flaccida

and the Altai; also in NW China and Mongolia, by streams and on wet scree at 2500m and above, flowering in May–July. Leaf blade to 16cm long, oblong, elliptic or oblong lanceolate, usually with white farina, serrate. Stems to 40cm. Flowers purple, 1.5–2.5cm across. Difficult to grow, requiring well-drained soil, wet in summer, dry in winter. Hardy to −25°C.

Primula tanneri King subsp. *tsariensis* (W. W. Sm.) Richards var. *alba* Richards syn. *?. tsariensis* W. W. Sm. (s. *Petiolares*) Native of S Xizang and C Bhutan, growing on damp mountainsides, by streams and on the edge of bamboo forest, at 3500–5000m, flowering in May–June. Plant tufted, with leaves elliptic to ovate-lanceolate, dark green, shining, without farina. Flowering stem 2–12cm, with 1–8 flowers. Corolla usually deep purplish, rarely white in f. *alba*, 1.5–3cm across. For moist, peaty soil in a cool position. Hardy to −20°C or so.

Primula vialii Delavay ex Franch. (s. *Muscarioides*) syn. *P. littoniana* Forrest Native of NW Yunnan and SW Sichuan, growing in marshy fields at up to 2800m, flowering in July–August. Leaves 20–30cm long, 4–7cm broad, softly hairy. Stems 30–60cm tall; the inflorescence usually *c*.8cm long. For moist, but well-drained soil in a cool position. Hardy to −20°C.

Primula chionantha subsp. *sinopurpurea*

Primula × chunglenta
'Lillemor'

Primula prolifera

Primula prolifera

Primula japonica
'Miller's Crimson' (p. 162)

Primula japonica
'Postford White'
(p. 162)

Primula
pulverulenta
(p. 163)

Primula japonica
(p. 162)

Primula
× chunglenta

Primula chungensis

Specimens from Sandling Park, Kent, 10 May. Life size

Primula 'Inverewe' at Sandling Park, Kent

Primula prolifera at Sandling Park, Kent

Primula 'Red Hugh'

Primula cockburniana

Primula bulleyana

Primula bulleyana Forrest (*Primulaceae*)
Native of Yunnan, especially the Lijiang range, growing by streams in wet mountain meadows at 3000–3200m, flowering in June–July. Leaves 12–35cm × 3–10cm with red petioles. Stem to 70cm, with 5–7 whorls of flowers, farinose at the nodes and on the pedicels. Calyx lobes very narrow, acute. Flowers orange; red in bud. For wet, peaty soil. Hardy to –20°C. *P. aurantiaca* W. W. Sm. & Forrest is from the edges of streams at *c.*3500m in W Yunnan. It differs in having less farina, stems to 30cm, and broader, acute or obtuse calyx lobes.

Primula chungensis Balf. fil. & Forrest
Native of Yunnan, Sichuan and on the borders of Assam and Bhutan, growing in marshes and in forest at 3000–3200m, flowering in May–June. Leaves elliptic to oblong or oblong-ovate, shallowly lobed 10–30cm × 3–10cm, without farina. Stem to 80cm, farinose at the nodes, with 2–5 whorls of up to 10 flowers. Pedicels 2cm. Flowers pale orange 1.5–2cm across, monomorphic or dimorphic. Early flowering in gardens, and best in sun or part shade and moist peaty and sandy soil. Hardy to –15°C. The closely related *P. cockburniana* has dark-orange flowers, corolla tube at most twice as long as the calyx, leaves with a distinct petiole, and flowers always monomorphic.

Primula cockburniana Hemsl.   Native of SW Sichuan, especially around Kanding (Tatsienlu), growing in marshy alpine meadows at 2900–3200m, flowering in June–July. Leaves

to 15 × 4cm, with a definite stalk and regularly finely toothed. Stem slender, to 40cm, farinose at the nodes with 2–3 whorls of flowers. Flowers monomorphic, 1.5cm across, with tube 1cm long. For well-drained but moist soil in partial shade, usually monocarpic, so must be raised to seed regularly. Hardy to –20°C.

Primula prolifera Wall. syn. *P. helodoxa* Balf. fil., *P. smithiana* Craib, *P. imperialis* Junghuhn, *P. sumatrana* Merrill   Native of Assam, N Burma, W China in Yunnan, and Indonesia in Java and Sumatra, growing by streams and in wet meadows and marshes, at around 2000m, flowering in May–June. Leaves more or less evergreen, usually without farina, to 50cm. Stems to 120cm, often with farina at the nodes and on the upper stem. Flowers yellow, to 2.5cm across, with the tube 1.5cm long, heterostylous or homostylous. Easily grown, preferring very wet ground. Hardy to –20°C. *Primula ianthina* Balf. fil. & Cave (see p. 162) is sometimes included in *P. prolifera*.

Candelabra Primula hybrids   Many of the species of the *Candelabra* section can cross freely, and different colour forms have been raised in shades of salmon, pale pink and scarlet. Among the earliest were those raised at Lissadell, then the garden of Sir Jocelyn Gore-Booth, in Co. Sligo, by crossing *P. pulverulenta* with *P. cockburniana*. One of these, 'Red Hugh' (O'Donnell, brother-in-law of the O'Neill), is still grown, and comes true from seed. 'Inverewe', also called 'Ravenglass Vermilion', is another bright red, raised from

Primula bulleyana (Brickell & Leslie 12320)

P. pulverulenta. It is very robust, but is sterile and has to be propagated by division. Beautiful soft colours appear from the cross between *P. beesiana* and *P. bulleyana*, including mauve, salmon pink and creamy yellow. All these hybrid primulas are easily grown in wet, peaty soil, and flower in June. *P.* × *chunglenta*, a hybrid of *P. chungensis* and *P. pulverulenta*, was raised at Wisley in 1929; its flowers are red, fading to pink. All are hardy to –20°C.

Primula pulverulenta and 'Bartley Pink' at Littlewood Park, Aberdeenshire

Primula pulverulenta at Sandling Park, Kent

Primula pulverulenta 'Lady Thursby'

Primula beesiana (*Primulaceae*) Forrest Native of Yunnan, especially the Lijiang mountains and SW Sichuan, growing in wet mountain meadows and by streams at *c*.2600m, flowering in July–August. Leaves to 22 × 6cm at flowering; in fruit to 40cm. Stems to 75cm, with 2–8 whorls of flowers, farinose at the nodes. Pedicels 1–3cm, not or slightly farinose. Flowers with orange tube and 'rose-carmine' petals with yellow eye, *c*.2cm across, deeply emarginate. Differs from *P. pulverulenta* in having leaves ovate-lanceolate, broadest near the middle, and yellow- not red-eyed flowers. Hardy to −20°C.

Primula burmanica Balf. fil. & Ward Native of NE upper Burma and NW Yunnan, growing in meadows and wet forests at rather low altitudes, flowering in July–August. Leaves oblanceolate,

to 30 × 8cm. Stems to 60cm, without farina, with up to 6 whorls of 10–18 flowers, on pedicels *c*.2cm. Flowers purplish with a yellow eye, dimorphic. Close to *P. beesiana* but differs by being without farina except on the inside of the calyx. A good plant for a wet position in shade or partial shade. Hardy to −15°C.

Primula ianthina Balf. fil. & Cave Native of the Himalayas in Sikkim, growing in damp meadows and scrub at *c*.3200m, flowering in June–August. Plant forming rosettes of oblanceolate leaves up to 25cm long, usually *c*.15cm. Flowering stem to 60cm, powdered at the nodes with yellowish farina, with 1–3 whorls of up to 12 violet or pinkish flowers, 1.5–2cm across, with wide corolla lobes. Less easy to grow than others of the group. For moist soil,

preferably by a stream on a slope. Hardy to −20°C or so.

Primula japonica A. Gray. (s. *Candelabra*) Native of Japan on all the islands and in Taiwan, growing along streams in the mountains, flowering in June–July. Plant without farina, except on the inside of the calyx. Leaves to 25 × 8cm, obovate-oblong to broadly spathulate. Stems to 50cm, with up to 6 whorls of flowers; flowers monomorphic, 2cm across, usually purplish red, but white in the form 'Postford White', the seed of which comes true. 'Miller's Crimson' is a good red, with less magenta in it than the usual form (p. 160). A good perennial, easily grown in partial shade, in rich heavy soil; in sun the flowers tend to bleach in an ugly way. Hardy to −20°C.

Primula ianthina

Primula wilsonii at the Royal Botanic Garden, Edinburgh

Primula japonica 'Miller's Crimson'

Primula beesiana

Primula poissonii Franch.   Native of
Yunnan, where it is common especially above
Dali and in Sichuan, growing by streams and
springs at 2000–3000m, flowering in May–July.
Leaves silvery, evergreen, oblong-obovate to
18cm × 4cm. Stem to 45cm with 2–6 whorls of
flowers. Flowers purplish to crimson, with a
yellow eye, flat, 2–3cm across. Calyx with red
lines, and lobed to ⅓ to ½, with large teeth. For
moist soil in full sun or partial shade, and wet
but well-drained soil. Hardy to −20°C.

Primula pulverulenta Duthie   Native of W
Sichuan near Kanding (Tatsienlu), growing in
wet places and by streams, flowering in
June–July. Leaves to 30 × 10cm obovate or
oblanceolate, dentate. Stem to 100cm, covered
with farina, as are the pedicels and calyx, with
c.10 whorls of flowers. Flowers 2–3cm across,
dimorphic, red with a dark eye, or pink in
'Bartley Pink'. 'Lady Thursby' is a good, pale
selection of the 'Bartley Strain'. For wet, peaty
soil. Hardy to −25°C.

Primula wilsonii Dunn syn. *P. poissonii* subsp.
wilsonii (Dunn) W. W. Sm. & Forrest   Native
of Yunnan and W Sichuan especially around
Kanding, in wet places in the mountains. Plant
aromatic, less silvery than *P. poissonii*. Leaves
evergreen, oblanceolate up to 20 × 5cm,
rounded at apex. Stem to 90cm, with 3–6
whorls of flowers, which are up to 1.5cm across,
with short calyx teeth. For moist but well-
drained soil. Hardy to −25°C. Var. *anisodora*
(Balf. fil. & Forrest) Richards differs in having
dark crimson to black cup-shaped flowers with
a green central ring. From Sichuan and N
Yunnan.

Primula poissonii (Brickell & Leslie 12307)

Primula japonica 'Postford White'

Primula burmanica at Sandling Park, Kent

Armeria pseudarmeria

Armeria alliacea at Edington, Wiltshire

Anagallis monellii in SW Spain

Cortusa matthioli

Anagallis monellii L. syn. *A. linifolia* L. (*Primulaceae*)   Native of Portugal and S, SE & C Spain, growing in open pine woods, vineyards and waste places, or as here on sand dunes, flowering in March–May, but in July–September in gardens. Stems 10–50cm long, sprawling; flowers 1–2cm across, usually blue with a reddish eye, or brilliant red in 'Sunrise'. For well-drained soil, in a warm, dry position, probably hardy only to −10°C and best raised from cuttings taken in late summer and wintered under cover.

Armeria alliacea (Cav.) Hoffman. & Link syn. *A. plantaginea* Willd. (*Plumbaginaceae*)   Native of W Europe, from Jersey, France and Germany, south to Spain, Portugal and Italy, growing in dry meadows, often in the mountains, flowering in June–September. Plant forming small clumps of narrowly oblanceolate or linear spathulate leaves 50–130mm long, 3–14mm wide. Flower stems 20–50cm, with heads 1–2cm across, with brownish or reddish bracts. Petals purplish, reddish, pink or white. Easily grown in well-drained soil in full sun. Hardy to −20°C. The varieties of *A. maritima* (Mill.) Willd., the common thrift, are more suitable for the rock garden, and always have narrow leaves to 2.5mm wide.

Armeria pseudarmeria (Murray) Mansfield syn. *A. latifolia* Willd.   Native of C Portugal, on the Cabo da Roca, growing on grassy granite slopes near the sea, flowering in May–June. Plant with stout, branched stems from the base, forming dense clumps. Leaves 10–20cm long, 15–20mm wide, flat. Flowering stems 25–50cm, with flower heads 3–4cm across. Flowers usually white, also pink in cultivation. Hardy to −15°C perhaps.

Cortusa matthioli L. syn. *C. altaica* A. Los. (*Primulaceae*)   Native of Europe, from the SW Alps in France, east to Bulgaria, the Urals and across Siberia to the Altai in Mongolia and N China (Sinjiang) with var. *yezoensis* in Japan, growing in shady places and rocky woods in the mountains, usually on limestone, flowering in April–June. Plant forming small clumps of rounded leaves to 25cm tall; blade up to 12cm across. Flowers 5–20 in an umbel, *c*.1cm long. For moist, very loose leafy soil in partial shade. Hardy to −20°C or less.

Dodecatheon clevelandii Greene (*Primulaceae*)   Native of W California, from San Francisco south to N Baja California, growing in grassy places below 600m, flowering in January–April. Roots white, without bulbils.

Leaves 5–11cm long, oblanceolate, toothed and with wavy margins. Stems 18–40cm, with an umbel of 5–16 flowers. Petals 10–20mm long. An early flowering species for heavy soil, moist in spring, dry in summer. Hardy to −10°C.

Dodecatheon meadia L. Shooting Star Native of E North America, from Pennsylvania west to Manitoba, and south to Georgia and Texas, growing in prairies and on moist cliffs, flowering in April–May. Plant with white roots, forming small clumps of stems 20–60cm tall. Leaves oblong to ovate, 7.5–30cm long. Flowers 1.8–3cm long, pale pink, purplish or white in f. *album* Macbride, shown here. For rich, moist soil in sun or partial shade, kept moist in summer. Hardy to −20°C or less.

Dodecatheon pulchellum (Raf.) Merr. syn. *D radicatum* Greene   Native of W North America, from Alaska south to Wisconsin, in the Rockies, and to N Mexico and in the E Sierra Nevada, growing in marshes and wet meadows and open woods at up to 3000m, flowering in April–May. Plant with white roots, forming clumps of upright stems to 50cm. Leaves 4–25cm long, oblanceolate to ovate. Umbel with 2–25 flowers, the petals 9–20mm long, magenta to pale purple. For well-drained or moist soil in sun. Hardy to −20°C.

Hottonia palustris L. (*Primulaceae*) Water Violet   Native of most of Europe, from Scotland and Sweden east to Siberia, south to C Italy, Romania and NW Turkey, growing in fresh water, in ponds (sometimes seasonal) and ditches, flowering in April–June. Submerged leaves soft, in whorls, deeply pinnately divided into linear lobes, to 10cm long. Flowering stems emerging from the water, to 40cm long. Flowers 2–2.5cm across, in 3–9 whorls. A beautiful plant for a small pond requiring pure, more or less neutral water, unshaded, becoming rare in the wild because of pollution and the draining of ponds. It can tolerate partial drying out in summer, when it forms tight rosettes of bright green feathery leaves, on wet mud.

Menyanthes trifoliata L. (*Menyanthaceae*) Bogbean or Buckbean   Native to the whole of the northern hemisphere, from Ireland and most of Europe to Japan, and in North America from Alaska to Greenland, south to California in the Sierra Nevada, to Nebraska and to Long Island, growing in bogs and on the margins of lakes, ponds and canals, flowering in April–July, and sometimes later. Plant wide spreading by long-creeping, thick, surface rhizomes. Leaves 3-foliate, bean-like, fleshy, to 4–8cm long.

Hottonia palustris

Hottonia palustris near Wye, Kent

Dodecatheon clevelandii

Dodecatheon pulchellum near Bishop, E California

Menyanthes trifoliata

Flowering stems to 40cm. Flowers *c*.15mm across, pink in bud, white when open, with long-ciliate petals. Easily grown in wet, peaty soil or shallow water. Hardy to −25°C.

Nephrophyllidium cristagalli (Menzies ex Hook.) Gilg. syn. *Fauria cristagalli* (Menzies ex Hook.) Mak. Native of Japan in Hokkaido and Honshu, of the Kurile Islands and NW North America, on the Olympic peninsula, growing in damp meadows, flowering in June–August. Plant forming dense mats of rather fleshy leaves to 30cm tall, but usually *c*.20cm. Blade 4–10cm across. Flowering stem is 15–40cm, with a rounded head of flowers *c*.12mm across without the ciliate petals of *Menyanthes*. For moist, peaty soil in a cool position or partial shade. Hardy to −20°C or less.

Nephrophyllidium at Wisley

Dodecatheon meadia f. *album*

Polemonium caeruleum at Sellindge, Kent

Polemonium caeruleum subsp. *himalayanum* at Gadsar, Kashmir

Polemonium caeruleum L.   Native of N & C Europe from Scotland and France eastwards across Siberia, to the Himalayas and of W North America from Alaska to the Sierra Nevada in California, and in the Rockies (subsp. *amygdalinum*), flowering in May–August. Very variable, but with usually rather few stems to 120cm from a tufted rootstock. Stems usually glandular above, and leafy. Flowers rotate, 8–15mm long, usually blue, lobes ovate, usually rounded. Easily grown in a good moist soil in full sun or partial shade. Hardy to −20°C and below. Easily raised from seed, and sometimes said to become a pest through self-seeding. This should also be a good plant for the wild garden as it survives in lush grass. Several subspecies or closely related species are cultivated: subsp. *himalayanum* (Baker) Hara is a delicate plant, found in damp places among rocks from Pakistan to W Nepal, at 2400–3700m. Stems 30–100cm. Flowers to 2cm long.

Polemonium caeruleum L. var. *nipponicum* (Kit.) Koji Ito syn *P. acutiflorum* Willd. var. *nipponicum* (Kit.) Ohwi (*Polemoniaceae*) Native of the mountains of Honshu, growing in damp scrub, by rivers and meadows, flowering in July–August, earlier in cultivation. Plant forming tufts of basal leaves, with leafy stems 40–80cm, usually with not more than 8 pairs of leaflets. Flowers stalked, rather few in a loose head, 18–22mm long. For moist peaty soil and a cool position in sun or partial shade. Hardy to −20°C.

Polemonium carneum A. Gray   Native of California, around San Francisco north to Washington, growing in scrub and grassy places, near the coast and in the hills up to 1800m, flowering in April–August. Plant forming slowly spreading mats, with glandular-pubescent flowering stems 40–80cm tall, usually less in cultivation. Leaves with the 3 terminal leaflets often joined at the base. Flowers 1–2.5cm across, purplish to pink. For a sunny position and well-drained, leafy soil; tolerant of summer drought. Hardy to −10°C, perhaps lower. Crossed with *P. reptans* this has produced the very pretty 'Lambrook Manor'.

Polemonium foliosissimum A. Gray   Native of Colorado, Utah, New Mexico and Arizona, growing in moist places by streams in the mountains, flowering in July. Stems few from a tufted rootstock up to 100cm tall, pubescent. Leaflets elliptic to oblong-ovate. Flowers purplish, 12–15mm long, the petals obtuse or mucronate. Easily grown in a good garden soil. Hardy to −20°C or below.

Polemonium 'Northern Lights'   A hybrid between *P. caeruleum* and *P. reptans*, forming clumps of shortly creeping rhizomes, and with numerous glandular-pubescent stems to 25cm. Flowers c.2.5cm across, pale blue. For good soil in sun or partial shade, moist in summer and probably best split and replanted every 3 years or so. Hardy to −20°C.

Polemonium pauciflorum S. Wats.   Native of SE Arizona and N Mexico, growing along streams in the mountains at 2000–3000m, flowering in June–August. Plant with few stems, 30–45cm from a thin rootstock. Leaflets lanceolate; flowers 4cm long, with a long, narrow tube, pale yellow. For rather moist, but well-drained soil in sun or partial shade. Hardy

Polemonium caeruleum var. *nipponicum*

Polemonium 'Northern Lights' at Alford, Aberdeenshire

Polemonium pauciflorum

Polemonium carneum

Polemonium foliosissimum

to −20°C or so. An elegant, quiet plant with its hanging tubular flowers. *P. flavum* Green, also from Arizona, has brighter-yellow flowers, without a long tube, and acuminate lobes.

Polemonium reptans L. Greek Valerian Native of E North America, from New York to Minnesota, south to Kansas and Georgia, growing in woods, flowering in April–May. Plant with a short rootstock and spreading usually glabrous stems up to 30cm. Leaflets oblong, ovate-oblong or lanceolate-oblong. Flowers 10–16mm across, blue. For leafy soil in sun or partial shade. Hardy to −20°C. There are several named cultivars or hybrids of this species, such as 'Sapphire', 'Pink Beauty' and 'Blue Pearl'.

Polemonium reptans 'Sapphire'

Polemonium reptans

HACKELIA

Hackelia setosa near Silver Lake, California

Borago pygmaea

Hackelia uncinata in Kashmir

Myosotis sylvatica

Myosotis scorpioides

Borago pygmaea (DC.) Chater & W. Greuter, syn. *B. laxiflora* Poiret (*Boraginaceae*) Native of Corsica, Sardinia and the island of Capraia (NE of Elba), growing in shady, rocky places, especially rampant after forest fires, flowering in May–July. Plant with a rosette of obovate, bristly leaves and several branched creeping and ascending stems to 60cm. Flowers pale blue, nodding, 5–8mm long. For a warm but partially shaded position, moist in summer. Hardy to −10°C, but often self-seeding if killed by frost. The unfortunate change of name is caused by Poiret's oversight of De Candolle's *Campanula pygmaea*, which was really this borage!

Hackelia setosa (Piper) Jtn. (*Boraginaceae*) Native of California, in the coast ranges from Lake Co. northwards, and in the Sierra Nevada, from Sierra Co. north to Oregon, growing in open grassy places in the conifer forest zone at 300–1800m, flowering in June–July. Plant forming dense clumps of upright stems to 50cm. Basal leaves bristly-hairy, linear-oblanceolate, blunt, upright, 5–10cm long. Flowers blue, 10–15mm across. For well-drained, sandy soil in sun or partial shade. Hardy to −15°C perhaps.

Hackelia uncinata (Royle ex Benth.) C. Fisher   Native of the Himalayas from Pakistan to SW China, growing in open places in forest and in scrub, at 2700–4200m, flowering in June–August. Perennial with few upright stems from a stout rootstock. Basal leaves long-stalked, ovate, acuminate, with a cordate base. Stems 30–60cm, branched. Flowers to 1.3cm across, pale blue. Fruits hooked, with bristles. For a rather dry position in leafy soil and partial shade. Hardy to −20°C or less?

Myosotis scorpioides L. (*Boraginaceae*) Water Forget-me-not   Native of most of N Europe, south to Romania and the Crimea, east across Siberia to N India, and as an escape from cultivation in E North America south to New York, Pennsylvania and Tennessee, in California, and in Japan. It grows in streams, by rivers and lakes and in marshes, flowering in May–September. Plant forming mats of creeping and rooting stems in shallow water or on wet soil, with yellowish-green, rather fleshy leaves. Flowering stems up to 100cm, usually *c*.30cm. Flowers 5–10mm across, bright blue. A beautiful and long-lived perennial with a long flowering season, growing by water or in moist borders, and easily propagated by planting rooted shoots. Hardy to −20°C or less.

Myosotis sylvatica Hoffm. Forget-me-not Native of most of Europe and SW Asia eastwards to the Himalayas and Japan, growing in open woods, flowering in May–June. Plant tufted with several ascending stems to 45cm from a central rootstock, usually short-lived, often biennial. Plant rather bristly-hairy, with dark-green leaves. Flowers up to 8mm across, pale blue or rarely white, and often pink if the plants are moved while in flower. For any moist soil in sun or partial shade; often disfigured by powdery mildew in dry conditions. Hardy to −20°C. Self-seeds freely.

Omphalodes cappadocica 'Cherry Ingram' at Washfield Nurseries, Kent

Omphalodes cappadocica (Willd.) DC. (*Boraginaceae*)   Native of Georgia and NE Turkey west to Ordu, growing on shady rocks and cliffs and by streams in forests of chestnut, hazel or other deciduous trees, at up to 1000m, flowering March–May. Vegetative stems, produced in summer, shortly creeping; flowering stems 10–15cm. Leaves ovate, cordate; blade 4.5–9cm, to 5cm wide. Flowers 4–8mm across. A delicate and beautiful plant; evergreen, but with leaves killed by hard frosts. Two slightly hardier clones have been selected: 'Anthea Bloom' survives well in the open in England.

'**Cherry Ingram**' has narrower leaves than usual and good large flowers. A typical large leaf can have a lanceolate blade 17 × 4.8cm, long-acuminate and barely cordate. All forms, however, are best in a sheltered position in partial shade, with protection from frost.

Omphalodes moupinense Franch.   Native of W China, especially Sichuan, growing in scrub and damp shady places, at *c.*2000m, flowering in May. Plant with a few broadly heart-shaped basal leaves and trailing flowering stems to 20cm. Flowers *c.*8mm across, pale blue. For moist, leafy soil in shade and shelter. Hardy to –15°C.

Omphalodes verna Moench   Native of the SE Alps, south to the Apennines in C Italy, and C Romania, but often naturalized elsewhere in W & C Europe, growing in damp mountain woods, flowering in March–May. Vegetative stems long-creeping. Leaves with ovate to cordate blade, 5–20cm × 2–6cm mucronate or acuminate. Flowering stems 5–20cm. Flowers 8–10mm across. Requires a moist shady position: because of its creeping stems and usually smaller flowers, this is less showy than *O. cappadocica*. A white-flowered form is known in cultivation. Hardy to –15°C.

Omphalodes moupinense at Wolong, Sichuan

Omphalodes verna at Wisley, Surrey

Echium russicum with *Stipa pulcherrima* on the Steppes near Stavropol, S Russia

Echium russicum J. F. Gmelin syn. *E. rubrum* Jacq. (*Boraginaceae*)   Native of E Europe, from Austria southwards to Bulgaria and NW Turkey, and eastwards to Russia, the Caucasus and NE Turkey, growing on grassy steppes, open pine forest and rocky hills, at up to 2200m in Turkey, flowering in June–July. Plant with several stems to 60cm, but usually *c*.30cm, from a deep rootstock. Leaves lanceolate to narrowly elliptical. Flowers 9–12mm long, dark red with 4–5 exserted stamens. Although this is usually described as a biennial, it has proved reliably perennial at Edington, Wilts., and flowered for several years, planted in well-drained sandy soil in full sun. Hardy to −20°C or less.

Symphytum asperum Lepechin syn. *S. orientale* L. p.p. (*Boraginaceae*)   Native of NE Turkey, the Caucasus, N & NW Iran, growing in spruce forests, meadows, by streams and in scrub, at up to 2200m in Turkey, flowering in May–August. Plant with upright stems to 1.2m, from a deep rootstock. Lower leaves cordate or rounded at the base. Flowers at first pink, later blue or purplish, 12–15mm long. For moist, deep, rich soil in sun or partial shade. Hardy to −20°C.

Symphytum caucasicum M. Bieb.   Native of the Caucasus, growing in waste places, by streams, in scrub and on grassy roadsides, flowering in April–July. A very invasive plant, spreading by slender underground rhizomes, producing rosettes of leaves and upright, then sprawling, stems to 1m. Flowers pure blue, to 12mm long. For any good soil in sun or partial shade. This plant will smother anything but the largest perennials, but is very pretty for a long season, flowering again in late summer if the old stems are cut down.

Symphytum ibericum Stev. syn. *S. grandiflorum* auct. non DC.   Native of NE Turkey and Soviet Georgia, growing on shady banks and in *Rhododendron* scrub at up to 1350m in Turkey, flowering in March–July. Plant with creeping stolons forming extensive patches. Stems 15–40cm. Leaves ovate to ovate-lanceolate, subcordate or rounded at the base, stalked. Flowers cream, 14–16mm long, rarely pinkish, with a small calyx 3–6mm long. 'Hidcote Pink' is a form with good pink flowers, possibly a hybrid. 'Variegatum' has leaves very irregularly marked with cream. For moist or shady places; hardy to −20°C or so. The true *S. grandiflorum* DC., from the Caucasus, has large flowers, the calyx 6–8mm, the corolla 20–24mm long.

Symphytum orientale L.   Native of S Russia and the Caucasus, west to Istanbul and NW Turkey, growing on shady stream banks in pine

Symphytum × *uplandicum* 'Variegatum'

forest at up to 1500m in Turkey, flowering in April–June. Stems upright to 70cm. Leaves ovate or oblong-ovate, shortly hairy, not bristly. Calyx 6–9mm, divided to ⅓ or ½. Corolla 15–17mm long, pure white. *S. kurdicum* Boiss. & Hausskn. from SE Turkey, N Iraq and W Iran has white flowers 16–19mm long, but thinner, more bristly leaves. It is similar in habit. Both are attractive early-flowering species, tolerant of dry shade. Hardy to −15°C, perhaps less.

Symphytum 'Rubrum'   This is possibly a hybrid between *S. ibericum* and *S. officinale* and has rather small flowers of a good red, on upright stems.

Symphytum tuberosum L.   Native of Europe, from Scotland, where it is common in the east, south to France and Spain, and east to Russia and Turkey, growing in woods, scrub and by rivers, flowering in May–June. Plant creeping to form extensive patches, with a tuberous rhizome. Stems arching 15–40cm, little branched. Flowers pale yellow, 15–20mm long, the scales not exserted, as they are in *S. bulbosum* C. Schimper. Easily grown in shade or a cool position in sun. Early flowering, and dormant in summer. Hardy to −20°C or so.

Symphytum × uplandicum Nyman **'Variegatum'**   *S. × uplandicum* is the hybrid between *S. asperum* and *S. officinale*. It is naturalized over much of N Europe, and is usually found by roadsides and in waste places in damp soil. The flowers are usually pinkish, becoming purple or blue as they mature, and 12–18mm long. The variegated form is especially beautiful in autumn and spring, when the basal leaves are fresh, as shown here. Hardy to −20°C or less.

Symphytum orientale

Symphytum caucasicum at Sellindge, Kent

Symphytum tuberosum at Alford, Aberdeenshire

Symphytum asperum

Symphytum 'Hidcote Pink'

Symphytum ibericum

Symphytum 'Rubrum'

Anchusa azurea 'Opal'

Anchusa azurea near Ronda, S Spain

Anchusa azurea 'Opal' (foreground) and 'Loddon Royalist' (background)

Lithodora diffusa in S Spain

Cynoglossum nervosum at Dali, Yunnan

Alkanna tinctoria in S France

Alkanna tinctoria (L.) Tausch (*Boraginaceae*)
Native of S Europe, from Spain and France
eastwards to Romania, Turkey, Syria and North
Africa, growing in rocky places, open woods,
scrub, steppes and sand dunes at up to 1300m,
flowering in April–July. Plant with several
spreading or creeping stems to 30cm long, from
a central rootstock which exudes deep-reddish
juice when bruised. Leaves greenish or greyish,
1–7cm long. Flowers blue, 4–10mm across. For
well-drained sandy soil in a hot dry position.
Hardy to −10°C, perhaps less.

Anchusa azurea Mill. syn. *A. italica* Retz
(*Boraginaceae*)   Native of Europe, from France,
Spain and Portugal eastwards, North Africa and
Turkey, eastwards to Iran and Arabia and into
C Asia, growing on the edges of arable fields, by
roadsides, and on steppes and stony hills, up to
2500m, flowering in May–July. A common and
conspicuous plant of roadsides throughout the
Mediterranean region and C Asia. Plant with
upright stems to 1.5m, from a stout rootstock.
Leaves 10–30cm long. Flowers purplish or deep
blue, 10–15mm across. There are many named
cultivars, propagated by root cuttings: 'Loddon
Royalist' is a good deep blue, and 'Opal' is
rather shorter and paler. 'Little John' is only
45cm tall. All are short-lived perennials
requiring deep but well-drained soil, and
tolerant of drought. Hardy to −15°C, perhaps
lower.

Buglossoides purpureocaerulea (L.)
Johnston syn. *Lithospermum purpureocaeruleum*
L. (*Boraginaceae*)   Native of most of Europe,
from England where it is rare and found on
limestone only in S Wales, N Somerset and
S Devon, to Spain and east to Russia and
Turkey, the Caucasus and N Iran, growing in
scrub and maquis, and on the edges of woods,
flowering in March–June. Plant forming
spreading colonies from a creeping rhizome,
with ascending flowering stems to 60cm, and
long, spreading sterile shoots. Leaves 3.5–8cm
long. Flowers 14–20mm long, opening purple,
becoming deep blue. For dry soil in a warm
position in partial shade. Hardy to −20°C
or less.

Cynoglossum nervosum Benth. & Hook.
(*Boraginaceae*)   Native of the Himalayas from
Kumaon to Yunnan, growing on grassy banks,
and by rice fields, flowering in April–August.
Stems several to 60cm, from a stout rootstock.
Basal leaves narrowly lanceolate to 30cm long.
Flowers *c*.10mm across. For well-drained soil
in full sun. Graham Thomas recommends not
too good soil for this, or the stems will flop,
and I have found it tricky and short-lived in
heavy soil. Hardy to −15°C, possibly less.
C. amabile Stapf. & Drummond from Yunnan
and Sichuan, is closely related, but is
usually biennial, with larger, paler-blue
flowers.

Lindelofia longiflora (Benth.) Baillon
(*Boraginaceae*)   Native of the Himalayas, from
Pakistan to W Nepal, and common in Kashmir,
growing on open, grassy slopes, at 3000–3600m,
flowering in June–August. Plant forming
patches of upright stems to 60cm or more from
a rhizome. Basal leaves long-stalked, lanceolate.
Stem leaves narrowly lanceolate, clasping the
stem at the base. Flowers deep blue to purple,
up to 1.5cm across. For well-drained, rich and
moist soil in full sun. Hardy to −20°C, possibly
less.
L. anchusoides (Lindl.) Lehm. has upper leaves
narrowed to the base, not clasping, and bright-
blue flowers.

Lithodora diffusa (Lagasca) Johnson syn.
Lithospermum diffusum Lagasca (*Boraginaceae*)
Native of W France, Spain and Portugal,
growing in pine woods, heathery scrub, and sand
dunes, flowering in March–June. Plant sprawling
to 1m or more, with creeping and rooting stems,
subshrubby at the base. Leaves linear to oblong
or elliptical. Flowers up to 20mm long. This
species is commonly grown as a rock garden
plant, but is happiest on heathy bank in acid soil
or sprawling among low shrubs or heather. The
commonest cultivar is 'Heavenly Blue', with
deep-blue flowers. 'Cambridge Blue' is a very
pale-blue form; there is also a rare white, 'Alba'.
'Grace Ward', an old variety, is said to be lime-
tolerant, unlike the other varieties, which prefer
acid soil. Hardy to −20°C.

Lindelofia longiflora near Vishensar, Kashmir

Buglossoides purpureocaerulea

Lithodora 'Heavenly Blue'

Antirrhinum australe on a road cutting near Ronda, S Spain

Antirrhinum 'Black Prince'

Scrophularia auriculata 'Variegata'

Asarina procumbens

Scrophularia sambucifolia among limestone rocks in S Spain

Synthyris missurica

Mimulus ringens at Beth Chatto's garden

Parahebe perfoliata

Antirrhinum australe Rothm.
(*Scrophulariaceae*)   Native of S & SE Spain,
growing on limestone rocks and walls, flowering
in April–June. Plant with several upright stems
to 120cm. Leaves opposite or in whorls of 3.
Flowers 40–45mm long, usually pinkish purple,
with pedicels shorter than the bracts. Although
they are usually grown as annuals, most
Antirrhinum species are perennial, and of the 17
or so species, 16 are found in Spain. *A. majus* L.,
from which the cultivated forms have been
bred, is found in S Europe, from Spain and
North Africa to Italy: it usually has pinkish-
purple flowers.
'Black Prince', shown here, is an old perennial
cultivar which flowers throughout the summer.
It has dark-purple leaves, and forms a low bush
about 30cm in diameter. *A. graniticum* Rothm.
usually has white flowers on pedicels longer
than the bracts, and is found in Spain and
Portugal on acid rocks. In cultivation the
perennials require very well-drained, poor soil.
Hardy to −10°C, perhaps less if kept dry.

Asarina procumbens Mill. syn. *Antirrhinum
asarina* L. (*Scrophulariaceae*)   Native of S
France and NE Spain, growing on shady acid
rocks in the mountains, flowering in
June–September. Plant with trailing stems to
30cm or more. Leaves *c.*5 × 6cm, softly sticky-
hairy. Flowers 30–35mm long. Easily grown in
rather dry, shady places, in sandy soil. Hardy to
−10°C, possibly less, i.e. it survives outdoors in
S England, with overhead protection.

Mimulus ringens L. (*Scrophulariaceae*)
Square-stemmed Monkey-flower   Native of
E North America, from Nova Scotia south to
Virginia and west to Manitoba, Nebraska and
Texas, growing in wet places and along streams,
flowering in June–September. Stems upright to
1m, from a tufted rootstock. Leaves sessile,
auriculate at the base, to 10cm long. Flowers
pale purplish blue, rarely white, *c.*2.5cm long
and wide. For good wet soil in sun or partial
shade. Hardy to −20°C or less. Other species of
Mimulus are shown in vol. 2, pp. 116–17.

Parahebe perfoliata (R. Br.) B. G. Briggs syn.
Veronica perfoliata R. Br. (*Scrophulariaceae*)
Native of SE Australia, especially on Mount
Victoria and on the Blue Mountains, flowering
in early summer. Plant with a subshrubby base
and trailing, sparingly branched stems to 75cm.
Leaves *c.*5cm across. Flowers 6mm across. For a
warm, sheltered position in full sun, looking best
sprawling through low shrubs. Hardy to −10°C.

Scrophularia auriculata L. 'Variegata' syn.
S. aquatica auct. (*Scrophulariaceae*)   Native of
most of Europe and North Africa eastwards to
Crete, growing in damp places, usually by
streams and rivers, flowering in
June–September. Plant with several upright,
4-winged stems to 100cm. Leaves simple or
with 1 or 2 pairs of small lobes. Flowers 7–9mm
long, brownish and much visited by wasps. The
variegated leaves are very beautiful from spring
onwards.

Scrophularia sambucifolia L.   Native of
S Spain and C & S Portugal and North Africa,
growing in damp places and among rocks at
*c.*1800m, flowering in April–June. Plant with
several stems to 80cm. Leaves lyrate,
pinnatisect. Flowers 12–20mm long. This
species has the largest flowers of any of the
European figworts, but is not often cultivated.
It should succeed in any good soil. Hardy to
−15°C, perhaps less.

Synthyris missurica (Raf.) Penn. syn.
S. stellata Penn. (*Scrophulariaceae*)   Native of
W North America, in Idaho, Washington,
Oregon and N California, growing in moist
places in the mountains and foothills, flowering
in April–July. Plant tufted, with stems to 60cm.
Leaf blades with blunt or sharp teeth, 2.5–8cm
across. Flowers 4–7mm long, in a loose spike-
like inflorescence, with large or small bracts
below the flowers. *S. reniformis* (Dougl.) Benth.
is smaller, to 15cm high, with curving stems not
exceeding the leaves, found in coniferous forests
south to San Francisco Bay. *S. schizandra* Piper
has stems to 30cm, with 2 leafy bracts and
fimbrate petals. It is found in moist, shady
habitats in Washington and Oregon.
S. pinnatifida Wats. is found from Washington
east to Idaho, Wyoming and Montana, growing
in rocky places in the mountains. It has pinnate
leaves and stems to 20cm. All species need
moist soil in a cool position, with *S. schizandra*
and *S. reniformis* needing more shade. Hardy to
−20°C perhaps.

Veronica spicata subsp. *incana*

Veronica spicata 'Heidekind'

Veronica exaltata

Veronica spicata subsp. *spicata*

Veronica gentianoides

Veronica filiformis

Veronica austriaca 'Shirley Blue' at the Royal Botanic Garden, Edinburgh

Veronica austriaca 'Crater Lake Blue'

Veronica austriaca L. subsp. *teucrium* (L.)
D. A. Webb (*Scrophulariaceae*)   Native of most
of Europe, the Crimea, the Caucasus (?) and
NW Turkey, growing in open woods and stony
meadows and hills, flowering in April–July.
Plant with numerous upright or ascending
stems to 1m. Leaves 2–7cm long, more or less
amplexicaul, crenate or serrate. Flowers
10–14mm across, bright blue. For any good soil
in sun or partial shade. Hardy to −20°C or less.
There are several cultivars of this species.
'Crater Lake Blue'   Tall, 45cm, upright with
deep-blue flowers.
'Shirley Blue'   Shorter, to 20cm, with
creeping, then ascending stems. There is also a
pink form.

Veronica exaltata Maund   Said to be native
of Siberia, flowering in gardens in June–August.
Plant with several upright stems to 120cm.
Leaves 15cm long. Flowers pale blue, *c*.8mm
across. For any good soil in full sun. Hardy to
−20°C and below.

Veronica filiformis J. E. Smith   Native of the
Caucasus, the Crimea, N Iran and N Turkey,
along the Black Sea coast growing in damp
meadows, grassy places in the forest, by streams
and on disturbed ground at up to 2200m,
flowering in March–August. Naturalized also in
much of Europe, especially on riverbanks and in
short grass and lawns. Plant creeping, soon
covering many square metres, with flowering
stems up to 15cm. Leaves more or less round,
5–13mm across. Flowers 8–14mm across,
usually pale sky blue in cultivation, but in the
wild often white or deeper mauve-blue. Easily
grown in any moist soil. Hardy to −15°C.

Veronica gentianoides Vahl   Native of the
Caucasus, the Crimea and N & C Turkey,
growing in mountain meadows and open
woods, at 1000–3600m, flowering in
May–August. Plant forming mats of gentian-like
leaves, 2–6cm long, with upright flowering
stems 5–60cm tall. Flowers 8–16mm across,
usually pale blue, but in Turkey sometimes dark
blue, rarely white. For moist but well-drained
soil in full sun. Hardy to −20°C or less.

Veronica spicata L. subsp. *incana* (L.)
Walters   Native of E Europe, east to Siberia
and NW China, growing in dry meadows and
steppes, flowering in June–July. Plant with
upright stems to 30cm, the whole plant silvery-
hairy. Flowers 4–6mm across, bright blue. For
well-drained rather dry soil in full sun. Hardy to
−20°C or less. Hybrids between subsp. *spicata*
and subsp. *incana* are frequently cultivated, and
combine the tall stems of *spicata* (especially the
form *V. hybrida* L.) with the grey leaves of
subsp. *incana*. 'Heidekind', with deep-pink
flowers, is one of these; it has stems to 30cm.
'Wendy' is a taller, pinkish cultivar.

Veronica spicata L. subsp. *spicata* (including
V. hybrida L.)   Native of Europe, from
England, where it is very rare, to Russia, Siberia
and NW China, growing in grassland and on
rocky hills, usually on limestone, flowering in
June–September. Plant with upright stems to
60cm. Leaves linear-lanceolate to ovate, almost
sessile, opposite, 2–8cm long. Flowers 4–6mm
across, usually bright blue. For well-drained soil
in full sun. Hardy to −20°C or less.

Veronicastrum virginicum (L.) Farwell syn.
Veronica virginica L. Beaumont's Root   Native
of E North America, from Ontario to Manitoba
south to Massachusetts, Alabama and Texas,
growing in meadows, woods and scrub,
flowering in June–September. Stems several,
upright to 2m tall. Leaves in whorls of 3–9,
lanceolate or oblong-lanceolate. Flowers tubular
4mm long with short lobes, white or bluish. For
any good moist soil. Hardy to −20°C or less.

Veronicastrum virginicum var. *sibiricum*
(L.) B. Boivin (*Scrophulariaceae*)   Native of
Japan in all the islands, Korea, N China,
Sakhalin and E Siberia, growing in grassy places
in the mountains and plains, flowering in
July–September. Plant with several upright
stems to 1.8m. Leaves in whorls of 4–6, broadly
lanceolate, 10–15cm long, to 5cm wide. Flowers
tubular with corolla lobes shorter than the tube.
For any good soil in full sun or partial shade.
Hardy to −20°C or less.

Veronicastrum virginicum var. *sibiricum* at Wisley, Surrey

Veronicastrum virginicum

Incarvillea emodi in Pakistan

Incarvillea mairei at Inshriach, Aviemore, Scotland

Incarvillea mairei near Lijiang, Yunnan

Incarvillea delavayi

Niedzwedzkia semiretschenskia in Tashkent Botanic Garden

Incarvillea arguta Royle (Royle) syn.
Amphicome arguta Royle (*Bignoniaceae*)   Native
of the Himalayas, from NW India to Nepal, SE
Xizang, and SW China in Yunnan and Sichuan,
growing in dry valleys on rocky slopes and
cliffs, often limestone, at 1800–3500m,
flowering in May–August. Plant with many
rather weak stems from a subshrubby base.
Leaves with 5–9 leaflets, the terminal c.5cm
long. Flowers 2.5–3.8cm, pale pink. For very
well-drained soil or a crevice in a wall. Hardy to
−15°C, perhaps lower if in a very dry position.

Incarvillea delavayi Bur. & Franch.   Native of
SW China, in Yunnan, growing in grassy places
and scrub at c.2000m, flowering in May–July.
Plant with deep fleshy roots and a rosette of
pinnate leaves to 20cm long. Stems to 60cm,
with rather few, large flowers, c.8cm across.
Easily grown in deep, sandy but rich soil in full
sun, the crown protected in winter from slugs
and extreme cold. Hardy to −15°C, less with
protection.

Incarvillea emodi (Wallich ex Royle)
Chatterjee   Native of Afghanistan to W Nepal,
growing on cliffs and rocks, at 600–2500m,
flowering in March–April. Plant with a woody
rootstock. Leaves pinnate, with 9–11 leaflets
1–4cm long, ovate; mostly at the base of the
stem. Flowering stems to 50cm, not branched,
with 1-sided clusters of flowers 3.5–5.8cm long.
Capsule thin, to 18cm long. For a dry position
on a wall or raised bed. Hardy to −15°C,
perhaps. Photographed by Andrew Paterson in
N Pakistan.

Incarvillea mairei (Léveillé) Grierson   Native
of the Himalayas from W Nepal to Xizang and
SW China in Yunnan, growing on stony slopes,
often on limestone, in dry valleys, flowering in
May–June. Plant with deep, fleshy root and a
rosette of pinnate leaves, with a large terminal
lobe. Flowers 4–6cm long, often stemless when
first open, the stems elongating to c.50cm in
fruit. Clones in cultivation include 'Frank
Ludlow', with large, very deep-pinkish-crimson
flowers, from Bhutan, and pink forms with
paler flowers such as 'Bees' Pink'. For very

Ourisia 'Loch Ewe'

Ourisia coccinea at Washfield Nurseries, Kent

Ourisia macrophylla at Inshriach, Aviemore, Scotland

well-drained deep, sandy soil in full sun, with protection from slugs. Hardy to −20°C or less.

Niedzwedzkia semiretschenskia B. Fedtsch. syn. *Incarvillea semiretschenskia* (B. Fed.) Grierson (*Bignoniaceae*) Native of C Asia, growing on dry rocky hillsides, flowering in May–June. Plant with numerous wiry, upright stems to 45cm from a subshrubby base. Leaves deeply dissected with linear lobes. Flowers *c*.6cm long, 4cm across. Fruits *c*.5cm long, with *c*.6 very wavy wings. For very well-drained, dry soil in a warm position in full sun. Hardy to −15°C, perhaps less.

Ourisia coccinea Pers. (*Scrophulariaceae*) Native of S Chile, growing in valleys in the mountains, flowering in June in northern gardens. Plant with fleshy creeping rhizomes, forming mats of coarsely toothed, ovate leaves, with blades *c*.5cm long. Flowering stems to 18cm. Flowers *c*.3cm long. An elegant plant for moist, cool peaty soil in partial shade. Hardy to −15°C, less with snow cover.

Ourisia 'Loch Ewe' A hybrid between *O. macrophylla* and *O. coccinea*, forming mats of coarsely crenate leaves, and whorls of 2–4 flowers on upright stems to 30cm. For moist peaty soil in partial shade. Hardy to −20°C, or less with snow cover.

Ourisia macrophylla Hook. New Zealand Mountain Foxglove Native of New Zealand, on North Island on Mount Egmont, and from East Cape southwards at up to 1500m, growing in damp shady places, flowering in October–January, or in June in the north. Plant with creeping rhizomes forming spreading mats of leathery, shallowly crenate, ovate leaves. Pedicels glandular. Flowers 12–18mm across, in 3–7 whorls, on upright stems to 60cm.
O. macrocarpa Hook. fil., from South Island, has fewer larger flowers to 2.5cm across, on longer glabrous pedicels, with broader calyx lobes, and leaves up to 15cm long. It grows in damp places (and along streams) in scrub and herbfields. Both require peaty, moist soil in partial shade and a cool position. Hardy to −20°C.

Incarvillea arguta near Dali, Yunnan

Aster falconeri at Gadsar, Kashmir

Aster tongolensis

Celmisia spectabilis

Bellis sylvestris in S Spain

Celmisia coriacea

Anthemis punctata Vahl subsp. *cupaniana* (Tod. ex Nyman) R. Fernandes syn. *A. cupaniana* Tod. ex Nyman (*Compositae*) Native of Sicily, growing on cliffs and rocky places, flowering in April–June. Plant with ascending stems to 60cm from a subshrubby base. Leaves almost glabrous, or white and silky in the commonly cultivated clones, pinnatisect with thin segments. Flowers up to 6cm across, with a hemispherical-conical disc. A valuable, early-flowering daisy for a warm, dry and sunny position. Hardy to −10°C perhaps.

Aster falconeri (C. B. Clarke) Hutch. (*Compositae*) Native of the Himalayas, from N Pakistan to W Nepal, growing in alpine meadows at 3000–4200m, flowering in June–August. Plant with few rosettes of oblong-lanceolate basal leaves to 15cm long and upright densely-leafy flowering stems to 15–35cm tall. Flowers solitary to 8cm across, the rays with a white base and a 3-lobed apex. For moist, well-drained soil in full sun. Hardy to −15°C or less.

Aster tongolensis Franch. Native of W China, growing in stony alpine meadows at *c.*3500m, flowering in June. Plant forming spreading mats of hairy, dark-green leaves, with numerous, almost leafless, flowering stems to *c.*45cm. Flowers *c.*6cm across. There are now several named clones of this species, such as 'Napsbury' and 'Lavender Star'. For well-drained soil in full sun. Hardy to −20°C. *Aster forrestii* Stapf. is very similar, but has broader basal leaves and leafier stalks.

Bellis sylvestris Cyr. (*Compositae*) Native of S Europe, from Spain and France to Bulgaria, Mediterranean Turkey and North Africa, growing in grassy places and ditches, moist in winter and spring, flowering in October–March. Plant forming rosettes of leaves to 18cm long, 2.5cm across, with 3 veins; flower stalks 10–45cm. Flowers 2–4cm across, often pinkish. Differs from the common daisy *B. perennis* in its larger flowers and 3-veined leaves. For any good soil. Hardy to −10°C perhaps. Winter flowering. *B. perennis* L., the Common Daisy, has been long cultivated, as well as being a common lawn weed. Large, pinkish and double-flowered forms are often grown as annuals, though they are good perennials and very pretty in wild grass. Hardy to −20°C.

Celmisia coriacea (Forster fil.) Hook. fil. (*Compositae*) Native of New Zealand, throughout South Island, growing in alpine and subalpine herbfields and grassland, flowering in December–February, or May–June in the north. Plant forming single rosettes of leaves or loose clumps. Leaves 20–60cm long, silky-silvery above and beneath. Flower stems to 60cm. Flowers 5–12cm across. For moist but well-drained, peaty, sandy soil in full sun, but a cool position. These New Zealand alpine daisies are easy to grow in cool climates such as Scotland, where *C. coriacea* is often seen in cottage gardens, but are more difficult to grow in the south of England, as they dislike summer heat. Hardy to −15°C.

Erigeron karvinskianus

Erigeron karvinskianus on the walls of Flora's garden in the Villa Torrigiani, near Lucca, Italy

Celmisia spectabilis Hook. fil.   Native of New Zealand, in South Island, from Mount Kikurangi southwards, growing in subalpine or alpine herbfields or tussock grassland, flowering in December–February. Plant forming single rosettes, or loose clumps. Leaves very tough and leathery, often shining green above, or hairy, densely woolly beneath, to 15cm long, 5cm across. Flowers to 5cm across, smaller than *C. coriacea*. For well-drained but peaty, sandy soil in full sun but a cool position. Hardy to −15°C or less.

Corethrogyne californica DC. (*Compositae*) Native of California, from San Francisco to Monterey (with var. *obovata* (Benth.) O. Kuntze north to Oregon), growing on grassy slopes near the coast, often on serpentine, flowering in April–July. Plant with spreading rootstock and leafy decumbent stems to 40cm from a woody base. Leaves 2–4cm long, linear or oblanceolate, greyish-hairy. Flowers purple to pinkish, with 30–40 rays, to 3cm across. For a dry position in full sun. Hardy to −5°C, perhaps less.

Erigeron karvinskianus DC. syn. *E. mucronatus* DC (*Compositae*)   Native of Mexico, and often naturalized in S Europe, growing on rocks and in crevices in walls, flowering throughout the summer. Plant forming delicate clumps of slender stems to 50cm from a woody rootstock. Flowers *c.*2cm across, pinkish. An attractive plant for warm, dry places, which will seed itself freely in old walls. Hardy to −10°C, but often regenerating by seed if the parent plants are killed by frost.

Leucanthemum vulgare L. syn. *Chrysanthemum leucanthemum* L. (*Compositae*) Ox-eye Daisy   Native of most of Europe except the Azores, the Balerics, Crete and Spitsbergen, and of N Turkey, east to China, and naturalized in North America, growing in hay fields, old grassland and roadside banks, flowering in April–June. Plant with a creeping rootstock and upright flowering stems to 1m, usually *c.*40cm. Flowers 2.5–5cm across, solitary. For any soil in full sun. Hardy to −20°C or less. A very good plant for long grass, to flower after daffodils have finished, nor to be entirely neglected for the herbaceous border as an earlier and more refined version of the common *L.* × *superbum*.

Leucanthemum vulgare with *Sisyrinchium striatum* (p. 417), at Symnel Cottage, Kent

Anthemis punctata subsp. *cupaniana*

Corethrogyne californica

Convallaria majalis
(tall form)

Convallaria majalis
'Prolificans'

Convallaria majalis
var. *rosea*

Convallaria majalis
'Fortin's Giant'

Speirantha convallarioides

*Maianthemum
bifolium*

Smilacina stellata

Specimens from Wisley, 15 May. ½ life size

Convallaria majalis

Convallaria majalis var. *rosea*

Smilacina racemosa at Wisley

Smilacina stellata in California

Smilacina purpurea at Kew

Smilacina racemosa in fruit

Convallaria majalis L. (*Convallariaceae*) Lily of the Valley   Native of Europe, from N England south to the Caucasus and NE Turkey, and eastwards to Japan, and in North America in the Appalachians in Virginia, North and South Carolina, growing in woods, in scrub, on limestone pavement and meadows in the mountains, flowering in May–June. Plant forming spreading mats by rhizomes which creep on the soil surface, beneath the leaf layer. Stems with 1–4 leaves, 3–20cm long, 0.5–10cm wide. Inflorescence arising from the lower sheaths, to 20cm tall, with 5–13 wonderfully scented flowers. Several varieties are found in the wild, and other variants are cultivated. Shown here are var. *rosea* Reichb., which is common in parts of C and E Europe, and has small pinkish flowers; 'Prolificans', with numerous small flowers on a branched inflorescence, and 'Fortin's Giant', a large clone. Double-flowered white and pink clones and a clone with white striped leaves, 'Variegata', are also grown.

Maianthemum bifolium (L.) F. W. Schmidt (*Convallariaceae*)   Native of Europe, from England and Norway eastwards, to N Japan, usually growing in coniferous woods on acid soils, flowering in April–July according to altitude and latitude. Plant forming spreading mats by creeping underground rhizomes. Flowering stems hairy above, 5–25cm tall, usually around 15cm, usually with 2 cordate leaves. Petals 2–3mm. Berries red. A delicate, if invasive, plant, useful for groundcover in cool shady places. *M. canadense* Desf., from E North America, differs in its narrower, shorter-stalked, shallowly cordate leaves and often glabrous stems.

Smilacina purpurea Wallich   Native of the Himalayas from NW India to SW China, growing in forests at 2400–4200m, flowering in April–June. Plant with creeping rhizome. Stems 20–40cm; leaves 3–9. Flowers in narrow spikes, sometimes branched at the base; usually dark purplish, sometimes white. Easily grown in a moist, shady position and leafy soil. Hardy to −15°C, perhaps less (Grey-Wilson 150).

Smilacina racemosa (L.) Desf. syn. *Maianthemum racemosum* (L.) Link (*Convallariaceae*)   Native of North America, from British Columbia east to Nova Scotia, Georgia and Missouri, with var. *amplexicaulis* (Nutt.) Wats. in California to the Rockies, growing in damp coniferous and deciduous woods, flowering in March–July, according to latitude and altitude. Plant with a tufted rhizome, forming dense clumps of stems 30–90cm tall. Leaves rounded at the base, or clasping in var. *amplexicaulis*, pubescent beneath. Flowers with petals 1–2mm long. Berries red, spotted with purple.

Smilacina stellata (L.) Desf. syn. *Maianthemum stellatum* (L.) Link   Native of California north to British Columbia, and eastwards to Newfoundland, Virginia and Kansas, in wet places in woods and scrub, flowering in April–June. Plant with a creeping rhizome, forming extensive patches. Stems 30–60cm tall. Flowers 3–15 in a loose raceme; petals 5–7mm long. Berries reddish purple, becoming black. *Smilacina trifolia* Desf., from N North America and Siberia, usually has only 3 narrowly ovate leaves, and dark-red berries. Easily grown in moist, leafy soil. Hardy to −25°C.

Speirantha convallarioides Baker syn. *S. gardenii* Baillon (*Convallariaceae*)   Native of SE China, in Jiangxi (Kiangsi) growing in woods, flowering in ?April–May. Plant with thick rhizomes, spreading by stolons. Leaves evergreen to 15cm long. Flowering stems to 15cm. Flowers scented; petals 4–6mm long. For leafy soil in shade. Hardy to −10°C perhaps.

Polygonatum odoratum
'Flore Pleno'

Polygonatum odoratum

Disporum sessile 'Variegatum'

Polygonatum falcatum
'Pumilum'

Polygonatum multiflorum

Polygonatum falcatum
'Variegatum'

Polygonatum humile

Polygonatum × hybridum

Specimens from Kew and Wisley, 14 May. ⅓ life size

Polygonatum odoratum (Furse & Synge 435) at Kew

Disporopsis pernyi (Hua) Diels syn. *Polygonatum cyrtonema* hort. (*Convallariaceae*) Native of China, in Yunnan, Guangxi and Gizhou, in forests at 1800–7500m, flowering in June. Plant evergreen, with stiff stems to 20cm from a shortly creeping rhizome, forming dense patches. Flowers solitary or in pairs, with petals diverging and almost reflexed in the lower part when open. For leafy soil in shade or partial shade. Hardy to −10°C, perhaps less

Disporum sessile (Thunb.) D. Don (*Convallariaceae*)   Native throughout Japan and in Sakhalin, growing in woods in the hills, flowering in April–May. Plant forming colonies from underground creeping rhizomes. Stems 30–60cm. Flowers 1–3, greenish white, about 3cm long. Berries blue-black. 'Variegatum'   A clone with white-striped leaves, shown here, is frequent in gardens. For other *Disporum* species see pp. 82–3.

Polygonatum biflorum (Walt.) Ell. (*Convallariaceae*)   Native of North America, from New Brunswick west to Michigan, south to Tennessee, West Virginia and Florida, growing in deciduous woods and scrub, flowering in April–July. Stems up to 90cm. Leaves 5–10cm long, pubescent, especially on the veins beneath. Flowers usually in pairs, 8–12mm long, greenish. Filaments papillose. The smaller of the two North American species, usually found in dryish places in woods. *P. canaliculatum* Purs, syn. *P. commutatum* (Schult.) Dietr., usually found in damp places can reach 2.5m high and is totally glabrous.

Polygonatum curvistylum Hua   Native of Sichuan and Yunnan, growing in stony places as scrub on limestone at *c.*3000m, flowering in June. Rhizomes shortly creeping. Stems dark purple to 80cm. Flowers pinkish, purple inside, narrowest at the throat.

Polygonatum falcatum A. Gray   Native of most of Japan and Korea, growing in woods in the hills, flowering in May–June. Rhizomes short, creeping, so the plant forms clumps of stems 50–85cm tall. Leaves 8–20cm long, 1.8–2.5cm wide, usually rough on the veins beneath. Flowers 1.1–2.2cm, in groups of 2–5. Berries small, 3–4mm across. 'Variegatum' is the clone commonest in cultivation, an attractive plant with reddish stems and a white edge to the leaf. *P. humile* (q.v.) is often wrongly called *P. falcatum*, and *P.* 'Pumilum', shown here, is a small form of *P. falcatum*.

Polygonatum humile Fisch.   Native of N China (Heilongjiang), E Siberia, Korea and Japan, in Hokkaido, N Honshu and Kyushu, growing in meadows and open woods at low altitudes, flowering in June–July. Rhizomes slender, creeping, forming spreading colonies of angled, upright stems 15–30cm tall; leaves 4–7cm long, hairy on the veins beneath. Flowers solitary or in pairs. Usually a dwarf plant with upright stems. Hardy to −20°C.

Polygonatum × hybridum Brugger   A hybrid between *P. multiflorum* and *P. odoratum*, common in gardens and sometimes naturalized in N & W Europe. Rhizomes stout, shortly creeping, especially above. Stems to 90cm, scarcely angled. Leaves glabrous beneath, up to 20 × 8cm; flowers mostly in groups of 4 in the axils of all except the uppermost 2 or 3 leaves. Filaments papillose. Seldom sets more than 1 or 2 berries. Easily grown and elegant with its

Polygonatum sewerzowii near Tashkent

Polygonatum biflorum in New Jersey

arching stems. The leaves are often stripped by the grey larvae of a sawfly.

Polygonatum multiflorum (L.) All.   Native of Europe, from W England eastwards to Turkey and European Russia, and W Siberia, growing in woods, usually on limestone, flowering in May–June. Rhizome stout, short, creeping; stems 30–90cm, not angled. Leaves 5–15cm, glabrous beneath. Flowers 9–20mm long, in groups of 2–6, usually confined to the lower half of the stem.

Polygonatum odoratum (Miller) Druce Angular Solomon's Seal   Native of most of Europe, including W England, eastwards to the Caucasus, N Iran, Siberia and Japan, growing in woods, usually on limestone, flowering in April–June. Rhizome long, creeping, forming colonies. Stems 30–85cm, angled, leaves 3–15cm; flowers solitary or in groups of 2–4. 'Flore Pleno' has attractive double flowers, and white-striped and -edged forms are also cultivated. Hardy to −25°C.

Polygonatum sewerzowii Regel   Native of C Asia, in the Tien Shan, Pamir Alai and Kopet Daǧ, growing in scrub and among shady rocks, flowering in April–June. Rhizome shortly creeping. Stems 20–100cm. Leaves whorled, the upper with curled tips. Flowers 15–20mm long. Berries first red, later purple. *P. verticillatum* (L.) All., from Europe and N Turkey to W Siberia and the Himalayas, is similar, but has flowers only 8–10mm long and leaves not curled at the tips. *P. sibiricum* Delaroche, from N China, Mongolia and E Siberia, has stems to 3m, climbing through the scrub and flowers in groups of up to 30.

Disporopsis pernyi at Harry Hay's, Surrey

Polygonatum curvistylum at Harry Hay's

The habitat of *Iris confusa* in low hills near Baoxing, Sichuan, W China

Iris confusa 'Martyn Rix'

Iris confusa (white form)

Iris lazica from the Black Sea coast, near Of, NE Turkey

Iris confusa Sealy (s. *Lophiris* (Evansia)) Native of W China, in Yunnan and W Sichuan, growing on steep rocky slopes among rocks and scrub, flowering in May. Like *I. japonica*, but with the fan of leaves on a stiff, bamboo-like stem up to 60cm high. Leaves *c.*5m wide. Flowers 4–5cm across, normally white, with yellow and purple spotting. For a sheltered and warm position in partial shade; hardy to −5°C perhaps, and only really satisfactory outdoors in warm parts of the USA such as S California. Brian Mathew recommends planting it in a tub which can be brought indoors during cold spells in winter. The darker-flowered form shown here, called '**Martyn Rix**', was growing in W Sichuan, at Baoxing, where the species is very common, with flowers of all shades of colour.

Iris cristata Solander (s. *Lophiris*) Native of Maryland west to S Ohio, and Indiana south to Georgia, Tennessee and Missouri in the Appalachians and Ozark mountains, growing in moist oak woods and along streams, flowering in April–May. Rhizomes creeping on the surface and branching freely to make a radiating mat. Stems, including the flower, to 7cm. Leaves soft, glabrous, bright green, 10–20cm tall. Flowers 3–4cm across, usually bluish, rarely pink or white. Easily grown in leafy soil in partial shade, but requires protection from slugs, frequent division, and replanting every other year if it is to thrive and persist. Hardy to −20°C. *Iris lacustris* Nutt. is an even dwarfer plant from the shores of Lake Huron, Michigan and Superior; its floral tube is shorter than the bracts.

Iris japonica Thunb. (s. *Lophiris*) Native of Japan (except Hokkaido) and China westwards to Sichuan, on grassy and rocky slopes, in woods in the hills, and among rocks by streams, flowering in April–May. Plant with a creeping aerial rhizome, rooting at intervals. Leaves 30–80cm long, 2.5–5cm wide, evergreen, shining green in a broad fan; stems 30–80cm, branched; the flowers opening in succession, white, pale to mid-blue or purplish, 5–6cm across. 'Ledger's Variety' seems to be the common one in cultivation in Europe. It is triploid, and another in cultivation, the 'Capri form', which has crests with paler-orange markings, is possibly of hybrid origin and is highly sterile. The robust variety 'Burne Graceful', raised in 1966, is a cross between these two. It has stems to 120cm and flowers 6–7.5cm across. Easily grown in a sheltered warm site in sun or partial shade. The flowers are susceptible to damage by late spring frosts and the plant will fail to flower after an exceptionally cold winter.

Iris lazica Albov (s. *Unguiculares*) Native of NE Turkey and Georgia, from Giresun eastwards, growing on sandy shady banks, beneath bracken or in scrub at near sea level to 250m, flowering in February–April. Plant forming a slowly spreading clump. Leaves evergreen, dark green, 15–32cm long, 8–15mm wide. Flowers deep purplish blue, to 8cm across, 2–4 on a short branching inflorescence *c.*5cm long, with overlapping spathe-like bracts. Capsules on a *c.*6cm stalk. For a warm, sunny or partially shaded position on well-drained, but leafy soil. Related to *I. unguicularis*, but the area where this grows is very warm, wet and cloudy in summer. It flowers best in a warm position in England. Hardy to −15°C or so: the leaves are killed at −10°C.

Iris unguicularis 'Walter Butt' at Washfield Nurseries. Kent

Iris tectorum in Sichuan

Iris unguicularis (Algerian form)

Iris unguicularis (white form)

Iris tectorum

Iris unguicularis subsp. *carica* var. *angustifolia*
from Greece

Iris cristata in Virginia

Iris confusa

Iris tectorum Maxim. (s. *Lophiris*)   Native of
Burma and SW & C China, and naturalized in
Japan, though commonly cultivated throughout
this area, on the roofs of thatched houses, the
tops of old walls, and found also in shady rocky
slopes and in scrub, flowering in May. Stems to
50cm, usually *c*.30cm tall, with few branches,
each with 2–3 flowers. Leaves semi-evergreen,
30–60cm long, 2.5–5cm wide. Flowers 8–10cm
across, purplish blue or white. Although seldom
seen in gardens in Europe, *I. tectorum* is not
difficult, though I have not found it grows or
flowers as prolifically as in its native habitat.
There it would have dry, cold winters and
warm, wet summers, with perfect drainage;
loose, leafy soil in a warm but partially shaded
position should suit it best.

Iris unguicularis Poiret syns. *I. stylosa* Desf.,
I. cretensis Janka   Native of Algeria, Tunisia,
S & W Turkey and W Syria, Greece and Crete,
growing in rocky places and woods usually of
pine at up to 1000m, flowering in March–April,
but often as early as December in cultivation.
Plant forming dense clumps. Leaves greyish
green, to 75cm long, and 1.8cm across (the
Algerian subsp.); the Greek subsp. to 7mm
across. Flowers pale to deep bluish mauve,
rarely white; to 8cm long, stemless, on a tube
9–28cm long. Capsules hidden among the
leaves. The Cretan subspecies, subsp. *cretensis*,
is very dwarf, with leaves less than 3mm across,
and often less than 15cm long: the flowers may
be pale bluish, with narrow falls and standards.
Narrow-leaved forms are found in the

Peloponnese and on the south coast of Turkey,
called subsp. *carica* (W. Schultz) A. Davis &
Jury, but have larger flowers. The North
African plants, which have the largest flowers,
are the ones generally cultivated. Easily grown
in a dry, sunny position, and requiring a warm
place, with rich, well-drained soil to flower
freely. Hardy to −15°C.
'Mary Barnard'   A good deep purplish blue,
said to be from Algeria, of the same colour as is
commonest in the Peloponnese. Free-flowering.
'Walter Butt'   A most beautiful pale lavender
blue, with a large flower. Free-flowering. White
forms are also in cultivation, but the commonest
has narrow-petalled flowers, and is always
infected with virus.

Iris scariosa near Karamay, NW China

Iris scariosa

Iris lutescens from S France, near St Tropez

Iris attica from Parnassos Oros, Greece

Iris aphylla L. (s. *Iris* – pogon)   Native of C & E Europe, from SE France to S Poland and the N Caucasus, growing on rocky slopes, flowering in May. Plant deciduous; stems 15–30cm; leaves to 2cm wide. Flowering stems branched at or below the middle, often near the base. Flowers 1–5, purple or violet, 6–7cm across. Bracts green. The form shown here is from the westernmost locality of the species, in the Alpes Maritimes, where it has been called *I. perrieri* Simonet ex P. Fournier.

Iris attica Boiss. & Held. syn. *I. pumila* subsp. *attica* (Boiss. & Held.) Hayek   Native of S Yugoslavia, Greece and NW Turkey, growing in rocky places usually on limestone, flowering in April–May. Plant deciduous in winter, forming small but spreading mats; stems very short; height 5–10cm, including the flowers, the recurved leaves 4–7mm wide. Flowers solitary, 3.5–4.5cm across, varying in colour, even in the same population, from purple to yellow and reddish with various bicolours, as shown here. Easily grown in a bulb frame, but not reliably hardy outside in N Europe or NE North America.

Iris lutescens Lam. syn. *I. chamaeiris* Bertol. Native of NE Spain, S France and Italy, growing on bare rocky or sandy hills, often on granite, or in open pine woods, flowering in March–April. Plant evergreen, forming dense mats. Stems 5–20cm; leaves 0.5–2.5cm wide. Flowers 1 or 2 per stem, 6–7cm across, often with standards rather larger than the falls, yellow, dark purple or bicoloured, with a yellow beard. Easily grown in a bulb frame or well-drained soil in a warm sheltered place. Hardy to −15°C perhaps. Plants shown here from SW France, west of St Tropez.

Iris pseudopumila Tineo   Native of SE Italy, W Yugoslavia and Sicily, growing on rocky hills and in dry scrub, flowering in March–April. Plant evergreen, forming small mats. Stems *c*.3cm, including the flowers, to 25cm. Leaves 1–1.5cm wide, slightly curved. Flowers yellow, purplish, white or bicoloured, 6–8cm across. Beard white with yellow tips. Probably best in a bulb frame or very sheltered sunny position. Hardy to −10°C perhaps.

Iris scariosa Willd. ex Link   Native of Asia, from the Urals eastwards to the Tien Shan in NW China, growing on rocky hillsides or steppes, sometimes in nearly desert or saline conditions, up to 3000m, flowering in May–June. Plant deciduous (?), forming dense mats. Stems 5–30cm; leaves greyish, recurved,

Iris subbiflora

1–2.5cm wide. Flowers 2 per stem, 4–5cm across, with loose, rather thin-textured bracts, usually bluish or purplish, with white or yellow forms rarer. In NW China the flowers were always purplish and it was very dwarf, but a striking sight on bare and apparently totally dry hills, taller and lusher on rocky hillsides with paeonies (p.96), tulips and fritillaries. Beard white. Probably easily grown in dry soil, with most water in spring. Should be very tolerant of dry cold.

Iris schachtii Markgraf   Native of C Turkey, especially on the Anatolian plateau east of Ankara and between Kayseri and Malatya, growing on rocky hillsides and open steppes, at up to 1800m, flowering in May. Plant deciduous, forming small clumps. Height 10–30cm, stem usually branched; leaves up to 1.5cm wide. Flowers 1–3, 5–6cm across, usually yellowish, though often purple, with green purple-tinted bracts which are transparent on the margins. Beard yellow. This species requires good soil and full sun, dry in summer if it is to flower freely. Hardy to −20°C perhaps.

Iris subbiflora Brot. syn. *I. lutescens* subsp. *subbiflora* (Brot.) Webb & Chater   Native of C & NE Portugal and SW Spain, with one locality near Antequera, growing on rocky hills and open scrub often on limestone, flowering in April. Plant evergreen, forming dense clumps. Stems 20–40cm. Leaves 0.5–2.5cm wide, upright. Flowers 7–8cm across, usually purple. Beard white or purple. An attractive plant which grows and flowers regularly in S England in well-drained, sandy soil. Hardy to −15°C.

Iris taochia Woron. ex Grossh.   Native of NE Turkey, growing on rocky screes at 1500–1700m, flowering in May–June. Plant deciduous, forming dense clumps. Stems 25–35cm tall, with 1–3 branches. Leaves 1.5–2.5cm wide, upright. Flowers 5–7cm across, purple, yellow or brownish-red in the same population. Beard yellowish or white, tipped yellow. This requires bulb-frame treatment to flower in S England, but would grow outside in hotter, drier parts of Europe and the USA. Hardy to −20°C. This species appears to be confined to the environs of Tortum: I have seen it making large dense clumps on otherwise barren, steep volcanic screes.

Iris hybrid   This old garden variety is probably a hybrid between *I. lutescens* and *I. germanica*, and is a forerunner of the intermediate bearded irises. It has 1–2 flowers on a stem.

Iris, unnamed hybrid

Iris shachtii near Malatya, C Turkey

Iris aphylla (*I. perrieri*)

Iris pseudopumila near Brindisi

Iris taochia from near Tortum

Iris taochia near Tortum, NE Turkey

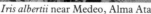

Iris albertii near Medeo, Alma Ata

Iris pallida at Sellindge, Kent

Iris albertii Regel (s. *Iris* – pogon)   Native of C Asia, in the Tien Shan and Pamir Alai, at 1700–2000m, growing on rocky hillsides and grassy mountain steppes, flowering in May. Plant forming spreading clumps. Stems up to 1m in cultivation, to 70cm in the wild, widely branched. Leaves 2–3cm across; bracts green with papery edges. Beard white tipped yellow. Flowers 6–8cm across, purplish blue. Easily grown, especially in a bulb frame, for protection from winter wet, requiring full sun to flower well. The widely branching stems are typical.

Iris albicans Lange   Native of Saudi Arabia and the Yemen, growing in dry, rocky places at up to 2200m, flowering in February–May. This iris was brought northwards by the Arabs and planted on their cemeteries, and is now found more or less wild, often still on abandoned cemeteries in much of the S Mediterranean, especially in Turkey, S Spain and Crete. Plant forming spreading clumps. Stems 30–60cm with, at most, 1 very short branch and usually 2 terminal flowers. Leaves very glaucous, incurved at the tips. Bracts broad, blunt, green or purplish below, papery on the margins. Flowers usually white, sometimes pale blue, sweetly scented. Easily grown in full sun and dry, well-drained soil. Source: S Arabia, John Marr 147. *I.* 'Florentina' (see p. 196) differs in its bracts, which are all papery at flowering, its stalked lateral branches, and slightly blue-flushed flowers.

Iris germanica L. 'Nepalensis' syn. 'Purple King', 'Atropurpurea'   This is one of the many named clones of *I. germanica*. It is distinct in its

entirely red-purple flowers, with the hairs of the beard white towards the apex, yellow tipped towards the base of the falls. Introduced in the 19th century from Kathmandu. Early flowering in gardens.

Iris imbricata Lindl.   Native of Azerbaijan and N Iran in the Talysh and Elburz mountains, growing on grassy alpine slopes, screes and in damp rocky places at 1400–3000m, flowering in May–June. Plant forming dense clumps. Stems 30–60cm, branched, with 2 or 3 flowers. Leaves flat, upright, grey-green, 2–3cm wide. Bracts inflated, pale green, transparent only at the tip. Beard dark yellow. Flowers 7–9cm across, pale yellowish. This species is beautifully illustrated in Brian Mathew's *The Iris*, growing with scarlet Oriental poppies in the alpine meadows of the high Elburz.

Iris pallida Lam. subsp. *pallida*   Native of W Balkans, growing on rocky limestone hillsides and the sides of gorges leading down to the Adriatic, flowering in May. Plant forming spreading clumps. Stems up to 1.2m, much branched. Leaves very glaucous, 1–4cm or more wide, up to 60cm high. Bracts entirely silvery and papery at flowering. Flowers 3–6, pale lilac blue, 9–11cm across. Easily cultivated in ordinary garden soil in a sunny position, and very free flowering. This species is beautiful not only for its flowers but also for its very pale glaucous leaves which remain healthy through the whole summer. Source: Montenegro near Podgorica (formerly Titograd).
I. pallida 'Variegata' is an excellent garden plant, with the advantage of the variegated

leaves when the flowers have finished; there are said to be 2 forms, 'Argentea', with white stripes on the leaf edges, and 'Aurea', with golden stripes. In practice, one tends to see a whitish-yellow form.
Subsp. *cengialtii* (Ambr.) Foster, from NE Italy, has stems only to 45cm, browner bracts, and greener leaves. The darker purple flowers have a white or orange-tipped beard. Photographed by Brian Mathew.

Iris purpureobractea Mathew & T. Baytop Native of NW & C Turkey, notably on Honaz Dağ, growing in dry rocky places, in cedar or pine forest at 60–1600m, flowering in April–May. Plant forming clumps. Stems 20–50cm. Leaves 1.5–2.5cm wide. Bracts purplish. Flowers pale yellow veined with greenish brown, or pale-blue veined darker blue, 10–12cm from top to bottom. For well-drained soil in full sun. Hardy to −15°C perhaps.

Iris variegata L.   Native of C & E Europe, from S Germany and Austria, eastwards to the W Ukraine and south to Montenegro and Bulgaria, growing in open woods, scrub and rocky places, flowering in May–June. Plant forming dense clumps. Stems 15–40cm, branched towards the top. Leaves dark green, to 30cm tall and 3cm wide, distinctly ribbed. Bracts green or purplish. Flowers 3–6, 5–7cm across, with pale-yellow standards, and nearly horizontal red- or purple-striped falls. Beard yellow. Easily grown in ordinary garden soil and more shade-tolerant than most species of this group. This is a parent of many of the bicoloured bearded irises.

Iris pallida subsp. *cengialtii*

Iris pallida 'Variegata'

Iris purpureobractea at Brian Mathew's

Iris albicans from Arabia, at Kew

Iris germanica 'Nepalensis'

Iris imbricata at Kew

Iris variegata

Iris 'Bromyard'

'Summer Nights'

'Sarah Taylor'

'Saltwood'

'Darkover'

'Sunny Smile'

'Truly'

'Bibury'

'Double Lament'

'Low'

'Royal Emblem'

Specimens from Wisley, 14 May. ½ life size

Iris 'Smarty Pants'

Iris 'Arctic Fancy'

Iris 'Partridge'

Iris 'Double Lament'

Iris 'Bibury'

'Arctic Fancy' (intermediate, bearded)
Registered by A. Brown 1964. Parents: 'Dale
Dennis' × 'Rococo'. Plicata, standards white,
stitched violet; falls white, stitched violet; beard
pale violet with yellow tips. Height 50cm. Early
season.

'Bibury' (standard dwarf, bearded)   Registered
by J. D. Taylor 1975. Parents: 'Saltwood' ×
seedling. Standards white; falls white with pale
yellow hafts; beard orangy. Height 30cm. Early
season.

'Bromyard' (standard dwarf, bearded)
Registered by J. D. Taylor 1979. Parents:
'Saltwood' × seedling. Standards blue-grey;
falls blended, maroon with yellow centres;
beard golden. Height 28cm. Early season.

'Darkover' (standard dwarf, bearded)
Registered by N. K. Stopes 1983. Parents:
74/73 (35/71m ('Blueberry Muffin' × 36/69m) ×
'Gingerman') × unknown. Deep maroon self
with bluish beard. Height 25cm. Early season.

'Double Lament' (standard dwarf, bearded)
Registered by J. D. Taylor 1969. Parents:
('Green Spot' × *pumila*) × 'Velvet Caper'.
Violet self with dark flush on the falls; beard
pale tipped orange. Height 30cm. Mid-season.

'Low' (standard dwarf, bearded)   Registered
by A. Brown 1969. Parents: (sibling of 'Sunny
Heart' and 'Cartwheel') × 'Lilli-Var'. Standards
bright chrome-yellow; falls deep oxblood-red
with a narrow margin of chrome yellow about
4mm, is solid and smooth; beard bright orange.
Height 30cm. Early season.

'Partridge' (intermediate, bearded)
Registered by J. D. Taylor 1973. Parents:
seedling C43 × ('Staten Island' × 'Dandy').
Standards gold; falls maroon. Height 60cm.
Late season.

'Royal Emblem' (standard dwarf, bearded)
Registered by L. W. Brummitt 1978. Parents:
'Blueberry Muffin' × 'Purple Landscape'.
Standards red-purple; falls red-purple (velvety);
beard more violet. Height 30cm. Early to mid-
season.

'Saltwood' (standard dwarf, bearded)
Registered by J. D. Taylor 1971. Parents:
'Sunny Heart' × Taylor seedling J42/1.
Standards lemon; falls yellow with lemon ring
round. Height 33cm. Early season.

'Sarah Taylor' (standard dwarf, bearded)
Registered by J. D. Taylor 1979. Parents: Jones
M212/3 × 'Stockholm'. Standards cream; falls

pale primrose; beard blue. Height 30cm. Early
season.

'Smarty Pants' (low border, bearded)
Registered by A. White. Parents: 'Sans Souci'
× unknown. Reddish toned. Mid-season.

'Summer Nights' (standard dwarf, bearded)
Registered by L. Boushay 1979. Parents:
('Honey Talk' × 'Grace Note') × 'Stockholm'.
Ruffled blend of bluebird-blue and olive self,
bluer at the base; beard the same colour. Height
29cm. Early to mid-season.

'Sunny Smile' (standard dwarf, bearded)
Registered by N. K. Scopes 1977. Parents:
('Eye Shadow' × 'Lenna M.') × 'Sapphire
Heart'. Standards pale golden yellow; falls
slightly deeper colour; beard white. Height
30cm. Early season.

'Truly' (standard dwarf, bearded)   Registered
by B. Warburton 1977. Parents: 'Daughter' ×
'Dear Love'. Very pale-blue self with darker
veining; beard white-cream. Height 30cm.
Early season.

193

Iris 'Happy Mood'

'Devilry'

'Anne Elizabeth'

'Amphora'

'Sky Caper'

'Downland'

'Austrian Sky'

'Little Suki'

'Langport Carnival'

Iris germanica (p. 196)

Specimens from Wisley, 14 May. ⅔ life size

Modern bearded irises

Iris 'Small Wonder'

Iris 'Owlet'

Iris 'Jeremy Brian'

'Amphora' (standard dwarf, bearded) Registered by J. D. Taylor 1972. Parents: 'Sunny Heart' × seedling 242. Standards white; falls white with clear yellow spot; beard yellow. Height 30cm. Mid-season.

'Anne Elizabeth' (standard dwarf, bearded) Registered by J. D. Taylor 1973. Parents: 'Circlette' × 'Plicatree'. Plicata white with blue-violet edges and veining; beard white. Height 28cm. Early to mid-season.

'Austrian Sky' (dwarf, bearded) Registered by G. W. Darby 1957. Parents: (seedling × 'Welch') × 'Blue Ensign'. Blue self with darker blue thumbprint and veins on falls and sky blue standards. Height 30cm. Mid-season.

'Devilry' (standard dwarf, bearded) Registered by J. D. Taylor 1969. Parents: seedling E96/10 × 'Lemanis'. Purple self with brown beard. Height 33cm. Mid-season.

'Downland' (intermediate) Registered by R. Usher 1969. Parents: 'Little Rosy Wings' ×

'Captain Gallant'. Standards plum red; falls burgundy-red, edge plum-red; beard bronze. Height 48cm. Mid-season.

'Happy Mood' (intermediate, bearded) Registered by A. Brown 1967. Parents: 'Knotty Pine' × 'Rococo'. Standards white with light-blue markings; falls white with a band of blue markings; beard ivory, tipped orchid. Height 56cm. Early season.

'Jeremy Brian' (standard dwarf, bearded) Registered by B. Price 1975. Parents: 'Blue Denim' × 'Sparkling Champagne'. Pale silver-blue self; beard yellow tipped. Height 25cm. Early to mid-season.

'Langport Carnival' (intermediate, bearded) Introduced by Kelway & Son prior to 1940; parents not known. Smoky violet with a distinct large brown patch on the falls; beard violet with orange tips. Height 56cm. Early season.

'Little Suki' (standard dwarf, bearded) Registered by N. K. Scopes 1970. Parents:

'Robert Melrose' × 'Velvet Capers'. Standards creamy tan with purple shadows at base; falls deeper tan. Height 30cm. Early season.

'Little Vanessa' (standard dwarf, bearded) Registered by J. D. Taylor 1968. Parents: (Langdale seedling × seedling) × 'Red Dandy'. Standards magenta; falls magenta, with white beard. Height 30cm. Mid-season.

'Owlet' (standard dwarf, bearded) Registered by J. D. Taylor 1976. Parents: 'Jane Taylor' × seedling. Standards lavender; falls lavender with darker spot. Height 33cm. Early season.

'Sky Caper' (miniature dwarf, bearded) Registered by Warburton 1962. Parents: 'Fairy Flax' × AM-5 (blue *pumila*). Pale purplish-blue self; beard white. Height 15cm. Early season.

'Small Wonder' (semi-dwarf, bearded) Registered by G. Douglas 1953. Parents: 'Helen McGregor' × *pumila* blue. Medium-French-blue self; beard yellow. Height 28cm. Early to mid-season.

'Green Spot'

'Canary Bird'

'Langport Wren'

'Langport Honey'

'Amethyst Flame'

'Florentina'

Langport Chief'

'Langport Finch'

'Langport Chapter'

'Blue Pansy'

Iris germanica

Iris germanica 'Nepalensis'

Specimens from Eccleston Square, 20 May. ⅕ life size

'Amethyst Flame'

Iris germanica

Iris germanica L. (*Iridaceae*)   Origin unknown, probably of hybrid origin, but perhaps native in the E Mediterranean. Widely cultivated as an old garden plant and also for the perfume extracted from its rhizome. Commonly naturalized in dry, rocky places. Flower stems stout and well branched, 40–90cm, branches to 5cm. Leaves 30–70cm × 2–3.5cm, somewhat glaucous, straight. Flowers with lavender-purple standards 5.5–9cm × 4–6cm; falls deep velvety purple with distinct white haft-markings, 5.5–9cm × 4–6cm; the beard white or whitish. An excellent plant for dry town gardens, where it will flower happily in light deciduous shade in March–May. Scented.

Iris germanica 'Florentina' syn. *Iris florentina* auct. vix L. Orris Root   Flowers white, flushed with very pale blue, with distinct haft markings and a yellow beard, fragrant. The bracts are almost wholly brown and papery at flowering time. Now considered to be a form of *I. germanica*. Cultivated in Italy especially in the area around Florence for perfume. Early-flowering, and easily grown in ordinary garden soil and full sun. The root must be dried before the scent, which resembles violets, is released.

Iris germanica 'Nepalensis' syn. *I. germanica* 'Atropurpurea'   An ancient variety that crops up in old gardens and can be found naturalized; it has deep-purple-violet standards and falls with a white beard. Scented. (See also p. 190.)

'Amethyst Flame' (tall, bearded)   Registered by B. R. Schreiner 1957. Parents: 'Crispette' ×

('Lavandesque' × 'Pathfinder'). Amethyst-violet self; beard pale yellowish. Height 97cm. Mid-season.

'Blue Pansy' (tall, bearded)   Kelway & Son 1966. 'Black Hills' × 'Knight Valiant'. Deep-violet-blue self with golden beard. Height 102cm. Mid-season.

'Canary Bird' (tall, bearded)   Kelway & Son 1957. 'Berkeley Gold' seedling. Lemon-yellow. Height 97cm. Early to mid-season.

'Green Spot' (intermediate, bearded)   Registered by P. H. R. Cook 1951. Parents: seedling × yellow *pumila*. Whitish self with green spot on falls; yellow beard and markings. Height 25cm. Very early in season.

Irises at Claude Monet's garden at Giverny in late May

'Langport Chapter' (intermediate, bearded)
Medium blue with purple markings; beard
purplish. Height 45cm. Early season.

'Langport Chief' (intermediate, bearded)
Introduced by Kelway & Son prior to 1940.
Parents not known. Purplish-blue with darker
markings on the falls; beard tipped gold. Height
40cm. Early season.

'Langport Finch' (intermediate, bearded)
Introduced by Kelway & Son prior to 1940.
Light-blue self with darker veining on the falls;
beard whitish with yellow tips. Height 45cm.
Early season.

'Langport Honey' (intermediate, bearded)
Introduced by Kelway & Son prior to 1940.
Parents not known. Orange-yellow with strong
purple-brown markings on the falls; beard gold.
Height 66cm. Early season.

Iris 'Plicata' at Myddelton House

'Langport Wren' (intermediate, bearded)
Introduced by Kelway & Son prior to 1940.
Parents not known. Deep magenta-brown with
black veining on falls and standards; beard
yellow. Height 66cm. Early season.

'Plicata' Is extremely similar to I. pallida
(p.190), the difference being that it is a semi-
albino form with purple colour on the veins at
the edges of the standards and falls. The beard
is yellow.

'White May' (intermediate, bearded)
Introduced by P. B. J. Murrell 1939. Parents:
'Orange Queen' × 'Senlac'. Standards pure
white. Early season.

Iris 'White May'

'Brown Trout'

'Big Day'

'Spring Festival'

'Dante'

'Headlines'

'Helen McGregor'

'Gold Flake'

'Argus Pheasant'

'Golden Planet'

Specimens from Eccleston Square, 6 June. ½ life size

'Argus Pheasant' (tall, bearded)   Registered by N. De Forest 1947. Parents: 'Casa Morena' × 'Tobacco Road'. Golden-brown self; beard deep yellow. Height 100cm. Mid-season.

'Big Day' (tall, bearded)   Introduced by Kelway & Son prior to 1940. Parents not known. Medium blue with white haft markings; beard white. Height 90cm. Mid-season.

'Brown Trout' (tall, bearded)   Registered by Kelway & Son 1959. Parents: 'Magic Carpet' × 'Ranger'. Standards copper; falls deep red. Height 90cm. Mid-season.

'Bruno' (tall, bearded)   Introduced by A. J. Biss 1922. Parents: 'Dominian' × unknown. Dark-yellow blended bicolour. Fragrance grape-like. Height over 76cm. Mid- to late season.

'Dante' (tall, bearded)   Registered by R. Kelway 1958. Parents: 'Mexico' × unknown. Standards golden bronze; falls blood-red with bronze edge. Height 76cm. Mid-season.

'Gold Flake' (tall, bearded)   Registered by O. D. N. and P. B. J. Murrell 1933. Parents: 'W. R. Dykes' × unknown. Ruffled golden bronzy-yellow with a cream patch and bronze veining on the falls. Height 102cm. Mid-season.

'Golden Planet' (tall, bearded)   Registered by Kelway & Son 1956. Parents: 'Desert Song' × unknown. Yellow self with deep-gold haft markings; beard yellow. Height 86cm. Early to mid-season.

'Gracious Living' (tall, bearded)   Registered by L. W. Brummitt 1966. Parents: 'Melodrama' × 'Mary Randall'. Standards cream; shaded colour of the falls at base of midrib; falls imperial-purple-shaded lilac below beard; hafts sepia. Height 90cm.

'Headlines' (tall, bearded)   Registered by L. Brummitt 1953. Parents: 'Extravaganza' × 'Louise Blake'. Standards pure white; falls velvety, deep purple, purple; beard yellow. Height 90cm. Late season.

'Helen McGregor' (tall, bearded)   Registered by N. Graves 1943. Parents: 'Purissima' × 'Cloud Castle'. Clear, bright-pale-blue self; beard whitish or touched with yellow. Height 100cm. Mid-season.

'Lady Mohr' (tall, bearded – Arilbred)   Registered by Salbach 1943. Parents: (seedling × 'William Mohr') × Ib–MAC. Standards pale violet with purple markings; falls cream with purple markings; beard brown. Height 90cm. Mid-season.

'Muriel Neville' (tall, bearded)   Registered by H. Fothergill 1963. Parents: ('Queechee' × 'Great Day') × ('Sequatchie' × 'Blood Cornelian') × ('Mexican Magic' × 'Benton Mocha') × 'Ebony Echo'. Crimson. Height 107cm. Mid-season.

'Orange Dawn' (tall, bearded)   Registered by S. Linnegar for A. Howe 1981. Parents: 'May Melody' × unknown. Standards buff-orange; falls apricot orange. Height 96cm. Mid- to late season.

'Spring Festival' (tall, bearded)   Registered by D. Hall. Parents: seedling × 'Mary Hall'. Standards light pink; falls medium pink; beard red. Height 94cm. Mid-season.

'Staten Island' (tall, bearded)   Registered by K. D. Smith 1947. Parents: 'The Red Admiral' × 'City of Lincoln'. Yellow with pink tones. Height 97cm. Mid-season.

'Wheatear' (tall, bearded)   Registered by B. L. C. Dodsworth 1984. Parents: 'Ultrapoise' × 'Radiant Light'. Ruffled apricot self with tangerine beard. Height 97cm. Late season.

Iris 'Lady Mohr' (showing viral streaks)

Iris 'Wheatear'

Iris 'Muriel Neville'

Iris 'Staten Island'

Iris 'Bruno'

Iris 'Gracious Living'

Iris 'Orange Dawn'

IRIS

'Passport'

'Out Yonder'

'Derwentwater'

'Lady Ilse'

'Fantasy Fair'

'Valimar'

'San Leandro'

'Mary Frances'

'Lovely Letty'

Specimens from Claire Austin, Albrighton, 20 June. ⅓ life size

'Actress' (tall, bearded)   Registered by K. Keppel 1975. Parents: 'Ford Wish' × 69-41c: (('Marquesan Skies' × 'Babbling Brook') × 'Touche'). Wisteria-violet self; beard pale with a lavender-blue tip, throat Indian-orange. Height 90cm. Early to mid-season. Remontant.

'Arcady' (tall, bearded)   Registered by H. Fothergill 1959. Parents: 'Jane Phillips' × 'Pegasus'. Standards pale blue; falls pale blue, slightly darker in the centre; beard white-tipped, pale yellow. Height 122cm. Mid- to late season.

'Babbling Brook' (tall, bearded)   Registered by Keppel 1965. Parents: 'Galilee' × 'Symphony'. Light-blue self; beard white-touched yellow. Ruffled. Height 97cm. Mid-season.

'Blue Rhythm' (tall, bearded)   Introduced by C. G. Whiting 1945. Parents: 'Annabel' × 'Blue Zenith'. Mid-blue-toned self. Height 100cm. Lemon scented. Mid-season.

'Blue Sapphire' (tall, bearded)   Registered by B. Schreiner 1953. Parents: 'Snow Flurry' × 'Chivalry'. Light silvery-blue self; beard white. Height 102cm. Early season.

'Derwentwater' (tall, bearded)   Registered by H. J. Randall 1953. Parents: 'Helen McGregor' × 'Cahokia'. Delicate-pale-blue self; beard creamy white. Height 86cm. Mid-season.

'Fantasy Fair' (tall, bearded)   Registered by J. Nelson 1977. Parents: ('Flame and Sand' × 'Pink Taffeta') × 'Buffy'. Ruffled and heavily laced smoky-pink-orchid, blended a touch rosy-tan on the haft; beard red. Height 90cm. Mid-season.

'Gilston Gwyneth' (tall, bearded)   Registered by H. Fletcher 1963. Parents: 'Pegasus' × ('Cascadian' × 'Keene Valley'). Standards mid-blue, ruffled; falls lighter blue. Height 86cm. Mid-season.

'Jane Phillips' (tall, bearded)   Registered by N. Graves 1946. Parents: 'Helen McGregor' × ('Pale Moonlight' × 'Great Lakes'). Delicate-blue self; beard white. Height 102cm. Mid-season.

'Lady Ilse' (tall, bearded)   Registered by K. Smith 1950. Parents: 'Jane Phillips' × 'Keene Valley'. Soft-blue-violet self with slight yellowish haft markings; beard creamy white. Height 104cm. Late mid-season.

'Lovely Letty' (tall, bearded)   Registered by D. Hall 1960. Parents unknown. Pale-violet-blue self with a tangerine beard. Height 80cm. Mid-season.

'Mary Frances' (tall, bearded)   Registered by L. Gaulter 1971. Parents: 'Town and Country' × ('Marie Phillips' × 'Sterling Silver'). Ruffled light-blue-orchid self; beard white with a hint of yellow. Height 98cm. Mid-season.

'Out Yonder' (tall, bearded)   Registered by G. Wickersham 1969. Parents unknown. Standards very pale blue with a touch of darker veining; falls violet-indigo; beard white or a touch yellowish. Height 90cm. Mid-season.

'Passport' (intermediate, bearded)   Registered by J. Ghio 1970. Parents: unknown × 'Oracle'. Lightly ruffled pale blue-purple white self with a darker area with dark-purplish-blue veins on

the falls; beard white. Height 60cm. Early season.

'San Leandro' (tall, bearded)   Registered by L. Gaulter 1968. Parents: [(('Fuchsia' × 'Party Dress'] × ['Frost and Flame' × sibling]) × ('Arctic Flame' × sibling)] × 'Rippling Waters'. Light-purple self; beard tangerine. Height 90cm. Mid-season.

'Valimar' (tall, bearded)   Registered by J. R. Hamblen 1956. Parents: ('Helen McGregor' × 'Radiation') × 'Palomino'. Ruffled, standards pinky violet; falls the same with orange haft markings; beard orange-red. Height 90cm. Mid- to late season.

'Blue Rhythm'

'Jane Phillips'

'Blue Sapphire'

'Actress'

'Gilston Gwyneth'

'Babbling Brook'

'Arcady'

Part of the classic iris collection at Myddelton House, Middlesex

'**Annabel Jane**' (tall, bearded)   Registered by B. Dodsworth 1973. Parents: 'Sterling Silver' × 'Champagne Music'. Standards pale lilac; falls medium lilac; beard white with yellow tips. Height 120cm. Mid-season.

'**Black Swan**' (tall, bearded)   Registered by Fay 1960. Parents: 'Sable Night' × 53-68. Reddish-black self; beard brown. Height 90cm. Mid-season.

'**Brummitt's Mauve**' (tall, bearded) Registration not found but presumed to be L. Brummitt. Parents not known. Violet-brown self, the edges of the falls brown and the centre vibrant violet, orangy markings on the haft; beard golden yellow. Height 97cm. Late season.

'**Deep Pacific**' (tall, bearded)   Registered by E. Burger 1975. Parents: 'Cup Race' × 'Royal Touch'. Navy-blue self with a medium-blue beard. Height 70cm. Mid- to late season.

'**Los Angeles**' (tall, bearded)   There is some confusion about this name. It is sometimes spelt 'Los Angelus'; also, as far as I can tell, it was registered by either W. J. Rudill 1926 or by S. B. Mitchell in 1927; these two registrations make it most confusing. My specimens have rich-violet-blue self, with browny-purple haft markings; beard white tipped yellow. Height 80cm. Mid-season.

'**Magic Man**' (tall, bearded)   Registered by B. Blyth 1979. Parents: [([('Fanfare Orchid' × ('Arctic Flame' × 'Morning Breeze')] × 'Latin Tempo')] × 'Cabaret Royale'. Standards light blue, with a deeper infusion of colour around the midrib; falls velvety purple with 3mm band of light blue around the edges; beard tangerine. Height 98cm. Mid- to late season.

'**Night Raider**' (tall, bearded)   Registered by C. Burrell 1976. Parents: ('Licorice Stick' × 'Rawlins' 68-17) × [('Dark Fury' × ('Black Hills' × 'Velvet Dusk')]. Velvety blue-black self, including the beard. Height 84cm. Early to mid-season.

'**Ninevah**' (tall, bearded)   Registered by Keppel 1965. Parents: 'Bang' × 'Capitola'. Standards purplish, flushed brown at base; falls red-violet washed warm brown; beard dark brown. Height 76cm. Early season.

'**Raspberry Ripples**' (tall, bearded) Introduced by O. D. Niswonger 1967. Parents: ('Pink Fulfilment' × 'Orchid Jewel') × 'Rippling Waters'. Frilly edged deep-rose-purple self with browny-orange beard. Height 90cm. Mid-season.

'**Royal Ruffles**' (tall, bearded)   Registered by E. Purviance 1962. Parents: 'Black Forest' × 'Chivalry'. Marine-blue self with a blue beard. Height 74cm. Early to mid-season.

'**Royal Touch**' (tall, bearded)   Registered by Schreiner's 1966. Parents: [J219-A 'Blue Ensign' × ('The Admiral' × 'Great Lakes')] × 'Randolph' × ['Pierre Menard' × ('Distance' × 'Sylvia Murray')]. Dark-marine, blue-violet self; beard navy-blue. Height 90cm. Late season.

'**Sable**' (tall, bearded)   Registered by P. H. Cook 1938. Parents: [{[('Innocenza' × 'Blue Boy') × 'Cinnabar'] × ['Cinnabar' × ('Innocenza' × 'Blue Boy')]} × 'Cinnabar'] × ('Seminole' × 'Cinnabar'). Standards dark purple-blue; falls darker velvety violet; beard orange and white. Height 84cm. Mid-season.

'**Sign of Leo**' (tall, bearded)   Registered by L. Zurbrigg 1976. Parents: 'Jet Black' × 'Lovely Again'. Standards violet with some red influence; falls violet with red influence and blackish overlay; beard bronze. Height 90cm. Early season, remontant in late summer.

Iris 'Sign of Leo'

Iris 'Night Raider'

Iris 'Royal Touch'

Iris 'Magic Man'

'Ninevah'

'Raspberry Ripples'

'Los Angeles'

'Deep Pacific'

'Brummitt's Mauve'

'Royal Ruffles'

Specimens from Claire Austin, 12 June. ⅓ life size

Iris 'Black Swan'

Iris 'Sable'

Iris 'Annabel Jane'

Iris fields at Claire Austin, Abrighton

Iris 'Joyce Terry'

Iris 'Star Shine'

Iris 'Golden Encore'

Iris 'Debby Rairdon'

Iris 'Lime Crystal'

Iris 'Grace Abounding'

'Aunt Martha' (border, bearded)   Registered by J. Allen 1970. Parents: ('Snow Goddess' × 'Limelight') × 'Yellow Dresden'. Heavily laced light-yellow self with a white area around the tip of the light-yellow beard. Height 60cm. Mid-season.

'Debby Rairdon' (tall, bearded)   Registered Kuntz 1964. Parents not recorded. Standards subdued yellow with white on reverse side; falls pearly white with white on reverse, side edges yellowish; beard golden. Height 90cm. Mid- to late season.

'Frost and Flame' (tall, bearded)   Registered by D. Hall 1956. Parents unknown. White self with a touch of purple, and yellow markings on the haft; beard red. Height 90cm. Early season.

'Gala Crown' (tall, bearded)   Registered by P. E. Corey 1958. Parents: (('Bureau' × seedling) × 'Anthea') × 'Pink Tea'. Pale melon colour blended with a touch of pink; beard orange. Height 90cm. Mid-season.

'Gold Alps' (tall, bearded)   Registered by L. Brummitt 1952. Parents: 'Admiration' × seedling. Standards creamy white with pale-yellow veining; falls deepish golden yellow, with darker veins at the haft; beard golden yellow. Height 90cm. Mid-season.

'Golden Encore' (tall, bearded, remontant) Registered by F. Jones 1972. Parents: (('Happy Birthday' × 'Fall Primrose') × 'Fall Primrose') × 'Renaissance'. Vivid-yellow self with a small white blaze on the falls; beard bright gold. Height 90cm. Early, and again in late summer.

Iris 'Spirit of Memphis'

Iris 'Lemon Brocade'

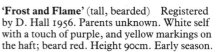

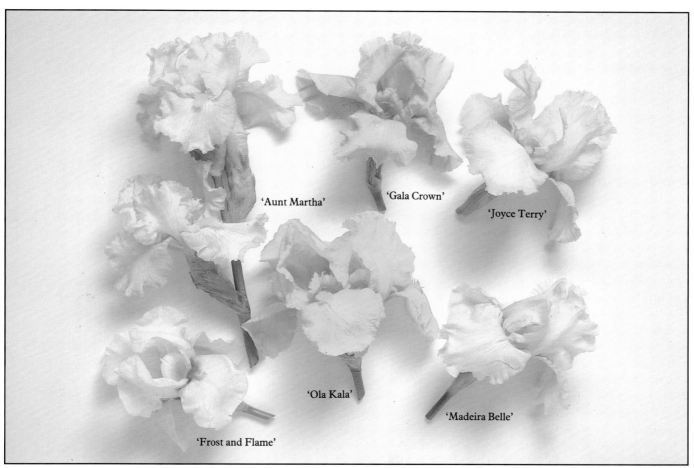

'Aunt Martha'   'Gala Crown'   'Joyce Terry'

'Frost and Flame'   'Ola Kala'   'Madeira Belle'

Specimens from Claire Austin, 15 June. ⅓ life size

Iris 'Pale Primrose'

Iris 'Gold Alps'

'Grace Abounding' (tall, bearded) Pauline M. McCormick on behalf of H. Fothergill 1976. ('Cream Crest' × sibling of 'Gilded Minaret') × sibling. Lemon-yellow self, lightly ruffled; cinnamon hafts; brilliant-yellow beard. Height 98cm. Mid-season.

'Joyce Terry' (tall, bearded) T. Muhlestein 1974. 'Charmaine' × 'Launching Pad'. Lightly ruffled, standards yellow, paler in the centre; falls white with a yellow edge and deeper yellow haft markings; beard deeper yellow. Height 98cm. Mid- to late season.

'Lemon Brocade' (tall, bearded) N. Rudolph 1973. 'Cream Taffeta' × 67-54. Ruffled lemon-yellow self with whitish-green patches on the falls; beard white tipped yellow-orange. Height 86cm. Mid-season.

'Lime Crystal' (tall, bearded) B. Blyth 1975. Parents: 'Apropos' × 'Twist and Shout'. Standards lime-yellow; falls a shade darker; beard yellow. Height 86cm. Mid- to late season.

'Madeira Belle' (tall, bearded) Registration not found. Ruffled, white self, standards tinged with a hint of violet. Height 80cm. Late season.

'Ola Kala' (tall, bearded) Registered by J. N. Sass 1942. Parents: ('Prairie Sunset' × unknown) × ('Golden Age' × unknown). Rich deep-yellow self; beard deep yellow. Height 86cm. Late season.

'Pale Primrose' (tall, bearded) N. Whiting 1946. 'Happy Days' × 'Midwest Gem'. Pale yellow self with a small white patch on the falls and darker haft markings; beard golden yellow. Height 76cm. Late season.

'Spirit of Memphis' (tall, bearded, remontant) Registered by L. Zurbrigg 1976. Parents: ('Miss Illini' × 'Grand Baroque') × 'Halloween Party'. Medium-yellow self, ruffled and heavily laced; beard yellow. Height 90cm. Mid-season, and again in late summer.

'Star Shine' (tall, bearded) Registered by N. Wills 1947. Parents: ('Hermitage' × 'Hernani') × 'Song of Gold'. Standards pale yellow; falls white with yellow edges and veining; beard yellow. Height 90cm. Mid- to late season.

'Jungle Shadows'

'Autumn Leaves'

'Little Sheba'

'Flareup'

'Strawberry Sundae'

'Carnaby'

'Olympic Torch'

'Firecracker'

'Etched Apricot'

Specimens from Claire Austin, 12 June. ⅓ life size

'Autumn Leaves' (tall, bearded) Registered by K. Keppel 1972. Parents: 'Vaudeville' × 'Radiant Apogee'. Standards blended pale brown; falls yellowish brown, strongly marked with red purple veining; beard orange-yellow. Height 86cm. Mid-season.

'Carnaby' (tall, bearded) Registered by Schreiner's 1973. Parents: 'Wine and Roses' × Y 1307-A: (R 118–BX 'Rippling Waters'). Standards ruffled light wine-pink; falls deep rose-pink in the centre, edges light wine-pink; beard orange. Height 90cm. Mid- to late season.

'Chartreuse Ruffles' (tall, bearded) Registered by N. Rudolph 1975. Parents: (seedling × Blocher 233) × 'Louise Watts'. Ruffled, standards pale lilac-pink with a deeper flush, chartreuse edge; falls greenish white with wide chartreuse edge; beard tipped yellow. Height 86cm. Mid-season.

'Deputé Nomblot' (tall, bearded) Registered by Cayeaux et Le Clerc 1929. Parents not recorded. Standards pink; falls pink, darker veining over a lighter patch on the haft; beard golden yellow. Height 74cm. Late season.

'Etched Apricot' (tall, bearded) J. Gibson 1967. 'Henna Stitches' × 'Wild Ginger'. Ruffled, standards brownish apricot; falls white ground etched apricot with a hint of purple; beard golden. Height 76cm. Mid-season.

'Firecracker' (tall, bearded) Hall 1942. ('Morning Splendour' × 'Legend') × ('Dauntless' × 'Rameses'). Standards red-brown over a yellow ground; falls yellow with red-brown veining and etching, around the edge; beard deep golden. Height 74cm. Early to mid-season.

'Flareup' (tall, bearded) J. Ghio 1977. 'Coffee House' sib × (('Ponderosa' × 'Travel On') × 'Ponderosa'). Ruffled, standards yellowy brown; falls same colour with yellow haft markings; beard yellowy brown. Height 97cm. Mid-season.

'Jungle Shadows' (intermediate, bearded) E. Sass and H. Graham 1959. 'Black Delight' × seedling 54-95. Rich blended golden-brown self with a violet patch on the falls; beard golden orange. Height 66cm. Mid-season.

'Lady River' (tall, bearded) Kelway 1966. 'Melody Fair' × 'Party Ruffles'. Apricot-pink self, ruffled with bronzy-violet veining on the haft; beard orangy-red. Height 75cm. Mid-season.

'Little Sheba' (tall, bearded) T. M. Abell. 'Saffron Charm' × 'Arabi Pasha'. Small-flowered, pale-oyster self with greenish yellowish veining; beard pale with touches of cobalt violet. Height 74cm. Mid-season.

'Olympic Torch' (tall, bearded) R. Schreiner 1956. 'Inca Chief' × (Schr. 49–46 × 'Watchfire'). Light golden-bronze self; beard bronze-yellow. Height 97cm. Mid-season.

'Sabre Dance' (tall, bearded) Registered by O. Brown 1970. Parents: ('Grandiflora' × (pink seedling × 'Gypsy Lullaby' sibling)) × 'Barcelona' sibling. Standards touched light blue blending to flesh at outer edges; falls champagne-brushed lavender-rose deep on shoulders, with a copper lustre overall; beard red. Height 97cm. Mid-season.

'Strawberry Sundae' (tall, bearded)

Iris 'Deputé Nomblot' at Myddelton House, Middlesex

Iris 'Sabre Dance'

Iris 'Chartreuse Ruffles'

Iris 'Witch of Endor'

Iris 'Lady River'

Registered by H. Schmelzer 1977. Parents: ('Harem Silk' × 'Wine and Roses') × 'Wine and Roses'. Standards creamy ruffled; falls strawberry–wine colour, edge creamy; beard red. Height 80cm. Mid-season.

'Wild Ginger' (tall, bearded) Registered by J. Gibson 1960. Parents: 'Tohdah' × 'Floradora Flounce'. Plicata, standards burnt-umber-shaded orchid; falls white with golden-brown stitching-shaded-orchid at the edges. Height 90cm. Early to mid-season.

'Witch of Endor' (tall, bearded, remontant) B. Miller 1977. 'Rainbow Promised' × 'Cayenne Capers'. Black-crimson self with a white area with dark-crimson veining on the hafts; beard golden, ruffled. Height 97cm. Early to mid-season, and again in late summer.

Iris 'Wild Ginger'

Bearded irises in the garden at Eccleston Square, London

Iris 'Stepping Out'

Iris 'Lovely Again'

'Flaming Sword' or **'Flammenschwert'** (tall, bearded)   Registered by Goos and Koenemann 1920. Parents not recorded. Standards yellow; falls dark purple-brown with very strong white veining on the hafts; beard yellow. Height 76cm. Mid-season.

'Lovely Again' (tall, bearded, remontant) Registered by R. G. Smith 1963. Parents not recorded. Lavender self with a yellow beard. Height 76cm. Mid-season, and again in late summer.

'Mary Vernon' (tall, bearded)   Registered by N. McKee 1941. Parents: (No. 3814 × 'Janet Butler') × 'Chosen'. Standards good yellow; falls red-brown with creamy yellow edge and haft markings; beard yellow. Height 74cm. Mid-season.

'Melbreak' (tall, bearded)   Registered by H. J. Randall 1957. Parents: ('Cherie' × 'Angela Borgia') × 'Mary Randall'. Ruffled; standards violet pink with deeper veining and a lighter orange patch at the haft; beard tangerine. Height 97cm. Mid- to late season.

'Needlecraft' (tall, bearded)   Registered by L. Zurbrigg 1976. Parents: ('Ribbon Round' × R. G. Smith E5AR) × 'Cross Stitch'. White ground plicata. Height 86cm. Mid-season.

'Sea Venture' (tall, bearded)   Registered by Bennett Jones 1971. Parents: 'Avis' × 'Eternal Love'. Ruffled; standards pale-blue-flushed, deep marine-blue at the base; falls pale blue; beard yellow. Height 86cm. Mid-season.

'Stepping Out' (tall, bearded)   Registered by Schreiner's 1964. Parents not known. Plicata, with large white areas with sharply patterned edges of blue-black-violet. Height 97cm. Mid- to late season.

'Sultry Sky' (border, bearded)   Registered by L. W. Neel 1952. Parents: 'Fair Elaine' × 'Wabash'. Standards pinky cream, yellowing at the base; falls straw-coloured ground with purple-brown centre; beard yellow. Height 97cm. Mid-season.

'Wabash' (tall, bearded)   Registered by E. B. Williamson 1936. Parents: 'Dorothy Dietz' × 'Cantabile'. Bicolour, standards white; falls velvety purple with white veining at the haft; beard bright yellow. Height 86cm. Mid-season.

'Whoop 'em Up' (border, bearded) Registered by D. Brady 1973. Parents: ('Bang' × 'Plunder') × 'Extravaganza'. Standards golden yellow; falls maroon with golden yellow on reverse side extending to the top as an all-round edge; beard yellow. Height 68cm. Mid-season.

Iris 'Needlecraft'

Iris 'Whoop 'em Up'

Iris 'Flaming Sword'

Iris 'Mary Vernon'

Iris 'Sultry Sky'

Iris 'Wabash'

Iris 'Melbreak'

Iris 'Sea Venture'

'Tyrian Robe'

'Royal Trumpeter'

'Rose Violet'

'Foggy Dew'

'My Smoky'

'Royal Oak'

'Gracchus'

'Superstition'

'Frontier Marshall'

'Ultrapoise'

Specimens collected, 4 June. ⅓ life size

Iris 'Gracchus'

Iris 'Blue Duchess'

'Blue Duchess' syn. 'Crystal Blue' (tall, bearded)   Registered by Kelway & Son 1966. Parents: 'Jane Phillips' × 'Blue Cameo'. Light-blue self. Height 97cm.

'Blue-Eyed Brunette' (tall, bearded) Registered by C. C. Hall. Parents: 'Queechee' × 'Carnton'. Standards cigar-brown; falls brown with a blue spot. Height 90cm.

'Dancer's Veil' (tall, bearded)   Registered by P. Hutchinson 1959. Parents: (plicata seedling × 'Dancing Waters') × 'Rosy Veil'. White ground plicata etched blue-purple. Height 90cm. Mid- to late season.

'Dovedale' (tall, bearded)   Registered 1980 by B. L. C. Dodsworth. Parents: 'Raspberry Ripples' × 'San Leandro'. Mid pinkish-lilac self. Height 82cm. Late season.

'Dusky Dancer' (tall, bearded)   Registered by Watt Foulger in 1952 and released by W. Luihn in 1966. Parents: 'Dark Fury' × 'Black Swan'. Very dark violet-black self, ruffled; beard dark-blackish. Height 90cm. Mid- to late season.

'Foggy Dew' (tall, bearded)   Registered by Keppel 1968. Parents: 'Siva Siva' × 'Diplomacy'. Plicata, standards pastel blend of greyish cream and lavender; falls white ground with soft-violet border with darker markings; beard white, tipped yellow. Height 97cm. Mid-season.

'Frontier Marshall' (tall, bearded)   Registered by Schreiner's 1964. Parents: ('Trim' × 'Tall Chief') × 'Gypsy Jewels'. Uniform crimson lake, red self; beard with a bronzy cast. Height 90cm. Early to mid-season.

'Gracchus' (tall, bearded)   Introduced by T. S. Ware 1884. Parents unknown: probably a hybrid of *I. variegata*. Standards light yellow; falls strongly veined reddish. Height 74cm.

'My Honeycomb' (tall, bearded)   Registered by J. M. Gibson 1958. Parents: seedling of 'Taholah'. Standards light brown; falls brown with rich brown veining, white patch on centre; beard yellow. Height 89cm. Mid-season.

'My Smoky' (tall, bearded)   Registered by Kelway & Son 1956. Parent: 'Magic Carpet' seedling. Plicata, white with faint yellowish touches; falls edged rose-brown. Height 87cm. Mid-season.

'Rose Violet' (tall, bearded)   Introduced by J. H. Kirkland 1939. Parents not recorded. Red self. Mid-season.

'Royal Oak' (tall, bearded)   Registered by C. C. Hall 1962. Parents: 'Queechee' × 'Carnton'. Standards cigar brown; falls bluish-mauve, edge brown. Height 76cm. Mid-season.

'Royal Trumpeter' (tall, bearded)   Registered by C. Reynolds 1969. Parents: ((59-27('Savage') × Ib-Mac) × 'Red Slippers')) × L.P. 65-03 ('Barbizon' × 'Fire Ruby'). Red self; beard brown-red. Height 74cm. Late season.

'Superstition' (tall, bearded)   Registered by Schreiner's 1977. Parents: (v435-1 × 1560-15) × 'Navy Strut'. Ebony-hued self; beard blue-black. Height 90cm. Mid-season.

Iris 'Dovedale'

Iris 'Blue-Eyed Brunette'

Iris 'Dancer's Veil'

Iris 'Dusky Dancer'

Iris 'My Honeycomb'

'Tyrian Robe' (tall, bearded)   Registered by C. C. Hall 1968. Parents: 'Redbourne' × seedling V178. Violet-purple self. Height 90cm. Mid-season.

'Ultrapoise' (tall, bearded, plicata)   Registered by Noyd 1961. Parents: ([(C. 'Honeyflow' × 'Tobacco Road') × 'Cliffdell'] × [('Salmon Shell' × Hall 44-09) × 'Pink Formal']) × 'Garden Gold'. Straw-yellow self with a pink flush in the standards; beard tangerine. Height 86cm. Mid-season.

Part of the classic iris collection at Myddelton House, Middlesex

Iris 'Emerald Fountain'

Iris 'I Do'

Iris 'Dream Lover'

'Bewick Swan' (tall, bearded)   Registered by B. L. C. Dodsworth 1980. Parents: 'Crystal Blaze' × 'Rippling Waters'. White self, yellow hafts; red beard. Height 102cm. Mid-season.

'Brother Carl' (tall, bearded, remontant) Introduced by L. A. Zurbrigg 1983. Parents: 'Sister Helen' × 'I Do'. White self with delicate darker veining on the falls; beard white with yellow tip. Height 76cm. Mid-season.

'Christmas Angel' (tall, bearded)   Registered by R. De Forest 1959. Parents: 'Frances Kent' × 'Paradise Pink'. White self with bright-gold haft. Height 97cm. Mid-season.

'Cliffs of Dover' (tall, bearded)   Registered by O. W. Fay 1952. Parents: 'New Snow' × 'Cahokia'. Pure-white self; beard yellow. Height 90cm. Mid-season.

'Cup Race' (tall, bearded)   Registered by Buttrick 1962. Parents: ('Bluebird Blue' ×

'South Pacific') × 'Concord Town'. White self, ruffled, with mauve and yellowish tints. Height 90cm. Mid- to late season.

'Dream Lover' (tall, bearded)   Registered by E. Tams 1970. Parents: 'Miss Indiana' × ('Melodrama' × 'Rippling Waters'). Ruffled. Standards blue-white; falls dark bluish purple; beard blue. Height 91-97cm. Mid- to late season.

'Emerald Fountain' (tall, bearded)   Registered by D. Brown 1960. Parents: ['Blue Sapphire' × ('Hit Parade' × 'Pink Formal')] × ('Mary Randall' × 'Limelight'). Standards pale uranium-greenish with a blue infusion, ruffled; falls flax-blue, edges brushed uranium-green; beard yellow. Height 97cm. Mid- to late season.

'English Cottage' (tall, bearded, remontant) Registered by L. Zurbrigg 1976. Parents: [('Crinkled Ivory' × 'Autumn Sensation') × 'Grand Baroque'] × 'Cross Stitch'. Standards

white with some very pale plicating of violet; falls white with light-violet plicata markings at haft only; beard near white. Height 87cm. Early season, and again in late summer.

'Gudrun' (tall, bearded)   Registered by Mrs W. R. Dykes 1930. Parents not known. White self with yellow veining on the haft; beard orange-yellow. Height 100cm. Mid-season.

'I Do' (tall, bearded, remontant)   Registered by L. Zurbrigg 1973. Parents: 'Grand Baroque' × 'Amy'. Standards white with a slight cast of violet and greenish yellow, green at the midrib; falls white, with some green texture veining in the centre; beard white-tipped, pale yellow, ruffled. Height 81cm. Early to mid-season, and again in late summer.

'Vanity' (tall, bearded)   Registered by B. Y. Morrison 1928. Parents not recorded. Blended with pale-pink tones; falls lighter; beard red. Height 94cm. Mid-season.

Iris 'Gudrun'

Iris 'Christmas Angel'

Iris 'Cliffs of Dover'

Iris 'English Cottage'

Iris 'Cup Race'

Iris 'Brother Carl'

Iris 'Vanity'

Iris 'Bewick Swan'

'Banbury Welcome'

'Pacific Moon'

'Banbury Beauty'

'Banbury Fair'

'Banbury Gem'

'Phillida'

'Lavender Royal'

'Banbury Velvet'

Irises from Wisley, 21 May. ½ life size

Iris douglasiana Herbert (s. *Californicae*)
Native of the Pacific coast, from S California to Oregon, growing on open, grassy slopes, flowering in March–May. Plant forming loose clumps. Leaves evergreen, dark green, ribbed, to 2cm wide. Stems to 80cm tall, usually with 1–4 side branches, with 1–3 leaves. Flower colour varying from pale cream to bluish or deep reddish-purple. Flowers with tube 1.5–2.8cm long; falls oblanceolate to obovate, 5–8.7cm long; standard oblanceolate 4–7cm long, to 1.8cm wide. Style 1–2cm long, coarsely toothed. Capsule sharply triangular in section. This is the tallest of the Pacific coast irises and the commonest species along the California coast; it is easily grown in rather moist, peaty and sandy soil. Hardy to −15°C perhaps.

Iris innominata Henderson (s. *Californicae*)
Native of NW California (in del Monte Co.) and in SW Oregon, growing on sunny or partially shaded hillsides, in mixed forest, on the inner side of the coast ranges, flowering in May–June. Plant forming loose clumps. Leaves dark-shiny-green, paler beneath, 2–4mm wide. Stems to 20cm tall, with 2–4 leaves. Bracts opposite, subequal, with scarious margin enclosing 2 flowers. Flower colour variable, from yellow to pale bluish or deep purple. Flowers with tube 1.5–3cm long; falls 5–8.5cm long; standards 4.5–7cm long, oblanceolate; style crests 0.9–1.4cm long, squarish, toothed. This and many other species are variable in colour, and hybrids are common in the wild, so the species of these Pacific Coast irises are difficult to name with confidence. They are all, however, easily grown in well-drained, preferably acid, sandy soil in sun or light shade.

Iris purdyi Eastw. (s. *Californicae*)   Native of NW California, growing in Redwood forest and mixed forest along the coast ranges, in open woods and on roadside banks, flowering in May–June. Plant forming loose clumps. Leaves evergreen, dark green above, greyish beneath, to 8mm wide. Stems to 35cm tall, unbranched, with many short overlapping leaves. Bracts opposite, inflated, enclosing 2 flowers. Flower colour from creamy yellow to pale bluish, variously veined. Flowers with tube 2.8.–4.8cm long; falls 5.5–8.4cm long, oblanceolate; standards 5–7cm × 0.9–2cm; style crests 0.9–2.1cm long, narrowly ovate. Easily grown in well-drained and rather dry sandy soil in partial shade.

Iris tenuissima Dykes (s. *Californicae*)   Native of N California from Butte to Siskiyou and Humboldt counties, growing in clearings in dry woods of oak, pine or mixed evergreens, often on roadside banks, flowering in April–June. Plant with a slender rhizome; leaves *c*.6mm wide, often reddish at the base, to 40cm long. Stems usually 2-flowered, around 20cm. Flowers usually pale cream, with purplish or brownish veins, but less veined in var. *purdyiformis* R. C. Foster which is probably the plant shown here. Falls 4.7–7.5cm, 1.1–1.8cm wide, narrowly ovate. Standards 4.4–6.4cm long, 0.6–1.4cm wide. Perianth tube slender below, dilated above. Style crests 1.1–2.3cm long, recurved. For well-drained soil in partial shade, dry in summer. Hardy to −15°C, perhaps less.

Pacific Coast Irises   This group is derived from hybrids of the *Californicae* irises and all are

Iris tenuissima near Mount Shasta, California

Iris 'Restless Native'

Irises near Mount Shasta, California

Iris purdyi

Iris 'Purple Dream'

Iris 'Banbury Beauty'

rather similar in everything except flower colour, which varies from deep purple and yellow to cream, brown, pink and white. They form spreading clumps, with usually evergreen leaves up to *c.*20cm and large numbers of flowers on stems 30–50cm high. They prefer well-drained, acid, fertile sandy soil and a warm, sheltered position in sun or partial shade. Most are hardy to around −15°C and so require protection from hard winter frosts in continental climates.

'Banbury Beauty' (Pacific Coast) Registered by M. Brummitt in 1960. Parents: *douglasiana* 'Amaguita' × (*innominata* × *douglasiana* seedling). Light lavender with a purple zone on the falls. Height 53cm.

'Banbury Fair' (Pacific Coast) Raised by M. Brummitt in 1967.

'Banbury Gem' (Pacific Coast) Raised by M. Brummitt in 1974.

'Banbury Velvet' (Pacific Coast) Registered by M. Brummitt in 1969. Parents: seedling × seedling. Standards violet; falls deep violet, velvety. Height 30cm. Mid-season.

'Banbury Welcome' (Pacific Coast) Registered by M. Brummitt in 1964. Parents: *douglasiana* 'Amaguita' × 'Lenz'. Deep raspberry, with gold and buff at the throat. Height 46cm.

'Lavender Royal' (Pacific Coast) Registered by M. Brummitt in 1982.

'Pacific Moon' (Pacific Coast) Registered by B. Hager in 1973. Parents: 'Ojai' × 'Grubstake'. Standards cream with pale-lavender veining, falls cream with lavender veining. Height 38cm. Early season.

'Phillida' (Pacific Coast) Raised by N. Scopes in 1985.

'Purple Dream' (Pacific Coast) Raised by N. Scopes in 1983.

'Restless Native' (Pacific Coast) This appears to be a perpetual-flowering cultivar, photographed here in the Santa Barbara Botanic Garden in February, long before the normal hybrids begin to flower.

Iris innominata (yellow form)

Iris douglasiana at Salt Point, California

Iris innominata (pale blue form)

Iris 'Lavender Royal'

IRIS

Iris kerneriana (B. Mathew 9001) at Kew

Iris masia near Gaziantep, SE Turkey

Iris masia

mid-winter, a deceitful invitation to birds which may think they are edible, like holly. A white-seeded form, which must be very beautiful, is in cultivation, but is very rare; a yellow-seeded form is also rumoured to exist and there is a form with white-striped leaves. The evergreen leaves are not very hardy, being killed by cold winds around −15°C, even in S England in severe winters.

Iris halophila Pallas (s. *Spuriae*) syn. *I. spuria* subsp. *halophila* (Pall.) Mathew & Wendelbo Native of S Romania and the E Ukraine to Siberia and NW China and south to the N Caucasus, growing in wet places in the steppes and by rivers often in saline soils, flowering in June. Stems 40–90cm. Leaves 7–12mm wide. Flowers 6–7cm across, pale to deep yellow; probably one of the hardiest of the spurias, and easily grown in moist heavy soil in full sun. Hardy to −25°C.

Iris kerneriana Aschers. & Sint. ex Baker (s. *Spuriae*)   Native of N Turkey from Bolu east to Erzurum and south to Kaz Dağ and Ankara, growing in dry, grassy turf, oak scrub and open pine forest at 300–2300m, flowering in May–July. Stems 20–45cm, rarely to 50cm. Leaves 2–4mm wide, rarely to 1cm. Flower 7–10cm across. Bracts with wide transparent margins, scarious after anthesis. Easily grown in a sunny position, in good but well-drained soil. This species has often been confused with *I. halophila* Pallas (q.v.), which has wider leaves 7–12mm wide, and bracts which do not become scarious after anthesis. At flowering the tube of *I. kerneriana* extends at least 2cm beyond the spathe, but the spathe extends almost to the base of the segments in *I. halophila*.

Iris masia Stapf ex Foster syn. *I. grant-duffii* Baker subsp. *masia* (Stapf.) Dyke (s. *Syriacae*) Native of SE Turkey from Gaziantep to Diyabakir, and of N Syria and Iraq, growing in fields and on rocky basalt steppe, especially on Mount Masia (today Karaça Da.), at up to 1050m, flowering in April–May. Plant tufted with sharp almost spiny fibres around the rhizome. Stems to 35–70cm. Leaves 3–6mm across, tough. Flowers always purplish. *I. grant-duffii*, with which this species has sometimes been confused, has greenish-yellow flowers and is found near the Mediterranean coast in Israel and Syria, in wet or marshy ground. Hardy to −15°C perhaps.

Iris milesii Foster (s. *Lophiris* evansia) Native of the Himalayas from Kashmir to Uttar Pradesh (west of Nepal), growing in conifer forests at 1600–2700m, flowering in June. Stems branched, 30–100cm. Rhizome short for the 'evansia' section, green. Leaves pale green, 30–60cm long, 4–7cm wide, with sterile fans produced in summer. Flowers 6–8cm across. Beautiful but rarely seen, though apparently not difficult in a sunny border in sandy, peaty soil. Hardy to −15°C, perhaps less for short periods.

Iris sintenisii Janka (s. *Spuriae*)   Native of SE Europe, from S Italy and Yugoslavia to Greece and NW Turkey, east to Kutahya, growing in grassy places and scrub, at up to 1350m in Turkey, flowering in June–July. Stems 8–25cm. Leaves evergreen, dark green, tough, 1–5mm across and up to 50cm long. Flowers 5–6cm across, not scented. Easily grown in semi-shade, but can disappear if neglected. Hardy to −15°C. Subsp. *bradzae* (Prodan) D. A. Webb & Chater, grows in wet, saline soils in N and E Romania and Moldavia; it has narrow 1.5–3.5mm wide leaves and an inflated spathe.

Iris foetidissima L. (s. *Foetidissimae*) Gladdon or Roast Beef Plant   Native from S England to the Azores to Spain, Portugal and North Africa and the Canaries, east to Italy and Sicily, growing in open woods, scrub and sunny hedge banks, especially on chalk and limestone, flowering in May–July. Stems 30–90cm. Leaves evergreen, shining, pungent. Flowers normally purplish, but yellow forms are frequent, especially in cultivation. The main garden value of the Gladdon is in its beautiful orange-red seeds which remain attached in the open pods in

Iris foetidissima (yellowish form)

Iris milesii at Kew

Iris foetidissima seeds in winter

Iris sintenisii near Bolu, NW Turkey

Iris halophila on the steppes near Stavropol, S Russia

Iris setosa

Iris setosa alba

Iris chrysographes
(text p. 221)

*Iris
chrysographes*
'Black Knight'

Iris pseudacorus
(pale form)

Iris graminea

Iris versicolor

Specimens from Beth Chatto, Unusual Plants, 9 June. ½ life size

IRIS

Iris chrysographes Dykes (s. *Sibericae*) See p.221.

Iris graminea L. var. *pseudocyperus* (Schur) Beck (s. *Spuriae*) Native of S Europe, from France and NE Spain east to Poland, Bulgaria and the N Caucasus, growing in grassy places in scrub and in open woods, flowering in May–June. Var. *pseudocyperus* is a larger plant with unscented flowers said to be from E Europe, but Brian Mathew records a similar variety from Spain. Stems 20–40cm; leaves 35–100cm long, to 1.5cm wide. Flower of the normal variety said to smell like plums, 7–8cm across; easily grown in leafy soil in partial shade. A larger, softer-leaved plant than *I. sintenisii* (p.217). Hardy to −20°C

Iris hexagona Walt. (s. *Hexagonae*) Native of South Carolina and Georgia to Florida and Texas, growing in swamps, flowering in March–May. Stems 30–90cm. Leaves 1.2–3cm wide, bright green; flowers to 10–12cm across, purplish with a yellow patch on the falls. Easily grown in wet soil; shown here by a small stream on the rock garden at Kew. Hardy to −15°C perhaps.

Iris pseudacorus (pale form) See p.229.

Iris setosa Pall. ex Link (s. *Tripetalae*) Native from Newfoundland to Ontario and Maine, then from Alaska west to E Siberia, NE China and Japan, in Hokkaido and Honshu, growing in wet peaty meadows, sometimes in brackish marshes in N Japan, by rivers and in open woods, flowering in June–August. Many varieties have been described, but all can be recognized by the very small, bristle-like standards. A beautiful white *alba* is frequent in cultivation. One of the tallest is subsp. *hondoensis* Honda, up to 75cm, with purple flowers. Stems normally 15–90cm; leaves 1–2.5cm wide. Flowers 6–9cm across. Capsule inflated, rounded at the apex. Easily grown in moist places by water or in a border in rich peaty soil. In my experience acid soil is not essential for the form from N Hokkaido. Hardy to −25°C.

Iris hookeri Penny syn. *I. setosa* Pall. ex Link subsp. *canadensis* (Foster) Hulten Native of NE America, from Newfoundland and Labrador, to Quebec, Ontario and Maine, growing in grassy and rocky places on the sea coast, flowering in June–August. Stem usually short, but up to 60cm, unbranched, with 1–2 flowers. Petals bluish. Often a rather small plant, easily grown in moist soil.

Iris versicolor L. syn. *I. virginica* L. (s. *Laevigatae*) Native of Newfoundland, to Manitoba south to Florida and Arkansas, and naturalized in Europe, e.g. on Ullswater and in Perthshire, growing in swamps, wet meadows, scrub and by lakes and rivers, flowering in May–July. Stems 20–80cm; leaves 1–2.5cm wide; flowers 6–8cm across, usually bluish purple but reddish purple in var. *kermesina*. Easily grown in wet soil by water, or in a moist border in rich soil. Hardy to −25°C.

Iris 'Gerald Darby' A form of *I. versicolor*, raised in the 1960s, with purple bases to the leaves and bluish-purple flowers of good shape. Leaves *c.*2cm wide. Easily grown on the edge of a shallow pond or a moist border, flowering in early summer.

Iris setosa at Beth Chatto

Iris hookeri

Iris hexagona at Kew

Iris 'Gerald Darby'

Mixed irises by the waterside

Iris chrysographes (black form)

Iris chrysographes at the Royal Botanic Garden, Edinburgh

Iris delavayi on the rock garden at Kew

Iris aff. *delavayi* SBEC 1063

Iris 'Holden Clough'

Iris forrestii hybrid

Iris chrysographes Dykes (s. *Sibiricae*)
Native of NE Burma, Yunnan and Sichuan, growing in wet meadows and marshes, at 1300–4500m, flowering in June–September. Plant forming spreading clumps. Leaves 35–45cm, equalling the stems, 1–1.5cm wide. Stems unbranched, with 2 flowers. Flowers reddish purple to almost black, usually with yellowish veining on the falls. Standards at an oblique angle, not upright. Easily grown in rich, moist peaty soil, in full sun or partial shade. Hardy to −15°C. Shown here are the black form, possibly the same as 'Black Knight' and 'Black Velvet', and a rich purple form. All the dark forms look especially beautiful with the morning sun shining through the flowers. See also p.218.

Iris clarkei Baker ex Hook. fil. (s. *Sibiricae*)
Native of E Nepal, Sikkim, Bhutan, SE Xizang (Tibet) and Manipur, growing on damp, grassy hillsides and marshes, sometimes at the edge of *Rhododendron* and *Abies* forest, often in great quantity, at 2500–4300m, flowering in May–July. Plant forming loose clumps. Stems 30–60cm, sometimes with 1–3 branches, usually with 2 flowers per branch. Leaves 1.3–2cm wide. Flowers to 7.5cm across, bluish purple to dark blue or reddish purple. Standards horizontal, giving the flower a flat shape. Falls with a pale patch shading from yellow or white. An attractive plant, rare in cultivation, and sometimes confused with dwarf forms of *I. setosa* (q.v.). For a moist, peaty soil in sun or light shade. Hardy to −15°C.

Iris delavayi Micheli (s. *Sibiricae*)   Native of W Yunnan and SW Sichuan, growing in wet meadows at 3000–4000m, flowering in July–August (June in cultivation in S England). Plant forming large clumps. Leaves to 90cm, shorter than the stems. Stems up to 1.5m tall, with 1–3 branches; flowers 2 per branch, light to dark purplish-blue, with a large white patch on the blade of the falls. Standards at an oblique angle, not upright. Easily grown in wet ground, and handsome with its tall stems held well above the leaves. Hardy to −15°C.

Iris forrestii Dykes (s. *Sibiricae*)   Native of W Yunnan, NE Burma and S Sichuan, growing in alpine meadows at 2900–4300m, flowering in June. Plant forming dense clumps, with stems usually 35–40cm tall. Leaves shorter than the flowering stems, glossy on one side, greyish on the other. Stems with 2 flowers, 5–6cm across, yellow with brownish-purple lines. Standards erect, soon becoming curled (as here). Pedicels short, less than 7.5cm long in fruit, compared with more than 10cm in *I. wilsonii*, the other yellow-flowered species of this group. Easily grown in moist peaty soil. This species hybridizes in gardens with purple-flowered species of the section, producing brownish or greenish flowers with various combinations of yellow and purple.
Iris 'Charm of Finches'   raised by Hansford Morris is a selected form or hybrid of *I. forrestii*.

Iris 'Holden Clough'   A chance hybrid between *I. chrysographes* and *I. pseudacorus*, which arose among a batch of seedlings of *I. chrysographes* in the Holden Clough nursery in Yorkshire, England, in the 1960s. This unusual parentage is confirmed by the chromosome number of the plant. The leaves are about 65cm high, usually longer than the flower stems. This grows well in ordinary good garden soil, as well as by water, flowering in June.

Iris clarkei (Chamberlain 1631)

Iris 'Splash Down'

Iris 'Splash Down'   Raised by Hansford in 1972. Stems c.120cm. Parentage: *I. sibirica* × *I. bulleyana*.

Iris wilsonii C. H. Wright   Native of W China, in W Hubei, W Yunnnan and probably also in Sichuan and Shensi, growing by streams and in wet meadows at 2300–4000m, flowering in July. Plant forming dense clumps. Leaves 60–75cm, often rather floppy, greyish-green. Stems little longer than the leaves, to 80cm tall, unbranched with 2 yellow flowers, 6–8cm across. Standards held at an oblique angle. Falls pale yellow, veined and dotted with brown or purple. Easily grown in moist peaty soil or by water. Hardy to −15°C.

Iris wilsonii at Crathes Castle

Iris 'Charm of Finches'

Iris forrestii

'Royal Blue'

Iris sibirica 'Alba'

'Cambridge'

'Savoir Faire'

'Perry's Blue'

'Ego'

'Sky Wings'

Iris sibirica specimens from Beth Chatto, Unusual Plants, 9 June. ½ life size

Iris sibirica (wild form) with *Primula japonica*

Iris sibirica 'Silver Edge'

Iris sibirica 'Alba' at Beth Chatto's

Iris sibirica, like a white form of 'Flight of Butterflies'

Iris sibirica 'Ewen'

Iris sibirica 'Ruffled Velvet'

Iris sibirica 'Caezar'

Iris sibirica L. (s. *Sibiricae*)　Native of Europe, from W France (in one place only) and Switzerland, eastwards to Russia, Yugoslavia and Bulgaria, N Turkey and the Caucasus, east to Lake Baikal, growing in wet meadows, reed swamps by lakes, and by streams, flowering in May–June. Plant forming dense clumps of narrow, upright leaves. Stems 50–120cm. Leaves to 80cm tall, 1cm wide. Flowers 1–3, to c.9cm from top to bottom, bluish violet, rarely white (in f. *alba*). Easily grown in moist soil by water, or in a normal border in rich soil which does not dry out in summer. Hardy to −20°C and below.

Iris sibirica cultivars
'Caezar'　Registered by F. Cleveland Morgan in 1930.
'Cambridge'　Registered by M. Brummitt 1964.
'Ego'　Registered by McGarvey 1965.
'Ewen'　Registered by C. McEwen 1970.
'Flight of Butterflies'　Registered by J. Witt 1972, it has small blue flowers, like the white form shown here.
'Perry's Blue'　Raised by A. Perry.
'Royal Blue'　Registered by Taylor 1932.
'Ruffled Velvet'　Registered by C. McEwen 1973.

'Savoir Faire'　Registered by S. DuBose 1974.
'Silver Edge'　Registered by C. McEwen 1973.
'Sky Wings'　Registered by W. Peck 1971.

Iris orientalis 'Shelford Giant'

Iris crocea at Sissinghurst Castle, Kent

Iris orientalis

Iris spuria (English wild form)

Iris xanthospuria (Rix 1306) from Kalkan

Iris spuria 'A. W. Tait'

Iris spuria subsp. *musulmanica* at Erevan Botanic Garden, Armenia

Iris crocea Jacq. syn. *I. aurea* Lindl. (s. *Spuriae*) Native distribution uncertain, but found, usually near cemeteries, in the Kashmir valley at 1600–2000m, flowering in June. Stems to 1.5m, or to 2m in gardens. Leaves 1.5–2cm wide. Similar to a yellow *I. orientalis* but with larger flowers, 12–18cm across. Easy to grow in good rich soil and full sun. Hardy to −20°C.

Iris lactea Pallas (s. *Ensatae*) Native of C Asia, from Kazakhstan eastwards to Korea, in N and W China and in Mongolia, extending southwards to the E Himalaya from Afghanistan to N India and Xizang, growing on banks by rivers, by roadsides, between irrigated fields and by sandy lake margins and dry river beds, at 800–3700m, flowering between May and July according to altitude. Plant forming dense clumps. Leaves greyish green, to 6mm wide, rather stiff. Stems 15–30cm, 1–2 flowered. Flowers usually pale bluish, sometimes white, 4–6cm across, scented. This rather modest species is likely to be exceptionally hardy, and easily grown in climates with warm summers, in moist, sandy soil.

Iris missouriensis Nutt. (s. *Longipetalae*) Native of W North America, from Mexico northwards to British Columbia, eastwards to South Dakota and Alberta, and common in inland California, especially on the eastern side of the Sierra Nevada. It grows in wet meadows and marshes, pine woods or by streams, at up to 3000m, flowering in May–July, according to altitude, in areas wet until flowering, but often dry later. Plant forming extensive dense clumps, often covering large areas. Leaves grey-green, 3–6mm wide. Stems 20–50cm tall, branched, with pale-bluish or whitish flowers, solitary or in pairs; bracts transparent, papery, greenish at the base and on the keel. Falls to 6cm long, 2cm wide; standards *c.*1cm wide. Easily grown in a sunny position, kept wet in spring. Brian Mathew recommends transplanting this species in spring or early autumn, not in summer.

Iris orientalis Mill. syn. *I. ochroleuca* L., *I. spuria* L. subsp. *ochroleuca* (L.) Dykes Native of NE Greece near Alexandropoulos and W Turkey, east to Kayseri, and on Lesbos and Samos, growing in damp meadows, marshes, and ditches up to 1400m, flowering in May–June. Stems 50–100cm. Basal leaves 1–2cm wide. Flowers 8–10cm across.
'**Shelford Giant**' An extra large clone, originating near Ephesus, with stems to 2m. Easily grown in warm, heavy soil, but not always free-flowering in gardens. Like all the *spuria* irises, it takes some years to flower freely after being moved.

Iris spuria L. subsp. ***musulmanica*** (Fomin) Takht. Native of N and NW Iran, the S Transcaucasus and Turkey westwards to Kayseri, growing in damp meadows, often in saline soil, on grassy plains by rivers, often in huge colonies, at 800–1900m, flowering in May–July. Stems 50–100cm. Leaves 8–17cm broad. Flowers *c.*10cm across, usually bluish, but white plants are common among the blue, with the haft of the falls equal to or little longer than the blade. Easily grown in warm, rich soil, but susceptible to slug damage, so less robust than *I. orientalis* or *I. xanthospuria*.

Iris spuria L. subsp. ***spuria*** Native of Europe, from England, in Dorset and Lincolnshire, to S Sweden, and east to Hungary and Czechoslovakia, growing in wet meadows and saline marshes, flowering in June–July.

Iris missouriensis in NE California in a marsh

Iris missouriensis

Iris missouriensis

Stems 30–80cm; flowers 6–8cm across, with the haft of the falls much longer than the blade. 'A. W. Tait' is an attractive form, more free-flowering in gardens than most, and easy in normal garden soil.

Iris xanthospuria B. Mathew & T. Baytop syn. 'Turkey Yellow' Native of SW Turkey near the coast east of Muğla, and in Hatay, and possibly also near Ankara, growing in marshy fields, in *Eucalyptus* plantations and by streams, which may dry out in summer, flowering in April–May. Stems to 1m or even 2m in gardens. Leaves 1.5–2cm across. Flowers 9–11cm across. Easily grown in good, heavy garden soil in full sun. Hardy to −15°C at least.

Iris lactea

IRIS

Iris 'Cambridge Blue' at Hidcote Manor, Gloucestershire

Iris 'Custom Design'

Iris monnieri

Iris monnieri DC. (*Iridaceae*)   This is now considered by Brian Mathew to be an ancient hybrid between *I. orientalis* and *I. xanthospuria*, introduced to France and there known as 'Iris de Rhodes', when painted by Redouté in the early 19th century. The flowers are pale lemon yellow, but the plant is otherwise similar to *I. orientalis*. *Iris* 'Ochracea', the hybrid between *I. orientalis* and *I. crocea*, has deeper-yellow flowers, and tall stems to 1.5m.

Iris spuria cultivars   These cultivars all form strong-growing upright plants around 2m tall, flowering mainly in June. They require good, rich, moist soil and full sun if they are to flower freely and do better in continental climates with hot summers. They require a year or two to settle down and flower freely after planting, but are then good perennials. Because of their hardiness and tolerance of heat, as well as saline or alkaline soils, *spuria* iris hybrids are popular in the inland parts of the United States. Most of the modern hybrids have been raised in America, and the colour range and flower shapes are continually being improved. The species from which these hybrids were derived are shown on the previous page. Numerous new cultivars have been named, including bicolours, and flowers which contain brown and red-purple shades. 'Adobe Sunset', 'Imperial Bronze', 'Red Clover' and 'Cherokee Chief' sum up the newer hybrids. Most of these plants were photographed at Wisley, where they may be seen growing in a trial.

'Cambridge Blue'   Introduced by Barr and Sons in 1924. The original hybrid between *I. monnieri* and *I. spuria*, 'Monspur', was made by Sir Michael Forster, and from this cross, Thomas Barr bred 'Cambridge Blue', 'Premier', and 'A. J. Balfour'.

'Clarke Cosgrove'   Raised by B. Hager in the USA in 1974.

'Custom Design'   Raised by B. Hager.

'Dawn Candle'   Raised by Ferguson in 1965.

'Media Luz'   Raised by B. Hager in 1967.

'Norton Sunlight'

'Protégé'   Raised by B. Hager in 1966.

Iris 'Cambridge Blue'

Iris 'Clarke Cosgrove'

Iris 'Dawn Candle'

Iris 'Norton Sunlight'

Iris 'Media Luz' in the Trial at Wisley

Iris 'Protégé'

Iris 'Sano-no-Yuki'

Iris ensata 'Rose Queen' at Beth Chatto's

Iris 'Shihainami'

Iris 'Mandarin'

Iris 'Haro-no-umi'

Iris 'Nari-hera'

Iris pseudacorus at Gibbon's Brook, Sellindge, Kent

Iris laevigata

Iris ensata Thunb. syn. *I. kaempferi* Siebold (s. *Laevigatae*)   Native of NE Asia, in Japan, Korea, NE China and E Siberia, growing in marshes, ditches and wet, grassy places, flowering in June–July. Plant forming dense clumps of narrow, upright leaves to 60cm tall, 1.2cm wide, with a distinct thickened midrib. Flowering stems 40–80cm, with few branches. Flowers purple, *c.*10cm across, with small erect standards. Hardy to −20°C or less. For wet soil or shallow water, if possible rather drier in winter. The wild form is sometimes called var. *spontanea* (Mak.) Nakai; the plant shown here was collected by Brian Halliwell (BH 407X), and has typical reddish-purple flowers. Bluer-flowered forms were photographed in the wild by Roy Lancaster in N China.

'Kaempferi' *Irises*   These are the large-flowered cultivated forms of *I. ensata*, some possibly hybrids with *I. laevigata*, most of which were bred in Japan. They generally have larger, flatter flowers, often with both inner and outer segments rounded and ruffled. Mauve-blue is the commonest colour, but there are also pinks, a near crimson, white, and a pale yellow, 'Aichi-no-Kagayaki', a hybrid with *I. pseudacorus*, which, however, is rather a poor grower with leaves golden in the spring. All the cultivars require moist, peaty soil, preferably with the rhizomes above the water level, but the roots growing down into wet soil. They flower in mid-summer. The following is a small selection of the cultivars established in cultivation in Europe:

'Haro-no-umi'   Red-purple with a pale edge.

'Mandarin'   Pinkish purple.

'Nari-hera'   Deep purplish blue, double.

'Rose Queen'   Pale pink, otherwise like the wild type in size and shape.

'Sano-no-Yuki'   Double white.

'Shihainami'   Deep purple, double.

Iris laevigata Fischer (s. *Laevigatae*)   Native of Japan, Korea, N China and Siberia from Lake Baikal and the Altai eastwards, growing in marshes, by lakes and rivers, flowering in May–July, usually before *I. ensata*. Plant forming loose clumps, with rather spreading rhizomes. Leaves 40–60cm long, to 4cm wide, without a distinct midrib. Stems 30–70cm, usually 3-flowered. Flowers 8–10cm across, bluish, rarely white. Easily grown in wet ground or shallow water. The commoner clone in gardens, shown here, often has flowers again in the autumn, and there is also a striking variegated form. Hardy to −20°C and below.

Iris pseudacorus L. (s. *Laevigatae*) Yellow Flag   Native of Europe, from the Faeroes, Ireland and Scotland, south to North Africa and east to W Siberia, the Caucasus, Turkey, Iran and Syria, naturalized in North America; it grows in wet fields and marshes, and by rivers and lakes, flowering April–August. Stems to 150cm. Leaves 1.5–3cm across. Flowers 7–10cm across. There is a pale-yellow-flowered form, and var. *bastardii*, in which the flowers lack the brownish markings. This has been hybridized with *I. chrysographes* to give 'Holden Clough' (see p.221), and with *I. ensata* (see above). There is also a stripy-leaved form of *I. pseudacorus*, 'Variegata', with leaves yellow-centred with pale-green edges when they emerge. Later the whole leaf becomes pale greenish. A double-flowered form is also in cultivation.

Iris ensata (wild form)

Grasses and sedges collected at Wisley, 15 May. ¼ life size

Melica
altisimma
'Atropurpurea'

Phalaris
arundinacea
'Picta'

Carex elata
'Aurea'

Carex
comans
'Frosted Curls'

Milium
effusum

Carex
muskinguemensis

Melica altissima L. 'Atropurpurea' (*Graminae*)   Native of E Europe from Czechoslovakia and Russia southwards to E Turkey and C Asia, growing in scrub and on rocks by streams, flowering in May–August. Plant forming loose clumps of stems to 2.5m. Leaves to 15mm wide, flat. Flowering panicle 10–20cm, dense or open at the base. Spikelets 7–10mm long. For woodland soil and partial shade or sun. Hardy to −20°C.

Milium effusum L. 'Aureum' (*Graminae*) **Bowles' Golden Wood Millet Grass**   Native of Europe, from the British Isles south to Spain and east to Siberia and the Himalayas, and of North America from Maine to Ontario, south to Massachusetts and Illinois, growing in damp woods, flowering in June–July. Plant tufted from a thin rootstock, short-lived. Leaves 5–10mm wide, golden yellow in 'Aureum', which comes true from seed. Stems 50–120cm, with the flowering part 10–25cm, pyramidal with often deflexed branches. Spikelets 2–3mm. An elegant and beautiful grass for a shady position. The leaves of the golden form are beautiful in mild winters. Hardy to −20°C or less.

Panicum virgatum L. 'Rubrum' (*Graminae*) **Switch Grass**   Native of North America, from Maine west to Saskatchewan, south to Florida, Arizona and Costa Rica, and in the West Indies, growing in both wet and dry places, flowering in August–September. Plant with creeping rhizomes and upright stems to 1.2m. Leaves 6–12mm wide, red in late summer in 'Rubrum'. Spikelets 3–5mm long. For any good soil in full sun. Hardy to −20°C or less.

Phalaris arundinacea L. var. *picta* 'Picta' (*Graminae*)   Native of Europe, including the British Isles, where it is very common, eastwards to Siberia, and North America, south to New Jersey and to Colorado, growing in wet places and shallow water, flowering in June–July. Plant with creeping rhizomes. Stems upright 60–200cm. Leaves *c.* 10mm wide. Spikelets *c.* 5mm, crowded. A fine plant for any large border, growing well in normal garden soil. Hardy to −20°C or less.

Stipa gigantea Link (*Graminae*)   Native of C & S Spain and Portugal, growing on dry, rocky slopes at *c.* 1500m, flowering in April–May. Plant forming massive clumps of tough but floppy leaves. Stems to 2.5m tall. Awns 2–12cm long, scabrid. For well-drained, dry, sandy or chalky soil. Hardy to −15°C, but likely to be damaged by colder winters, especially on heavy soils. Also in danger from slugs, which eat the soft bases of the shoots.

Stipa pulcherrima C. Koch   Native of most of Europe, from C France and N Germany eastwards to Sicily and S Russia, the Caucasus and the Kopet Dağ, growing in steppes and dry, rocky and stony meadows, flowering in June–August. Plant forming small clumps. Leaves lax but scabrid and tough, 1mm in diameter. Flowering stems to 1m, with a short panicle 10–15cm long. Awns to 50cm with a short corkscrew base and long seta with silky hairs to 7mm long. Hardy to −25°C, if dry. See also p.170.

Panicum virgatum 'Rubrum'

Carex comans Berggren 'Frosted Curls' (*Cyperaceae*)   Native of New Zealand, growing in pastures, where it is a common weed, and in damp places at up to 1300m. Plant forming dense tufts of fine lax leaves to 1mm wide and slender stems to 70cm long, usually green but whitish in this form shown here, or brownish. An unusual plant, like a mop of long, pale hair. Hardy to −10°C.

Carex elata 'Aurea'   See p. 232.

Carex muskinguemensis Schweinitz   Native of E North America from Ohio to Manitoba south to Missouri and E Kansas, growing in moist woods and scrub, flowering June–August. Plant with a creeping rhizome and upright stems to 60-90cm. Leaves to 5mm wide. Spikes 16–26mm long. For any moist soil in sun or partial shade. Hardy to −20°C.

Stipa gigantea with *Cotinus coggygria* 'Foliis Purpureis' at Withersdane Hall, Wye, Kent

Phalaris arundinacea 'Picta' at Cedar Tree Cottage, Sussex

Milium effusum 'Aureum' (young leaves in spring)

Stipa pulcherrima

Carex elata 'Aurea' at Longstock Park Gardens, Hampshire

Carex elata 'Aurea'

Carex pendula

Cyperus longus by the Seven Acres Lake, Wisley

Carex elata All. 'Aurea' syn. *C. stricta* Good. (*Cyperaceae*) Bowles' Golden Sedge   Native of most of the British Isles and Europe to North Africa and the Caucasus, growing in shallow, usually alkaline water and wet fens, flowering in April–June. Plant forming clumps about 1.5m across. Stems to 1.2m tall, slightly arching. Leaves 2–6mm across. Male spikes 1–2; female spikes 2–4, 30–70cm long, erect in fruit. The clone usually grown in 'Aurea', said to have been found by E. A. Bowles in the Norfolk Broads, or perhaps Wicken Fen, near Cambridge. The clumps are bright in spring, greener in late summer. *C. flava* L. with stems up to 50cm tall and short spikes of deflexed fruit is sometimes sold in place of *C. elata* 'Aurea'. It grows in similar habitats in N Europe and North America.

Carex pendula Hudson   Native of most of the British Isles and Europe, except the far north, south to North Africa and Turkey, growing in woods and damp shady places, usually on heavy soils, flowering in April–June, fruiting in July–August. Plant forming large clumps about 2m across. Flowering stems arching to 150cm. Leaves 15–20mm wide, deep green. Female spikes 4–5, pendulous, 7–16cm long, with numerous small fruits. Hardy to −25°C. An elegant, evergreen, large plant for a partially shaded position. The male spikes (shown here) are conspicuous in flower in spring; the female hanging spikes in fruit in summer.

Carex pseudocyperus L. Cypress Sedge   Native of most of Europe, including the British Isles, and across Europe and N Asia to Japan; of North America, from Nova Scotia west to Saskatchewan and south to Connecticut and Michigan and of New Zealand (South Island), growing on the edges of rivers, canals and lakes and in wet bogs, flowering in June–August. Stems upright to 1m tall; leaves 5–10mm wide, longer than stems. Male spikes 1; female spikes 3–5, nodding, 2–6cm long, 8–12mm in diameter, the fruits with a long, pointed beak. Beautiful for the edge of a pond or lake.

Cyperus longus L. (*Cyperaceae*)   Galingale   Native of Europe, from England, where it is confined to the south from Cornwall and Pembrokeshire to Kent, to Hungary and southwards to Spain and Portugal and east to Turkey and SE Russia, growing in marshy places and shallow water by ponds, often under trees, flowering in July–September. Stems forming loose clumps to 150cm. Leaves 2–10mm wide. Spikelets 4–25mm × 1–2mm, dark brown or reddish. An elegant and graceful plant for the waterside.

Glyceria maxima (Hartm.) Holmberg 'Variegata' (*Graminae*) Reed Grass   Native of Europe, from the British Isles, where it is common, to S France and east to the Caucasus, C Asia and NW China, growing in shallow water by ditches, canals and slow rivers, flowering in July–August. Plant with a creeping rhizome and erect stems to 2m. Leaves to 2cm wide. Spikelets 5–8mm long, narrowly ovate, dark brown, rather hard. Hardy to −20°C.

Helictotrichon sempervirens (Vill.) Bess. ex Pilg. (*Graminae*)   Native of SE France and NW Italy, in the SW Alps, growing on rocky and stony hillsides, flowering in June–July. Plant forming dense clumps of upright, blue-grey leaves to 60cm. Flowering stems to 1.2m, the branched inflorescence with 30–55 spikelets, each to 10–14mm long. For a sunny position in well-drained soil. Hardy to −15°C. *Leymus*

Imperata cylindrica 'Rubra'

Schoenoplectus lacustris subsp. *tabernaemontani* 'Zebrinus'

arenarius (L.) Hochst. Lyme Grass. Found wild on sand dunes in the south of England and S Europe has broader, equally blue leaves to 1cm or more wide, 150cm long, but has a spreading invasive root system.

Imperata cylindrica (L.) Beauv. **'Rubra'** (*Graminae*) Native of China, Korea and Japan, growing in waste places at low altitudes, flowering in May–June. Plant forming a tuft of flat upright leaves 20–50cm tall, 7–12mm wide, a beautiful red in 'Rubra'. Inflorescence 30–80cm, with hairy nodes, and silvery, spike-like, erect panicles of spikelets 3.5–4.5cm long, with a tuft of silvery hairs. One of the most distinct and striking of all small ornamental grasses. For sun or partial shade. Hardy to −15°C.

Miscanthus sinensis Anderss. **'Zebrinus'** (*Graminae*) This form of *Miscanthus sinensis* (see p.451) has been long cultivated in Japan. The unusual horizontal bands of variegation are also seen in *Scirpus* 'Zebrinus'.

Schoenoplectus lacustris L. subsp. *tabernaemontani* (C.C. Gmel.) Á. & D. Löve **'Zebrinus'** syn. *Scirpus tabernaemontani* C.C. Gmel. (*Cyperaceae*) Native of Europe, from the British Isles, south to Portugal and east to Siberia and NW China, in Sinjiang, growing in streams, canals, ditches, ponds and bogs, especially near the sea, flowering in June–July. Plant with a creeping rhizome. Stems rather slender to 1.5m tall, glaucous and banded in 'Zebrinus'. Spikelets 5–6 mm long. A striking plant for shallow water. Hardy to −25°C or less.

Scirpus sylvaticus L. Wood Club Rush Native of Europe, from the British Isles, east to the Caucasus, Siberia, NW China and North America, from Maine and Michigan south to Georgia, growing in wet places by streams and in open woods, flowering in June–July. Plant with a creeping rhizome and arching stems to 1m. Leaves green, flat, 2cm wide. Spikelets 3–4 mm long. A graceful plant for the waterside or bog garden. Hardy to −20°C or less.

Helictotrichon sempervirens

Scirpus sylvaticus

Glyceria maxima 'Variegata'

Carex pseudocyperus

Miscanthus sinensis 'Zebrinus'

A moss garden at Ryoan-ji, Kyoto, Japan

Eriophorum vaginatum near Aviemore

Leucobryum glaucum

Hakonechloa macra 'Aureola'

Carex fraseri Andr. (*Cyperaceae*)   Native of E North America, in SW Virginia, West Virginia, E Tennessee and North Carolina, growing in moist woods, flowering in May–July. Plant forming dense clumps. Stems 15–45cm long. Leaves 2.5–5cm wide, deep green, evergreen. Spike terminal, solitary, male at apex, with white female fruits below. For moist soil and shade. One of the most striking sedges with broad leaves and white fruits. Some other American sedges, such as *C. platyphylla* Carey, have equally broad leaves, but several spikes, the male and female usually separate.

Carex ornithopoda Willd. '**Variegata**'   From Europe, is superficially similar to *C. oshimensis* but has narrower leaves to 4mm wide, and small female spikes 3–10mm long. It is suitable for dry, sunny places on sandy or chalky soils.

Carex oshimensis Nakai '**Evergold**'   Native of Japan in W Honshu, Shikoku and Kyushu, growing in woods at low altitudes, flowering in April–May. Plant forming dense clumps, to 1m across, of evergreen leaves, to 9mm wide, with a pale yellowish or white centre in 'Evergold' or a narrow white edge in 'Variegata'. Flowering stems 20–50cm, with 1 terminal male spikelet and 2–4 female spikelets to 2.5cm long. Fruits sparsely puberulent. For moist, leafy soil in shade or partial shade. Hardy to −10°C. 'Evergold' is sometimes listed under *C. morrowii* Boott.

Eriophorum vaginatum L. (*Cyperaceae*) Sheathing Cottongrass   Native of N Europe, from Scotland and Ireland, southwards to Spain, N Italy and Greece and eastwards to Siberia, and N Japan, growing in peaty wet bogs, mainly in the mountains, flowering in April–May, and fruiting (shown here) in May–June. Plant forming dense clumps. Stems 30–50cm. Leaves very narrow, to 1mm wide. Flower heads solitary, with white silky bristles *c.* 2.5cm long. A beautiful plant for a moist peaty

Luzula nivea 'Schneehaschen'

Luzula sylvatica at the base of a beech hedge, Kildrummy Castle, Aberdeenshire

Carex ornithopoda 'Variegata'

Carex fraseri

Carex oshimensis 'Evergold'

position, to associate with heathers. *E. scheuchzeri* Hoppe, from N Europe, North America and the Alps, is similar, but less densely tufted, and with bristles up to 3cm. *E. callithrix* Cham., from Newfoundland and Alaska, and south to Massachusetts and Wisconsin, has similar loosely sheathing stem leaves. *E. angustifolium* Honck., with several nodding flower heads, has long creeping rhizomes; it is the common cottongrass in N Europe.

Hakonechloa macra Mak. ex Honda **'Aureola'** (*Graminae*)   Native of Japan, in the Tokaido district of SE Honshu, growing on wet cliffs in the mountains, flowering in August–October. Plant with shortly-creeping rhizomes forming dense clumps. Stems arching, 40–70cm long. For moist, peaty soil in shade or partial shade. Hardy to −15°C. A beautiful grass for the front of a cool border.

Leucobryum glaucum (Hedw.) Schp. (*Dicranaceae*)   Native of Europe, including Britain, of Asia and of North America, growing

on open woodland, in bare acid woods, or even as an epiphyte on trees in wet areas. A moss, forming rounded hummocks to 20cm across, then becoming flattened, pale green when fresh, white when dry. Individual shoots 20cm long, *c*.6mm across, with crowded scale-like leaves. For damp or wet, very acid soil in shade or a cool position in the open. Mosses are rarely planted in European gardens, though they may be tolerated or even encouraged, and good examples of *Leucobryum* 'lawns' can be seen at Knightshayes Court in Devonshire, and at the Savill Gardens, Windsor. In Japan, however, moss culture is an important aspect of gardening. They are especially useful in forming neat, slow-growing, green ground-cover in places where it is too dark for grass to survive. The modern gardener has one great advantage when growing moss: it is not killed, and even seems positively to be encouraged, by paraquat, so it becomes easy to grow, requiring no mowing or fertilizer, and hardly increasing in height. Other mosses worth encouraging are *Mnium hornum* and various *Polytrichum* species.

Luzula nivea (L.) DC. **'Schneehaschen'** or **'Snow Leveret'** (*Juncaceae*)   Native of N France south to the Pyrenees, C Italy and N Yugoslavia, growing in subalpine woods, scrub, and shady slopes, flowering in June–July. Plant forming loose tufts to 60cm across, spreading by stolons. Flowering stems to 60cm. Leaves 3–4mm wide, with scattered white hairs. Flowers 5mm long. For a hardy, moist position, and leafy soil. Hardy to −20°C.

Luzula sylvatica (Huds.) Gand. syn. *L. maxima* (Reich.) DC.   Native of Europe, from the British Isles south to Spain and eastwards to Turkey and the Caucasus, growing in damp acid woods, and on rocky slopes in moorland, flowering in May–June. Plant forming dense clumps of soft, bright leaves *c*.12mm wide. Flowering stems 30–80cm, arching. Flowers in clusters of 3–4, dark brown, 3–3.5mm long. For a shady position, or a cool peaty place in full sun. Hardy to −20°C. 'Marginata' has a narrow white margin to the leaf, but is less beautiful than the wild type.

Clematis integrifolia 'Hendersonii'

Clematis integrifolia at Harry Hay's, Surrey

Clematis integrifolia f. rosea

Clematis texensis at Harry Hay's, Surrey

Anemonopsis macrophylla Sieb. & Zucc.
(*Ranunculaceae*) Native of Japan, in C
Honshu, growing in woods in the mountains,
flowering in July–September. Plant with a thick
rootstock and upright stems to 80cm. Leaves
much divided, 2- to 3-ternate, with leaflets
4–8cm long. Flowers with 7–10 sepals, and
about 10 petals, nodding, 3–3.5cm across. For a
very sheltered and shady position and leafy, acid
soil. Hot, dry wind soon causes the leaves to die,
although the root may survive. Hardy to −15°C.

Clematis addisonii Britton (*Ranunculaceae*)
Native of E North America, from S West
Virginia and North Carolina, possibly to
Tennessee, growing on scrubby slopes,
flowering in May–June, in July in cultivation.
Plant with several annual climbing stems to 2m.
Leaves obtuse, bluish green, ovate, sessile or
the uppermost stalked with a few tendrils,
5–10cm long. Flowers 1.8–3cm long with thick,
fleshy sepals. For any good soil in sun or partial
shade. Hardy to −15°C.

Anemonopsis macrophylla

Clematis fremontii

Clematis recta f. purpurea

Clematis addisonii at Harry Hay's, Surrey

Clematis heracleifolia var. davidiana 'Wyevale'

Clematis × jouiniana 'Praecox'

Clematis fremontii S. Wats.   Native of North America, in Kansas, Nebraska and Missouri, growing on limestone hills, flowering in April–May. Plant with hairy stems 15–45cm tall, from a stout rootstock. Leaves sessile, glabrous except on the veins and edges; flowers c.2.5cm long. For well-drained soil in full sun. Hardy to –20°C or less.

Clematis heracleifalia DC var. **davidiana** (Franch). Hemsl.   Native of China, from the northeast, west to Hubei, growing in rocky places, flowering in July–September. 'Wyevale' is now considered a selection of var. davidiana and is named after the nursery in Hereford. The flowers of 'Wyevale' are a good pale sky-blue, well scented, c.4cm across. Stems upright to 1m, requiring staking. Hardy to –20°C or less. Other varieties, and C. stans, have more tubular, paler flowers; see Shrubs p. 199.

Clematis integrifolia L.   Native of Europe, from Austria south to Bulgaria and east to C Asia and the Caucasus, growing in grassland and steppes, flowering in June–August. Plant with several upright or sprawling stems to 1m from a stout rootstock. Leaves to 9cm long, ovate. Flowers nodding, with 4 sepals to 5cm long. Forma rosea has pink flowers and was distributed by the Plantsmen in the 1960s. 'Hendersonii' has blue flowers, around 6cm long. 'Olgae' has scented flowers with wavy margins to the sepals. For good soil in full sun and exposure. Hardy to –20°C or less.

Clematis × jouiniana C. K. Schneid. 'Praecox'   A hybrid between C. heracleifolia 'Davidiana' and C. vitalba, raised in c.1900 in Metz. Stems to 3m in a year, often from a woody base. Flowers each about 2cm long, produced in great quantity in July–September, scented. For sun or partial shade, either on a wall or scrambling through scrub. Hardy to –20°C or less.

Clematis recta L.   Native of Europe, from France and Spain, east to Poland, Bulgaria, Russia and the Caucasus, growing in scrub and sunny hills, flowering in June–July. Plant forming a clump of hollow stems to 1.5m. Leaves I-pinnate, the leaflets to 9cm long. Flowers 1–4cm across. Forma purpurea (shown here) has purple leaves; the intensity of colour varies with the season and the clone. For any soil in fully sun. Hardy to –25°C.

Clematis texensis Buckley   Native of E North America, in Texas, between Colorado and the Rio Grande, growing in rich soil on shady limestone ledges, often along streams, flowering in July–September. Stems often annual, sometimes persistent near the base in warm winters, to 3m from a stout rootstock. Leaves glaucous, simple or 3-foliate, apiculate, cordate. Flowers 2–3cm long, scarlet to reddish purple. For a warm position; hardy to –15°C.

Delphinium nudicaule at Axeltree Nursery, Kent

Delphinium barbeyi in the mountains above Flagstaff, Arizona

Delphinium × *belladonna* 'Lamartine'

Delphinium × *belladonna* 'Moerheimii'

Delphinium × *ruysii* 'Pink Sensation'

Delphinium tatsienense at Crathes Castle, Aberdeenshire

Delphinium cardinale

Delphinium barbeyi Huth (*Ranunculaceae*)
Native of E Arizona, Wyoming, Colorado, Utah
and New Mexico, growing in grassy subalpine
'parks', flowering in July–August. Plant with
stems to 2.5m from a stout rootstock. Leaves
with 5 divided lobes. Flowers with lanceolate-
acuminate sepals, *c*.2cm across. Rhachis of the
inflorescence glandular. For any good soil in a
sunny position. Hardy to –20°C perhaps.

Delphinium × belladonna (Kelway)
Bergmans These more delicate branched
Delphiniums are the result of crossing *D. elatum*
hybrids and a branching species, such as *D.
grandiflorum* L., from Siberia and N China, very
similar to *D. tatsienense*. The early crosses were
done by Kelways, Ruys and Lémoine in around
1900; a few of these are still grown today.
Shown here are: 'Lamartine', raised by
Lémoine in 1903, and 'Moerheimii', raised by
Ruys in 1906.

Delphinium cardinale Hook. syn. *D.
coccineum* Torr. Scarlet Larkspur Native of S
California from Monterey Co. to San Diego
Co., and in Baja California, growing in open
places in dry scrub and chaparral, and in open
woods, flowering in May–July. Stems upright,
to 2m, unbranched or with smaller racemes at
the base of the inflorescence, from a thick,
woody rootstock. Leaves appearing in autumn,
5-lobed to the base, the lobes each divided into
3. Flowers on short ascending pedicels 2–6cm
long, scarlet, rarely yellowish, 2–3cm across;
spur stout 1.5–2cm long. For well-drained soil
in a warm position, dry in summer. Hardy to
–10°C perhaps.

Delphinium elatum L. Native of Europe,
from the E Pyrenees and Provence east to the
Caucasus, and in C Asia, Siberia and NW
China, growing in grassy places and open
woods, from 1500–1900m in the Alps, flowering
in June–August. Plant with a stout, woody
rootstock and numerous stout stems to 2m.
Leaves 5-lobed and toothed; sepals to 1.6cm
long; spurs *c* 1.7cm. For ordinary well-drained,
rather moist soil in sun or partial shade. This is

Delphinium elatum in the Order Beds at Kew

the main species from which the garden
delphiniums have been raised. It was
introduced into cultivation in 1597, probably
from Siberia via St Petersburg, but most of the
early breeding work was done by Kelways at
Langport from 1875 onwards, and more
recently by Blackmore and Langdon of
Pensford, near Bristol.

Delphinium nudicaule Torr. & A. Gray
Native of California and S Oregon, from
Monterey Co. northwards in the Coast Ranges
and from Mariposa and Plumas Cos,
northwards in the Sierra Nevada, growing in
chaparral and in open woods and on rocky
banks below 2200m, flowering in May–June.
Plant with an elongated rootstock and swollen
roots. Stems to 60cm, usually sparsely branched
with few flowers. Flowers with long pedicels
and spurs 2.5–3.2cm long, the sepals forming a
cup, usually red, sometimes orange or
yellowish. For well-drained soil in a warm
position in sun or partial shade, dry in summer.
Hardy to –15°C perhaps.

Delphinium × ruysii hort. ex Möllers '**Pink
Sensation**' syn. 'Rosa Uberraschung' A
hybrid between a garden delphinium and *D.
nudicaule*, raised by Ruys in the 1920s.
Thousands of seedlings were raised, using
D.nudicaule as the seed parent, but all appeared
to be pure *nudicaule*, until, after the programme
had been abandoned, one seedling was found
which appeared to be a hybrid. In the second
generation 'Pink Sensation' was raised, and it
proved to be tetraploid and fertile. Stems
branching to 90cm. Hardy to –15°C, perhaps
less.

Delphinium tatsienense Franch. Native of
W China, in S Sichuan, growing on rocky and
grassy slopes at *c*.4000m, flowering in June–
July. Plant with a woody rootstock and several
branched stems to 60cm. Flowers *c*.2.5cm
across, bright blue, on slender ascending
pedicels. Spur 3cm. For well-drained, sandy soil
in sun or partial shade. Rather short-lived but
easy to raise from seed. Hardy to –15°C or
less.

Delphinium brunonianum by a stream near Gadsar, Kashmir

Delphinium brunonianum

Delphinium brunonianum Royle (*Ranunculaceae*) Native of the Pamirs and the Himalayas from Afghanistan and N Pakistan to E Nepal and SE Xizang, growing on cliffs, screes and stony slopes, at 4300–5500m, flowering in July–September. A glandular-hairy plant, with few stems to 20cm from a stout rootstock. Leaves rounded in outline, 3–8cm across, lobed to ⅔. Flowers 3–5cm long, purplish with a broad, blunt spur. For well-drained soil in full sun, moist in summer. Hardy to −20°C or less. Very similar to *D. cashmerianum*, but usually dwarfer with larger flowers and with glandular hairs, or hairs with swollen yellow bases on the inflorescence.

Delphinium caeruleum Camb. Native of Sikkim and Bhutan, growing on cliff ledges and grassy, rocky slopes at 4000–4500m, flowering in August–October. Plant with widely branching stems 5–15cm tall, to 30cm in gardens. Flowers widely separated, on pedicels 2–8cm long. Petals and sepals *c.*15mm long; spur 18–22mm. For well-drained soil in full sun. Hardy to −20°C.

Delphinium cashmerianum Royle Native of the Himalayas, from Pakistan to N India, growing on alpine slopes (and recorded on irrigated land in Ladakh by O. Polunin), at 2700–4500m, flowering in July–September. Plant not glandular-hairy, with flowers usually 2–3cm long with a more slender spur to 1.5cm long. Stems to 30cm; leaves 3–5cm across, deeply lobed. For well-drained soil in sun or partial shade. Hardy to −20°C or less.

Delphinium glaucum Wats. syn. *D. scopulorum* Gray var. *glaucum* Native of California north to Alaska, and in the Rockies, growing in wet meadows near streams at 1500–3000m, flowering in July–September. Plant with upright stems to 2.5m, from a stout woody rootstock. Leaves 8–15cm broad, much divided. Flowers 16–24mm across; spur 8–10mm long. A tall, robust plant for any good moist soil. Hardy to −20°C or less.

Delphinium patens Benth. Native of California, in the coast ranges and the W Sierra Nevada, growing in open woods and scrub at up to 1200m, flowering in March–May. Stems to 40cm, rather thick and fistulose, from a tuberous rootstock. Inflorescence single or branched, 6–15 flowered. Flowers to 3cm across: spur 8–11mm long, rather stout. For well-drained soil in full sun, dry in summer. Hardy to −10°C.

Delphinium pyramidale Royle Native of the Himalayas, from Pakistan to C Nepal, and common in Kashmir, growing on stony slopes by streams and in scrub at 2000–3600m, flowering in July–September. Plant with few upright stems to 90cm from a stout rootstock. Leaves with lobes not overlapping. Flowers *c.*3cm long, hairy. For well-drained but moist soil in sun or partial shade. Hardy to −20°C or less.

Delphinium semibarbatum Bienert ex Boiss. syn. *D. zalil* Aitch. Native of NE Iran, Afghanistan, and C Asia from the Kopet Dağ and Badghis to the Dzungarian Ala Tau and Tienshan in NW China, growing on grassy steppes, flowering in April–July. Plant with upright stems to 80cm from a thickened rootstock. Leaves divided into threadlike segments. Flowers *c.*1cm across; spur *c.*1cm. This unusually coloured species should be perfectly hardy to cold, but resents warm, damp conditions in winter and summer. For a hot, dry position, with water only in spring. Hardy to −20°C or less.

Delphinium trolliifolium Gray Native of NW California and W Oregon, growing in moist, shady places below 1200m in the evergreen forest zone, flowering in April–July. Plant with upright stems to 1.5m from a deep woody rootstock. Lower leaves 10–15cm wide, much-divided. Inflorescence lax, with divergent pedicels to 5cm long. Flowers 3–5cm across; spur 15–20mm. An attractive species for a cool, semi-shaded position. Hardy to −15°C perhaps.

Delphinium trolliifolium in the University Botanic Garden, Cambridge

Delphinium semibarbatum

Delphinium glaucum in the Order Beds at Kew

Delphinium cashmerianum

Delphinium patens near Silver Lake

Delphinium pyramidale in Kashmir

Delphinium caeruleum

Delphinium 'Guy Langdon'

Delphinium 'Lilian Bassett'

Delphinium 'Strawberry Fair'

Delphinium 'Fanfare' in the trials at Wisley

Delphinium 'Shasta'

Delphinium 'Blue Tit'

Delphinium 'Macaz'

Delphinium 'Spindrift'

Delphinium 'Leonora'

Delphiniums in Beryl Pye's garden at Eccleston Square, London

New Delphinium hybrids

'Blue Tit'   Raised by Blackmore and Langdon in 1960. Height to 1.4m; flowers 7cm across.

'Crown Jewel'   Raised by Blackmore and Langdon in 1979. Height to 2.8m; flowers 2.8cm across.

'Fanfare'   Raised by Blackmore and Langdon in 1960. Height to 1.8m; flowers 7.5cm across.

'Guy Langdon'   Raised by Blackmore & Langdon in 1955. Height to 2.0m; flowers 8.75cm.

'Leonora'   Raised by Latty in 1969. Height to 1.5m; flowers 7.5cm across.

'Lilian Bassett'   Raised by Bassett in 1984. Height to 1.5m; flowers 7.1cm across.

'Macaz'   Raised by McIntosh. A. M. 1984.

'Purple Triumph'   Raised by Blackmore and Langdon in 1960. Spike to 72cm long; flowers 7.5cm across.

'Sandpiper'   Raised by Latty in 1977. Height to 1.2m; flowers 8cm across.

'Shasta'   Raised by Bott. A. M. 1983.

'Spindrift'   Raised by Cowan in 1971. Height to 2m; flowers 8cm across.

'Strawberry Fair'   Raised by Blackmore and Langdon in 1967. Height to 2m; flowers 7cm across.

Delphinium 'Sandpiper'

Delphinium 'Purple Triumph'

Delphinium 'Crown Jewel'

Delphinium 'Honey Bee'

Delphinium 'Butterball'

Delphinium 'Can-Can'

Delphinium 'Blackmore's Blue'

Delphinium 'Turkish Delight'

Delphinium 'Loch Maree'

Delphinium 'Charles Gregory Broan'

Delphinium 'High Society'

The new red *Delphinium* seedlings behind bars in an experimental house at Wisley

An old, reliably perennial Blackmore and Langdon hybrid

New Delphinium hybrids at Wisley Attempts to breed a hardy red border delphinium are still continuing. Ruys's breeding programme, begun in the 1920s, failed, but did produce the dainty 'Pink Sensation' (see p. 17). In 1953 Dr R. A. Legro began his breeding experiments at Wageningen in Holland, and this programme was moved to the Royal Horticultural Society's garden at Wisley in 1980. The original plants used were white cultivars of *D. elatum*, crossed with *D. nudicaule*, *D. cardinale* and *D. semibarbatum* (syn. *D. zalil*), to try to raise a yellow. The first stage in the programme was to produce tetraploid forms of the three wild species, but crosses between these and the already tetraploid *elatum* cultivars proved disappointing. Success was finally achieved by producing allotetraploid, and therefore fertile, seedlings of *nudicaule* × *cardinale* and *semibarbatum* × *cardinale*. When these were crossed with the *elatum* cultivar 'Black and White', a range of bluish seedlings was produced, but other colours appeared in the second generation, including an orange and a semi-double red, creams and yellows. The plants themselves were very beautiful, but short-lived, difficult to propagate and unreliable from seed as they produced a large proportion of inferior plants. To be valuable commercially, the new coloured plants have to be reliably perennial, hardy and able to be propagated in large quantities. This has finally been achieved, again with great difficulty, by tissue culture, and the first plants of the new hybrids should be ready for sale to the public by spring 1992, 39 years after the breeding programme was begun.

Delphinium cultivars

'Blackmore's Blue' Raised by Blackmore and Langdon. Height to 1.65m; flowers 7.5cm across. A. M. 1947.

'Butterball' Raised by Blackmore and Langdon before 1969. Height to 1.9m; flowers 7cm across.

'Can-Can' Raised by McGlashan in 1986. Height to 2.0m; flowers 8.5cm across.

'Charles Gregory Broan' Raised by Broan in 1967. Height to 1.2m; flowers 6.5cm across.

'High Society' Raised by Pye before 1985. Height to 1.63m; flowers 9.2cm across.

'Loch Maree' Raised by Cowan in 1968. Height to 2.4m; flowers 7.5cm across.

'Stalwart' An old variety of great elegance, preserved at Kew. Height to 1.8m; flowers *c*.2cm across.

'Turkish Delight' Raised by Blackmore and Langdon in 1967. Height to 1.7m; flowers 6.2cm across.

Blackmore and Langdon's hybrid A seedling from Blackmore and Langdon, dating from the 1940s. This old one we have treasured in our own garden; it is reliably perennial, with rather small flowers of a good sky-blue, and stems to 2m.

Delphinium 'Stalwart' at Kew

Nymphaea alba near Maam Cross, Connemara

Nymphoides peltata

Nuphar lutea

Nuphar lutea (L.) Sm. (*Nymphaeaceae*) Yellow Water Lily   Native of Europe and N Asia, east to Japan, growing in lakes and rivers, often in moving water, flowering in June–August. Plant very invasive with creeping rhizomes. Leaves either submerged, floating or emergent; when floating ovate, thick or leathery, 12–40cm long. Flowers 4–6cm across, with 4–6 sepals, smelling of brandy and fruit decanter-shaped, hence the colloquial name 'Brandy-bottle'. For water up to 3m deep. Hardy to −20°C or less.

Nuphar polysepala Englem.   Native of W North America, from California to Alaska, and east to Colorado and South Dakota, growing in ponds and slow rivers, flowering in April–September. Differs from the European *N. lutea* by having 7–9 sometimes reddish sepals, to 5cm long, and broadly oval leaves to 40cm long, either floating or emergent. A striking plant in shallow water, with its large emergent leaves. Hardy to −20°C.

Nymphaea alba L. (*Nymphaeaceae*)   Native of Europe, from W Ireland and NW Africa eastwards to Turkey, Russia and Kashmir, growing in ponds, lakes and slow rivers, flowering in June–August. Plant with a stout rhizome, forming loose patches of floating leaves 10–30cm across. Flowers 5–20cm across, usually scented for the first day after opening, white. (The wild red form originated from Sweden, around Nerike.) Subsp. *occidentalis* Ostenf. is merely a small form, with flowers 5–12cm across and globose fruit, described from Connemara and Perthshire. Best in water 1–3m deep. Hardy to −20°C or less.

Nymphaea 'Froebelii'   Raised by a Zurich nurseryman, Otto Froebel, in around 1898, by repeated selection of *N. alba* var. *rubra*. Leaves purplish. Flowers rather small but scented. Best in water 45–60cm deep.

Nymphaea 'Laydeckeri Fulgens'   Raised by Marliac-Latour in 1895, and named after his foreman and son-in-law Maurice Laydecker. The 'Laydeckeri' hybrids are smaller than the 'Marliacea' hybrids, and are probably derived from *N. tetragona* Georgi, a dwarf species with flowers *c*.2.5cm across. In 'Laydeckeri Fulgens' the flowers are around 8cm across. For small pools and shallow water 3–60cm deep.

Nymphaea 'Marliacea Carnea' syn. 'Marliac Flesh'   Raised by Marliac-Latour in 1887. Flowers large, *c*.20cm across, scented. Leaves large, purplish when young. Best in water 45–150cm deep.

Nymphaea 'Marliacea Chromatella' syn. 'Marliac Yellow'   Raised by Marliac-Latour in 1887. Flowers yellow, 15cm across. Leaves speckled with maroon. Probably a hybrid with *N. mexicana* which has speckled leaves and yellow flowers. There are several 'Marliacea' hybrids, ranging in colour from deep-crimson 'Ignea' to white 'Albida'.

Nymphaea odorata Dryander **'William B. Shaw'**   Raised by Dreer in *c*.1900. Flowers well scented, raised slightly above the water. *N. odorata* itself is native of North America from Newfoundland and Cape Cod to Kansas, Mexico and cuba, growing in lakes, bog pools and slow rivers, flowering in June–September. Plant forming large clumps, with long, creeping rhizomes; leaves and flowers variable in size.

Nymphaea 'Marliacea Carnea'

Nuphar polysepala

Nymphaea 'Marliacea Chromatella'

Nymphaea 'Froebeli'

Nymphaea odorata 'William B. Shaw'

'William B. Shaw' requires water 45–60cm deep. Others require variable depths, according to their size.

Nymphoides peltata (Gmel.) O. Kuntze (*Menyanthaceae*)   Native of Europe, from N England and S Sweden eastwards to the Caucasus, N Asia, and Japan, growing in lakes and slow rivers, flowering in June–August. Plant with a creeping rhizome, and floating leaves 3–10cm across. Flowers in 2–5-flowered groups, supported by a pair of leaves. Corolla *c*.3cm across, with wavy and ciliate lobes. Fruits flattened, with grey, flattened ciliate seeds. Related to Bogbean (p.165), rather than water lilies, but so similar in habit to a miniature water lily that it is put on this page.

Nymphaea 'Laydeckeri Fulgens'

Nymphaea 'Gladstoniana' at Inverewe

'Madame Wilfron Gonnère'

'Gonnère'

Hardy Water Lily hybrids   It is a measure of the indestructible nature of water lilies, and the lack of modern interest in the hardy varieties, that of the 90 or so hybrids commonly available in Europe at present, 66 were bred by M. Marliac-Latour, who had a nursery near Temple-sur-Lot, and raised hybrids between 1880 and 1920. More recent work has been done, mainly in America, and has concentrated on the spectacular subtropical species, whose tuberous roots require protection from frost in winter. Much of the early work was done by George Pring at the Missouri Botanical Garden from 1913 to 1930, and other hardy cultivars have been produced in North Carolina by Perry Slocum, whose first hybrid, 'Pearl of the Pool', was patented forty years ago, and who is still producing new hybrids.

'Amabilis' syn. 'Pink Marvel'   Raised by Marliac-Latour in 1921. Flowers large, to 25cm across. Best in 45–60cm depth of water.

'Charles de Meurville'   Raised by Marliac-Latour in 1931. Flowers large. Best in 60–120cm of water.

'Escarboucle' syn. 'Aflame'   Raised by Marliac-Latour in 1906. The best large red; flower large, up to 30cm across, scented. Best in deep water, 60–185cm deep.

'Fabiola'   Raised by Marliac-Latour in 1910. Flowers with a deep-red centre, pale on the edge. Best in 45–75cm depth of water.

'Gladstoneana' syn. 'Gladstone'   Raised by Richardson in 1987. A hybrid of *N. tuberosa*. Flowers very large. Best in deep water, 60–250cm deep.

'Gonnère' syn. 'Crystal White'   Raised by Marliac-Latour. Compact growing. Best in 45–75cm of water.

'James Brydon' syn. 'Brydonia Elegans'   Raised by Dreer in 1902. Flowers large, scented. Leaves speckled. Best in water 45–90cm deep.

'Madame Wilfron Gonnère'   Flowers large, with an extra-large number of petals. Best in 45–75cm of water.

'Masaniello'   Raised by Marlica-Latour in 1908. Flowers scented, pink with crimson speckles. Best in 45–90cm of water.

'Norma Gedye'   Raiser not recorded. Plant with very long flowering season. Best in 30–45cm of water.

'Pink Opal'   Raised by Fowler in 1915. Recognized by its spherical buds. Leaves brownish. Best in 45–75cm of water.

'Sioux'   Raised by Marliac-Latour in 1908. Flowers open yellowish and become crimson as they age. Leaves with purple speckles. Best in 30–45cm depth of water.

'Fabiola'

'Escarboucle'

Nymphaea 'James Brydon' in the water lily collection at Kew

'Charles de Meurville'

'Pink Opal'

'Masaniello'

'Sioux'

'Amabilis'

'Norma Gedye'

Papaver orientale 'Goliath' at Sissinghurst

Papaver orientale 'Harvest Moon' from Blooms

Papaver orientale 'Ladybird'

Papaver orientale 'Picotee'

Papaver bracteatum Lindl. Syn. *P. lasiothrix* Fedde   Native of NW Iran and the northern Caucasus, growing on moist screes and in grassy valleys at around 2500m, flowering in July. Stems to 1m, with large leafy bracts below the flower. Petals usually 6, dark crimson-red, with a large dark blotch, longer than broad, reaching the base. Anthers blackish-purple. Recent photographs in Iran by J. C. Archibald show this spectacular species in huge stands. The large, dark red varieties such as 'Goliath' and 'Ladybird' are closest to this species.

Papaver orientale L. syn. *P. paucifoliatum* (Trautv.) Fedde, *P. orientale* L. var. *parviflorum* Busch (*Papaveraceae*)   Native of the Caucasus, NW Iran and NE Turkey south to Lake Van,

growing in mountain hay meadows, grassy slopes and sheltered screes at 2100–2400m, flowering in July–August, but earlier in cultivation. Stems 30–90cm, without bracts below the flowers. Buds pendulous. Petals 4, pale orange, unspotted or with a pale blue or white blotch at the base. Anthers yellow or pale violet. *P. orientale* L. is the oldest name for a poppy of this group, but most of the cultivars are closer to other species. In the supplement to *The Flora of Turkey* (1988), only three wild species are now recognized.

Papaver pseudo-orientale (Fedde) Medw. Native of the S Caucasus, NW Iran and E Turkey south to Hakkari, growing in mountain meadows, steppe, and rocky slopes, especially

by streams at 1450–2100m, flowering in June–August. Stems to 80cm, without bracts or sometimes with small, undivided bracts below the flower. Buds erect. Petals 4 or 6, deep orange to vermilion, with a large dark blotch, broader than long, above the base. Anthers dark purple. This is the commonest species in Turkey, conspicuous on the southern side of the Pontus mountains in July, but usually growing singly, rather than in dense stands.

Papaver cultivars

'Allegro Vivace'   Orange flowers with 4 petals; unspotted without bracts, fairly dwarf to 90cm.

'Goliath'   Very large, blood-red flowers with bracts and a dark spot. Close to *P. bracteatum*.

Papaver 'May Queen'

Papaver orientale with cow parsley among long grass on a roadside in Scotland

Papaver 'Olympia'

'Harvest Moon' Flowers rather small, orange, unspotted. Stems *c.*1m.

'Ladybird' Flowers very large with bracts and with a black blotch. 60cm. Early season.

'May Queen' Double, orange-red flowers with quilled petals and flexuous stems without bracts.

'Olympia' Semi-double flowers with flat petals. Stems flexuous, without bracts.

'Picotee' Petals frilled, with a white base and pinkish-orange tip; the proportion of orange and white is variable.

Papaver 'Allegro Vivace'

Papaver 'Picotee'

Papaver 'Picotee'

Papaver 'Ladybird'

Papaver orientale specimens from Wisley, 1 June. ¼ life size

'Glowing Embers'

'Blue Moon'

'Pale Face'

'Sultana'

'Cedric Morris'

'Beauty of Livermere'

'Princessin Victoria Louise'

Papaver orientale specimens from Wisley, 1 June. ⅓ life size

Papaver orientale 'Mrs Perry' at Crathes Castle, Aberdeenshire

Papaver 'Turkish Delight'

Papaver 'Cedric Morris'

Papaver 'Curlilocks'

Oriental Poppies Cultivated oriental poppies, are now found in all shades of red, orange, pink, almost mauve and white. They were all bred from the three wild species from Turkey and the Caucasus, notably by Amos Perry at Enfield. In the 1930s even more colours and shapes were available than can be found today, including 'Waterloo', dark-crimson-suffused purple, with woolly leaves; 'Mahony'and 'Darkness', deep maroon like 'Patty's Plum'; and 'Tulip', with long, tapering buds. All are easily grown in any good moist soil in full sun and are beautiful in a herbaceous border or in grass. They die back after flowering, are best moved or planted in autumn, and are easily propogated by root cuttings. Even small pieces of broken root will make new plants. Hardy to −20°C or less.

'Beauty of Livermere' Flowers blood-red, with black blotch and large bracts to 120cm. Close to *P. bracteatum*, and probably the same as 'Goliath', p. 23.

'Black and White' Flowers white with black blotches. Stems *c*.80cm.

'Blue Moon' Flowers very large to 25cm across; blush pink with basal blotches and large bracts. Stems to 100cm.

'Cedric Morris' Flowers very large, pale pink, with frilled petals and a large black centre; stems to 80cm, with bracts.

'Curlilocks' Flowers orange, somewhat nodding, with deeply separated petals, with black blotches; stems *c*.70cm.

'Glowing Embers' Flowers orange-red with black blotches; stems to 110cm, with large bracts.

'Mrs Perry' Flowers medium, pale salmon pink with black blotches; stems *c*.90cm, with small bracts.

'Pale Face' Flowers very pale pink, with a white centre; stems *c*.90cm, without bracts.

'Princessin Victoria Louise' Flowers very large, pale pink with dark blotches.

'Sultana' Flowers mid-pink with a faint darker base; stems *c*.60cm.

'Turkish Delight' syn. 'Turkenlouis' Flowers medium, pale salmon pink, unspotted; stems *c*.80cm, without bracts.

Papaver 'Black and White'

Meconopsis 'George Sherriff 600'

Meconopsis 'George Sherriff 600' at Inshriach, Aviemore

Meconopsis × *beamishii* at Branklyn, Perth

Meconopsis grandis

Meconopsis quintuplinervia

Meconopsis × beamishii Prain
(*Papaveroceae*)   A hybrid between *M. grandis*
and *M. integrifolia*, and one of the few hybrids
to have remained in cultivation for some time. It
was first raised in Co. Cork in 1906, is often
monocarpic and has large pale-yellow flowers in
the axils of the upper leaves. *M.* × *sarsonii*, the
cross between *M. betonicifolia* and *M.
integrifolia*, is taller, with smaller flowers.

Meconopsis betonicifolia Franch. syn. *M.
baileyi* Prain   Native of SE Xizang, NW
Yunnan and NE Burma, growing in woods and
scrub, and along streams in alpine meadows at
3000–4000m, flowering in June–August. Stems
to 1.5cm. Basal leaves oblong, truncate or
slightly cordate at the base, usually obtuse or
rounded at the apex. Upper stem leaves usually
auriculate or cordate at base, amplexicaul in a
whorl at the top of the stem. Flowers 1–6 in the
uppermost whorl of leaves; petals *c.*5cm across
and long, often purplish, on pedicels *c.*10cm at
first opening, elongating in fruit. This species
differs from *M. grandis* most clearly in its basal
leaves, which are truncate or cordate at the base,
not tapering into the narrow stalk. Easily raised
from seed, and prefers a sandy, peaty soil, moist
in summer. Sometimes this species is
monocarpic, and it is said that preventing it
flowering in its second year encourages the
production of side shoots at the base. Hardy to
−20°C.

Meconopsis grandis Prain   Native of Bhutan
and Sikkim, extending to W Nepal and S
Xizang, growing on rocky hillsides and in scrub
at 3650–4800m, flowering in June–August.
Reputed to be cultivated around shepherds'
huts in Sikkim where the seeds are used for oil.
Plant forming large clumps of stems to 120cm.
Basal leaves elliptic, 15–25cm long, acute,
cuneate or attenuate at base. Stem leaves
become sessile and whorled at the top of the
stem, sometimes cordate. Flowers 1–4 per stem,
on pedicels 10–15cm; petals 4–7cm, often
purplish. G. Sherriff 600 is a clone of this
species, collected SW of Sakden in E Bhutan,
and very close to *M.* × *sheldonii*. There is much
discussion as to which of the cultivated forms
are 'pure' *M. grandis*, and which are hybrids
with *M. betonicifolia* (see *M.* × *sheldonii*).
Generally *M.* × *sheldonii* has leafier stems, with
the stem leaves cordate at the base, and more
than 4 flowers per stem. *M. grandis* usually has
longer pedicels, and narrower basal leaves
which taper gradually with the stalk. For sandy,
peaty soil, cool and moist in summer. Hardy to
−20°C.

Meconopsis punicea Maxim.   Native of NE
Xizang, S Gansu and NW Sichuan, growing in
damp hay meadows with willows or
Rhododendron, and on grassy slopes, at 2800–
4500m, flowering in June–August, usually in
the shade. Plant forming small clumps, with
leaves all basal, to 30cm long, but usually
*c.*15cm. Flower stems to 6 for each rosette, up
to 75cm, but usually *c.*30cm at flowering,
elongating in fruit. Petals to 10cm long. This
species was found by Rock & Wilson, but had
died out in gardens until recently reintroduced
into cultivation by Roy Lancaster under the

Meconopsis × *sheldonii* at Kildrummy Castle Garden, Aberdeenshire

Meconopsis 'Branklyn' at Branklyn

Meconopsis 'Crewdson Hybrids'

Meconopsis 'Slieve Donard'

Meconopsis betonicifolia

Meconopsis *punicea* at Inshriach

number 1630. Requires a very cool position and moist shade: it is likely to grow best in Scotland or in cool gardens in the mountains elsewhere. Hardy to −20°C.

Meconopsis quintuplinervia Regel   Native of NE Xizang, S Gansu, NW Sichuan to C Shensi, growing in alpine meadows on limestone, often among dwarf *Rhododendron* scrub, at 2200–4300m, flowering in ?June–August. Plant forming extensive clumps, with leaves up to 25cm long. Flower stems to 90cm, usually *c*.30cm. Flowers 1 per rosette, with petals 3.75cm long, pinkish to azure-blue. This dainty alpine species is happiest in places such as the peat beds in the Royal Botanic Garden, Edinburgh, growing in the open but shaded from the south, among dwarf shrubs. Hardy to −20°C.

Meconopsis × ***sheldonii*** G. Taylor   Many of the finest blue poppies in cultivation at present probably belong to this cross between *M*.

grandis and *M. betonicifolia*. It was first raised at Oxted in Surrey in 1937 and is a strong-growing perennial, with stems to 1.5m. Easy to grow, but liable to die if it becomes too hot and dry in summer. In warmer climates, such as E North America and SE England, a cool, shaded and sheltered position is required if it is to survive. Several named clones or forms are grown in gardens:

'Branklyn'   A robust plant to 1.8m, often with a hint of mauve in the very large flowers, and with leafy stems. Originally 'Branklyn' was a selection of 'G. Sherriff 600', a form of *M. grandis*, itself very close to *M.* × *sheldonii*; the plant shown here growing at Branklyn is possibly not the original.

'Crewdson Hybrids'   A good form with a neat habit derived from *M. betonicifolia*, and dark-blue flowers.

'Slieve Donard'   One of the earliest crosses, increased and sold by the Slieve Donard nursery in Northern Ireland. An elegant form with longer, more pointed petals than most.

Eschscholzia californica

Eomecon chionanthum at Edington, Wiltshire

Meconopsis villosa at Inverewe

Meconopsis cambrica in Derbyshire

Meconopsis cambrica 'Flore Pleno'

Meconopsis chelidonifolia at Sellindge, Kent

Glaucium flavum

Papaver lateritium at Inshriach, Inverness-shire

Eomecon chionanthum Hance (*Papaveraceae*)
Native of E China, in Guangzi (Kwangsi)
growing on the banks of the Bamboo River,
presumably under trees, flowering in April–July.
Plant forming wide mats by far-creeping
rhizomes. Leaves fleshly, with yellow juice, on
petioles to 30cm, with blade 10cm across.
Flower stems with few branches to 40cm;
flowers 3.5–4cm across. Easily grown in moist,
leafy soil, and can become a pest if it grows too
well, but dislikes drought and cold, heavy soil.
Hardy to −20°C or so.

Eschscholzia californica Cham.
(*Papaveraceae*) Native of California, west of
the Sierra and the west part of the Mojave
desert, and of Washington and Oregon from the
Columbia River southwards, growing on dunes,
rocky hills and roadside banks at up to 200m;
commonly naturalized in S & W Europe and the
Canaries; flowering in February–September.
Usually perennial, although flowering in the
first year from seed. Stems usually prostrate,
20–60cm high. Leaves glaucous. Petals deep
orange to yellow, 2–6cm long. Capsule 3–8cm
long. Variable and common in many habitats;
the flowers often large and orange in spring,
paler and smaller in late summer, and in shades
of pink in cultivated annual strains. Easily
grown as an annual, and perennial in mild
winters and with well-drained soil. Hardy to
−10°C.

Glaucium flavum Crantz (*Papaveraceae*)
Native of the coasts of most of Europe except
the far north, in Ireland and in Britain from
Arran southwards; naturalized inland in
Switzerland,? Hungary, Austria,
Czechoslovakia, and Poland. Native also in the
E Mediterranean, NW Africa and the Black
Sea, growing on sandy shores and shingle
banks, flowering from May–August. Perennial
or sometimes biennial. Stems to 90cm, sparsely
bristly-pubescent. Leaves greyish green.
Flowers 6–9cm across. Seed pods linear,
15–30cm long. This species usually has yellow
flowers. Red or orange flowers are found in the
annual *G. corniculatum* (L.) Rud. which is
common in S Europe, and in the perennial *G.
grandiflorum* Boiss. & Huet, from Greece, east
to Iran, a plant of semi-deserts, with flowers
8–12cm across, and red, black-spotted petals.
All species require very well-drained, poor soil
to survive the winter as perennials. Hardy to
−10°C.

Meconopsis cambrica (L.) Vig. (*Papaveraceae*)
Native of Britain, chiefly in Wales and also on
Exmoor; and in Ireland, mainly in the Wicklow
Mountains, in Co. Sligo, and on the Antrim
coast; of W France and N Spain, and
naturalized in Germany, Switzerland and
Holland, growing in woods by rocky streams,
on old walls and mountain rocks at up to 600m,
flowering in June–August. A long-lived
perennial with branching taproots. Stems
30–60cm. Flowers 4–8cm across.
'**Aurantiaca**' Flowers orange. Common in
cultivation, coming true from seed, in various
shades of orange.
'**Flore Pleno**' Flowers orange or yellow,
double, coming true from seed.
'**Francis Perry**' Flowers reddish-orange. All
three are easily grown in cool gardens, especially
in north-facing shade.

Meconopsis chelidonifolia Bur. & Franch.
Native of W China, in W Sichuan, at 1800–

2750m, especially from Mount Omei to around
Kangding (Tatsienlu), growing in scrub,
flowering in July–August. A long-lived
perennial, with stems to 1m, with leafy bulbils
in leaf axils. Petals *c.*2.5cm long and wide.
Capsule ellipsoid, splitting by 5–6 valves, not
often produced in cultivation. *M. oliverana*
Franch. & Prain from E Sichuan and W
Hubei has a capsule rather like that of *M. villosa*
(q.v.), but is otherwise very similar to *M.
chelidonifolia*. An elegant and attractive plant,
requiring a moist position, sheltered from
drying winds in summer, which shrivel and
blacken the leaves. The stem bulbils form a
convenient means of propagation. Hardy to
−15°C, perhaps less.

Meconopsis villosa (Hook. fil.) G. Taylor syn.
Cathcartia villosa Hook. Native of E Nepal,
Sikkim and Bhutan, often forming large clumps
on shady rocks and by streams in *Tsuga* and
Abies forest, and in forest clearings, at
2700–4000m, flowering in May–July. Stems
60–150cm. Basal leaves palmately 3–5-lobed,
the lobes toothed. Flowers 1–5 per stem. Petals
2.5–3cm long and wide. Capsule cylindric,
40–80mm × 5–7mm, 4–7 valved, the valves
splitting almost to the base. It is because of its
distinct capsule that this species is sometimes
placed in the genus *Cathcartia*. Easily grown in
a moist, shaded and sheltered position, but not
often seen in cultivation. It is liable to damage
from warm, wet weather in winter.

Papaver lateritium Koch (*Papaveraceae*)
Native of NE Turkey, in the Çoruh valley at
1200–3000m, on hillsides, meadows and screes,
flowering in July–August. Stems 30–60cm,
usually *c.*40cm in cultivation. Leaves narrowly
lanceolate, deeply double-toothed. Flowers
orange, *c.*5cm across. Similar to *P. monanthum*
Trautv. and *P. oreophilum* Rupr. from the
Caucasus. 'Fireball' syns. 'Nana Plena' or
'Nana Flore Pleno' is possibly a double form or
hybrid of this species, not of *P. orientale*. Both
are long-lived perennials forming spreading
clumps. For any well-drained soil. Hardy to
−15°C.

Papaver spicatum Boiss. & Bal. syn. *P.
heldreichii* Boiss. Native of W & S Turkey,
from Manisa to Anamur, on limestone screes
and rocky mountains at 600–1400m, flowering
in June. Stems 60–75cm. Leaves greyish white
with appressed hairs, serrate-crenate. Flowers
sessile or short-stalked towards the base, the
terminal opening first; petals orange, unspotted;
capsules glabrous. Easily grown in well-drained
soil in full sun.

Papaver spicatum at Windsor

Papaver lateritium 'Fireball'

Argemone munita above Death Valley, California

Argemone munita

Capparis spinosa near Tarsus, S Turkey

Argemone munita Dur. & Hilg. (*Papaveraceae*) Prickly Poppy   Native of California in the Coast Ranges from San Luis Obispo Co. southwards to Baja California, and on the dry eastern side of the Sierra Nevada north to Shasta Co. and eastwards to Arizona, Nevada and Utah, growing in scrub, chaparral, open pinyon pine woodland and roadside desert margins at up to 2500m, flowering in March–September. Plant usually perennial with prickly, upright or spreading stems to 150cm. Leaves prickly, usually greyish. Flowers 5–13cm across. The subspecies, four of which are covered in *A California Flora*, differ primarily in the size and distribution of their prickles. For very dry soil in full sun. Hardy to −15°C, possibly less. *A. mexicana* is a commonly cultivated annual, with yellow flowers, now found throughout the tropics.

Capparis spinosa L. (*Capparidaceae*) Caper Native of the E Mediterranean and now found throughout the Mediterranean region east to Kashmir, growing in old walls, cliffs and rocky roadsides, flowering in July–August. Plant with annual usually spiny, trailing stems from a shrubby base. Leaves rounded up to 4cm long. Flowers *c.*7cm across. Much cultivated for its aromatic buds which are eaten in sauces. For a dry position in full sun. Hardy to −10°C perhaps. *C. ovata* Desf., which has flowers with much longer lower petals than upper, and elliptic leaves, is possible hardier.

Eucnide urens (Gray) Parry (*Loasaceae*) Rock Nettle   Native of SE California, around Death Valley, eastwards to Utah, Arizona and Baja California, growing in dry rocky places and open scrub at up to 1500m, flowering in April–June. Plant with a woody base and stems to 60cm, forming a round bush. Stems and leaves with long, barbed, stinging hairs. Flowers with 5 petals, each 2.5–4cm long. For a very dry position in sandy, rocky soil and full sun. Hardy to −10°C or lower if dry. Most of the family *Loasaceae* have stinging hairs, but very beautiful flowers. 'Blazing Star', *Mentzelia*, is the commonest genus in California, with 19 species including *M. lindleyi* (syn. *Bartonia aurea*), a commonly grown annual.

Hypericum cerastoides (Spach) Robson syn. *H. rhodoppeum* Friv. (*Hypericaceae*)   Native of S Bulgaria, Greece and NW Turkey, growing in stony places and woods at up to 1500m, flowering in April–July. Plant forming spreading mats or with ascending stems to 30cm. Leaves 8–30mm, oblong to ovate, finely pubescent. Flowers 2–4cm across, deep yellow. Easily grown in well-drained, sandy soil, preferably slightly acid. Hardy to −15°C or less.

Hypericum olympicum L. f. *minus* Hausskn. 'Sulphureum' syn. *H. polphyllum* 'Citrinum' hort.   Native of S Greece, in parts of Thessaly, Euboea, Attica and the Peloponnese, growing on rocky slops and in dry scrub, flowering in May–July. Plant with erect or sprawling stems to 35cm from a woody base. Leaves glabrous, narrowly elliptic, acute to rounded, greyish. Flowers *c.*6cm across, deep yellow or pale in 'Sulphureum'. For well-drained soil in full sun. Hardy to −15°C perhaps. Forma *uniflorum* D. Jord. & Kuz. has rounder leaves and fewer flowers (1–3) per stem. It also has a pale-yellow form, 'Citrinum'.

Macleaya cordata (Willd.) R. Br. syn. *Bocconia cordata* Willd. (*Papaveraceae*)   Native of Japan, from Honshu southwards, of E China and Taiwan, growing in grassy places, open meadows and on the grassy floors of *Cryptomeria* plantations, flowering in June–August. Plant with spreading underground rhizomes and upright stems to 2m or more. Leaves rounded, deeply lobed, usually white beneath, to 25cm long. Flowers whitish, with 2 sepals *c.*10mm long, and 25–30 stamens. Capsules 2cm long. *M. microcarpa* (Maxim.) Fedde has smaller pinkish-brown or pinkish flowers, red in 'Kelways' Coral Plume', with 8–12 stamens, and a more invasive root. Both are easily grown in sun or partial shade. Hardy to −15°C or less.

Romneya coulteri Harvey (*Papaveraceae*) Matilija Poppy   Native of S California from Ventura Co. and the Santa Ana mountains south to Baja California, growing in canyons and dry riverbeds below 1200m, flowering in May–July and later if watered. Plant with creeping underground rhizomes and upright or leaning stems to 2.5m; flowers to 20cm across. Two varieties are recognized in California: var. *coulteri*, which is not found along the coast, has glabrous sepals, rather bare peduncles, and lobes of leaves less than 12mm wide; var. *trichocalyx* (Eastw.) Jepson has more slender stems, narrower leaves, with lobes 3–10mm wide, peduncles leafy to the top and bristly buds. Most of the plants in cultivation are probably hybrids between the two varieties. For well-drained soil in a warm position in full sun. Hardy to −15°C, or less if the rootstock is covered.

Eucnide urens

Eucnide urens above Death Valley, California

Hypericum cerastoides

Hypericum olympicum 'Sulphureum'

Macleaya cordata in Honshu

Romneya coulteri in a garden near Cambridge

Megacarpaea orbiculata at Amankutan, near Samarkand

Megacarpaea polyandra at Keillour Castle

Megacarpaea orbiculata (fruit)

Crambe cordifolia in the University Botanic Garden, Oxford

Erysimum scoparium on Mount Teide, Tenerife

Crambe cordifolia Stev. (*Cruciferae*) Native of the N Caucasus, growing in steppes and open stony places, flowering in May–July. Plant with a very thick, woody rootstock, from which come a few much-branched stems making a huge frothy mass to 1.8m in diameter, with small, white flowers. Basal leaves thin, heart-shaped, bristly, shallowly lobed, *c*.35cm long. Flowers 12–14mm across, scented. Fruit firm, 4.5–5mm across. A fine plant for a huge border, in well-drained but good soil in full sun. Hardy to −20°C or less.

Crambe kotschyana Boiss. Native of C Asia, in the Tien Shan, the Pamir-Alai, the Dzungarian Ala-tau, and in NW China (Sinjiang); also in SW Asia in the Badgis, in NE Iran and perhaps in Afghanistan, growing on rocky slopes, grassy foothills and screes at 1400–4000m, flowering March–May. Plant with several much-branched stems from a deep, woody rootstock. Basal leaves thick, less deeply lobed than *C. cordifolia*. Inflorescence to 2.5m tall and as much across. Fruit spongy, *c*.6mm across. *C. orientalis* L., which is widespread in Turkey and Iran, is similar but it forms a mound to 120cm in diameter, with small flowers 8–12mm across. For deep, well-drained, rather dry soil in full sun. Hardy to −20°C.

Crambe maritima L. Seakale Native of Europe, including the British Isles, on the shores of the Baltic, the Black Sea and the Atlantic, but not the Mediterranean, on shingle beaches near the high-tide line, flowering in May–June. Stems and leaves form a mound to 50cm across from a hard, woody rootstock. Flower shoots to 60cm. Leaves very fleshy, fluted and wavy edged, with a glaucous bloom. Flowers 10–16mm across, scented. The fruiting stems break off and blow like a tumbleweed. Fruits spongy, 12–14mm across, able to float in seawater without damage to the seed. Often grown as a vegetable but is also an attractive border plant, recommended by Gertrude Jekyll, growing best in sandy, very well-drained soil. Easily propagated by root cuttings. Hardy to −20°C.

Erysimum scoparium (Willd.) Wettst. (*Cruciferae*) Native of the Canary Islands, especially Tenerife, growing on rocky volcanic slops at *c*.3000m, flowering most of the year. Shrubby at the base to 30cm; stems to 50cm. Leaves thick and fleshy to 12.5cm long, 1cm wide, not toothed or with distinct fine teeth. 'Bowles' Mauve' (p. 47) is very similar to this species but has shorter, broader leaves and large flowers. For very dry, poor soil in full sun. It will grow easily in richer, damper soil, but then is liable to rot in winter. Hardy to −15°C or lower when dry.

Megacarpaea orbiculata B. Fed. (*Cruciferae*) Native of C Asia, in the Tien Shan and the Pamir Alai, growing on rocky limestone hills at *c*.1800m, flowering in March–April. Rootstock thick and deep. Stems 50–100cm, widely branched. Young leaves fan-shaped, glaucous; plant probably monocarpic, growing for several years before flowering. Fruits almost circular, 2.5–3cm across. For well-drained but deep, rich soil and full sun, dry in summer. Hardy to −15°C.

Megacarpaea polyandra Benth. Native of Kashmir to C Nepal, growing in alpine meadows and open forests, at 3000–4300m, flowering in June–July. Stems 1–2m. flowers 1cm across; fruit 3.5–5cm across, of 2-headed lobes. Plants taking many years to flower from seed, perhaps monocarpic. Leaves pinnate, lobes 10–20cm long. Hardy to −20°C. Most of the eight or so *Megacarpaea* species are from C Asia.

Stanleya pinnata (Pursh) Britton (*Cruciferae*) Native of California, especially on the east side of the Sierra Nevada and in the south, east to North Dakota, Kansas, Arizona and Texas, growing in dry, stony places and desert slopes at up to 1800m, flowering in April–September. Plant subshrubby at the base, with many tall, upright stems to 1.5m. Lower stem leaves pinnatifid. Inflorescence remarkably *Eremurus*-like. Petals with the inner surface hairy, 12–16mm long. Seed pods 5–8cm long, curling or recurved. For dry, poor soil in full sun. Hardy to −20°C or less. This plant grows well in a warm, dry border at Kew.

Crambe kotschyana near Ferghana, C Asia

Crambe maritima at Dungeness, Kent

Stanleya pinnata in Arizona

Sphaeralcea fendleri var. *venusta* at Kew

Alcea excubita Iljin (*Malvaceae*)   Native of N
Iran and E Turkey westwards to Malatya,
growing on rocky hillsides at 600–2000m,
flowering in June–July and later in gardens.
Stems to 1.5m, few to several from a woody
rootstock. Leaves and stems with dense stellate
hairs. Upper leaves deeply 5–7-lobed. Petals
white or pale yellow, to 5.5cm long. For a dry,
sunny, well-drained position in full sun. Hardy
to −20°C or less.

Alcea rugosa Alef.   Native of S Russia and the
Caucasus, south to Georgia and Armenia, east to
N Iran and the Kopet Daǧ, growing on dry hills
and steppes, and in open woods, flowering in
June–August. Stems to 2.5m from a stout,
woody rootstock, purple spotted, bristly-hairy
with stellate hairs. Upper leaves shallowly 3–5-
lobed, the middle lobe longest. Flowers to 12cm
across, pale yellow. For dry, well-drained soil in
a full sun. Hardy to −20°C or less.

Sidalcea candida A. Gray (*Malvaceae*)   Native
of Nevada to Wyoming, south to S New
Mexico, growing along streams and in moist
mountain meadows, flowering in June–
September. Stems upright or leaning to 90cm.
Basal leaves rounded with 7 shallow lobes,
upper deeply 7-palmate. Flowers c.2.5cm
across, in an often dense spike. For any good
soil in sun or partial shade. Hardy to −20°C or
less.

Sidalcea malviflora (DC.) A. Gray ex Benth.
Native of the coast of California, from Los
Angeles north to Mendocino Co., growing on
open grassy slopes and mesas (moist grassy
hollows), flowering in May–July. Other
subspecies (there are at least 10) grow at higher
elevations northwards to Oregon. Stems several
from a tough rootstock, to 60cm. Leaves 7–9-
lobed. Petals to 2.5cm long, usually with pale
veins. About 24 cultivars are grown now,
including: 'Elsie Heugh', petals attractively
fringed; 'Rose Queen', large, pink flowers and
stems to 1.2m; 'Sussex Beauty', flowers very
pale pink; 'William Smith', flowers deep pink.
For any good soil in sun or partial shade. Hardy
to −20°C perhaps.

Sidalcea oregana (Nutt.) Gray subsp. **spicata**
(Repel) C. L. Hitchc.   Native of W North
America from Oregon south to N California
(Modoc to Siskiyou Cos.), growing in
coniferous forests in damp grassy places,
flowering in June–August. Stems several, 80cm
to 1m in cultivation, from a stout tap-root.
Inflorescence many-flowered, spike like. Petals
10–20mm long. For moist soil in sun or partial
shade. Hardy to −15°C or less.

Sphaeralcea emoryi Torr. (*Malvaceae*)
Native of W North America, from N Baja
California east to S Nevada and S Arizona,
growing by fields and roadsides at below 1000m,
flowering in March–May. Stems several,
upright to 120cm, sometimes greyish. Leaves
3-lobed, usually twice as long as wide. Petals
10–20mm long, usually reddish, sometimes
pinkish. *S. ambigua* Gray is similar, but has a
more open inflorescence and leaves as long as
wide. For well-drained, dry soil in full sun.
Hardy to −10°C perhaps.

Sphaeralcea fendleri Gray var. **venusta**
Kearney   Native of N Mexico to Arizona (with
other varieties in S Colorado and W Texas)
growing in pine forest and evergreen oak scrub,
usually along streams, at up to 2599m, flowering
in June–October. Stems several from a stout
rootstock to 1.5m. Leaves silky-silvery, with
few but long-rayed stellate hairs. Petals 15–
20mm, pinkish, rarely reddish. For well-
drained, dry soil in a sunny, sheltered position.
Hardy to −15°C, perhaps lower when dry.

Sphaeralcea laxa Woot. & Standl.   Native of
W Texas and Arizona, growing in scrub and on
open hillsides on limestone at 600–1800m,
flowering in March–November. Stems several,
sprawling, from a stout rootstock. Leaves
usually silvery, tomentose, often deeply
dissected. Flowers in an open, long-branched
panicle, to 5cm across. For well-drained, dry
soil in full sun. Hardy to −15°C, perhaps less in
dry climates.

Alcea rugosa at Leeds Castle, Kent

Sphaeralcea emoryi in Arizona

Alcea excubita near Lake Van, Turkey

Alcea rugosa

Sidalcea candida with *Melianthus major*

Sidalcea oregana subsp. *spicata*

Sidalcea malviflora 'William Smith'

Sphaeralcea laxa

Sidalcea malviflora 'Rose Queen'

Lavatera 'Barnsley' with *Phlox* and *Nicotiana* at Cockermouth Castle, Cumbria

Malva moschata

Althaea officinalis L. (*Malvaceae*) Marsh Mallow   Native of Europe, from S Ireland eastwards to C Asia and Afghanistan and south to Israel, growing in grassy places by the sea, and by ditches and salt marshes inland, flowering in June–September. Plant with lax stems to 2m from a stout rootstock. Leaves softly whitish, hairy. Flowers in groups in the leaf axils, 1.2–3cm across. For good, moist soil. Hardy to −25°C.

Kitabela vitifolia Willd. (*Malvaceae*)   Native of Yugoslavia and recorded also in the Kopet Dağ (Göktepe), growing in scrub, grassy places and in vineyards, flowering in June–August. Plant with a great clump of tall stems to 3m from a huge rootstock. Leaves up to 18cm across with 5–7 toothed, pointed lobes. Flowers *c*.4cm across, pinkish. For any soil in sun or partial shade. Hardy to −20°C perhaps.

Lavatera cachemeriana Cambess. (*Malvaceae*)   Native of the W Himalayas, from Pakistan to N India, growing in meadows and open places in forest at up to 3600m, flowering in July–September. Stems much branched, to 2m from a stout rootstock. Leaves 3–5 lobed. Flowers 5–8cm across, in the commonly cultivated variety with narrow, widely separate, petals with a pale centre. For any good soil in sun or partial shade. Hardy to −20°C perhaps. Now often considered a minor variant of *L. thuringiaca*.

Lavatera olbia L.   Native of SW Europe, from Italy and Sicily westwards to Spain, Portugal and North Africa, growing in hedges, by rivers and in damp places, flowering in May–September. Plant shrubby at the base, with stems to 2m or more in gardens. Lower leaves 3–5-lobed, upper leaves 3-lobed, with the lower lobes much reduced. Flowers pink, 3.5–7cm across, on very short stalks 2–7mm long. For well-drained soil in sun. Hardy to −15°C perhaps.

Lavatera thuringiaca L.   Native of Europe from C Italy and Germany, eastwards to Russia and NW China and south to Turkey and NW Iran, growing in scrub by roadsides and by streams at up to 2800m in Turkey, flowering in July–October. Plant with annual stems to 1m.

Lavatera 'Barnsley'

Malva sylvestris 'Primley Blue'

Lavatera triloba in S Spain

Kitabela vitifolia at Axeltree Nursery, Kent

Lower leaves 3–5-lobed, upper leaves weakly 3-lobed. Flowers 4.5–10cm across on stalks 10–22mm long. For any good garden soil. Hardy to –20°C, perhaps less. The following are considered by Alan Leslie to be hybrids with *L. olbia*:
'**Barnsley**' A semi-albino form found by Rosemary Verey in a garden in Gloucestershire in *c*.1985. It is one of the best plant introductions of recent years. It will revert to pink if the top growth is killed.
'**Kew Rose**' A deep-pink flowered form, with purplish stems. A pure white is also known. The old variety 'Rosea' syn. *L. olbia* 'Rosea' differs from 'Kew Rose' in its paler flowers, hairier stems and paler leaves.

Lavatera triloba L. Native of C, S & E Spain, S Portugal and Sardinia, with subsp, *agrigentina* (Tineo) R. Fernandes in S Italy and Sicily, growing on rocky hillsides, often in damp, heavy or saline soils, flowering in April–June. Plant musk-scented, glandular, woody below, with upright stems to 1.5m with broad stiples. Leaves slightly 3-lobed, woolly or bristly-hairy. Flowers in clusters of 3–7, purplish pink or yellow, 4–7cm across. For rich soil in full sun. Hardy to –15°C perhaps.

Malva moschata L. (*Malvaceae*) Musk Mallow Native of Europe, from England and Poland south to Spain, NW Africa and Turkey (where it is rare), growing in grassy places, especially on road verges, flowering in June–September. Plant with several decumbent stems from a branching taproot. Leaves very deeply divided. Flowers pink or white in *f. alba*, 4–7cm across. Easily grown in any good soil in full sun. Hardy to –25°C or less.

Malva sylvestris L. Native of most of Europe, North Africa and Asia eastwards to NW China, growing in grassy places, on roadsides, flowering in May–October. Plant perennial or biennial, with upright or trailing stems to 150cm. Leaves with 3–7 rounded lobes. Flowers to 6cm across, usually pinkish purple, but bluish in 'Primley Blue' (shown here), a recent introduction. A large, upright form with fine, deep-purple flowers has been called *M. mauritanica* L. but is now considered a subsp. of *M. sylvestris*. For any soil in full sun. Hardy to –20°C or less.

Lavatera olbia

Lavatera cachemeriana

Lavatera 'Kew Rose'

Althaea officinalis on Romney Marsh

Euphorbia schillingii

Euphorbia longifolia

Euphorbia schillingii at Washfield Nurseries, Hawkhurst, Kent

Euphorbia kotschyana Fenzl (*Euphorbiaceae*) Native of W & S Turkey, W Iran, W Syria and Lebanon, growing in fir and cedar forest, oak scrub and on mountain steppes, at up to 2500m, flowering in May–August. Plant with several stems to 80cm from a woody rootstock. Leaves glossy above, glaucous beneath, to 8cm long. Raylet leaf cups 1–4cm across. Fruits pubescent or glabrous. Differs from *E. macrostegia* Boiss. mainly in its taller stems and narrower glossier leaves. For well-drained soil in sun or partial shade. Hardy to −15°C perhaps. J. & J. Archibald 47900.

Euphorbia longifolia D. Don   Native of the Himalayas, from W Nepal to Bhutan, growing

in mountain meadows and clearings in forest at 1680–3600m, flowering in May–June, according to altitude. Plant with creeping rhizomes and stems to 1m, forming spreading clumps. Stem leaves linear-lanceolate, 6–11cm long, 1–1.8cm across. Bracts yellow, ovate. Fruits warty. Styles deeply bifid. Close to *E. griffithii* (see vol. 1, p. 51), but without the red leaves and bracts. For moist soil in sun or partial shade. Hardy to −15°C, perhaps less. Schilling 2069.

Euphorbia palustris L.   Native of Europe, from Sweden and Spain, east to Siberia, the Caucasus and Turkey, growing by rivers and lakes, and in marshes, flowering in March (in the south) to August. Plant forming large clumps of stems to 1.5m, from a stout, woody rootstock. Rays and raylet leaves bright yellowish when young, with willowy side branches developing after flowering. Fruit tuberculate. For moist or wet soil in sun or partial shade. Hardy to −20°C or less.

Euphorbia schillingii A. Radcliffe-Smith Native of E Nepal, in the Dudh Kosi valley south of Everest, growing on rocky slopes at 2500–3000m, flowering in July–September. Plant clump forming, with many branching stems to 1.0m tall, 30cm across. Leaves to 12cm long, *c*.2cm across. For moist but well-drained soil in sun or partial shade. Hardy to −20°C, perhaps less.

Euphorbia seguieriana Necker subsp. **niciciana** (Borbás) Rech. fil. syn. *E. niciciana* Borbás   Native of Yugoslavia, Greece and

Turkey, east to Pakistan, growing in dry scrub, by roadsides and on rocky hills, flowering in March–October. Plant with several upright stems to 60cm from a woody rootstock. Leaves rather leathery, linear or oblong-linear, acute, 1–4cm long, spreading. Rays up to 30. Differs from the rather similar *E. nicaeensis* (see vol. 1, p. 49) in its narrower leaves, more upright stems and more numerous rays. For any dry position in full sun. Hardy to −15°C, possibly less.

Euphorbia sikkimensis Boiss.   Native of the Himalayas in Sikkim and possibly Bhutan, growing in scrub and clearings in forest, at 2700–3300m, flowering in July. Plant with far-creeping rhizomes and glabrous stems to 1.2m. Young shoots beautifully marked, reddish. Stem leaves lanceolate, 10–12cm long, 2cm wide. Bracts rounded at apex, yellow. Close to *E. griffithii* but taller, with yellow, not red, rounded bracts and later flowering. For moist soil. Hardy to −20°C perhaps.

Humulus lupulus L. **'Aureus'** (*Cannabidaceae*) **Golden Hop**   Found wild throughout Europe, W & C Asia (but native distribution uncertain), growing in scrub or hedges, flowering in June–August. Plant with a stout rootstock and annual climbing stems to 6m or more. Male and female flowers on separate plants, the male with conspicuous stamens, the female only forming hops. The golden-leaved form shown here has been known since 1889. It is male. For any soil, preferably in a warm, sheltered position. Hardy to −20°C or less.

Euphorbia sikkimensis

Euphorbia sikkimensis (young shoots)

Humulus lupulus 'Aureus' with *Lysimachia ciliata* at Cobblers, Sussex

Euphorbia seguieriana subsp. *niciciana*

Euphorbia palustris

Euphorbia kotschyana at Coldham, Kent

Persicaria bistorta 'Superba' with *Allium giganteum* at the Culpepper Gardens, Leeds Castle, Kent

Persicaria macrophylla

Persicaria bistorta subsp. *carnea* above Kasbegi, C Caucasus

Persicaria tenuicaulis

Eriogonum compositum Douglas ex Benth. (*Polygomaceae*)   Native of W North America, from Idaho to Washington and south to California, growing on dry, rocky slopes at 1900–3500m, flowering in May–July. Plant branched and rather woody at the base, with flowering stems 10–50cm. Leaves with blades 2–10cm long, whitish beneath, cuneate to cordate. Primary umbel with lanceolate bracts; secondary umbels many-flowered. For dry, well-drained soil, in full sun. Hardy to −15°C, or less if dry. There are at least 150 species of *Eriogonum*, mostly in W North America, ranging from low shrubs to herbaceous perennials, annuals and cushion-like alpines. Flowers are commonly yellow, but may be red, or white to pink.

Persicaria affinis (D. Don) R. Deer. syn. *Polygonum affine* D. Don, *Bistorta affinis* (D. Don) Greene (*Polygonaceae*)   Native of Afghanistan, east to Nepal and Sikkim, growing on rocky slopes and screes at 3000–4800m, flowering from June–September. Plant forming leafy mats, often up to 1m across. Stems 15–30cm. Leaves lanceolate, elliptic, the blade 4–8cm long. Flower-head 5–7.5cm long, with pink or red flowers. Best in rather shallow, peaty, but well-drained soil. Hardy to −20°C. 'Donald Lowndes' is a deep-pink form. 'Superbum' is said by Graham Thomas to be an even better clone.

Persicaria amphibia (L.) S. F. Gray, syn.
Polygonum amphibium L.   Native of Europe
and Asia, from Ireland eastwards to Japan,
south to the Mediterranean, and in North
America from Quebec and Alaska south to
Kentucky and California, growing in lakes,
ponds, rivers and canals, flowering in July–
September. Either an aquatic plant with floating
ovate-oblong leaf blades and an emerging flower
stalk, or a leggy marsh plant with oblong-
lanceolate leaves. Flower-head 2–4cm, with
pink or red flowers. An attractive aquatic for
water from 1–3m deep. The leaves are often
attacked by the black and yellow larvae of the
water-lily beetle. Hardy to −25°C and less.

Persicaria bistorta (L.) A. Samp., syn.
Polygonum bistorta L., *Bistorta vulgaris* Hill
Native of Europe, from Ireland eastwards to
Japan, southwards in the mountains to Turkey,
growing in subalpine meadows, by rivers and on
grassy roadsides, flowering from June–August.
Plant forming extensive colonies, with a very
thick rhizome. Stem 25–50cm. Leaves 5–15cm,
broadly ovate, obtuse, truncate or subcordate at
base. Flowers pink or white, on a spike 3–6cm
long. Hardy to −25°C or less. An attractive
clump-forming perennial for a moist border.
'Superbum' is a garden selection.

Persicaria bistorta L. subsp. *carnea* (Koch)
Coode & Cullen syn. *Polygonum carneum* Koch
Native of Caucasus and NE & E Turkey,
growing in mountain meadows and open woods,
at 1800–3600m in Turkey, flowering June–
August. Similar to *P. bistorta*, but generally
smaller, with deep-pink, stalked flowers, in a
more rounded, oblong-globose head. For moist
soil in a cool position. Hardy to −20°C or less.

Persicaria macrophylla (D. Don) Trehane,
syn. *P. sphaerostachyum* auct. non Meissn.
Native of the Himalayas, from N India and
Nepal to SW China, growing in damp alpine
meadows at 1700–4870m, flowering in
May–September. Plant forming spreading
clumps. Stems 5–30cm; leaf blades ovate-
lanceolate, 4–12cm × 2–3cm, or sometimes
narrower, rounded or cordate at base. Flower
spikes 2–7cm, erect; flowers 2–5mm, pink,
pendent on the spike. For moist, peaty soil in
sun or partial shade. Flowering in gardens in
mid-summer. Hardy to −20°C. Dwarf forms,
with narrower leaves and short flower spikes,
are found at high altitudes.

Persicaria milletii (Léveillé) Trehane syn.
Polygonum milletii Léveillé   Native of the
Himalayas, from W Nepal to SW China,
growing in scrub and on cliff ledges at
300–4700m, flowering in June–November.
Plant tufted with many stems 20–60cm tall.
Leaves lanceolate, 8–15cm × 0.7–4.5cm,
acuminate, decurrent at base into the stalk.
Flowers 5–6mm, crimson, on spikes 2.5–6cm
long. Differs from *P. macrophylla* in its larger
crimson flowers, and long leaf sheaths up to
10cm. For moist, well-drained soil in sun or
partial shade. Hardy to −20°C.

Persicaria tenuicaulis (Biss. & Moore)
Trehane syn. *Polygonum tenuicaule* Biss. &
Moore   Native of Japan, in Honshu, Shikoku
and Kyushu, growing in woods and on shady
banks, flowering in April–June. Plant mat-
forming, with short, thick rhizomes. Leaves
3–8cm × 2–3cm, oblong-ovate. Stems 7–15cm.
Flower spikes 2–3.5cm long. For a moist,
shaded position; an attractive small ground-
covering plant. Hardy to −15°C perhaps.

Persicaria affinis

Persicaria amphibia

Eriogonum compositum in N California

Persicaria milletii

Gypsophila 'Rosenschleier' in the ruins at Cockermouth Castle, Cumbria

Gypsophila paniculata 'Flamingo'

Gypsophila acutifolia Stev. ex Spreng.
(*Caryophyllaceae*)   Native of the N Caucasus
and southern Russia northwards to Romania
(introduced) and the Ukraine (possibly
introduced), growing in dry, sandy places and
on stony slopes, flowering in July–September.
Plant with a stout, deep rootstock, and
branching stems to 170cm long. Leaves linear-
lanceolate to lanceolate, acuminate.
Inflorescence glandular, the pedicels 1–4mm
long. *G. perfoliata* L. has similar flowers, but
longer pedicels which are glabrous and ovate,
amplexicaul leaves. For well-drained soil in full
sun. Hardy to −20°C or less.

Gypsophila bicolor Freyn & Sint. syn. *G.
paniculata* L. subsp. *bicolor* Freyn & Sint.
Native of E Turkey, the S Caucasus, Iran and C
Asia, growing in steppes, in open woods and
cornfields, flowering in May–July. Differs from
G. paniculata in its green, not glaucous leaves,
denser inflorescence and calyx teeth orbicular-
cordate, finely toothed. For dry, well-drained
soil in full sun. Hardy to −20°C or less.

Gypsophila paniculata L.   Native of E
Europe, from C Austria and Bulgaria eastwards
to the Caucasus, C Asia and NW China,
growing in grassy sandy steppes and stony
places, flowering in July–August. Stems few to
several from a deep, stout rhizome, forming a
mound of stiff, thin stems 1.5m high. Leaves
usually glaucous and glabrous. Pedicels 3–6mm
long. Flowers white or pink, double in
'Flamingo' (pink) and **Bristol Fairy** (white);
the petals linear-spathulate, 3–4mm long. For
well-drained soil in a dry and sunny position.
Hardy to −20°C or less, but intolerant of winter
damp.

Gypsophila 'Rosenschleier' syn. 'Rosy Veil'
A hybrid between *G. paniculata* and *G. repens*
'Rosea' raised by K. Foerster in 1933. It forms

Gypsophila acutifolia

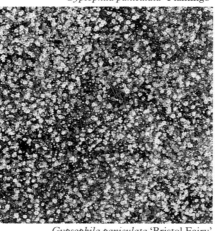

Gypsophila paniculata 'Bristol Fairy'

Saponaria ocymoides in S France

Gypsophila bicolor in a cornfield near Lake Van, SE Turkey

a mound of trailing stems to 100cm across, with double flowers opening white, becoming very pale pink, produced in July–August. For very well-drained soil in full sun. Hardy to −20°C or less.

Saponaria × lempergii hort. 'Max Frei' (*Caryophyllaceae*)   A hybrid between *S. cypria* and *S. haussknechtii*, with numerous softly glandular-hairy stems to 30cm and masses of flowers *c.*1.5cm across. For well-drained soil in a dry position in full sun. Hardy to −15°C perhaps.

Saponaria ocymoides L.   Native of Europe, from N Spain and S France to Italy, S Germany and Yugoslavia, growing on sunny slopes and rocks, usually limestone, in the foothills up to *c.*2300m in the Alps, flowering in July. Stems creeping to 50cm or more. Flowers purplish-pink or rarely white, 7–12mm across. For a well-drained, sunny, dry position on a wall or edge of border creeping over a path. Hardy to −15°C, perhaps less.

Saponaria officinalis L. Soapwort   Native of most of Europe, though often an escape from cultivation, eastwards to Turkey and the Caucasus, growing most commonly on grassy roadsides but also by streams and in damp woods, flowering in June–August. Naturalized in North America. Plant with upright stems to 70cm from creeping underground rhizomes, forming spreading patches. 'Rosea Plena' is the commonest with double, pale-pink flowers. 'Rubra Plena' has dark-pinkish-red flowers. There is also a double white. Flowers sweetly scented, to 20mm across. Easily grown but invasive, though intolerant of shade in cultivation. Hardy to −20°C. Used in the past as soap and still valuable for treating especially delicate, ancient fabric.

Saponaria × lempergii 'Max Frei' at Kew

Saponaria officinalis 'Rubra Plena'

Saponaria officinalis

Saponaria officinalis 'Rosea Plena'

A form of *Dianthus deltoides* at Coldham, Kent

Dianthus deltoides in Finland

Dianthus superbus

Dianthus superbus on grassy dunes near Shari, Hokkaido

Dianthus 'White Loveliness'

Dianthus gratianopolitanus at Cheddar

Dianthus knappii at the Royal Botanic Garden, Edinburgh

Dianthus 'Glory Lyonnaise'

Dianthus 'Green Eye'

Dianthus 'Ursula Le Grove'

Dianthus deltoides L. (*Caryophyllaceae*)
Maiden Pink   Native of most of Europe from
Scotland eastwards to Finland and N Russia,
but absent from the Mediterranean region,
growing in dry, grassy places, flowering in
June–September. Plant with very many
sprawling stems to 45cm, from a slender,
creeping rootstock. Leaves usually green; on
sterile shoots oblanceolate 10–15mm long, on
flowering shoots longer and more acute.
Flowers usually solitary, *c*.1.8cm across,
unscented. For light soil in full sun. Hardy to
−20°C or less. Several named cultivars are
grown, including a pure white, and a fine red,
'Steriker', introduced by Valerie Finnis.

Dianthus ferrugineus Mill.   Native of the
Mediterranean region, from S France to
Yugoslavia and Albania, growing on stony hills
and scrub, flowering in June–July. Plant with
several lax stems to 50cm from a woody
rootstock. Leaves very narrow. Flowers in
dense heads, *c*.3cm across. Epicalyx scales with
a long point. There are numerous very similar
species with tall stems and heads of reddish-
magenta flowers; *D. carthusianorum* L. is the
commonest, and differs from *D. ferrugineus* in
its broader, short, pointed epicalyx scales. For
any well-drained soil in full sun. Hardy to
−15°C perhaps.

Dianthus gratianopolitanus Vill. Cheddar
Pink   Native of Europe from England, only
found in Cheddar Gorge, east to Poland and
the W Ukraine, growing on limestone rocks and
cliffs, flowering in June–July. Plant tufted with
sterile rosettes and flowering stems to 20cm.
Leaves glaucous. Flowers to 3.5cm across,

clove-scented. For well-drained soil in a sunny
position. Hardy to −20°C.

Dianthus knappii (Pant.) Aschs. & Karnitz ex
Borbás   Native of W Yugoslavia, growing in
grassy places and scrub, flowering in
June–August. Plant with few rather lax stems to
40cm. Inflorescence with usually 2 heads, each
crowded with several flowers, *c*.2cm across.
This untidy plant, interesting as the only yellow-
flowered *Dianthus*, was used in breeding the
yellow-flowered pinks. For well-drained soil in
sun or partial shade. Hardy to −15°C.

Old *Dianthus* cultivars
'Glory Lyonnaise'   An old cultivar of
unknown origin. Stems to 30cm.
'Green Eye'   Origin unknown. Stems to 20cm.
'Ursula Le Grove'   Raised by the Revd. C.
Oscar Moreton and named after his daughter.
Stems to 30cm.
'White Loveliness'   Stems *c*.25cm; well
scented. Probably a hybrid of *D. superbus*, raised
by Allwoods in 1928.

Dianthus superbus L.   Native of Europe,
from France and Holland eastwards to Russia
and E Siberia, south to Japan and Taiwan,
growing in damp, grassy places, on dunes, in
open woods and in mountain meadows,
flowering in June–October. Plant with usually
green leaves, decumbent sterile shoots and
flowering stems to 90cm. Flowers 3.5–6.5cm
across; largest in subsp. *speciosus* (Rchb.) Pawl,
the montane subspecies; the petals always
deeply laciniate. For any well-drained, peaty soil
in sun or partial shade, and a cool position.
Hardy to −20°C and below.

Dianthus ferrugineus

DIANTHUS

'Pheasant's Eye'

'Eileen'

'Lady Glanville'

'Painted Beauty'

'Queen of Sheba'

'Kesteven Chambery'

'Hollycroft Fragrance'

'Farnham Rose'

'Gravetye Gem'

'Dewdrop'

'Glory Lyonnaise'

'Musgrave's Pink'

'Brympton Red'

'Inchmery'

'Arthur'

Specimens from Ramparts Nursery, 4 June. ⅔ life size

Dianthus cultivars (pinks) These have been bred for many centuries from *D. caryophyllus* and *D. plumarius*.

Double-flowered pinks
'Alice' Raised by Allwoods in 1930. Stems *c*.32cm. Well scented.
'Bat's Double Red' Raised by T. Bat in the 18th century. Stems *c*.17cm.
'Bridal Veil' Known since the 17th century. Stems *c*.35cm. Well scented.
'Heidi' C. Frickart 1959. Stems *c*.20cm.
'Hope' Raised by Allwoods in 1946. Stems *c*.25cm. Well scented.
'Laced Joy' Raised by Allwoods in 1947. Stems *c*.30cm.
'Laced Romeo' Raised by Allwoods in 1963. Stems *c*.30cm. Well scented.
'London Delight' Raised by F. R. McQuown before 1946. Stems *c*.25cm. Well scented.
'London Poppet' Raised by F. R. McQuown in 1946. Stems *c*.25cm. Variable.
'Mrs Sinkins' Raised by J. Sinkins in 1868. Stems *c*.20–25cm. Flowers untidy but wonderfully scented.
'Old Crimson Clove' Known since the 16th century. Stems *c*.25cm. Well scented.
'Old Pink Clove' An old cultivar of unknown origin. Stems weak, to 40cm. Well scented.
'Paisley Gem' Raised by J. Macree around 1798. Stems *c*.30cm. Well scented.
'Prudence' Raised by Allwoods before 1953. Stems *c*.30cm.
'Rose de Mai' C. 1820. Stems *c*.25cm.
'Sam Barlow' An old variety, known since the early 19th century, resembling Mrs Sinkins in form. Compact.
'Sops-in-wine' An old cultivar of unknown origin. Stems *c*.17cm.
'Sweetheart Abbey' An old cultivar from Sweetheart Abbey in SW Scotland; *c*.25cm.
'White Ladies' An old cultivar of unknown origin. Stems *c*.25cm. Well scented.

Single and semi-double pinks
'Arthur' Raised by Allwoods in 1920. Stems *c*.28cm. Well scented.
'Brympton Red' Raiser not recorded, pre-1960. Stems *c*.25cm. Well scented.
'Dewdrop' Raised by Allwoods before 1932. Stems *c*.15cm. Well scented.
'Eileen' Raised by Allwoods before 1927. Stems *c*.25cm. Well scented.
'Fair Folly' syn. 'Constance Finnis' Well scented. White, with clear crimson markings.
'Farnham Rose' Soft maroon, with flecks and blotches. Well scented.
'Glory Lyonnaise' An old cultivar of unknown origin. Stems *c*.30cm.
'Gravetye Gem' Raised by W. E. Th. Ingwersen before 1940. Well scented.
'Hollycroft Fragrance' Raised by Hollycroft Nurseries before 1979. Stems *c*.15cm. Well scented.
'Inchmery' Raised in the 18th century. Stems *c*.28cm. Well scented.
'Kesteven Chambery' Raised by A. E. Robinson *c*.1970. Stems *c*.15cm.
'Lady Glanville' Raised in *c*.1840. Stems *c*.25cm. Well scented.
'Musgrave's Pink' syn. 'Charles Musgrave' Raised *c*.1730. Stems *c*.20cm. Well scented.
'Painted Beauty' An old cultivar of unknown origin. Stems *c*.20cm.
'Pheasant's Eye' An old cultivar known since 1671. Stems *c*.30cm. Well scented.
'Queen of Sheba' Early 17th century. Stems *c*.25cm. Well scented.

'White Ladies'

'Sam Barlow'

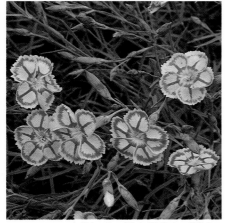

Dianthus 'Fair Folly' at Wisley

Dianthus 'Rose de Mai' at Bressingham Gardens

Dianthus 'Old Pink Clove'

Dianthus 'Bat's Double Red'

A collection of pinks with *Allium christophii* at Northbourne Court, Kent

'Prudence'

'London Delight'

'Paisley Gem'

'Alice'

'London Poppet'

'London Poppet'

'Laced Joy'

'Old Crimson Clove'

'Heidi'

'Hope'

'Laced Romeo'

'Sweetheart Abbey'

'Sops-in-wine'

'Bridal Veil'

'Mrs Sinkins'

Specimens from Ramparts Nursery, Essex, 4 June. ⅔ life size

Dianthus 'Doris', one of the most popular pinks

'Diane'

'Doris'

'Constance'

'Helen'

'Achievement'

'Iceberg'

'Brilliance'

'Haytor White'

'Widecombe Fair'

'Show Ideal'

'Freckles'

'Freckles'/'William of Essex'

'William of Essex'

Specimens from Ramparts Nursery, Essex, 4 June. ⅔ life size

Modern garden pinks

'Achievement' Raised by Allwoods before 1959; stems 22cm, well scented.

'Annabelle' Raised by Th. Charli. before 1957, stems 30cm.

'Anthony' Raised by P. A. Fenn in 1967; stems 20cm.

'Brilliance' Raised by P. A. Fenn in 1975; long flowering season, stems 20cm.

'Constance' Raised by Allwoods before 1955; stems 30cm.

'Desmond' Raised by Mrs D. Underwood in 1978, strong-growing, stems 25cm.

'Diane' Raised by Allwoods in 1964; a sport of 'Doris', stems 26cm.

'Doris' Raised by Allwoods before 1954; vigorous and well scented, stems 26cm.

'Freckles' Raised by C. H. Fielder in 1948. Well scented, stems 20cm.

'Gaiety' Raised by Lindabruce Nurseries in around 1955, stems 25cm.

'Golden Cross' Raised by J. Galbally before 1972; stems 25cm.

'Gran's Favourite' Raised by Mrs D. Underwood; well scented, stems 25cm.

'Haytor White' Raised by C. Wyatt in 1971; well scented, robust, stems 33cm.

'Helen' Raised by Allwoods before 1948; well-scented, stems 30cm.

'Houndspool Cheryl' syn. 'Cheryl' Raised by J. Whetman in 1980; stems 27cm.

'Houndspool Ruby' syn 'Ruby Doris' Raised by J. Whetman in 1977; stems 27cm.

'Iceberg' Raised by C. H. Fielder in 1950; well scented, with a second crop of flowers; stems 33cm.

'Kesteven Kirkstead' Raised by A. E. Robinson; stems 15cm.

'Pink Bouquet' Raised by Mrs D. Underwood in 1958; well scented, with a second crop of flowers; stems 22cm.

'Pink Mrs Sinkins' Raised by C. Turner before 1908; well scented, stems 30cm.

'Polly Piggott' A modern variety of unrecorded origin; stems 25cm.

'Portrait' A modern variety of unrecorded origin; good on light soil, stems 25cm.

'Ruth' Allwoods before 1933; stems 27cm.

'Show Ideal' Raised by Allwoods in 1945; strong-growing, stems 30cm.

'Thomas' Raised by C. Wyatt in 1977; stems 25cm.

'Valda Wyatt' Raised by C. Wyatt in 1977; stems 25cm.

'Widecombe Fair' Raised by C. Wyatt in 1974. Well scented and an unusual apricot colour; stems 30cm.

'William of Essex' Raised by Ramparts Nursery in 1982, a sport of 'Freckles' (q.v.); well scented, stems 10cm.

'Winsome' Raised by C. H. Fielder in 1947; strong-growing, stems 25cm.

Dianthus 'Golden Cross' at Wisley

Dianthus 'Thomas'

Dianthus 'Haytor White'

Dianthus 'Pink Mrs Sinkins'

'Gaiety'   'Houndspool Ruby'   'Annabelle'

'Pink Bouquet'   'Winsome'

'Portrait'   'Anthony'   'Houndspool Cheryl'

'Polly Piggott'   'Gran's Favourite'

'Desmond'   'Valda Wyatt'   'Ruth'

Specimens from Ramparts Nursery, Essex, 4 June. ⅔ life size

Dianthus 'Kesteven Kirkstead' at Wisley

Sedum spectabile 'Carmen' with Small Tortoiseshell butterflies

Sedum telephium subsp. *telephium* in NW England

Sedum 'Sunset Cloud' at Wisley

Sedum telephium subsp. *maximum*
'Atropurpureum'

Sedum alboroseum 'Medio-variegatum'

Sedum 'Ruby Glow'

Cotyledon orbiculata L. var. *oblonga* (Haw.)
DC. (*Crassulaceae*)   Native of S Africa, from the
N Transvaal to Lesotho and SE Cape Province,
growing in rocky places on cliffs and in dry scrub
at up to 3000m, flowering throughout the year.
Plant forming rosettes of obovate, fleshy, white
leaves to 20cm long; flowering stems to 1m, with
pendent flowers *c.*3cm long. For well-drained soil
in full sun. Hardy to −10°C, or probably less,
with the protection of a pane of glass.

Sedum aizoon L. 'Euphorbioides' syn.
'Aurantiacum' (*Crassulaceae*)   Native of N
Japan in Hokkaido and Honshu, in E Siberia,
Mongolia and in N and NW China (N
Sinjiang), growing on dry grassy slopes, in scrub
and by rocky streams, flowering in
July–September. Stems to 50cm from a stout,
branching rhizome forming spreading clumps.
Leaves usually alternate. Flowers 10–13mm
across in heads about 6cm across, yellow, or
reddish in bud and fruit in 'Euphorbioides'. For
good soil in sun or partial shade, moist in
summer. Hardy to −25°C.

Sedum alboroseum Baker 'Medio-variegatum'
syn. *S. erythrostictum* Miq.   Native of E Siberia,
N China and ? Japan, flowering in July–October.
Similar to *S. spectabile* (q.v.), but differing in its
greenish flowers, alternate or opposite leaves and
inflorescence with longer lowest branches. The
variegated form is the one usually seen.

Sedum 'Ruby Glow' syn. *S. cauticola*
'Robustum'   A hybrid between *S. cauticola*
Praeger and *S. telephium* L.; it forms sprawling
clumps of stems to 25cm, very grey leaves, with
deep purplish flowers in July–August. Hardy to
−15°C.

Sedum spectabile Boreau   Native of Korea
and NE China (Heilonjiang), flowering in
July–September. Stems to 70cm from a stout,
branched rootstock, forming dense clumps.
Leaves fleshy, glaucous, opposite or whorled.
Flowers in a head *c.*12cm across, with flowers
each 10mm across, with stamens longer than
the petals; much visited by butterflies. 'Carmen'
is one of several cultivars in various shades of
mauve-pink. 'Iceberg' has white flowers. All do
best in rich, sandy soil, with ample water in
summer. Hardy to −20°C.

Sedum 'Sunset Cloud'   A hybrid between
'Ruby Glow' (q.v.) and *S. telephium* subsp.
maximum 'Atropurpureum' (q.v.) raised by Jim
Archibald of The Plantsmen in around 1970.
Leaves purplish grey; stems to 30cm, sprawling.
'Vera Jameson' is similar.

Sedum telephium L. subsp. *maximum* (L.)
Krosker.   Native of Europe, from France
eastwards to N Turkey and the Caucasus,
growing in dry, rocky places and open pine
forest at up to 2300m, flowering in July–
September. Stems few, erect to 45cm, from a
stout rootstock. Leaves broadly ovate,
amplexicaul, to 4cm wide. Inflorescence very
dense; flowers 6–10mm across, usually greenish
white, rarely pink. In 'Atropurpureum' the
leaves are deep purple. Hardy to −15°C.

Sedum telephium L. subsp. *telephium*
Native of Europe, from Ireland and Spain
eastwards to China, Siberia and Japan, growing
in open grassy places in woods and scrub,
flowering in August–September. Stems few, to
50cm tall, usually erect, from a stout rootstock.
Leaves oblong, toothed, truncate at its base.
Flowers purplish pink, rarely white. For good,
well-drained soil not too dry. Hardy to −20°C.

Cotyledon orbiculata var. *oblonga* at 3000m on Carlyle's Hoek, NE Cape Province

Sedum aizoon 'Euphorbioides'

Sedum telephium subsp. *maximum*

Lathyrus grandiflorus, a rampant weed in a border

Lathyrus japonicus subsp. *maritimus* growing on shingle at Dungeness, Kent

Lathyrus sylvestris at Dungeness, Kent

Lathyrus grandiflorus Sibth. & Sm. (*Leguminosae*)   Native of S Italy, Sicily, Greece and the S Balkan peninsula, and NW Africa, growing in scrub in the mountains, flowering in May–July. Stems from a suckering and invasive rootstock, pubescent, ridged but not winged, to 1.5m. Leaves with 1 pair of ovate leaflets and a simple or 3-branched tendril. Flowers 1–4 on a stalk 2.5–3cm across. Pods with 15–20 seeds, but rarely formed in gardens. A pretty but invasive plant, difficult to remove once it is established. It is best in a narrow bed at the base of a hedge, or where it can hang down over a wall, and not be in danger of swamping other plants.

Lathyrus japonicus Willd. subsp. *maritimus* (L.) P. W. Ball Sea Pea   Native of the colder coasts of the N Hemisphere, south to the Scilly Isles, to New Jersey and to Del Norte Co., California, and by the Great Lakes, growing on shingle and on sand dunes (var. *acutiformis* (Bab.) Pedersen) flowering in June–August. Stems to 90cm, creeping, from a deep rootstock. Stipules broadly hastate. Leaves rather fleshy and leathery when growing by the sea, but losing this character when growing in gardens, glaucous, with 3–4 pairs of obovate leaflets, usually with small tendrils. Flowers up to 15cm on a stalk, around 1.8cm across, purplish or bluish. For deep, moist and well drained soil in a cool position.

Lathyrus latifolius L. Everlasting Pea   Native of Europe, except the north, from France to Spain and Portugal, east to Poland, S Russia and the Caucasus (commonly naturalized in England, Belgium and Germany, in E North America, and N California) growing in scrub, grassy roadsides and waste places, flowering in May–July. Stems scrambling or climbing to 3m, from a stout and sometimes suckering rootstock, glabrous or pubescent, winged. Leaves with 1 pair of linear to ovate leaflets, to 15 × 5cm, and branched tendrils. Flowers 5–15 on a stalk, 2–3.5cm across, usually purplish pink, but also white, white with pink veins or pale pink with darker veins. Pale-coloured forms have been give various names such as 'White Pearl' ('Weisse Perle'), 'Pink Pearl' ('Rosa Perle'), 'Blushing Bride', etc., and can be grown with difficulty from cuttings, but similar plants can be raised from seed. Easily grown in any soil in warm position. A beautiful plant with a very long flowering season.

Lathyrus laxiflorus (Desf.) Kuntz.   Native of Europe from S Italy to Greece, SW Russia, the Caucasus, Turkey, Syria and N Iran, growing in woods, scrub and shady roadsides, flowering in June–July. Plant forming clumps from a tuberous rootstock. Stems scrambling to 50cm, with leaf-like stipules. Leaves with 1 pair of broadly elliptic or lanceolate leaflets 1–4cm long without a tendril. Flowers 1.5–2cm long, usually bicoloured. For well-drained soil in sun or partial shade. Hardy to −15°C.

Lathyrus mulkak Lipsky   Native of C Asia, in the Pamir-Alai, in the districts of Saravshan, Hissar, Darvas, etc., growing in scrub at around 3000m, flowering in June–August. Plant with climbing stems to 2m, from a deep, branched rhizome. Flowers 25–30mm across. This beautiful species is not easy to grow, and requires a very well-drained but deep, rich, sandy soil in full sun. Hardy to −15°C or less.

Lathyrus latifolius with Santolina at Cockermouth

Lathyrus rotundifolius

Lathyrus laxiflorus

Lathyrus latifolius 'White Pearl'

Lathyrus mulkak

Lathyrus latifolius, a veined seedling at Dungeness, Kent

Lathyrus tuberosus

Lathyrus latifolius

Lathyrus rotundifolius Willd. Native of the Crimea, growing in pine forests, flowering in June–July. Subsp. *miniatus* (Bieb. ex Stev.) Davis, from the Caucasus, N Iran and N & E Turkey, grows in scrub, wet meadows and corn fields, flowering in June–July. Stems glabrous to 2m, from a perennial stock. Leaves with 1 pair of rounded obovate, elliptic or suborbicular leaflets, and branched tendrils. Flowers up to 10 on a stalk, deep pinkish purple or reddish, 1.5–2.5cm across. Subsp. *miniatus* is said to have longer leaflets, stouter, more broadly winged stems and a larger clayx with longer teeth. It is not clear to which subspecies the cultivated plants shown here belong, but the bright-reddish-flowered plant is probably subsp. *miniatus*. For any soil in sun or partial shade.

Lathyrus sylvestris L. Narrow-leaved Everlasting Pea Native of most of Europe, including England, NW Africa, N Turkey and the Caucasus, growing in woods, scrub, shady woodside banks and on shingle by the sea, flowering in June–August. Stems winged, climbing, from a stout rootstock, to 2cm or more; stipules narrowly lanceolate leaflets to 15cm long, 2cm wide, with branched tendrils. Flowers usually flesh-pink, 1.3–2cm across, up to 12 on a stalk. As rampant as the commoner *L. latifolius*, but with smaller flowers.

Lathyrus tuberosus L. Fyfield Pea Native of most of Europe, from France and Spain eastwards to Russia and Siberia and southwards to Turkey and W Iran, growing in grassy places, water meadows, hedges or corn fields, flowering in June–August. Plant spreading by thin underground rhizomes which have small edible tubers. Stems not winged, to 100cm. Leaflets 1 pair, elliptic to broadly oblanceolate, *c.*30cm long, with one tendril. Stipules lanceolate, semi-sagittate. Stems with 3–9 flowers, 12–20mm across. For any soil in full sun; slightly invasive but with a long flowering period; suitable for meadow gardens or for a rough bank. Called Fyfield pea because it once grew wild, though probably naturalized, near Fyfield in Essex.

Galega officinalis 'His Majesty'

Galega orientalis

Hedysarum coronarium with a lead tank at Edington, Wiltshire

Hedysarum hedysaroides above St Luc, the Valais

Galega officinalis L. syn. *G. bicolor* Hausskn., *G. coronilloides* Freyn & Sint. (*Leguminosae*) Goat's Rue   Native of C & S Europe, the Caucasus, Turkey and Lebanon, east to C Asia and W Pakistan, growing in scrub, woods, marshy fields and roadsides, flowering in June–September. Often naturalized on roadside banks in England. Plant with rather lax stems to 1.5m. Leaflets in 4–10 pairs. Inflorescence with 30–50 flowers, 10–15mm across, variable in colour from white, to purple or bicoloured. 'His Majesty' is one of the selected clones of *G.* × *hartlandii*, a hybrid between *G. bicolor* and *G. officinalis*. *G. bicolor* Hausskn. is now considered merely a colour form of *G. officinalis*, so the name *G.* × *hartlandii* is unnecessary. Other colour selections are 'Alba', 'Candida' and 'Lady Wilson'. Easily grown in sun or partial shade.

Galega orientalis Lam.   Native of the Caucasus, growing in subalpine meadows, on riverbanks, in scrub and open forest, flowering in May–June. Plant with upright stems to 1.5m, and spreading by creeping underground rhizomes. Leaflets 30–60cm long, acuminate. Flowers bluish, usually larger than *G. officinalis*. Pods deflexed. A beautiful, if rather invasive, plant for the large herbaceous border or meadow, flowering in late May or June, and growing well in E Scotland. Hardy to −20°C.

Hedysarum coronarium L. (*Leguminosae*) Native of the W Mediterranean east to Sicily, and naturalized elsewhere, growing in grassy places, most in spring, flowering in March–May. Plant with erect or leaning stems to 1m. Leaflets 15–35mm long, in 3–5 pairs. Flowers 12–15mm long, reddish purple or carmine. Pod splitting into rounded, prickly segments. For well-drained soil in a sunny position. Sometimes grown as a fodder crop in S Europe. Hardy to −15°C perhaps. Photographed in the Old Vicarage Garden, Edington, Wiltshire.

Hedysarum hedysaroides (L.) Schinz & Thell. syn. *H. obscurum* L. (*Leguminosae*)   Native of the Alps and Carpathians, east to Romania, Siberia and Japan (Rebun Island), growing in subalpine meadows, stony mountainsides or cliffs at 1200–2500m in the Alps, flowering in July–August. Plant forming spreading clumps, with single stems up to 20cm tall. Leaflets in 4–6 pairs. Flowers 15–25mm long. For well-drained soil, moist in summer. Hardy to −20°C.

Ononis spinosa L. Spiny Restharrow (*Leguminosae*)   Native of England and most of Europe except the far north and north-east south to Turkey, Syria and east to Iran and Pakistan, growing in chalk and limestone grassland, stony hillsides and open pine forests, flowering in May–August. Plant with few stems to 80cm, woody and spiny towards the base, often sticky with glands. Leaflets *c*.1.5cm long. Flowers 10–20mm long. Shown here is subsp. *spinosa*, found mainly in N & W Europe. Easily grown in well-drained soil, or in a sunny meadow. Other species of Restharrow are shrubby with yellow or pink flowers, annuals or creeping perennials e.g. *O. repens* L.

Trifolium rubens L. (*Leguminosae*)   Native of C Europe, from N Spain to C Russia, Romania, and Albania, growing in dry, open woods and scrub, flowering in June. Plant with numerous upright stems from rhizomes, to 60cm tall. Leaflets up to 7cm long. Flower-heads to 8cm long, cylindrical, with purple or white flowers. One of the showiest clovers, easily grown in a sunny rather dry position. Hardy to −20°C or lower. Other native species are good for meadow gardens. *T. pratense* L., the common red clover, is easily grown and very common as a fodder crop. *T. medium* L., the Zigzag Clover, forms spreading clumps by underground stems. It is tolerant of more shade and usually found on rather heavy soil.

Vicia canescens Lab. subsp. *variegata* (Willd.) Davis syn. *V. variegata* Willd. (*Leguminosae*)   Native of E & NE Turkey, Armenia and NW & N Iran, growing in grassy places, abandoned fields, and on banks at 1600–2800m, flowering in June–July. Plant forming patches of erect stems to 80cm. Leaves greyish hairy, though even more silvery in other subspecies. Flowers lilac or bluish, 17–25mm long, 3–18 in a long-stalked, dense raceme. Seed pods usually hairy. For well-drained soil in a sunny position; shown here growing on a ledge on the rock garden at Kew. Hardy to −20°C. Related to *V. cracca*, the tufted vetch, a beautiful and common climbing plant of hedges throughout Europe.

Vicia sylvatica L. Wood Vetch   Native of Europe, from Ireland and Scotland east to Siberia, and south in the mountains to France, Albania and S Russia, growing on wood edges, scrub and on coastal cliffs and shingles, in June–August. Plant climbing with stems to 2m. Leaflets 5–12 pairs, usually 6–9, oblong-elliptic. Tendrils branched. Flowers up to 18 on the raceme, 15–20mm long, white with bluish veins. For well-drained moist soil and a cool position. Hardy to −20°C and below.

Vicia unijuga A. Br. (*Leguminosae*)   Native of E Siberia, N China, Korea, Sakhalin and throughout Japan, growing in scrub and grassy places, flowering in June–October. Plant with many stems, 60-100cm tall, without tendrils. Leaflets 2, 4–7cm long. Flowers 12–15mm long, bluish purple. For a sunny or partly shaded position, moist in summer. Hardy to −20°C.

Trifolium rubens, one of the largest clovers

Vicia sylvatica in Finland

Vicia unijuga at Kew

Ononis spinosa on chalk downs in Wiltshire

Vicia canescens subsp. *variegata* on the rock garden at Kew

Aruncus dioicus by the Japanese Bridge at Wisley

Cardiandra alternifolia near Kyoto, Japan

Filipendula ulmaria 'Aurea'

Aruncus dioicus (Walter) Fernald syn. *A. silvester* Kostel, *A. vulgaris* Raf. (*Rosaceae*) Native of E North America, from Pennsylvania to Iowa, south to Georgia and Missouri, and in Europe from Belgium and the Pyrenees eastwards to the Caucasus and Siberia, N China and Japan (where it is particularly variable), growing in damp woods, in shady places and by streams usually in mountain areas, flowering in June–August. Plant forming very large clumps of stems to 2m. Leaves to 1m long, 2-pinnate, with ovate leaflets. Flowers 5mm across, usually unisexual. For any moist soil in partial shade. Hardy to –20°C or less. A handsome plant, like a giant *Astilbe*.

Cardiandra alternifolia Sieb. & Zucc. (*Hydrangeaceae*)   Native of S Honshu, Shikoku and Kyushu, growing in moist woods in the mountains, flowering in July–September. Plant with erect stems to 70cm, like an herbaceous hydrangea, with alternate, narrowly ovate, acuminate leaves. Calyx lobes 2–3, petal-like, on sterile flowers around the margin of the inflorescence. Fertile flowers *c.*6mm across. For moist, peaty soil in partial shade. Hardy to –15°C perhaps.

Deinanthe caerulea Stapf (*Hydrangeaceae*) Native of Hubei, growing in wet places on shady cliffs, flowering in July–August. Stems few to 45cm, from a tufted rootstock. Leaves *c.*15cm long. Flowers 2cm across white, pale blue or purple. For a cool, sheltered, moist position in shade, protected from drying wind. Hardy to –20°C perhaps.

Filipendula kamtschatica (Pall.) Maxim. (*Rosaceae*)   Native of Japan in Hokkaido and N Honshu and of E Siberia, growing along streams in the mountains, often in large quantity, flowering in June–September. Plant forming large clumps of stems to 2m. Leaves with a large, round terminal leaflet, 15–25cm across, palmately 5–lobed, deeply double-toothed. Lateral leaflets very small or absent. Flowers 6–8mm across, white or pale pink. For moist soil in sun or partial shade. Hardy to –25°C.

Filipendula ulmaria (L.) Maxim. 'Aurea' Golden-leaved Meadow Sweet   Native of Europe, from Iceland south to Portugal and east to SE Turkey (Hakkari), the Caucasus, Siberia and NW China, growing in grassy bogs, wet ditches and by streams often in willow scrub, flowering in May–September. Plant forming clumps, and often covering large areas. Stems to 2m. Leaves aromatic, emerging golden in 'Aurea', with 3–5 pairs of leaflets. Flowers to 10mm across, creamy-white. For moist soil; the golden-leaved form needs shade if the leaves are not to scorch. All need ample moisture. Hardy to –20°C or less.

Filipendula rubra (Hill) Robinson 'Venusta' syn. 'Magnifica' Queen-of-the-Prairie   Native of E North America, from Pennsylvania to Michigan and Illinois, south to Georgia and Kentucky and Iowa, and naturalized in New England, growing in meadows and prairies, flowering in June–August. Plant with several stems to 2.5m. Leaves irregularly pinnate, with the terminal leaflet large, 7–9 lobed, incised and toothed. Lateral leaflets also incised into 3–5

Kirengeshoma koreana

Francoa ramosa

Francoa sonchifolia

Kirengeshoma palmata

Deinanthe caerulea in Sussex

lobes. Flowers bright pink. For good, moist soil in full sun. Hardy to −20°C or less.

Francoa ramosa D. Don (*Francoaceae*)
Native of Chile, in the region of Valparaiso, flowering in December–January. Plant forming small clumps of softly-hairy evergreen leaves, sometimes producing a leafy stem to 20cm. Flowering stems to 90cm, branched below, with loosely arranged white flowers; petals often spotted. For a warm sheltered position. Hardy to −5°C perhaps. It is likely that this species, *F. sonchifolia* and *F. appendiculata* Cav. are merely forms of one very variable species.

Francoa sonchifolia Cav.   Native of Chile, growing in rather dry areas, in rock crevices on the sides of gorges overhanging water, flowering in December–January. Plant forming mats of softly hairy evergreen leaves from creeping rhizomes. Flowering stems to 60cm unbranched, with a rather compact inflorescence of pink flowers. For a warm sheltered position in sun or partial shade. Hardy to −10°C perhaps. The hardiest species.

Kirengeshoma palmata Yatabe
(*Hydrangeaceae*)   Native of Japan in Shikoku and Kyushu, growing in woods in the mountains, flowering in August. Plant with several stems to 120cm from a stout rhizome. Leaves 10–20cm long and as wide, with shallow, long-pointed lobes. Flowers with fleshy petals c.3cm long. *Kirengeshoma koreana* Nakai from Korea is little different, often more erect to 2m or more, with more open flowers. Both require moist leafy soil in partial shade, with ample water in late summer. Hardy to −20°C.

Filipendula kamtschatica

Filipendula rubra 'Venusta'

'Bressingham Beauty'

'Weisse Gloria'

'Cattleya'

'Betsy Cuperus'

'Federsee'

Astilbe rivularis

Specimens from the Savill Gardens, Windsor, 20 July. ¼ life size

Astilbe rivularis var. *myriantha*

Astilbe 'Deutschland'

Astilbe 'Fanal'

Astilbe 'Jo Ophurst'

Astilbe All Astilbes require wet or moist peaty soil in partial shade, and make valuable late-flowering plants for the bog garden, with delicate leaves to contrast with bold foliage plants such as *Hosta*, the closely related *Rodgersia* and *Ligularia*. All are hardy to −20°C and less.

Astilbe × *arendsii* Arends (*Saxifragaceae*) A group of hybrids between *A. chinensis* var. *davidii*, *A. astilboides*, *A. japonica* and *A. thunbergii*, raised by George Arends at Ronsdorf, Germany, from 1909 until 1955. Cultivars include:
'Betsy Cuperus'   Very graceful, spreading habit, to 1.2m high. Raised by B. Ruys in 1917. A hybrid of *A. thunbergii*.
'Bressingham Beauty'   Rich pink with horizontal or slightly dropping side branches; stems to 1m. Raised by Alan Bloom.
'Cattleya'   Raised by G. Arends in 1953. Height *c.*90cm.
'Fanal'   Raised by G. Arends in 1933. Height *c.*60cm. Early-flowering.
'Federsee' Stems around 60cm.   Raised by P. Theobolt in 1939.
'Granat' Raised by G. Arends in 1920.
'Jo Ophurst'   Upright side branches give this a
'Weisse Gloria' syn. 'White Gloria' Raised by G. Arends in 1924. Height *c.*60cm. Early-flowering.

Astrilbes at Longstock Park Gardens, Hampshire

stiff effect; stems to 90cm. Close to *A. chinensis* var. *davidii*, and late-flowering. Raised by B. Ruys in 1916.

Astilbe japonica (Morr. & Decne.) A. Gray Native of Japan, in S Honshu, Shikoku and Kyushu, growing on moist rocks in ravines in the mountains, flowering in May–June. Stems to 80cm; flowering panicles 10–20cm long, dense; flowers white. Cultivars include: **'Deutschland'** Stems around 50cm; flowers pure white. Raised by G Arends in 1920.

Astilbe rivularis Buch.-Ham. ex D. Don Native of the Himalayas, from Pakistan to SW China, Yunnan, growing in scrub by streams at 1800–3300m, flowering in July–September. Plant with few stems 1–2m tall, from a stout rootstock. Leaves 2–3 pinnate, with ovate, pointed leaflets 2.5–10cm long. Inflorescence pyramidal, 30–60cm, with unbranched, upward-pointing side branches. Sepals and stamens 5, petals absent, carpels 2. In habit like *Aruncus dioicus*, but that is dioiceous, has 5 petals, numerous stamens in the male flowers, and 3 carpels in the female. *Astilbe rivularis* var. *myriantha*, from SW China, differs in the more branched and drooping side shoots of the inflorescence. It makes a very large and graceful late-flowering specimen.

Astilbe 'Granat' on the rock garden at Kew

Astilbe chinensis 'Purpurlanze'

Astilbe simplicifolia 'Bronce Elegans'

Astilbe chinensis 'Pumila'

Rodgersia pinnata 'Superba'

Astilbe chinensis (Maxim.) Franch. & Sav. var. *taquetii* (Léveillé) Vil. **'Purpurlanze'** (*Saxifragaceae*)   Native of E China, growing in damp woods and along shady streams, flowering in August, the last of the *Astilbes* to flower. Plant with upright stems to 1.2m. Leaflets broadly lanceolate with brownish stalks. Inflorescence with erect side branches; flowers magenta-purple. 'Pumila', sometimes considered a hybrid, has paler-pink flowers and stems to 45cm, and is close to the wild type of *A. chinensis*. For moist soil in sun or partial shade. Hardy to −20°C.

Astilbe simplicifolia Mak.   Native of Honshu, found only in Sunya and Sagama prefectures, where it is rare. A dwarf plant with simple basal leaves to 8cm long, with 3 or 5 lobes, deeply double-toothed. Inflorescence loose to 30cm, with spreading branches and white flowers. Numerous crosses have been made using this species, e.g. **'Bronce Elegans'**, which has pink flowers but retains the loose inflorescence and lobed, sharply toothed leaflets. For a moist, sheltered position, in partial shade. Hardy to −15°C perhaps.

Darmera peltata (Torr.) Voss syn. *Peltiphyllum peltatum* (Torr.) Engl. (*Saxifragaceae*)   Native of California, from Tulare Co. northwards to S Oregon, growing by the banks of mountain streams below 1800m, in yellow pine and mixed evergreen forest, flowering in April–July before the leaves emerge. Stems 30–100cm, from a stout, creeping rhizome. Leaves 30–60cm across, peltate. Petals 5–7mm long. There is a dwarf form, 'Nana', with leaves only 30cm high, 25cm across. *Astilboides tabularis* (Hemsl.) Engl. (syn. *Rodgersia tabularis*) (not shown), from NE China and North Korea, has rather similar peltate leaves, paler, of a smoother texture, up to 90cm across. The flowers are *Astilbe*-like, in a plume to 1.5m tall, produced in June–July.

Rodgersia aesculifolia Batalin (*Saxifragaceae*)   Native of W China, in Gansu, Hubei and Sichuan, growing in damp woods and along streams in scrub at 1500–3200m, flowering in June–July. Plant with a creeping rootstock and basal leaves to 45cm across. Leaflets 7, to 25cm long, coarsely toothed. Inflorescence to 1.8m,

with white flowers. For moist, peaty soil in sun or partial shade. Hardy to −20°C. Leaves like *R. pinnata*, but always palmate; sepals accrescent after anthesis; leaf with idumentum along the veins and on the teeth beneath. Sepals not accrescent after anthesis and leaves with indumentum on the veins only are the distinguishing characters of *R. henrici*.

Rodgersia pinnata Franch. **'Superba'** syn. *Astilbe pinnata* (Franch.) Franch.   Native of W China, in Yunnan and S Sichuan, growing in moist, grassy places in scrub, open forest and by streams at 2100–3650m, flowering in June–July. Plant with a stout, shortly creeping rhizome. Leaves to 1m, usually partially pinnate, with 5–9 rugose leaflets, to 20cm long, glabrous above. Inflorescence 60–120cm; flowers white, pink, yellowish or reddish. For peaty soil in sun or partial shade. Hardy to −20°C. 'Superba' is a good form, with bright-pink flowers and leaves purplish when young. It often has palmate leaves, and may be a hybrid with *R. aesculifolia*.

Rodgersia podophylla A. Gray, syn. *Astilbe podophylla* (A. Gray) Franch.   Native of Japan, in Hokkaido and Honshu, and of Korea, growing in moist woods in the mountains at 700–2000m, flowering in June–August. Plant with a stout, creeping rhizome, in time forming large clumps. Leaves palmate with 5 rather thin shallow lobes towards the apex. Flowering stems to 1.3m; flowers white, with long acuminate sepals. For most soil in shade or a cool, sunny place by water, away from hot, drying wind. Hardy to −20°C or less.

Rodgersia sambucifolia Hemsl.   Native of W China, in Yunnan and S Sichuan, growing on mossy rocks often of limestone, in pine forest at 2700–3350m, flowering in June–July. Plant with shortly creeping rhizomes. Leaves pinnate or rarely irregularly pinnate, with 8–11 leaflets, with glandular hairs on the surface. Flowers white or pink; stamens and styles equal to or shorter than the sepals at anthesis. For moist, rich soil in sun or partial shade. Hardy to −20°C perhaps. The leaves of this really do look like *Sambucus*, with 6 pairs of sharply toothed leaflets and a sessile terminal one.

Rodgersia podophylla by a stream in Kent

Rodgersia sambucifolia

Darmera peltata (leaves)

Darmera peltata (flowers only)

Rodgersia podophylla in autumn colour at Kildrummy Castle

Rodgersia aesculifolia by a stream near Baoxing, Sichuan

289

Lythrum salicaria in a wet meadow in Connemara

Epilobium angustifolium f. *albiflorum* at Bracken Hill, Kent

Lythrum salicaria 'Feuerkerze'

Lythrum virgatum at the Royal Botanic Garden, Edinburgh

Epilobium dodoneaei

Cuphea cyanea Mocino & Sesse (*Lythraceae*) Native of Mexico in the Sierra Madre Oriental, flowering in July–September. Stems to 45cm from a woody rootstock. Leaves evergreen in mild climates. Flowers *c.*20mm long. For a warm, sheltered position in full sun. Hardy to −10°C, especially in very well-drained soil. Most *Cuphea* species are more tender and require protection from frost, but may be used for summer bedding.

Epilobium angustifolium L. syn. *Chamaenerion angustifolium* (L.) Scop. (*Onagraceae*) Rosebay Willowherb   Native of most of Europe, N Asia and North America, south to Carolina and Arizona in the mountains, growing in woods and on grassy roadsides, especially in areas recently cleared of trees or burned, flowering in June–September. Plant with stems to 2m or more from strongly creeping underground rhizomes, forming large patches. Leaves to 20cm long, narrowly lanceolate, up to 5.5cm broad in var. *macrophyllum* (Hausskn.) Fern. Flowers with petals 21–22cm long, normally magenta, more rarely in shades of pink, and occasionally white in f. *albiflorum* (Dumort.) Hausskn. (shown here) with whitish sepals; flowers also white, but with red sepals in f. *spectabile* (Simmons) Fern.

Rosebay Willowherb appears to be more variable in North America than in Europe, though pink-and white-flowered forms are recorded in both continents. The white form is an attractive plant for a wild garden or a position where its invasive rhizomes will not become a nuisance. Hardy to −20°C or less.

Limonium chrysocephalum in a cold desert near Sairam Nor, Sinjiang

Epilobium dodoneaei Vill. syn. *E. rosmarinifolium* Haenke. Native of Europe, from Germany and S France to W Russia and Greece, growing on river gravel and in moist screes, at up to 1500m in Turkey, flowering in August–September. Stems 30–85cm from a creeping rootstock, forming spreading patches. Leaves 2–2.5cm long, to 3.5mm wide, linear, sparsely pubescent with spreading hairs. Flowers 3–3.5cm across. The closely related *E. stevenii* Boiss., from the S Caucasus, N Iran and Turkey, has wider, 4–8mm, silky-hairy leaves. For any good, well-drained soil in full sun. Hardy to –20°C.

Epilobium wilsonii Petrie syn. *E. glabellum* hort. Native of New Zealand, in South Island, growing in grassland and herbfields, flowering in November–February, or June–August in the northern hemisphere. Stems to 30cm, creeping or upright from a slender rootstock. Leaves ovate, finely toothed, opposite or alternate. Flowers 6–25mm across, white or yellowish in 'Sulphureum'. For moist soil in a cool position in sun or partial shade. Hardy to –15°C perhaps.

Limonium chrysocephalum (Regel) Lincz (*Plumbaginaceae*) Native of C Asia in NW China (Sinjiang), growing in dry, stony steppe and desert, flowering in May. Plant with many upright stems to 30cm from a tough, woody rootstock. Leaves linear. Flowers *c.*10mm long. For well-drained, dry soil in full sun. Hardy to –25°C or less, and tolerant of summer heat and drought.

Limonium latifolium (Sm.) Kuntz. Native of SE Europe from Bulgaria and Romania to S Russia, growing in steppe and dry grassland, flowering in July–September. Plant with rosettes of spathulate to elliptical leathery, evergreen leaves, to 60cm long and 15cm wide, from a tough, deep rootstock. Flowering stems to 80cm, much branched, with whitish hyaline bracts and a small purple corolla *c.*6mm long. For sandy, well-drained soil in full sun. Hardy to –15°C, possibly less in a dry climate.

Lythrum salicaria L. (*Lythraceae*) Purple Loosestrife Native of Europe, from Ireland south to North Africa and eastwards to India, China and Japan, growing in wet meadows, shallow water and reed swamps, flowering in July–September. Stems several from a stout rootstock, to 180cm tall. Leaves ovate to narrowly lanceolate, opposite or in whorls of 3, truncate or semi-amplexicaul at the base. Flowers with 12 stamens, and petals 10mm long. 'Feuerkerze' syn. 'Firecandle' has more pinkish-red, less magenta flowers than the usual wild form. For wet soil in sun or partial shade. Hardy to –25°C or less.

Lythrum virgatum L. Native of C Europe, from NW Italy and E Russia, southwards to Greece, Turkey, the Caucasus and east to C Asia and NW China, growing in marshes and shallow water, flowering in June–August. Stems several from a stout rootstock to 200cm, branched above. Leaves linear-lanceolate, tapered towards the base. Petals 6–9mm long. A much more graceful plant than the commoner *L. salicaria*. For wet soil in sun or partial shade. Hardy to –20°C or less. Less purple- and more pinkish-flowered named clones are cultivated, such as 'Rose Queen'.

Epilobium glabellum

Cuphea cyanea at Sissinghurst Castle

Limonium latifolium with *Artemisia* 'Powys Castle' at Wisley

Oenothera fruticosa subsp. *glauca* 'Clarence Elliott' at Edington, Wiltshire

Oenothera missouriensis

Oenothera fruticosa

Oenothera fruticosa subsp. *glauca*

Oenothera acaulis Cav. syn. *O. taraxifolia* hort. (*Onagraceae*)   Native of C Chile, from Coquimbo to Concepción, where it is common, growing in gravelly places and disturbed ground, flowering in November–March, or May–September in the north. Plant with short, branching stems to 15cm high, forming a twiggy mass or sometimes stemless, and deeply cut, dandelion-like leaves. Flowers opening in the late evening, *c.*9p.m., fading to pinkish by daybreak, to 7.5cm across, on a tube 5–12.5cm long. For poor soil, well-drained, in full sun. Hardy to −10°C perhaps.

Oenothera caespitosa Nutt.   Native of N Mexico and from California northwards on the east of the Sierras to Utah and E Washington, growing on dry stony slopes, in open scrub and pinyon pine woods in very dry areas, at 1000–3000m, flowering in April–August. Plant tufted with a thick rootstock and stemless or with short stems to 20cm. Leaves usually hairy, linear-lanceolate, toothed and wavy edged, tapering into a winged stalk. Flowers opening at night, white, fading pink, with a tube up to 10cm long and petals to 4cm long, pollinated by hawkmoths. A very beautiful plant for a sheltered and dry, sunny position. Hardy to −15°C or less, but intolerant of winter damp and often short-lived. Shown here is subsp. *caespitosa*, which includes var. *eximea*.

Oenothera fruticosa L. subsp. *fruticosa* Native from Florida to Oklahoma north to New England, New York, Tennessee and Missouri, growing in marshes, meadows and wood margins, in sandy places and even in coastal salt marshes, flowering in May–August. Plant with erect or ascending stems to 100cm from a compact rootstock. Leaves lanceolate, oblong or linear. Flowers with calyx pubescent but not glandular. Flowers 3–5cm across. Capsule clayate, tapering to a slender stalk. For any good soil in sun or partial shade. Hardy to −20°C or less.

'Clarence Elliott'   A distinct form of *O. fruticosa* subsp. *glauca* with purplish foliage and red buds; flowers yellow, *c.*6cm across. 'Fyrverkeri' ('Fireworks') and 'Glaber' are

Oenothera acaulis

Oenothera speciosa at Edington, Wiltshire

similar but less purple. Stems *c.*50cm. For good soil in full sun. Hardy to −20°C or less. Subsp. *glauca* (Michx.) Straley syn. *O. tetragona* Roth, differs in having few hairs, often glaucous leaves and glands on the calyx and ovary. There are numerous cultivars, some of which have reddish stems.

Oenothera missouriensis Sims   Native of Missouri and Kansas, south to Texas, growing in rocky or sandy places, flowering in May–September. Plant with a deep root and short, decumbent leafy stems to 30cm. Flowers 6–12cm across; fruit ellipsoid to suborbicular, 5–8cm long, with broad wings. Seeds in one row, crested. A fine dwarf species with large flowers for well-drained soil in full sun. Hardy to −15°C.

Oenothera rosea Ait.   Native of S Arizona and Texas, south through Mexico to Bolivia and naturalized elsewhere, e.g. South Africa, growing in canyons and river valleys, flowering in April–August. Stems to 60cm, upright or sprawling, flowering the first year. Leaves shallow-toothed to pinnatifid. Flowers pink, open in the daytime, small, up to 2cm across. For a hot, sunny position. Hardy to −10°C perhaps, but easily raised from seed.

Oenothera speciosa Nutt.   Native of Missouri and Kansas, south to Texas and Mexico, and naturalized in other parts of SE United States, from Virginia to Florida, growing in dry fields and prairies, flowering in May–July. Plant with creeping underground rhizomes and stems to *c.*30cm Leaves oblong-lanceolate to linear, with large triangular teeth or almost pinnatifid; flowers nodding in bud, opening in the evening, 4–8cm across, white or pale pink. Capsule obovoid, 9-ribbed; seeds in more than 2 rows. For well-drained soil in full sun. Hardy to −15°C or less, but intolerant of winter damp, especially in rich soil. 'Siskiyou' and 'Rosea' are good pink-flowered varieties

Oenothera caespitosa subsp. *caespitosa* at Edington, Wiltshire

Oenothera rosea

Aciphylla aurea

Aciphylla squarrosa (inflorescence)

Heracleum mantegazzianum

Aciphylla squarrosa

Levisticum officinale

China (Heilonjiang), growing in grassy places and open woods in the mountains, flowering in August–September. Stems few from a thick rootstock, 1–2m tall. Leaves with inflated purplish sheaths. Flowers deep purple, in umbels to 12cm across. Fruits 8 × 5mm. For good, leafy soil, moist in summer, flowering in 2 years from seed. Usually monocarpic. Hardy to −20°C or below.

Gunnera magellanica Lam. (*Gunneraceae*) Native of the Falkland Islands, SW Argentina, S Chile to 35°30′S and along the Andes to 1°N, growing in damp grassy places, flowering in October–February. Plant creeping to form extensive patches. Leaf stalks 1.5–20cm; leaves up to 5.5cm × 9cm, toothed. Male flowers (shown here) on slender stalks to 12cm, the female stouter, finally with scarlet fleshy fruits. Hardy to −10°C or lower.

Gunnera manicata Lindl. ex Andre   Native of S Brazil, in the Serro do Mar, growing by streams in grassland and on wet rocks in the mountains at 700–1200m, flowering in May–June in gardens in the north, December in the wild. Plant huge, with a large creeping rhizome and leaves 1.5–5m across, on prickly petioles to 2.5m tall. Differs from *G. tinctoria* in its larger size and slender, flexuious inflorescence branches, over 15cm long. For rich, wet soil. Hardy to −10°C, with protection.

Gunnera tinctoria (Molina) Mirbel syn. *G. chilensis* Lam.   Native of Chile, from Valparaiso southwards, reported also from Ecuador and Columbia, and naturalized in W Ireland, W France and the Azores, growing in damp places and by streams and lakes, flowering in June–August. Plant slowly spreading, forming dense clumps. Leaf stalks to 1.5m, with stiff spines. Leaf blades, to 1.5m across, cordate, deeply lobed and toothed. Flowers minute, on *c.*12 cm long branches on a compound inflorescence to 1m. The rootstock is rather tender, surviving *c.*−10°C, and so requires protection in autumn by piling the dying leaves over the growing points.

Heracleum mantegazzianum Somm. & Lév. (*Umbelliferae*) Giant Hogweed   Native of the Caucasus, growing in damp places by streams, flowering in June–August and often naturalized by rivers in the rest of Europe. Often perennial, but sometimes biennial or monocarpic. Stems to 5m, up to 10cm in diameter, red-spotted. Leaves to 3m long, pinnate, coarsely toothed. Umbels to 1.5m across. A statuesque place for the wild garden, indeed one of the largest of all hardy perennials. The plant contains a poison which can cause the skin to burn when exposed to sunlight, but it is less dangerous than wild hemlock or the common rue.

Hydrocotyle verticillata Thunb. (*Umbelliferae*) Native of North America, from California to Texas and from Massachusetts to Florida, mainly in the south and along the coast; and widespread in C & S America, growing in marshy places, and in shallow water, flowering in April–September. Plant creeping to form large patches. Leaves to 5cm across.

Levisticum officinale Koch Lovage (*Umbelliferae*)   Native of S E Iran and Afghanistan, growing by streams and in wet places at 2500–3400m, but widely naturalized in Europe, especially in the mountains. Plant forming clumps of stems to 2.5m. leaves strongly aromatic, rather curry-like, lobes long-cuneate at the base, toothed and lobed at the apex.

Aciphylla aurea W. R. B. Oliver (*Umbelliferae*) Native of New Zealand, in South Island, growing on the east of the mountains in subalpine and mountain grassland, flowering in November–February. Plant forming rosettes of leaves with flat segments *c.*7mm across, usually golden-green, finely toothed. Inflorescence *c.*80cm. For well-drained, peaty soil in sun. Hardy to −15°C.

Aciphylla squarrosa Forster & Forster, Common Spaniard.   Native of New Zealand, in North and South Islands, from East Cape to N Canterbury, growing in subalpine tussock grassland, by roadsides and on abandoned meadows, flowering in November–January, or June–July in the northern hemisphere. Plant forming large spiny tussocks of several rosettes, up to 1m tall; flower stalk 60–200cm; male and female flowers on separate inflorescences, sweetly scented. Easily grown in moist but well-drained soil in full sun. Hardy to −15°C or less.

Angelica gigas Nakai (*Umbelliferae*)   Native to Japan (Shikoku and Kyushu), Korea and N

Gunnera tinctoria

Gunnera manicata at Wisley

Gunnera magellanica

Gunnera tinctoria naturalized in Connemara

Angelica gigas

Gunnera by the lake at Stancome Park, Gloucestershire

Hydrocotyle verticillata

Pimpinella major 'Rosea' at Old Rectory Cottage, Berkshire

Myrrhis odorata by the River Don, Aberdeenshire

Chaerophyllum hirsutum 'Roseum'

Selinam wallichianum

Chaerophyllum hirsutum L. 'Roseum' (*Umbelliferae*) Native of S Europe, from France and Spain to Poland, SW Russia and Greece, growing in grassy places and scrub in the mountains, flowering in June–July. Plant with several stems from a deep branching rootstock up to 120cm. Leaves softly hairy, with overlapping segments. Umbels *c.*6cm across; flowers white or pink in 'Roseum', with ciliate petals. *C. roseum* M. Bieb., from the Caucasus, Armenia and Georgia, regularly has pink flowers; it is almost glabrous, with stems to 70cm. Both are easily grown in rich, moist soil in sun or partial shade. Hardy to −20°C or less.

Ferula communis L. syn. F. *chiliantha* Rech. fil. (*Umbelliferae*) Native of the Mediterranean region from Spain, North Africa and the Canary Islands east to the Lebanon, growing in rough ground, in rocky places, and by roadsides, often in soil which is damp in spring, flowering in April–June. Stems usually solitary from a stout root, up to 2.5m. Leaves with linear lobes up to 5cm long, all green and up to 0.8mm wide in subsp. *communis*; glaucous beneath and 1–3mm wide in subsp. *glauca* (L.) Rouy & Camus; leaf sheaths of uppermost leaves very large, inflated and leathery. Umbels without bracts (the related genus *Ferulago* has well-developed bracts and bracteoles), *c.*8cm across. Fruit elliptic to suborbicular, flattened. Easily grown in a well-drained border, but sometimes dying after flowering. Hardy to −10°C, possibly lower without protection for the top of the rootstock.

Ferula kuhistanica Korov. syn. F. *jaeschkeana* auct. non Vatke Native of C Asia in the Tien Shan, and Pamir Alai, in both of which it is widespread, growing in grassy places among limestone rocks, in soil moist in spring, dry in summer, at 1200–3500m, flowering in May–June. Plant with robust stems to 2m or more from a stout tuberous root. Leaf segments flat, rather thin in texture, *c.*5cm wide. Umbels to 20cm across. A fine plant for a sunny position, dry in summer, when it becomes quite dormant. Hardy to −20°C or less. *F. jaeschkeana* Vatke, from the W Himalayas at 2400–3600m, is very

similar, but taller and more slender, with narrower leaf segments 1–2cm wide. I had a plant increasing in size for several years before flowering spectacularly and then dying.

Myrrhis odorata (L.) Scop. (*Umbelliferae*) Sweet Cicely   Native of the Alps, Pyrenees, Apennines and W Greece, Albania and W Yugoslavia, commonly naturalized elsewhere in N Europe, growing in damp woods and hedges, by streams and rivers and on damp, grassy roadsides, flowering in May–July. Plant with several stems from a deep-branching rootstock, up to 120cm tall and wide. Leaves softly hairy, smelling sweetly of aniseed. Umbels *c.*5cm across. Hardy to −20°C or below. A beautiful plant for a cool position, more reliably perennial, with longer-lasting, fresh, green leaves, and at the same time less invasive than the common Cow's Parsley or Queen Anne's Lace, *Anthriscus sylvestris* (L.) Hoffm. A black-leaved form of *A. sylvestris*, called 'Raven's Wing', has appeared recently.

Pimpinella major (L.) Huds 'Rosea' (*Umbelliferae*) Native of most of England, SW Ireland and S Scotland, south to Portugal and east to the Caucasus, growing on grassy roadsides, in hedges and scrub, flowering in June–July. Stems several, 50–120cm, from a stout rootstock. Basal leaves simply pinnate, the segments toothed, subcordate. Upper leaves small, with sheath-like petioles. Flower umbels 6cm across. Easily grown in any good soil, preferring rather moist conditions. Hardy to −20°C.

Selinum wallichianum (DC.) Nasir syn. *S. tenuifolium* Wall. ex C. B. Clarke (*Umbelliferae*) Native of the Himalayas, from Kashmir east to Bhutan, growing in scrub and mountain meadows, at 2700–4000m, flowering in July–September. Plant with many stems to 150cm, forming handsome clumps. Leaves very finely divided into elliptical segments. Umbels 5–8cm across, with white-edged, toothed bracteoles as long as the flowers. A fine plant for the border or for growing in damp grass. Hardy to −20°C.

Ferula kuhistanica in the Amankutan hills near Samarkand, overlooking the Oxus valley

Ferula communis near Ronda, S Spain

Ferula kuhistanica (young inflorescence)

'Rosea'

'Rubra'

'Rosensinphonie'

Astrantia major

'Sunningdale Variegated'

'Shaggy'

Astrantia major
subsp. *involucrata*

Astrantia maxima

Specimens from Beth Chatto and Wisley, 20 June. ½ life size

Astrantia major 'Rosea'

Astrantia major at Cedar Tree Cottage, Sussex

Alepidea natalensis in the Drakensberg

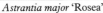

Astrantia major 'Rubra'

Sanicula caerulescens near Ya-an, Sichuan

Alepidea natalensis Wood & Evans (*Umbelliferae*) Native of South Africa in the Drakensberg mountains in Natal, growing in damp, rocky grassland, on bare rock and peat and in shallow streams at up to 2400m, flowering in January–February. Plant with few stems of 45cm rising from a rosette of ovate leaves. Flower-heads *c.*1cm across. With its tight head of small flowers and petal-like bracts this genus of *c.*25 species, mainly in South Africa, resembles the northern hemisphere *Astrantia*. For moist, peaty soil in full sun.

Astrantia major L. subsp *involucrata* Koch syn. *A. major* subsp. *carinthiaca* Arcangeli (*Umbelliferae*) Native of the Alps, Pyrenees and NW Spain, growing in alpine meadows, flowering in July–September, or June in gardens. Subspecies *involucrata* differs from subsp. *major* in its longer bracteoles, around twice as long as the umbel. The commonest cultivar is called 'Shaggy' syn. 'Margery Fish', with its whitish bracteoles, sharply toothed, to 3.5cm with green edges. Another form, shown here, with paler flowers and only the tips of the bracteoles green, is sometimes wrongly labelled 'Carniolica'. *A. carniolica* Jacq., from the SE Alps in Austria, Italy and Yugoslavia, has bracteoles shorter than the umbel, and central leaf lobes not divided to the base.

Easily grown in good soil in sun or partial shade. Hardy to −20°C.

Astrantia major L. subsp. *major* Masterwort Native of much of Europe from NW Spain, the Pyrenees and Alps and from the Black Forest south to Bulgaria and east to W Russia, and sometimes naturalized in Britain, growing in damp meadows and open woods, flowering in June–September. Plant forming large clumps of upright stems to 1m, branched near the top. Basal leaves 3- to 5-lobed, the lobes themselves lobed and coarsely toothed. Bracteoles petal-like, white, greenish or pinkish, surrounding and more or less equalling the dense umbel of small greenish flowers. Easily grown in good soil, moist in summer, in sun or partial shade. Hardy to −20°C. There are several selected varieties of this subspecies in cultivation; shown here are:
'Alba' With white, green tipped bracteoles.
'Rosea' Deeper pink.
'Rosensinfonie' A good rose pink.
'Rubra' The darkest, purplish-red.
'Sunningdale Variegated' An excellent foliage plant with a neat mound of leaves with a good white edge and patches of pale green. Fresh new leaves are produced throughout the summer.

Astrantia maxima Pallas Native of the Caucasus, south to NW Iran and NE Turkey,

west to Ordu, growing in woods and damp meadows at 1300–2400m in Turkey, flowering in July–August. Plant forming widely spread mats of leaves 3-lobed to the base; lobes toothed, 3–10cm long. Bracteoles 9–12, elliptic to ovate, pinkish, 1–3m long, 3–12mm wide, longer than the umbel. Usually a rather small plant with 3-lobed leaves and a short, often unbranched flowering stem. Subsp. *haradjianii* (Grintz) Rech. fil. From C Turkey from Ladik and Ulu Dağ south to Adana and Isparta has 3- or 5-lobed basal leaves, shorter, narrower bracteoles which are green and white, and more branched stems. It grows in drier places, in conifer forests and scrub, flowering in June–July. Both are easily grown in sun or partial shade, subsp. *maxima* preferring a cool position. Hardy to −20°C.

Sanicula caerulescens Franch. (*Umbelliferae*) Native of China, in W Sichuan and Yunnan, growing in damp scrub and woodland, flowering in May. Plant with a compact rootstock. Leaves deeply 3-5 lobed, with the lobes toothed, 5–8cm across. Flowers very small, sky-blue. Hardy to −15°C perhaps. For a moist and sheltered woodland position in shade. *S. europaea* L., a native of Europe, is found in woods and shady banks, especially on chalk and limestone soils. It has attractive dark-green leaves and white flowers.

ERYNGIUM

Eryngium variifolium

Eryngium billardieri near Erzurum, E Turkey, October

Eryngium billardieri B. Delaroche syn. *E. orientale* Stapf & Wettst. (*Umbelliferae*)   Native of E Turkey, Lebanon and Armenia east to Kashmir, growing on mountain steppes and rocky slopes at 1400–3810m in Turkey, flowering in July–October. Basal leaves bluish green, leathery, in a rosette, the blades deeply divided with broad linear segments, to 15cm long. Stems several, 40–75cm, stiff, with tripartite leaves. Bracts 5–7, 2.5–5cm long, linear-lanceolate, with a spiny tip. For dry, well-drained soil in full sun. Hardy to −25°C.

Eryngium bourgatii Gouan   Native of the Pyrenees, to Spain and NW Africa, with subsp. *heldreichii* (Boiss.) Davis in S Turkey and Lebanon, growing in dry rocky places, usually on limestone, at up to 2400m in Turkey,

flowering in July–August. Basal leaf blades much divided and spiny, 3–7cm across. Stem leaves similar. Stems 15–45cm. Bracts 7–15, linear-lanceolate, spiny, 3–5-veined, 2–5cm long in subsp. *bourgatii*, 7-veined and to 6cm long in subsp. *heldreichii*. Heads 1.5–2.5cm across, ovoid-globose, or depressed-globose (1.2–1.5cm across in subsp. *heldreichii*). For well-drained soil in full sun. Hardy to −15°C, perhaps less. 'Picos Blue' has especially good colour.

Eryngium horridum Malme.   Native of Brazil and Argentina, in wet or dry grassland, and on the Pampas, flowering in November–January, in summer in the north. Plant to 3m; basal leaves to 1m long, 3cm wide. Heads nearly globose, 9–12mm across. For any good soil in full sun. Hardy to −10°C perhaps.

Eryngium maritimum L.   Native of the coasts of W Europe, the Mediterranean and the Black Sea, growing on sand dunes, flowering in June–September. Leaves leathery, glaucous, with large, triangular, spiny teeth. Stems widely branched, to 35cm. Bracts 5, ovate, with broad teeth tipped with spines. Flower-heads 1.5–3cm across. A familiar seaside plant, but good in the garden too, needing deep, well-drained, sandy soil in a hot, dry position. Hardy to −15°C, perhaps less.

Eryngium pandanifolium Cham. & Schlecht syn. *E. decaisneanum* Urban   Native of South America, in S Brazil, Argentina, Uruguay and Paraguay, growing in marshes and wet fields, flowering in gardens in late summer. Stems 1.5–4m. basal leaves sword-shaped, 1.5–2.5m long, 2.5cm wide, undivided, with slender spines along the edge. Flower-heads 6–10mm long, 4–8mm across, often purplish. Bracts *c*.2cm. For any good, rich soil in full sun. Hardy to −10°C.

Eryngium paniculatum Cav. & Domb.   Native of S. Chile and Argentina in Patagonia, growing in grassy places, flowering in summer. Stems to 1.5m. Basal leaves spiny on the edge, to 35cm long, 1.5cm wide. Flower heads 8–15mm across. For any good soil in full sun. Hardy to −10°C perhaps.

Eryngium variifolium Coss.   Native of North Africa, in Morocco, growing in the mountains, flowering in June–August. Plant with a clump of rosettes of fleshy leaves, green through the winter. Leaf blades ovate, cordate, crenate, *c*.5cm long, with pale veins. Stems *c*.45cm, stiff, upright. Bracts 6–7, *c*.4cm long, unequal, linear, white, with a stiff terminal spine and 1–2 lateral spines. Flower-heads rounded, *c*.1.5cm wide. For any good, moist soil in full sun. Will grow in short grass. Hardy to −15°C, perhaps less, but then not evergreen.

Eryngium decaisneanum at the Chelsea Physic Garden

Eryngium paniculatum at the Chelsea Physic Garden

Eryngium maritimum

Eryngium horridum

Eryngium bourgatii

Eryngium
× tripartitium

Eryngium amethystinum

Eryngium
agavifolium

Eryngium × zabelii

Eryngium eburneum

Specimens from Beth Chatto, Unusual Plants, 7 August. ¼ life size

Eryngium agavifolium at Wakehurst Place, Sussex

Eryngium eburneum with white *Agapanthus*

Eryngium alpinum with variegated mint

Eryngium agavifolium Griseb. (*Umbelliferae*) Native of Argentina, in the province of Cordoba, growing on stony hills and river banks, flowering in January–March, and in summer in the north. Stems *c*.2m. Leaves 75–50cm long, spiny-toothed. Bracts small. Flower-heads 5cm long, 2.5cm across. For well-drained but not dry soil in full sun. Hardy to −10°C perhaps.

Eryngium alpinum L. Native of the Jura and the Alps, from France to C Yugoslavia, growing in subalpine meadows usually on limestone at 1500–1800m, flowering in July–August. Plant with a rosette of stalked basal leaves with the blade 8–15cm × 5–13cm, ovate-cordate, toothed. Stems 30–70cm, with deeply cut leaves. Bracts 3–6cm, more than 25, very finely divided, 2–4cm long. For well-drained, stony soil in full sun, but not too dry. Hardy to −20°C or less.

Eryngium amethystinum L. Native of SE Europe, from Italy to Greece and Crete, growing in dry, stony places, flowering in July–August. Plant with tough, leathery basal leaves with lamina 10–15cm long, below, palmate-lobed above, pinnate below with a broadly winged stalk. Bracts 5–9, 2–5cm long, linear-lanceolate, with 1–4 pairs of spines. For dry, well-drained soil in full sun. Hardy to −15°C perhaps. The best forms are a very good blue.

Eryngium eburneum Decne. Native of S Brazil, Argentina, Paraguay and Uruguay, growing in marshes and wet, grassy places, flowering in October–May, but in late summer in the north. Stems to 1.5m. Leaves to 1m long,

3–5cm wide, with thin spines, evergreen. Flower-heads 15–20mm long. For good, moist soil in full sun. Hardy to −15°C perhaps.

Eryngium planum L. Native of Europe, from Germany and Austria eastwards to Russia, the Caucasus and C Asia, growing in dry places, roadsides and rocky slopes, flowering in July–September. Plant forming large clumps of stems to 1m or more in gardens. Basal leaves with blade 5–10cm × 3–6cm, oblong to ovate-oblong, cordate, toothed. Middle leaves undivided; upper leaves only deeply lobed. Bracts 6–8, 1.5–2.5cm long. Flower head ovoid-globose, 1–2cm long. For well-drained soil in a sunny position. If grown in too rich soil, the plant needs staking before the stems have flopped. Hardy to −25°C or less.

Eryngium × tripartitum hort. non L. Probably a hybrid between *E. planum* and a species with divided basal leaves such as *E. amethystinum*. The basal leaves are more coarsely toothed than those of *E. planum*; the stem leaves are deeply 3–5-lobed. The small heads are a good blue. For sunny, dry soil. Hardy to −20°C perhaps.

Eryngium × zabelii hort. ex Hegi A group of hybrids between *E. alpinum* and *E. bourgatii*, named in 1926. They differ from *E. alpinum* in having variably lobed basal leaves and more rounded flower-heads, produced in July–August. The old selections, 'Jewel' and 'Violette', both raised in 1913, are still occasionally available; both have large, blue flower-heads.

Eryngium planum

Galax urceolata in the Valley Gardens, Windsor Great Park

Lysimachia ephemerum at Edington, Wiltshire

Lysimachia clethroides

Lysimachia nummularia 'Aurea'

Lysimachia thyrsiflora in Finland

Galax urceolata (Poir.) Brammitt syn. *G. aphylla* auct. non L. (*Diapensaceae*) Beetleweed Native of E North America, from Virginia and West Virginia, south to Georgia and Alabama, growing in dry, open woods, mainly in the mountains, flowering in late May–July. Plant forming mats of creeping rhizomes, with red roots and leathery evergreen leaves 3–16cm wide, on slender petioles. Flowering stems to 80cm; flowers 3–4mm across. For leafy soil in shade or partial shade, and acid soil. Hardy to −20°C.

Lysimachia ciliata L. syn. *Steironema ciliata* (L.) Raf. (*Primulaceae*) Native of North America, from Quebec to British Columbia, south to Florida, Texas and Colorado, growing in damp woods and by lakes and rivers, flowering in June–August. Plant spreading by underground rhizomes with stems to 1.2m. Leaves ciliate on the petioles. Flowers 1.5–2.8cm across, on thin axillary shoots. For any moist soil in sun or shade. Hardy to −25°C or less. There are five other species in this group in North America, mostly with narrower leaves, and seldom seen in gardens.

Lysimachia clethroides Duby Native of Japan, in all the islands, or Korea, N & E China and Indochina, and naturalized in Holland, growing on sunny, grassy hills at low altitudes, flowering in June–July. Plant with upright flowering stems to 100cm, and creeping rhizomes, forming large clumps. Leaves alternate, acuminate often chlorotic when young. Flowers 8–12mm across. Distinct in the raceme which is nodding in bud, becoming erect as the flowers open. Hardy to −25°C or less. For any good soil. *L. barystachys* Bunge, also from E Asia, has obtuse, or subacute, not acuminate leaves, but is otherwise very similar.

Lysimachia ephemerum L. Native of W Portugal, S, C & E Spain and SW France, in the Pyrenees and Corbières, growing in damp, grassy places, especially by springs, and by streams, flowering in June–July. Plant forming clumps of upright stems to 1m or more. Leaves glaucous in 4 rows. Flowers *c.*1cm across. For any good soil that is not too dry, in sun or partial shade. Hardy to −15°C or less. A very handsome plant for a moist border.

Lysimachia nummularia L. 'Aurea' Creeping Jenny Native to most of Europe, south to Spain and Turkey in Europe, and east to Russia and the Caucasus, growing in damp woods, in fens, and on the banks of streams and lake shores, flowering in April–September. Naturalized in North America. Stems creeping and rooting to 70cm long or more. Leaves 12–25mm long, bright yellowish green in 'Aurea'. Flowers yellow, on short stalks in the leaf axils, 9–12mm long, cup-shaped. Hardy to −25°C or less. A distinct leaf shape and colour to contrast with other shade-loving foliage plants.

Lysimachia punctata L. Native to SE & EC Europe, from W Austria and N Italy eastwards to W Turkey and widely naturalized elsewhere in Europe and in NE North America, growing in shallow water in ditches, marshes and on river banks, flowering in May–September. Plant with shortly creeping rhizomes and upright stems to 150cm, forming large patches. Leaves in whorls of 2–4. Flowers 20–24mm across, 2–7 in a whorl. For any good, moist soil in sun or partial shade. Hardy to −20°C or less. *L. verticillaris* Spreng., sometimes included in *L. punctata*, is found in N & E Turkey, the Caucasus, Crimea and N Iran. It differs in its longer petioles, broader leaves 27–45mm wide, and 4–14 flowers in each whorl.

Lysimachia thyrsiflora L. syn. *Naumbergia thyrsiflora* (L.) Reichb.   Native of Europe, from England eastwards across Siberia to Japan, and of North America, from Alaska to Quebec south to California, Colorado and West Virginia, growing in marshes, bogs and cold swamps, flowering in May–July. Stems to 80cm from creeping rhizomes. Leaves lanceolate to elliptic. Flower 3–5mm long, crowded into dense spikes. For wet soil in sun or partial shade. Hardy to −25°C or less.

Lysimachia vulgaris L. Yellow Loosestrife Native of most of Europe and NW Africa, east to Turkey, N Iraq, Siberia and China, to Japan (var. *dahurica* (Ledeb.) Kunth), and naturalized in North America, growing in marshes, streams and in shallow water in reedswamps, flowering in April–September. Stems to 120cm, from a creeping rootstock, spreading by stolons. Leaves opposite or in whorls of 3–4. Flowers 12–15mm across, cup-shaped. Easily grown in wet soil in sun or partial shade. Hardy to −25°C or less.

Pyrola asarifolia Michx. (*Pyrolaceae*)   Native of North America, from Newfoundland west to Yukon, south to Prince Edward Island and New England, and along the Rockies from Indiana to New Mexico, growing in woods and scrub, usually on limestone, flowering in June–August. Plant with creeping underground rhizomes and round leaves to 6.5cm across. Flowering stems to 35cm with up to 20 flowers. Flowers 8–16mm across, crimson to pale pink, with rather thin calyx and petals. Style curved. For moist, loose, leafy soil, not too acid, in shade or partial shade. Hardy to −25°C or less.

Pyrola rotundifolia L.   Native of NE North America, from Greenland to Quebec and Nova Scotia, with var. *americana* (Sweet) Fern south to South Dakota and Georgia; and of Europe, from Iceland and Scotland, south to C Spain and east to the Altai and Siberia in the north, to Turkey and the Elburz Mountains in N Iran, growing in bogs, fens and woods, especially of beech, often on limestone, and in dune slacks (subsp. *maritima* (Kenyon) E. F. Warburg) in NW Europe, flowering in June–September. Plant with creeping underground rhizomes and rosettes of rounded leaves to 5cm across. Flowering stems to 40cm. Flowers white, scented, 12–18mm across with a thick calyx and stiff, leathery petals. Style curved, 7–8mm long (5–7mm is subsp. *maritima*). For peaty or leafy soil, moist in summer. Hardy to −20°C or less.

Lysimachia vulgaris

Lysimachia ciliata

Lysimachia clethroides

Lysimachia punctata

Specimens from Sellindge, Kent, 20 August. ⅓ life size

Pyrola rotundifolia

Pyrola asarifolia in Arizona

Lysimachia vulgaris

Asclepias incarnata

Asclepias tuberosa

Asclepias cordifolia in N California

Asclepias syriaca at Logan Botanic Garden

Asclepias cordifolia (Benth.) Jeps. (*Asclepiadaceae*) Native of California in the Coast Ranges and the Sierra Nevada, from Kern Co. northwards to Oregon and in W Nevada, growing in chaparral, scrub and pine forest, at up to 1800m, flowering in May–July. Stems to 80cm, sprawling, from a stout, woody rootstock. Leaves mostly opposite, cordate-amplexicaul, ovate, acute. Flowers dark red-purple, 16–18mm across. For dry, well-drained soil in full sun and a warm position. Hardy to −10°C perhaps.

Asclepias incarnata L. Swamp Milkweed Native of North America, from Quebec west to Manitoba and Wyoming, south to Long Island, South California, Texas and New Mexico, growing in marshes, wet scrub and on lake shores, flowering in July–September. Plant with few or several upright stems to 1.5m. Leaves oblong-lanceolate to ovate, with ascending, not transverse, veins. Umbels usually several. Flowers c.8mm across, pink, purplish or rarely white. Hoods 2–3mm high. For any good soil in full sun. Hardy to −25°C or less.

Asclepias syriaca L. Common Milkweed Native of North America, from New Brunswick west to Saskatchewan, south to North Carolina,

Kansas and Georgia, growing in scrub, by roadsides and in waste places, flowering in June–August. Stems softly pubescent, to 2m from stout creeping rhizomes. Leaves lanceolate-oblong to broadly oval, to 26cm long, to 18cm across, greyish with fine hairs beneath. Flowers scented, in rounded umbels, each flower 12–18mm across, purplish or greenish, with obtuse hoods, 3–4mm high. For any good soil in full sun. Hardy to −25°C and less. The young shoots and half-grown seed pods are edible.

Asclepias tuberosa L. Butterfly-Weed Native of North America, from S Ontario and New York west to Minnesota, south to Colorado, Arizona and N Mexico, and to Florida in the east, growing in dry, grassy places, flowering in June–September. A variable species with stems upright, roughly hairy, to 90cm from a tuberous rootstock. Leaves from linear to lanceolate or oblong-ovate, sessile or with a short petiole. Flowers yellowish to orange, or red, c.12mm across; hoods erect, oblong. For dry soil in full sun. Hardy to −20°C.

Calystegia pulchra Brummitt & Heywood (*Convolvulaceae*) Native habitat unknown but

probably from NE Asia or a garden hybrid; now naturalized in Europe from Ireland and Scotland, eastwards to Poland, Sweden and Czechoslovakia, growing in hedges and scrub, flowering in July–September. Plant with fleshy underground rhizomes and climbing stems to 3m or more. Leaves sagittate, the sinus oblong with more or less parallel sides. Bracteoles overlapping, saccate at the base, obtuse to emarginate at the apex. Flowers pink, 50–70mm long. Very similar to *C. sepium* subsp. *americana* (Sims) Brummitt, which is found in similar habitats in W Europe; it also has pink flowers, but only 40–55mm long. A double-flowered form of the Chinese *C. pubescens* Lindl. is also grown in gardens. All require careful siting in the garden because of their rampant roots. Hardy to −20°C, probably less.

Convolvulus althaeoides L. (*Convolvulaceae*) Native of S Europe and around the Mediterranean, but commoner in the west and naturalized in S California, growing on roadsides, and rocky slopes usually on limestone, flowering in April–May and later in gardens. Plant with creeping underground rhizomes and trailing or climbing twining stems to 1m or more. Lowest leaves produced in winter, hastate; upper leaves, on the twining

Solanum xantii var. *montanum* above Bishop, California

Ipomopsis subnuda in Arizona

Calystegia pulchra in Ireland

Ipomopsis aggregata

Ipomopsis aggregata in California

Convolvulus althaeoides in S Spain

stems, deeply lobed, but lobes not reaching the midrib. Flowers 27–38mm long, rich pink; outer sepals 8–10mm. Subsp. *tenuissimus* (Sibth. & Smith) Stace syn. *C. elegantissimus* Mill., from the E Mediterranean, has more silky-hairy leaves, divided to the midrib, shorter outer sepals (4–7mm long), and usually paler pink flowers. Both need very well-drained soil in full sun and will happily naturalize in old walls, though they are rather too rampant for a choice position. Hardy to −15°C perhaps.

Ipomopsis aggregata (Pursh) V. Grant syn. *Gilia aggregata* (Pursh) Spreng. (*Polemoniaceae*) Skyrocket   Native of W North America, from Oregon to S California, east to W Texas and N Mexico, and north to North Dakota, growing on dry, rocky slopes in sagebrush, scrub and clearings in pine forest at up to 3000m in California, flowering in June–September. A very variable plant, usually a short-lived perennial, sometimes biennial, with a rosette of deeply divided pinnate leaves with a musky scent and flowering stems to 80cm. Flowers 2–3.5cm long, varying in colour from magenta and crimson to red with yellow mottling or all yellow (pale pink or white in subsp. *attenuata* (Gray) V. & A. Grant). For well-drained, dry soil in sun or partial shade. Hardy to −15°C,

or less if dry in winter. Easily raised from seed.

Ipomopsis subnuda (Torr.) V. Grant syn. *Gilia subnuda* Torr.   Native of N Arizona, New Mexico, Utah and Nevada, growing on sandy or rocky hills at 1500–2500m, flowering in June–July. Plants often biennial with stems to 60cm. Leaves glandular-pubescent, entire to shallowly pinnatifid. Flowers in small groups, the corolla tubular, 12–20mm long. For dry, well-drained soil in full sun. Hardy to −15°C, or less if dry.

Solanum xantii Gray var. ***montanum*** Munz (*Solanaceae*)   Native of E California, from San Bernadino north to Nevada Co. on the east of the Sierra Nevada, growing on dry slopes in the conifer forest zone at 1500–2750m, flowering in May–September. Stems to 40cm, often prostrate from a woody rootstock. Leaves greyish, pubescent, ovate. Flowers 1.5–2.5cm across. Berries greenish, 9–10mm across. For well-drained, dry soil in full sun. Hardy to −15°C if dry. Other varieties of *S. xantii* found in S California, Arizona and Baja California are subshrubby, up to 90cm high and found in scrub and chaparral at lower altitudes.

'Mother of Pearl'

'Cherry Pink'

'Rijnstroom'

'Mary Fox'

'Dodo Hanbury-Forbes'

'Fujiyama'

'Sandringham'

'Skylight'

Phlox specimens from the Savill Gardens, Windsor, 28 August. ½ life size

Phlox 'Fujiyama'

Phlox 'Prospero' in the Culpepper Garden, Leeds Castle, Kent

Phlox paniculata L. often called *P. decussata* Introduced to Europe from North America in 1730. Several cultivars were developed during the 19th century, some possibly by hybridization with *P. carolina*, but mainly by selection of colour forms of the original species and varieties. The greatest advances in the raising of new cultivars were made by Capt. B. Symons-Jeune in the 1950s. He aimed not only for large flowers, but also for pure colours, scent and disease resistance. All the large-flowered border *Phlox* require full sun, rich soil and plenty of water, with liquid feed at the root. Mildew, which can be a problem, can best be avoided by making sure that air circulation is good, and that the roots do not suffer from drought. All are hardy to at least −25°C, and flower in July–September. (See also p.67.)

'Alison Jane'   Raised by A. Goatcher & Son, Sussex, before 1960. Stems to 70cm. Flowers 3.8cm across. Panicles 7.5–10cm long.
'Cherry Pink'   Raiser not recorded. Height up to 90cm.
'Dodo Hanbury-Forbes' (syn. 'Dorothy Hanbury-Forbes')   Raised by Capt. B. Symons-Jeune and introduced by Bakers Nurseries. Flower stems stout, *c*.90cm; panicles *c*.15cm long and wide. Flowers 4–4.5cm across.
'Europe'   Raiser nor recorded. Height to 75cm.
'Fujiyama' (syn. 'Mount Fuji')   Raised in the USA, this has sturdy stems up to 1m, with large heads of pure-white flowers from mid-September onwards.
'Le Mahdi'   A strong grower, and an old variety, known since 1933. Flowers deep purplish blue.
'Mary Fox'   Raised by Alan Bloom; stems to 80cm, healthy and robust.
'Mother of Pearl'   Raised by Alan Bloom. Height to 120cm. Flowers 3.75cm across, freely produced, in panicles to 20cm long and wide.
'Prospero'   Raised by K. Foerster in 1956. Height to 90cm.
'Rijnstroom'   An old, and reliable, variety. Height up to 80cm.
'Sandringham'   An old variety, raised by R. M. Bath Ltd of Wisbech before 1953, with stems up to 1m.
'Silver Salmon'   Raised in Germany before 1965. Height to 90cm.
'Skylight'   Raiser unrecorded. Height to 90cm.

Phlox 'Le Mahdi'

Phlox 'Europe'

Phlox 'Alison Jane'

Phlox 'Silver Salmon'

Onosma tauricum at Edington, Wiltshire

Onosma frutescens in S Turkey

Solenanthus circinnatus near Frunze

Onosma albo-roseum at Edington, Wiltshire

Macromeria viridiflora in Arizona

Moltkia doerfleri

Arnebia densiflora on limestone hills near Malatya, C Turkey

Arnebia densiflora (Nordb.) Ledeb. syn.
Macrotonia cephalotes (DC.) Boiss.
(*Boraginaceae*)   Native of Greece, in the
Peloponnese (Aroania Oros), and of Turkey,
from Bursa south to Adana and east to
Erzinçan, growing on limestone and igneous
rocks and cliffs, at 750–2600m, flowering in
May–August. Plant tufted with several dense
rosettes of narrowly lanceolate basal leaves, and
flowering stems to 40cm. Flowers 12–16mm
across, 35–45mm long. A beautiful plant, but
very difficult to grow; although I have collected
seed and raised seedlings on several occasions,
the plants have always rotted before flowering.
They will require well-drained soil in full sun,
kept, if possible, dry and cold in winter. Hardy
to −25°C, probably less.

Arnebia pulchra (Roem. & Schult.)
Edmondson syns. *A. echioides* (L.) Boiss.,
Echioides longiflora (K. Koch) I. M. Johnston
Native of the N Caucasus, N Iran and NE
Turkey, growing in rocky places and roadsides
at 1525–3000m in Turkey, flowering in June–
July. Plant with stout rootstock, and few
sprawling stems to 45cm. Leaves stiffly hairy.
Flowers 18–25mm across, 20–24mm long, with
blackish spots which fade as the flower ages. For
well-drained soil in full sun. Hardy to −20°C or
less.

Macromeria viridiflora DC. (*Boraginaceae*)
Native of New Mexico and E Arizona to N
Mexico, growing on rocky slopes and in valleys
in pine forest and in scrub, at 1000–2750m,
flowering in July–September. A bristly plant
with several stems to 90cm. Flowers to 4cm
long, with stamens shortly exserted. Leaves
5–12cm long, broadly lanceolate. For well-
drained soil in full sun. Hardy to −15°C. Used

by the Hopi Indians, dried and mixed with wild
tobacco, for rain-bringing ceremonies.

Moltkia doerfleri Wettst. (*Boraginaceae*)
Native of NE Albania, growing in rock crevices,
flowering in May–June. Plant with a horizontal
rhizome and several upright stems to 50cm.
Leaves lanceolate, acute. Flowers 19–25mm
long, deep purple, the anthers not exserted. For
well-drained soil in full sun. Hardy to −20°C or
so.

Onosma albo-roseum Fisch. & Mey.
(*Boraginaceae*)   Native of Turkey, N Syria and
N Iraq, growing on rocky slopes and cliffs on
limestone, at up to 2550m, flowering in April–
July. Plant with erect or ascending stems from a
central rootstock. Leaves obovate to oblong,
whitish, with dense appressed bristly hairs.
Flowers 18–30mm long, broadly campanulate.
For well-drained soil in full sun, in a crevice,
wall, or in a scree garden. Hardy to −15°C.

Onosma frutescens Lam.   Native of C & S
Greece, W & S Turkey, and W Syria, growing
on limestone slopes and rocks at up to 1600m,
flowering in March–June. Plant bristly, with
somewhat woody, spreading stems and oblong-
lanceolate leaves. Flowering stems several, more
or less upright. Flowers 18–20mm long. For
well-drained soil in full sun, in a crevice or
similar position. Hardy to −10°C perhaps.

Onosma tauricum Pallas ex Willd.   Native of
Yugoslavia and Romania, south to Turkey and
Syria, and east to the Caucasus and the Crimea,
growing on rocks, old walls, stony slopes and
steppes, flowering in March–June. Plant with
bristly stems and leaves, and several spreading
flowering stems from a central rootstock. Stem

leaves linear-lanceolate or linear-oblong.
Flowers 22–25mm long, white, yellow or cream.
For well-drained soil in full sun, preferably in a
crevice in paving, in a wall or in a scree garden.
Hardy to −15°C.

Solenanthus circinnatus Ledeb.
(*Boraginaceae*)   Native of E Turkey and N Iraq
eastwards to Afghanistan and Siberia in the
Tien Shan and the Altai, and in NW China,
growing in scrub and alpine meadows in rich
soil, at up to 2800m in Turkey, flowering in
May–June. Plant with several stems to 100cm,
from a stout rootstock. Basal leaves broadly
ovate, 10–30cm long, to 20cm wide. Flowers
purplish, 5–7mm long, with whitish, long-
exserted stamens and style. For well-drained,
rich soil, dryish in summer. Hardy to −20°C or
less.

Arnebia pulchra in the Caucasus

Verbena macdougallii in Arizona

Verbena bonariensis with *Crocosmia* 'Lucifer' at Bressingham Gardens, Norfolk

Chelone glabra L. (*Scrophulariaceae*) Balmony, Turtle-head   Native of Newfoundland, west to Ontario and Minnesota, south to Georgia, Alabama and Missouri, growing in wet places, in woods, clearings and by streams, flowering in late July–October. Stems to 2m, from a stout rootstock, finally forming large patches. Leaves tapering or rounded at base, with almost no petiole. Sepals with scarious margins. Flowers usually white. For moist, rich soil in sun or partial shade. Hardy to −20°C or less.

Chelone obliqua L.   Native of Tennessee south to Florida and Mississippi, growing in wet woods and cypress swamps, flowering in late August–October. Differs from *C. glabra* in its lanceolate, slender-stalked leaves, purplish flowers, and sepals with very faint scarious margins and rounded, not acuminate bracts. For moist, good soil in sun or partial shade. Hardy to −20°C perhaps. The very similar *C. lyonii* Pursh has broader leaves, rounded at the base, on longer stalks, and a more sharply ridged upper lip to the flower.

Verbena bonariensis L. (*Verbenaceae*)   Native of South America, in S Brazil, Argentina, Uruguay and Paraguay, growing in wet fields and waste places, flowering in late summer. Stems few, upright, square in section to 100cm tall. Leaves few, sessile, clasping the stem. Inflorescence with long, leafless branches. Flowers purple *c.*1mm across, in flat-topped cymes. For any good soil in full sun. Hardy to −10°C, possibly less, and often appearing again the following spring after sowing itself, if killed in a cold winter.

Verbena corymbosa Ruiz & Pav.   Native of S Chile and Argentina, flowering in June–August in the north. Plant with upright stems to 100cm with far-creeping underground rhizomes. Leaves oblong or ovate, to 6cm long, sometimes lobed near the base. Flowers pale bluish mauve. Best in moist soil in full sun.

Verbena corymbosa at Axeltree Nursery, Rye, Kent

Chelone glabra in New York State

Verbena hastata in New York State

Chelone obliqua in Harry Hay's garden, Surrey

Verbena tenuisecta at Wisley

Verbena hastata L. Simpler's Joy   Native of North America, from Nova Scotia and New Brunswick south to Florida, Texas and from British Columbia to California, growing in marshes, damp scrub and by lakes and rivers, flowering in June–September. Stems erect from a tufted rootstock, to 150cm. Lowest leaves sometimes hastate, but often lanceolate to narrowly ovate. Inflorescence of numerous narrow spikes. Flowers violet blue, pink in f. *rosea*, or white, 3–4.5mm across. For good, moist soil in full sun. Hardy to −20°C or less.

Verbena macdougallii Heller.   Native of Arizona, New Mexico and W Texas to S Wyoming, growing in grassy places in open pine forest at around 2000m, flowering in June–October. Plant with erect, stiffly hairy stems to 90cm. Leaves coarsely toothed to 10cm long. Flowers 6mm across. For any rich soil in full sun. Hardy to −20°C.

Verbena rigida Spreng. syn. *V. venosa* Gillies & Hook.   Native of Argentina and S Brazil. Plant with many upright stems to 60cm from tuberous roots. Leaves oblong, sessile, amplexicaul, rough, irregularly toothed. Flower spikes in threes, congested, the lateral being long-stalked. Flowers purple to magenta, about 8mm across. For any good soil in full sun. Hardy to −10°C, but the tubers should be protected from freezing.

Verbena tenuisecta Brig.   Native of southern South America, in Argentina and Chile, and commonly naturalized in Mexico, Arizona and ? California, growing on roadsides and bare rocky places, flowering in summer. Stems slender, trailing, rooting at the nodes. Leaves dissected into linear lobes, bipinnatifid. Flowers blue to purple, in flat heads; limb of corolla *c.*1cm across. *V. tenera* Spreng. is similar, but has more downy leaves, less finely divided, and pinkish-purple flowers. Hardy to −10°C if rather dry.

Verbena rigida at Hawstead, Suffolk

Eremostachys lehmanniana

Eremostachys laciniata

Eremostachys speciosa near Tashkent

Phlomis bracteosa, avoided by grazing ponies, in Kashmir

Phlomis russelliana at the Chelsea Physic Garden

Phlomis lychnitis in S France

Phlomis tuberosa on the steppes near Stavropol, growing with *Paeonia tenuifolia* and *Plantago media*

Eremostachys laciniata (L.) Bunge (*Labiatae*)   Native of S & E Turkey, W Syria, Transcaucasia and Iran east to C Asia, growing on steppes, in oak scrub and dry meadows at up to 2200m in Turkey, flowering in May–July. Stems 1–2m from a tuberous rootstock. Leaves deeply laciniate, hairy, 15–30cm long. Flowers white, cream or pinkish, often speckled with red on the lip, 3–4cm long. Calyx not enlarging in fruit. (In *E. molucelloides* Bunge, from C Turkey east to Mongolia, the calyx becomes large and bell-shaped and acts as an aid for the dispersal of the seeds by the wind.) For dry, well-drained, but good soil in full sun, with water in autumn and spring only. Hardy to −25°C.

Eremostachys lehmanniana Bunge   Native of C Asia, growing on dry, rocky hillsides, flowering in May–June. Plant with a clump of stems to 1m from a tuberous rootstock; leaves *c*.15cm long, hairy, deeply lobed. Flowers deep pink. For dry, well-drained soil in full sun. Hardy to −25°C.

Eremostachys speciosa Rupr.   Native of C Asia and the W Himalayas, growing on rich, grassy slopes and steppes, flowering in May–June. Stems few to 60cm, from a tuberous rootstock. Leaves green, pinnatifid, serrate. Flowers on stout spikes in condensed whorls. Calyx very woolly; corolla hairy. For a well-drained, sandy soil, rather dry in summer and winter. Hardy to −25°C.

Phlomis bovei Noë subsp. *maroccana* Maire syn. *P. samia* L. subsp. *maroccana* Maire   For illustration see p. 318. Similar to *P. samia*, but differing in its mostly unbranched stems, and in its larger flowers over 3.5cm long, with the central lobe of the lower lip over 2cm wide, and the upper lip only 5mm above the lower. Native of the mountains of Morocco and Algeria. Hardy to −10°C.

Phlomis bracteosa Royle ex Benth. (*Labiatae*)   Native of the Himalayas, from Afghanistan to SW China, growing in grassy places among rocks at 1200–4000m, flowering in July–August

Stems several, 20–80cm, from a stout rootstock. Leaves 5–10cm long. Flowers 1.5–2cm long, with a short tube and a large, elongate upper lip. For good, but well-drained soil in full sun, with water in summer. Hardy to −25°C.

Phlomis lychnitis L.   Native of S France, as far north as the Ardêche, of Spain and Portugal, growing in dry scrub, garrigue and on rocky hills, flowering in May–July. Plant spreading by underground suckers. Stems 30–50cm, from a woody base. Leaves puberulent, with stellate hairs, to 7.5cm long. Flowers in whorls of 4–10, *c*.2.5cm long. For dry, well-drained soil. Hardy to −10°C, perhaps less.

Phlomis russelliana (Sims) Benth. syn. *P. viscosa* hort.   Native of Turkey, mainly in the north, from Istanbul to Rize, growing in woods and clearings, and in hazel scrub, at up to 1700m, flowering in May–September. Plant with stems 30–90cm, spreading above and below ground. Leaves ovate, cordate, crenate. Whorls distant on the spike; calyx stellate tomentose, with spreading teeth; corolla yellow, 30–35cm long. For any good soil in sun or partial shade. Hardy to −20°C.

Phlomis samia L.   Native of Greece, S Yugoslavia and SW & S Turkey, growing in pine and cedar forest, usually on volcanic soil, flowering in June–August. Plant forming large clumps of spreading and branching stems to 1m. Leaves 8–20cm long, lanceolate-ovate to broadly ovate, crenate or serrate. Flowers 30–35mm long, with upper lip helmet-shaped. A vigorous species for fairly dry, partially shaded places as well as in full sun.

Phlomis tuberosa L.   Native of C & SE Europe, N & E Turkey, N Iran and Siberia, growing on steppes, dry meadows and stony hills, flowering in June–July. Plant with spherical tubers formed as nodules on the root system, and stems to 120cm or more tall. Leaves green, ovate, cordate, to 25cm long. Flowers 14–40 per whorl, with the corolla 15–20mm long, the upper lip longer than the lower. Easily grown and totally deciduous in winter. Hardy to −25°C.

Phlomis tuberosa (detail)

Phlomis samia

Nepeta grandiflora

Stachys officinalis 'Rosea' (p. 97)

Nepeta govaniana

Nepeta × faassenii

Nepeta 'Six Hills Giant'

Specimens from Wisley, 20 July. ⅓ life size

Melissa officinalis L. (*Labiatae*) Lemon Balm
Native of S Europe and North Africa, east to
the Caucasus and N Iran, but commonly
naturalized in disturbed ground further north,
growing in open woods, scrub and on rocky
slopes by streams, flowering in June–September.
Plant with upright stems to 1m, from a shortly
creeping, woody rootstock. Leaves rough,
usually lemon-scented. Flowers 9–14mm long.
For any soil in sun or partial shade, and useful
in dry difficult places, though it can seed so
freely as to be a nuisance. 'Aurea' has golden-
variegated leaves. Hardy to −15°C, perhaps less.
For *Melittis* see p. 430–1.

Nepeta × *faassenii* Bergmans ex Stearn
(*Labiatae*) A hybrid between the Caucasian *N.
racemosa* Lam. syn. *N. mussinii* Spreng. ex
Henckel and *N. nepetella* L., a species from
Europe and North Africa. It is a useful edging
plant for hot, dry borders on an alkaline soil,
with silvery leaves, and stems around 30cm,
flowering throughout the summer.
'Six Hills Giant' Taller and tougher, with
stems to 1m, and deep-blue flowers.

Nepeta govaniana Benth. Native of the
Himalayas, from Pakistan to N India (Uttar
Pradesh), growing in moist places in open
woodland, flowering in August–September. A
sweetly aromatic plant of great beauty with
branched stems to 1m, and flowers to 30mm, on
long pedicels, often in pairs. For moist, mildly
acid soil in a cool position. Hardy to −15°C.

Nepeta grandiflora M. Bieb. Native of the
Caucasus, growing in grassy meadows and
scrub, flowering in May–June. Plant with
several stems to 1m; leaves 5cm long, cordate,
crenulate. Flowers in an elongated spike,
lavender-blue, 1.5cm long. For any good soil in
full sun. Hardy to −20°C.

Nepeta persica Boiss. Native of Iran, growing
on dry, rocky hills, flowering in June–August.
Plant compact, to 10cm, with grey, hairy, ovate
leaves to 1.5cm long. Flowers in tight whorls.
For dry soil in full sun. Hardy to −10°C. (See
also p. 430.)

Nepeta sibirica L. syn. *N. macrantha* Fisch. ex.
Benth. Native of Siberia, growing in grassland,
flowering in June–July. Stems to 1m, with
smooth lanceolate leaves, 8cm long.
Inflorescence branched. Flowers *c.*4cm long,
with a straight corolla tube. For good soil in full
sun. Hardy to −25°C.
'Souvenir d'André Chaudron' syn. 'Blue
Beauty' A short stocky form of *N. sibirica*, with
a longer flowering season.

Scutellaria amoena C. H. Wright (*Labiatae*)
Native of China, particularly in Yunnan around
Kunming and Lijiang, growing in dry scrub on
limestone at *c.*1500m, flowering in April–May.
Stems upright, tufted, to 20cm, from a shortly
creeping rootstock. Leaves oblong, obtuse.
Flowers *c.*15mm long. For well-drained soil in
sun or partial shade. Hardy to −15°C perhaps.

Scutellaria incana K. Spreng. syn. *S. canescens*
Nutt. Native of E North America, from New
Jersey south to North Carolina, west to Kansas
and Alabama, growing in open woods, scrub
and grassland, flowering in June–August. Stems
to 120cm; leaves grey, ovate, 7.5–12cm long.
Flowers 15–25mm long. For any soil in sun or
light shade. Hardy to −25°C.

Nepeta 'Six Hills Giant' at Crathes Castle, Aberdeenshire *Nepeta persica*

Nepeta sibirica *Nepeta* 'Souvenir d'André Chaudron'

Melissa officinalis *Nepeta govaniana*

Scutellaria incana at Wakehurst Place, Sussex *Scutellaria amoena* near Lijiang, Yunnan

Stachys thirkei

Ballota pseudodictamnus

Nepeta cataria

Marrubium peregrinum

Stachys byzantina 'Primrose Heron'

Stachys byzantina (two forms)

Phlomis bovei subsp. *maroccana* (text p. 315)

Specimens from the Chelsea Physic Garden, 11 July. ¼ life size

Stachys officinalis 'Rosea'

Stachys coccinea at Harry Hay's, Surrey

Hyssopus officinalis 'Rosea'

Ballota pseudodictamnus (L.) Benth. (*Labiatae*) Native of Crete, Kithira and Cyrenaica, growing on rocks and rough ground, flowering in May–July. Plant very woolly, yellowish grey. Calyces conspicuous, 7–8mm across; corolla small, usually white, 14–15mm. Subsp. *lycia* Hub.-Mor., from SW Turkey, has the fruiting calyx 8–10mm across. *Ballota acetabulosa* (L.) Benth. from S Greece, the Aegean islands and SW Turkey, has flatter calyces to 20mm across and larger flowers 15–18mm, white with purple spots; the whole plant is greyer and larger. Both need well-drained position in full sun. Hardy to −10°C.

Hyssopus officinalis L. 'Rosea' (*Labiatae*) Hyssop Native of S Europe, east to the Caucasus and N Iran, growing in dry hills and on rock ledges, at up to 2200m in N Turkey, flowering in July–August. Plant very variable in hairiness, calyx and leaf shape. Stems numerous, to 60cm. Leaves linear, aromatic, to 5cm long. Flowers 7–13mm long, usually bluish, but also purplish, pink or white. The pink form, shown here, was grown by Philip Miller in the Chelsea Physic Garden in the 18th century. For a dry, sunny place. Hardy to −25°C.

Marrubium peregrinum L. (*Labiatae*) Native of SE Europe, from Austria to Greece and Russia south to the N Caucasus and W Turkey, growing in dry, open places, flowering in June–August. Stems yellowish, to 60cm. Leaves whitish hairy, especially beneath. Flowers small, hairy outside. For a dry place in full sun. Hardy to −25°C.

Nepeta cataria L. (*Labiatae*) Catnip or Catmint Native of Europe, from S England east to Siberia, the Himalayas, China and Korea, and naturalized in North America and Japan, growing in scrub, hedges and on dry, grassy banks, often on limestone, flowering in July–August. Plant much loved by cats, with upright stems to 1m. Leaves grey-pubescent, c.5cm long. Flowers white with bluish spots, 6–7mm long. 'Citriodora' has lemon-scented foliage. For well-drained soil in a warm position. Hardy to −25°C.

Stachys macrantha (bicoloured form)

Stachys byzantina at Crathes Castle, Aberdeenshire

Prunella grandiflora

Prunella grandiflora subsp. *pyrenaica*

Stachys macrantha

Prunella grandiflora (L.) Scholler (*Labiatae*) Native of most of Europe, growing in grassland, usually on alkaline soils, flowering in June–September. Plant forming spreading mats with upright stems to 60cm, usually *c*.30cm. Flowers 25–30mm long, usually bluish, but also reddish, pink and white in garden forms. The inflorescence, without a pair of leaves at the base, distinguishes this species. Subsp. *pyrenaica* (Gren. & Godr.) A. & O. Bolos syn. *P. hastifolia* Brot., found on acid soils in SW France, Spain and Portugal, has larger flowers and hastate leaves; both need good, moist soil in full sun. Hardy to −25°C.

Stachys byzantina C. Koch syns. *S. lanata* Jacq., *S. olympica* Briq., (*Labiatae*) Lambs' Ears Native of N Turkey, the S Caucasus and N Iran, growing on rocky hills, in juniper scrub and waste places, flowering in June–September. Whole plant densely woolly, with rosettes of basal leaves to 10cm long, and ascending flowering stems to 1m. Flowers pink, 12–14mm long. Calyx teeth erect, sometimes slightly recurved. For a hot, dry, sunny position. Hardy

to −20°C. Several distinct forms are grown in gardens: 'Primrose Heron' has yellowish leaves under the wool; 'Cotton Boll' syn. 'Sheila Macqueen' has flowers proliferating to form woolly balls up the stem.

Stachys coccinea Jacq. Native of W Texas, New Mexico, S Arizona and Mexico, growing in canyons and by streams in rich soil at up to 2400m in Arizona, flowering in March–October. Plant usually forming spreading patches of stems to 30cm tall. Leaves triangular-ovate, sparingly hairy. Flowers 18–21mm long. For good, well-drained soil in full sun. Hardy to −10°C, perhaps less.

Stachys macrantha (C. Koch) Stearn syn. *S. grandiflora* Benth. non Host Native of the Caucasus, NE Turkey and NW Iran, growing in meadows, on rocky slopes and in scrub, at 1600–3000m, flowering in June–September. Plant spreading slowly to form dense clumps, with upright stems to 45cm. Flowers 30–35mm long, purplish pink, rarely pure, pale pink. For any good soil in sun or light shade. Hardy to

−20°C. There are pink 'Rosea', white 'Alba', and a bicoloured form in cultivation, and 'Robusta'.

Stachys officinalis (L.) Trevisan syn. *Betonica officinalis* L. Wood Betony Native of Europe, from Ireland and Scotland east to Siberia and south to Turkey and N Iran, growing on moist grassy banks, in meadows and in openings in forest, flowering in June–September. Plant with slender, erect stems to 45cm. Flowers in dense spikes, usually reddish purple, rarely pink. An attractive plant for the wild garden or meadow, and characteristic of heathy roadside banks on heavy soils. Hardy to −25°C or less.

Stachys thirkei C. Koch Native of the Balkan peninsula and Italy to W Turkey, growing on bare hills and waste ground, flowering in May–September. Plant with mats of tight rosettes of grey-green or densely white-tomentose leaves, with a rugose upper surface. Calyx teeth longer than those of *S. byzantina*, spreading. Flowers magenta. For a dry position in full sun, and dislikes winter wet. Hardy to −15°C.

Salvia nemorosa 'Superba'

Salvia buchananii

Salvia buchananii Hedge (*Labiatae*)   Found in the 1950s in a garden of an English family in Mexico City. Provenance unknown, but probably S Mexico or C America. Stems to 60cm. One of the most beautiful half-hardy species, with distinct dark-green, ovate, leathery leaves and flowers to 5cm long, velvety-hairy above. Flowers from July onwards, and best in rich, moist soil. Hardy to −10°C.

Salvia chamaedryoides Cav.   Native of the mountains of Mexico. A low creeping plant, with stems herbaceous below ground, becoming hard and woody above; stems *c.*30cm, spreading 60cm or more. Leaves elliptic, with fine hairs *c.*1cm long. Flowers with a short tube and bottom lip widely open. For hot, dry rocky places, flowering in late summer. Hardy to −10°C.

Salvia farinacea Benth. Mealy Cup Sage Native of Texas and New Mexico, growing on dry hillsides, flowering in summer. Stems to 45cm; leaves ovate-lanceolate, 2.5–7.5cm long. Flowers in tight whorls, 1.2cm long, hairy. 'Alba' has green bracts and white, hairy flowers. For dry soil in full sun. Hardy to −15°C.

Salvia miltiorhiza Bunge   Native of NE China, and common near Beijing, growing in light woodland and clearings, flowering in May. Plant to 1m, with a large, orange-red tuber below ground and recognized by its leaves, which are pinnate with 5 leaflets. It is praised for its alleged medicinal qualities, which include a remedy for cancer.

Salvia nemorosa L. '**Superba**'   The clone 'Superba' was selected at the turn of the century from the species which is native of C & E Europe and SW Asia, from E Turkey and Iran to the Caucasus and Afghanistan, growing on rocky slopes, in dry meadows and rough ground, flowering in June–September. Stems forming clumps to 1m or more tall, with a stiff, upright habit; flower spikes to 15cm long, with dark-blue flowers and reddish-purple bracts. Flowering in gardens is from midsummer onwards and the effect is prolonged by the persistence of the bracts. Hardy to −20°C.

Salvia pratensis L. Meadow Sage or Common Clary   Native of most of Europe, including Britain, where it is not as common as it used to be, south to Morocco, and east to Russia, growing in meadows, flowering in June–July and spasmodically later. Stems to 90cm, usually less; leaves wrinkled 7.5–15cm long. Flowers with calyx often tinted dark blue, and with

Salvia × *sylvestris* 'Mainacht'

Salvia pratensis in a subalpine meadow in Switzerland

Salvia chamaedryoides

Salvia farinacea 'Victoria'

corolla rich blue, pink or white, the upper lip prominently curved, to 2.5cm long. For well-drained but good soil. Hardy to −25°C.

Salvia sclarea L. Clary Sage   Native of SE Europe and SW Asia, growing in dry rocky places, flowering in July–August. A short-lived perennial or biennial; in its first year from seed it produces a rosette of pubescent leaves which are broadly ovate, wrinkled and up to 22cm long. Flowering stem to 1m, very large and much branched, produced the following year. Bracts very prominent, pinkish, lilac or white, sometimes with a greenish tinge. Flowers to 2.5cm long, with the upper lip strongly curved downwards. *S. sclarea* is known as Clary Sage on account of its alleged value as an aid to clear sight. Var. *turkestanica* Moltet is a form with exceedingly large bracts, probably not in cultivation. The whole plant is strongly aromatic. For dry, well-drained soil in full sun. Hardy to −20°C.

Salvia spathacea Greene Pitcher Sage   Native of California, from Solano Co. near San Francisco along the Coast Ranges south to Orange Co., growing in scrub, chaparral and open woods, flowering in March–May. Plant viscid, forming low, ground-covering mounds by means of creeping underground rhizomes. Leaves hastate, 10–15cm long, rugose above and hairy beneath. Flower-spikes 60–90cm high; corolla 4cm long, deep reddish-purple. Sometimes called 'Hummingbird Sage' in reference to its pollinator. For any soil in sun or partial shade. Hardy to −10°C perhaps.

Salvia × *sylvestris* L. '**Mainacht**' syn. 'May Night'   Sometimes found under the name *S. nemorosa*, this German hybrid between *S. pratensis* and *S. nemorosa* has given some excellent clones; 'Mainacht' has larger flowers than *S. nemorosa*, of rich indigo-violet, enclosed in reddish-purple bracts, in mid- to late summer. Hardy to −20°C.

Salvia uliginosa Benth.   Native of Brazil, Uruguay and Argentina, growing in damp grassland, flowering in August–October in the north. Stems to 2m high, forming large clumps a metre or more thick by means of fleshy underground stolons. Leaves lanceolate, to 7cm long, both stems and leaves slightly viscid. Flowers on small spikes at the top of each branch; corolla mid-blue 2cm long, the lower lip having a white patch. For any good sandy soil that is not dry in summer. Hardy to −10°C, possibly less, but in danger from slugs in winter, which eat the fleshy rhizomes.

Salvia spathacea in Santa Barbara Botanic Garden

Salvia miltiorhiza near Beijing

Salvia uliginosa

Salvia sclarea

Salvia campanulata on the plain at Lijiang, early May

Salvia forskahlei

Salvia campanulata Benth. (*Labiatae*)
Native of the Himalayas, from N India to SW
China, growing on rocky hillsides or grassy
meadows at 2500–4000m, flowering in May–
July. Plant with a tuberous rootstock. Leaves
ovate, to 12cm long. Flower spike to more than
30cm. Flowers in pairs with large calyces.
Flower colour very variable, ranging from cream
to yellow, pink or blue. For well-drained soil in
full sun, moist in summer. Hardy to –15°C
or less?

Salvia castanea Diels   Native of the
Himalayas in W China, described from Lijiang,
growing in open turf on limestone, flowering in
July–August. Plant forming clumps 90cm tall,
60cm across. Leaves ovate, glutinous, softly
hairy, to 15cm long. Flowers dark brownish-
maroon, 2.5cm long, with an expanded corolla
tube. For well-drained soil, with plenty of
moisture in the growing season, but may suffer
from too much moisture when dormant in
winter. Hardy to –20°C.

Salvia flava Diels var. **megalantha** Diels
Native of W China, in Yunnan, in the Dali and
Lijiang mountains, growing in rocky meadows,
flowering in June–July. Plant forming clumps of
leaves 60–90cm across, the blades cordate or
hastate 2–7cm long. Flowering stems 20–50cm,
with flowers in 4s. Calyx 1.3–1.5cm. Corolla
yellow c.3cm long, the lower lip brown or
purple, mimicking a bumble bee. In var. *flava*,
which also occurs in Sichuan, the tip is yellow.
S. bulleyana Diels has purple-blue flowers. For
well-drained soil in full sun. Hardy to –15°C,
perhaps less.

Salvia forskahlei L.   Native of Bulgaria and
N Turkey along the Black Sea, growing on dry
hillsides, at up to 1900m, flowering in
June–September. Plant forming large, almost
woody, ground-covering clumps, with ovate or
cordate rather rough leaves. Flowers in spikes to
100cm high. Corolla violet-blue with white
streaks on the lower lip, which is strongly
deflexed. For rich soil in sun or partial shade.
Hardy to –15°C.

Salvia glutinosa L.   Native of Europe, from
the Alps east to the Caucasus, Turkey and N
Iran, growing in scrub and in moist places in
deciduous forest, flowering in July–October.
The closely related *S. nubicola* Sweet, from
C Asia, can scarcely be regarded as a separate
species, as it differs only in the more reflexed
lower lip. This plant is very sticky all over,

Salvia flava var. megalantha

Salvia glutinosa

Salvia hians

Salvia hians in Kashmir, July

in common with many herbaceous species from Asia. Plant making a handsome clump to 1m high and wide. Leaves heart-shaped, large, to 20cm long. For full sun or partial shade in any good soil. Hardy to −20°C or less?

Salvia hians Royle   Native of the Himalayas, from Pakistan to Bhutan, and common in Kashmir, growing on rocky open slopes at 2000-3000m in single clumps, flowering in June–September. Plant covered in sticky glands, producing an aromatic oil which is very pleasantly scented. Leaves ovate, cordate, 8–13cm long; flower spikes normally 60cm high. Flowers to 3cm long, with an inflated tube and spreading lips. For good, rich soil in full sun. Hardy to −20°C.

Salvia hydrangea DC. ex Benth.   Native of NE Turkey, Armenia and Iran, growing on dry, rocky slopes, pastures and roadsides, at up to 2000m, flowering in June–August. Plant spreading by stems running below the ground, and layering itself from horizontal branches above ground, creating a mat to 60cm across, from which many flowering branches emerge to 50cm tall. Leaves pinnatisect, with 2–3 pairs of small lobes and a large lanceolate or linear terminal lobe to 4cm long. Flowers *c.*22mm long, pink to magenta. For dry, well-drained soil in full sun. Although cold-tolerant, this species often dies in damp temperate winters. Hardy to −25°C if dry.

Salvia multicaulis Vahl   Native of SW Asia, from Iran and Turkey to Syria and Sinai, growing is dry scrub, on steppes and rocky limestone slopes, at up to 2600m, flowering in April–July. Plant shrubby, nearly deciduous in winter. Stems to 15cm high; leaves oblong to suborbicular, *c.*4cm long, wrinkled and a good substitute for garden sage for cooking. Flowers pink or violet, enclosed in large reddish calyces which expand when the seeds develop. For well-drained, dry soil in full sun. Hardy to −25°C or less?

Salvia przewalskii Max.   Native of China, especially in W & NW Sichuan, growing on rocky slopes and seasonal stream beds, in rather dry valleys, flowering in August–September. Plant with several hairy stems to 1.2m. Leaves ovate, cordate, to 15cm long, hairy on both surfaces. Calyx glandular, viscid; corolla tube swollen to 2.5cm long, pale pink to rose-purple coloured. For well-drained soil in full sun. Hardy to −20°C or less?

Salvia multicaulis

Salvia castanea

Salvia hydrangea

Salvia przewalskii

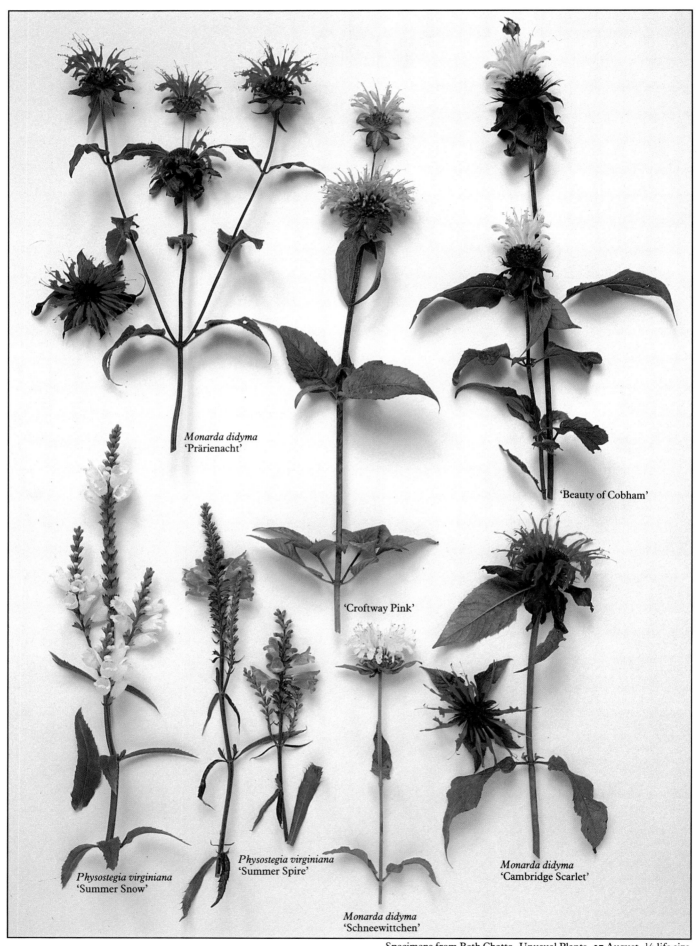

Monarda didyma
'Prärienacht'

'Beauty of Cobham'

'Croftway Pink'

Physostegia virginiana
'Summer Spire'

Monarda didyma
'Cambridge Scarlet'

Physostegia virginiana
'Summer Snow'

Monarda didyma
'Schneewittchen'

Specimens from Beth Chatto, Unusual Plants, 17 August. ⅓ life size

Monarda didyma L. (*Labiatae*) Bergamot, Oswego Tea   Native of E North America, from New York to Michigan, and in the mountains south to Georgia and Tennessee, growing in moist woods and scrub, flowering in late June–August. Plant pleasantly aromatic, forming clumps of upright stems to 1.5m. Leaves softly hairy or smooth, toothed, to 14cm long, with a short stalk. Flowers in a terminal head, with red-tinged bracts. Corolla 3–4.5cm long, vermilion to scarlet, glabrous or nearly so. For a border or partial shade in a wild garden, in good, rich soil. Hardy to −25°C, or less. The cultivars, most of which are probably of hybrid origin, include the following. They are more tolerant of dry conditions than the wild species, but are still likely to suffer from mildew when too dry at the root.
'Beauty of Cobham'   Pink flowers and purplish foliage.
'Cambridge Scarlet'   Raised by Prichard before 1913. Stems 90cm.
'Croftway Pink'   Stems around 90cm.
'Prärienacht' syn. 'Prairie Night' Raised by Kayser & Siebert in 1955. 'Blaustrumpf' syn. 'Blue Stocking' is another purple.
'Schneewittchen' syn. 'Snow Maiden'   Raised by K. Foerster in 1956. Stems *c*.60cm.

Monarda fistulosa L. Wild Bergamot   Native of NE North America from Quebec to Minnesota, south to Georgia, Alabama, Louisiana and E Texas, growing in dry scrub and wood edges, flowering in July–August. Var. *menthaefolia* (Graham) Fern. is found further west to British Columbia and along the Rockies to N Mexico. Plant forming clumps of stems 50–150cm tall. Leaves greyish, triangular-ovate to lanceolate, sessile. Bracts often pink-tinged. Flowers lilac, pink or whitish, pubescent, with the tip of the upper lip bearded. For any good soil in sun of part shade. Hardy to −25°C or less.

Monardella purpurea Howell (*Labiatae*)   Native of California in Del Norte Co., north to SW Oregon, growing on dry, stony slopes at 300–1200m, flowering in July–September. Plant small, glabrous, with stems to 15cm from a woody base. Leaves 1.5–3cm long. Flower-heads 1.5–2cm across. Bracts purplish; flowers *c*.2cm long. For a dry, warm position in full sun. Hardy to −10°C perhaps.

Physostegia virginiana L. (*Labiatae*) False Dragonhead   Native of E North America, from Quebec to Minnesota, south to North Carolina, Tennessee and Missouri, growing on river banks, in damp scrub and wet meadows, flowering in June–September. A rampant plant, spreading by white, fleshy stolons to form clumps several metres across when happy. Stems upright to 1m. Leaves to 12.5cm lanceolate, sharply toothed. Flowers 2–3cm long, inflated at the mouth. The pedicels are malleable, remaining fixed when moved, hence the name 'Obedient Plant'. There are several named clones:
'Summer Snow'   Shorter than most, 45–60cm.
'Summer Spire'   Stems to 1m; 'Vivid' (not shown) has stiffer stems, *c*.50cm, and deep-pink flowers. 'Bouquet Rose' has paler flowers. For good, moist soil in full sun. Hardy to −25°C.

Monarda didyma (pink form) in North America

Monarda 'Cambridge Scarlet'

Monarda fistulosa at Harry Hay's, Surrey

Monardella purpurea from Del Norte Co. at Harry Hay's, Surrey

Penstemon jamesii

Penstemon baccharifolius

Penstemon isophyllus (p. 107)

Penstemon clutei

Penstemon superbus

Penstemon strictus

Penstemon glaber

Specimens from Green Farm Plants, 4 August. ⅕ life size

Penstemon barbatus

Penstemon barbatus 'Coccineus'

Penstemon alluviorum Pennell (*Scrophulariaceae*) Native of S Indiana and S Illinois to Missouri and south to Mississippi and Arkansas, growing in marshes, river valleys and damp hillsides, flowering in May–June. Stems to 1.5m. leaves pubescent, the lowest acuminate, serrate. Inflorescence sparsely glandular. Flowers 1.7–2.3cm long, upper lobes curved upwards. *P. digitalis* Nutt. is similar but has a very glandular inflorescence and flowers to 3cm long. For moist, rich soil in full sun. Hardy to −15°C or less.

Penstemon baccharifolius Hook. Native of Texas, in the Trans-Pecos area, and in Mexico to San Luis Potosi, growing in crevices of limestone rocks, flowering in June–July? Plant subshrubby at the base, with flowering stems to *c.*60cm. leaves 2.5–5cm long, thick and leathery. Inflorescence glandular. Flowers 2.5–3.2cm long, the staminode glabrous. For well-drained, dry soil in full sun. Hardy to −10°C or lower if dry.

Penstemon barbatus (Cav.) Roth. Native of Colorado to Nevada and south to Mexico, at up to 3000m, growing on low hills and dry canyons, in pinyon pine, oak or aspen forest, flowering in June–October. Plant with several stiff, upright stems to 90cm. Leaves often glaucous, sometimes hairy. Flowers bright red, rarely pink. Corolla strongly 2-lipped, the lower lip reflexed usually hairy; upper lip projecting. Anthers hairy of glabrous. For well-drained soil in warm position in full sun. Hardy to −20°C if dry. 'Coccineus' is the clone commonly grown. It has fewer glaucous leaves and more branching stems than the type.

Penstemon centranthifolius Benth. Scarlet Bugler Native of California, in the Coast Ranges from Lake Co. southwards, and in Lower California, growing in dry places in chaparral, often with *Romneya*, below 2000m, flowering in April–July. Stems woody to 120cm tall. Leaves entire, glaucous, lanceolate, the upper amplexicaul. Flowers 25–35mm, to 6mm wide, the lobes scarcely spreading. Staminode glabrous. For dry soil in full sun. Hardy to −10°C.

Penstemon clutei A. Nelson Native of Arizona, around Sunset Crater, growing in volcanic ash at *c.*1900m, flowering in June–July. Stems to 1.8m. leaves finely toothed, perfoliate above, glaucous. Flowers inflated from a narrow base, 9–12mm wide. Staminode not exserted. For dry, well-drained soil in full sun. Hardy to −15°C perhaps, if dry.

Penstemon glaber Pursh Native of South Dakota, to Nebraska, Wyoming and ?Arizona, growing in dry, open places, grasslands, and prairies in stiff, stony soil and on limestone, often with *Artemisia*, flowering in June–July. Plant forming small clumps of several stems 30–60cm tall. Leaves oblong to lanceolate, 5–10cm long. Flowers *c.*3cm long, deep blue. Staminode glabrous or spreading, finely hairy. For any good, well-drained soil in full sun. Hardy to −20°C, or less if dry.

Penstemon jamesii Benth. Native of SW Colorado, S Utah, W New Mexico and N Arizona, growing in sandy places, in pinyon pine Juniper and *Pondorosa* pine forests at 1300–2000m, flowering in May–June. Stems to 60cm. Leaves scattered, linear, sometimes with few teeth. Corolla to 22mm long, swollen at the throat, and hairy inside. For dry, well-drained soil in warm position. Hardy to −20°C perhaps.

Penstemon ovatus Dougl. ex Hook. Native of S British Columbia, Washington and N Oregon, growing on limestone rocks and in open woods below 1000m, flowering in May–June. Stems 30–100cm, from a rosette of stalked, leathery leaves. Flowers glandular outside, 15–22mm; staminode bearded. For good, well-drained soil. Hardy to −15°C, perhaps.

Penstemon palmeri Gray Native of California in the mountains west of Death Valley at up to 1800m, and in S Utah and Arizona, growing in dry, rocky places, by roadsides and in seasonal stream-beds, flowering in March–September. Stems several to 120cm, from a tufted rootstock. Leaves spiny-toothed, the lower lanceolate-ovate, amplexicaul, the upper perfoliate. Flowers scented, 22–35mm long, to 12mm wide; staminode exserted, shaggy-bearded. For dry, well-drained soil. Hardy to −15°C if dry.

Penstemon rostriflorus syn. *P. bridgesii* Gray Native of E California, to Arizona, SW Colorado and W New Mexico, growing on dry, open, stony hillsides at 1500–3300m and among pinyon and *Pondorosa* pines, flowering in May–September. Plant with several stems to 1m from a slightly woody base. Leaves linear oblanceolate at the base, linear above, not glaucous. Calyx and pedicel glandular. Flowers 22–35mm long, the lower lip reflexed. Staminode glabrous. For well-drained soil in warm position in full sun. Hardy to −15°C.

Penstemon strictus Benth. Native of S Wyoming and Utah, and south to NE Arizona and N New Mexico, growing in canyons and mountains at up to 3000m, among sagebush, flowering in June–July. Stems to 60cm. Leaves oblanceolate, deep green. Inflorescence not glandular. Pedicels appressed to the stem. Flowers deep blue, with a short tube and a swollen throat, 2-lipped at the mouth.

Penstemon superbus A. Nelson Native of SE Arizona and New Mexico (Chihuahua), growing in rocky canyons, along seasonal streams, in sandy or gravelly places, at 1000–1700m, flowering in April–May. Stems to 2m, often many from a stout rootstock. Stem leaves oblong-ovate, blackening on drying. Flowers 20–25mm long, with 7 equal rounded, spreading lobes and stalked glands. Staminode bearded. For well-drained soil in full sun. Hardy to −15°C perhaps, if kept dry in winter.

Penstemon venustus Dougl. ex Lindl. Native of Idaho, Washington and Oregon, growing in open rocky slopes and dry river channels, flowering in May–August. Stems to 80cm high, shrubby at the base, from a stout taproot. Leaves sessile, lanceolate, serrate, 4–10cm long, 1–3cm wide. Flowers lavender to purple or violet, 2.5–3.8cm long, c.1cm wide at the mouth; staminode with a long white beard near the tip. For well-drained soil in full sun. Hardy to −15°C.

Penstemon whippleanus A. Gray Native of Montana, Wyoming, E Idaho to Utah, New Mexico and Arizona, growing in dry, grassy places, scrub or open woods, into the alpine zone, flowering in July–August. Stems 20–60cm from a branching rootstock. Leaves entire, sessile, oblong or lanceolate. Inflorescence and outside of flowers glandular. Flowers blue or violet to deep purplish black, sometimes cream. Staminode bearded at the tip. For good well-drained soil in full sun. Hardy to −20°C or less.

Penstemon whippleanus at Edington, Wiltshire

Penstemon ovatus

Penstemon venustus

Penstemon centranthifolius

Penstemon rostriflorus

Penstemon palmeri

Penstemon alluviorum

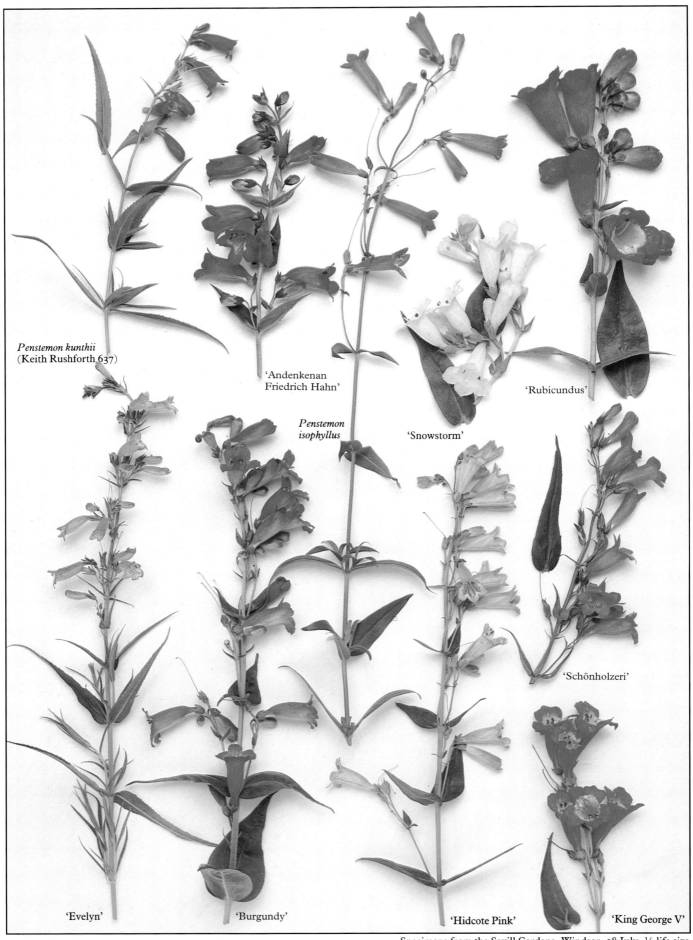

Penstemon kunthii
(Keith Rushforth 637)

'Andenkenan
Friedrich Hahn'

*Penstemon
isophyllus*

'Snowstorm'

'Rubicundus'

'Schönholzeri'

'Evelyn'

'Burgundy'

'Hidcote Pink'

'King George V'

Specimens from the Savill Gardens, Windsor, 28 July. ⅓ life size

Penstemon 'Stapleford Gem' with *Lychnis coronaria* 'Alba'

Penstemon 'Burgundy'

Penstemon 'Flame'

Penstemon 'Catherine de la Mare'

Penstemon 'Thorn'

Penstemon 'Alice Hindley'

Penstemon **'Catherine de la Mare'** A low plant to 30cm, with narrow, toothed leaves and small, blue-purple flowers. Close to *P. heterophyllus*, a native of California. 'Blue Bedder' is rather similar, too.

Penstemon **'Evelyn'** A bushy, pink form or hybrid of the blue-purple *P. campanulatus* Willd., native throughout the mountains of Mexico, in meadows and rocky places. Differs from *P. kunthii* in flower colour and in its corolla being abruptly expanded towards the mouth. Hybrids between the two species are frequent in the wild. 'Evelyn' is very free-flowering from June onwards in S England.

Penstemon × *gloxiniodes* hort. (*Scrophulariaceae*) This is the name given to the large-flowered hybrids between *P. hartwegii* and *P. cobaea*. Many were raised by the 1840s, soon after *P. hartwegii* was introduced from Mexico. They flower from July–September or the first hard frost. They vary in hardiness, but all are killed by temperatures of *c.*−15°C, and often die in warmer winters, probably because they rot at the root. Cuttings should be taken in August and wintered under glass.
'Alice Hindley' syn. 'Gentianoides' A tall plant to 120cm, with pale bluish-lilac flowers about 4.4cm long. The leaves are undamaged by −10°C. Flowering usually from mid-July. Raised by Forbes of Hawick in 1931.
'Andenken an Friedrich Hahn' syn. 'Garnet' A rich purplish-red.
'Burgundy' syn. 'Burford Purple' Close to 'Garnet' but more purple.
'Flame' A good red, with a dark throat.
'King George V' Height to 80cm. Flowers

from July–October. Raised by Forbes in 1911.
'Rubicundus' Raised at Lyme Park, Cheshire, in 1906. Height and width 60cm. The large flowers are produced in July–September.
'Schönholzeri' syn. 'Ruby', 'Firebird' A vigorous plant, up to 1m. Flowers 4cm long, from early July. Hardy in warm areas only.
'Snowstorm' Stems to 65cm. Leaves darkish green. Flowers pure white, with a slightly cream tube, *c.*4cm long and dark anthers. Flowers from late July.
'Thorn' Flowers *c.*4cm long. 'Peace' is similar. 'Beech Park' is larger.

Penstemon **'Hidcote Pink'** A hybrid (possibly between *P. campanulatus* and *P. hartwegii*) raised at Hidcote. Stems to 75cm. Flowers produced from July–September.

Penstemon isophyllus Robson Native of Mexico. Stems to 2m, subshrubby at the base. Leaves rather thick and fleshy. Flowers pale in the throat, with dark lines, *c.*5cm long. Hardy to −15°C perhaps, in a dry position.

Penstemon kunthii G. Don Native of S & W Mexico, growing in disturbed ground and by roadsides in the mountains at 1500–2000m, flowering in summer. Stems *c.*60cm. Flowers red, the corolla narrowly tubular to gradually ampliate. Hardy to −10°C.

Penstemon **'Stapleford Gem'** A rather small-flowered plant, with lilac and cream flowers, close to *P. hirsutus* (L) Willd., a native of NE North America, from Quebec and Ontario, to Wisconsin, Virginia, Kentucky and N Tennessee. Sometimes incorrectly labelled 'Sour Grapes'. For well-drained soil in full sun.

Linaria repens in Harry Hay's garden, Surrey

Linaria purpurea 'Canon Went'

Linaria triornithophora

Verbascum bugulifolium

Alonsoa warscewiczii Regel (*Scrophulariaceae*) Native of Peru, flowering in late summer. Plant with several branched upright stems to 60cm. Leaves ovate, short-stalked. Flowers intense scarlet, *c*.2.5cm across. There is also a pale-orange-pink form, 'Peachy-Keen', found in gardens. Hardy to −5°C perhaps, but often self-seeding if killed by cold.

Linaria dalmatica (L.) Mill. syn. *L. genistifolia* (L.) Mill. subsp. *dalmatica* (L.) Maire & Petit (*Scrophulariaceae*) Native of S Italy, Romania, Yugoslavia to Greece, C Turkey and S Russia, growing in sandy and stony places and roadsides, flowering in June–August. Naturalized in Kashmir and North America. Plant forming patches of decumbent or upright stems to 100cm. Leaves up to 4cm wide, ovate to lanceolate (narrower in *L. genistifolia*). Flowers 2–5cm long. For well-drained soil and sun in a warm position. Hardy to −20°C. *Linaria grandiflora* Desf., which is found scattered throughout Turkey, has rather shorter stems, ovate, thick, glaucous leaves and deflexed bracts; the pedicels are short and stout.

Linaria purpurea (L.) Mill. **'Canon Went'** Native of C & S Italy and Sicily, but naturalized in England and Ireland, growing on grassy roadsides, flowering in June–August. Stems to 90cm, erect from a tufted rootstock. Leaves linear, alternate above, verticillate below, glaucous. Flowers in a slender raceme, 9–12mm, usually purple, but in 'Canon Went' (shown here) pink, and white in 'Springside White'. For any good soil in sun. Hardy to −20°C or less.

Linaria repens (L.) Mill. Native of S Europe, from N Spain to NW Italy and NW Germany, but widely naturalized elsewhere in Europe, including England, and in NE North America, growing in grassy places, on roadsides and waste ground, flowering in June–August. Plant with creeping underground rhizomes, forming spreading patches. Stems to 120cm, erect, much branched. Leaves linear. Flowers 8–15mm, white to pale lilac. Hardy to −20°C. *L.×dominii* Druce, the hybrid between *L. repens* and *L. purpurea*, has a longer flowering season and lilac or pinkish flowers.

Linaria triornithophora (L.) Willd. Native of Spain and Portugal, except the south, growing in hedges and scrub, flowering in June–August. Plant with several upright stems to 130cm, often branched. Leaves lanceolate to ovate-lanceolate, to 7.5cm long, in whorls of 3–4. Flowers in whorls of 3–4, 35–55mm long, purplish or pinkish, marked with yellow. For well-drained soil in sun in a warm position. Hardy to −15°C.

Verbascum blattaria L. (*Scrophulariaceae*) Native of S Europe and North Africa, east to Afghanistan and Siberia, and naturalized in England and North America, growing in waste places, by roads, in dry scrub and on sand dunes, flowering in May–July. A biennial or short-lived perennial, with a rosette of lower leaves, pinnate with rounded lobes. Stems to 150cm, glabrous below, glandular above. Flowers 20–30mm across, with a slender pedicels longer than the bracts. Filaments with purple hairs; stamens 5. For well-drained, rather dry soil in full sun. Hardy to −20°C. A very elegant and dainty plant.

Verbascum bugulifolium Lam. syn. *Celsia bugulifolia* (Lam.) Jaub. & Spach Native of S Bulgaria and extreme NW Turkey, growing in open woods, scrub and waste places at up to 450m, flowering in April–June. Plant very glandular with usually simple stems to 75cm. Basal leaves with a long petiole and ovate lamina. Inflorescence rather few flowered. Flowers yellowish or bluish green, 2–3.5cm across. An unusual species, for a sunny or partly shady, well-drained, warm position. Hardy to −15°C.

Verbascum hybrids Most of the larger *Verbascum* species are biennials, but a large group of hybrids has been raised by crossing the perennial purple *V. phoeniceum* with a yellow species. They are not long lived, and should be propagated regularly by root cuttings. They flower in June–August. Shown here are:
'Cotswold Beauty' Stems to 130cm.
'Cotswold Queen' Stems to 120cm.
'Helen Johnson' Stems to 120cm.
All are best in well-drained, warm soil, and grow well on chalk. Hardy to −20°C. 'Mont Blanc' (not shown) has white flowers.

Linaria dalmatica

Verbascum 'Helen Johnson' at Kew

Verbascum blattaria from Turkey

Verbascum 'Cotswold Queen'

Alonsoa warscewiczii at Edington, Wiltshire

Verbascum 'Cotswold Beauty'

Glumicalyx goseloides at Sellindge, Kent

Zaluzianskya microsiphon near Cathedral Peak, Natal

Diascia anastrepta Hilliard & Burtt (*Scrophulariaceae*)   Native of the Drakensberg in Natal, Transkei and Lesotho, growing in moist, grassy places below cliffs of basalt or among boulders by streams at 1800–3000m, flowering in December–March. Plant with long, slender stems up to 40cm. Leaves are ovate, subcordate or cuneate at the base, 10–25cm long, on stalks up to 8mm long. Flowers with corolla, *c.*25mm across, the lowest lobe *c.*12mm × 12mm with dark glands in a loose patch across its base, with two stamens pointing upwards and two downwards. Spurs 6–7mm long, curving outwards. Easily grown in moist soil. Hardy to −10°C perhaps.

Diascia megathura Hilliard & Burtt Native of the S Drakensberg in Natal and Lesotho, growing in short, moist, grassland or on stony slopes at 1800–2400m, flowering in December–February. Plant with spreading, ascending and very glandular stems to 45cm, rooting at the base. Leaves 15–30mm × 11–20mm, ovate, obtuse, cuneate at base, sometimes shallowly toothed. Flowers slightly nodding, in loose racemes, on stalks 15–20mm. Corolla 20mm across, the lowest lobe 9mm × 11mm, the other lobes much smaller, with 2 patches of dark glands on either side of the style and stamens; yellow patch elongated. Spurs 6–8mm, spreading, with dark glands inside. 2 stamens ± sterile, pointing upwards; 2 fertile stamens pointing downwards with green pollen. Easily grown in well-drained but moist, sandy soil. Hardy to −10°C perhaps.

Diascia patens (Thunb.) Fourcade   Native of South Africa, in Cape Province, on the Rooiberg and the hills near Willowmore,

growing on rocky slopes and by streams and waterfalls, at *c.*800m, flowering in March–August. Plant bushy, and sometimes scrambling through shrubs. Leaves linear to lanceolate. Flowers 17mm across, deep red to orange; spurs 4–5mm long, straight, diverging. Hardy to −10°C perhaps. An attractive, almost shrubby species with a long flowering period, in autumn and early spring.

Diascia purpurea N. E. Br.   Native of the Drakensberg around Mont-aux-Sources and south to the upper Loteni valley, growing on bare patches in moist grassland at 2350–2440m, flowering in January–April. Plant with rather few creeping shoots and upright flowering stems to 45cm. Leaves deep purple beneath, ovate, obtuse, cuneate at base, margins smooth or slightly crenate, on stalks to 2mm long. Flowers nodding in a loose spike-like raceme on ascending stalks 13–25mm long. Corolla 18–20mm long, with the lower lobe very short (*c.*2.5cm), the two upper lobes forming an elongated upper lip *c.*13mm × 16mm, so that the flower appears upside down. Spurs curved, short, 3–4mm long, white; 2 ± sterile stamens erect; 2 projecting forwards, fertile, with green pollen. This species is more difficult to grow, requiring moist, well-drained soil, and high humidity in summer. Hardy to −15°C perhaps.

Glumicalyx goseloides (Diels) Hilliard & Burtt (*Scrophulariaceae*)   Native of the Drakensberg in Natal and Lesotho, growing in damp, rocky grassland and by streams at 1800–2800m, flowering in December–January. Plant aromatic with creeping leafy stems and ascending flowering shoots to 40cm. Leaves 3–4cm long, obtuse, tongue-shaped, sessile. Flowers in dense

nodding heads with overlapping, leafy bracts. Corolla 25mm, buff outside, bright orange inside. Easily grown in well-drained soil; hardy to −10°C, flowering in late spring and until late summer if dead-headed and watered. Source: CD&R 228, from Sani Pass area, Natal.

Nemesia caerulea Hiern (*Scrophulariaceae*) Native of the Drakensberg, in Natal, Transkei and Lesotho, growing on grassy slopes, by roadsides and among rocks at 1800–2900m, flowering in December–February. Plant with glandular-hairy creeping and ascending stems to 30cm. Leaves ovate-lanceolate, toothed on short, 1–3mm stalks. Flowers bluish with a white, red-edged patch in the throat and a single downward-pointing spur with 2 yellow furry bosses almost blocking its throat. Corolla 15mm.

Nemesia fruticans (Thunb.) Benth. syn. *N. foetens* Vent. is very similar, but does not have furry bosses in the throat. Both are easily grown in ordinary, well-drained soil. Hardy to −10°C perhaps. Photographed on the Sani Pass, C Natal. *Nemesia strumosa* Benth. is commonly grown as an annual. Other perennials such as the pink-flowered *N. denticulata* (Benth.) Fourcade are now popular.

Sutera breviflora (Schltr.) Hiern (*Scrophulariaceae*)   Native of the Drakensberg in Natal and Lesotho and on high ground in C Natal, growing on grassy slopes and ridges at 1800–2800m, flowering in January–March. Plant with sprawling stems to 30cm from a thin rootstock. Flowers *c.*1.5cm across, bright red. Forms hybrids in the wild with *S. pristisepala*. For well-drained but not dry soil in full sun. Hardy to −15°C perhaps.

Sutera pristisepala

Sutera breviflora

Diascia anastrepta

Diascia patens at Kew

Diascia purpurea near Mont-aux-Sources

Diascia megathura

Nemesia fruticans at Green Farm Plants

Nemesia caerulea on the Sani Pass in the Natal Drakensberg, South Africa

Sutera pristisepala Hiern   Native of the Drakensberg in Natal, NE Cape Province, Lesotho and Transvaal, at 1980–2900m, growing on cliffs, rocky slopes and screes, flowering in December–February. Plant spreading and almost shrubby at the base to 80cm high and across, glistening glandular-hairy and strongly aromatic. Leaves silvery, pinnate with toothed lobes, c.3cm long. Flowers with a yellow, red-edged spot in the throat, 12mm across, with a bent tube 1cm long. An attractive silvery plant for a well-drained, warm, sunny position. Easily grown from cuttings in late summer. Hardy to −10°C perhaps.

Zaluzianskya microsiphon (O. Kuntze) K. Schum. (*Scrophulariaceae*)   Native of the Drakensberg in Natal, Transkei, Lesotho and the NE Cape Province, growing in stony grassland at 1800–2750m, flowering in January–March. Plant with few upright stems to 30cm. Inflorescence elongated, with overlapping, appressed bracts; corolla tube 15–50mm reddish outside, whitish on the inside of the limb which opens in sunlight.

DIASCIA

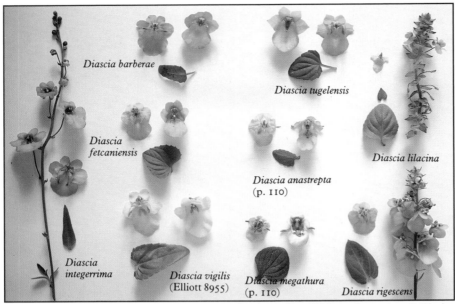

Specimens from Wisley, 5 September. ½ life size

Diascia (*Scrophulariaceae*)   These have recently become popular garden plants as they are easily propagated and flower throughout the summer if dead-headed and kept moist. There are altogether around 50 species, mostly annuals, in the summer-dry Cape region of South Africa, but about 18 from the summer-rainfall area of the Drakensberg are perennials. Most of these will tolerate up to $c.-10°C$, especially if protected from wet in winter, but are easily overwintered as rooted cuttings kept in a frame or cold greenhouse. All species are easy to propagate from basal shoots taken off in the autumn or spring and kept moist until rooted. The species are rather similar in general appearance, but differ in details of the flower structure. Hilliard & Burtt (1984).

Diascia barberae Hook. fil.   Native of the mountains of Lesotho, and of one or two valleys in C Drakensberg, growing in wet, stony or silty places among rocks in the beds of streams, or in marshy ground at 1980–2000m, flowering in January–February. Plant with low spreading stems to 45cm. Leaves 10–25mm × 5–20mm, ovate or ovate-lanceolate, subcordate, rounded or almost truncate at base. Flowers in very loose racemes. Corolla 23–27mm × 20–24mm, lowest lobe 11–13mm × 13–16mm, with a white patch at the base and 2 patches of dark glands on either side. Spurs 7–8mm long, pointing outwards and downwards, tips slightly incurved with dark glands inside. 'Ruby Field' is a commonly grown and richly coloured clone of *D. barberae*, though it is often listed as *D. barberae × cordata*. *D. barberae* itself has been long cultivated since Mrs Barber sent seeds to Kew in 1870.

Diascia fetcaniensis Hilliard & Burtt syn. *D. felthamii* hort.   Native of the S Drakensberg, in the NE Cape, in Lesotho and in Transkei, at 1675–3000m, growing in damp, grassy places below cliffs and by streams, often in shade, flowering in January–March. Plant with many creeping glandular stems to 40cm. Leaves ovate, cordate, rounded or obtuse at apex, 15–24mm long. Corolla 20–24mm × 15–21mm, mid-pink; lowest lobe with a patch of dark glands across the base. Spurs curved downwards and inwards. One of the easiest and hardiest species.

Diascia integerrima Benth. syn. *D. moltenensis* Hiern   Native of Lesotho and South Africa, in Natal, Orange Free State, Transkei and NE Cape Province, growing on cliffs, in rock crevices, in loose, gritty soil and by streams, at 1800–3000m, flowering in November–March. Plant forming clumps of thin, wiry stems and far spreading underground by long stolons. Stems up to 1m, but usually $c.30$cm unsupported. Leaves linear to oblong lanceolate, sometimes with a few shallow teeth. Flowers in loose spike-like racemes, 17–24mm × 15–24mm, the lowest lobe 7–11mm × 9–15mm, with a zone of dark glands towards the base and on a shallow keel. Spurs 4–6mm, directed downwards, the tips incurved. More tolerant of dry conditions and hardier than other species, to $-15°C$ perhaps.

Diascia lilacina Hilliard & Burtt   Native of NE Cape Province, at Saalboom Nek pass near Barkly East, growing on cliffs at $c.2000$m, flowering in January. Plant softly glandular-hairy, with stems to 30cm. Leaves ovate, $c.15$mm in diameter. Flowers $c.12$mm across, without spurs, but with the 'window' forming a cone $c.3$mm long. For moist, well-drained soil.

Diascia 'Ruby Field' at Edinburgh

Diascia integerrima on Sani Pass

Diascia barberae from Sani Pass

Diascia integerrima at Carlyle's Hoek, NE Cape

Diascia tugelensis

Diascia rigescens Benth.   Native of South Africa, in S Natal, the Transkei and the E Cape west to the Great Winterberg, growing in moist places, especially along the edges of forest and in grassland at 100–1525m, flowering in November–April. Plant forming dense mats. Stems up to 1.3m, usually *c*.30cm in gardens. Leaves sessile, usually crowded, opposite or alternate above, 15–60mm × 10–35mm, broadly ovate. Flowers crowded into spike-like racemes. Corolla 11–18mm across, the lowest lobes 5–8mm × 7.5–11mm with stalked yellow glands on a keel. Spurs *c*.3mm long, directed downwards and inwards. Hardy to −10°C.

Diascia tugelensis Hilliard & Burtt   Native of the NE corner of the Drakensberg mountains, around Mont-aux-Sources, growing in rocky stream beds, in rock crevices and on wet basalt cliffs, at 1800–3000m, flowering in January–March (June–August in northern gardens). Plant forming spreading mats with long, thin stems ascending to 45cm, with stolons. Leaves mostly at the base, 8–25mm × 6–15mm, ovate-cordate, apex subacute, serrate. Flowers in very loose racemes 20–23mm × 18–20mm, the lowest lobe 9–11mm × 10–11mm with a pale patch beneath the projecting stamens. The yellow and maroon patch on the upper lobe is Y-shaped and sunken. Spurs 5–7mm directed downwards and outwards, with swollen ends, with dark-greyish glands wide. Hardy to −10°C perhaps.

Diascia vigilis Hilliard & Burtt   Native of the NE Drakensberg around Mont-aux-Sources, south to Cathedral Peak, on the Platberg near Harrismith and in W Lesotho, growing in low scrub and among rocks in moist places, at 1800–3000m, flowering in December–March. Plant with many creeping and ascending stems to 50cm. Leaves ovate or ovate-lanceolate, subacute, rounded at the base. Flowers usually pale pink in loose racemes. Calyx lobes not reflexed. Corolla 22–28mm × 17–23mm, with a patch of black glands in the centre of the lowest lobe. Spurs 7–9mm long, curved downwards and slightly inwards. Elliott 8955 is a good, large form.

Diascia rigescens at Aldington, Kent

Diascia fetcaniensis

Diascia vigilis

Phygelius capensis in a typical streamside habitat at Naude's Nek, NE Cape Province

Phygelius aequalis Harvey ex Hiern (*Scrophulariaceae*)   Native of Drakensberg, the mountains of C Natal, e.g. Nngeli mountain, northwards to the NE Transvaal (Zoutpansberg), growing in grassland on the margins of streams and on wet rocks, at 1200–2200m, flowering in October–April. Plant with stems to 1.5cm, shrubby only at base. Leaves triangular, cuneate at the base, the blade around 10cm long, 6cm across. Inflorescence cylindrical. Corolla *c.*4cm long, pale brownish red, or dusky pink, the tube curved slightly downwards, or straight, the lobes spreading but not deflexed; visited by sunbirds. For any good moist soil in full sun, requiring ample water in summer. Hardy to −10°C, perhaps less.
'Yellow Trumpet' syns. 'Cream Delight', 'Alba'   This distinct, pale-yellow form was discovered on Mawahqua mountain, between Underberg and Bulwer in Natal, and introduced by B. L. Burtt and Harold Hillier. Yellow forms have been seen in other areas also.
'Sensation' syn. 'Sani Pass', collected in the Sani pass area in Natal, has purple flowers.

Phygelius capensis E. Meyer ex Benth. Native of Drakensberg in Lesotho and NE Cape Province, to Orange Free State, more rarely in Natal, from Mont-aux-Sources southwards to the Boschberg, and Koudeveldberg, growing on rocks by mountain streams, and on moist slopes at above 2000m, flowering in October–April. Plant with subshrubby stems to 2m and underground stolons. Leaves rounded at the base. Inflorescence pyramidal. Corolla 3.75cm long, orange or red, yellow on the lobes inside, the mouth facing downwards, the tube curved forwards and the lobes reflexed; visited by sunbirds. A yellow form is recorded from the Mokhotlong valley in Lesotho at 2100m, but is probably not in cultivation. For any good soil in full sun. Hardy to −15°C or less with protection for the roots.

Phygelius × *rectus* Coombes   A group of hybrids between *P. aequalis* and *P. capensis*, originally raised by Peter Dummer, the chief propagator at Hillier Nurseries in around 1985. They combine the hardiness of *P. capensis* with the more compact inflorescence of *P. aequalis*. Five cultivars were named, as follows:
'African Queen' (not shown)   Raised by John Ray in 1969 from *P. aequalis* × *P. capensis* 'Coccineus'.

'Devil's Tears' ('Winchester Fanfare' × *P. capensis* 'Coccineus')   Stems *c.*1.2m. Panicle *c.*45cm.

'Moonraker' ('Yellow Trumpet' × 'Winchester Fanfare')   Stems to 95cm. Panicle *c.*25cm. Flowers all round the stem.

'Pink Elf' (not shown) ('Yellow Trumpet' × 'Winchester Fanfare')   Has shorter stems to 75cm; panicle *c.*15cm. Flowers with the tube pale pink and lobes deep crimson.

'Salmon Leap' (not shown)   Has corolla tube orange, with deeper lobes. Stems *c.*1.2m. Panicle 45cm, open.

'Winchester Fanfare' syn. 'Winton Fanfare' ('Yellow Trumpet' × *P. capensis* 'Coccineus') Stems *c.*1m. Panicle *c.*30cm.

Phygelius aequalis 'Yellow Trumpet'

Phygelius aequalis at Cathedral Peak

Phygelius 'Moonraker' at Wisley

Phygelius 'Winchester Fanfare'

Phygelius capensis

Phygelius 'Devil's Tears'

337

Mimulus 'Wisley Red'

Mimulus 'Magnifique'

Mimulus cardinalis

Mimulus 'Western Hills'

Mimulus lewisii in Oregon

Mimulus 'Fire Dragon'

Mimulus lewisii from Kelways' Nurseries

Mimulus moschatus at Kew

Mimulus naiandinus at Kew

Mimulus luteus by a chalk spring in Sussex

Mimulus guttatus

Mimulus cardinalis Dougl. ex Benth. Native of Oregon to California, east to Nevada and Arizona and south to Mexico, growing along streams and in wet places, often in shade, at up to 2500m, flowering in March–October, but usually June–August in gardens, and again if cut down after the first flowering. Stems to 80cm glandular-hairy, from a creeping stock. Flowers 4–5cm long, the upper lip arched upwards, the lower reflexed. Pollinated by hummingbirds. For moist but not waterlogged soil in sun or partial shade. Hardy to −15°C.

Mimulus guttatus DC. Native of Alaska south to Mexico and east to Montana, and widely naturalized in Europe and E North America, growing in streams and wet places below 3000m, flowering in March–August. Plant with creeping and rooting stems and ascending inflorescence to 100cm, usually c.50cm. Leaves 1–8cm long, toothed. Inflorescence pubescent and glandular. Flowers yellow, spotted red, the throat nearly closed by hairy ridges. For wet soil or shallow running water in sun or partial shade. Hardy to −20°C or less.

Mimulus × hybridus These are mainly selected from crosses between *M. luteus*, *M. guttatus* and *M. cupreus* Regel from S Chile. **'Fire Dragon'** Stems to 30 cm. Flowers large.

'Magnifique' Stems to 30cm. Flowers large, c.60cm across.
'Wisley Red' Possibly a form or hybrid of *M. cupreus*, raised at Wisley. Stems c.15cm tall, flowering in June–August. 'Whitecroft Scarlet is an older, very similar cultivar. 'Malibu' (not shown) is a vigorous seed strain, with stems to 15cm and deep-orange flowers.

Mimulus lewisii Pursh Native of W North America, from Alaska south to California (Tulare Co.) in the Sierra Nevada, and east to Colorado, growing by streams at 1200–3000m, flowering in June–September. Plant with erect, glandular-hairy stems to 80cm from a creeping rootstock. Leaves oblong-elliptic, 2–7cm long, with wavy teeth. Flowers pink, often blotched maroon, 3–5cm long. Graham Thomas mentions a beautiful white form which I have never seen. For moist or wet soil in sun or partial shade. Hardy to −15°C.

Mimulus luteus L. Native of Chile, and naturalized in Scotland, growing in streams and wet places, flowering in December–March. Very similar to *M. guttatus* from NW North America, and commonly hybridizing where the two species are naturalized, but with calyx and pedicels glabrous, and flowers with an open throat and large red blotches and patches of colour. Flowers usually yellow, but sometimes

creamy or pinkish in the wild as well as in selected cultivars. Hardy to −20°C.

Mimulus moschatus Dougl. ex Lindl. Musk Native of North America, from Alaska to C California eastwards to Newfoundland, south to North Carolina and West Virginia, but probably introduced in much of E North America, growing in damp places and by streams, flowering in June–September. Plant softly glandular and sticky. Flowers 18–25mm long. This plant was valued in the past for its musky smell, but plants in cultivation are scentless. There is no mention of the scent in Munz's *Flora of California*, and Fernald's edition of *Gray's Manual of Botany* says: 'Plant only rarely with musky odour.' The scented plant should be sought in the wild.

Mimulus naiandinus J. M. Wats. & C. von Bohlen, usually called **'Andean Nymph'** Native of C Chile, growing on moist rocks and cliffs at 800–1100m, flowering most of the summer. Plant forming spreading mats of hairy stems to 50cm or more across. Flowers pink, with a yellow throat marked with numerous small spots. For moist soil in sun or partial shade. Hardy to −5°C.

Mimulus 'Western Hills' A presumed hybrid between *M. cardinalis* and *M. lewisii*, with stems to 1m and vermilion flowers more open than those of *M. cardinalis* and with less-reflexed corolla lobes.

Digitalis grandiflora

Digitalis grandiflora, naturalized in Kashmir

Digitalis lamarkii from NE Turkey

Digitalis laevigata

Digitalis ferruginea

Digitalis purpurea subsp. *heywoodii*

Digitalis obscura

Digitalis × purpurascens at Kew

Digitalis purpurea in Wales

Digitalis ferruginea L. (*Scrophulariaceae*) Native of Europe, from Italy eastwards to Romania, Turkey, the S Caucasus and Lebanon, growing in woods, grassy clearings and scrub, and on rocky slopes and roadsides at up to 2700m in turkey, flowering in June–September. Plant short-lived or sometimes biennial; flowering stems to 1m, unbranched. Stems leaves oblong to linear; sepals glabrous with a scarious border. Flowers 18–34mm long, the lower lip *c.*8mm broad. For well-drained, dry soil in sun or partial shade. Hardy to −15°C.

Digitalis grandiflora Mill. Native of C Europe, from Belgium eastwards to Siberia and the Altai, south to Turkey-in-Europe and naturalized in Kashmir, growing in open woods and grassy places by streams, flowering in June–July. Stems often several, to 100cm. Leaves to 25cm × 6cm, ovate-lanceolate. Sepals lanceolate, acute, glandular-pubescent. Flowers 4–5cm long. For any good soil in partial shade. Hardy to −20°C or less. In around 1925 the hybrid *D. purpurea × D. grandiflora* was treated with colchicine and formed the new hybrid tetraploid species *D. × mertonensis* Buxton & Darlington. It is a short-lived perennial with rather hairier leaves than *D. grandiflora* and large pinkish-buff flowers, raised at the John Innes Horticultural Institution, then at Merton, Surrey.

Digitalis laevigata Waldst. & Kit. Native of SE Europe in Yugoslavia, Albania, Bulgaria and Greece, growing in woods and scrub, flowering in June–August. Stems several from a tufted rootstock to 100cm, glabrous. Leaves oblong-lanceolate to lanceolate. Sepals ovate, acute or acuminate. Flowers 15–35mm long, over 25mm in the north of its range, less than 25mm in the south (subsp. *gracea* (Ivan.) Werner), from Thessaloniki southwards. For well-drained soil in partial shade or sun; and a warm position. Hardy to −15°C.

Digitalis lamarkii Ivan. syn. *D. orientalis* Lam. Native of Turkey mainly in dry valleys in the north and north-east, growing on dry, rocky slopes, in open forest and scrub or in steppe, at up to 1500m, flowering in May–August. Plant forming tufts of rosettes of linear leaves to 20cm long, 8mm wide from a rather woody rootstock. Stem leaves to 1cm wide. Sepals mucronate, glandular-pubescent. Flowers 25–30mm long, hairy outside. For a dry position in poor, well-drained soil. Very susceptible to warm damp in winter. Hardy to −20°C if dry.

Digitalis obscura L. Native of E & S Spain and of North Africa, growing in dry open woods, often on limestone, flowering in May–July. Plant with branched shrubby stems to 1m. Inflorescence to 50cm, with narrowly oblong to lanceolate, entire or toothed evergreen leaves. Flowers orange-yellow to brownish red, 2–3cm long. For a warm position in dry soil in sun or partial shade. Hardy to −10°C perhaps.

Digitalis × purpurascens Roth. This hybrid between *D. lutea* L. and *D. purpurea* is reported occasionally where the parents grow together, i.e. from Belgium to Germany and in Spain. Stems to *c.*100cm, much branched. Flowers *c.*3.5cm long in June–August. Hardy to −20°C.

'Glory of Roundsay' is similar, with slightly larger flowers, and is possibly *D. lutea × D. × mertonensis*.

Digitalis purpurea L. Foxglove Native of W Europe, from Ireland south to Spain and Morocco, east to Finland, Czechoslovakia and in Corsica and Sardinia, widely naturalized elsewhere in Europe, in North America and on mountains in North Africa, growing in woods and on rocky slopes, usually on acid soils, flowering in June–September. Plant usually biennial, but often perennial in SW Europe and Corsica. Stems to 180cm. Flowers 40–55mm long, purplish, pink or white. For any soil except pure limestone in partial shade. Hardy to −25°C.

Digitalis purpurea subsp. **heywoodii** P. & M. Silva Native of S Portugal, around Reguengos de Monsaraz, growing on granite rocks, flowering in June. Plant with rosettes of very woolly, white leaves, the lowest ovate-lanceolate to lanceolate, tapered into the petiole. Flowering stems to 75cm. Flowers creamy white, sometimes yellowish or pinkish, sparsely hairy outside. A beautiful plant for well-drained soil in sun or partial shade, not too dry at the root. Susceptible to warm damp in winter. Hardy to −15°C. Subsp. *mariana* (Boiss.) Rivas Goday (not shown) has white woolly leaves but purplish-pink flowers, glabrous outside. It is native of SC Spain and NE Portugal, growing on rocky slopes and plains, flowering in June–August. *Digitalis thapsi* L. from E Portugal and C & W Spain is rather similar: covered with yellowish glandular hairs and the inflorescence is branched. The purplish-pink flowers are pubescent outside.

Acanthus hungaricus

Acanthus spinosus at Nymans, Sussex

Acanthus mollis var. *latifolius* at Kew

Acanthus dioscoridis Willd. (*Acanthaceae*)
Native of Turkey, from Kastamonu southwards
and eastwards, of Lebanon, N Iraq and W Iran,
growing on dry hillsides, steppes, rocky slopes
and abandoned fields at up to 2200m, flowering
in May–August. Plant with creeping
underground rhizomes and rosettes of leaves,
narrowly lanceolate and unlobed in var.
dioscoridis, to pinnatifid with spiny lobes in var.
perringii (Siehe) E. Hossain. Flowering stem to
40cm, but only 10–15cm in var. *brevicaulis*
(Freyn) E. Hossain from Kastamonu. Bracts
green; corolla pink or purplish. For dry, well-
drained soil in full sun. Hardy to −15°C.

Acanthus hirsutus Boiss.   Native of Turkey,
from the Mediterranean islands eastwards to
Sivas, at up to 1800m, growing on bare steppes,
on banks between cornfields and in pine forest,
often on non-limy soils, flowering in May–July.
Plant with deep, fleshy roots, without long
underground stolons. Leaves in a basal rosette,
spiny, deeply lobed, lanceolate in outline.
Flowering stems 10–35cm, densely hairy.
Bracts hairy, delicately spiny, 7–13 veined.
Corolla pale yellow or whitish, rarely pink. For
well-drained, sandy soil in full sun in a dry,
warm position. Hardy to −15°C, perhaps less.

Acanthus hungaricus (Borbas) Baenitz syns. *A.
balcanicus* Heywood & Richardson, *A.
longifolius* Host   Native of Yugoslavia,
Romania, southwards to Greece, growing in
woods, scrub and on rocky hills, flowering in
June–July. Plant forming dense clumps. Leaves
not spiny, lanceolate in outline with deep lobes
narrowed at the base and with only broadly
winged midrib between the central lobes.
Flowering stems to 150cm, usually *c*.60cm, with
flowers often in 4 rows. Bracts purplish, corolla
white. For well-drained soil in full sun. Hardy
to −15°C.

Acanthus mollis L.   Native of S & SW
Europe, from Portugal to Italy, Sicily and
Yugoslavia, and in NW Africa, growing in
rocky woods and beneath old walls, flowering in
June–August. Leaves dark green, shining
above, lobed or pinnatisect, but not spiny; the
broadest form, var. *latifolius* (hort. ex Goeze),
which appears to be native of Spain and
Portugal, has shallowly lobed leaves to 20cm
wide, ovate in outline. Flowering stems up to
2m, usually suffused with purple. Corolla
white, sometimes with pinkish veins. For a
deep, well-drained soil in a warm position in full
sun. This plant always looks best associated
with old stone or brickwork. Hardy to −15°C.

Acanthus hirsutus at Wisley

Acanthus syriacus near Gaziantep, S Turkey, photographed by Brian Mathew

Acanthus dioscoridis from Hakkari

Strobilanthes atropurpurea

Acanthus spinosissimus at Kew

Acanthus spinosissimus Desf. This is now considered merely a form of *A. spinosus* L., but it is distinct enough to be worth illustrating separately. Native of the E Mediterranean in SW Turkey, Rhodes and possibly Crete, growing in dry scrub, on roadsides and in pine forest at up to 600m, flowering in May–June. Plant with a tufted rootstock, forming clumps. Leaves ovate in outline to 40cm long, and 30cm broad, deeply dissected to the midrib, with stiff white spines on all edges. Flowering stems to 1.2m with a very long, dense inflorescence. Bracts greenish, tipped with purple. For a hot dry position in well-drained soil. Hardy to −15°C. Not free-flowering even in S England, except in hot summers.

Acanthus spinosus L. Native of the E

Mediterranean area, from Italy and Yugoslavia southwards, growing in scrub and grassy places, flowering in May–July. Plant forming dense clumps. Leaves lanceolate in outline, dissected to the midrib, with scattered, rather soft spines, flowering stem to 1.5m, not very dense; bracts purple; corolla white. For well-drained soil in full sun. Hardy to −15°C and free-flowering.

Acanthus syriacus Boiss. syn. *A. hirsutus* subsp. *syriacus* (Boiss.) Brummitt Native of SE Turkey from Adana to Urfa, W Syria, Lebanon and Palestine, growing in abandoned fields, scrub and on rocky limestone slopes at 500–1900m, flowering in April–June. Plant with creeping underground rhizomes. Leaves to 32cm long, lanceolate in outline, very spiny, deeply dissected and hairy. Flowering stems to 60cm,

with a short and rather compact inflorescence. Bracts deep purple, 7–11 veined. Corolla white. For dry, well-drained soil in full sun. Hardy to −15°C perhaps. *A. caroli-alexandri* Hausskn., from N Greece, is very similar but usually taller.

Strobilanthes atropurpurea Nees syn. *Pteracanthus urticifolius* (Kuntz.) Bremek (*Acanthaceae*) Native of the Himalayas, from Kashmir to C Nepal, growing in forests and scrub at 1200–2700m, flowering in July–October. Plant forming a large clump of upright stems to 2m. Leaves ovate, toothed and strongly veined, acuminate. Inflorescence glandular; bracts soon withering. Flowers *c.*3.5cm long, blue to purplish. For any good soil in partial shade. Hardy to −20°C.

Centranthus ruber at Cockermouth Castle, Cumbria

Valeriana phu 'Aurea' in spring

Valeriana pyrenaica

Phuopsis stylosa

Triosteum pinnatifidum at Kew

Asperula taurina L. subsp. **caucasica** (Pobed.) Ehrend. syn. *A. caucasica* Pobed. (*Rubiaceae*)   Native of the Caucasus, N Turkey and N Iran, with subsp. *taurina* in SE Europe and N Turkey, growing in woods, scrub and on rough banks at 550–2100m, flowering in April–August. Plant suckering to form loose patches. Leaves hairy on both surfaces, 3–8cm long. Flowers 8–14mm long, pale lilac to bluish, or usually white or very pale in subsp. *taurina*. For leafy soil in partial shade. Hardy to −20°C.

Centranthus ruber (L.) DC. (*Valerianaceae*) Red Spur Valerian   Native of the Mediterranean region, but widely naturalized further north, growing in rocky places, old walls and on coastal shingle, flowering in May–August. Plant with a tough, woody rootstock and stems to 80cm. Flowers 9–10mm, with a spur 5–7mm long, red, pinkish or white. For a very well-drained position. Hardy to −15°C.

Galium odoratum (L.) Scop. syn. *Asperula odorata* L. (*Rubiaceae*) Sweet Woodruff   Native of Europe, but rare in the south, and of North Africa and W Asia to S Turkey, east to E Siberia, Korea and N Japan, growing in rich deciduous woods and hedges, flowering in May–July. Plant with wiry, creeping, underground rhizomes and upright stems to 45cm, usually *c.*20cm. Leaves 2.5–4cm, in whorls of 6. Flowers 4–6mm long. For a shady position in good not very acid soil. Hardy to −25°C or less.

Patrinia triloba Miq. var. **palmata** (Maxim) Hara (*Valerianaceae*)   Native of Japan, in W Honshu and Kyushu, growing in grassy places in the mountains, flowering in July–August. Plant with shortly creeping stolons. Stems 20–

Asperula taurina subsp. *caucasica* at Sellindge, Kent

Valeriana phu in flower

Galium odoratum

Thladiantha dubia at Kew

Patrinia triloba var. *palmata*

Thladiantha olivieri near Baoxing, Sichuan

60cm. Leaves orbicular, 5-angled, palmate, 4–8cm long. Flowers 7–8mm across, spurred at the base. For moist soil in a cool position. Hardy to −15°C, perhaps less.

Phuopsis stylosa (Trin.) B. D. Jackson (*Rubiaceae*) Native of the Caucasus and N Iran, in the Elburz near Chalus, flowering in June–September. Plant with a characteristic pungent scent, forming spreading patches. Stems to 30cm from an underground branching and creeping rootstock. Flowers pale pinkish, deeper purplish-pink in 'Purpurea', with a tube *c.*1cm long. For moist, sandy soil in sun or partial shade. Hardy to −20°C or less.

Thladiantha dubia Bunge. (*Curcubitaceae*) Native of Korea and N China and naturalized in C Japan, growing in scrub and rocks flowering in June–July. Plant with a large tuberous rootstock and climbing stems to 3m, with simple tendrils. Leaves ovate-cordate. Flowers 6–7mm across; the males solitary in the leaf axils. For any soil in a sheltered position with protection for the young shoots. Hardy to −20°C or less.

Thladiantha olivieri Cogn. ex Oliv. Native of SW China, in Hubei and Sichuan, growing in hedges and on rock ledges by streams, flowering in May–June. Plant with a stout rootstock and climbing or hanging stems to 4m or more. Leaves to 25cm long on a stalk to 10cm long. Tendrils branched. Flowers *c.*5cm across. For a warm, sheltered position moist in summer. Hardy to −15°C perhaps.

Triosteum pinnatifidum Maxim. (*Caprifoliaceae*) Native of N China and Japan

(where it is very rare), growing in scrub, flowering in July–August. Stems few, 45–60cm, from a stout rootstock. Leaves slightly hairy, glandular. Flowers *c.*10mm long; fruit a white berry, *c.*8mm across. For well-drained but humus-rich soil in sun or partial shade. Hardy to −20°C perhaps less. The genus is interesting as one of the few herbaceous genera in the Honeysuckle family. *T. perfoliatum* L., the Feverwort, with orange fruit in the leaf axils, is native of E North America, and *T. himalayanum* Wall., with red fruit, is found in dry scrub and forest W China and N India.

Valeriana phu L. 'Aurea' (*Valerianaceae*) Native of Europe (perhaps) and Turkey (one record) (but native distribution uncertain because it was widely grown for the drug 'Valerian'), growing on rocky slopes flowering in July–August. Plant with a thick, woody rhizome. Basal leaves golden when young in the commonly grown 'Aurea', simple or compound. Stem leaves amplexicaul, the upper pinnatifid. Stems to 1.5m. Flowers white, with a tube 4mm long. For good soil in sun or partial shade. Hardy to −20°C or less.

Valeriana pyrenaica L. Native of the Pyrenees in France and Spain, and in the Cantabrian mountains, growing in damp woods and subalpine meadows; flowering in May–July. Sometimes also found naturalized in Scotland and Ireland. Plant with a short, stout rhizome and upright stems to 110cm. Basal leaves ovate-cordate, toothed. Flowers 5–6mm long. For moist, peaty soil or a rich border in partial shade. *V. alliarifolia* Adams, from Euboea, the Caucasus and N Turkey, is similar but has all leaves simple, the upper ovate or lanceolate.

Catananche
caerulea

Knautia
macedonica

Scabiosa caucasica
'Clive Greaves'

Stokesia laevis
(p. 153)

Cephalaria gigantea

Scabiosa ochroleuca

Scabiosa caucasica
'Bressingham White'

Specimens from Beth Chatto, 17 August. ½ life size

Catananche caerulea L. (*Compositae*)   Native of SW Europe, from Spain to France and Italy, and North Africa, growing in dry, grassy places, flowering in June–August. Plant with many wiry upright stems to 45cm from a compact rootstock. Leaves linear, entire or with up to 4 narrow teeth. Flowers 3cm across, with transparent, papery, overlapping bracts, usually bluish, sometimes white, with a dark centre. For sandy soil in full sun. Hardy to −15°C.

Cephalaria alpina (L.) Roem. & Schult. (*Dipsacaceae*)   Native of the SW & C Alps, Jura and N Apennines, from France to Austria and Italy, growing in rocky meadows at up to 1800m, flowering in June–July. Stems to 2m, usually *c.*1.2m. leaves pinnate or lyrate with 3–8 pairs of leaflets. Flower-heads *c.*2cm across. Flowers *c.*12mm long. Receptacular scales spiny. For any well-drained, moist soil in sun or partial shade. Hardy to −20°C or less.

Cephalaria gigantea (Ledeb.) Bobrov. syn. *Scabiosa tartarica* M. Bieb.   Native of the Caucasus and N Turkey, growing by streams, in wet meadows and on rocky slopes at 1350–2600m, flowering in July–August. A huge perennial with stems to 3.5m. Lower leaves to 40cm long, lyrate or pinnatisect. Flower-heads 4–6m across. Flowers 15–18mm long. Receptacular scales acuminate, not spiny. For any rich, moist soil in sun or partial shade. Hardy to −20°C or less.

Knautia arvensis (L.) Coult. (*Dipsacaceae*)   Field Scabious   Native of Europe eastwards to the Caucasus and W Siberia, growing in meadows, and on grassy hills, especially on limestone, flowering in July–September. Plant with a deep taproot and branched stems to 100cm. Leaves oblanceolate or pinnatifid at the base; stem leaves pinnatifid. Flower-heads 3–4cm across, bluish. For any well-drained soil and good for meadow garden. Hardy to −25°C or less.

Knautia macedonica Griseb. syn. *Scabiosa rumelica* hort.   Native of Yugoslavia to Albania, Bulgaria and SE Romania, growing in scrub and open woods, flowering in July–August. Sometimes biennial, but usually perennial. Basal leaves undivided, but withered by flowering time. Upper leaves pinnate with an ovate, serrate terminal lobe. Flower-heads 1.5–3cm across, dark red, but sometimes lilac; the unusual dark-red colour is also found in the annual or biennial *Scabiosa atropurpurea* L. For well-drained soil in a warm position. Hardy to −20°C or less.

Scabiosa caucasica M. Bieb. (*Dipsacaceae*)   Native of the Caucasus, N Iran and NE Turkey, growing in subalpine meadows and sunny, rocky slopes at 1900–2900m in Turkey, flowering in July–August. Plant with simple stems to 60cm, sometimes with a few branches. Lower leaves lanceolate, entire, upper pinnatisect. Flower-heads 4–6cm across, bluish-lavender, the outer flowers with finely toothed petals. Two cultivars are shown here. 'Bressingham White', raised by Alan Bloom; 'Loddon White' and 'Miss Willmott' are also white. 'Clive Greaves', raised in 1929, is lavender-blue. 'Moonbeam Blue' is darker. For well-drained, chalky or limy soil in full sun. Hardy to −20°C or less, but short-lived on acid or wet soils. Easily raised from seed.

Scabiosa ochroleuca L. syn. *S. columbaria* L. var. *ochroleuca* (L.) Coulter   Native of C and S Europe, W Russia, North Africa, Lebanon to

Turkey, the Caucasus and Siberia, growing in dry meadows and rocky slopes, flowering in May–September. Basal leaves obovate-lanceolate, crenate. Stem leaves lyrate or 1-pinnatisect. Flower heads 15–26mm across. For well-drained soil in full sun. Hardy to −20°C or less.

Succisa pratensis Moench. (*Dipsacaceae*)   Devil's Bit Scabious   Native of most of Europe, and of North Africa, eastwards to W Siberia, the Caucasus and N Turkey, growing in wet, heathy, grassy places among heather and in open forest, flowering in June–October. Plant with few stems from a short rootstock. Leaves 5–30cm in a basal rosette, obovate-lanceolate. Flowering stems to 100cm. Flower-heads 1.5–3cm across, purplish blue, rarely pink or white (even rarer). For moist, preferably peaty soil in sun or partial shade. Hardy to −20°C.

Catananche caerulea

Catananche caerulea

Cephalaria alpina

Succisa pratensis

Knautia arvensis

Knautia macedonica

Morina coulteriana near Gadsar, Kashmir

Acanthocalyx delavayi (Franch.) Cannon syns. *Morina bulleyana* Forrest & Diels, *M. delavayi* Franch. (*Morinaceae*) Native of SW China, especially Yunnan, growing on rock ledges and grassy, stony places on limestone at *c*.3000m, flowering in May–June. Plant with rosettes of barely spiny, linear leaves to 10cm long. Stems to 15cm. Flowers in a loose head, with a curved tube *c*.2cm long. For well-drained soil in sun or partial shade. Hardy to −20°C. *A. nepalensis* (D. Don) Cannon syn. *Morina nepalensis* D. Don is very similar, but appears to be taller, with narrow leaves, with a margin of 2 rows of stiff hairs.

Morina coulteriana Royle (*Morinaceae*) Native of Pakistan to NW India and Xizang, and locally abundant in Kashmir, growing on steep grassy slopes in rather dry valleys, at 2400–3600m, flowering in June–August. Plant with several stems to 90cm, from a deep, fleshy rootstock. Leaves to 15cm, with slender spines on the edges. Flowers with a tube 2cm long, and lobes 8mm long, sweetly scented. A long-lived perennial, for well-drained but rich, deep, sandy soil in full sun. It resents disturbance, so is best established from seedling plants. Hardy to −20°C or less.

Morina kokanica Regel   Native of C Asia, in the region of Kokand and Ferghana, growing in conifer forests, flowering in May–June. Stems several, upright, to 1.2m, from a fleshy rootstock. Leaves narrowly lanceolate, smooth and spineless. Inflorescence with spines only on the bracts. Flowers *c*.3cm long, opening white, becoming pale pink with a red blotch. For good, well-drained soil in full sun. Hardy to −15°C, perhaps less. *M. subinermis* Boiss., recorded once from W Turkey, is similar in being spineless, except on the inflorescence.

Morina longifolia Wall. ex DC.   Native of the Himalayas, from Kashmir, where it is common, to Bhutan, growing on moist but steep slopes, on open hillsides or in clearings in woodland, at 3000–4000m, flowering in June–September. Plant with few stems to 1m, from a deep, fleshy root. Leaves spicily aromatic, to 20cm long, with short, rather weak spines on the toothed edges. Flowers with a tube 2.5cm long, and lobes 6mm long, opening white, becoming pink at maturity. A beautiful plant for a moist but well-drained border, not difficult to grow but often short-lived. Hardy to −15°C, but liable to rot in cold, damp conditions.

Morina persica L.   Native of Greece, Turkey and the Lebanon, eastwards to C Asia, growing in dry steppes, on rocky slopes and roadsides, and on screes at 300–2750m in Turkey, flowering in May–August. Plant with several stiff, upright stems to 1.5m. Leaves very spiny, lanceolate. Flowers scented, white, becoming pink or reddish. For a very dry position in well-drained, poor soil. Hardy to −20°C, but likely to die of damp in winter. This species is not often grown; I have collected seed several times, but never succeeded in germinating it.

Stellera chamaejasme L. (*Thymelaeaceae*) Native of the Himalayas from N India to Nepal, Bhutan and N & W China in Yunnan and Xizang, growing on stony slopes and plains, and on abandoned fields, at 2700–4300m, flowering

Morina coulteriana at Edington, Wiltshire

Morina kokanica in Tashkent BG

Acanthocalyx delavayi at Lijiang

Morina persica near Kayseri, Turkey

Morina longifolia

Stellera chamaejasme at Branklyn

Stellera chamaejasme near Lijiang, Yunnan

Morina longifolia near Vishensar, Kashmir

in May–July. A herbaceous relative of *Daphne*.
Plant with several simple leafy stems from a
very stout, long-lived rootstock. Flowers
1–1.5cm long in a terminal head, either white,
pink in bud (in the Himalayas) or yellow (in
Yunnan). For very well-drained soil in full sun.
This plant is very rare in gardens because it is so
hard to propagate except from seed. Very old
plants are found in gardens in E Scotland, e.g.
in Branklyn in Perth, and in the Royal Botanic
Garden, Edinburgh. Hardy to −20°C.

Campanula latiloba at Hidcote Manor, Gloucestershire

Campanula carpatica Jacq. (*Campanulaceae*) Native of the Carpathians, in Poland, Czechoslovakia, Romania and W Russia, growing on mountain rocks, flowering in June–August. Plant with a tuft of thin, white rhizomes and many stems to 45cm. Basal leaves rounded, cordate, the upper rather narrower. Flowers solitary on 10–15cm stalks, *c*.3cm wide in 'Chewton Joy', a good blue with a pale centre, white in 'Hannah', or deep blue in 'Isabel', among numerous named forms. For a well-drained position in full sun but moist soil. Hardy to −25°C or less.

Campanula lactiflora M. Bieb. Native of the Caucasus, NE Turkey and NW Iran (and naturalized in Scotland), growing in forests, scrub and subalpine meadows at 600–2400m, flowering in July–October. Stems several, to 1.5m or more in gardens, from a stout rootstock. Leaves numerous up the stem, ovate-oblong or oblong. Flowers 1.5–2.5cm long, bluish purple, pale blue or white, pinkish in cv. 'Loddon Anna'. For moist, rich soil in sun or partial shade. Hardy to −20°C or less. 'Pouffe' and 'White Pouffe' are dwarf forms which lack the good points of the normal form. 'Prichard's Variety' has dark purple flowers and is rather shorter (*c*.75cm) than the normal type.

Campanula latiloba DC. syn. *C. persicifolia* L. subsp. *sessiliflora* (K. Koch) Velen. ex W. Greuter & Burdet Native of N Turkey, from Ulu Dağ, near Bursa, east to Samsun, growing in meadows at 200–1200m, flowering in June–August. Stems thicker than *C. persicifolia*, 10–15mm thick, to 100cm tall, stiff. Stem leaves broadly lanceolate, acute, attenuate. Flowers sessile, 2–3 in each axil, shallower and wider open than *C. persicifolia*, bluish or in 'Hidcote Amethyst' pinkish mauve. Other cultivars include 'Alba' and 'Percy Piper', a dwarf variety. For any good soil in sun or partial shade. Hardy to −20°C or less.

Campanula persicifolia L. Native of most of Europe from Belgium and Holland eastwards, to C & S Russia, and NW Turkey, growing in meadows, open woods and on the edges of forest at up to 2000m in Turkey, flowering in June–August. Plant forming rosettes of narrow leaves from shortly running rhizomes. Stems 40–70cm, glabrous with scattered narrow leaves. Flowers horizontal or slightly drooping, 4–5cm long, 5cm across the mouth. Numerous varieties of this species are cultivated, including whites, pinks, semi-doubles, doubles and a 'cup-and-saucer' white, 'Hetty'; 'Hampstead White' is similar, if not the same. For any good garden soil; easy and very long-lived. Hardy to −25°C or less.

Campanula rhomboidalis L. Native of Europe in the Jura, SW & C Alps, from France to Switzerland and Italy and naturalized in Belgium, Holland, Germany and Austria, growing in alpine and subalpine meadows, flowering in July–September. Plant with a

Campanula persicifolia f. *alba*

Campanula rhomboidalis in the Valais

Campanula lactiflora above Trabzon

Campanula lactiflora at Withersdane Hall, Wye, Kent

Campanula carpatica

Campanula trachelium near Wye, Kent

Campanula trachelium 'Alba'

stout, deep taproot and upright stems to 60cm. Stem leaves ovate to broadly lanceolate, acute, toothed. Buds erect. Flowers *c.*2cm long, few, in a loose raceme. For any good, well-drained soil in full sun. Hardy to −20°C or less.

Campanula sarmatica Ker-Gawl. Native of the Caucasus, growing on dry cliffs and on rocky slopes at up to 1800m, flowering in June–July. Plant with a deep, branching taproot and roughly hairy, narrowly ovate, cordate basal leaves. Flowering stems several, spreading, to 30cm. Flowers pale blue, *c.*20mm long. A long-lived plant for a very well-drained, rather dry position. Hardy to −20°C or less.

Campanula trachelium L. Nettle-leaved bell-flower Native of most of Europe, including England, North Africa, Turkey and West Syria, N Iran and W Siberia, growing on wood margins, in hedges and in forests, often on chalky soils, flowering in July–September. Stem to 100cm or more. Leaves ovate, cordate, sharply toothed. Flowers 2.5–3.5cm long, usually mid-blue to mauve, short-stalked, or sessile in subsp. *athoa* from Greece and Turkey. For any good soil in sun or partial shade and tolerant of dry shade. The white form, 'Alba', is very beautiful; there is also a double white in cultivation. Hardy to −20°C or less.

Campanula latiloba 'Hidcote Amethyst'

Campanula sarmatica from the N Caucasus

Campanula ossetica at Washfield Nurseries

Campanula glomerata 'Superba' at La Vesterival, near Dieppe

Campanula alliarifolia at the Royal Botanic Garden, Edinburgh

Campanula crispa near Erzurum

Campanula alliarifolia Willd.
(*Campanulaceae*) Native of the Caucasus and
N Turkey, from Ordu eastwards, growing on
wet cliffs and steep banks in Spruce forest, and
in scrub, at up to 1830m, flowering in
June–September. Plant with several simple or
branched stems to 70cm from a tufted
rootstock. Leaves roughly hairy, broadly
triangular-cordate, obtuse or acute. Flowers
nodding on a one-sided stem, *c.*20mm long,
always white. For a moist position in sun or
partial shade, but does well amongst shrubs in a
border. Hardy to −20°C perhaps.

Campanula 'Burghaltii' Probably a hybrid
between *C. punctata* and *C. latifolia*, with *C.
punctata* on the seed parent. Rhizome not
creeping. Stems to 60cm spreading. Flowers
greyish mauve, 7–10cm, long. Calyx lobes
declined and spreading.

Campanula crispa Lam. Native of NE
Turkey and adjacent Armenia and Azerbaijan,
growing on dry rocks and low cliffs, at
1500–2500m, flowering in June–August. Stems
upright to 50cm from a fleshy rootstock,
sometimes monocarpic. Leaves glabrous, shiny.
Flowers white or blue, deeply 5-lobed, to 3cm
across. An unusual species, rather like a
Michauxia in appearance. For a dry, well-
drained position. Hardy to −25°C, or less if dry.

Campanula glomerata L. Native of most of
Europe, from England, where it is frequent on
chalk downs, south to Spain and east to Siberia
and SW Asia, growing in scrub and mountain
meadows, flowering in May–September. Plant
suckering to form spreading clumps. Stems
30–60mm. Flowers in clusters in the axils of
leafy bracts, and in a terminal head, 15–20mm
long, dark purplish blue. For any good, well-
drained soil in sun or partial shade. 'Superba',
raised by G. Arends, is a large form, similar to
that shown here. There are also several named
white forms. Hardy to −25°C.

Campanula latifolia L. Native of most of
Europe, including England, where it is
commonest in the north-west, the Caucasus, N
Turkey, N & C Iran and W Siberia, growing in
hedges, scrub, forests and meadows often on
limestone, at up to 2600m in Turkey, flowering
in June–August. Plant with a compact, tufted
rootstock with upright stems to 100cm. Lower
leaves ovate, cordate, doubly serrate. Flowers
40–55cm, with lobes, pale to deep blue; rarely, a
beautiful pure white in 'Alba'. Var. *macrantha*
DC. is a coarser plant with long, *c.*55mm,
mauve-blue crowded flowers, which is
sometimes cultivated: it lacks the charm of the
ordinary variety. For any heavy soil in shade or
partial shade. Hardy to −25°C or less.

Campanula ossetica M. Bieb. Native of the
Caucasus, growing on rocks and in ravines,
flowering in June–July. Plant with trailing or
almost climbing stems to 60cm. Basal leaves
cordate, double-toothed. Flowers *c.*3cm long.
Calyx teeth narrowly lanceolate. Introduced to
cultivation by Bill Baker. Hardy to −20°C.

Campanula punctata Lam. f. *rubriflora*
Native of Japan, in all the islands, growing on
grassy slopes at low altitudes and in foothills,
flowering in June. Plant with creeping
underground rhizomes, sometimes with stolons.
Lowest leaves ovate-cordate. Flowering stems
40–80cm, usually simple. Flowers *c.*5cm long,
reddish, sometimes very pale, spotted and long-
hairy inside. For moist, leafy soil in sun or part
shade; it may require protection from slugs.
Hardy to −15°C, perhaps less.

Campanula takesimana Nakai Native of
Korea and of Ullung-Do, an island off the east
coast of Korea, growing in grassy places,
flowering in July–September. Plant with
creeping rhizomes and rosettes of leaves, with a
blade *c.*8cm long. Stems to 36cm, leafy. Flowers
*c.*5cm long, pale blue to pink, spotted inside.
For moist, leafy soil in part shade. Hardy to
−20°C perhaps. The fleshy rhizomes are liable
to attack by cockchafer grubs or slugs, but
otherwise the plant appears easy to grow.

Campanula 'Van Houttei' Probably a hybrid
between *C. latifolia* and *C. punctata*, of
uncertain origin before 1878. Stems up 45cm.
Flowers mauve or greyish blue, 10cm long, but
also variously described as deep indigo or
lavender. Calyx lobes spreading and reflexed,
closer to *C. latifolia*, which is said to be the seed
parent. Both this hybrid and 'Burghaltii' will
grow in an ordinary, rather moist border, or
among shrubs. Hardy to −20°C perhaps.

Campanula 'Van Houttei'

Campanula takesimana

Campanula punctata f. *rubriflora*

Campanula latifolia seedlings with the leaves of *Diphylleia*

Campanula 'Burghaltii'

Campanula latifolia var. *macrantha*

Codonopsis lanceolata near Kyoto, Japan

Codonopsis lanceolata

Codonopsis tangshen at Windsor

Codonopsis ovata in Kashmir, with the leaves of *Bergenia stracheyi* behind

Adenophora triphylla in Hokkaido

Wahlenbergia undulata on Ngeli Mountain, Natal

Platycodon grandiflorus

Ostrowskia magnifica in Tashkent

Adenophora triphylla (Thunb.) A. DC. var. **japonica** (Regel) Hara (*Campanulaceae*) Native of Japan, in all the islands, growing in grassy places in lowlands and mountains, and on the edges of woods, flowering in July–October. Plant with deep, thick roots and stems to 90cm, usually *c.*50cm. Leaves in whorls of 4, oblong or ovate-elliptic. Flowers 13–22mm long, arranged in whorls on the inflorescence. For moist, peaty soil in sun or partial shade. Hardy to −20°C. *Adenophora* differs from *Campanula* in having a tubular or cup-shaped disc around the base of the style. *A. confusa* Nannfeldt has broader leaves and short-stalked flowers scattered up a tall inflorescence.

Codonopsis lanceolata (Sieb. & Zucc.) Trautv. (*Campanulaceae*) Native of Japan, in all the islands, with var. *emaculata* Honda in E Siberia, Korea and N China, growing in scrub, bamboo, on the edges of woods and in clearings on low mountains and hills, flowering in August–October. Plant with large, fleshy tuberous roots. Stems climbing, to 2m or more. Leaves narrowly oblong to ovate, glabrous, glaucous beneath. Flowers 3–3.5cm long, 6–10mm wide; calyx lobes acuminate, 2–2.5 cm long. Seeds white, winged on one side (var. *emaculata* has flowers without spots inside). Pollinated by large wasps. For moist, leafy soil among shrubs. Hardy to −20°C, possibly less.

Codonopsis ovata Benth. Native of the Himalayas, from Pakistan to Kashmir, where it is common, growing on rocky, grassy slopes at 3000–4200m, flowering in July–August, often in June in gardens. Plant with fleshy roots and few to several upright stems to 20cm. Leaves 1–3cm long, tubular campanulate often expanded at the mouth with spreading calyx lobes. For moist but well-drained soil in full sun, but not easy to grow. Hardy to −20°C or less. *C. clematidea* (Schrenk) C. B. Clarke, from C Asia to N India, is found in similar habitats, but is taller, to 60cm, and has rounded bells, narrow at the mouth, and recurved calyx lobes. Easier to grow.

Codonopsis tangshen Oliver Native of W China, growing in scrub, flowering in August–September. Plant with long, fleshy roots and climbing stems to 2m or more. Leaves ovate to ovate-lanceolate. Calyx lobes ovate, 5–6mm long. Flowers to 3.5cm long, veined inside towards the base of the bell. For loose, peaty soil in sun or partial shade. Hardy to −20°C perhaps.

Ostrowskia magnifica Regel (*Campanulaceae*) Native of C Asia, in the Pamir-Alai, growing on rocky hillsides, flowering in May–June. Stems few, to 1.5m, from a tuberous rootstock. Leaves in whorls of 4 or 5, ovate-lanceolate, 10–15cm long. Flowers 12–15cm across, rather few at the top of the stems. For well-drained, sandy, leafy soil in full sun, dry in late summer and with protection from excess wet in winter. Hardy to −20°C or less.

Platycodon grandiflorus (Jacq.) A. DC. (*Campanulaceae*) Native of Japan, in all the islands, of Korea, N China and E Siberia, growing on grassy slopes in hills and mountains, flowering in August–September. Plant with a tufted rootstock and thick roots. Stems 40–100cm, usually *c.*20cm in the commonly cultivated 'Apoyama'. Flowers 4–5cm across, blue, or, in 'Mother-of-Pearl', pale pink. For any good, moist, sandy soil in sun or partial shade. Hardy to −20°C or less.

Wahlenbergia undulata (Thunb.) A. DC. (*Campanulaceae*) Native of South Africa, from E Cape Province northwards to Natal, growing in dry places among rocks at up to 1800m in Natal, flowering in November–March. Plant with branched stolons from a tufted rootstock, forming many-stemmed clumps, often flowering in a year from seed. Stems to 40cm. Leaves wavy-edged, obtuse. Flowers *c.*3cm across, pale blue, mauve or white. Hardy to −15°C, perhaps less if dry in winter.

Lobelia siphilitica near New York

Lobelia × *speciosa* 'Queen Victoria' at the Savill Gardens, Windsor

Lobelia × *gerardii* 'Vedrariensis'

Lobelia cardinalis

Lobelia cardinalis hybrid at Wisley

Lobelia tupa (detail)

LOBELIA

Lobelia tupa in SE Chile, photographed by Martin Gardiner

Lobelia cardinalis L. (*Campanulaceae*) Cardinal Flower Native of North America, from New Brunswick, S Quebec and Minnesota, south to Florida and E Texas, with subsp. *graminea* (Lam.) McVaugh syn. *L. splendens* Willd. from Arizona to California and southwards to Mexico and C America, growing by lakes, in damp meadows and along streams, flowering in June–October. Plant with a tufted rhizome and stems to 1.8m; leaves lanceolate to ovate-lanceolate, or narrow-lanceolate to linear in subsp. *graminea*. Flowers 3–4.5cm long. For good soil in sun or partial shade, by water or in a moist border. Hardy to –25°C and less.

Lobelia × gerardii 'Vedrariensis' A hybrid between *L. cardinalis* and *L. siphilitica*, known in the wild. Several colour forms are in cultivation: 'Vedrariensis' is rich purple; 'Tania' is redder, described as crimson-purple, 'Blauzauber', presumably more blue.

Lobelia laxiflora H., B. & K. var. *angustifolia* DC. Native of S Arizona, Mexico and much of C America, growing in oak woodland at *c.*1500m in Arizona, flowering in May. Var. *angustifolia* is the plant found in Arizona. Plant forming spreading clumps of stems to 60cm. Leaves linear-lanceolate, *c.*7cm long. Flowers *c.*3.5cm long, red and yellow or pure yellow. For well-drained, sandy but moist soil in a warm position. Hardy to –10°C, or less for short periods.

Lobelia siphilitica L. Native of E North America, from Maine and South Dakota, southwards to Missouri and east Kansas and Texas, growing in moist woods and marshes, flowering in August–September. Plant with a tufted rootstock and stems to 1.3m. Leaves ovate, thin. Flowers 2.3–3.5cm long, usually blue, rarely white. For moist soil in sun or partial shade. Hardy to –25°C or less.

Lobelia × speciosa Sweet A hybrid race derived from *L. cardinalis*, *L. fulgens* Willd. from Mexico and *L. siphilitica*. All require rich, moist, peaty soil in sun or partial shade. Best with protection from cold, wet winters, and well mulched.
'**Cherry Ripe**' Leaves green; flowers cherry-red.
'**Queen Victoria**' An old variety, with deep-red leaves and stems. Flowers intense red. Stems to 1m.

Lobelia tupa L. Native of Chile, growing on sandy hills near the sea, flowering in December–April, or July–October in the north. Plant with a large tufted rootstock and numerous stems to 2.5m. Leaves softly hairy to 20cm. Flowers thick and fleshy, *c.*6cm long, doubtless pollinated by hummingbirds. For really well-drained but good soil, kept moist in summer. Hardy to –10°C, and lower if the rootstock is protected against wet and frost in winter. Grows well along the west coasts of Europe and North America.

Lobelia laxiflora var. angustifolia

Lobelia × speciosa 'Cherry Ripe'

Anthemis tinctoria 'E. C. Buxton'

Anthemis tinctoria

Echinacea purpurea

Anthemis tinctoria L. (*Compositae*) Native of most of Europe, Turkey, the Caucasus, W Syria and Iran and naturalized in the British Isles and North America, growing on roadsides, steppes, waste places and in scrub, flowering in May–July. Plant with several branching upright stems to 45cm. Leaves 2–3 pinnatisect, oblanceolate or obovate in outline, 1–5cm long. Flowers 2.5–4.5cm across, yellow or white or cream in var. *pallida* DC., pale yellow in 'E.C. Buxton', paler still in 'Wargrave'. For well-drained soil in full sun; good on chalk. Hardy to −25°C, perhaps less.

Arnica montana L. (*Compositae*) Native of most of Europe from Belgium and Holland eastwards to Russia, and south to S Portugal, C Italy and Yugoslavia, growing in meadows, heaths and subalpine meadows, mainly on acid soils, at up to 2500cm in the Alps, flowering in June–August. Plant with short rhizomes and stems 25–60cm tall. Basal leaves obovate to oblanceolate, glandular-pubescent. Stem leaves in pairs, linear-lanceolate. Flowers 5–6.5cm across, 1–3 per stalk. For well-drained, sandy or peaty soil in full sun. Hardy to −25°C.

Coreopsis verticillata L. (*Compositae*) Native of E North America, from Florida to Alabama and Arkansas, north to Maryland and Virginia, growing in open woods and clearings in rather dry soil, flowering in June–July. Plant bushy with short rhizomes and much-branched stems to 110cm, usually *c.*60cm in gardens. Leaves with hair-like segments, 0.3–1.5mm wide. Flowers 4–6cm across, usually bright yellow, but a beautiful pale lemon yellow in 'Moonbeam'. For well-drained soil in sun or partial shade. Hardy to −25°C or less.

Echinacea purpurea (L.) Moench (*Compositae*) Native of Virginia west to Ohio, Michigan, Illinois and Iowa, and south to Georgia and Louisiana, growing in prairies and dry, open woods, flowering in June–October. Plant with a short, spreading rootstock and stems to 1.2m. Leaves rough, the lowest ovate, the rest ovate-lanceolate. Flowers purplish, rarely white, to 12cm across. Several (*c.*10) named cultivars are available: 'White Lustre', raised in America, is said to have drooping petals. 'Robert Bloom' is a rich mauve-crimson; this is now usually sold as seedlings or

Arnica montana

Echinacea tennesseensis

Leucanthemum × superbum 'Wirral Supreme'

Leucanthemum × superbum 'Everest'

Senecio doronicum in Switzerland

'Bressingham hybrids'. For good, light soil in a border, where it makes a bold feature. Hardy to −20°C, perhaps less.

Echinacea tennesseensis (Beadle) Small   A rare plant found in Tennessee and Arkansas in the Interior and Ozark plateaux, growing on gravelly hillsides. Differs from *E. purpurea* in its vertical, nor spreading, rootstock, linear leaves, and smaller 'petals', to 2.5cm long.

Eriophyllum lanatum (Pursh) Forbes (*Compositae*)   Native of S California, north to British Columbia and the Rockies, growing in dry scrub at up to 3000m, flowering in April–August. A variable plant with stems up to 80cm, usually *c.*50cm. Leaves usually toothed, often woolly. Flowers with 8–13 petals, *c.*2.5cm across. For a dry position in full sun. Hardy to −25°C, if introduced from a cold area.

Leucanthemum × superbum Bergman ex Ingram syn. *Chrysanthemum maximum* hort. (*Compositae*)   The large garden Shasta daisies formerly listed under *L. maximum* (Rem.) DC., a Pyrenean species, are now considered hybrids between *L. maximum* and *L. lacustre* (Brot.) Samp., from the Estremadura in WC Portugal, a very similar but slightly smaller-flowered species. Numerous cultivars have been raised and named, and 48 are listed in Trehane's *Index Hortensis*. Shown here are '**Everest**', large-flowered to 10cm across, on stems around 90cm, and '**Wirral Supreme**', a double with stems again *c.*90cm. 'Snowcap' is a short-stemmed single, *c.*50cm tall. 'Phyllis Smith' has the petals interestingly recurved and twisted, on stems to 90cm. 'Cobham Gold' has pale-yellow flowers, and stems 60cm, but is now very rare. All flower in late summer, in June–September.

Senecio doronicum L. (*Compositae*)   Native of C & S Europe, from Spain and France to Greece and Romania, growing in grassy and rocky places in the mountains at 1500–2700m, usually on limestone, flowering in June–August. Plant variable, but stems usually *c.*30cm. Leaves thick, usually white and cottony beneath. Stem leaves few, alternate, lanceolate. Flowers orange-yellow, 3–6cm across, 1–3 per stem. For well-drained soil in sun or partial shade. Similar in general appearance to *Arnica*, but that has stem leaves in pairs. Hardy to −20°C or less.

Coreopsis verticillata

Eriophyllum lanatum

Coreopsis verticillata 'Moonbeam'

Achillea 'Coronation Gold'

Tanacetum ptarmiciflorum 'Silver Feather' in the White Garden at Sissinghurst Castle

Achillea tomentosa

Achillea filipendulina 'Gold Plate'

Achillea 'Taygetea'

Achillea ageratum 'W. B. Childs'

Achillea ptarmica

ACHILLEA

Achillea 'Cerise Queen'

Achillea 'Galaxy hybrids'

Achillea 'Paprika'

Achillea ageratum L. 'W. B. Childs' syn. *A. decolorans* Schräd. (*Compositae*) Native of Spain, the Balearic islands and Italy, growing on grassy hills, flowering in June–August. Stems to 80cm. Lower leaves pinnatifid; stem leaves with forward-pointing teeth. Hardy to −15°C, perhaps.

Achillea 'Coronation Gold' A hybrid between *A. clypeolata* and *A. filipendulina*, a chance seedling in the garden of Miss R. B. Pole. Stems *c.*90cm. Leaves greyish, flower-heads looser than those of *A. filipendulina*. Hardy to −25°C or less.

Achillea filipendulina Lam. 'Gold Plate' Native of the Caucasus and SE Turkey to Iran, C Asia and Afghanistan, growing in wet meadows, by streams or lakes and on rocky slopes, flowering in June–August. Plant forming dense clumps or upright stems to 120cm. Leaves green, densely hairy, 10–20cm long 3–7mm wide, oblong, deeply divided. Flower-heads 4–10cm or more across; flowers 2.5–3.5mm across, rich golden yellow. For any good soil in full sun and, in cool climates, tolerant of summer drought. Hardy to −25°C. *A. clypeolata* Sm., from Greece and European Turkey to Romania, has woolly, narrower leaves to 4cm wide and smaller heads of flowers.

Achillea 'Galaxy hybrids' A group of hybrids between *A. millefolium* and the yellow-flowered *A.* 'Taygetea' (itself a hybrid between *A. clypeolata* and *A. millefolium*), raised by A. Kikillus in Germany and introduced by Blooms of Bressingham. The main named colour forms are as follows:

'Apfelblüte' ('Apple Blossom') Flowers pink; *c.*90cm.
'Fanal' ('The Beacon') Bright red, *c.*75cm.
'Hoffnung' ('Great Expectations') Sulphur-yellow *c.*60cm.
'Lachsschönheit' ('Salmon Beauty') Pale salmon-pink, fading to cream.
'Paprika' *c.*60cm, appears to be of similar parentage.
All are easily grown in full sun and tolerate poor soil. Hardy to −25°C or less.

Achillea millefolium L. Native of most of Europe and W Asia east to the Himalayas and naturalized in North America, Australia and New Zealand, growing in meadows and dry, grassy places, flowering in June–September. Plant forming spreading mats of rosettes of deeply divided leaves and erect flowering stems to 60cm. Middle stem leaves 2-pinnatisect, lanceolate in outline. Flowers usually white, sometimes pale pink, deep pink or crimson; there are many named forms, including 'Cerise Queen', bright pinkish-red; all have petals (ligules) 1–2.5mm long. Pale-pink flowers and very hairy leaves are common in subsp. *sudetica* (Opiz) Weiss, from the mountains of central Europe. A drought-resistant plant for a sunny border, and common in old lawns where it stays green after the grass has gone brown. Hardy to −25°C and less. *A. asplenifolia* Vent., closely related to *A. millefolium*, is a tall plant, to 100cm, found in wet meadows in SE Europe, from Austria to Romania. It has glabrous, finely cut leaves and pink or purplish-red flowers.

Achillea ptarmica L. Native of N Europe to N Spain, N Italy and SW Romania, eastwards to Siberia and naturalized in North America, growing in wet meadows, marshes and heaths, flowering in July–September. Plant with a creeping rhizome, forming loose patches. Leaves 1.5–8cm long, linear-lanceolate, finely toothed. Stems floppy, 20–60cm. Flowers 12–18mm across, rather dirty white, but pure white and perfectly double in 'Boule de Neige', syns. 'The Pearl' and 'Schneeball', which is commonly cultivated. For a moist, rich border in sun or partial shade. Hardy to −25°C or less.

Achillea 'Taygetea' A hybrid of uncertain origin, probably between *A. millefolium* and *A. clypeolata*. Leaves green, flatter and less divided than *A. millefolium*. Stems *c.*60cm tall. Flowers pale yellow. *A. ochroleuca* Ehrh, from Czechoslovakia to the Ukraine, appears very similar. *A. taygetea* Boiss. & Held., from S Greece, is greyish-hairy, has yellow flowers and is considered in *Flora Europaea* to be synonymous with *A. aegyptiaca* L.

Achillea tomentosa L. Native of SW Europe, from C France and C Italy to Spain, growing on dry hills and waste ground, flowering in May–June. Plant forming mats of woolly or silky leaves with linear lobes, with flowering stems to 40cm. Flowers *c.*3mm across. Petals 2mm. For dry soil in full sun. Hardy to −15°C.

Tanacetum ptarmiciflorum (Webb & Berth.) Schulz-Bip. (*Compositae*) 'Silver Feather' Native of Gran Canaria, where it is very rare, growing on rocks and cliffs in the mountains. Often grown as an annual for bedding.

361

Erigeron specimens from Kelways' Nurseries, 24 June. ¼ life size

Osteospermum jucundum

Erigeron 'Dunkelste Aller'

Erigeron cultivars   These have been raised from the American species *E. speciosus* (Lindl.) DC., crossed with *E. speciosus* var. *macranthus* (Nutt.) Cronquist, *E. glaucus* (q.v.) and *E. aurantiacus* Regel, with orange-yellow flowers. About 50 named cultivars are now extant. Shown here are:
'Adria'   Lavender-blue; stems *c.*75cm, raised by H. Goetz in 1954.
'Amity'   Lilac-pink; stems *c.*60cm, raised by Alan Bloom.
'Dignity'   Violet-blue; stems to 45cm, raised by Alan Bloom.
'Dunkelste Aller' syn. 'Darkest of All'   Deep purplish blue, stems to 60cm, raised by Benary in 1951.
'Felicity'   Bright pink; stems to 60cm, raised by Alan Bloom.
'Foerster's Liebling'   Deep reddish pink; stems to 45cm, raised in Germany in 1951.
'Prosperity'   Lilac; stems to 45cm, raised by Alan Bloom.
'Quakeress'   Pale lilac-pink; stems to 45cm, an old variety.
All flower in late June–July and require good, well-drained soil in full sun. Hardy to –25°C or less.

Erigeron glaucus Ker-Gawl. (*Compositae*) Native of California, from San Luis Obispo north to Oregon and naturalized in Europe, especially by the sea, growing on coastal bluffs and cliffs, sand dunes and on beaches, flowering in April–August. Plant forming wide, spreading mats of obovate to oblanceolate, obtuse leaves. Stems glandular-hairy, 10–40cm tall. Flowers 4–6m across, usually pale purplish, but pinkish in 'Roseus'. 'Elstead Pink' is possibly a hybrid. For sandy, dry soil in full sun. Hardy to –10°C, perhaps less. Common in gardens near the coast.

Osteospermum jucundum (E. P. Phill.) T. Norl. syn. *Dimorphotheca jucunda* E. P. Phill. (*Compositae*)   Native of South Africa, from the Transvaal south to Lesotho and Natal, growing on rocks and in moist grassland at up to 3200m, flowering in December–February, or July–September in the north. Plant forming mats of narrowly oblanceolate leaves. Flowering stems to 30cm. Flowers *c.*6cm across. For well-drained sandy, peaty soil, moist in summer, dry in winter. This should be the hardiest *Osteospermum*, as it comes from such high altitudes in the Drakensberg. Hardy to –10°C or less if dry.

Tanacetum cultivars   The garden Pyrethrums are selections of *Tanacetum coccineum* (Willd.) Grierson, syn. *Pyrethrum roseum* (Adams) M. Bieb., *Chysanthemum roseum* Adams, a native of subalpine meadows in the Caucasus. In the wild it has pale-pink flowers and stems *c.*60cm tall. The garden selections have brighter flowers, often double or semi-double. They do best in well-drained, slightly acid, sandy soil in an open, sunny position, and flower in June–July. Shown here are:
'Brenda'   Bright cerise-pink; stems *c.*60cm.
'Eileen May Robinson'   Pale pink; stems *c.*60cm.
'Mont Blanc'   White double; stems *c.*60cm.

Erigeron glaucus

Tanacetum coccineum 'Brenda'

Pyrethrums in a Cambridgeshire garden

Tanacetum coccineum 'Eileen May Robinson'

Tanacetum coccineum 'Mont Blanc' at Bridge of Alford, Aberdeenshire

Cicerbita alpina

Cicerbita bourgaei at Edington, Wiltshire

Syneilesis aconitifolia

Adenostyles alpina near Samaden, Switzerland

Lactuca perennis at St Luc, the Valais

Liatris spicata 'Alba'

Hieraceum lanatum at Wisley

Adenostyles alpina (L.) Bluff & Fingerh. (*Compositae*)   Native of the Jura, the Alps, Apennines and Corsica (subsp. *briquetii*) eastwards to Yugoslavia, growing in woods, by streams, in alder scrub and on damp, rocky slopes usually north-facing, usually on limestone at up to 2400m, flowering in June–September. Plant with large, rounded basal leaves, *c.*15cm across and few upright stems to 50cm. Flowers in a loose, flat-topped inflorescence. For a cool, rich position in shade or partial shade. Hardy to −20°C or less. *A. alliariae* (Gouan) A. Kerner has more branched, woolly flowering stems and usually sessile upper-stem leaves. It has darker purplish-pink flowers.

Cicerbita alpina (L.) Wallr. (*Compositae*) Native of Europe, from Scotland (where it is *very* rare) and Norway to the Alps, the Pyrenees and Carpathians, eastwards to Russia and Bulgaria, growing on shady, moist cliffs and in alder scrub flowering in July–September. Plant with few simple or branched stems to 250cm. Lower leaves to 25cm, with a large, triangular terminal lobe and a few pairs of small lateral lobes. Upper leaves clasping the stem. Flowers in a rounded, then elongated head. *c.*2cm across. For moist, rich soil in partial shade. Hardy to −20°C or less.

Cicerbita bourgaei (Boiss.) Beauv.   Native of NE Turkey, from Giresun eastwards, and of Georgia, growing in forest clearings, by streams and in hazel scrub at 1050–1820m, flowering

in August–September. Plant forming clumps or erect stems to 3m from a tufted rootstock. Leaves elliptic, unlobed or with 2–4 rounded lateral lobes. Flowers 1.7–1.9cm long. For moist, rich soil in sun or partial shade. Hardy to −25°C or less. *C. macrophylla* (Willd.) Wallr. from C Russia and the Caucasus south to the Talysh has a far-creeping rhizome and is naturalized in N & C Europe. It often persists as a roadside weed after it has been thrown out of a nearby garden. It has stems to 180cm and flowers to 3cm across in a loose, rather flat-topped inflorescence. *C. plumieri* (L.) Kirschl. is shorter, to 1.3m, hairless, and the leaves have a triangular terminal lobe and several pairs of lateral lobes. Native of the Pyrenees, W Alps and Bulgaria.

Hieraceum lanatum Vill. (*Compositae*) Native of France and N Italy, in the Alps and the Jura, growing on limestone rocks and cliffs at 300–2100m, flowering in May–July. Plant with a rosette of densely white-felted leaves, the blade to 10cm long, ovate, elliptical or lanceolate, usually ovate in cultivated plants. Flowers with the involucre 12–15mm long. For a very well-drained, sunny position such as on this old wall. Hardy to −20°C, perhaps less.

Lactuca perennis L. (*Compositae*)   Native of Europe, from Spain to France, Germany and Belgium east to Romania, growing on sunny banks and among dry rocks in the hills, usually on limestone, flowering in June–August. Plant with a rosette of pinnatifid or pinnatisect rather

glaucous leaves, with lanceolate segments. Stems several, to 80cm, much branched. Flowers *c.*2.5cm across, blue to lilac. For dry, well-drained soil in full sun. Hardy to −25°C perhaps. A delicate and attractive garden plant.

Liatris spicata (L.) Willd. (*Compositae*) Native of E North America, from Pennsylvania and New Jersey west to Michigan and Wisconsin, and south to Florida and Louisiana, growing in damp meadows, the edges of marshes and in savannahs, flowering in July–September. Plant with stiff, upright stems to 1.8m, from corm-like rhizomes. Leaves glabrous, linear to linear-lanceolate, to 40cm long, 2cm wide. Involucral bracts with appressed tips (tips spreading in *L. pycnostachya* and *L. scariosa*). For good, moist soil in full sun. Hardy to −25°C or less. Various colour forms are cultivated in shades of bluish purple, violet and white.

Syneilesis aconitifolia (Bunge.) Maxim. (*Compositae*)   Native of N Honshu and NE China, north of Beijing, where it is common, growing in dry woods and scrub in low hills, flowering in August–October. Plant with a tufted rootstock. Leaves silky when young, on upright stalks to 60cm, peltate, deeply divided and with jaggedly toothed lobes to 30cm across. Flowering stems to 1m or more, with pinkish flowers without rays. For sun or partial shade in leafy soil. Hardy to −25°C or less. The leaves are exciting, the flowers a disappointment.

Ligularia 'Gregynog Gold' in the stream garden at Leeds Castle, Kent

Ligularia 'Zepter' in the Savill Garden, Windsor

Ligularia stenocephala 'The Rocket' in the Wild Garden at Wisley

Ligularia macrophylla at Kew

Ligularia dentata (A. Gray) Hara syn. *L. clivorum* Maxim. (*Compositae*)   Native of China, from W Sichuan eastwards, and in Japan in Honshu, growing in scrub, forest clearings, by ditches and in mountain meadows, flowering in July–August to October in the wild. Plant with a tufted rootstock and long-stemmed leaves to 30cm long, 38cm wide, cordate. Stem leaves usually 2; stems to 1.2m; flower-heads *c*.11cm across. For moist, rich soil in shade or partial shade. Hardy to −25°C or less. Several cultivars have been named: 'Othello' (1915) was the earliest of the purple-leaved cultivars; 'Moorblut' is said to have even darker leaves; 'Desdemona', surprisingly, is similar to 'Othello'. These purple-leaved forms come more or less true from seed.

Ligularia 'Gregynog Gold'   A hybrid between *L. dentata* and *L. veitchiana*, raised by Hess in 1950. This is one of the finest of the *Ligularias*, with large flowers, rich orange-yellow, the lowest *c*.10cm across, in a loose spike. Stems to 1.8m. For rich, moist or boggy soil in sun or partial shade. Hardy to −20°C.

Ligularia macrophylla (Ledeb.) DC.   Native of C Asia, in Kazakstan and NW China in Sinjiang, growing on dry but fertile hillsides, flowering in July–August. Leaves very glaucous, upright from a deep rootstock, the blades broadly ovate, finely toothed. Inflorescence to 1.5m, of numerous small flowers 3–5cm across. For deep, rich but well-drained soil in full sun. This requires moisture in spring but can be dry in the latter part of the summer. Hardy to −25°C or less. Very rare in gardens but the fine clump in the order beds at Kew shown here is often illustrated, e.g. in Graham Thomas' *Perennial Garden Plants* and elsewhere. It covers the foothills of the Tien Shan above Alma Ata and in NW China.

Ligularia × palmatiloba Hesse syn. *L. × yoshizoeana* (Mak.) Kitam., the hybrid between *L. dentata* and *L. japonica*, has fewer deeply lobed leaves, but better flowers than *L. japonica*, *c*.7cm across. *L. japonica* (Thunb.) Less. itself is a native of W China in Hubei and Sichuan and in Korea, Taiwan and in Japan, in W Honshu, Shikoku and Kyushu, growing in rich, moist meadows and clearings in the mountains, flowering in June–August. Plant with a stout rootstock and large, orbicular

Ligularia veitchiana

Ligularia sibirica by a forest stream near Kyoto, Japan

Ligularia × palmatiloba

Ligularia dentata at Wallington, Northumberland

cordate lobed leaves, the lobes variably lobed or jaggedly deeply toothed. Inflorescence to 1.5m rather flat-topped, corymbose with flower stalks 2.5–20cm long. Flower-heads 2–8, about 10cm across. Both need moist, deep soil in shade or partial shade. Hardy to −20°C, perhaps less.

Ligularia sibirica (L.) Cass. Native of Europe, from C France and Bulgaria eastwards to the Caucasus, Siberia, China and Japan (var. *speciosa* DC.), growing in wet woods, meadows and scrub by streams, flowering in July–October. Plant forming a large clump of rounded cordate leaves to *c*.32cm long and wide, sometimes densely hairy beneath. Flowering stems to 2m tall, usually *c*.1.5m. Flower-heads 4–5cm across, with 7–11 'petals'.

Ligularia stenocephala (Maxim.) Matsum. & Koidz. **'The Rocket'** Native of Japan in all the islands except Hokkaido, N China and Taiwan, growing in wet places in the mountains, flowering in June–September. Plant forming large clumps of triangular leaves with narrow, elongated points and fine, irregular teeth to 24cm long, 20cm wide. Flowering stems often blackish, tall and slender to 1.2m. Flower-heads with 1–3 'petals', each 2–2.5cm long. For moist, rich soil in partial shade. Hardy to −25°C or less. *Ligularia przewalskii* (Maxim.) Diels has jagged, deeply toothed and lobed leaves, with a rather similar inflorescence. It is native of NW China.

Ligularia veitchiana (Hemsl.) Greenman Native of W China, in Hubei growing in wet

places at 1100–1800m, flowering in July–September. Plant forming a large clump of soft, rounded leaves to 60cm across with solid stalks. (Leaf stalks hollow in the similar *L. wilsoniana* (Hemsl.) Greenm.). Inflorescence to 1.8m, of numerous flower-heads *c*.6cm across, with broad bracts. For rich, moist soil in partial shade and shelter. Hardy to −20°C or less.

Ligularia 'Zepter' This is the hybrid between *L. veitchiana* and, it is said, *L. przewalskii*, raised by K. Partsch in 1975. A striking plant for rich, moist soil in partial shade. If 'The Rocket' was the parent instead of the true *L. przewalskii* then the plant shown here would be a likely outcome. The leaves show no lobing; the black stalk takes after 'The Rocket'.

Telekia speciosa with *Myrrhis odorata*

Inula racemosa at the Savill Garden, Windsor

Inula hookeri

Inula royleana in Kashmir

Inula hookeri C. B. Clarke (*Compositae*)
Native of the Himalayas, from C Nepal east to
Burma and SW China, growing in scrub at
2400–3600m, flowering in August–October.
Plant forming spreading patches with numerous
slender, rather lax leafy stems to 75cm tall.
Leaves elliptic-lanceolate, 8–15cm long, hairy.
Buds covered with shaggy hairs. Flower-heads
3.5–6cm across. For moist but well-drained soil
in sun or partial shade. Hardy to −20°C,
perhaps less.

Inula racemosa Hook. fil. Native of NW
China and Afghanistan to C Nepal, usually
growing near habitations, at 2000–3200m,
flowering in July–September. It is cultivated
because its roots are used for medicine. Stems to
2m or more from a stout rootstock. Lower
leaves elliptic-lanceolate, to 45cm long. Flower-
heads 4–8cm across. For deep, rich soil in sun
or partial shade. Hardy to −25°C or less.

Inula royleana C. B. Clarke Native of the W
Himalayas, from Pakistan to Kashmir, where it
is common, growing in scrub and grassy
clearings in forest at 2100–4000m, flowering in
July–September. Plant with few, rather stout,
upright stems to 60cm. Leaves few, large,
elliptic-lanceolate. Flower-heads 10–12.5cm
across, usually solitary. For moist but well-
drained soil in sun or partial shade. Hardy to
−20°C or less.

Senecio bicolor (Willd.) Tod. subsp. **cineraria**
(DC.) Chater (*Compositae*) Native of the W
Mediterranean region, Portugal and North
Africa, and naturalized in the British Isles,
growing in rocky and sandy places by the sea,
flowering in July–August. Plant with leafy,
cottony stems to 50cm, somewhat shrubby at
the base. Leaves ovate to ovate-lanceolate in
outline, deeply divided, with the ultimate lobe
longer than wide, subacute. In subsp. *bicolor*,
from the E Mediterranean, the leaves are ovate,
often lyrate, with the ultimate lobe as wide as
long and obtuse. Flower-heads on short
peduncles, with very short 'petals'. For well-
drained, sandy soil in full sun. Hardy to −10°C,
perhaps less in some cultivars.

Senecio doria L. syn. *S. macrophyllus* M.
Bieb. Native of most of Europe from France,
Spain and North Africa, east to Bulgaria and the
Caucasus growing in wet meadows and marshes,
flowering in June–July. Plant with several
upright stems to 1m from a tufted rootstock.
Lower leaves linear-elliptical to oblong-obovate,
usually 3–7cm wide, dentate or entire. Flower-
heads small, 12–25mm across with 5–6 'petals'.
For moist or wet soil in full sun. Hardy to
−25°C. This species has been sold in error
under the name *Ligularia macrophylla*!

Senecio jacquemontianus (Decne.) Benth. ex
Hook. Native of the W Himalayas, from
Pakistan to Kashmir, where it is locally
common, growing in alpine meadows at 3000–
4000m, flowering in July. Plant with thick,
upright stems and *Ligularia*-like habit. Basal
leaves heart-shaped, to 20cm across. Stem
leaves with a sheathing stalk. Flower-heads to
4cm across with rather few (12–15) 'petals',
c.1.5cm long. For moist soil in full sun or partial
shade. Hardy to −20°C or less.

Senecio pseudoarnica

Senecio pseudoarnica on the coast of Hokkaido

Sinacalia tangutica at Inverewe

Senecio jacquemontianus in Kashmir

Senecio doria in Kent

Senecio pseudoarnica Juss. Native of Korea, N China, Japan in Hokkaido and N Honshu, E Siberia, Kamschatka and Alaska south to British Columbia, growing on shingle by the sea, flowering in July–October. Plant forming clumps of fleshy leaves with stout, hairy stems to 50cm; flower-heads 1–30 per plant, 3.5–4.5cm. For well-drained, sandy soil in full sun. Hardy to −15°C, perhaps less.

Sinacalia tangutica (Maxim.) P. Nord. syn. *Senecio tanguticus* Maxim. Native of NW China in Gansu, growing in meadows, flowering in August–October. Plant with tall, black stems to 3m. Leaves 12–18cm, ovate in outline, deeply cut into jaggedly toothed lobes. Flower-heads very small, with 3–4 ray florets and 3–4 disc florets. For moist, peaty soil in shade or partial shade. Hardy to −25°C or less.

Telekia speciosa (Schreb.) Baumg. syn. *Bupthalmum speciosum* Schreb. (*Compositae*) Native of C Europe, from Poland and Yugoslavia east to the Caucasus and Turkey, and naturalized elsewhere in NW Europe, growing in clearings in forest and by streams in scrub, at 300–1700m, flowering in July–September. Plant with a stout, shortly spreading rhizome and upright stems to 2m. Basal leaves ovate, on long stalks, rather thin, aromatic. Flower-heads 7.5–10cm across. For deep, moist soil in partial shade. Hardy to −25°C or less. A bold, tough plant with large *Hosta*-like leaves.

Senecio bicolor subsp. *cineraria*

Rudbeckia laciniata

Rudbeckia 'Goldquelle'

Rudbeckia hirta

Grindelia maritima at Santa Barbara

Rudbeckia fulgida var. speciosa

Rudbeckia 'Goldsturm'

Rudbeckia laciniata in Arizona

Grindelia maritima (Greene) Steyerm. (*Compositae*) Gum Weed   Native of California, on the coast around San Francisco, growing in scrub or on rocky bluffs by the sea, flowering in August–September. Plant woody at the base, to 80cm. Leaves rather thick, the lowest narrowly oblanceolate, to 18cm long. Flower-heads 2.5–4cm across, excluding the 'petals' which are 10–13mm long. Bracts with green, mostly erect tips (recurved tips are found in other species including *G. squarrosa* (Pursh) Dunal from the Great Plains). For well-drained soil in full sun. Hardy to –10°C, perhaps less. *G. chiloensis* (Corn.) Cabr. is rather similar to the above. The white gum on the buds is characteristic of *Grindelia*, of which there are 11 species in California.

Ratibida columnifera (Nutt.) Wooton & Standley var. *pulcherrima* (DC.) Wooton & Standley syn. *Lepachys columnaris* (Pursh) Torrey & Gray (*Compositae*) Mexican Hat Native of North America, from Alberta south to Mexico east to Manitoba, Minnesota, Illinois, Arkansas and Texas, growing in prairies, dry grassy valleys and gorges usually on limestone, flowering in June–September. Plant with stems to 80cm, branching from the base. Leaves pinnate, with 5–9 oblong, narrowly linear leaflets. Flower-heads with the column 3–6cm high; 'petals' rather few, 1.3–2cm long, yellow or reddish-brown in f. *pulcherrima*. For dry, well-drained soil in full sun. Hardy to –25°C or less.

Ratibida pinnata (Vent.) Barnh. syn. *Lepachis pinnata* (Vent.) Torr. & Gray   Native of E North America, from S Ontario and New York west to Minnesota and Nebraska, south to Georgia and Oklahoma, growing in dry places,

flowering in June–September. Column *c.*2cm high. 'Petals' drooping, *c.*5cm long, pale yellow.

Rudbeckia fulgida Ait. var. *speciosa* (Wend.) Perdue syn. *R. newmannii* Loud. (*Compositae*) Native of E North America from New York to Georgia, Alabama and Missouri, growing in woods and marshy valleys, flowering in late July–September. Stems to 1m from an elongated rhizome. Basal leaves ovate, with a long stalk; stem-leaves lanceolate, deeply toothed; '**Goldsturm**' is the common garden clone of this variety and has stems usually *c.*60cm. Flowers 5–9cm across. For any soil in full sun. Hardy to –25°C or less.

Rudbeckia hirta L.   Native of E North America, from Massachusetts to Illinois, south to Georgia and Alabama, growing in open woods, scrub and rough meadows, flowering in June–October. Plant with several stems to 1m, from spreading rhizomes. Basal leaves ovate, to 7cm across. Stem leaves ovate, coarsely toothed. Flower-heads orange-yellow, 5–8cm across. For any good soil in full sun. Hardy to –25°C.

Rudbeckia laciniata L. Cut-leaved Coneflower   Native of North America, from Quebec west to Montana and south to N Florida, Texas and through the Rockies to Arizona, growing in moist meadows in valleys and on grassy hills, flowering in July–October. Plant forming loose clumps of stems 60–120cm tall. Leaves deeply lobed into 3–7 pointed and toothed segments. Flowers 7.5–15cm wide, with a conical centre, or double in 'Goldquelle', a common garden form with stems to 1.2m. For any good soil in full sun. Hardy to –25°C.

Ratibida columnifera var. *pulcherrima*

Ratibida pinnata

Artemisia stelleriana on the coast of Hokkaido, near Shari

Artemisia ludoviciana with *Salvia aethiopis* at the Royal Botanic Garden, Edinburgh

Anaphalis margaritacea in Hokkaido

Artemisia lactiflora, a bit too dry

Anaphalis margaritacea

Anaphalis triplinervis

Artemisia schmidtiana

Artemisia 'Canescens'

Helichrysum 'Schwefellicht'

Anaphalis margaritacea (L.) Benth. & Hook. syn. *A. cinnamomea* DC. (*Compositae*) Pearly Everlasting Native of North America, from Newfoundland to Alaska, of N. Asia and of the Himalayas, growing on sand dunes, dry, stony lake shores, dry meadows and subalpine slopes, flowering in July–September. Plant with spreading rhizomes, forming dense patches. Stems 10–90cm, usually *c*.40cm, white, woolly. Leaves very variable, 3–20mm wide, variably hairy; green or greyish above, white beneath. Bracts rounded, erect at flowering. Shown here are: a wild form in Japan, probably var. *margaritacea*, the broadest-leaved variety; and an old garden variety, close to the American var. *subalpina* Gray, which has leaves hairy above, rather blunt at the apex. For any well-drained soil in full sun, not too dry in summer. Hardy to −25°C.

Anaphalis triplinervis (Sims) Sims ex. C. B. Clarke Native of the Himalayas, from Afghanistan to SW China, growing in meadows and clearings in forest at 1800–3300m, flowering in July–October. Var. *intermedia* (DC.) Airy Shaw is found at higher altitudes, at 2900–4100m. Plant forming spreading clumps of rather lax stems 30–60cm tall, with leaves green above, 5–10cm long. Bracts spreading, acute. Var. *intermedia* has shorter (*c*.3cm) woolly leaves on shorter stems to 30cm. In gardens two named varieties are 'Silberregen' and 'Sommerschnee' (syn. 'Summersnow'), a dwarfer variety which seems to fall between *intermedia* and *triplinervis*. This is perhaps the same as *A*. 'Nubigena' of gardens. All need well-drained soil in full sun, but not too dry in summer. Hardy to −25°C or less.

Artemisia absinthium L. (*Compositae*) Wormwood Native of Europe eastwards to W Asia and Siberia, and of North Africa, growing in grassy places by streams, in steppes, dry fields and by roadsides, flowering in June–September. Plant somewhat shrubby at the base. Flower-heads 3–5mm across in a branched, narrow or broad inflorescence up to 1m tall. 'Lambrook Giant', selected by Margery Fish, is a tall form; '**Lambrook Silver**', a smaller one with stems to 75cm. For any dry soil in full sun.

Artemisia 'Canescens' syn. *A. armeniaca* hort. A garden plant of uncertain origin, but distinct in its very fine curling leaf segments which join at right angles, giving the shoots a characteristic spiky look. Flowering stems narrow, to 45cm. Flower-heads globose, 6mm wide. For any well-drained soil in full sun.

Artemisia lactiflora Wall. ex DC. Native of W China, in Sichuan, and recorded by Roy Lancaster on Omei Shan, growing in scrub and forest clearings, flowering in August–October. Plant forming large clumps of graceful stems to 1.8m, blackish in 'Guizhou'. Leaves green, coarsely toothed. Flowers creamy yellow. For moist, peaty soil in sun or partial shade. Hardy to −20°C, perhaps less.

Artemisia ludoviciana Nutt. Western Mugwort Native of North America, from Michigan to Washington south to Texas and Mexico, and naturalized further east, growing in prairies, dry, open ground or light woodland, flowering in July–September. Plant spreading by long, thin stolons to form loose patches. Stems 30–100cm. Leaves variable, green or white above, often with a few large teeth, but extra white in cultivar '**Silver Queen**', which has stems to 75cm, and lanceolate leaves.

Artemisia ludoviciana 'Silver Queen'

Artemisia 'Powis Castle'

Artemisia ludoviciana

Artemisia absinthium 'Lambrook Silver'

Artemisia pontica

Artemisia stelleriana 'Boughton Silver'

Specimens from the Savill Garden, Windsor, 28th August. ¼ life size

Artemisia pontica L. Native from Germany and Austria eastwards to Russia, Bulgaria and C Asia, growing on dry, grassy and rocky hills, flowering in May–July. Plant forming clumps of stems 40–80cm. Flower-heads in a very narrow inflorescence, nodding, *c*.2.5mm across. For any soil in full sun. Hardy to −25°C or less.

Artemisia 'Powis Castle' This is probably a hybrid between *A. absinthium* and the shrubby *A. aborescens*, which has finely divided leaves with segments to 2mm wide. 'Powis Castle' can form a shrub, as can be seen in the picture of the original plants in *Shrubs*, p. 160, but is also a quick-growing perennial, often killed by hard winters, but very easily raised from cuttings. Longest-lived when planted in the poorest soil.

Artemisia schmidtiana Maxim. Native of Japan, in Hokkaido and N Honshu, and of Sakhalin and the S Kurile Islands, growing in bare soil in the mountains, and by the sea, flowering in August–October. Plant with creeping vegetative shoots forming hummocks or mats of soft, silvery, hair-like leaves.

Flowering stems to 30cm, usually *c*.15cm. Flower-heads nodding, *c*.8mm across. For well-drained, sandy soil in full sun. Hardy to −20°C or less. Usually called 'Nana', but all *A. schmidtiana* are dwarf.

Artemisia stelleriana Bess. Native of E Siberia, N Japan, in Hokkaido and N Honshu, Korea, Sakhalin and the Kurile Islands, and widely naturalized in North America on the east coast, growing on sand dunes and on coastal cliffs, flowering in July–October. Plant with stolons and more or less prostrate vegetative shoots. Flowering stems to 65cm. Leaves thick, ovate to oblong, greyish or white with obtuse lobes. Flower-heads 8–10mm wide. For sandy soil in full sun. '**Boughton Silver**' syn. 'Mori' is an extra-white and more prostrate form, introduced from Japan by Kazno Mori.

Helichrysum '**Schwefellicht**' syn. 'Sulphur Light' (*Compositae*) Raised by H. Klose. A tufted plant with upright stems 20–30cm tall, and softly woolly leaves. Hardy to −15°C, perhaps less.

Centaurea argentea

Centaurea macrocephala

Centaurea montana 'Alba'

Centaurea montana

Centaurea dealbata 'Steenbergii'

Centaurea atropurpurea

Centaurea argentea L. (*Compositae*) Native of Crete and Kithira, growing on mountain rocks, and in gorges, flowering in June–July. Leaves silvery, lyrate. Flower-heads 5–7mm across, solitary on stalks 10–45cm high. For a dry, sunny position on a wall or in some crevice. Hardy to −15°C perhaps.

Centaurea atropurpurea Waldst. & Kit. Native of Yugoslavia, Albania and Romania, growing on rocky slopes in the mountains, flowering in June–July. Stems to 150cm, branched above. Flowers dark reddish purple, above 4cm across. For well-drained soil in full sun. Hardy to −20°C perhaps. This species is striking mainly for its colour, like that of *Cirsium rivulare* 'Atropurpureum' or *Knautia macedonica* (see pp. 376 and 347).

Centaurea dealbata Willd. Native of the Caucasus to NE Turkey, growing in subalpine meadows and on rocky slopes, flowering in June–August. Plant forming clumps of green leaves, pinnatisect with lobed or pinnatifid segments, greyish beneath. Stems *c*.50cm, but can grow up to 100cm. Flowering stems leafy, often with leaves surrounding the pinkish flower. 'Steenbergii' syn. 'Skanbergii' has deep-reddish-purple flowers, and stems *c*.30cm. For well-drained soil, in full sun. Hardy to −25°C or less. *Centaurea hypoleuca* DC., from the S Caucasus, NW Iran and N Turkey, is very similar, but, in the commonly cultivated form 'John Coutts', has slender, branched stems with lanceolate upper leaves with perhaps 1 or 2 lobes near the base, flowers bright pink, with a pale centre, *c*.6cm across, and dark-brown appendages with whitish hairs on the margins.

Centaurea declinata M. Bieb. Native of the Caucasus and the Crimea, growing in dry, rocky subalpine meadows and subalpine woods, flowering in June–July. Plant forming mats of leaves, greyish above and below, with rounded segments. Flowering stems 10–30cm. Flower-heads *c*.5cm across, short and thick, bracts with spreading, pointed appendages. For well-drained soil in full sun, or a crevice on a wall. Hardy to −25°C or less.

Centaurea declinata

Stokesia laevis 'Wyoming'

Stemmacantha rhapontica

Centaurea macrocephala Muss.-Puschk. ex Willd. Native of the Caucasus and extreme NE of Turkey, growing in subalpine meadows at 2000–2300m, flowering in July–August. Plant with several stout, upright stems to 1m. Stems densely leafy. Flowers yellow, the flower-heads 4.5–5.5cm across, with large, to 2cm broad, rounded papery appendages on the bracts. For rich soil in full sun, moist in summer. Hardy to −20°C.

Centaurea montana L. Native of Europe, from the Ardennes in Belgium south to the Pyrenees in Spain and east to Poland and C Yugoslavia, growing in subalpine meadows and open woods, flowering in May–July. Plant with creeping rhizomes forming spreading patches. Stems to 60cm usually simple. Leaves undivided, softly silky beneath. Flowering *c*.5cm across, blue or sometimes white in 'Alba', pink in 'Carnea' and mauve in 'Violetta'; three colour forms grown in gardens. For moist but well-drained soil in sun or partial shade. Hardy to −20°C or less.

Centaurea simplicaulis Boiss. & Huet Native of NE Turkey and S Caucasia, growing in rock crevices and on screes at 400–2600m in Turkey, flowering in May–June. Plant forming mats of pinnatisect leaves, green above, whitish beneath, but variable in shape. Flowering stem 5–35cm, usually *c*.20cm in gardens. Flower-heads *c*.5cm across, rather long and slender with characteristic white-tipped appendages on the bracts. For a well-drained position in full sun, at the front of a border or on a wall. Hardy to −25°C or less.

Stemmacantha rhapontica (L.) Dittr. subsp. *rhapontica* syn. *Leuzea rhapontica* (L.) J. Holub, *Centaurea rhapontica* L. Native of the SW & C Alps, growing in mountain meadows, flowering in July–August. Stems 40–150cm. Leaves grey hairy beneath, the lowest variably divided. Flower-heads 5–7cm across. For any rich, moist, well-drained soil. Hardy to −20°C. *Centaurea* 'Pulchra Major' probably belongs to this species.

Stokesia laevis (Hill) E. Greene (*Compositae*) Native of SE North America, from Florida and Louisiana to South Carolina, growing in moist pinelands on acid soil, flowering in April–July. Stems to 50cm, usually woolly. Lower leaves elliptic or narrowly lanceolate. Flowers purplish blue or white. For sandy soil in full sun. Hardy to −15°C, perhaps less.

Centaurea simplicaulis at Coldham, Kent

Centaurea hypoleuca 'John Coutts' at Wisley

Berkheya purpurea with *Eucomis*

Cirsium falconeri in Kashmir

Cirsium rivulare 'Atropurpureum'

Senecio smithii in the Royal Botanic Garden, Edinburgh

Echinops exaltatus

Echinops ritro

Carlina acaulis at Powys Castle

Cynara scolymus with *Crambe maritima*

Cynara cardunculus in the long border at Great Dixter

Berkheya purpurea (DC.) Masters (*Compositae*)   Native of South Africa, in the Drakensberg, Natal and NE Cape Province (Winterberg) growing on moist, rocky, grassy slopes at 1800–2800m, flowering in December–February. Plant with few upright, thistle-like stems to 80cm. Basal leaves to 45cm long, white cottony beneath. Flower-heads *c*.7.5cm across, purple to white. For moist, peaty but well-drained soil in full sun. Hardy to −15°C.

Carlina acaulis L. (*Compositae*)   Native of Europe from C France and C Spain to Poland, W Russia and Greece, growing in rather dry alpine and subalpine meadows at up to 2500m, flowering in July–August. Plant usually short-lived or monocarpic, with rosettes of thistle-like leaves to 60cm across. Flowering stems variable in height: in subsp. *acaulis* usually stemless, but if grown in rich soil or partial shade with a short stem, to 15cm or so; in subsp. *simplex* (Waldst. & Kit.) Nyman, with an often branched stem up to 60cm, with up to 6 flowers. Flower-heads 8–12cm across, with silvery-white or pale-pink shining bracts. Hardy to −20°C.

Cirsium falconeri (Hook. fil.) Petrak (*Compositae*)   Native of the Himalayas, from Pakistan to SE Xizang (Tibet), growing in grassy places and clearings in forest at 2700–4300m, flowering in July–September. Plant with few upright stems to 1.5m. Whole plant covered with whitish spines. Flower-heads nodding, 7–8.5cm across in Kashmir as shown here; upright and purple-flowered in Nepal to SE Xizang. For moist but well-drained soil in sun or partial shade. Hardy to −20°C or less.

Cirsium rivulare (Jacq.) All. 'Atropurpureum' Native of C Europe, from the Pyrenees in Spain and France eastwards to Yugoslavia and W

Russia, growing in damp meadows usually on acid soils, flowering in June–July. Plant forming spreading clumps by shortly creeping rhizomes. Stems to 120cm or more in gardens. Flower-heads in clusters, *c*.3cm across, purple or deep crimson-purple in commonly cultivated 'Atropurpureum'. For a moist, sandy border in sun or partial shade. Hardy to −20°C or less.

Cynara cardunculus L. (*Compositae*) Cardoon Native of SW Europe, from Portugal to S France, Italy, Greece and North Africa, growing on stony slopes and in dry grassy places, flowering in June–August. Stems to 100cm, in the wild, to 2m or more in gardens. Leaves greyish, to 1m long, deeply dissected, usually with some spines. Flower-heads 5–8cm across, with spiny, spreading bracts. For deep, well-drained soil in full sun. Hardy to −10°C or less with protection. *C. hystrix* Ball, from North Africa is sometimes grown in gardens. It has very spiny, narrow leaves and stems *c*.100cm; flower-heads with reddish-purple bracts.

Cynara scolymus L. Artichoke   The cultivated Artichoke is usually grown as a vegetable, but makes a handsome plant for a border if it is allowed to flower. It is unknown in the wild, and is almost certainly a form of the Cardoon (see above), long cultivated for its edible flower-head, which in a good cultivar may be 12cm or more across.

Echinops exaltatus Schrad. syn. *E. commutatus* Jur. (*Compositae*)   Native of Europe, from Italy and Poland, eastwards to W Russia and Bulgaria, growing in grassy places and scrub, flowering in August–September. Plant forming huge clumps of upright stems to 2m. Leaves ovate to elliptical in outline, green above, hairy beneath; segments triangular with few slender

spines and a very rough margin. Flower-heads white or greyish, 3.5–6cm across. For good soil in full sun or partial shade. Hardy to −20°C or less. *E. sphaerocephalus* L. is a similar huge, white-flowered plant, but has leaves with smooth margin.

Echinops ritro L. incl. *E. ruthenicus* M. Bieb. Globe Thistle   Native of Europe from S France and Spain eastwards to Siberia and C Asia, growing in scrub, on rocky slopes and in bare, stony places, flowering in July–October. Plant with a tufted rootstock and several white-hairy stems 30–60cm. Leaves stiff, leathery, very spiny, green above, white beneath, pinnatifid, with segments 4mm wide or more at the base; leaves more finely divided and segments less than 2mm wide in subsp. *ruthenicus* (M. Bieb.) Nyman. Flower-heads blue, 3.5–4.5cm across. For well-drained, dry soil in full sun. Hardy to −20°C or less. Another dwarf species worth growing is *Echinops emiliae* O. Schw. from limestone screes in SW Turkey. It has stems to 60cm, but huge pale jade-green flower-heads to 15cm across. It was discovered by Peter Davis in 1947, but still awaits introduction!

Senecio smithii DC. (*Compositae*)   Native of W Argentina north to 46°S and S Chile north to 43°S, growing in marshes, wet grassy places, along the coast and by streams crossing shingle beaches, flowering in December–April, or July–August in the north, where it is naturalized in Shetland, and other parts of W Scotland, growing by streams across bogs. Plant forming large clumps of stalked leaves with blade 8–25cm long, white-hairy beneath. Flowering stems to 120cm. Flower-heads 3–5cm across. For wet, peaty soil or shallow water in sun or partial shade. Hardy to −25°C, perhaps less. Often damaged by slugs.

Veratrum nigrum with Cimicifuga racemosa in Kent

Veratrum mengtzeanum at Windsor

Amianthium muscaetoxicum (Walt.) A. Gray (*Melanthiaceae*) Fly-poison   Native of E North America, from Long Island and E Pennsylvania, south to Florida, Missouri and Oklahoma, growing in open, sandy woods, bogs and wet, sandy fields, flowering in May–July. Plant with a slender, bulbous rootstock and linear basal leaves to 3cm wide. Stems 45–120cm tall, not branched. Flowers 5–7mm across, without nectaries. Hardy to −20°C.

Stenanthium gramineum (Ker-Gawl.) Morong. (*Melanthiaceae*)   Native of E North America, from Virginia to Kentucky, south to Missouri, Florida and E Texas, at up to 1800m in North Carolina, growing in dry, open woods in the mountains, in scrub and on the edges of swamps (var. *robustum* (S. Wats.) Fern.), flowering in mid-June–September. Plant with a slightly bulbous rootstock and upright stems to 1.9m. Leaves numerous, to 3cm broad, rather lax. Inflorescence with a spike-like terminal branch, and several, usually nodding, side branches, but ascending and more densely flowered in var. *robustum*. Flowers usually whitish, but sometimes greenish or bronze-purple. Rare in cultivation, but grows well in the Royal Botanic Garden, Edinburgh.

Veratrum album L. incl. *V. lobelianum* Bernh., *V. oxysepalum* Turcz. and *V. grandiflorum* (Maxim.) Loes. (*Melanthiaceae*)   Native of Europe, from Norway, France and Spain, eastwards to the Caucasus, Siberia, China, Japan and Alaska, growing in moist, grassy, subalpine meadows and open woods, flowering in June–July. Plant with a short, stout rootstock and upright stems to 2m. Leaves hairless above, hairy beneath on the veins. Flowers 1.5–2.5cm across, whitish, yellowish or green. The distinction between green forms of this species and the E American *V. viride* Ait. is not clear. *V. viride* is said to have leaves hairy beneath, and more drooping side branches to the inflorescence. It grows in wetter places than are usual for *V. album*.

Veratrum mengtzeanum Loes. fil. syn. *V. wilsonii* C. M. Wright   Native of W China, in Yunnan, Sichuan and Guizhou, growing in stony pastures, scrub and forest, flowering in June–September. Stems to 1.5m. Leaves linear

Stenanthium gramineum

Stenanthium gramineum at Edinburgh

Veratrum leaves with *Phalaris arundinacea* 'Picta'

Veratrum album (green form)

Veratrum album at Wisley

Veratrum taliense at Edinburgh

Zigadenus elegans at Wisley

or linear-lanceolate to 50cm long, 1.5–3.5cm wide, hairless. Flowers 1.5–2.5cm across, on long, 7–15mm, pedicels; with 2 conspicuous nectaries on each petal. For moist, peaty soil in partial shade. Hardy to −20°C perhaps.

Veratrum nigrum L. fil. syn. *V. ussuriense* (Loes. fil.) Nakai   Native of Europe, from France and Poland eastwards to Siberia, N China and Korea, growing in subalpine meadows, scrub and openings in woods, flowering in June–August. Plant with short, stout rootstock and stems to 130cm. Leaves glabrous on both sides, pleated when young. Flowers 9–15mm across, blackish purple to reddish brown, smelling of rotten fruit and visited by flies. For any good, moist soil in sun or partial shade. Hardy to −25°C or less.

Veratrum taliense Loes. fil.   Native of W China, in Yunnan and Sichuan, growing in alpine meadows, flowering in June–July (to September in gardens). Stems to 1.5m. Leaves narrowly lanceolate, acuminate, 30–50cm long, to 2.5cm wide. Flowers 1.5–2.2cm across, glabrous inside and out, with a small 2-lobed nectary. Introduced by Roy Lancaster from the mountains near Dali, Yunnan.

Xerophyllum tenax (Pursh) Nutt. (*Melanthiaceae*) Indian Basket Grass   Native of W North America, from California, in Monterey Co., north to British Columbia, and in the Rockies in Idaho and Montana, growing on dry, sunny hills and in open woods, flowering in May–August. Plant with a short, thick, rootstock and solitary upright stems to 150cm. Basal leaves to 4mm wide, with numerous narrower stem leaves. Raceme 10–60cm long. Flowers 12–20mm across. For well-drained soil in full sun. Hardy to −20°C.

Zigadenus elegans Pursh syn. *Anticlea elegans* (Pursh) Rydb. (*Melanthiaceae*)   Native of E North America, from New Brunswick to Vermont, New York and Missouri and in the Rockies south to New Mexico and Arizona, growing in pine woods, and moist places at up to 3000m, flowering June–August. Plant with slender bulb, forming small clumps. Stems to 90cm. Flowers 16–20mm across, with an obcordate nectary.

Xerophyllum tenax

Amianthium muscaetoxicum at Harry Hay's

379

Paradisea liliastrum near St Luc, the Valais

Paradisea lusitanica at Sellindge, Kent

Anthericum ramosum in NW Italy

Paradisea liliastrum

Paradisea lusitanica

Anthericum ramosum L. (*Liliaceae-Asphodelaceae*)   Native of S Sweden and N France south to the Pyrenees, C Italy, Bulgaria, the Crimea and NW Turkey, growing in dry sunny meadows and open scrub, flowering in May–July. Stems to 90cm. Flowers starry, on a branched stem; petals 10–14mm long. *A. liliago* L., from Europe and S Turkey, and especially the clone 'Major', have larger petals to 22mm long, on usually unbranched stems, like a smaller-flowered *Paradisea*. Both species are easy to grow in well-drained soil in a sunny position.

Asphodeline liburnica (Scop.) Reichb. (*Asphodelaceae*)   Native of Austria and Italy east to Greece, Crete and Turkey-in-Europe, growing in dry scrub and open woods, flowering in June–July. Stems to 100cm, few , upright, from fleshy roots. Leaves mostly on the lower half of the stem. Inflorescence simple or with 1 or 2 branches; flowers 5–6cm across. For dry, well-drained soil in full sun. Hardy to −15°C.

Asphodeline lutea (L.) Reichb.   Native of the Mediterranean area, from C Italy to Romania, Greece and Turkey east to Trabzon (and North Africa?), growing on rocky slopes and in scrub, usually on limestone, at up to 1650m in Turkey, flowering in March–June. Stems to 150cm, covered with narrow, grassy leaves. Bracts *c.*10mm wide. Flowers numerous, 20–30mm long. This is the commonest species in cultivation. For well-drained soil in full sun, and a warm position. Hardy to −15°C perhaps.

Asphodeline taurica (Pall.) Kunth   Native of Greece, the Crimea, the Caucasus, Turkey and W Syria, growing on rocky hills, in dry meadows and in open woods, at 500–2500m, flowering in May–July. Stems to 80cm, glaucous, leafy throughout. Flowers white, 2.5–3cm across. For dry, well-drained soil in full sun. Hardy to −15°C.

Asphodelus albus Mill. (*Asphodelaceae*)   Native of S & W Europe, from NW France and Portugal to Hungary and North Africa, growing in rocky places, scrub, open woods and heathland, flowering in April and May. Roots swollen and fleshy. Leaves 1–2cm wide, flat. Stems 30–100cm, usually not branched. Bracts dark brown in subsp. *albus*, whitish and papery in subsp. *villarsii*. Petals 15–20mm long. *A.*

Asphodeline liburnica

Asphodeline taurica in the Tauros Mountains, south of Kayseri, Turkey

ramosus L. is rather similar but has much-branched candelabra-like flowering stems and roots tuberous towards their ends. It is common from Spain, Portugal and North Africa, east to Greece and NW Turkey. Hardy to −15°C. *A. aestivus* Brot. syn. *A. microcarpus* Viv. is like *A. ramosus* but fruits are obovoid, smaller, with lateral branches shorter. Tuber narrowing to a point.

Bulbinella hookeri (Colenso ex Hook.) Cheeseman syn. *Chrysobactron hookeri* Colenso ex Hook. (*Asphodelaceae*)   Native of New Zealand, in North and South Islands, from Lake Taupo and Mount Egmont southwards, growing in subalpine grassland, flowering in October–January. This has become much more common in the wild because it is not grazed and can survive burning. Leaves many in a tuft, from a clump of fleshy, edible roots. Stem 25–45cm. Flowers 6–8mm across. For moist, peaty soil in full sun. Hardy to −5°C, possibly less.

Paradisea liliastrum (L.) Bertol. (*Asphodelaceae*) St Bruno's Lily   Native of the Alps, Jura, Pyrenees and N & C Apennines, from Spain to Italy and Yugoslavia, growing in subalpine meadows, flowering in June–July. Plant forming small clumps. Leaves to 5mm wide. Stems 30–60cm, with usually 4–10 flowers, each 30–50mm long. Not easy to grow; moist but well-drained soil and a sunny position. Photographed near St Luc, in the Valais, S Switzerland. 'Major' or 'Magnificum' is a large clone or selection.

Paradisea lusitanica (Cout.) Samp.   Native of N Portugal and adjacent parts of Spain, growing in woods, marshes and damp meadows, flowering in May–June. Plant forming clumps to 50cm across. Leaves to 2cm wide; stems 50–150cm, with 20–25 flowers, each 20–35mm long and 40mm across. Easily grown in rich, moist soil in sun or partial shade. Hardy to −10°C and below? This elegant species has been distributed by Dr J. Smart from his garden at Barnstaple, N Devon.

Bulbinella hookeri with meadowsweet

Asphodeline lutea at Kew

Asphodelus albus on limestone rocks near Ronda

Kniphofia caulescens at 2800m on Carlyle's Hoek, above Rhodes, NE Cape Province

Kniphofia rooperi

Kniphofia breviflora Harv. ex Baker (*Liliaceae-Asphodelaceae*) Native of South Africa in Natal and Orange Free State, in the foothills and slopes of the Drakensberg, at 1800–1900m, growing singly in thick mountain grassland, flowering in January–March. Flowers normally a uniform clear yellow, but a form with white flowers is found in Natal. *K. buchananii* Baker also has white flowers and is similar to *K. breviflora*, but with shorter flowers 3–7mm long (7–11mm in *K. breviflora*). Hardy to −15°C.

Kniphofia caulescens Baker Native of South Africa, from NE Cape Province, E Orange Free State, Lesotho and the crest of Natal Drakensberg at 1800–3000m, growing often in colonies on peaty soil overlying rock along

Kniphofia rooperi at Wisley, in autumn

Kniphofia linearifolia

Kniphofia linearifolia in a marsh at the foot of the Sani Pass, Natal

Kniphofia northiae on Bustervoedpad, NE Cape Province

Kniphofia breviflora at Mont-aux-Sources

seepage lines, flowering in January–March. This species produces short, almost woody stems, often branching. The glaucous leaves with serrulate margins and bicolorous flowers on an inflorescence 60cm tall make it easily identifiable. It is hardy to −20°C

Kniphofia linearifolia Baker syn. *K. uvaria* var. *maxima* Baker Native of South Africa, Swaziland and Zimbabwe, this is the most widespread of all *Kniphofias* and is closely related to several other robust 'Red-hot Pokers'. From it are raised some well-known garden cultivars. It is found in large clumps in damp grassland. Flower colour is usually bright pinkish red in bud, opening to orange or yellow. The bright inflorescence is large, elongate or rhomboid in shape as opposed to globose in *K.*

uvaria (L.) Hook., and the plant is larger with stiffer leaves. *K. praecox* Baker is also similar but has narrow bracts with an acuminate tip. Hardiness variable, to −10°C perhaps, in the hardiest forms.

Kniphofia northiae Baker. Native of South Africa in NE Cape Province, Natal and Lesotho, growing in steep, grassy gullies in wet, peaty soil, sometimes in large colonies at 1600–3000m, flowering in November–February. This is a solitary non-clump-forming species which produces thick stems. These can be more than 1m tall and are crowned by a rosette of wide, evergreen, strap-shaped leaves, up to 1.5m long × 5–10cm wide. Most forms of *K. northiae* have a U- rather than V-shaped keel as the section of the leaf. Inflorescence ovoid, dense with

pinkish-red buds, opening whitish or yellow, flowering in December–February. Hardy to −10°C.

Kniphofia rooperi (Moore) Lem. Native of E Cape Province and S Natal, growing in marshy places near the coast, flowering in June–September, but at other times of year in gardens. Plant robust, with broad acuminate leaves. Inflorescence large and globose. Flowers 32–44mm long. *K. uvaria* is similar, but usually less robust, often with a more cylindrical inflorescence. Intermediates are found in the wild, but *K. uvaria* is commonest in the S & W Cape, flowering at any time of year. Hardy to −15°C perhaps.

Kniphofia thodei on Ngeli Mountain

Kniphofia thodei near Mont-aux-Sources

Kniphofia triangularis in Natal

Kniphofia porphyrantha

Kniphofia ritualis near Mont-aux-Sources

Kniphofia rufa (yellow form)

Kniphofia thomsonii var. *snowdenii* at Beth Chatto's

Kniphofia laxiflora Kunth (*Liliaceae-Asphodelaceae*)   Native of South Africa, mainly in Natal and Transvaal. This clump-forming species is found from sea level to 2400m on the Natal Drakensberg. It is a variable species and plants known as *K. natalensis* Baker are now included in *K. laxiflora*. Flower colour varies from yellow, yellow-green, orange, salmon and orange-red. Some plants are found on grassy slopes, others among rocks flowering in February–May.

Kniphofia parviflora Kunth   Native of South Africa, from the coast of Transkei to the mountains of Natal. A solitary species growing in marshy ground and wet grassland up to

Kniphofia laxiflora near Himeville, Natal

Kniphofia parviflora on Ngeli Mountain

1800m, flowering in January–March. Unique in South African species is the secund inflorescence (flowers borne on one side of the stem only). Inflorescence narrow, 6–28cm long, with many small greenish flowers. Difficult to discern on the landscape but for its delicious fragrance, not dissimilar from that of carnations. There are a few other fragrant, small-flowered species, the most spectacular of which is *K. typhoides* Codd. This has a tall, narrow inflorescence up to 30cm long, with many fragrant purple-brown flowers. Hardy to –10°C perhaps.

Kniphofia porphyrantha Baker Native of South Africa in NW Natal, E Orange Free State, S Transvaal and W Swaziland. This clump-forming species is usually found growing in groups in grassland at 1000m–2500m in the Orange Free State Drakensberg. The inflorescence is shortly cylindrical, almost globose, with reddish buds opening to yellow flowers tinted with pale yellowish green. A most attractive small species. Leaves smooth-margined. Flowering October–December, but later higher up in the mountains. Hardy to –15°C.

Kniphofia ritualis Codd Native of South Africa in Orange Free State, Natal and Lesotho, and in N Transvaal on the Wolkberg, usually at 2100–3000m on the Drakensberg escarpment and outlying sandstone hills, growing in clumps in damp grassland, flowering in January–

March. Leaves strongly serrulate, flower buds orange-red, becoming greenish yellow as they open. *K. sarmentosa* (Andr.) Kunth is similar, but has orange-red flowers and leaves with smooth margins. Hardy to –10°C.

Kniphofia rufa Baker Native of South Africa mainly along the Natal Drakensberg, growing beside mountain streams and in wet grassland at up to 2100m, flowering from November until early April. There are three distinct colour forms; coral red, white and yellow. The yellow form resembles the closely related *K. ichopensis* Baker ex Schinz. which is generally larger with longer flowers 3–4.2cm long (1.9–3cm in *K. rufa*). Both species have characteristically lax inflorescences with the individual flowers hanging down gracefully. Hardy to –15°C perhaps.

Kniphofia thodei Baker Native of South Africa in E Orange Free State, Natal, Transkei and Lesotho, growing as solitary plants in moist grassland at 1500m–2800m, flowering in January–February. The typical form is bicolorous with reddish buds opening into waxy white flowers in a short globular inflorescence. Another form on Ngeli mountain has narrow, red, tubular flowers with a white rim at the end of the tube. Hardy to –15°C perhaps.

Kniphofia thomsonii Baker var. *snowdenii* (C. H. Wright) Marais Native of C Africa, in Uganda and Kenya. A solitary species found in

wet grassland at 1800m–3900m, flowering in November–April. The tall, lax inflorescences carry pendulous flowers which are yellow, orange or red. This is one of several species found on the slopes of the high Central African mountains. Now considered a variety of *K. thomsonii*, var. *snowdenii* has hairs in the lower part of the flower tube whereas var. *thomsonii* is quite smooth. This plant is grown outside in sheltered areas of Britain with fair success provided the soil is not wet and cold in winter. It has the great advantage of sending up a succession of flowers from midsummer until the frost. Hardy to –10°C perhaps.

Kniphofia triangularis Kunth Native of South Africa, from E Cape Province, E Orange Free State, C & S Natal, in the Drakensberg, and Lesotho, growing in moist, peaty grassland at 1800–2000m, flowering in January–April. A variable species with red concolorous inflorescences which now includes plants previously known as *K. nelsonii* Mast. and *K. macowanii* Baker. Plants with narrow leaves 1–3mm wide, with serrulate margins come under subsp. *triangularis*, whilst plants with broader leaves 3–10mm wide with smooth margins come under subsp. *obtusiloba* (Berger) Codd. One of the hardiest species, forming small clumps, which flowers very freely with adequate summer rain. Hardy to –15°C perhaps.

'Orange Torch'

'Limeade'

Kniphofia
fluviatilis

'Yellow
Hammer'

'Little Maid'

Seedling 1

'Green Jade'

'Strawberries
and Cream'

Seedling 2

Specimens from Beth Chatto, 17 August. ¼ life size

Kniphofia cultivars or red-hot pokers   Most species of *Kniphofia* cross very easily and numerous garden hybrids have been raised and named. The following is a selection mostly of the smaller hybrids. All do best in moist, sandy soil in full sun and are hardy to −10°C or less for short periods.

'Brimstone'   A late-flowering hybrid, with stems to 1m and a slender inflorescence. Graham Thomas reports that it is of 'imperturbable hardiness'.

'Green Jade'   This is a seedling selected from plants in Sir Cedric Morris's Suffolk garden grown at the Beth Chatto Gardens in 1968. Beth Chatto has since raised other green cultivars but regards this original very highly. It is a robust, clump-forming plant producing rich-green spikes of flowers on 120cm-tall stems. Flowering in late summer.

'Ice Queen'   This seedling was selected by Alan Bloom. The stems can reach 1.5m, and are produced late in the season, usually in October, until the frost. The flowers are at their palest in cool weather.

'Limeade'   A hybrid of medium height, about 1.2m, raised by Beth Chatto; flowers intense green.

'Little Maid'   A Beth Chatto favourite, this little *Kniphofia* was selected from her garden in the late 1960s. It is a small, clump-forming plant with narrow, grassy leaves and flower spikes up to 60cm tall. The buds are pale-green, sometimes faintly pink-tinged, opening to clear-white flowers. It flowers from late summer onwards.

'Mount Etna'   Previously known as 'Wallenden's Mount Etna', named after a northern breeder. This has *K. linearifolia* in it and makes a large clump-forming plant. Tall stems to 120cm with red buds, flowers creamy; inflorescence long and dense.

'Orange Torch'   A tall orange-yellow, raised by Beth Chatto. Stems to 1.5m.

'Painted Lady'   A hybrid of medium height, about 1.5m, flowering in late summer. Flowers orange in bud, opening creamy white.

'Spanish Gold'   A tall, stout hybrid to 1.5m; flowers green in bud, opening rich yellow.

'Strawberries and Cream'   A dwarf, with stems c.60cm, raised by Beth Chatto.

'Yellow Hammer'   A plant of medium height, c.1m, raised by Slieve Donard Nursery in Northern Ireland. A good, rich yellow.

Unnamed seedling 1   Called 'Red and maize yellow'; this is a seedling of medium height, c.1.2m. Possibly 'Toasted Corn'.

Unnamed seedling 2   This has stems around 1.2m, with a rather short head of flowers, of clear bicolour, red and yellow.

Kniphofia fluviatilis Codd. (*Asphodelaceae*) Native of South Africa in Natal, NE Orange Free State, E Transvaal. A clump-forming species usually found with its feet in water (*fluviatilis* = of rivers) growing on streamsides from 1000–2500m in the sandstone foothills and main range of the Drakensberg mountains, flowering in November–January. Inflorescence conical up to 80cm tall. The buds are orange or flame-yellow, with the long tubular flowers apricot or greenish yellow. The flowers may be 4.5cm long, longer than in most species.

Kniphofia 'Ice Queen'

Kniphofia 'Mount Etna'

Kniphofia 'Spanish Gold' at Wisley

Kniphofia 'Painted Lady' at Abbey Dore Court

Kniphofia 'Little Maid' in Beth Chatto's nursery

Kniphofia 'Brimstone' with a *Verbascum*

Kniphofia 'Green Jade' at Wisley

Kniphofia 'Lord Roberts'

Kniphofia 'Underway'

Kniphofia 'Atlanta'

Kniphofia 'Gold Else'

Kniphofia 'Atlanta' (*Asphodelaceae*)   Found in the garden of Atlanta Hotel, Tintagel, Cornwall. This is a large clump-forming cultivar with a bicoloured inflorescence of red and cream above glaucous foliage. Early summer flowering, the stems reach 120cm high.

Kniphofia 'Erecta'   An oddity in the *Kniphofia* world with flowers which turn upside down, giving the inflorescence a curious shape. It was sent from France in 1903 and has been cultivated ever since. The strong reddish-pink colour is constant on spikes 100cm high above large clumps of leaves.

Kniphofia 'Goldelse'   Raised by Wallace in 1906. A dwarf hybrid between the endangered *K. pauciflora* Baker and the more robust globular-headed *K. citrina* Baker. A diminutive species with small yellow inflorescences to 75cm, making small clumps which flower in mid-summer.

Kniphofia 'Lord Roberts'   A fine, old, clump-forming cultivar close to, if not synonymous with, 'John Benary'. The scarlet buds and flowers create a uniformly coloured elongated inflorescence, which may reach 120cm in height, flowering in late summer.

Kniphofia 'Lye End'   Flower spikes 100cm, with long inflorescences consisting of pinkish-red buds on top of white flowers. Raised by A. M. Pole in 1976, flowering from July onwards above large clumps of stiff, green leaves.

Kniphofia 'Royal Standard'   Raised by Prichard in 1921, with stout stems to 100cm high and bicoloured pokers of scarlet buds opening to bright-yellow flowers. A handsome clump-forming plant which flowers in midlate summer.

Kniphofia 'Samuel's Sensation'   Justifiably one of the best cultivars in recent years. Free-flowering, bright-scarlet flowers with a hint of yellow on the oldest flowers near the base. Tall, uniformly elegant spikes which are elongate in shape, stems 150cm high above green leaves. Plants in large clumps, flowering from late summer onwards.

Kniphofia 'Underway'   Raised by the great gardener Norman Hadden in Somerset between the World Wars, probably a cultivar of *K. triangularis*. A grassy-leaved plant which makes small clumps with slender spikes of pale orange to 80cm in autumn.

Kniphofia 'Erecta'

Kniphofia 'Lye End' in the monocot borders at Wisley

Kniphofia 'Royal Standard'

Kniphofia 'Samuel's Sensation' in the trial at Wisley

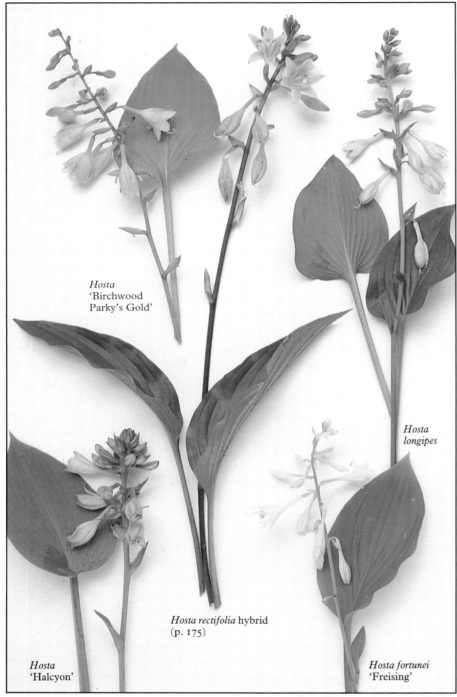

Hosta
'Birchwood
Parky's Gold'

Hosta
longipes

Hosta rectifolia hybrid
(p. 175)

Hosta
'Halcyon'

Hosta fortunei
'Freising'

Specimens from Wisley, 17 August. ⅓ life size

Hosta minor

Hosta tardiflora at Washfield Nurseries

Hosta 'Birchwood Parky's Gold'   Leaves heart-shaped, 10cm × 5cm, golden green with wavy edge, 5–6 pairs of veins. Plant forming a mound *c*.46cm high. Shade to three-quarters sun. Flowers pale purple, in August.

Hosta fortunei (Baker) Bailey 'Freising' (*Liliaceae-Hostaceae*)   Native of Honshu. Leaves green 36cm × 20cm, puckered; plant forming a mound 80cm high; for shade to half-shade; flowers white, in July.

Hosta 'Halcyon'   Leaves blue-grey, 18cm × 10cm. Plant forming a large mound 30cm high. Veins 10–12. Fades in colour if it gets too much sun, so best in full shade. Flowers violet, in August.

Hosta hypoleuca Murata   Native of C Honshu, growing in crevices on damp cliffs. Leaves thin textured, 38cm × 30cm, pale green, with distinctive powdery-white coating on the underside, with 8 pairs of veins. Plant forming a mound 30cm high. For shade to partial shade. Flowers on tall stems almost white, in July.

Hosta longipes (Franch. & Sav.) Matsumura   Native of Japan. Leaves dark green, 15cm × 8cm, with 7–8 pairs of veins. Plant forming a mound 15cm high. Flowers and leaf stems with dark-brown spots. For shade to three-quarters sun. Drought-tolerant. Flowers pale lilac and sometimes bluish, in late August–September.

Hosta minor (Baker) Nakai   Native of S Japan and Korea. Leaves 8cm × 5cm, winged, broadly ovate, dark green, with 4 or 5 pairs of veins, petioles winged. For shade to half-shade. Flowers bluish purple.

Hosta tardiflora (Irving) Stearn   Not known in the wild. Leaves 10–15cm long, 3–4cm wide, tapering into the stalk; deep green, with 4–5 pairs of veins. Flowers late, with a dense head of flowers 4–4.5cm long.

Hosta ventricosa Stearn   Native of China. Leaves 18cm × 12cm, heart-shaped, pointed, dark glossy green, with 8–9 pairs of veins. Plant forming a mound 60cm high. For shade to half shade. Inflorescence tall, to 90cm, rising far above the leaves; without vestigial leaves; flowers dark violet, in August.

Hosta ventricosa var. *aureomaculata* Henson syn. *H. ventricosa* 'Maculata'   Leaves with a yellowish-green centre with a dark-green margin, but the central colour darkens in the summer until the leaves are uniform dark green. For shade to half-shade. Flowers violet, in August.

Hosta ventricosa 'Aureo-marginata'   Leaves 18cm × 15cm, heart-shaped, twisted, with an irregular yellowish margin which matures white. Plant forming a mound 45cm high, and persisting until the first frosts. Shade to three-quarters sun. Flowers mauve, in July.

Hosta ventricosa in the Wild Garden at Wisley

Hosta ventricosa var. *aureomaculata*

Hosta species on a wet cliff in C Honshu

Hosta hypoleuca in Honshu

Hosta ventricosa 'Aureo-marginata'

Hosta 'Halcyon'

Specimens from Goldbrook Nurseries, 20 August. ⅓ life size

Hosta crispula Maekawa (*Liliaceae-Hostaceae*) Leaves 10cm × 20cm, oval with a long point often twisted back underneath, dark green with a broad white margin and wavy edges, with 7–8 pairs of veins. Wide mound up to 40cm tall, but subject to damage from cold winds. Flowers 30 or more on a green scape, pale lavender. Shade to half-shade, flowering in late June–July.

Hosta 'Fall Emerald'   Introduced by Alex Summers. Close to *H. sieboldii* with large, bright-green leaves which hold their colour longer. Flowers in June–July.

Hosta fortunei 'Albo-marginata'   Leaves sage green with a white edge. Mound 35cm high. Stays in good condition until the first frost. Shade to three-quarters sun. Flowers lavender, in July.

Hosta fortunei var. *albopicta*   Leaves bright yellow, edged with pale green, gradually fading until the yellow is nearly the same as the edge by mid-summer. Mound 60cm high. Shade to three-quarters sun. Flowers elegant, pale lavender, in July–early August.

Hosta fortunei var. *aureomarginata*   Leaves with a distinct wide golden edge. Shade to three-quarters sun.

Hosta fortunei 'Francee'   Introduced by Klopping. Leaves 15cm × 13cm, forest-green with white margins. Rapid grower to mound of 30cm high. Shade to three-quarters sun. Flowers lavender in August–early September.

Hosta fortunei 'Goldbrook'   Registered by Mrs S. Bond. Leaves mid-green with a wide creamy white margin and a rather wavy edge. Shade to three-quarters sun. Flowers violet, in July.

Hosta fortunei 'Spinners'   Registered by Peter Chappell. Leaves with a very wide irregular white margin. Shade to three-quarters sun. Flowers violet, in July.

Hosta lancifolia (Thunb.) Engler   Native of Japan. Leaves lance-shaped 15cm × 5cm, dark glossy green, with 4–5 pairs of veins. Mound

Hosta fortunei var. *albopicta*

Hosta fortunei var. *aureomarginata*

30cm high. Needs shade, or not more than half-shade at most. Flowers purple, in August.

Hosta 'Northern Halo' Registered by Walters Gardens in 1984. *H. sieboldiana* 'Elegans' sport. Leaves 26cm × 30cm, blue-green with an irregular creamy white margin, slightly cupped upward, with puckering between the 14 pairs of veins. Shade to half-shade. Flowers on one-sided scapes, white with a hint of purple, in late June–July.

Hosta sieboldiana (Hook.) Engler & Prantl Native of Honshu. Leaves large and sumptuous, bluish grey-green 30cm × 35cm, heavily puckered with a lovely bloom at first, forming large mound. Shade to three-quarters sun. Flowers white with just a hint of violet on short stems, in July.

Hosta sieboldiana var. *elegans* Leaves round, bluish, heavily puckered, 30cm × 35cm, forming a magnificent clump. Shade to half-shade. Flowers white with just a hint of lilac on rather short stems that nestle attractively among the leaves, in July.

Hosta sieboldiana 'Frances Williams' Leaves bluish green with wide irregular yellowish margins 36cm × 20cm, puckered. Forms a magnificent mound 80cm high. Shade to half-shade. Flowers pale lavender, in July.

Hosta sieboldii var. *alba* syn. *H. albomarginata* var. *alba* The word 'alba' refers to the colour of the flowers which are white. Leaves bright green, 13cm × 4cm, with 3–4 pairs of veins. Mound 30cm high. Shade to half-shade. Flowers white, on rather tall scapes, in August.

Hosta 'True Blue' Registered by Paul Aden. Leaves broad, 20cm × 18cm, a good blue-green, puckered, with 11–14 pairs of veins. Keeps its colour well in sun, a quarter to three-quarters sun. Flowers delicate mauve with white edges, in July–early August.

Hosta undulata var. *albomarginata* syn. 'Thomas Hogg' Leaves lanceolate, green, with an irregular creamy white margin which continues down the stem, 20cm × 8cm. Mound 30cm high. Shade to half-shade. Flowers lilac, on tall scapes in late June–July.

Hosta 'Fall Emerald'

Hosta sieboldiana

Hosta sieboldiana var. *elegans*

Hosta sieboldiana 'Frances Williams'

Specimens from the Savill Gardens, Windsor, 10 July. ⅕ life size

Hosta sieboldii var. *alba*

Hosta 'True Blue'

Hosta decorata
f. decorata

Hosta 'Ginko Craig'

Hosta fortunei
'Phyllis Campbell'

Hosta montana
'Aureomarginata'

Hosta fortunei
'Gold Standard'

Hosta fortunei 'Green Gold'

Specimens from the Savill Gardens, Windsor, 17 July. ½ life size

Hosta montana 'Aureomarginata' at Wisley

Hosta fortunei 'Gold Standard' at Goldbrook Plants, Suffolk

Hosta 'Zounds' at Goldbrook Plants, Suffolk

Hosta 'Sum and Substance' at Goldbrook Plants, Suffolk

Hosta decorata Bailey f. *decorata* (*Hostaceae*) Leaves 8cm × 13cm, oval, pointed with a narrow, white, slightly wavy margin, with 5–6 pairs of veins. The variegated form came to Europe before the all-green form, which is called *H. decorata* f. *normalis*. Plant 26cm high. Stem tall with dark-lilac flowers in July–early August; the seed heads are good for flower arranging. Shade to half-sun.

Hosta fortunei 'Gold Standard' Introduced by Pauline Banyai in 1976. Yellow leaves with green edges or tending to green in the shade, blotched, 18cm × 13cm. Plant 60cm high; a rapid grower which gives the best colour when mature. A quarter to three quarters sun. Flowers pale lavender, in July–early August.

Hosta fortunei 'Green Gold' Leaves with a satin sheen, heart-shaped, with a gold margin

which fades gradually with age. A quarter to three-quarters sun. Flowers pale lavender, in July–early August.

Hosta fortunei 'Phyllis Campbell' Leaves green, firm, not wavy edged, splashed with yellow in the centre. Shade to half-sun. Flowers lavender, in July.

Hosta 'Ginko Craig' Introduced by Alex Craig-Summers, who reputedly found it in a Japanese market. It is named for his Japanese wife. Leaves frosted green with a narrow white edge. Makes an attractive flat rosette even when young, in older plants the leaves are larger. Flowers good, purple on tall stems.

Hosta montana Maekawa **'Aureomarginata'** Leaves large, 35cm × 26cm, elongated, heart-shaped, rich green with irregular yellow

margins, deeply veined with 13–17 pairs. Plant 65cm tall, 100cm wide. Shade to three-quarters sun. Stems 100cm with densely grouped pale-lavender flowers in July–August.

Hosta 'Sum and Substance' Registered by Paul Aden in 1980. Leaves strong golden yellow, more greenish if not in strong light, 30cm × 26cm, thick and tough. Plant up to 75cm across, pest-resistant. Flowers lavender, in August–early September.

Hosta 'Zounds' Introduced by Paul Aden. Leaves golden metallic colour 20cm × 18cm. Plant up to 35cm. A quarter to three-quarters sun. Flowers pale lavender, in July–early August.

HOSTA

Hosta rohdeifolia

Hosta sieboldii f. *kabitan*

Hosta sieboldii f. *shiro-kabitan*

Hosta kikutii var. *polyneura*

Hosta sieboldii

H. sieboldii 'Emerald Isle'

'Brian Martin'

Hosta sieboldii 'Inaho'

Hosta longissima

Hosta undulata var. *univittata*

Hosta capitata

'Gloriosa'

Specimens from Goldbrook Plants, 20 August. ⅓ life size

Hosta capitata (Koidzumi) Nakai (*Hostaceae*) Heart-shaped green leaves, 13cm × 8cm, with wavy edges, 6–8 pairs of veins, forming a 26cm-high mound. Shade to three-quarters sun. Flowers purple on a purple dotted, ridged stem, in July–August.

Hosta fortunei (Baker) Bailey   Nothing definite is known of its origin and it probably should really be regarded as a hybrid. Leaves green, 18cm × 12cm, with 9–11 pairs of veins, edges rather wavy. A rapid grower to a mound 35cm high. Shade to three-quarters sun. Flowers profuse, violet, in July.

Hosta 'Green Fountain'   Registered by Paul Aden in 1979. A cultivar of *H. kikutii*. Leaves 25cm × 8cm, shiny green in a dense mound 90cm high. Pest-resistant and sun-tolerant. Flowers lavender, in August–September.

Hosta japonica (Lam.) Asch. syn. var. *grandiflora* (Sieb.) A. & G.   Native of China. Leaves 20cm × 30cm, cordate, large without bloom, glossy, bright yellowish green. Flowers white, scented, large with vestigial leaves on a 75cm-high scape, in August. This plant will stand quite a lot of sun. *H. plantaginea* 'Honeybells' has pinkish flower buds and a faint pink flush to the flowers. Flowers late August–September.

Hosta kikutii Maekawa   Native of Kyushu. Leaves 23cm × 3cm, glossy green, with 8–10 veins, stems short. Plant 30cm high, drought-resistant. Shade to three-quarters sun. The white flowers are on a tall, light-green stem, with bird-head-shaped bracts covering the buds, flowers in August.

Hosta longissima (Honda) Honda   Native of W Honshu. Leaves very narrow, 18cm × 2cm, with 3 pairs of veins, forming an arching mound 15cm high. This is a bog *Hosta*, and is flood-tolerant but not drought-tolerant. Shade to half-sun. Flowers few on each stem, pale violet, in September.

Hosta rectifolia 'Tallboy'   Named by Sir Eric Savill in 1968, registered in 1983. Possibly *H. rectifolia* × *H. ventricosa*. Leaves 23cm × 41cm, bright green, making a 75cm upright mound. Shade to three-quarters sun. Flowers dark lilac, about 20 on each; 90cm-tall scape, with vestigial leaves, in August–September.

Hosta 'Royal Standard' at Wisley

Hosta plantaginea var. *japonica*

396

Hosta rohdeifolia Maek. syn. *H. helonioides* hort. f. *albopicta*   Leaves elongated, 18cm × 3cm, bright green with a broad, creamy yellow margin, with 3–4 pairs of veins. Plant 26cm high. Flower stems tall, up to 60cm, with horizontal purple-striped flowers. Shade to three-quarters sun, flowering in August–early September. *H.* 'Brian Martin' is very similar, and has broader leaves with broad white or cream margin.

Hosta 'Royal Standard'   Registered by Wayside Gardens. Leaves heart-shaped, 26cm × 18cm, rich green, shiny, deeply veined and puckered with wavy edges, forming a mound 60cm high. Flowers, like its parent *H. plantaginea*, are white and fragrant, in August–September.

Hosta 'Shade Fanfare'   A sport of *H.* 'Flamboyant', introduced by Paul Aden. Leaves come early and are a good golden green in the centre, with creamy margins 20cm × 15cm. Plant 50cm high. For shade to full sun, but colours best in sun. Rapid grower, pest-resistant. Flowers beautiful lavender, in July–early August.

Hosta sieboldii (Paxton) Ingram syn. *H. albomarginata* (Hook.) Ohwi   Leaves 13cm × 4cm, wavy, dark green with a narrow white edge, with 3–4 pairs of veins. Plant 30cm high. Likes wet soils, shade to half sun. Flowers violet, in August.

Hosta sieboldii 'Emerald Isle'   Has more pointed leaves than *sieboldii*. Shade to half-sun. Flowers white, in August.

Hosta sieboldii 'Inaho' syn. *H. tardiva* hort. non Nakai   Leaves 13cm × 4cm, moss-green blotched with golden green. Shade to half-sun. Flowers purple, in August.

Hosta sieboldii f. *kabitan* Maekawa   Leaves small, yellow with a green margin, lance-shaped, 13cm × 3cm, undulate on the margins. Shade to three-quarters sun. Flowers whitish with purple veins, in August. Forma *shiro-kabitan* has leaves white, with a green margin.

Hosta undulata (O. & D.) Bailey var. *univittata* (Miq.) Hyland.   Leaves small, 4cm wide, twisted towards the tip, with a white median stripe surrounded by blue-green, both colours run down the wavy stem wings. Plant 45cm high. Shade to half-sun. Flowers rich lilac, in July.

Hosta fortunei

Hosta plantaginea 'Honeybells'

Hosta rectifolia 'Tallboy' at Wisley

Hosta 'Shade Fanfare'

Hosta 'Green Fountain' at Goldbrook Plants, Suffolk

Pontederia cordata at Wisley

Sagittaria latifolia

Dianella tasmanica

Astelia nervosa Hook. fil. (*Asteliaceae*)
Native throughout New Zealand, growing
in moist places in lowland and subalpine
forest, flowering in October–January. Plant
forming tussocks of stiff silvery leaves, to
200cm long, usually *c.*60cm in gardens. Flowers
on a short, branched inflorescence to 60cm,
green or reddish, scented. Fruits berry-like,
orange, in yellow cups formed by the persistent
petals, but seldom produced in gardens. For
moist, peaty or clay soil in shade or partial
shade. Hardy to –10°C, but best in moist,
coastal gardens in Europe and NW North
America.

Commelina tuberosa L. (*Commelinaceae*)
Native of Mexico, flowering in mid-summer.
Plant with fleshy, swollen roots. Stems to 75cm.
Leaves linear, *c.*2.5cm across; flowers usually
closing by evening. For a warm position in full
sun. Hardy to –10°C, provided the rootstock is
protected from freezing.

Dianella tasmanica Hook. (*Phorminaceae*)
Native of SE Australia, in New South Wales,
Victoria and Tasmania, growing in cool, damp,
shady forest, flowering in August–October,
fruiting in January–February, or spring and
summer in the north. Plant forming clumps of
stiff leaves to 120cm tall, 3cm wide, with rough
edges. Flowering stems to 150cm. Flowers
pale blue; anthers brownish yellow. Berries
1–2cm long. For a sheltered position in shade
with a peaty soil. Hardy to –10°C for short
periods.

Phormium cookianum Le Jolis syn. *P. colensoi*
Hook. fil. (*Phormiaceae*) Mountain Flax,
Wharariki   Native of New Zealand, and
naturalized on the Scilly Isles, growing on
coastal rocks and cliffs, and in the mountains at
up to 1500m, on rocky outcrops, flowering in
December–January. Plant with soft, lax leaves

to 1.6m long, 3.5–6.5cm wide. Flowering stems
1.3–1.6m. Flowers yellowish; fruits hanging and
usually twisted. Recommended for coastal
planting in exposed sites. Hardy to –10°C
perhaps.

Phormium tenax J. R. & G. Forst. New
Zealand Flax, Harakeke   Native of New
Zealand and Norfolk Island, and naturalized in
W Ireland, SW England and the Azores, as well
as on other Atlantic Islands such as Tristan da
Cunha where it has become a pest, growing in
lowland marshes and bogs, flowering in
November–January, or July–August in the
north. Leaves tough and leathery, evergreen, to
3m long, 5–12.5cm wide. Inflorescence to 5m.
Flowers 2.5–5cm long. Fruits erect. For any
deep soil that does not dry out, but most
striking in a warm, wet and sheltered position.
Hardy to –10°C or less for short periods.

Phormium cultivars   There are numerous
named varieties of *Phormium*, many of hybrid
origin between the two species. Most were
grown by Duncan and Davis in New Zealand
and introduced by them to Europe.
'Dazzler'   A hybrid with particularly brightly
coloured leaves, raised by W. B. Brockie in
*c.*1940.
'Sundowner'   A colour form of *P. tenax*, with
good greyish purple leaves.
Other colour forms available are indicated by
their names: 'Cream Delight', 'Apricot Queen',
'Bronze Baby', 'Yellow Wave', etc.

Pontederia cordata L. (*Pontederiaceae*)
Pickerelweed   Native of E North America,
from Prince Edward Island west to S Ontario,
south to N Florida, Missouri and Oklahoma,
growing in shallow water, flowering in June–
November. Plant forming spreading patches by
a thick, creeping rhizome. Stems fleshy to
120cm. Leaves varying from broadly ovate to

linear-lanceolate, cordate or truncate at the
base, sometimes with submerged, linear leaves
only. Flowers 8mm long, blue, in a dense spike.
For shallow water by a pond or stream. Hardy
to –25°C or less.

Sagittaria latifolia Willd. (*Alismataceae*)
Wapato, Arrowhead   Native of North
America, from New Brunswick to S British
Columbia, south to South Carolina, Alabama,
Louisiana, Arizona and California, growing in
shallow water in lakes and rivers, flowering in
July–September. Plant with a tuberous
rootstock and upright stems to 150cm. Leaves
variable in shape, sagittate, usually with a broad
main lobe and smaller, narrower basal lobes.
Flowers white, with petals unmarked; stamens
yellow. For wet soil or shallow water. Hardy to
–20°C or less. This is the common North
American Arrowhead; the European differs in
its usually narrower leaves, flowers with purple
blotches at the base of each petal, and purple
anthers.

Tradescantia × andersoniana Ludwig &
Rohweder   Most of the cultivars are said to
belong to this hybrid group, between *T.
virginiana* and other species, of which there are
ten in E North America. Colours vary from
almost blue to magenta, nearly red, pink and
white. They all require good, moist soil in sun
or light shade and flower from midsummer to
autumn. Hardy to –20°C or less.

Tradescantia virginiana L. (*Commelinaceae*)
Spiderwort   Native of E North America, from
Connecticut east to Wisconsin, south to NW
Georgia, Tennessee and Missouri, growing in
woods, scrub and meadows, flowering in
April–July. Stems many, to 35cm, from a tufted
rootstock with fleshy roots. Petals 12–18mm
long, blue to pink or white, on pedicels
1.5–3.5cm long.

Phormium 'Sundowner'

Phormium tenax naturalized in Connemara, near Ballynahinch

Phormium cookianum

Phormium 'Dazzler'

Tradescantia virginiana

Commelina tuberosa

Astelia nervosa

Tradescantia × *andersoniana*

Yucca flaccida 'Ivory'

Yucca filamentosa

Yucca 'Vittorio Emmanuele'

Beschorneria yuccoides

Yucca gloriosa 'Variegata' at Wisley

Beschorneria yuccoides Hook. subsp. **dekosteriana** (C. Koch) Garcia-Mendoza (*Agavaceae*)   Native of Mexico, in Hidalgo and Veracruz states, growing in *Liquidambar* and *Alnus* woodland in the mountains, flowering in May–June. Plant forming large clumps. Leaves 60–100cm long, green or glaucous. Inflorescence up to 2.5m, reddish. Flowers 3.5–6cm long, green, tubular. For any good soil in sun or partial shade. Hardy to −5°C.

Yucca filamentosa L. (*Agavaceae*)   Native of E North America, from S New Jersey to Florida, growing on dunes, rocky bluffs, sandy fields and dry pine forest along the coastal plain, flowering in June–September. Plant with a short, mostly underground stem. Leaves usually hooded below the spine, oblanceolate, with curled threads on the margins. Inflorescence 1.5–2m. Flowers 5–7cm long.
'Variegata''   Leaves striped with pink and cream. For dry, well-drained soil in full sun. Hardy to −20°C.

Yucca flaccida Haworth   Native of E North America, from North Carolina to Alabama, especially along the Blue Ridge and Appalachian mountains, growing in dry, stony places, flowering in May–July. Plant stemless. Leaves tapering from base to apex, with straight or slightly curled threads. Flowering stem hairy to 1.5m. Flowers 5–8cm long. For well-drained, sandy soil in full sun. Hardy to −15°C.
'Ivory'   A short form with stems to 1.2m, very free-flowering, raised by G. R. Jackman.

Yucca gloriosa L. 'Variegata'   Native of SE North America, from South Carolina to NE Florida, growing on sand dunes and stony places by the sea, flowering in July–August. Plant with a sometimes branched woody trunk to 8m, usually up to *c.*1m. Leaves 40–60cm long, 5–7.5cm wide, with a sharp, stiff point. Flowers to 5.5cm long, often tinged purple. For a dry, sunny and sheltered position. Hardy to −25°C perhaps.

Yucca recurvifolia Salisb.   Native of E North America, from Georgia to Missouri and E Louisiana, growing on dunes on the coastal plains, flowering in July–September. Stems in clumps, woody, to 5m, usually less than 2m. Leaves soft, recurved towards the apex, *c.*5cm wide. Inflorescence to 120cm. Flowers 5–7cm long. For a warm, dry position in well-drained soil. Hardy to −15°C perhaps.

Yucca 'Vittorio Emanuele II'   Close to *Y. gloriosa*, with exceptionally heavily marked flowers. Similar purplish-flowered cultivars have been raised in Tashkent Botanic Garden.

Yucca whipplei Torr. Our Lord's Candle   Native of S California, north to Monterey Co., and in Baja California, growing on dry, grassy hills and in scrub and chaparral, flowering in April–June. Plant stemless, often monocarpic, with a bulbous base, but in subsp. *percursa* suckering to form young plants, and in subsp. *caespitosa* and subsp. *intermedia* forming clumps of rosettes. Leaves to 100cm long, 10mm wide, with a terminal spine 1–2cm long. Inflorescence 1.5–2.5m, sometimes to 3.5m. Flowers pendent 2.5–3.5cm long, often purplish outside, sweet-scented. For a warm, sunny, sheltered position in full sun. Hardy to −10°C for short periods; has survived to flowering outside at Kew and at Bodnant in North Wales. *Yucca newberryi* McKelvey from NW Arizona is very similar.

Yucca filamentosa 'Variegata'

Yucca whipplei near New Cuyama, California

Yucca flaccida

Yucca recurvifolia

Agapanthus campanulatus subsp. *patens* on Mont-aux-Sources, Orange Free State

Agapanthus campanulatus subsp. *patens*

Agapanthus caulescens

Agapanthus nutans 'Albus'

Agapanthus inapertus subsp. *hollandii*

Agapanthus campanulatus subsp. *patens* F. M. Leighton (*Alliaceae*) See p. 405.

Agapanthus caulescens Spreng.   Native of Swaziland, with subsp. *angustifolius* in NE Natal, in the Ubombo area, growing in grassy places, flowering in January–February. Plant with distinct leek-like stems to the leaves, with short, lower leaves to 15cm, and upper leaves, usually stiff, to 60cm and 4cm or more broad. Inflorescence to 130cm, with a dense head of spreading and drooping flowers. Flowers 3–5cm long, with the tube 1–2cm, and wide-spreading petals, recurved in subsp. *gracilis* Leighton. This last is similar to *A. campanulatus*, though separated in the wild, and usually with larger flowers in a more crowded umbel. For any good soil in full sun. Hardy to −10°C perhaps.

Agapanthus dyeri Leighton   Native of the Transvaal, in the Blaauberg, on the Mohlakeng plateau, and of S Mozambique, at *c.*1800m perhaps, flowering in January–February. Plant clump-forming, with stems to 90cm. Leaves deciduous, to 1.5cm broad. Flowers in umbels of *c.*35, ascending in bud, but more or less hanging when open. The tube 1.3–1.4cm long, sometimes curved; the segments to 11mm long, usually rather pale blue. Like *A. inapertus* but with a shorter tube and more spreading lobes. For well-drained soil in a warm position. Hardy to −10°C perhaps, as it survives at Kew.

Agapanthus inapertus Beauv. subsp. *hollandii* Leighton   Native of the E Transvaal in the Lydenberg area. This differs from the other subspecies in its narrower but more wide-spreading petals, which are generally blue. Hardy to −10°C perhaps.

Agapanthus inapertus Beauv. subsp. *intermedius* Leighton   Native of the Transvaal and Swaziland, mainly on the periphery of the area of the other subspecies; flowers 2.5–4.5cm long, opening at the mouth, with the lobes and tube about equal. It seems likely that it is the result of hybridization with other species in the wild, and the photograph shown here, of a garden plant, is possibly another such hybrid.

Agapanthus inapertus subsp. *pendulus* (L. Bol.) Leighton   Native of the E Transvaal in the Lydenberg, Belfast and Dullstroom areas, often above 2000m, growing in grassy veldt or in clearings in forest, flowering in January–February. Plant forming clumps of rather upright deciduous leaves, 2–3cm across. Flowering stems tall, to 180cm. Flowers fleshy, hanging, 2.5–4cm long, the tube making up ⅔ of the flower, often purplish and sometimes very dark in colour; the segments are barely open at the mouth. For any good garden soil. Hardy to −10°C, or less with protection. The dark-coloured forms of this species are particularly fine.

Agapanthus nutans Leighton   Native of scattered localities in Natal and C Transvaal, growing on grassy slopes and cliff ledges, flowering in January–February. Plant forming clumps; leaves usually erect, often glaucous, 20–50cm long, to 4cm broad. Inflorescence to 90cm, usually not greatly exceeding the leaves. Umbels few or many-flowered. Flowers blue or white in 'Albus' (shown here): tube 1.3–2.7cm long, segments 2.2–3.3cm, spreading gradually to the mouth, not reflexed. For any good soil in full sun. Hardy to −15°C, or less with protection. Generally a rather low plant with broad leaves and long, slender flowers without reflexed petals.

Agapanthus nutans

Agapanthus dyeri at Kew

Agapanthus inapertus subsp. *intermedius*

Agapanthus inapertus subsp. *pendulus* in Natal

Agapanthus inapertus subsp. *pendulus*

Agapanthus
'Buckingham Palace'

Agapanthus
'Rosemary'

Agapanthus
'Luly'

Agapanthus
comptoni subsp.
longitubus

Agapanthus
'Diana'

Agapanthus campanulatus
subsp. patens

Agapanthus 'Molly Howick'

Agapanthus campanulatus
subsp. campanulatus

Specimens from the Savill Gardens, Windsor, 28 August. ⅓ life size

Agapanthus 'Ben Hope'

Agapanthus 'Loch Hope' at the Savill Garden, Windsor

Agapanthus campanulatus F. M. Leighton subsp. *campanulatus* (*Alliaceae*) Native of South Africa, in Natal, and N Cape Province, at no great altitude, growing in grassy and rocky places, often among bracken and in moist, peaty soil, flowering in December–February, or July–August in the northern hemisphere. Plant forming large clumps of thick, fleshy roots in gardens, often more or less solitary in the wild. Leaves deciduous, up to 2.5cm wide, forming a short leek-like stalk. Flowering stems up to 1m or more. Flowers 2–3.5cm long, blue, or white in 'Albus', which is most beautiful. Petals spreading to 45°. For rich, well-drained, sandy soil in full sun, with water in summer. Hardy to −15°C, or less if the rhizomes are protected. *Agapanthus campanulatus* subsp. *patens* F.M. Leighton differs in its more widely spreading petals and short tube. It is found at higher altitudes, up to 2400m, throughout the Drakensberg and north to the Transvaal. Stems 40–70cm. Probably the hardiest of the species, to −15°C, at least.

Agapanthus comptoni F. M. Leighton subsp. *longitubus* F. M. Leighton Native of South Africa, in E Cape Province, on the coast around East London, Port Elizabeth, and Grahamstown, flowering in January–February. Plant forming clumps in gardens. Leaves evergreen, to 2cm across. Flowers up to 6.5cm long, with the tube 2–2.5cm, in a few to many-flowered, but not dense, inflorescence, on a stem to 100cm. For well-drained soil, on full sun, with water in summer. Hardy to −10°C, perhaps less.

Agapanthus 'Headbourne Hybrids' Most hardy (z.6–9) *Agapanthus* are sold under the name 'Headbourne Hybrids'. These were raised by the Hon. Lewis Palmer in his garden at Headbourne Worthy, Hampshire, in the late 1940s from seeds which originated in the *Agapanthus* collection in Kirstenbosch Botanic Gardens in Cape Town. He raised around 300 seedlings, all of which proved to be hybrids, and from these selected the named varieties listed below. The best were sent for trial at Wisley, and judged there over a period of several years, but, good though they are, they are not generally available because they are slow to propagate. Seedlings called 'Headbourne

Agapanthus campanulatus 'Albus'

Agapanthus 'Bressingham Blue'

Hybrids' are usually deciduous like *A. campanulatus*, but with larger flowers. Named varieties shown here were all raised by Lewis Palmer, with the exception of 'Bressingham Blue', which was raised by Alan Bloom.
'Ben Hope' Height to 1.2m.
'Bressingham Blue' Height 70–80cm. An exceptionally deep blue, with rather tubular flowers, showing the influence of *A. inapertus* subsp. *pendulus*.
'Buckingham Palace' Height to 1.8m.
'Delft' Height to 1m.
'Diana' (AM 1977) Height to 45cm.
'Loch Hope' (AM 1977) Height to 1.5m.
'Luly' (FCC 1977) Height to 75cm.
'Molly Howick' (AM 1977) Height to 75cm.
'Rosemary' (AM 1977) Height to 1.4m.

Agapanthus 'Delft'

Hemerocallis flava

Hemerocallis minor

Hemerocallis yezoensis

Hemerocallis flava 'Major'

Hemerocallis forrestii

Specimens from Beth Chatto's, 9 June. ¼ life size

Hemerocallis dumortieri at the Royal Botanic Garden, Edinburgh

Hemerocallis middendorfii

Hemerocallis altissima Stout (*Liliaceae*) The plant shown here appears to be close to *H. thunbergii*, with tall stems to 1.5m and pale-yellow, long-tubed flowers, flowering in July–September. Several cultivars have been raised from this, now incorporating different flower colours on strong slender stems up to 1.8m. Examples are 'Autumn Minaret', golden yellow; 'Challenger', brick-red with a yellow throat; and 'Statuesque' with pale-yellow flowers of a good shape.

Hemerocallis citrina Baroni   Native of China, but wild distribution uncertain, flowering in gardens in June–July. Plant forming large clumps of leaves 70–80cm long. Flowering stems longer than the leaves. Many-flowered (20–65 flowers). Flowers 9–12cm long, with narrow, lemon-yellow petals, scented, opening at night; tube ⅓ the length of the flower. For any good soil with ample water in summer. Hardy to −20°C or less.

Hemerocallis dumortieri Morr.   Native of Japan in Hokkaido and N & C Honshu, E Siberia, NE China and Korea, growing in meadows in the mountains, flowering in May–June. Plant forming large clumps of flopping leaves. Flowering stems 25–50cm, as long as, or slightly shorter than, the leaves. Flowers few, ascending, with very short stalks hidden by broad bracts, 5–7cm long with a tube *c*.1cm long. Inner petals less than 2cm, usually *c*.1.2cm wide. For any good, moist soil in sun or partial shade. Hardy to −20°C or less.

Hemerocallis exaltata Stout   Native of Tobishima Island, off the west coast of N Honshu, growing in meadows, flowering in June–July. Plant similar to *H. middendorfii* (q.v.), but with taller stems to 1m or more, and longer pedicels, almost forming an umbel. Flowers orange-yellow. For any good, moist soil. Hardy to −15°C, possibly less.

Hemerocallis forrestii Diels   Native of SW China, especially in the Lijiang range at *c*.3000m growing in grassy places, flowering in June–July. Roots cylindrical, swollen towards the ends. Leaves rather lush and broad to 1.5cm wide. Inflorescence about equalling the leaves, or shorter. Flowers *c*.7cm long, with the tube less than ¼ the length. Anthers blackish. For moist soil in sun or partial shade.

Hemerocallis fulva L.   Probably native of China and Japan but not known in the wild state (all plants are sterile triploids); widely naturalized in Europe and North America by

Hemerocallis fulva var. *littorea*

Hemerocallis fulva 'Kwanso'

spread of pieces of rhizome. Plant forming large clumps of bright, pale leaves. Stems to 120cm. Flowers 7–10cm, the tube about 2.5cm long, brownish orange with darker markings inside. '**Kwanso**' has double flowers, very strongly marked inside. For any position in rich soil or near water. Hardy to −20°C or less.

Hemerocallis fulva L. var. *littorea* Mak. Native of Japan, in W Honshu and Kyushu, growing in grassy places near the sea, flowering in August–October. Plant similar to *H. fulva*, but smaller with leaves dark green, and narrower, up to 15mm wide. Flowers 10–12cm long, the tube 1.5–2cm long. Inner petals subacute, about 2cm wide. Seeds fertile. For any good soil in full sun. Hardy to −15°C perhaps. This may be one of the diploid parents of *H. fulva* itself.

Hemerocallis lilioasphodelus L. syn. *H. flava* L.   Native of E Siberia and N China, growing in grassy places, flowering in May–June. Roots tuberous, with spreading rhizomes. Leaves 50–60cm long, 1–1.4cm wide. Flowers scented, 7–8cm long, or larger in 'Major'; tube about ¼ the length of the flower. Capsule large, broadly elliptic. For any good, moist soil in sun or partial shade. Hardy to −25°C or less.

Hemerocallis middendorffii Trautv. & Mey. Native of Japan, in Hokkaido and of E Siberia, N China and Korea, growing in mountain meadows, flowering in June–July, later than *H. dumortieri*. Plant forming large clumps. Flowering stems to 70cm or more, longer than the leaves. Flowers 8–10cm long, orange-yellow, the inner petals 2–2.5cm wide, obtuse.

Hemerocallis minor Mill.   Native of N China, growing in scrub on rocky hillsides, flowering in May–June. Recorded by Roy Lancaster growing along the Great Wall north of Beijing. Roots not tuberous, slender, cylindrical and fibrous. Rhizomes not spreading. Leaves narrow, 30–45cm long, 5–9mm wide. Flowers 5–7cm with a long tube, more than ¼ the length of the flower. Capsule narrowly elliptic. For moist, sandy soil in full sun. Hardy to −25°C or less.

Hemerocallis yezoensis Hara   Native of Japan in Hokkaido, growing in grassy places and marshy meadows near the sea, flowering in May–June. Roots slender, not swollen. Leaves broad, pale green to 1.5cm wide. Inflorescence to 50–80cm. Flowers opening in the day, 7–8cm long, with a rather short tube. For moist soil in full sun. Hardy to −25°C or less.

Hemerocallis fulva

Hemerocallis altissima

Hemerocallis citrina

Hemerocallis exaltata

Hemerocallis 'Hyperion'

Hemerocallis 'Golden Chimes'

Hemerocallis 'Burford'

Hemerocallis 'Stella d'Oro'

Hemerocallis 'Marion Vaughan'

Hemerocallis 'Astolat'

Hemerocallis 'Astolat'   Introduced by V. L. Peck in 1974. Height 71cm. Flowers 16cm across, near-white self with a green throat. Parents: 'Tetra Catherine Woodbery' × seedling. Tetraploid. Mid- to late season.

'Burford' Details not known.

'Cherry Ripe'   Introduced by L. W. Brummitt in 1959. Height 90cm. Flowers orangey red with a yellow stripe. Parents: 'Royal Ruby' × 'Pink Prelude'. Mid-season.

'Golden Chimes'   Introduced by H. A. Fischer in 1954. Height tall, 115cm. Flowers chrome, yellow self. Parents: 'Bijou' × 'Kraus'. Early to mid-season.

'Hope Diamond'   Introduced by M. McMillan in 1968. Height 36cm. Flowers 10cm across, nearly pure-white self. Parents: 'President Giles' × seedling. Remontant. Early to mid-season.

'Hyperion'   Raised in 1925 by Franklin B. Mead. Rigid stems to 100cm. Flowers pale yellow. Scented. Early to mid-season. Deciduous.

'Luminous Jewel'   Introduced by F. Childs in 1974. Height 71cm. Flowers 15cm across, near-white self with mint-green throat. Remontant. Mid-season.

'Marion Vaughn'   Introduced by K. D. Smith in 1951. Height tall, 105cm. Flowers lemon-yellow with a white midrib on the petals. Mid-season.

'Pardon Me'   Introduced by D. A. Apps in 1982. Height 60cm. Flowers bright-red, self with yellow-green throat. Parents: 'Little Grapette' × seedling. Remontant. Fragrant. Mid-season.

'Red Precious' syn. 'Red Diamond' Introduced by R. H. Coe in 1969. Height 55cm. Flowers 9cm, brilliant-red self. Evergreen. Mid- to late-season.

'Stafford'   Introduced by H. J. Randall in 1959. Height 71cm. Flowers glowing crimson, with greenish yellow throat. Mid-season.

'Starling'   Introduced by C. Klehm in 1979. Height 71cm. Flowers 15cm across, brown-purple blend. Tetraploid. Early to mid-season.

'Stella d'Oro'   Introduced by W. Jablonski in 1975. Height to only 28cm. Flowers 5.6cm, gold self, with very small green throat. Deciduous, fragrant. Remontant. Mid-season.

Hemerocallis 'Cherry Ripe'

Hemerocallis 'Red Precious'

Hemerocallis 'Stafford'

Hemerocallis 'Pardon Me'

Hemerocallis 'Starling'

Hemerocallis 'Luminous Jewel'

Hemerocallis 'Hope Diamond'

'Wally Nance' 'Princess Lilli' 'Ed Murray'

'Fancy Folly' 'Elizabeth Ann Hudson' 'Dancing Sheva'

'Berlin Red' 'Veiled Organdy' 'Little Red Hen'

'Joan Senior' 'Wild Song' 'Perennial Pleasure'

Day lilies from Wisley, 20 July. Life size

Hemerocallis 'Banbury Cinnamon'
Introduced by L. W. Brummitt in 1965. Height tall 93cm. Flowers 12.5cm across, cinnamon, with yellow base and a green throat. Parents: 'St George' × 'Flat Top'. Mid- to late-season.

'Berlin Melon' Introduced by Tomas Tamberg.

'Berlin Red' Introduced by Tomas Tamberg in 1983. Height to 88cm. Flowers 15cm across, bright red with yellow throat. Parents; 'Dundee' × 'Prussia'. Tetraploid. Deciduous. Mid-season.

'Burning Daylight' Introduced by H. A. Fischer in 1957. Height 71cm. Parents: 'Smiling thru' × seedling. Mid-season. Fragrant. Flowers, glowing orange self.

'Cynthia Mary' Introduced by C. C. Pole in 1982. Height 73cm. Flowers 11cm, deep red with darker edges and yellow-orange throat. Early to mid-season.

'Dancing Shiva' Introduced by S. C. Moldovan in 1974. Height 55cm. Flowers 12.5cm across, medium-pink blend with greeny yellow throat. Tetraploid. Remontant. Early season.

'Ed Murray' Introduced by E. T. Grovatt 1971. Height 75cm. Flowers 10cm across, black-red self with a green throat. Parents: 'Tis Midnight' × seedling. Mid-season.

'Elizabeth Anne Hudson' Introduced by R. W. Munson in 1975. Height 65cm. Parents: 'Bishop's Crest' × Tetra Sari'. Flowers to 14cm across, peach-rose edged purple with wine-coloured eye zone and gold throat. Tetraploid. Evergreen. Remontant. Early to mid-season.

'Fancy Folly' Details not known.

'Frans Hals' Introduced by W. B. Flory in 1955. Height 60cm. Flowers bright-rust and orange bicolor with a creamy orange midrib on the petals. Parents: 'Baggette' × 'Correll'. Mid- to late-season.

'Jake Russell' Introduced by H. M. Russell in 1956. Height 90cm. Flowers golden, self with a velvety sheen. Remontant. Early to late-season.

'Joan Senior' Introduced by K. G. Durio in 1977. Height 63cm. Flowers 15cm across, nearly white self with a lime-green throat. Parents: 'Loving Memory' × 'Little Infant'. Remontant. Early to mid-season.

Hemerocallis 'Wild Song'

Hemerocallis 'Ed Murray'

'Little Red Hen' Introduced by D. A. Apps in 1979. Height 75cm. Flowers 9cm across, red self with a yellow throat. Parents: 'Golden Chimes' × 'Rebel Thunder'. Mid-season.

'Mighty Mogul' Introduced by S. C. Moldovan in 1973. Height 55cm. Flowers sultry, maroon self, with a green throat. Tetraploid. Mid- to late-season.

'Neyron Rose' Introduced by E. J. Kraus in 1950. Height 75cm. Flowers light red. Parents include 'Gypsy Amaryllis' and 'Dauntless'. Mid-season.

'Nova' Introduced by Mrs H. W. Lester in 1962. Height 55cm. Flowers lemon-yellow, self with a green throat. Parents: 'Jack Frost' × seedling. Early to mid-season.

'Penelope Vestey' Introduced by R. H. Coe in 1969. Height tall, 90cm. Flowers 11cm across, pink with a deeper eye zone and lemon throat. Semi-evergreen. Late-season.

'Perennial Pleasure' Introduced by Mrs W. T. Hardy in 1968. Height 65cm. Flowers 14cm across, light-yellow self with a green throat. Remontant. Mid-season.

'Pink Damask' Introduced by J. C. Stevens in 1951. Height 90cm. Flowers mid-red self. Remontant. Mid-season.

'Princess Lilli' Introduced by M. Kasha in 1978. Height 50cm. Flowers 12.5cm across, light lavender with a rich-purple eye zone and a pale-yellow throat. Parents: 'Heavenly Haviland' × 'Prairie Blue Eyes'. Mid-season.

'Stoke Poges' Introduced by M. J. Randall.

'Veiled Organdy' Introduced by Brother Charles Reckamp in 1972. Height 75cm. Flowers 16cm across, pinkish apricot overlaid gold, with a greeny yellow throat. Parents: ('Minted Gold' × 'Noah's Ark') × 'Heavenly Harp'. Tetraploid. Mid-season.

'Wally Nance' Introduced by Wild in 1976. Height to 62cm. Flowers 15cm across, bright ruby red with small green throat. Early to mid-season.

'Wild Song' Introduced by A. J. & H. Wild in 1965. Height 71cm. Flowers 14cm across, golden-peachy self. Mid-season.

Hemerocallis 'Frans Hals'

Hemerocallis 'Joan Senior'

'Banbury Cinnamon'

'Cynthia Mary'

'Jake Russell'

'Frans Hals'

'Stoke Poges'

'Berlin Melon'

'Penelope Vestey'

'Burning Daylight'

'Neyron Rose'

'Nova'

'Pink Damask'

Day lilies from Wisley, 20 July. Life size

Hemerocallis 'Mighty Mogul'

Hemerocallis 'Cherry Cheeks'

Hemerocallis 'Pink Sensation'

Hemerocallis 'Siloam Purple Plum'

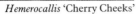

Hemerocallis 'Blushing Belle'

Hemerocallis 'Chicago Two Bits'

Hemerocallis 'La Pêche'

Hemerocallis 'May Colven'

Hemerocallis 'Chicago Petticoats'

Hemerocallis 'Chicago Royal Robe'

Hemerocallis 'Elizabeth Yancey'

Hemerocallis 'Nob Hill'

Massed day lilies in mid-summer at Wisley

Hemerocallis 'Catherine Woodberry'

Hemerocallis 'Come Hither'

Hemerocallis 'Luxury Lace'

Hemerocallis **'Blushing Belle'** Introduced by D. F. Hall in 1962. Height 71cm. Flowers melon-blushed rose. Early to mid-season.

'Catherine Woodberry' Introduced by F. W. Childs in 1967. Height 75cm. Flowers 15cm across, orchid self with green throat. Very fragrant. Mid- to late season.

'Cherry Cheeks' Introduced by Mrs R. C. Peck in 1968. Height 71cm. Flowers 15cm across, rose-pink blend with a greeny-yellow throat. Tetraploid. Mid- to late-season.

'Chicago Petticoats' Introduced by J. E. Marsh and C. Klehm in 1980. Height 60cm. Flowers 13cm across, pink blend. The parents were seedlings. Tetraploid. Deciduous. Early to mid-season.

'Chicago Royal Robe' Introduced by G. E. Lenington in 1978. Height 63cm. Flowers 14cm across, plum-purple self with a green throat.

Parents: 'Chicago Pansy' × seedling. Tetraploid. Semi-evergreen. Early season.

'Chicago Two Bits' Introduced by J. E. Marsh in 1972. Height 65cm. Flowers 15.5cm across, violet-purple with a deeper eye zone and a green throat. Semi-evergreen. Tetraploid. Mid-season.

'Come Hither' Introduced by D. F. Hall in 1960. Height 71cm. Flowers pink, with wine-purple eye zone. Early to mid-season.

'Elisabeth Yancey' Introduced by Yancey Harrison in 1973. Height 71cm. Flowers 14cm across, very light-pink self with a green throat. Remontant. Semi-evergreen. Early season.

'La Pêche' Introduced by R. W. Munson in 1976. Height to 60cm. Flowers 13cm across, peach-yellow self with yellow throat, fragrant. Tetraploid. Semi-evergreen. Early to mid-season. Remontant.

'Luxury Lace' Introduced by Miss E. Spalding in 1959. Height 80cm. Flowers mauve, orange self with a green throat. Remontant. Mid-season.

'May Colven' Introduced by Mrs R. C. Peck. Height 73cm. Flowers 15cm across, rose-pink blend with green throat. Parents: 'Mary Gray' × seedling. Tetraploid. Mid- to late-season.

'Nob Hill' Introduced by Mrs H. W. Lester in 1962. Height 90cm. Flowers pale pink bi-tone. Early to mid-season.

'Pink Sensation' Introduced by J. W. Terry in 1953. Height 75cm. Flowers light pinky-red self. Mid-season.

'Siloam Purple Plum' Introduced by Mrs R. Henry in 1970. Height 43cm. Flowers 7cm across, dark-red-purple self with a green throat. Early to mid-season.

413

'Princess Marie-Louise'

'Princess Sarah'

'Princess Margaret'

'Princess Frederika'

'Princess Bianca'

'Princess Sophia'

'Princess Diana'

'Princess Victoria'

'Princess Beatrix'

Alstroemeria specimens from Chanctonbury Nursery, Ashington, Sussex, July 20th. ½ life size

Alstroemeria aurea

Alstroemeria psittacina

Alstroemeria aurea Graham syn. *A. aurantiaca* D. Don (*Alstroemeriaceae*) Native of S Chile, including Chiloe, growing in moist woodland, flowering in December–March. Plant far-spreading by thin, fleshy roots. Stems to 1m or more. Leaves lanceolate. Flowers 3–4cm long, the outer petals tipped with green. For moist soil in sun or partial shade. The hardiest species, to –15°C or less with protection for the roots, which tend to be very invasive.

Alstroemeria haemantha Ruiz & Pavon Native of Chile, especially around Valparaiso, growing on well-drained, rocky hillsides, flowering in December–January. Plant spreading by fleshy roots to form large patches. Stems to *c*.1m. Leaves glaucous beneath. Flowers *c*.5cm long, red to orange. The outer petals oblong to obovate. Hardy to –10°C, perhaps less.

Alstroemeria ligtu L. Native of Chile, growing in dry scrub in rocky, sandy soil, flowering in November–January. Plant wide spreading by underground fleshy roots. Stems 60–100cm. Leaves narrowly linear or linear-lanceolate. Flowers variable in colour, usually pinkish lilac, reddish or whitish, *c*.3.75cm long. *A. ligtu* is said to be usually pink-flowered in the wild, and the 'ligtu hybrids' that are usually sold are hybrids between *A. ligtu* and *A. haemantha*, raised by Clarence Elliott in around 1927 when he and Balfour Gourlay introduced the parents from Chile. For well-drained soil in full sun. Hardy to –15°C.

Alstroemeria pelegrina L. Native of Chile and Peru, growing on sand dunes along the coast, flowering in December–January. Plant spreading by fleshy roots; stems 30–50cm. Leaves lanceolate. Flowers purplish or reddish, *c*.5cm long. For well-drained soil, moist in summer. Hardy to –10°C perhaps.

Alstroemeria psittacina Lehm. syn. *A. pulchella* L. fil. Native of Mexico and N Brazil, flowering in November–February. Plant forming clumps of stems to *c*.1m, from shortly spreading fleshy roots. Leaves oblong to oblong-spathulate. Flowers *c*.3.75cm long. For sun or partial shade in good, well-drained soil, moist in summer. Hardy to –10°C.

Alstroemeria hybrids Most of the large-flowered cultivars shown here have been raised for the cut-flower trade in Holland by Van Straaveren B. V. of Aalsmeer. They make, however, excellent garden plants, with a long flowering season, requiring rich, well-drained soil in full sun. They will probably survive temperatures of at least –10°C, if the fleshy roots are protected with a good mulch of dry peat in winter. They are hybrids between *A. aurea* and other species originally raised by J. Goemans, and are mainly triploid, so that they do not set seed and are not easily used for breeding by other growers! They have stems 50–75cm. Shown here are:
'Princess Beatrix' (syn. 'Stadoran');
'Princess Bianca' (syn. 'Zelblanca');
'Princess Diana' (syns. 'Stablaco', 'Mona Lisa');
'Princess Frederika' (syn. 'Srabronza');
'Princess Margaret'
'Princess Marie-Louise' (syn. 'Zelanon');
'Princess Sarah' (syn. 'Stalicamp');
'Princess Sophia' (syns. 'Stajello', 'Yellow King');
'Princess Victoria' (syn. 'Regina') all raised by Van Straaveren.
'Rosy Wings' An older cultivar of unknown origin. Height to 30cm.

Alstroemeria 'Princess Diana'

Alstroemeria pelegrina

Alstroemeria 'Rosy Wings'

Bomarea × *cantabrigiensis* at Great Dixter

Alstroemeria ligtu hybrids at Cobblers, Sussex

Bomarea × **cantabrigiensis** Lynch (*Liliaceae-Alstroemeriaceae*)   A hybrid between *B. hirtella* and *B. caldasiana* Herb., raised at the University Botanic Garden, Cambridge before 1920. This has grown outside in a bay between the glasshouses at Cambridge since 1922 and so should be quite hardy if the rootstock is covered. The twining leafy stems grow to 2m or more and the flower clusters are *c*.20cm across.

Bomarea hirtella Herb. syn. *B. edulis* (Tussac) Herb.   Native of Cuba, Mexico and Belize south to Peru, growing on the edge of forests at 1400–3000m, flowering in July–October in S England. Roots tuberous and edible, with slender stems scrambling and twining to 2m or more. Leaves lanceolate. Flower clusters *c*.15cm across, the flowers 2.5–3.7cm long. For any good soil in sun or partial shade. Hardy to −10°C or less.

Bomarea hirtella at Kew

Alstroemeria haemantha

Libertia formosa

Libertia formosa

Sisyrinchium striatum 'Aunt Mary'

Fascicularia bicolor

Diplarrena moraea

Sisyrinchium bellum

Sisyrinchium striatum syn. *Phaiophleps nigricans*

Aristea grandis

Olsynium biflorum in the Cruickshank Botanic Garden, Aberdeen

Belamcanda chinensis

Aristea grandis Weim. (*Iridaceae*)   Native of South Africa, in the Drakensberg mountains of S Natal, growing in moist grassland by rock outcrops and by streams at up to 2250m, flowering in January–February. Plant with solitary or few upright stems 60–80cm tall from a tufted rootstock. Flowers in stemless clusters of 3–8, blue, *c*.20mm across, each lasting only one day. For a sunny position, moist in summer, dryish in winter. Hardy to −10°C, perhaps less. *A. major* Andrews (syn. *A. thyrsiflora*), from the Cape, is a tall plant, to 2m, with a solid, spike-like inflorescence of hundreds of flowers. It is a beautiful waterside plant for a warm climate. Hardy to −5°C perhaps.

Belamcanda chinensis (L.) DC. (*Iridaceae*) Native of E Siberia, China, S Japan and the Himalayas to N India, and naturalized in Malaysia and in North America, from Connecticut south to Georgia, Indiana and Kansas, growing in scrub, open woods and grassy places, flowering in June–August. Plant with branched stems to 1m from a fan of *Iris*-like leaves. Flowers *c*.5cm across. Capsule 4cm long, splitting to reveal shining black seeds. For any soil in a warm position, moist in summer. Hardy to −15°C.

Diplarrena moraea Labill. (*Iridaceae*)   Native of Tasmania and SE Australia, in New South Wales and Victoria, growing in moist, grassy places in the mountains, flowering in October–December, or May–June in the north. Plant tufted. Stems 45–65cm. Leaves 8–12mm wide. Flowers 2 or 3 per bract, 4–6cm across, scented. For well-drained, sandy and peaty soil, moist in

summer. Hardy to −10°C for short periods. *D. latifolia* Benth. has wider leaves to 2.5cm and larger flowers 6–15cm across, 5 or 6 per bract.

Fascicularia bicolor (Ruiz & Pav.) Mez (*Bromeliaceae*)   Native of Chile, and naturalized in the Scilly Isles and off NW France, growing on rocks by the sea, flowering in June–August. Plant forming crowded rosettes of narrow leaves to 35cm long, glaucous, especially beneath. Leaves around the inflorescence becoming bright red at flowering time, then reverting to green. Flowers small, pale blue in a head *c*.5cm in diameter. For a position among rocks or on a wall. Hardy to −5°C.

Libertia formosa Graham (*Iridaceae*)   Native of Chile, flowering in spring. Plant forming large clumps. Leaves 15–45cm, to 1.2cm wide. Stems 50–120cm. Flowers in small umbels; longer petals 12–18mm. For well-drained soil and a sunny position. Hardy to −15°C. *L. ixioides* (Forster) Spreng. is a native of New Zealand and the Chatham Islands, and is later flowering, with the individual flowers on stalks longer than the minute bracts, and petals only 6–9mm long.

Olsynium biflorum (Thunb.) Goldblatt syn. *Phaiophleps biflora* (Thunb.) R. C. Foster, *Symphostemon narcissoides* (Cav.) Miers ex Klatt, *Sisyrinchium odoratissimum* Lindl. (*Iridaceae*) Native of W Argentina north to 46°S and Chile north to 50° 40′S, and common in Tierra del Fuego, growing in grassland and open scrub to 150m, flowering in November–January, or

May–June in the north. Plant with a short rhizome and 1–5 narrow, solid leaves to 22cm. Flowering stems 10–70cm, with 2–7 flowers each with a tube 7–20mm long, and reflexing petals to 18mm long, scented. Subsp. *lyckholmi* (Owen) D. M. Moore has purplish- or brownish-red to orange flowers, and is found at higher altitudes. For well-drained, sandy soil in full sun, moist in summer. Hardy to −15°C.

Sisyrinchium bellum S. Wats. (*Iridaceae*) Blue-eyed Grass   Native of California, from Humboldt Co. south to Ventura Co., growing in often-damp, grassy places below 1000m, in the coast ranges, flowering in February–May. Other forms of this species are found inland. Plant with several flattened and branched stems 40cm. Leaves greenish or glaucous, to 4mm wide. Flowers around 30mm across, usually deep blue. For moist, sandy soil, in full sun. Hardy to −15°C, though some plants from coastal areas may be tenderer. *S. idahoense* Bickn., from California to Washington and Idaho, differs in its leafless, unbranched stem.

Sisyrinchium striatum Smith syn. *Phaiophleps nigricans* (Phil.) R. C. Foster   Native of Argentina and Chile, growing in woods and scrub, and becoming especially prolific after forest fires, flowering in summer. Plant with few to several fans of leaves to 40cm from a short rhizome. Leaves to 18mm across, striped in 'Aunt May' syn. 'Variegatum'. Stems to 45cm. Easily grown in any good garden soil, preferably rather moist. Short-lived but self-seeds freely. The leaves are killed by −15°C or so, and are often blackened by slighter frosts.

'Hadspen Abundance'

'Prinz Heinrich'

Anemone tomentosa

Anemone vitifolia

'Honorine Jobert'

Specimens from Beth Chatto, Unusual Plants, 15 September. ⅙ life size

Anemone × lesseri

Anemone 'September Charm'

Anemone 'Honorine Jobert' at Cockermouth Castle

Anemone hupehensis (Brickell & Leslie 12470)
from Yunnan

Anemone 'Koenigin Charlotte'

Anemone × hybrida 'Hybrida'

Anemone vitifolia from Nepal

Anemone 'Koenigin Charlotte' at Trewidden, Cornwall

Anemone 'Luise Uhink'

Anemone hupehensis (Lémoine) Lémoine (*Ranunculaceae*)   Native of C & W China, from Hubei to Sichuan and Yunnan, growing in gorges on cliffs, among shady rocks in scrub and in open, stony places at 600–2500m, flowering in August–October, to November in the wild. Plant with a tufted rootstock, spreading by stolons. Leaves with 3 stalked leaflets, sparsely hairy, often purplish beneath, more or less evergreen. Stems 60–130cm, branched, with umbels of white, pale-pink or purplish-pink flowers; petals 5–6, rounded, crimson outside. For any good soil in sun or partial shade. Hardy to –15°C, possibly less. 'Hadspen Abundance' Introduced by Eric Smith of The Plantsmen, has stems *c*.60cm and 6–9 deep purplish-pink petals. Var. *japonica* (Thunb.) Bowles & Stearn has numerous (20–30 or more) narrow petals, and is widely grown in E China and Japan. It was introduced by Robert Fortune who collected it among the graves of the natives around the ramparts of Shanghai.

Anemone × hybrida Paxton 'Hybrida'   This is the old garden Japanese anemone, so valuable for its late flowering. It is a hybrid between *A. vitifolia* and *A. hupehensis* var. *japonica* and is generally sterile and often triploid. It has tall, 1.2–1.8m or more, stems, and tough, wiry roots, spreading to form large colonies. The pale-pink form, with 6–11 petals, is the original 'Hybrida'. Other cultivars shown here are:
'Honorine Jobert'   Raised in 1858; the commonest white, single; petals 6–9.
'Luise Uhink'   Flowers large, white; petals 6–10. Stems to 120cm.
'Prinz Heinrich' syn. 'Prince Henry'   Raised in 1902; deep rose-pink; 10–13 narrow petals.
'Koenigin Charlotte' syn. 'Queen Charlotte'

Raised in 1898; the best large-flowered, mid-pink, with 6–8 petals; stems *c*.80cm.
'September Charm' is a good selection, raised by Bristol Nurseries in 1932, with stems *c*.75cm.

Anemone × lesseri Wehrh.   A hybrid between the American *A. multifida* Poir, which may have red flowers (or green or yellowish), and *A. sylvestris* L., from Europe, which has white flowers. Stems to 45cm. Flowers 2–4cm across, in May–September. For deep, well-drained soil in sun or partial shade. Hardy to –25°C or less.

Anemone tomentosa (Maxim.) P'ei syn. *A. vitifolia* 'Robustissima'   Native of NE China, growing in scrub, open woods and among shady rocks, flowering in August–October. Plant forming a compact clump of much-branched stems to 1m or more, spreading by stolons. Leaves with 3 separate leaflets, lobed and toothed, densely white-hairy beneath. Flowers in umbels, 5–8cm across with 5–6 petals. For any good soil. Hardy to –25°C or less.

Anemone vitifolia Buch.-Ham. ex DC. Native of the Himalayas, from Afghanistan to N Burma and W China in NW Sichuan, growing in scrub and abandoned fields at 2000–3000m, flowering in August–September. Plant with a tufted rootstock, far spreading by underground stolons. Basal leaves 5–9 lobed and toothed, long, silky and woolly beneath, deciduous. Stems to 150cm, usually *c*.75cm, branched with umbels of few flowers, 3.5–5cm across; petals 5–6, usually white, though pink-flowered forms were recorded by Wilson in NW Sichuan. Hardy to –20°C or less.

Cimicifuga simplex 'Elstead' at Wisley

Cimicifuga simplex 'Elstead'

Cimicifuga simplex 'Brunette'

Cimicifuga rubifolia with *Veratrum nigrum*

Impatiens tinctoria subsp. *tinctoria* at Logan Botanic Garden

Cimicifuga japonica near Kyoto

Melianthus villosus at Kew

Melianthus major at Edington, Wiltshire

Cimicifuga japonica (Thunb.) Spreng. syn.
Actaea japonica Thunb. (*Ranunculaceae*)
Native of Japan, in C & W Honshu, growing in
woods, often among ferns in deep shade,
flowering in August–October. Plant with few,
upright stems 60–80cm tall. Leaflets broadly
ovate to orbicular, 6–10cm long and wide.
Flowering stems usually leafless. Flowers sessile,
usually crowded; stamens c.8mm long. For leafy
soil in shade or partial shade. Hardy to −15°C,
perhaps less. DNA studies by Dr J. A. Compton
have shown that *Cimicifuga* should be included
within *Actaea* (see p. 30).

Cimicifuga rubifolia Kearney syn. *Actaea
cordifolia* DC.   Native of E North America, in
Tennessee and parts of Illinois, growing in
rocky woods, flowering in June–July. Stems to
200cm. Leaves 2-ternate, with large leaflets
12–20cm long, ovate to suborbicular, irregularly
lobed. Follicles 1 or 2, 8–10mm long, glabrous,
prominently veined. For moist rich soil in shade
or partial shade. Hardy to −20°C or less.
   This species has commonly been called
C. racemosa var *cordifolia* (Pursh) Gray in
gardens.
   C. racemosa (L.) Nutt. Black Cohosh or
Black Snakeroot, the common North American
species, has small leaflets, 3–10cm long, and a
single follicle. It is found in damp woods from
Massachusetts and S Ontario south to Georgia
and Missouri.

Cimicifuga simplex Wormsk. syn. *Actaea
simplex* (DC.) Wormsk. ex Prantl 'Elstead'

Native of Japan, in all the islands, and of
Sakhalin, the Kurile Is. and Kamschatka,
growing in subalpine and alpine meadows,
flowering in August–October, usually in
October in gardens. Plants with shortly creeping
rhizomes and upright stems c.100cm, forming
patches. Leaflets ovate or narrowly ovate,
3–10cm long. Flowering stems arching, black,
little branched. Flowers on stalks 5–10mm long.
Petals shallowly 2-lobed, styles 2–7. For moist,
leafy soil in partial shade. Hardy to −25°C or
less. 'Elstead' has brownish-purple stems and
buds; 'White Pearl' has pure-white flowers from
green buds; 'Atropurpurea' has purplish leaves
and buds; '**Brunette**' has even darker leaves of
a rich purplish black, and pinkish-white flowers
on stems to 180cm. It was introduced by
Blooms from Denmark. *C. foetida* L. syn. *Actaea
cimicifuga* L. from Europe, W Asia and the
Himalayas to W China, has greenish-yellow
flowers in a long, nodding spike, with shorter
branches around its base.

Impatiens tinctoria A. Rich. subsp. *tinctoria*
(*Balsaminaceae*)   Native of C Africa, in E Zaire,
S Sudan, Ethiopia and N Uganda, growing in
damp mountain forests, shrub-filled gullies, by
streams and on shady banks at 750–3000m,
flowering in January, and in April–November;
in August–October in gardens in Britain. Plant
with large tuberous rootstock, and thick, fleshy
stems to 2m. Leaves with blade 10–20cm long,
narrowly ovate, elliptical or lanceolate. Flowers
with lower petals 3.5–5cm long. Spur very long,

8–12cm in subsp. *tinctoria*, 3.8–6.5cm long in
subsp. *elegantissima* from Mount Elgon and the
mountains of C & S Kenya, which also appears
to be in cultivation. For rich, leafy soil, moist in
summer in a sheltered position. Hardy to −10°C
and long-lived; a plant has been growing
between the glasshouses at Wisley for over 12
years.

Melianthus major L. (*Melianthaceae*)   Native
of South Africa, in the S Cape Province,
flowering in August–September, i.e. in Spring.
In the wild and in mild climates a shrub to 3m,
but herbaceous in colder climates, growing to
1.2m in one season. Leaves glaucous, smooth,
to 30cm or more long. Flowers deep blood-red;
fruits inflated. One of the most handsome
foliage plants for exotic effect. Hardy to −15°C
with protection for the rootstock; to −10°C
perhaps, for shorter periods for the aerial
parts.

Melianthus villosus Bol.   Native of South
Africa in the Drakensberg in Lesotho and Natal,
growing by streams, among rocks in scrub and
on the margins of forests at up to c.1950m,
flowering in December–January. In the wild a
shrub up to 2m, but herbaceous in colder
climates, and usually up to 1.5m. Plant hairy,
aromatic. Leaves c.15cm long. Flowers greenish;
fruits inflated, triangular. For any good soil in
full sun, moist in summer, but in a warm
position. Hardy to −10°C perhaps, for short
periods.

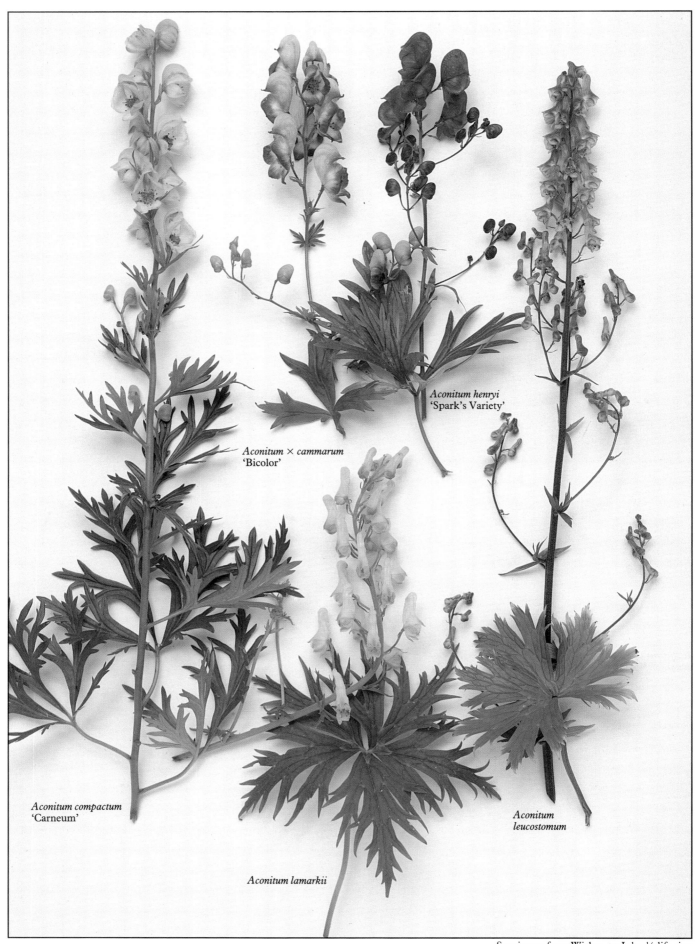

Aconitum henryi
'Spark's Variety'

Aconitum × cammarum
'Bicolor'

Aconitum compactum
'Carneum'

*Aconitum
leucostomum*

Aconitum lamarkii

Specimens from Wisley, 20 July. ½ life size

Aconitum × cammarum L. syn. *A. bicolor* Schult. (*Ranunculaceae*) A group of hybrids between *A. napellus* L. and *A. variegatum* L., with rather short spikes of large flowers and a helmet as high as wide. Flower colour basically blue. 'Bicolor' is the original form: stems to 1.2m, much branched; spikes rather short. 'Grandiflorum Album' is a beautiful pure white, with longer spikes and well-spaced flowers.

Aconitum compactum Rchb. 'Carneum' Native of the Pyrenees and W Alps in France and possibly Portugal to Switzerland, growing in woods and damp meadows, especially along streams, flowering in July–September. Plant with upright stems to 1.5m. Basal leaves divided to the base, with narrow, linear lobes; stem-leaves crowded below the unbranched inflorescence. Graham Thomas records that this form provides flowers of a better pink in cool climates. *A. compactum* is one of the *A. napellus* group.

Aconitum henryi E. Pritz. ex Diels 'Spark's Variety' Native of China, in Hubei and Sichuan, growing in scrub, flowering in July–September. Plant with tuberous roots and stems to 1.5m which begin upright but then twine or scramble, though in 'Spark's Variety', shown here, they are merely flexuous above. Leaves mainly 3-lobed, the middle lobe short-stalked. Flowers with a short, broad helmet. For any good soil in partial shade. Hardy to −20°C.

Aconitum japonicum Thunb. Native of Japan, in SW Hokkaido, Honshu, Shikoku and Kyushu, growing in hills and mountains, flowering in September–November. Plant forming large clumps of stems to 100cm, rarely climbing towards the top. Leaves 3–5 lobed, coarsely toothed, with broad lobes. Inflorescence much branched, with few-flowered, short spikes. Hardy to −20°C perhaps. Valuable for its handsome leaves and very late flowering.

Aconitum laeve Royle Native of the Himalayas, from Pakistan to W Nepal, growing in open forest and scrub at 2000–3300m, flowering in June–August. Plant forming clumps of tall stems to 2m. Basal leaves to 30cm across with broad lobes. Flowers to 2.5cm high, with a tall, narrow, curved helmet; variable in colour from white to pale yellow, or pinkish purple. Hardy to −20°C, perhaps less.

Aconitum lamarkii Rchb. syn. *A. lycoctonum* subsp. *neapolitanum* (Ten.) Nyman Native of S Europe, from France and Spain and Morocco, east to Bulgaria, N Greece and Romania, growing in mountain woods and meadows, often by streams, flowering in July–August. Plant with few or several upright stems to *c*.1m, from a tufted rootstock. Basal leaves 7–8-lobed, the lobes deeply cut to beyond the middle. Helmet 18–25mm. For moist, peaty soil in partial shade or sun. Hardy to −20°C.

Aconitum leucostomum Vorosch. Native of C Asia in the Saur Tarbagatau, Dzungarian Ala Tau and Tien Shan, both in Kirgizia and NW China (Sinjiang), growing in forest and juniper scrub in the mountains, flowering in June–July, and August in gardens. Plant with few stems to 1.5m. Basal leaves pale green, with 3–7 lobes, the lobes cut to above the middle. Flowers pinkish, the helmet *c*.15mm tall. For any good soil in sun or partial shade. Hardy to −25°C or less. *A. oriental*, Mill., from NE Turkey and the Caucasus, is similar in its leaves and flowers which are smoky lilac or pinkish, an

altogether interesting colour. It grows in clearings in coniferous forest.

Aconitum septentrionale Koelle 'Ivorine' syn. *A. lycoctonum* L. subsp. *lycoctonum* in *European Garden Flora* Native of N Europe from Norway to Russia, growing on forest margins and in rich meadows, flowering in June–July, or even late May in gardens. Plant forming clumps of upright stems to 90cm. Basal leaves deeply 4–6 lobed to ⅔, the lobes coarsely toothed. Inflorescence glandular, narrow; flower usually dark violet, but white in 'Ivorine', the helmet 18–25mm, tapering from a wide base. For any good, cool soil in sun or partial shade. This is the earliest Monkshood to flower and is very distinct in its dense narrow spikes of white flowers. Hardy to −25°C or less.

Aconitum japonicum at the Royal Botanic Garden, Edinburgh

Aconitum laeve in Kashmir

A. × cammarum 'Grandiflorum Album'

Aconitum septentrionale 'Ivorine'

Zauschneria californica subsp. *latifolia*

Zauschneria californica

Zauschneria californica subsp. *cana* at Wisley

Gaura lindheimeri Englemann & A. Gray (*Onagraceae*) Native of Louisiana and Texas, growing in prairies and pinelands, flowering in April–October. Plant with a tufted rootstock and numerous, rather stiff upright stems forming a low bush to 1m high and wide. Leaves oblanceolate or spathulate, to 7.5cm long. Flowers *c*.2.5cm across. For a warm sunny position in well-drained soil, tolerant of both heat and drought. Hardy to −20°C perhaps. *G. coccinea* (Nutt.) Pursh, widespread in North America, has stems to 50cm, and flowers to 16mm across, which may be deep pink on opening, becoming red. For an even drier, hotter position.

Lespedeza thunbergii (DC.) Nakai (*Leguminosae*) Native of Japan, Korea and China, growing on dry, grassy hills and scrub, flowering in June–September, and to November in gardens. Plant with a woody rootstock and arching stems to 180cm, sometimes woody at the base. Leaves with 3 narrowly oblong, ovate or elliptic leaflets, 3–5cm long. Flowers 18–25mm long, in spikes longer than the leaves. Calyx-teeth acuminate, 1-nerved, the lowest longer than the tube. *L. bicolor* Turcz., with short racemes of flowers and shorter calyx teeth, is shown in *Shrubs*, p. 169. For good soil in warm position in full sun. Valuable for its late flowering when pruned to the ground in spring. Hardy to −20°C.

Lychnis cognata Maxim. (*Caryophyllaceae*) Native of NE China (Heilongjiang) and Korea, growing in open woods and grassy places in the mountains, flowering in July–August. Stems few, bristly-hairy or nearly glabrous, 40–100cm tall, with ovate or elliptic leaves 5–8cm long. Bracts broadly lanceolate, ciliate, 10–15mm long, appressed to the calyx. Calyx 2.5–3cm long. Flowers 3 or more in a head, 5–6cm across, with a long tooth on the side of each petal and deep notch on the apex. Hardy to −20°C or less.

Lychnis miqueliana Rohrb. Native of Japan in S Honshu, Shikoku and Kyushu, growing in

Gaura lindheimeri

Gaura lindheimeri

Lespedeza thunbergii at Kew

Zauschneria californica 'Albiflora'

damp woods in the mountains, flowering in July–October. Plant with stems 50–80cm, sparingly branched. Flowers 5–6cm across with smooth, rounded petals. For moist soil in partial shade. Hardy to –10°C, perhaps less.

Zauschneria californica Presl. (*Onagraceae*) Native of California from Sonoma and Lake Cos. south to Baja California, growing in dry, open places, in cliffs and gravelly soil, flowering in August–October, with the occasional flower earlier. Plant usually with numerous stems to 90cm long, from a woody rootstock. Leaves green to greyish, ovate to linear. Flowers with a long tube 2–3cm long and petals 8–15mm long, usually scarlet, rarely pink or white in, for example, 'Albiflora'. For a warm position in dry, well-drained soil. Hardy to –15°C perhaps. A very variable species, divided into 3 subspecies, as follows. Subsp. *californica* has stems slightly woody at the base; leaves linear to lanceolate, 3–5mm wide, hairy but not white. Subsp. *angustifolia* Keck is woody at the base, has narrower linear leaves 2.5–3.5mm wide and flowers 30–40mm long. Both these are found below 1200m, mostly in the Coast Ranges. Subsp. *latifolia* (Hook.) Keck is entirely herbaceous, with leaves ovate to ovate-lanceolate, mostly opposite, green or silky, 7–17mm wide and often glandular. It is a mountain plant, found from Tulare Co. to SW Oregon, below 3000m. It is probably hardier than the coastal subspecies.

Zauschneria californica subsp. *cana* Greene Native of California, from Monterey to Los Angeles Co., growing on dry slopes and roadside cliffs, in chaparral and coastal scrub below 600m, flowering in August–October. Plant with several stems, somewhat woody at the base, to 60cm. Leaves white-hairy, linear-filiform, up to 2mm wide, clustered. Flowers with the tube 2–3cm long, and petals 8–10mm long. For dry, hot, sunny position in well-drained soil. Hardy to –10°C, perhaps less. All *Zauschneria* may now be found under the name *Epilobium canum* (Greene) P. H. Raven!

Lychnis miqueliana near Kyoto

Lychnis cognata

Fallopia japonica var. *compacta*

Persicaria mollis var. *rudis*

Specimens from Braken Hill, Platt, 28 July. ½ life size

Aralia cordata near Kyoto, Japan

Persicaria amplexicaulis

Fagopyrum dibotrys

Fallopia japonica var. *compacta*

Persicaria campanulata

Persicaria runcinata

Persicaria mollis

Aralia cordata Thunb. syn. *A. edulis* Sieb. &
Zucc. (*Araliaceae*)   Native of Japan, in all the
islands, of Sakhalin, Korea and China, growing
in scrub and open forest in ravines in the
mountains, flowering in August–October. Plant
with a large, fleshy rootstock and arching stems
to 1.5m. Leaves to 1m long, twice pinnate, the
leaflets ovate to oblong 5–30cm long,
acuminate. Flowers pale green. Fruits black,
fleshy *c*.2mm long. For moist, leafy soil in shade
and shelter. Hardy to −25°C or less.

Fagopyrum dibotrys (D. Don) Hara syn. *F.
cymosum* (Trev.) Meissn. (*Polygonaceae*)
Native of the Himalayas from Pakistan to SW
China, growing in open forest and near
cultivation at 1300–3400m, flowering in
June–October. Plant with upright, unbranched
stems to 2m or more, from a stout rootstock.
Leaf blades 6–15cm long, the lowest long-
stalked, the upper sessile. Flowers *c*.5mm
across; seed to 8mm long, used for food in the
Himalayas, along with the cultivated annual
buckwheats *F. esculentum* Moench and *F.
tartaricum* (L.) Gaertn. For good soil in partial
shade. Hardy to −20°C, perhaps less.

Persicaria amplexicaulis (D. Don) Decne
syn. *Polygonum amplexicaule* D. Don, *Bistorta
amplexicaulis* (D. Don) Greene (*Polygonaceae*)
Native of Afghanistan to SW China, growing in
scrub and mountain meadows by streams at
2100–4800m, flowering in July–September.
Stems to 1m or more. Leaves clasping. Flowers
white, pink, red, or purple. Spikes 5–15cm long,
usually erect, but nodding in var. *pendula* Hara
from C & E Nepal and Bhutan. 'Arun Gem',
introduced from Nepal in 1971, belongs to

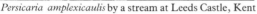
Persicaria amplexicaulis by a stream at Leeds Castle, Kent

Persicaria species amongst *Hostas*

Fallopia sachalinensis

Bistorta vaccinifolia

this var. A robust plant forming large clumps in moist ground. Hardy to −20°C.

Persicaria campanulata (Hook. fil.) R. D. syn. *Polygonum campanulatum* Hook. fil., *Aconogonum campanulatum* (Hook. fil.) Hara Native of N India, Nepal, Sikkim, Bhutan, N Burma and SW China, growing in damp places in *Abies* or *Tsuga* forest, and scrub at 2100–4100m, flowering in June–September. Plant forming large clumps with shortly creeping rooting stems and erect flowering stems, 60–120cm. Leaves elliptic-ovate, 5–12cm long, white or pale salmon beneath with parallel side ribs. Flowers bell-shaped, *c.*5mm long, pink or nearly white. A pretty plant for a very damp position. Tolerant of shade but not tolerant of drought in summer. Hardy to −15°C.

Fallopia japonica var. *compacta* (Hook. fil.) Trehane syn. *Polygonum cuspidatum* Sieb. & Zucc. var. *compactum* (Hook. fil.) Bailey Native of Japan, Korea, Taiwan and China, growing in mountain scrub and meadows, flowering in July–October. Plant with creeping underground rhizomes and upright stems to 90cm. Leaves *c.*10cm long, broadly ovate to ovate-elliptic, truncate at the base. Flowers 2.5–3mm long, male and female on different plants, white when fresh, turning pink; the clone of var. *compacta* in cultivation is female.

Var. *cuspidata* is a rampant, large plant with stems to 2m, still a little smaller than *P. sachalinense*. There is a slightly weaker variegated clone 'Spectabilis'. For moist soil in partial shade. Hardy to −25°C.

Persicaria mollis (D. Don) H. Gross var. *rudis* (Meissn.) Trehane syn. *Polygonum molle* D. Don D. Don var. *rude* (Meissn.) Hara, *Polygonum rude* Meissn. Native of the Himalayas from N India to SW China, growing in forests, scrub and damp ground at 900–4250m, flowering in May–November. Plant shrubby at the base, with stem to 2.5m. Var. *rudis* is distinguished from the other vars. by having appressed deflexed hairs on the stem, especially at the nodes (var. *molle* has ascending hairs). Leaves elliptic 10–18cm × 3–6.5cm, usually pubescent. Flowers yellowish white; fruits black, fleshy. Easily grown in sun or partial shade and moist soil. Valuable for its late flowering in gardens.

Persicaria runcinata (D. Don) H. Gross syn. *Polygonum runcinatum* D. Don Native of Bhutan and Sikkim, growing on cliffs and roadside banks, at 1000–3800m, flowering in May–October. Plant with soft, fleshy creeping and rooting stems to 30cm or more. Leaves *c.*7.5cm long. Flower-head *c.*1cm across. For moist, leafy soil in partial shade. Hardy to −10°C perhaps.

Fallopia sachalinensis (F. Schmidt) R. D. syns. *Polygonum sachalinense* F. Schmidt, *Reynoutria sachalinensis* (F. Schmidt) Nakai Native of Japan in Hokkaido and Honshu, Sakhalin and the S Kurile islands, growing in gorges, along shady streams and in damp clearings in woods in the mountains, flowering in August–September. Stems to 3m. Leaves 15–30cm × 10–20cm, glaucous and glabrous beneath, cordate. Inflorescence pubescent. A fine plant for a huge garden, especially where it can be viewed from above. Hardy to −25°C.

Bistorta vaccinifolia (Wall. ex Meissn.) Greene syn. *Polygonum vacciniifolium* Wall. ex Meissn. syn. Native of Kashmir to SE Xizang, growing on rocks and open mountains, at 3000–4500m, especially common in the wetter areas of the C Himalayas, flowering in August–September. Flowering stems up to 15cm. Leaves 1–2cm × 0.6–1cm. Flower spikes 3–8cm; flowers 6mm. Requires peaty soil, cool and moist in summer, but well-drained, and best trailing over rocks.

Persicaria species Plant with trailing stems to 30cm long. Leaves cut to the midrib, *c.*5cm long. Flower spikes 1.5cm in August–September. For moist, leafy soil in partial shade; pretty, as shown here, for its unique leaf shape.

Gentiana asclepiadea at Wallington, Northumberland

Gentiana asclepiadea (Turkish form)

Gentiana cruciata in NW Turkey

Gentiana septemfida on the peat banks at Wisley

Gentiana affinis Griseb. (*Gentianaceae*)   Native of North America, from the Rockies eastwards to W Minnesota and South Dakota, growing in damp grassland and marshy places, flowering in July–August. Plant with few upright stems to 45cm. Leaves 7–13 pairs below the flowers, 1.5–3cm long, linear-lanceolate. Flowers with calyx tube 5–7mm; corolla 2–3cm long, blue. For peaty soil in full sun. Close to the European *G. pneumonanthe*. Hardy to −20°C or less.

Gentiana asclepiadea L.   Native of the mountains of Europe, from the Jura and W Alps eastwards to the Caucasus, N & S Turkey and northern Iran, growing in mountain meadows and open woods at up to 2000m, flowering in July–September. Plant with several arching stems to 1m from a tufted rootstock. Leaves ovate-lanceolate to lanceolate. Flowers with corolla 30–50mm long, mid- or deep blue, commonly with a white throat in Turkey or Cambridge blue in Corsica, rarely pure white in 'Alba'. 'Knightshayes' has a pale throat similar to the Turkish form. For light shade or sun, in a cool position and leafy soil which does not dry out in summer. Hardy to −20°C or less.

Gentiana cruciata L.   Native of the Alps east to the Caucasus, N Iran, W Siberia and Turkey, growing in alpine meadows and scrub, flowering in July–September. Plant with few or several stems from a central rosette of leaves. Stem leaves to 10cm long, 3cm wide. Flowers with a 4-lobed corolla, 15–30mm long. A rather coarse, leafy plant, but easy to grow in any good soil. Hardy to −20°C or less. Photographed in NW Turkey by James Compton.

Gentiana septemfida Pallas syns. *G. freyniana* Bornm., *G. lagodechiana* (Kuzn.) Grossh. Native of the Crimea, the Caucasus, N Turkey and N Iran, growing in alpine meadows and grassy scrub, and open birch or fir forest, at up to 3200m in Turkey, flowering in July–August. Plant with several decumbent or creeping stems to 30cm. Leaves ovate, narrower towards the flowers. Corolla 30–40mm long, with hairs between the main lobes, blue or purplish. For any moist, peaty soil in sun or light shade. Hardy to −20°C perhaps. Very variable. *G. freyniana* from N Turkey was described as having 3-veined leaves and no hairs between the main corolla lobes. *G. lagodechiana*, described from the S Caucasus, has flowers mostly solitary on short leafy side branches. *G. gelida* M. Bieb., from dry meadows in N Turkey and the Caucasus, has yellow flowers and is often larger than *G. septemfida*.

Gentiana tianshanica Rupr.   Native of the Tien Shan in Soviet C Asia, and NW China south to Tibet (Xizang), growing in mountain meadows, flowering in August. Plant with several stems to 30cm from a basal rosette of leaves. Stem leaves sheathing at the base. Flowers with corolla *c*.2.5cm long, blue or purplish. An attractive plant for any good soil in a warm position. Hardy to −20°C or less.

Gentiana triflora Pall.   Native of E Siberia, NE China, Sakhalin, Korea and Japan (var. *japonica* (Kusn.) Hara), in N Honshu and Hokkaido, growing in grassy places, especially on roadsides, from sea level to the mountains, flowering in August–September. Plant with few or several upright stems to 80cm from a thick

Gentiana tianshanica

Swertia iberica on the Zigana Pass

Gentiana affinis

Tripterospermum japonicum

Gentiana triflora var. *japonica* near Shari, Hokkaido

rootstock. Leaves lanceolate. Flowers with corolla 4–5cm long, not opening wide, even in sun. For peaty, moist, but well-drained soil in sun or partial shade. Hardy to −20°C or less.

Swertia iberica Fisch. ex C. A. Meyer (*Gentianaceae*)   Native of the Caucasus and NE Turkey, growing in alpine meadows, by streams and in damp places in scrub and forest at 1600–2700m in Turkey, flowering in July–September. Plant with few upright stems 6.5–9cm tall, from a rosette of broad leaves. Stem leaves alternate. Flowers with bluish or reddish-purple petals, 11–15mm long. For moist, peaty soil in a cool position. Hardy to −20°C. Other species are found on mountains across the northern hemisphere.

Tripterospermum japonicum (Sieb. & Zucc.) Maxim. syn. *Crawfurdia japonica* Sieb. & Zucc. (*Gentianaceae*)   Native of E China, Taiwan, Korea, Sakhalin and Japan, in all the islands, growing in woods and grassy places, flowering in August–October. Stems very slender, twining, to 80cm, from slender, creeping rhizomes. Leaves broadly ovate to lanceolate, 4–8cm long. Flowers with corolla *c.*3cm long, rather pale blue. Fruits red-purple, fleshy. A delicate plant. For moist, peaty soil in partial shade with a low shrub to creep through. Hardy to −20°C perhaps. Shown here in Yakusima.

Nepeta clarkei by a lake in Kashmir

Nepeta clarkei

Nepeta connata

Calamintha nepeta

Nepeta subsessilis var. *yesoensis*

Calamintha grandiflora (L.) Moench. (*Labiatae*)   Native of Europe, from NE Spain east to NW Iran and the Caucasus, growing in damp woods and scrub, often on limestone, flowering in June–October. Plant pleasantly fragrant when bruised, with shortly creeping stolons and stems to 60cm. Leaves pale green, ovate, toothed. Calyx 12mm long, with a ciliate margin; corolla 25–40mm long, bright pink. *C. sylvatica* Bromf., from Ireland to North Africa east to the Caucasus, is similar, but with smaller, pink or lilac flowers, with purple spots on the lower lip, *c.*15mm long. For any good soil in sun or partial shade.

Calamintha nepeta (L.) Savi   Native of Europe, from S England east to S Russia and N Iran and south to Spain and North Africa, growing in scrub and on dry banks, usually on limestone, flowering in June–September. Plant aromatic, with ascending pubescent branched stems to 60cm. Leaves broadly ovate, 10–20mm long. Flowers white or lilac, sometimes purple spotted, 10–15mm long, much loved by bees. For a warm, sunny place. Hardy to –15°C.

Dracocephalum nutans L. (*Labiatae*)   Native of Siberia and NW China in Sinjiang, growing in dry, rocky places and scrub, flowering in May–July. Plant with a shortly creeping rhizome and stems to 70cm, though usually less. Leaves often reddish. Flowers nodding, 17–22mm long. For a sunny, well-drained position. Hardy to –25°C.

Dracocephalum ruyschianum L.   Native of Europe, from Norway and the Pyrenees eastwards to N Turkey, Siberia, C Asia and China, growing in steppes, dry meadows and rocky hills, flowering in June–July. Plant with upright stems to 60cm, but usually forming clumps 30cm high and wide. Leaves linear-lanceolate, 2–7cm long. Flowers in short spikes, in whorls of 2–6; corolla 2–2.8cm, blue to violet, rarely pink or white. For well-drained but good soil in full sun. Hardy to –25°C.

Lallemantia canescens (L.) Fisch. & Mey. syn. *Dracocephalum canescens* L. (*Labiatae*)   Native of E Turkey, the S Caucasus and Iran, growing in rough ground, abandoned fields, rocky slopes and screes, often on limestone at 1300–3250m, flowering in June–August. Plant with spreading, then upright stems to 50cm tall. Lower leaves toothed, 2–6cm long, greyish. Flowers purple or bluish, 28–40mm long. For well-drained, dry soil in full sun. Hardy to –25°C.

Meehania fargesii (Léveillé) Wu (*Labiatae*)   Native of W China in Yunnan and Sichuan, growing in woods, scrub and wet, shady ravines, at *c.*1500m, flowering in April–June. Plant usually not forming stolons, unlike *M. urticifolia* (see p. 75). Stems to 40cm, slightly hairy above. Leaves and lower bracts stalked, the blade *c.*6cm wide and long, cordate. Upper bracts not leafy. Flowers *c.*4.5cm long, in loose terminal spikes. Calyx teeth acute. For a moist position, in some shade. Hardy to –10°C, perhaps less.

Melittis melissophyllum L. (*Labiatae*) Bastard Balm   Native of Europe, from England south to Spain and Portugal, and east to Russia, Greece and just reaching NW Turkey, growing in hedges, scrub and mountain woods, flowering in May–June. Plant with a clump of upright stems 20–70cm tall. Leaves to 7cm in W Europe. Flowers 25–40mm, usually purple or pink in W Europe, white with a purplish lip

Dracocephalum nutans

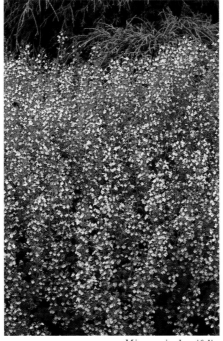

Micromeria thymifolia

Calamintha grandiflora

Meehania fargesii in Sichuan

Dracocephalum ruyschianum

Melittis melissophyllum

Lallemantia canescens at Harry Hay's, Surrey

in E Europe, and in subsp. *carpatica* and subsp. *albida*, which have larger leaves, to 15cm long. For any good soil in partial shade; the most attractive form in cultivation has white flowers with a pink lower lip. Hardy to −20°C.

Micromeria thymifolia (Scop.) Fritsch (*Labiatae*) Thyme-leaved Savory   Native of SE Europe, from Hungary and N Italy to Yugoslavia and Albania, growing in rock crevices, flowering in June–August. Stems to 50cm, branched. Leaves 5–20mm long. Flowers 5–9mm long, white and violet, with a 13-veined calyx. Hardy to −15°C, but dislikes wet soil in winter.

Nepeta clarkei Hook. fil. (*Labiatae*)   Native of the Himalayas from Pakistan to Kashmir, growing, often in great quantity, in rather dry valleys by streams and lakes at 2700–3300m, flowering in July–September. Plant forming large upright clumps to 80cm. Leaves ovate-lanceolate, 2.5–6cm long. Flowers pure blue (not purplish), with a white patch on the lower lip. Hardy to −25°C or less, but eaten by slugs in winter if not protected.

Nepeta connata Royle ex Benth.   Native of the Himalayas, from Pakistan to N India, growing in scrub and grassy places at 2100–3600m, flowering in July–September. Stems few, unbranched, to 60cm. Leaves 8–20cm, heart-shaped at the base. Flowers *c.*2cm long, purplish. For any good soil in full sun. Hardy to −25°C. *N. nervosa* Royle ex Benth. is similar, but has a spike of pale blue or, more rarely, purple flowers, 1.5cm long, and shorter linear-lanceolate leaves. It is common in Kashmir.

Nepeta subsessilis Maxim. var. *yesoensis* Fr. & Sav.   Native of Japan, in Hokkaido and C & N Honshu, growing on shady rocks by streams in the mountains, and on sheltered coastal cliffs, flowering in July–September. Stems several, to 100cm, but nearer 30cm in gardens, from a tufted rootstock. Leaves ovate, 6–10cm long, short-stalked. Flowers *c.*3cm long, usually bluish, rarely white. For moist, rich soil in partial shade. Hardy to −20°C perhaps.

Wild Marjoram *Origanum vulgare* on chalk downs near Wye, Kent

Origanum calcaratum Juss. syn. *O. tournefortii* Ait. (*Labiatae*)   Native of Crete, Amorgos, Ikaria and other C Aegean islands, growing on limestone rocks, flowering in April–October. Plant with many stems to 30cm from a woody rootstock. Leaves broadly ovate to orbicular, glaucous, pubescent. Bracts 8–13mm long, 4–10mm wide, acute. Calyx with a large entire or almost undivided upper lip, and lower lip either absent or of 2 very small teeth. Corolla 10–17mm long. Easy to grow in well-drained, dry soil in full sun, possibly planted in a wall. Hardy to −10°C, or less if dry.

Origanum laevigatum Boiss.   Native of S Turkey and Cyprus, growing in grassland, maquis, scrub and open woods at up to 2000m, flowering in April–October. Plant with upright stems to 70cm from a woody and suckering rootstock. Inflorescence very diffuse. Leaves ovate to elliptical, glaucous, glabrous. Bracts 3–6mm, lanceolate, acute, purple. Calyx with 5 equal teeth, 3–6mm long. Corolla 8–16mm long, purple. Stamens not exserted. For well-drained soil in full sun. Hardy to −15°C, probably less.

Origanum rotundifolium Boiss.   Native of NE Turkey, in the Çoruh gorge and near Erzurum and of Georgia, growing in walls, rocks and rocky slopes at up to 1300m, flowering in June–September. Plant with a woody base and creeping underground stolons. Flowering stems hairy, to 30cm long. Leaves roundish, with conspicuous veins. Bracts 8–25mm × 7–27mm, yellowish green. Calyx 5–9mm, 2-lipped, with 5 teeth. For well-drained soil in sun or partial shade, best growing out of a wall. Hardy to −10°C, perhaps less. *O. acutidens* (Hand.-Mazz.) Ietswaart is similar, but has longer glabrous stems and much branched to 50cm. The leaves are ovate, less

grey, with inconspicuous veins, and the calyx teeth are acuminate. It is found in E Turkey at up to 3000m, on rocky slopes and screes, but proved short-lived in cultivation in S England, probably killed by damp rather than cold.

Origanum scabrum Boiss. & Held.   Native of Greece, growing in rocky places in the Taygetos mountains of the Peloponnese (with subsp. *pulchrum* (Boiss. & Held.) P. H. Davis in Euboea), flowering in June–September. Plant with creeping underground rhizomes and flowering stems to 45cm. Leaves cordate at the base, glabrous. Bracts 7–8mm wide, ovate, purple. Upper lip of calyx with 3 teeth. In subsp. *pulchrum* the leaf margins are smooth, not scabrid, the calyx is more deeply divided and the bracts are ovate-elliptic. For well-drained, stony soil in full sun. Hardy to −15°C or less.

Origanum vulgare L. Wild Marjoram   Native of most of Europe, Turkey and C Asia eastwards to Taiwan, growing in dry grassy places or, in the south, in open woods, flowering in May–October. A very variable species, both in its wide natural distribution and in cultivation. Stems to 100cm or more from a woody base, but also with suckers. Leaves and stems variably hairy. Inflorescence compact or diffuse. Bracts 4–5mm purple. Calyx with 5 equal teeth, 2–4mm long. Corolla 3–10mm long, purple, pink or white. For well-drained soil in full sun. Hardy to −20°C or less. Some of the commoner cultivars are 'Aureum', with golden leaves; 'Compactum', with numerous short stems to 15cm, a very free-flowering and valuable plant; 'Prismaticum', with spicules 12–20mm long, often grown for cooking, as 'Oregano'; and 'Roseum' (shown here) which has pink flowers.

Origanum hybrids   Origanum species hybridize very readily both in the wild and in gardens. The following have been named and propagated, and others are likely to appear, between any of the species cultivated.

Origanum 'Barbara Tingey'   A hybrid between *O. calcaratum* and *O. rotundifolium*, raised in around 1980.

Origanum 'Emma Stanley'   A form or hybrid of *O. scabrum*, possibly with *O. amanum*, which appeared in the garden of Roger Poulett at North Mundham in Sussex in around 1985. A very striking plant with smooth, glaucous leaves and neat, particularly well-coloured spicules. Hardy to −15°C perhaps.

Origanum 'Hopleys'   Introduced by David Barker of Hopleys Nurseries in *c.*1980. This is probably a form of *O. vulgare*, close to subsp. *gracile* (syn. *O. tytthanthum* Gontsch.). It is native of Turkey and Iran east to Pakistan. It may, however, be a hybrid between *O. vulgare* and *O. laevigatum*, under which it has usually been listed. Stems to 70cm. Spicules slender, compact. Corolla *c.*6mm long. For well-drained soil in full sun. Hardy to −15°C perhaps.

Origanum 'Kent Beauty'   A hybrid between *O. scabrum* and *O. rotundifolium*, raised at Washfield Nurseries, Hawkhurst, Kent in around 1978. 'Kent Beauty' was selected from among a number of seedlings which appeared near where the parents were growing. It has much branched, semi-prostrate stems to 35cm from a woody and suckering rootstock. Stem leaves glaucous and glabrous. Bracts 1.6cm × 1.5cm, rounded. Corolla 13mm long. For well-drained soil in full sun, preferably on a raised bed. Hardy to −10°C.

ORIGANUM

Origanum vulgare 'Roseum'

Origanum 'Hopleys' at Windsor

Origanum calcaratum

Origanum 'Kent Beauty'

Origanum laevigatum

Origanum rotundifolium

Origanum scabrum

Origanum 'Emma Stanley'

Origanum 'Barbara Tingay'

Leonotis dysophylla (pale form)

Leonotis dysophylla near Cathedral Peak, Natal

Leonotis leonurus at Sissinghurst

Chelonopsis moschata at Sellindge, Kent

Agastache foeniculum

Agastache cana (Hook.) Woot. & Standl. (*Labiatae*)   Native of W Texas and S New Mexico, growing on dry slopes in the mountains, flowering in July–August. Plant aromatic, to 60cm. Stems branching; leaves ovate-lanceolate, serrate, to 4cm long. Flowers pink, 25mm long. For a hot, dry position in full sun. Hardy to −20°C.

Agastache foeniculum (Pursh) O. Kuntze syn. *A. anethiodora* Britt.   Native of North America, from Ontario west to Washington, south to Colorado, and naturalized in the east in New England, growing in fields, dry scrub and hills, flowering in June–September. Plant smelling of aniseed; stems to 1.5m, glabrous. Leaves ovate, whitish beneath. Bracts often tinged violet; flowers blue. For dry soil in full sun. Hardy to −25°C.

Chelonopsis moschata Miq. (*Labiatae*) Native of Japan, in Hokkaido, Honshu and Shikoku, growing in wet places along streams, flowering in August–September. Plant with numerous slender stems, 50–100cm, from a woody rootstock. Leaves narrowly ovate to broadly oblanceolate, 10–20cm long. Flowers 1–3 in the leaf axils, 4–4.5cm long. Nutlets 7–8mm long. For a moist, cool position in light shade. Hardy to −20°C.

Leonotis dysophylla Benth. syn. *L. ocymifolia* (Burm. fil.) Iwarsson var. *raineriana* (Visiani) Iwarsson   Native of South Africa, in the E Cape Province and into Natal and Transvaal, growing in grassland in the mountains, to 2000m in the Drakensberg, flowering in November–February. Plant 1–5m, sometimes woody at the base, and suckering underground. Leaves broadly ovate, 5–17cm long, the margins crenate. Calyx 15–30cm long, 2-lipped. Flowers 24–45mm long, velvety-hairy outside, orange or rarely very pale pink. Hardier than *L. leonurus*, but needing a hot, dry position. The albinistic form of this species is more cream-buff than white, with brownish-red pollen. Hardy to −15°C, perhaps.

Leonotis leonurus (L.) R. Br. Wild Dagga Native of South Africa from Cape Province to Natal and Transvaal, growing in grassy places, on the edge of scrub and on roadsides below 1800m, flowering in November–July. Plant with upright stems to 2m or more. Leaves linear, 5–10cm long. Calyx shorter than 15mm, teeth equal. Flowers 40–50mm long, rarely white in var. *albiflora* Benth., usually grown as the cultivar 'Harrismith White'. For a warm, dry, sunny position. Hardy to −10°C, perhaps less with frost protection for the root.

Perovskia atriplicifolia Benth. (*Labiatae*) Native of Afghanistan to S Xizang, growing in open, rocky places, flowering in July–September. Plant to 1m, with numerous stems from ground level. Leaves entire, ovate-oblong, to 4cm. Flowers with a blue-hairy calyx. For any dry soil in full sun. Hardy to −10°C, or less. (Not illustrated.)

***Perovskia* 'Blue Spire'**   Probably a hybrid between the entire-leaved *P. atriplicifolia* and the bipinnate-leaved *P. abrotanoides* Kar., raised by Notcutts. Plant spreading below ground and becoming woody at the base. Leaves deeply laciniate, nearer to *P. abrotanoides*. Flowers with very woolly calyces. For dry soil in full sun. Hardy to −25°C.

Perovskia 'Blue Spire' at the Royal Botanic Garden, Edinburgh

Perovskia 'Blue Spire'

Agastache cana

435

Helenium hoopesii in the Yellowstone National Park, Wyoming

Silphium perfoliatum

Helenium 'Wyndley'

Heliopsis 'Light of Loddon'

Heliopsis 'Spitzentänzerin'

Helenium autumnale L. (*Compositae*)   Native of North America, from Quebec south to Florida, and west to Manitoba, Oregon, Nevada and Arizona, growing in wet meadows and marshes, flowering in August–October. Plant forming large clumps of stems to 1.8m. Leaves elliptic oblong or lanceolate. Flowers 5–7cm across, with a yellow centre in wild *H. autumnale*, a brown centre in the closely related *H. nudiflorum*, from the Midwest. Most cultivars are probably hybrids between these and *H. bigelovii* from California, which also has a yellow centre. Typical cultivars are: 'Moerheim Beauty', flowers brownish-red; stems to 80cm; raised by Ruys in 1930. 'Riverton Beauty', flowers yellow; stems to 1.5m. **'Wyndley'**, flowers yellow marked with red; stems to 60cm.

Helenium hoopesii Gray   Native of California, in the Sierra Nevada, from Tulare Co. north to S Oregon, and east to Wyoming and New Mexico, growing in meadows along streams and on marshy hillsides at 2000–3000m, flowering in July–September. Plant with a handsome rosette of large oblanceolate leaves to 30cm long, from a thick aromatic rootstock. Poisonous to sheep and generally a sign of overgrazing in the parts of the Rockies where it is common. For any good soil. Hardy to −25°C or less.

Helianthus decapetalus L. (*Compositae*) Wild Sunflower   Native of NE North America, from SW Quebec to Minnesota and Nebraska, south to Georgia, Kentucky and Missouri, growing in open woods, clearings and scrub, flowering in August–October. Plant with a creeping rhizome, forming large patches of stems to 1.5m tall. Leaves ovate, acute, thin in texture, to 20cm long. Flower-heads 5–6.5cm across with 8–12 or more 'petals'. A large garden variety, 'Multiflorus', is sometimes considered a hybrid with *H. annuus*. 'Corona Dorica' is a form with enlarged central florets.

Helianthus salicifolius A. Dietrich syn. *H. orgyralis* DC.   Native of Nebraska to E Colorado south to W Missouri, Oklahoma and Texas, growing in meadows, clearings in forest and prairies, usually on limestone, flowering in August–October. Plant with long rhizomes, forming clumps of tall stems to 2m or more. Leaves linear to linear-lanceolate, recurved, usually 1–3mm across. Flower-heads *c.*5cm across. 'Lemon Queen' sounds more beautiful.

Heliopsis helianthoides (L.) Sweet (*Compositae*)   Native of New York and S Ontario west to Minnesota and south to North Carolina and Illinois, growing in open woods, scrub and dry hillsides, flowering in July–September. Plant forming clumps of stems to 1.5m. Leaves ovate-lanceolate to oblong-ovate. Flowers with 'petals' that remain attached when dead. **'Light of Loddon'** has single flowers; **'Spitzentänzerin'** (syn. 'Ballerina') semi-double; and 'Golden Plume' (syn. 'Goldgefieder') and 'Incomparabilis' have double zinnia-like flowers of brash orange-yellow. For any good soil in full sun. Hardy to −25°C or less.

Silphium perfoliatum L. (*Compositae*)   Native of E North America, from Ontario to South Dakota, south to Georgia, Missouri and Oklahoma, growing in damp woods on river banks, in scrub and moist meadows, flowering in July–September. Stems to 2.5m, forming a large clump. Lower leaves coarsely toothed, with winged petioles; upper leaves joined at their bases to form a cup. Flower-heads 5–7.5cm across. For rich, moist soil in sun or shade. Hardy to −25°C or less.

Helianthus salicifolius at Bressingham

Helenium autumnale

Helianthus decapetalus in New York State, near Purchase

Helianthus decapetalus

'Orlando'

'September Ruby'

'Lye End Beauty'

'Herbstschnee'
syn. 'Autumn Snow'

'Jenny'

'Andenken an
Alma Potschke'

'Harrington's
Pink'

'White Swan'

'Coombe Margaret'

'Carnival'

'Pink Zenith'

'Barr's Pink'

'September Glow'

'Ada Ballard'

'Mrs S. T. Wright'

'Lady-in-Blue'

'Chequers'

'Little Pink Beauty'

'Chatterbox'

Michaelmas daisy specimens from Wisley, 1 October. ⅔ life size

Wild asters in Wyoming

Aster thomsonii

Aster amellus L. (*Compositae*)   Native of
Europe, from NC France and Poland
southwards to N Italy and Bulgaria, eastwards
to Russia and C Asia, Turkey (subsp. *ibericus*)
and the Caucasus, growing in scrub and on the
edges of woods, flowering in June–August. Plant
with erect stems to 70cm. Leaves oblong to
lanceolate. Flower-heads large, solitary; petals
blue, white or occasionally red. Hardy to
−25°C.

Aster × dumosus hort.   This is a group of
dwarf Michaelmas daisies which form rounded,
bushy plants to *c*.40cm high. They are probably
hybrids between *A. dumosus* L., a species from
North America, and *A. novi-belgii*. Leaves linear
or linear-lanceolate, entire, to 8cm long.
Flower-heads up to 2cm across, white or pink,
to lavender-blue, produced in August–October.
Hardy to −25°C or less.

Aster × frikartii 'Mönch'   This is a very good
selection of *A. × frikartii*, which is a hybrid
between *A. amellus* and *A. thomsonii* (q.v.).
Raised by Frikart in Switzerland in *c*.1920, the
name 'Mönch' refers to a famous Swiss
mountain. This particular form is highly
regarded for its long flowering season. Plant to
120cm high. Flowers lavender-blue, *c*.6cm
across, freely produced in a loose panicle from
July–October. Hardy to −20°C.

Aster novae-angliae L.   Native of North
America, from Quebec to Alberta, south to
North Carolina, Kentucky, Arkansas, Kansas
and Colorado, growing in damp scrub,
meadows and on shores, flowering from
August–October. Also commonly cultivated and
seen as an escape elsewhere in North America
and Europe. Stems stout, up to 2m high. Leaves
lanceolate, to 12cm long, entire. Flower-heads
numerous, violet-purple or pink, to 5cm across.
Involucral bracts recurving, sticky. There are
several varieties available. Hardy
to −25°C.

Aster novi-belgii L.   Native of E North
America, from Newfoundland to Quebec and
Nova Scotia, south to Georgia, growing in
damp scrub, meadows, and on shores, usually
within 100 miles of the sea, flowering from late
July–October. The name '*novi-belgii*' comes
from 'New Belgium', the early name for New
York. Plant to 1.2m high. Leaves lanceolate to
linear-lanceolate, to 12cm long. Flowers blue-
violet. Involucral bracts spreading. There are
many garden varieties, with flowers ranging in
colour from white and pink through to light and
dark blue and purple; they need to be divided
every few years, preferably in the spring. Hardy
to −25°C or less.

Michaelmas daisy cultivars   (In brackets is
the species group to which the cultivar belongs.)
'**Ada Ballard**' (*novi-belgii*) 1m. Large flowers in
September.
'**Andenken an Alma Potschke**' (*novae-angliae*)

Aster 'King George'

Aster × frikartii 'Mönch'

105cm. September–October.
'**Barr's Pink**' (*novae-angliae*) 1.3m. Large
semi-double flowers in September.
'**Carnival**' (*novi-belgii*) 60cm.
'**Chatterbox**' (× *dumosus*)
'**Chequers**' (*novi-belgii*) 1m. Raised by R. A.
Lidsey *c*.1955. Flowers *c*.5cm across.
'**Coombe Margaret**' (*novi-belgii*)
'**Harrington's Pink**' (*novae-angliae*) 120cm.
Leafy growth. Clear-pink flowers in
September–October. Good for cutting.
'**Herbstschnee**' syn. '**Autumn Snow**' (*novae-
angliae*) 130cm. Recently introduced from
Germany, large flowers in bushy heads from
August–September.
'**Jenny**' (× *dumosus*) 30cm. August–September.
Raised by R. A. Lidsey at Gayborder Nursery,
Melbourne, Derbyshire in around 1965, and
named after his mother.
'**King George**' (*amellus*) 60cm. An old cultivar,
easy to grow. August–October.
'**Lady-in-Blue**' (× *dumosus*) 25cm. Compact
bush, with numerous semi-double flowers from
August–October.
'**Little Pink Beauty**' (× *dumosus*) 40cm. Good
semi-double. September–October. Raised by
R. A. Lidsey.
'**Lye End Beauty**' (*novae-angliae*) 130cm. This
occurred in a garden in the late 1950s. Rich
cerise-lilac flowers in August–September.
'**Mrs S. T. Wright**' (*novae-angliae*)   Named
after the wife of the first Superintendent of the
RHS gardens at Wisley.
'**Orlando**' (*novi-belgii*) 1.5m. Raised by Mr
Percy Picton. Flowers *c*.5cm across in
September–October.
'**Pink Zenith**' (*amellus*) 60cm. Upright habit.
August–October.
'**September Glow**' (*amellus*)
'**September Ruby**' (*novae-angliae*) 120cm.
September–October.
'**White Swan**' (*novi-belgii*)

Aster thomsonii C. B. Clarke   A native of the
W Himalaya, from Pakistan to Uttar Pradesh,
growing in forests and shrubberies, at
2100–3000m, flowering in July–September.
Stems erect, branched, to 1m. Leaves ovate to
elliptic, toothed, to 10cm long. Flower-heads
usually solitary, pale lilac, 3.5–5cm across. Best
increased by seeds or cuttings. Hardy to −20°C.

Aster novae-angliae

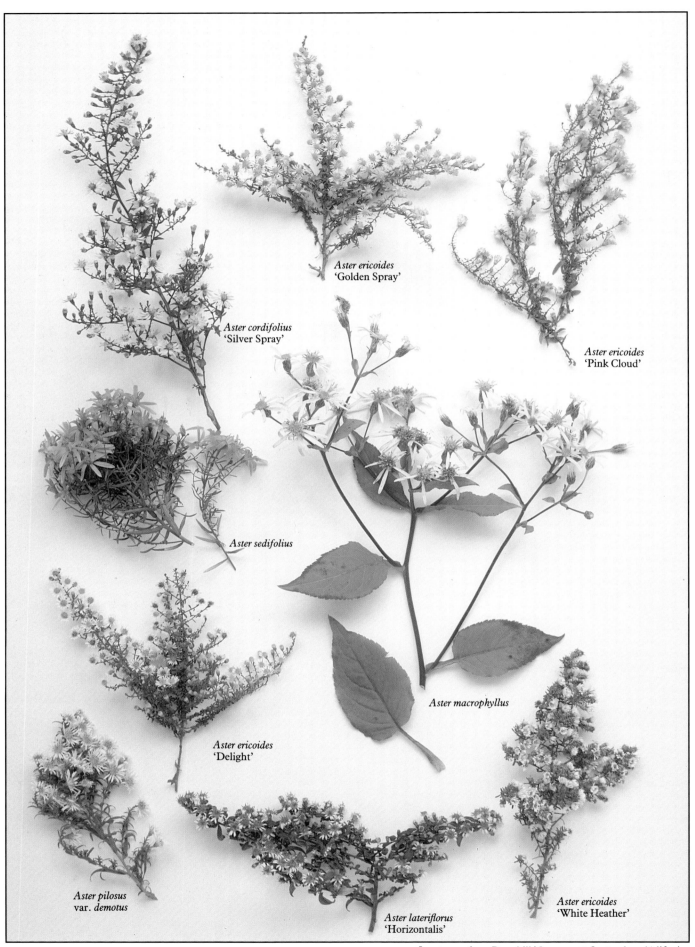

Aster ericoides
'Golden Spray'

Aster cordifolius
'Silver Spray'

Aster ericoides
'Pink Cloud'

Aster sedifolius

Aster macrophyllus

Aster ericoides
'Delight'

Aster pilosus
var. *demotus*

Aster lateriflorus
'Horizontalis'

Aster ericoides
'White Heather'

Specimens from Perryhill Nursery, 30 September. ½ life size

Aster species with Artemisia, in Idaho

Aster ericoides 'Hon. Vicary Gibbs'

Aster sedifolius

Aster divaricatus

Aster cordifolius L. (*Compositae*) Native of North America, from Nova Scotia and Quebec south to Wisconsin, Georgia, Alabama and Missouri, growing in open woods, thickets and clearings, flowering from August–October. Plant erect, much branched, with glabrous stems to 2m, arising from a creeping rhizome. Leaves broadly ovate, cordate, sharply toothed, to 12cm long. Flowers numerous, small, star-like, ranging in colour from violet or blue to nearly white, to 2cm across, borne in loose graceful sprays. Hardy to −25°C and less. *A. cordifolius* 'Silver Spray' grows to 1.5m and bears very pale lilac flowers in long arching sprays.

Aster divaricatus L. syn. *A. corymbosus* Ait. Native of North America, from S Maine west to Oregon, south to Georgia, Alabama and Tennessee, growing in dry woods and clearings, flowering in July–October. Very variable and easily confused with other species. Stems dark purple, to 1m high, from creeping rhizomes. Leaves cordate, lobed at the base, to 7cm long, coarsely toothed. Flowers white, with a pale-yellow disc. Flower-heads *c.*3cm across, in corymbs. Hardy to −25°C and less.

Aster ericoides L. Native of North America, from Maine west to British Columbia, south to New England, Georgia, Texas and Arizona, growing in dry open soil or thickets, flowering in July–October. Plant to 1m high, bushy. Stems slender, erect, much-branched above, arising from a short rhizome. Leaves almost rigid, linear, entire, to 7cm long. Flower-heads numerous, white or tinged rose, to 1cm across. Hardy to −25°C and less.
Aster ericoides cultivars include: '**Delight**', '**Golden Spray**' (80cm), '**Hon. Vicary Gibbs**', '**Pink Cloud**' (80cm), '**White Heather**' (1m).

Aster lateriflorus (L.) Britt. '**Horizontalis**' *A. lateriflorus* is native of North America, from Quebec, Nova Scotia, Ontario and Minnesota south to Georgia, Tennessee and Arkansas, growing in dry to moist fields, clearings, thickets and on shorelines, flowering from

August–October. Plant with slender, purplish or green stems, to 1.5m, with spreading branches. Leaves linear-lanceolate to broadly lanceolate, toothed, to 12cm long. Flower-heads numerous, white or pale purple, to 1.5cm across. '**Horizontalis**' is a common cultivar, with very wide-spreading branches.

Aster macrophyllus L. Native of North America, from Quebec west to Minnesota, south to North Carolina, Tennessee, West Virginia, Ohio, Indiana and Illinois, growing in dry to moist, open woods, thickets and clearings, flowering from August–September. A rather coarse plant, with reddish stems, to 1.5m high, from a thick rootstock. Basal leaves large, cordate, toothed; upper leaves variable, often smaller and narrower. Flowers lavender to violet, *c.*2.5cm across, borne in a broad corymb. A very variable plant, with many different forms. Hardy to −25°C.

Aster pilosus Willd. var. **demotus** Blake syn. *A. tradescantii* hort. This is the commonest variety of *A. pilosus* and is native from Maine west to Minnesota, and southwards throughout the USA, growing in dry thickets, clearings, fields and by roadsides, flowering from August–October. Plant to 1.5m high. Leaves linear-lanceolate. Small flower-heads (white or tinged rose) to 1.5cm across. Hardy to −25°C.

Aster sedifolius L. syn. *A. acris* L. Native of S Europe, from France, Spain and Portugal, eastwards to Russia and the Caucasus, growing on dry hills and waste places, flowering in August–September. Plant with branching stems, forming a rounded bush to 120cm, but usually *c.*50cm. Leaves very narrow, white-hairy in subsp. *canus* from E and SE Europe. Flowers blue to lilac, rather small, and spidery, with 5–10 'petals'. For dry soil in full sun. Hardy to −20°C or less. The cultivar 'Nanus' is said to be more compact, to 45cm, and so less likely to flop to one side.

Boltonia asteroides

Chrysanthemum serotinum at Kew

Chrysanthemum yezoense

Aster albescens

Aster albescens (DC.) Hand.-Mazz.
(*Compositae*) Native of the Himalayas, from
Kashmir to SW China and Burma, growing in
light forests, shrubberies and on open slopes, at
2100–3600m, flowering in June–September. A
rambling subshrub, to 2m, with large leaves to
12cm. Flower-heads *c*.8mm across, lilac, purple
or rarely white. Hardy to −10°C, perhaps.

Aster tartaricus L. fil. Native of Japan, N
China and Siberia, from Lake Baikal eastwards,
growing in subalpine meadows and wet places,
flowering in August–October. Plant with erect
stems, up to 2m. Leaves lanceolate or oval-
lanceolate, narrowed to the base, entire, the
lower ones up to 30cm long. 2.5–3.3cm across.

Aster tartaricus

Aster turbellinus

Chrysanthemum zawadskii 'Clara Curtis'

Chrysanthemum zawadskii 'Mary Stoker'

Aster turbellinus Lindl.   Native of North America, from Illinois to Nebraska, south to Louisiana, Arkansas and Kansas, growing in dry prairies, open woods and on rocky outcrops, flowering in September–October. Plant to 1m. Leaves lanceolate or oblong-lanceolate, entire, to 8cm long. Flower-heads *c.*2cm across, violet, usually solitary at ends of branches.

Boltonia asteroides (L.) L'Her. (*Compositae*) Native of North America, from New York and New Jersey to Ohio south to Maryland and the mountains of North Carolina, growing on gravelly shores and sandy thickets, flowering in mid-July–September. Plant to 2m. Leaves linear to oblanceolate, entire, to 12cm long. Hardy to −25°C.

Chrysanthemum zawadskii Herbich var.

latilobum (Maxim.) Kitam. (*Compositae*) Native of parts of Russia, in the Carpathians and the Urals, Czechoslovakia and Poland, and east across Siberia to Japan, Korea and N China, growing on stony slopes, somewhat calcicole, flowering in August–October. Plant woody at base, to 60cm. Leaves broadly triangular-ovate, much divided, to 5cm long, coarsely toothed or lobed. Flower-heads terminal, solitary, or rather few in a loose corymb, to 8cm across, fragrant. Petals pale pink, or white; disc yellow. Hardy to −20°C. There are a number of extremely free-flowering clones or hybrids of this plant, with stems *c.*60cm e.g.: '**Clara Curtis**' and '**Mary Stoker**'.

Leucanthemella serotina (L.) Tzveler, syn. *Chrysanthemum serotinum* L., *C. uliginosum* Pers.

Native of E Europe, from SE Czechoslovakia and EC Yugoslavia eastwards to N Ukraine and NE Bulgaria, growing in wet places, flowering in September–November. A bushy, erect plant, with stems to 2m. Leaves lanceolate to oblong-lanceolate, deeply divided. Flowers with green centres, to 7cm across, turning to the sun. Good for cutting.

Chrysanthemum yezoense Maek. syn. *Dendranthema yezoense* (Maek.) D. J. H. Hind Native of Japan, in Hokkaido and Honshu, growing on rocks near seashores, flowering from September–December. Plant to 40cm, stoloniferous, from long-creeping rhizomes. Leaves wedge-shaped, to 4cm long and wide, tapered at base. Flowers white, daisy-like in branching sprays. A good plant for well-drained soil in full sun. Hardy to −15°C.

Eupatorium perfoliatum

Eupatorium purpureum near New York

Solidago 'Goldengate'

Eupatorium cannabinum by the Stour in Dorset

Vernonia novaboracensis

Vernonia crinita

Eupatorium rugosum

Solidaster × *luteus*

Solidago 'Crown of Rays'

Eupatorium purpureum subsp. maculatum

Eupatorium cannabinum L. (*Compositae*)
Hemp Agrimony   Native of Europe, from
Scotland to North Africa and Spain, and east to
Turkey and C Asia, growing in moist places,
fens, on river banks and by streams, flowering in
July–September. Plant forming large clumps of
stems to 120cm with rather soft leaves, deeply
3–5 lobed. Flower-heads 2–5mm across in a
large, flat-topped inflorescence, usually mauve-
pink but a white form is listed by Monksilver
Nursery near Cambridge, England. Like the
American *Eupatoria*, this is much visited by
butterflies. For any rich, moist soil in sun or
partial shade. Hardy to −25°C or less.

Eupatorium perfoliatum L. Thoroughwort,
Boneset   Native of E North America, from
Quebec to Manitoba, south to Florida,
Louisiana and Texas, growing in wet woods,
scrub, fens and damp grassland, flowering in
July–October. Whole plant roughly hairy with
rather few stems to 1.5m. Leaves opposite, the
lower often joined at the base round the stem,
usually long acuminate. Flower-heads 10–40
flowered in a rather flat-topped inflorescence,
whitish or purplish. Hardy to −25°C.

Eupatorium purpureum L. Green-stemmed
Joe Pye Weed   Native of E North America,
from New Hampshire west to Minnesota and
Nebraska, and south to N Florida and
Oklahoma, growing in damp places in woods,
usually on basic soils, flowering in
July–September. Plant forming large clumps of
glaucous stems to 2m or more, purple only at
the nodes. Leaves lanceolate to ovate, in whorls
of 2–5. Flower-heads 3–7 flowered, in a large
pyramidal inflorescence, pale pinkish, mauve or

creamy white. For any rich, moist soil in sun or
partial shade. Hardy to −25°C or less. A fine
sight when covered with butterflies.

Eupatorium purpureum subsp. *maculatum*
L. Joe Pye Weed   Native of North America,
from Newfoundland west to British Columbia,
and south to New York and in the mountains of
North Carolina, New Mexico and Washington,
growing in damp places in open woods,
meadows and river and lake shores usually on
base-rich soils, flowering in July–September.
Plant forming large clumps of tall, purple stems
to 2m or more. Leaves simple, oblong-
lanceolate to narrowly ovate-lanceolate, in
whorls of 4–5. Flower-heads 8–20 flowered in a
large flat-topped inflorescence. Hardy to −25°C
or less. 'Atropurpureum' has rich-reddish-
purple flowers.

Eupatorium rugosum Houtt. syn. *E.
urticifolium* Reich. White Snakeroot   Native of
E North America from Quebec to S
Saskatchewan and south, in the mountains, to
Georgia and Texas, growing in woods and
especially scrub, flowering in July–October.
Stems to 1.5m from a tough, knobbly rhizome,
forming large clumps to 1.5m. Leaves ovate,
stalked, coarsely toothed, to 18cm long. Flower-
heads 15–30 flowered, pure white. For any good
soil in sun or partial shade. Hardy to −25°C.

Solidago 'Crown of Rays' (*Compositae*)   A
short plant to 50cm with small flowers on
radiating rays. Several wild species from N
America have an inflorescence of this shape, e.g.
S. juncea. For any soil in full sun. Hardy to
−25°C or less.

Solidago 'Goldengate'   Raised by Burleydam
in 1948. Stems to 30cm in a slowly spreading
clump. For any soil in full sun. Hardy to −25°C
or less.

× *Solidaster luteus* (Everett) M. L. Green ex
Dress syn. *Aster* 'Hybridus luteus'   A supposed
hybrid between *Aster ptarmicoides* and *Solidago
canadensis*, known since before 1910. Stems to
60cm; flowers *c*.5mm across, pale yellow
produced in July–September. 'Lemore' raised
by Thos. Carlisle Ltd in 1948 is probably the
plant shown here. For any good soil in full sun.
Hardy to −25°C or less.

Vernonia crinita Raf. (*Compositae*) Ironweed
Native of Missouri, Kansas, Arkansas and
Oklahoma, growing in wet meadows, marshes
and open woods, flowering in July–September.
Plant forming clumps of stout stems to 3m tall.
Leaves linear or linear-lanceolate, to 2cm wide.
Flower-heads 55–90 flowered, 1.2–2cm across,
with numerous curling threads on the bracts.
For any good, moist soil in sun or partial shade.
Hardy to −20°C or less.

Vernonia noveboracensis (L.) Michx.
Native of Massachusetts and S New York
south to West Virginia, Ohio, Georgia and
Mississippi, growing in marshy meadows and
clearings in woods, flowering in August–
October. Plant with branching stems to 2m.
Leaves lanceolate to oblong-lanceolate, to
4.7cm wide. Flower-heads 30–50 flowered,
around 10mm across, red-purple or white,
with threads on the bracts. For any good, moist
soil in sun or partial shade. Hardy to −25°C
or less.

Tricyrtis 'White Towers'

Tricyrtis 'White Towers' at Washfield Nurseries, Kent

Tricyrtis latifolia

Tricyrtis affinis

Tricyrtis hirta in Kagoshima, Kyushu

Tricyrtis hirta

Tricyrtis affinis Mak. (*Liliaceae*)　Native of Japan, in Hokkaido, Honshu, Shikoku and Kyushu, growing in woods and on mossy banks in the mountains, flowering in August–October. Stems few or several, spreading, from a tufted rootstock. Leaves hairy, acuminate, 8–18cm long, the upper clasping the stem. Flowers 1 to several in the leaf axils and terminal, *c.*2cm, long-stalked; petals spreading, not reflexed. For leafy or peaty soil in partial shade. Hardy to −20°C perhaps.

Tricyrtis formosana Baker syn. *T. stolonifera* Matsum.　Native of Taiwan, growing in forest and wet shady scrub, at up to 3000m, flowering in August–September. Plant often spreading by stolons, forming wide colonies of stems to 80cm. Leaves rather shining, deep green with darker spots, the upper clasping the stem. Flowers 2.5–3cm. For moist, loose, leafy soil in partial shade and shelter. Hardy to −15°C. Probably the most easily grown species.

Tricyrtis hirta (Thunb.) Hook.　Native of Honshu, Shikoku and Kyushu, growing on shady rocks, flowering in August–October. Stems 40–80cm, from a tufted rootstock, sometimes pendulous, hairy. Leaves narrowly ovate-oblong to broadly lanceolate, 8–15cm long. Flowers 2–3 in the leaf axils, and tufted and terminal, on stalks shorter than the 2.5–3cm-long flowers. For moist, leafy soil in partial shade and shelter. Hardy to −15°C.

Tricyrtis latifolia Maxim. syn. *T. bakeri* Koidz.　Native of Japan, in all the large islands, and of China, growing in woods in the mountains, flowering in July–September. Stems few, hairy, upright or arching, to 80cm. Leaves obovate, 8–15cm long, 4–9cm wide. Inflorescence cymose. Flowers 2–2.5cm long. For leafy soil in partial shade. Hardy to −15°C.

Tricyrtis '**Lilac Towers**' and '**White Towers**' These are very similar except for the flower colour and are perhaps hybrids between *T. hirta* and possibly *T. affinis*, having hairy stems and leaves, always stiffly upright, with several flowers on short stalks in the leaf axils. 'Lilac Towers' is often sold as *T. hirta*. Both are easily grown in leafy soil in partial shade. Hardy to −15°C.

Tricyrtis formosana at the Savill Gardens, Windsor

Tricyrtis formosana

Tricyrtis 'Lilac Towers'

Tricyrtis 'Lilac Towers'

Liriope muscari

Ophiopogon planiscapus 'Nigrescens'

Ruscus aculeatus

Prosartes smithii

Liriope muscari (Decne.) Bailey (*Convallariaceae*) Native of China, Japan, from C Honshu southwards, Taiwan, Korea and Vietnam, growing in woods, flowering in August–October. Plant tufted with grassy leaves 4–7 (–12)mm wide, up to 60cm long. Flower spikes often flattened, usually exceeding the leaves. Flowers 5–8mm across. Seeds exposed, black. For leafy soil in shade or partial shade. Hardy to –10°C perhaps.

Ophiopogon planiscapus Nakai (*Convallariaceae*)   Native of Japan, in Honshu, Shikoku and Kyushu, growing in woods and scrub at low altitudes, flowering in July–August. Plant with thickened tuberous roots, spreading by stolons to form loose patches. Leaves 15–50cm long, usually around 20cm, and 4–6mm wide.

Flowering stems 15–30cm, 3-angled, flattened. Flowers 6–7mm long. Seeds blue. For leafy or peaty soil in sun or shade. Hardy to –15°C, perhaps less for short periods. 'Nigrescens' syn. 'Arabicus' is an unusual form with blackish leaves. *O. japonicus* (L. fil.) Ker-Gawl, is smaller with narrower, 2–3mm-wide leaves. It is commonly planted as ground cover or as low-maintenance grass substitute. Hardy to –15°C.

Prosartes smithii (Hook.) Utech, Shinwari & Kawano syn. *Disporum smithii* (Hook.) Piper (*Liliaceae*)   Native of W North America, from C California to British Columbia, growing in moist, evergreen woods and redwood forest in the Coast Ranges, flowering in March–May, fruiting in August–October. Plant

with much-branched stems to 20cm, usually *c*.30cm from a tufted rootstock. Leaves ovate to ovate-lanceolate, 5–12cm long. Flowers whitish, in clusters of 1–5, 1.5–2.5cm long. Berries 12–15mm long. For a leafy soil in a shady, sheltered position. Hardy to –15°C, perhaps less.

Ruscus aculeatus L. (*Convallariaceae*) Native of Europe, from the Azores, North Africa and S England eastwards to the Caucasus and south to Turkey, with var. *angustifolius* Boiss. commoner in SE Europe and the Mediterranean area to the Caucasus, growing in oak woods, scrub and on rocky limestone slopes, flowering in February–May and September–October. Plant with stiff evergreen stems to 80cm from a slowly

Tricyrtis flava subsp. *ohsumiensis*

Ophiopogon planiscapus

creeping, tough rootstock, forming dense
thickets. Leaves (strictly flattened stems, called
cladodes) stiff, spiny, *c*.2.5cm long, 2–3 times as
long as wide in var. *aculeatus*, 3 times as long as
wide in var. *angustifolius*. Plants usually male or
female, but hermaphrodite and self-fertile
clones are valued in gardens for their free-
fruiting habit. Berries *c*.1cm across, long lasting
through the winter. For any dryish soil. Hardy
to −25°C or less.

Tricyrtis flava Maxim. subsp. ***ohsumiensis***
(Masam.) Kitam. (*Liliaceae*)   Native of
Kyushu, growing in woods in the mountains,
flowering in September–October. Plant with a
dense clump of stout stems to 50cm. Upper
leaves elliptic to oblong, 5–20cm long, glabrous.
Flowers 2.5–3.5cm long with minute spots. For
moist, peaty soil in partial shade. Hardy to
−15°C.

Tricyrtis macrantha Maxim.   Native of
Shikoku, with subsp. *macranthopsis* (Masam.)
Kitam. in C Honshu, growing on smooth, wet
rocks and cliffs in humid gorges where there is
permanently running water at least in summer,
flowering in August–October. Stems few with
pale-brown, coarse hairs, from a tufted
rootstock, with orchid-like fleshy roots running
across the rocks. Leaves cordate at the base,
7–17cm long. Flowers 3–4cm long, pendulous,
very fleshy. Subsp. *macranthopsis* has more
deeply cordate leaves and glabrous stems. For
careful cultivation in very well-drained, leafy
soil in shade and shelter, with ample water in
summer. Hardy to −15°C, perhaps less. *T.
ishiiana* (Kitag. & T. Koyama) Ohwi, from
Honshu, is very similar, but has 3–5 flowers in a
terminal corymb.

Tricyrtis perfoliata Masam.   Native of
Kyushu, growing on shady rock ledges,
flowering in September–October. Stems usually
pendulous, to 70cm, not branched, glabrous.
Leaves very shiny, the upper broadly lanceolate
to narrowly ovate-oblong, 7–18cm long,
perfoliate, long acuminate. Flowers upright,
solitary, 2.5–3cm long. For moist, leafy, well-
drained soil and shelter. Hardy to −15°C perhaps.

Tricyrtis macrantha at Washfield Nurseries, Kent

Tricyrtis perfoliata at Washfield Nurseries, Kent

Miscanthus sinensis by suphur springs in Hokkaido

Cortaderia selloana 'Rendatleri'

Cortaderia selloana 'Aureo-lineata'

Pennisetum orientale

Cortaderia richardii (Endl.) Zotov
(*Gramineae*) Toetoe   Native of New Zealand,
growing in swampy places and along rivers in
the lowlands, flowering in November–March.
Plant forming huge clumps with arching stems
to 6m. For moist, sandy soil in full sun. Hardy
to −15°C, perhaps. *C. fulvida* (Buchanan)
Zotov, from upland habitats, has more upright
stems to 2m, with a nodding head of flowers,
pinkish when young, and is possibly hardier.

Cortaderia selloana (Schult. & Schult. fil.)
Asch. & Graebn.   Native of South America,
growing in moist, sandy soils, flowering in late
summer, August–October in gardens. Plant
dioecious, forming huge clumps of lax leaves to
3m long, with very sharply toothed cutting
edges. Inflorescence to 3m; rather erect in the

Cortaderia richardii at Harry Hay's

Molinia caerulea 'Variegata'

Cortaderia selloana 'Pumila'

Cortaderia selloana 'Sunningdale Silver'

male, with spreading branches in the female. Spikelets *c*.15mm long, white or pinkish, shining. For deep, good soil in full sun. Hardy to −20°C. Several named clones are cultivated: **'Aureo-lineata'** syn. 'Gold Band' has yellow-striped leaves and stems to 2.5m. **'Pumila'** is a small form with erect plumes to 1.5m. **'Rendatleri'** has pinkish, spreading and drooping plumes to 3m tall. **'Sunningdale Silver'** has upright plumes around 2.2m.

Miscanthus sinensis Anderss. (*Gramineae*) Native of Japan, in all the islands, Taiwan and China, growing on hillsides and in sunny places in the mountains, flowering in August–October. Plant forming clumps of upright stems to 2.5m. Leaves with flat blades, 1–2cm wide. Inflorescence of numerous narrow racemes 15–

30cm long forming a corymb. Spikelets 5–7mm long, with a tuft of white or purplish hairs. For any soil in sun or partial shade. Hardy to −20°C. Numerous cultivars are grown in gardens. 'Zebrinus' has white patches across the leaves and stems at regular intervals. 'Silberfeder' ('Silver Feather'), has stems to 2.2m and white hairs on the spikelets. It is the most free-flowering form in cool climates. Some others do not get enough summer heat in England to flower freely. Var. *purpurascens* (Anders.) Rendle has reddish-purple leaves.

Molinia caerulea (L.) Moench (*Gramineae*) Native of N Europe eastwards to Siberia, south to N Turkey and the Caucasus and naturalized in North America, growing in bogs, heaths and on wet, peaty mountainsides, often covering

many square miles and colouring golden in winter, flowering in June–August. Plant forming large dense clumps. Leaves flat. Flowering stems to 130cm. Spikelets 6–9mm long. For acid, sandy, soil in full sun. 'Variegata', shown here, has white-striped leaves. Hardy to −25°C or less.

Pennisetum orientale (Willd.) Rich. (*Gramineae*)   Native of North Africa and Turkey east to the Kopet Dağ, south to Arabia, growing on dry, rocky hillsides, flowering in May–July. Plant forming tufts of narrow leaves with flowering stems to 100cm, forming a mound. Spikelets bristly hairy, purplish when young, later greyish brown. For a warm, sheltered position in full sun. Hardy to −15°C, perhaps less in dry areas.

Polystichum
aculeatum

Polystichum
polyblepharum

Polystichum
munitum

Polystichum setiferum
'Bevis'

Polystichum
rigens

Polystichum setiferum
Divisilobum 'Densum Erectum'

Specimens from Wisley, 28 July. ⅓ life size

Onoclea sensibilis

Asplenium scolopendrium L. (*Aspleniaceae*)
Hart's-Tongue Fern   Native of Europe,
including the British Isles, Asia and North
America, growing in various habitats but most
luxuriantly on banks in cool woodland, often on
lime-rich soils and in high-rainfall areas, also
occasionally in crevices in mortared walls.
Fronds evergreen, to 60cm but much smaller in
dry situations. Easily grown in a soil rich in leaf-
mould, in shade. As well as spores and division,
this may be propagated by inducing the base of
the leaf-stalk to form plantlets. Very variable
indeed and many varieties have been named.
Most fall into broad groups. Crispum group:
with strongly undulate and often rather broad
fronds. Muricatum group: frond surface
roughened. Cristatum group: fronds variously
forked at apex.

Matteuccia struthiopteris (L.) Todaro
(*Woodsiaceae*)   Native of Europe, W Asia, E
United States, Canada, China and throughout
Japan. The typical habitat is light shade on
rocky stream-banks, where it may form
extensive colonies. Rhizome short but
producing long stolons by which it spreads quite
rapidly once established. Fronds deciduous,
very erect, forming characteristic pale-green,
'shuttlecock', 60–120cm tall. Fertile fronds
shorter, from the centre of the crown. Hardy
and quick to establish, given light shade and a
moist but well-drained, leafy soil.

Onoclea sensibilis L. (*Woodsiaceae*)   Native
of much of North America east of the Rocky
Mountains, from Newfoundland south to
Florida and Texas, and to NE Asia from E
Siberia to Japan and Korea, growing in wet,
grassy places, open, damp woodland and
occasionally on open hillsides. Rhizome fairly
slender, far-creeping, throwing up fronds singly.
Fronds deciduous, rather long-stalked, up to 1m
tall but more often 45–70cm. Fertile fronds
erect, rather shorter than the sterile ones, with
the pinnae-lobes contracted to bead-like
structures. An easily grown fern, spreading
quite vigorously when well established in a
moist, light soil in light shade. The fronds die
quickly with the first frosts, providing attractive
autumn colour.

Polystichum aculeatum (L.) Roth
(*Dryopteridaceae*)   Native of Europe (including
the British Isles) and much of Asia, growing in
deciduous woodland, often on limy soil, and
sometimes on shaded limestone outcrops.
Fronds thick, leathery, evergreen, more or less
bipinnate; pinnules wedge-shaped at base, often
rather convex. Fronds forming a fairly upright
shuttlecock to 80cm tall. Very hardy and easily
grown in light shade in any reasonable soil.
Similar variation to *P. setiferum*, but fewer
cultivars.

Polystichum munitum (Kaulf.) Presl   Native
of W North America, often forming extensive
colonies in cool mountain forests. Rhizome
short; fronds to 1m or more, evergreen, fairly
erect, pinnate with finely serrate pinnae, each of
which has an enlarged basal lobe on the side
facing the frond tip. A robust clump-forming
species easily grown in light shade and a peaty
or leafy soil.

Asplenium scolopendrium 'Crispum'

Polystichum setiferum Divisilobum group

Polystichum polyblepharum (Roem.) Presl. Native to C & S Japan and S Korea, growing on the woodland floor in deciduous and mixed forest at low altitudes. Fronds erect, tufted, to 1m tall, very glossy on the upper side, bipinnate, with rather square pinnules. Apparently hardy and a very beautiful fern, easily grown in woodland conditions and a cool, leafy soil – probably dislikes limy soils.

Polystichum rigens Tagawa   Native of Japan in S Honshu, growing in woods. Fronds evergreen, leathery, shining, 30–45cm long, bipinnate, narrowly ovate-oblong; pinnules 10–12mm long. Scales on the stalk black-brown, lanceolate, 1–1.5mm wide, ciliate. For moist, acid soil in shade and shelter. Hardy to −10°C perhaps.

Polystichum setiferum (Forssk.) Woynar Native of Britain and N Europe with similar species in both Asia and North America, growing in deciduous woodland, most often in limy soils. Fronds thin-textured, bipinnate, evergreen to 1m long, arching to form an open shuttlecock. Pinnules distinctly stalked. Hardy and easily grown in light shade in cool, leafy, acid or alkaline soil. Young unfurling croziers have dense, often silvery scales. Propagated by division or spores. Many variations in frond shape have been found, most falling into distinct groups of similar cultivars. For example, Cristatum group: frond tip is repeatedly forked to produce a flat crest. Grandiceps group: a large crest in 3 dimensions, broader than rest of frond. Cruciatum group: each pinna is forked from the base to give a criss-cross or lattice effect. Acutilobum group: pinnules lanceolate-ovate, long pointed; fronds tending to lie flat; often proliferous. Divisilobum group: each pinna is bipinnate; sometimes proliferous. Plumosum group: pinnules are extra-finely divided and more leafy; usually sterile. 'Bevis' is an exceptionally fine clone of this group. Cultivars within these groups do not breed true from spores and so are treated as clones, propagated by division or by bulbils where present.

Matteuccia struthiopteris in the S Caucasus near Telavi, with Veratrum and Alchemilla

453

Athyrium niponicum in China

Athyrium nipponicum
'Pictum'

Athyrium filix-femina
(crested form)

*Hypolepis
millefolium*

Athyrium filix-femina
(heavily crested form)

Specimens from Wisley, 1 August. ⅓ life size

Onychium japonicum at Washfield Nurseries, Hawkhurst, Kent

Adiantum pedatum L. (*Adiantaceae*) Native of North America, from Quebec to Alaska, south to California and Georgia, and of E Asia, from Japan and Kamchatka to Sikkim and N India, growing in cool deciduous or coniferous forest, or on rocks by waterfalls. Fronds deciduous, on stalks 15–50cm high, usually about 25cm. Leaflets (pinnules) 2–4cm wide. Hardy and easily grown in a cool, moist and shady position. Lime-tolerant in that it grows on tufa. Slow to establish from the divisions of mature plants but easy from young plants. The rhizomes need to be covered by a layer of loose leaf mould or decaying leaves. Var. *aleuticum* Rupr. is found on the west coast of the USA, Utah and in Quebec. Forma *imbricatum* has overlapping pinnules. Var. *subpumilum* W. H. Wagner is a compact variety from Vancouver.

Adiantum venustum D. Don Native of the Himalayas and W China, growing on mossy banks and boulders, in light shade, at up to 3500m. Rhizomes slender, spreading quite widely but not so rapidly as to be troublesome. Fronds usually deciduous, 20–30cm tall, on a polished deep-brown stalk 10–15cm long. Blade broadly triangular and much divided into many triangular-obovate segments 6–10mm long. Sterile segments finely toothed along the apical margin, fertile ones with the sporangia under infolded flaps on the margin. Very hardy and quick to establish on peat banks or in rock crevices in light shade or, if not too dry, under trees. Readily propagated by division.

Athyrium filix-femina (L.) Roth. (*Woodsiaceae*) This species has one of the widest distributions found among ferns, occurring in Europe, Asia, North Africa, C North America. It is a characteristic species of deciduous woods on various, usually acidic soils, but may also be found in drier and more open habitats. Rhizome short; fronds deciduous, generally 60–100cm tall, pale green, bipinnate, with bluntly toothed pinnules. The rachis may be green or reddish – the latter forms are perhaps the more attractive. Innumerable aberrant forms were brought into cultivation and named in the 19th century and the species remains remarkably prolific of crested, plumose and other variants.

Athyrium niponicum (Mett.) Hance. Native of woodland habitats in NE Asia where it occurs in two colour forms. The commoner type has green fronds, but in 'Pictum' they are a light grey-green with a paler central band and purplish-pink midrib. The latter is the more popular garden plant and breeds largely true

Athyrium otophorum

Oreopteris limbosperma

from spores. Rhizomes shortly creeping and slender; fronds 30–50cm tall, loosely clustered, rather thick-textured but deciduous. Among plants raised from spores, individuals occur with somewhat crested fronds, but most gain little in attractiveness from this aberration.

Athyrium otophorum (Miq.) Koidz. Native of Japan and China, growing in deciduous woodland. Rhizome short, erect; fronds 60–80cm tall, thick textured but deciduous, bipinnate with toothed pinnules. Plants in cultivation mostly have greyish-green fronds with wine-red midribs to the frond and the pinnae. Hardy to −10°C perhaps and requiring a moist, shaded site to develop to its full luxuriance, forming a very handsome and decorative fern. Propagation is easy from spores, sown fresh, or by division of established clumps in early spring or in autumn.

Hypolepis millefolium Hook.
(*Dennstaedtiaceae*) Native of New Zealand, generally growing in fairly open situations on hills to over 1000m. Rhizome slender, long, forming extensive colonies. Fronds deciduous, 20–50cm tall, triangular and very finely divided, arising singly from the rhizome. Hardy to −15°C and easily grown in light shade and a leafy, acid soil. Propagated by division, but small pieces may fail to establish.

Onychium japonicum (Thunb.) Kunze. Widespread in E Asia, from the Himalayas to China, Japan, Taiwan and south to Malaysia. Rhizome creeping. Fronds more or less evergreen, to 60cm tall, very finely divided, with the ultimate segments linear-lanceolate. Hardiness varies depending on origin but plants from higher altitudes in China and Korea appear to be quite hardy, forming colonies of lacy fronds. For acid soil with plenty of humus and a situation in partial shade. Alternatively, it makes a fine specimen in a cold greenhouse.

Oreopteris limbosperma (All.) Holub. syn. *Thelypteris limbosperma* (All.) H. P. Fuchs Native of much of Europe and North America, with an allied species in NE Asia, growing on wet stream-banks on acid soils, in both lowland and upland areas and a characteristic species of acid 'flushes' on moorland. Rhizome fairly short, usually decumbent. Fronds erect, 30–90cm tall, deciduous; when young, bearing conspicuous silvery scales. The under-surface is covered with minute yellowish glands which release a lemony scent when the frond is brushed. Easily cultivated in cool, moist, acid soil but not tolerant of drought or lime.

Adiantum venustum at Wisley

Adiantum pedatum in Virginia

Athyrium filix-femina wild in Perthshire

Osmunda regalis

Polypodium australe

Polypodium australe
'Cornubiense'

*Blechnum
penna-marina*

Polypodium vulgare
'Bifidograndiceps'

Polypodium vulgare
'Longicaudatum'

Specimens from Wisley, 5 August. ⅓ life size

Osmunda cinnamomea in New Hampshire

Osmunda regalis (young fronds) at Wisley

Woodwardia fimbriata

Blechnum magellanicum at Logan

Osmunda regalis in Connemara

Blechnum chilense (Kaulf.) Mett. syn. *B. magellanicum* hort. (*Blechnaceae*) Native of S South America, growing in light forest and in more open situations up to *c*.500m. A robust evergreen fern with a slowly creeping rhizome, forming colonies of erect, very leathery pinnate fronds to 80cm tall; fertile fronds similar but with much narrower pinnae. The bristle-like scales at the base of the stalk differ from the ovate scales found on other similar species with which it has been confused. Hardy to −10°C. This species is sometimes cultivated as *B. tabulare*, which, however, is a distinct and somewhat more tender species from South Africa. *B. magellanicum* (Desv.) Mett. has tufted rhizomes forming a low trunk, narrow sterile pinnae, 7–13mm wide, and fertile fronds with still narrower pinnae. It is native of Tierra del Fuego and the Falkland Is.

Blechnum penna-marina (Poir.) Kuhn Native of South America, north to S Brazil, New Zealand and many subantarctic islands, growing in woods, on rocky slopes and in scrub. Rhizome creeping, with fronds at intervals, in clusters, to 17cm. Pinnae up to 8.5mm long. Fertile leaves usually longer than the sterile ones, taller with narrower pinnules with rolled margins. Hardy to −10°C, perhaps less.

Osmunda cinnamomea L. (*Osmundaceae*) Native of North, Central and South America and also in NE Asia (the latter sometimes distinguished as var. *fokiensis* Copeland), growing in a variety of habitats at low altitudes,

including moist woods, bogs and stream-banks. Rhizome large, slowly creeping. Fronds deciduous, 40–60cm or taller, of two sorts; sterile fronds loosely erect, bipinnatifid, with a conspicuous tuft of woolly reddish-brown scales at the base of each pinna. Fertile fronds stiffly erect, usually shorter than the sterile ones and confined to the centre of the crown, bipinnate, but with very contracted pinnules – normal green pinnules are usually absent. Hardy and easy to grow in damp woodland or by the margins of pools or streams.

Osmunda regalis L. Very widely distributed in Europe, North and South America, Africa and Asia, generally growing in swampy areas, fens and other damp woodland. Rhizome erect and becoming massive with age. Fronds erect, deciduous, 60–150cm tall, bipinnate, with the fertile pinnules confined to the contracted apex of the fronds. One of the better ferns for autumn colour, the fronds becoming a warm russet-orange. Easily cultivated, preferably from spores but, unlike most ferns, those of *Osmunda* remain viable for only a few days, so must be sown as soon as possible. A crested form 'Cristata' is grown, as is 'Purpurascens', with attractive 'stems' and young foliage.

Polypodium australe Fee (*Polypodiaceae*) Native of the British Isles, W Europe, Madeira and the Azores, growing in similar habitats to *P. vulgare*. Fronds to 30cm, broadly ovate: pinnae somewhat toothed, the lower ones inflexed. Fertile fronds appear in late summer.

Easily cultivated and quite hardy, this species has given rise to numerous cultivars (often attributed to *P. vulgare*). These include some very attractive foliose and plumose forms with much expanded, pinnately lobed pinnae. Examples include the Cambricum and Pulcherrimum groups.

Polypodium vulgare L. Native (as an aggregate of similar species) to Europe, Asia, North America and South Africa, growing in various habitats, including rocks, walls and trees as well as on the ground. Rhizome fairly thick, creeping and branching usually on or near the surface. Fronds evergreen, to 30cm long. Outline oblong, with the pinnae similar in length to the base of the frond. Hardy and easy to grow in most light soils but the rhizome should be scarcely buried. Crested cultivars and other types of variation occur.

Woodwardia fimbriata Rees syn. *W. radicans* var. *americana* Hook. (*Blechnaceae*) Native of W North America, from W British Columbia to California and east to Arizona and Nevada, growing in moist, shady places and on streambanks at up to 2500m. Rhizome short and stout. Fronds to 1.5m, more or less evergreen, leathery in texture and fairly short-stalked. Segments finely but sharply toothed. Plants from the northern part of the range should be hardy to −10°C. In western USA it is said to be easily grown and handsome, being well suited to a moist site in light shade.

Arachniodes aristata from Japan

Arachniodes standishii in a wood near Kyoto, Japan

Dryopteris filix-mas 'Cristata'

Dryopteris affinis 'The King'

Dryopteris marginalis

Dryopteris erythrosora

Specimens from Wisley, 5 October. ⅓ life size

Gymnocarpium dryopteris with *Endymion non-scriptus*

Arachniodes aristata (Forst.) Tindale (*Dryopteridaceae*) Widely distributed from India and E Asia to Australia, the more hardy forms are probably those from S Japan and China, growing as isolated plants on the woodland floor, generally in areas with a fairly high rainfall. Rhizome long-creeping; fronds evergreen, 30–60cm tall, including the long stalk, somewhat leathery and rather satiny in texture on the upper side, bi- to tripinnate with oblong, whiskery-toothed pinnules. Depending greatly on provenance it may be quite hardy and is a very handsome fern. *Arachniodes pseudoaristata* (Tagawa) Ohwi and *A. simplicior* (Makino) Ohwi are closely allied. A cultivar of the latter, 'Variegata', has yellowish bands down the centre of each frond and its pinnae. It is perhaps not very hardy and is grown as a house plant.

Arachniodes standishii (Moore) Ohwi Native almost throughout Japan and also in Korea, where it is often the dominant fern, forming extensive colonies in woodland in low mountains. Rhizome short; fronds 60–90cm tall, rather thin-textured but evergreen, bi- to tri-pinnate with coarsely toothed pinnules. Plants originating in N Honshu and Hokkaido will be very hardy but those in cultivation are probably from further south and require a sheltered site.

Dryopteris affinis (Lowe) Fraser-Jenkins syn. *D. borreri* Newman (*Dryopteridaceae*) Native of much of Europe, including the British Isles, growing in woods and on shady banks, usually

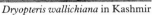

Dryopteris wallichiana in Kashmir

Dryopteris shiroumensis at Kew

on acid soils and most luxuriantly in areas of high rainfall. Rhizome short and erect. Fronds to 120cm tall, semi-evergreen, the midrib and stalk densely clothed with golden-brown scales which are particularly conspicuous on the unfurling fronds in spring. Rather similar to *D. filix-mas*, but differing in the almost untoothed, square-tipped pinnules and more abundant scales. Vigorous, easily cultivated and much more handsome than *D. filix-mas*. The cultivar 'The King' (Cristata group) is symmetrically crested and is common in gardens. Unlike many fern cultivars, it breeds 'true' from spores.

Dryopteris erythrosora (Eaton) O. Kuntze Widely distributed in NE Asia, from China to the Philippines and Taiwan and very common in C & S Japan, growing in woods and on banks at low altitudes and frequently self-sowing in gardens there. Rhizome short; fronds to 70cm tall, leathery and evergreen. The young fronds are often attractively tinged pink or bronze and the developing sori are frequently bright red. Hardy and easily grown but requiring constant moisture in the growing season. Best in light shade as the mature fronds may become a sickly yellow in a more exposed situation.

Dryopteris filix-mas (L.) Schott Native in many parts of the temperate northern hemisphere, including the British Isles, where it is one of the most common ferns. Found in a wide range of habitats but most luxuriant in damp woodland at low altitudes. Rhizome short and stout; fronds to 120cm or more, deciduous,

bipinnatifid; pinnules oblong, crenate or serrate, rounded at the tip but not narrowed at the base. The species is hardy and vigorous and will grow almost anywhere. In its wild form it is much less attractive than *D. affinis*, but it has given rise to many cultivars, some of which are highly garden-worthy. There are many types of variation, including the 'Cristata', 'Linearis', 'Plumosa' and 'Foliosa' groups.

Dryopteris marginalis (L.) A. Gray Native of North America, from Georgia to Canada westwards to the Rockies, growing in damp woods and swamps. Rhizome short; fronds to 60cm or more, bipinnate, deciduous. Pinnules deeply crenate-toothed; sori conspicuously near the margins as the specific epithet suggests. This, together with the rather erect bluish fronds, makes it quite distinctive. In the wild, this species has hybridized with numerous others and it is possible that some of the plants in cultivation are also hybrids.

Dryopteris shiroumensis Kurata & Nakamura Native of Japan, in C Hokkaido, growing in woods. Plants forming compact clumps. Rhizome stout. Fronds to 60cm or more. The pinnules overlap and are deeply divided to the midrib, and symmetrically curved. For shade and shelter. Hardy to −10°C, perhaps less.

Dryopteris wallichiana (Spreng.) Hylander Native of much of Asia, parts of Africa and of South America, although numerous names have

been applied to the different provenances. The usual habitat is woodland, generally at fairly low altitudes, but it also occurs on open stream-banks at higher altitudes, up to about 4000m in the Himalayas. Resembles *D. affinis* in size, vigour and frond shape, but the abundant scales are almost black, occasionally deep reddish brown. They are particularly conspicuous on the unfurling fronds in spring. The fronds are evergreen, usually collapsing at the base of the stalk during the winter but not turning brown. Hardy and easily cultivated in cool shade and leafy acid or neutral soil. Propagated by spores; even established plants are slow to produce offsets allowing division.

Gymnocarpium dryopteris (L.) Newman (*Dryopteridaceae*) Oak Fern Widespread in the temperate regions of North America, Europe and Asia, usually forming carpets in deciduous or mixed forests in cool areas and generally on acid soils. Rhizome very slender, black, far-creeping. Fronds deciduous, pale green and thin-textured, on stalks up to 30cm tall but usually less. Blade 10–25cm long, broadly triangular and held almost horizontally. Hardy and easily grown where the natural habitat can be emulated – it requires shade and a cool root-run in soil containing plenty of acid leaf mould in which the rhizomes should be just covered. The cultivar 'Plumosum' has broader pinnules, giving the fronds a more solid appearance.

Early spring in the woodland at the Pepsi-Cola Garden, New York, with *Dicentra spectabilis*, *Ajuga* and ferns

Gardening with Perennials

All the plants shown in this work will grow happily outside somewhere in Europe or North America, but gardeners on the east coast of America and in the colder parts of Europe have particular problems to contend with, different from those encountered near the milder west coasts of either continent. The possibility of intense cold in winter and extreme heat and humidity in summer restrict the range of exotic perennials that can be grown. Fortunately the North American native flora is very rich in perennials which naturally tolerate these extremes, and similar climatic conditions in parts of eastern Asia, Siberia and eastern Europe enlarge the range of plants from which to make a choice.

California and other Mediterranean regions, with hot, dry summers and mild winters, can grow a completely different range of plants; again the native floras of these areas are very rich. Plants from parts of the world with a Mediterranean climate, such as the Cape region of South Africa and southern Europe, and western Asia are among the most beautiful and diverse of any in the temperate zone. The advantage of growing plants which are adapted to climates with a summer drought is that they require little or no water from June onwards; indeed too much water in summer will often kill the plants altogether.

Many gardens in North America are made in clearings in woodland, not the primaeval forest of giant oaks, hickories and chestnuts which the first settlers found, but the trees which have grown up on abandoned farmland, often less than a hundred years old. Black cherry, ash, maples and Robinia, the Black Locust, are common examples of trees of secondary forest, and they often have greedy surface roots. Ash and lime and wild cherry, and the roots of a hedge, often produce similar problems in Europe.

Although this work deals only with herbaceous perennials, gardeners should not expect to achieve good results with perennials only. Bulbs and shrubs are the necessary companions of perennials in permanent and informal plantings; annuals, biennials and bedding plants are invaluable for filling gaps in borders, either where some perennial has died or not grown as it should, or where something has grown too well and had to be removed. The following notes put forward some ideas for gardeners in harsh climates, such as the east coast of America and California, and suggest plants suitable for situations they may find in their own gardens. Further very stimulating ideas, most wittily presented, can be found in *The Perennial Gardener* by Frederick McGourty (Houghton Mifflin, Boston 1989), who has his own perennial garden in Norfolk, Connecticut, and has long been a professional garden designer.

1. **Planting for beds around the house**   The plants in this area want to be neat and rather low, with good foliage and leaf contrasts. Sweet-smelling flowers are especially valuable, so the scent can come into the house on warm days. Suitable plants for the shady side of the house are violets, the smaller Hostas, ferns like *Adiantum pedatum* or small forms of *Polystichum*, *Ajuga reptans*, *Helleborus*, *Dicentra*, especially the forms of *D. formosa* and *D. eximea*, and dwarf and striped grasses and sedges like *Hakonechloa macra* 'Aureola'. Dwarf shrubs are also suitable in this sort of planting; those with scented flowers in early spring, such as *Daphne* or *Sarcococca* are especially valuable, and there are *Daphne* species suitable for every climatic zone. Patches of intense colour in summer can be produced by shade-tolerant annuals like *Impatiens* or *Begonia semperflorens*, and earlier by smaller spring-flowering perennials, such as *Pulmonaria*. Early flowering bulbs like snowdrops, aconites, and *Chionodoxa* are happy when grown in places which are covered, in summer, by the leaves of Hostas and similar perennials.

For sunny borders around the house, plants of similarly compact habit are needed, but they have to be tolerant of great heat. The shorter bearded irises, *Dianthus*, and low grey-leaved plants are suitable, as is lavender in areas where it will thrive. Sun-loving lilies will be happy in this area, as they appreciate the protection for their young shoots. All these plants require good drainage, so special preparation may be needed on heavy soils. No lily is more suitable here than the common *Lilium regale*, which will prove long-lived in poor, stony soil, and is wonderfully scented on summer evenings.

2. **Perennial borders in lawns and island beds, in full sunlight**
This is the area of the garden in which cultivars of popular herbaceous genera are appropriate; the borders can either be composed of collections of one genus, such as day-lilies, or contain a mixture of plants to give a long and effective display of colour. Large-flowered *Phlox*, border delphiniums, *Gypsophila paniculata*, paeonies, lupins, and other strong-growing perennials can be grouped in colour schemes to give either a powerful or subdued effect. Soils will need to be rich and well-manured and the plants will mostly need staking against heavy rain and summer storms. The essential feature of an island bed is that it can be admired from any direction. When it is being planted, the height of the plants must be carefully checked, so that the tallest are in the middle of the bed, and there is a gradient to the shortest around the edges.

3. **Perennials on banks and rock outcrops**   In many gardens among undulating areas of lawn or mown grass, are outcrops of rock or rocky banks which can be ugly if left bare. A large clump of a perennials alongside the rock will give it a sense of purpose, while the rock itself provides a good background for the perennial. If the surrounding soil is moist, a large clump of *Aruncus* makes a fine feature, while a tall bearded Iris will be suitable in a dry

position. The essential characteristic of a plant for this position is that it should be large and have a bold habit of growth. Irises are also suitable to clothe a rocky bank in the sun or even under slight shade of trees, as long as they get some direct sun during the day.

4. Borders along stone or brick walls and fences, hedges or shrubs These borders are best kept narrow, less than two metres wide, and they have the advantage of a definite background. I have seen attractive examples of this type of border planted entirely with one species or cultivar such as one of the smaller-flowered day-lilies, with a long flowering season, like 'Hyperion', or 'Golden Chimes'. Japanese anemones are suitable for a shady bed for late flowering; they can be mixed with early flowering bulbs and ferns, or with an early-summer flowering perennial such as *Aquilegia*. A low border on the north side of a wall can be planted with a combination of ferns and hostas; the golden and striped varieties will brighten what might otherwise be a dark area.

Where the border is backed by a hedge, or a bank of shrubs, it is advisable to leave a gap between hedge and border, both for weeding and so that the plants at the back of the border do not suffer from root competition. If tree roots are troublesome, it may be necessary to make a barrier to keep them at bay.

5. The woodland edge In this case the border forms the visual transition between the grass and the woodland. The bed should be rather narrow and sited so that its background is the shade under the trees; therefore it will often be on the north side of the wood, and the plants will be seen against the light. In this position plants with white, airy flowers create a beautiful effect from a distance, and dark reds and purples are lit up by the sun. White Astilbes, *Lysimachia clethroides*, *Thalictrum dipterocarpum*, *Physostegia virginiana* 'Alba', *Phlox carolina* 'Miss Lingard', *Campanula lactiflora*, *Papaver bracteatum* 'Goliath' and *Aquilegia atrata* are all striking in this sort of position.

6. Swamp gardens, lakeside beds, the edges of streams or creeks, and places with poorly-drained soil Soils which are wet and poorly drained are unsatisfactory for the majority of ordinary perennials, but there are numerous beautiful plants whose natural habitat is swampy, and which thrive in or even require such conditions. Many irises, *Lythrum*, *Caltha*, *Trollius*, *Rodgersia*, *Lobelia*, and many others need wet soils. Bog primulas, *Meconopsis* and other Himalayan plants are suitable in cooler climates.

Soils which are waterlogged in winter but dry out in summer pose a greater problem. *Iris spuria* grows naturally in this type of position, and a collection of its cultivars would be suitable, provided that the place is in full sun.

7. Perennials in woodland The native American flora is particularly rich in woodland perennials. Many of the most beautiful, such as the Virginian bluebell *Mertensia virginiana*, are spring flowering, and drifts of *Phlox stolonifera* in its various colour forms are equally lovely. There are, however several which flower later in the summer and will make a fine feature in a shady clearing; *Veratrum*, *Cimicifuga*, *Campanula*, and *Telekia* are all large perennials for this position in the garden, and they can be preceded by spring flowering bulbs such as snowdrops, *Scillia*, *Erythronium*, *Chionodoxa* and *Aenemone blanda*.

8. Meadow and prairie gardens The formation of a prairie or meadow garden may at first thought appear easy, but in practice it is often difficult to achieve the necessary degree of soil fertility, so that the ranker herbs and coarse grasses do not smother the more delicate flowers. The drier and poorer the site, the easier it is to establish an attractive meadow, and large numbers of one plant produce a fine effect. American *Asclepias tuberosa* and *Salvia campanulata* are lovely in drifts, and *Camassia* and *Fritillaria meleagris* can be planted in the wetter areas. European 'weeds' such as Queen Anne's Lace, Ox-eye Daisies and Chicory, with *Salvia pratensis* may prove easier to establish. Larger perennials such as Goldenrod, *Vernonia*, *Eupatorium* and Asters can make a fine show in the early autumn, and will do best in somewhat swampy ground.

9. Dry Mediterranean gardens The examples mentioned above apply mostly to gardens in northern Europe and on the east coast of America, or to areas which have rain in summer, and a freezing winter. As mentioned above, a different range of plants can be grown in California and southern Europe, and many are suited to parts of the garden which are not irrigated, or watered only occasionally in the summer. American shrubs such as *Ceanothus* are very good in these areas, and perennials such as *Romneya*, *Zauschneria*, *Yucca* and various *Penstemon* species will grow equally well and produce colour in summer. There are many attractive perennials from the European Mediterranean which grow as easily; *Acanthus*, *Phlomis*, *Origanum*, *Paeonia*, *Erigeron*, *Iris* and *Euphorbia* all contain good species tolerant of summer drought and heat.

Late summer in a woodland clearing in the Leonard J. Buck Garden, New Jersey with *Veronia novaboracensis* and Goldenrod (*Solidago*)

Some Gardens to visit, with good collections of Herbaceous Perennials

England

The times and dates of opening may change, especially of those gardens which are privately owned. An asterisk denotes a garden open only occasionally. Many are open under The National Gardens Scheme, which publishes yearly a 'yellow book' of Gardens of England and Wales Open, giving opening dates, times, and directions for finding each garden. Details of other gardens open may be found in *The Good Gardens Guide*, edited by Graham Rose and Peter King and published yearly by Barrie & Jenkins, London.

(Those gardens marked with an asterisk are open on only a few days in the summer.)

Arley Hall, near Knutsford, Cheshire
Beth Chatto Gardens, Elmstead Market, Suffolk
Bodnant Garden, near Colwyn Bay, North Wales (The National Trust)
Bressingham Gardens, Diss, Norfolk
Cambridge University Botanic Garden, Brookside
Chelsea Physic Garden, Royal Hospital Road, London SW3
Cobblers, Crowborough, Sussex*
Coldham, Little Chart, Ashford, Kent*
Garden House, Buckland Monachorum, Devon
Great Dixter, Northiam, Sussex
Harewood House Gardens, near Leeds, West Yorkshire
Hatfield House, Hertfordshire
Hidcote Manor, Chipping Camden, Gloucestershire (The National Trust)
The High Beeches, Handcross, Sussex
Highdown, Goring-by-Sea, near Worthing, Sussex
Jenkyn Place, Bentley, Hampshire
Kew, The Royal Botanic Gardens, near Richmond, Surrey
Knightshayes Court, Tiverton, Devon (The National Trust)
Leeds Castle, near Maidstone, Kent
Liverpool University Botanic Garden, Ness, Neston, South Wirral
Longstock Park Gardens, near Stockbridge, Hampshire*
Marwood Hill, Barnstaple, Devon
Myddelton House, Bulls Cross, Enfield, Middlesex
Old Rectory Cottage, Tidmarsh, Berkshire*
The Old Vicarage, Edington, Wiltshire*
Oxford University Botanic Garden, Oxford
Powis Castle, near Welshpool, Powys, Mid-Wales (The National Trust)
Sandling Park, near Hythe, Kent*
Savill Gardens, Windsor Great Park, Berkshire
Sissinghurst Castle, Cranbrook, Kent (The National Trust)
Stancombe Park, Dursley, Gloucestershire*
Wakehurst Place, Haywards Heath, Sussex (The National Trust)
Wallington, Morpeth, Northumberland (The National Trust)
Washfield Nurseries, Hawkhurst, Kent
Wisley, The Royal Horticultural Society's Garden

Scotland

Aberdeen, Cruickshank Botanic Garden of the University, St Machar Drive, Old Aberdeen
Branklyn Garden, Perth (The National Trust for Scotland)
Cluny, Aberfeldy, Perthshire
Crathes Castle, Aberdeenshire (The National Trust for Scotland)
Edinburgh, The Royal Botanic Garden, Inverleith Row
Inverewe, Poolewe, Wester Ross (The National Trust for Scotland)
Jack Drake, Inshriach Alpine Plant Nursery, Aviemore, Inverness-shire
Kildrummy Castle Garden, Strathdon, Aberdeenshire
Logan Botanic Garden, Port Logan, Dumfries and Galloway
Pitmedden Garden, Ellon, Aberdeenshire (The National Trust for Scotland)

Ireland

Beech Park, Clonsilla, Co. Dublin
Glenveagh Castle, Letterkenny, Co. Donegal
Mount Stewart, Newtownards, Co. Down (The National Trust)
Mount Usher, Ashford, Co. Wicklow
National Botanic Gardens, Glasnevin, Dublin

North America

Alabama
Birmingham Botanical Garden, 2612 Lane Park Rd., Birmingham, AL 35223, 205-879-1227

Arizona
Filoli Center, Canada Rd., Woodside, CA 94062, 415-364-2880

California
Huntington Botanical Gardens, 1151 Oxford Road, San Marino, CA 91108, 818-405-2100
Rancho Santa Ana Botanic Garden, 1500 North College Ave., Claremont, CA 91711, 714-625-8767
Regional Parks Botanic Garden, Tilden Regional Park, Berkeley, CA 94708, 415-841-8732
Santa Barbara Botanic Garden, 1212 Mission Canyon Rd., Santa Barbara, CA 93105, 805-682-4726
Strybing Arboretum & Botanical Gardens, Ninth Avenue at Lincoln Way, San Francisco, CA 94122, 415-559-3622
University of California Botanical Garden, Centennial Dr., Berkeley, CA 94720, 415-652-3343
University of California Botanic Gardens – Riverside, Dept. of Botany & Plant Science, Riverside, CA 92521, 718-787-4650
Western Hills Nursery, 16250 Coleman Valley Rd., Occidental, CA 95465, 707-874-3731

Colorado
Denver Botanic Gardens, 909 York Street, Denver, CO 80206, 303-575-2547

Connecticut
Hillside Gardens, Litchfield Rd., P.O. Box 614, Norfolk, CT 06058, 203-542-5345
White Flower Farm, Litchfield, CT 06759-0059, 203-496-9600

Delaware
Mt. Cuba Center, P.O. Box 3570, Greenville, DE 19807

District of Columbia
United States National Arboretum, Agricultural Research Service, U.S. Dept. of Agriculture, 3501 New York Ave., NE Washington, D.C. 20002, 202-472-9279

Idaho
University of Idaho, Plant Science Dept., Moscow, ID 83843

Illinois
Chicago Botanic Garden, Lake Cook Rd., Clencoe, IL 60022, 312-835-5440
Glen Oak Botanical Garden, Peoria Park District, 2218 N. Prospect Rd., Peoria, IL 61603, 309-685-4321

Maine
The Abby Aldrich Rockefeller Garden, Seal Harbor, ME. Open one day a week for a very short season only by reservation, if you know how to obtain the unlisted number.

Maryland
William Paca House & Garden, 1 Martin St., Annapolis, MD 21401, 301-269-0601/267-6656

Massachusetts
Berkshire Garden Center, Box 826, Rtes 102 & 183, Stockbridge, MA 10262, 413-298-3926
The Botanic Garden of Smith College, Lyman Plant House, Northampton, MA 01063, 413-584-2700, ext. 2748
Garden in the Woods of the New England Wild Flower Society, Hemenway Rd., Framingham, MA 01701, 617-888-3300

Michigan
Cranbrook House & Gardens, 380 Lone Pine Rd., P.O. Box 801, Bloomfield Hills, MI 48103, 313-645-3149
Matthaei Botanical Garden, University of Michigan, 1800 North Dixboro Rd., Ann Arbor, MI 48105, 313-764-1168

Missouri
Gilberg Perennial Farms, 2906 Ossenfort Rd., Glencoe, MO 63038
Missouri Botanical Garden, 4344 Shaw Rd., Glencoe, MO 63110, Mailing Address: P.O. Box 299, St. Louis, MO 63166, 314-577-5100
Woodland and Floral Garden, University of Missouri, Columbia, MO 62511

New York
Brooklyn Botanic Garden, 1000 Washington Ave., Brooklyn, NY 11225, 718-622-4433
The Cloisters, The Metropolitan Museum of Art, Fort Tryon Park, New York, NY 10040, 212-923-37700
Mary Flagler Cary Arboretum Institute of Ecosystem Studies, Box AB, Millbrook, NY 12545, 914-677-5358
The Conservatory Garden, Central Park, 105th St. & Fifth Ave., New York, NY 1003, 212-360-8236
Minn's Gardens, Dept. of Floriculture & Ornamental Hort., Cornell University, Ithaca, NY 14850
The New York Botanical Garden, Bronx, NY 10458, 212-220-8700
Old Westbury Gardens, 71 Old Westbury Rd., Old Westbury, NY 11568
Pepsico World Headquarters, Anderson Hill Rd., Purchase, NY 10577
Wave Hill, 675 W. 252nd St., Bronx, NY 10471, 212-549-2055

North Carolina
The North Carolina Botanical Garden & Coker Arb., UNC-CH Totten Center, 457-A Laurel Hill Rd., Chapel Hill, NC 27514, 919-976-2246
North Carolina State University Arboretum, Raleigh, NC 27695

Ohio
Gardenview Horticultural Park, 16711 Pearl Rd., Strongsville, OH 44136, 216-238-6653
Sunnybrook Farms & Homestead Garden, 9448 Mayfield Rd., Chesterland, OH 44026, 216-729-7232

Pennsylvania
Bowman's Hill Wild Flower Preserve, Washington Crossing Historic Park, Washington Crossing, PA 18977, 215-862-2924
Longwood Gardens, P.O. Box 501, Kennett Square, PA 19348, 215-388-6741

Tennessee
Memphis Botanic Garden, 750 Cherry Rd., Memphis, TN 38117, 901-685-1566

Virginia
Andre Viette Farm & Nursery, Rte 1, Box 16 (Route 608), Fisherville, VA 22939, 703-943-2315

Wisconsin
Boerner Botanical Gardens in Whitnall Park, 5879 South 92nd St., Hales Corners, WI 53130, 414-425-1130/529-1870

Canada
British Columbia
The Butchart Gardens, 800 Benvenuto Boulevard, Brentwood Bay, British Columbia V8X 3X4, (604) 652-4422
Website: www.butchartgardens.com
University of British Columbia Botanical Garden, 6804 S.W. Marine Drive, Vancouver, British Columbia V6T 1Z4, (604) 822-9666

Ontario
Niagara Falls Botanical Gardens, 2565 Niagara Parkway North, P.O. Box 150, Niagara Falls, Ontario L2E 6T2, (905) 356-8554. Website: www.niagaraparks.com
Royal Botanical Gardens, 680 Plains Road West, Highway 2, Burlington, Ontario L7T 4H4, (905) 527-1158
Website: www.rgb.ca

Quebec
Montreal Botanical Garden, 4101 Sherbrooke East, Montreal, Quebec H1X 2B2, (514) 872-1400
Website: www.ville.montreal.qc.ca/jardin

How to obtain Herbaceous Plants

Flower seeds can be imported into the United States and Canada without much difficulty, but the importation of living plants and plant materials requires special arrangements which will be detailed in suppliers' catalogs.

American regulations vary according to the country of origin and type of plant. Every order requires a phytosanitary certificate and may require a CITES (Convention on International Trade in Endangered Species of Wild Fauna and Flora) certificate. For more information contact:

USDA-APHIS-PPQ
Permit Unit
4700 River Road, Unit 136
Riverdale, Maryland 20727-1236
Tel: (301) 734-8645
Fax: (301) 734-5786
Website: www.aphis.udsda.gov

Canadians importing plant material must pay a fee and complete an "application for permit to import."

Contact:

Plant Health and Production Division
Canadian Food Inspection Agency
2nd Floor West, Permit Office
59 Camelot Drive
Nepean, Ontario K1A 0Y9
Tel: (613) 225-2342
Fax: (613) 228-6605
Website: www.cfia-agr.ca

Aimers
81 Temperance Street
Aurora, Ontario L4G 2R1
Tel: (905) 841-6226
Rare and unique seeds. Catalog available.

Andre Viette Farm and Nursery
P.O. Box 1109
Fisherville, Virginia 22939
Tel: (540) 943-2315
Website: www.viette.com
Over 3,000 varieties and cultivars of perennials. Specializes in daylilies and irises.

Bluestone Perennials
7211 Middle Ridge Road
Madison, Ohio 44057
Toll-free Tel: (800) 852-5243
Website: www.bluestoneperennials.com
Good selection. Does not ship to Canada.

Brickman's Botanical Gardens
R.R. 1
Sebringville, Ontario N0K 1X0
Tel: (519) 393-6223
Over 3,000 species of perennials, specializing in rare hostas, cosmos, daylilies, peonies and irises.

Busse Gardens
17160 245th Avenue
Big Lake, Minnesota 55309-9716
Tel: (763) 263-3400
Toll-free Tel: (800) 544-3192
Website: www.bussegardens.com
Over 1,200 perennials including more than 125 hostas. Catalog available.

NURSERIES – BIBLIOGRAPHY

Butchart Gardens Ltd.
Box 4010
Victoria, British Columbia V8X 3X4
Tel: (250) 652-4422
Website: www.butchartgardens.com
Old-fashioned perennials. Catalog available.

Canyon Creek Nursery
3527 Dry Creek Road
Oroville, California 95965
Tel: (530) 533-2166
Website: www.canyoncreeknursery.com
Good selection of perennials. Does not ship to Canada.

Carroll Gardens
P.O. Box 310
Westminster, Maryland 21157
Toll-free Tel: (800) 638-6334

The Crownsville Nursery
1241 Generals Highway
Crownsville, Maryland 21032
Tel: (310) 923-2212

Gardenimport
P.O. Box 760
Thornhill, Ontario L3T 4A5
Tel: (905) 731-1950
Toll-free Tel: (800) 339-8314
Fax: (905) 881-3499
Website: www.gardenimport.com
E-mail: flower@gardenimport.com
Ships to the United States.

Heronswood Nursery, Ltd.
7530 NE 288th Street
Kingston, Washington 98346
Tel: (360) 297-4172
Fax: (360) 297-8321
Website: www.heronswood.com
Rare and unusual perennials. Excellent catalog available.

McFayden Seed Company Ltd.
30-9th Street, Suite 200
Brandon, Manitoba R7A 6N4
Tel: 1(800) 205-7111
Website: www.mcfayden.com
Seeds and hardy perennial flower plants for short-season gardens. Free catalog.

The Perennial Gardens
13139 224th Street
Maple Ridge, British Columbia V4R 2P6
Tel: (604) 467-4218
Fax: (604) 467-3181
Website: www.perennialgardener.com
Wide selection of perennials, especially shade varieties. Does not ship to U.S.

Thompson and Morgan, Inc.
P.O. Box 1308
Jackson, New Jersey 08527-0308
Toll-free Tel: (800) 274-7333
Toll-free Fax: (888) 466-4769
Website: www.thompson-morgan.com
Excellent selection of seeds of common and unusual perennials. Parent company is British. Catalog available.

General

Beckett, Kenneth A., *Growing Hardy Perennials* Croom Helm and Timber Press 1981.
Clausen, R. R. and Ekstrom, N. H., *Perennials for American Gardens* Random House 1989.
McGourty, Frederick, *The Perennial Gardener* Houghton Mifflin, Boston 1989.
Thomas, Graham Stuart, *Perennial Garden Plants* 2nd ed. Dent 1982.
Trehane, Piers, *Index Hortensis volume 1: Perennials* (Obtainable by post from the publisher). Quarterjack Publishing, Wimborne, Dorset 1989.
Walters *et al.* eds., *European Garden Flora* Cambridge 1984.
Royal Horticultural Society Dictionary of Gardening, 2nd ed. revised, Oxford University Press 1977.

'Curtis's Botanical Magazine'; since 1974 'The Kew Magazine', London
'Journal of the Royal Horticultural Society', since June 1975 'The Garden', R.H.S. London
'The Plantsman', 1979 onwards, Royal Horticultural Society, London

Regional Floras

Europe
Coste, H., *Flore de La France* Paris 1901.
Heywood *et al.*, eds., *Flora Europaea* Cambridge University Press 1964–1980.
Komarov, V. L. *et al.*, eds., *Flora of the USSR* Moscow and Leningrad, 1933–1964 (translated by the Israeli Program for Scientific Translations).
Polunin, Oleg, *Flowers of Greece and the Balkans* Oxford University Press 1980.
Polunin, Oleg, *Flowers of Southwest Europe* Oxford University Press 1973.
Polunin, Oleg and Walters, Martin, *A Guide to the Vegetation of Britain and Europe* Oxford University Press 1985.
Strid, Arne, *Mountain Flora of Greece* vol.1, Cambridge University Press 1986.
Thompson, H. S., *Subalpine Plants* G. Routledge 1912.
Vvedensky A. I., ed. *Conspectus Florae Asiae Mediae* Tashkent 1971 onwards.

Africa
Bond, Pauline and Goldblatt, Peter, *Plants of the Cape Flora. A Descriptive Catalogue* Journal of South African Botany, supplementary volume no. 13 Cape Town 1984.
Hilliard, O. M. and Burtt, B. L., *The Botany of the southern Natal Drakensberg* National Botanic Gardens, Kirstenbosch Cape Town 1987.

Asia
Davis, P. H. *et al.*, *Flora of Turkey* Edinburgh University Press 1965–1987.
Grierson, A. J. C. and Long, D. G., *Flora of Bhutan* Edinburgh University Press 1983 onwards.
Ohwi, J., *Flora of Japan* in English, Smithsonian, Washington 1965.
Polunin, Oleg and Stainton, Adam, *Flowers of the Himalaya* Oxford University Press 1984.
Rechinger, K. H., *Flora Iranica* Graz 1963 onwards.
Wilson, E. H., *A Naturalist in Western China* Methuen 1913.

Northern America
Britton, N. L. and Brown, A., *An Illustrated Flora of the Northern United States and Canada* New York 1913.
Fernald, M. L., *Gray's Manual of Botany*, 8th ed. 1950.
Kearney T. H. and Peebles R. H. *et al.*, *Arizona Flora* University of California Press 1951.
Munz, P. A. and Keck, D. D., *A Californian Flora* University of California Press 1968.
Niering, A., *The Audubon Society Field Guide to North American Wildflowers, eastern region* Knopf, New York 1979.

Spellenberg, R., *The Audubon Society Field Guide to Northern American Wildflowers, western region* Knopf, New York 1979.

South America
Moore, David M., *Flora of Tierra del Fuego* Nelson and Missouri Botanical Garden, 1983.

New Zealand
Allan, H. H., *Flora of New Zealand*, volume I Govrt. Printer Wellington 1961, 1982.
Moore, L. B. & Edgar, E., *Flora of New Zealand*, volume II Wellington 1970.
Salmon, J. T., *New Zealand Plants and Flowers in Colour* Reed 1963

Plant Monographs
Campanulas Lewis, Peter and Lynch, Margaret, Christopher Helm, 1989.
Diascia, A Revision of Series Racemosae Hilliard, O. M. and Burtt, B. L., Jl. S. Afr. Bot. 5(3):269–340(1984)
Gentians Wilkie, David, revised edition Country Life 1950.
Geraniums, Hardy Yeo, Peter, Croom Helm and Timber Press 1985.
Geranium, A Revision of Geranium in Africa south of the Limpopo Hilliard, O. M. and Burtt, B. L. Notes from the Royal Botanic Garden, Edinburgh vol. XLII no. 2 1985.
Hellebores Mathew, Brian, Alpine Garden Society 1989.
Iris, The Mathew, Brian, Batsford 1981.
Iris, A taxonomic review of Iris L. series Unguiculares, Davis Aaron P. and Jury S. L., Bot. Journ. Linn. Soc. (1990), 103:218–300.
Kniphofia, The South African Species of Codd, L. E. *Bothalia* vol. 9, parts 3 & 4 1968.
Meconopsis, The genus Taylor, George, New Flora and Silva 1934.
Meconopsis Cobb, James S. L., Christopher Helm 1989.
Paeonia, A Study of the Genus Stern, F. C., The Royal Horticultural Society 1946.
Peonies of Greece Stearn, William T. and Davis, Peter H. The Goulandris Natural History Museum 1984.
Phlox, The genus Wherry, Edgar T., Morris Arboretum Monographs, 111 Philadelphia 1955.
Primula, the Genus Wright Smith, W., Forrest, G. and Fletcher H. R. (reprints of several papers from Trans. Proc. Bot. Soc. Edinb. 1941–49) J. Cramer Vaduz 1977.
Saxifrages of Europe Webb, D. A. and Gornall, R. J. Christopher Helm, 1989.
Waterlilies Swindells, Philip; Croom Helm and Timber Press 1983.

Books and articles of general interest, including planting and design
Brown, Jane, *Lanning Roper and his Gardens* Weidenfeld and Nicholson 1987
Buchan, Ursula, *An Anthology of Garden Writing* Croom Helm 1986
Chatto, Beth, *The Dry Garden*
Fish, Margery, *We made a Garden* Collingridge and Transatlantic Arts London and New York 1956
Fish, Margery, *Cottage Garden plants* Collingridge and Transatlantic Arts London and New York 1961
Gorer, Richard, *The Development of Garden Flowers* Eyre and Spottiswood 1970
Hobhouse, Penelope, *Colour in your Garden* Collins 1985
Jekyll, Gertrude, *Colour Schemes for the Flower Garden* Country Life 1919
Page, Russell, *The Education of a Gardener* Collins 1962
Lloyd, Christopher, *Foliage Plants* revised edition Viking 1985
Robinson, William, *The Wild Garden* reprinted by The Scolar Press 1977, but see: Elliott, B., *Some Sceptical Thoughts about William Robinson*, The Garden vol. 110 part 5 214–217(1985)!
Thomas, Graham, *The Art of Planting* Dent 1984
Thomas, Graham, *Plants for Ground Cover* revised ed. Dent 1977
Verey, Rosemary, *Good Planting* Frances Lincoln 1990

Glossary

* indicates a cross-reference

Acuminate gradually tapering to an elongated point

Acute sharply pointed, with an angle less than 90°

Amplexicaul with the base of the leaf encircling the stem

Anther the part of the *stamen which contains the pollen

Anthesis the time of opening of the flowers

Axil the angle between the leaf stalk and the stem

Bract a modified leaf below a flower

Bracteole a small *bract

Bulbil a small bulb, sometimes produced by a plant instead of a seed

Calyx the outer parts of a flower, usually green

Canaliculate with the sides turned upwards, channelled

Capsule a dry fruit containing seeds

Carpel the part of the flower which produces the seeds

Ciliate with a fringe of hairs on the margin

Clavate shaped like a club, narrow at the base, swelling towards the apex

Clone the vegetatively propagated progeny of a single plant

Cordate heart-shaped, with rounded lobes at the base

Corolla the inner parts of the flower, comprising the petals, usually used when the petals are united into a tube

Crenate with shallow, rounded teeth

Cultivar a cultivated variety, denoted by a fancy name in inverted commas, e.g. 'Loddon Pink'

Decumbent trailing loosely onto the ground

Dentate with sharp, regular teeth

Diploid containing twice the basic number of chromosomes (the usual complement)

Exserted sticking out, usually of the *style or *stamens from the flower

Filament that part of the *stamen which supports the *anther

Flexuous wavy, usually of a stem

Forma a minor variant, less different from the basic species than a *variety. Abbreviated to **f.** or **ff.** if plural

Genus a grouping of *species, such as *Iris* or *Paeonia*

Glabrous without hairs or glands

Glandular with glands, which are usually stalked, like hairs with a sticky blob on the apex

Glaucous with a greyish bloom, especially on the leaves

Globose more or less spherical

Hastate with a broad but pointed apex, and two diverging lobes at the base

Hyaline transparent, often soft or papery

Hybrid the progeny of two different species

Incised with deep cuts in the margin

Inflorescence the flowers and flower stalks, especially when grouped

Laciniate deeply and irregularly toothed and divided into narrow lobes

Lanceolate shaped like a spearhead, widest below the middle, with a tapering point

Leaflets the parts of a compound leaf

Linear long and narrow, with parallel sides

Lyrate with a broad, but pointed apex and lobes becoming smaller towards the leaf base

Monocarpic usually dying after flowering and fruiting

Nectary the part of the flower which produces nectar

Oblanceolate shaped like a spearhead, but widest above the middle

Obtuse bluntly pointed, with an angle greater than 90°

Orbicular almost round

Ovate almost round, but with a pointed apex, broader than lanceolate

Palmate with lobes or leaflets, spreading like the fingers of a hand

Panicle a branched *raceme

Pedicel the stalk of a flower

Peduncle the stalk of an *inflorescence

Peltate shaped like a round shield, with the stalk in the centre

Petal generally the coloured part of the flower

Pinnae leaflets of a *pinnate leaf

Pinnate with leaflets on either side of a central axis

Pinnatifid with lobes on either side of a central axis

Pinnule a small *pinna

Puberulent with a fine but rather sparse covering of hairs

Pubescent with a fine coating of hairs, denser than *puberulent

Raceme an *inflorescence with the flowers on a central stem, oldest at the base

Rhizome an underground modified stem, often swollen and fleshy

Rootstock the part of the plant from which the roots and the stems arise

Rosette an encircling ring of leaves

Scarious dry and papery, usually also transparent

Sepal the outer, usually green parts of the flower vs. petal

Serrate sharply and finely toothed

Sessile without a stalk

Spathulate with a broad, rounded apex and tapering into a narrow stalk

Species group of individuals, having common characteristics, distinct from other groups; the basic unit of plant classification. Abbreviated to **sp.** or **spp.** if plural

Stamen the pollen-bearing part of the flower, usually made up of *anther and *filament

Staminode a sterile *stamen, often a flattened *filament

Stigma the sticky part of the flower which receives the pollen

Stolon a creeping and rooting, usually underground stem which produces new plants

Style that part of the flower which carries the *stigma

Subcordate weakly heart-shaped at the base

Suborbicular almost round, but usually slightly narrower

Subspecies a division of a species, with minor and not complete differences from other subspecies, usually distinct either ecologically or geographically. Abbreviated to **subsp.** or **subspp.** if plural

Tetraploid with four times the basic number of chromosomes

Triploid with three times the basic number of chromosomes: these plants are usually sterile, but robust growers and good garden plants

Truncate ending abruptly, as if cut off at right angles

Umbel an *inflorescence in which the branches arise from a single point, usually forming a flat or gently rounded top

Undulate wavy, usually of the edges of a leaf

Variety a group of plants within a *species, usually differing in one or two minor characters. Generally referring to natural variations, the term *cultivar is used for man-made or chosen varieties. Adjective varietal, abbreviated to **var.** or **vars.** if plural

Index

INDEX

INDEX

INDEX

INDEX

INDEX

INDEX